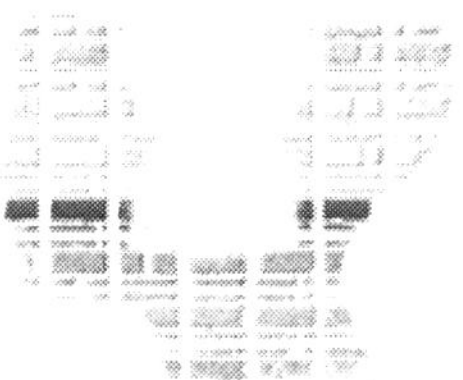

Prison Lives

ALMANAC

Prisoner Resource Guide

2017 Edition

If today's date is after **November 15, 2017**, this book is **outdated**.

Order the *2018 edition* of the *Prisoner Resource Guide* today at:

Prison Lives
PO Box 842
Exeter, CA 93221

www.PrisonLives.com

Copyright

To purchase an additional copy of this book, please make your payment of $25 by:

- money order or facility check mailed to *Prison Lives.*
- MoneyGram
- Credit/Debit card at: *www.PrisonLives.com* or by email at *info@prisonlives.com*
- PayPal payment sent direct to *info@prisonlives.com*.
- quick and easy payment by debit card, go to: *cash.me/$PrisonLives*

For further information, please contact:

Prison Lives
PO Box 842, Exeter, California, 93221

www.PrisonLives.com

info@PrisonLives.com (*Corrlinks* registered)

Prison Lives is a 501(c)(3) nonprofit corporation established to give prisoners the ability to be productive individuals and achieve self-sufficient freedom with a positive focus to effectively reduce national recidivism rates.

Printed in the United States

We're listening!

This is YOUR publication, full of the resources that you need, designed to help you to be productive. What are we missing? Tell us what you would like to see in the pages of our next edition of the largest and most comprehensive Prisoner Resource Guide. We want to know!

PRISON LIVES
PO Box 842
Exeter, California 93221

www.PrisonLives.com
info@PrisonLives.com (CorrLinks registered)

Table of Contents

Prison Lives was established as a bridge to all of the information prisoners find useful.

Our aim is to **provide you with the ultimate tools** to access the resources you need to successfully navigate the world outside of your cell or dorm bunk so that you can make the best use of your time inside.

Even if you don't quite know what direction you want to take while trapped behind bars, *Prison Lives* will prove that **life doesn't have to end or even stall with a prison sentence**.

Better still, to ensure that the opportunities keep presenting themselves, our publications are accurate, reliable, and regularly updated.

There's an entire world available to empower prisoners.

There's no reason for you not to be a part of it.

INTRODUCTION

Are you tired of having to depend on someone else to provide you with what you need?

Even the most ambitious prisoners, many who have been trapped in boxes for decades, struggle to find ways to do something positive or to accomplish any effort that was not designed to be accomplished from a prison cell. Those who believe that something should be different than it is and choose to fight for their ideas, those who want to write a book or sell their art, those who strive to become musicians, legal beagles, or to acquire an education, those who want to fight their unlawful incarceration, even those who simply want to be able to buy something or find a friend from the other side of the wall... every motivated prisoner struggles. The unfortunate truth is that doing anything positive from a reinforced concrete box will likely be the most difficult thing that most prisoners have ever done, not because they don't have the motivation, but, rather, due to the limitations of life in their box.

It shouldn't have to be that hard. It doesn't have to be that hard.

Prison Lives is a nonprofit organization established to provide a bridge to all the information and services that prisoners find useful. Our aim is to provide you with the ultimate tools to access the resources you need to successfully navigate the world outside of your cell or dorm bunk so that you can make the best use of your time inside.

Whatever your motivation, however you want to spend your time, we provide your ultimate resources. Whether you're hoping to improve your mind, your legal situation, your status with God, Allah, or your almighty prison spending account, we provide the means to accomplish it Even if you don't quite know what direction you want to take while trapped behind bars, Prison Lives will prove that life doesn't have to end or even stall with a prison sentence.

To ensure that the opportunities keep presenting themselves, that it is accurate, and up-to-date, this guide is updated *annually*.

There's an entire world available to empower prisoners. There's no reason for you not to be a part of it.

How This Book is Structured

Prison Lives Almanac is *full* of prisoner resources. So many resources, in fact, that it can be easy to get lost. Therefore, we wanted our Almanac to be organized in such a way that made it easy for you to pick it up when the need arises and to be able to find exactly what you are looking for with just a flip of the pages.

Here are some features that will help you get to the information you need when you need it.

- **DISTINCT SECTIONS**. Instead of listing all the resources in alphabetical order, we've clearly listed each resource under subject headings. But there are some subjects that require much more comprehensive information. While you'll find many resources listed in the *Resource Center*, and of course more by state in the *State-by-State Resources*, you'll notice that many topics have their own distinct sections so that we can give you the most comprehensive information for that topic.
- **INDEXING**. If you are looking for a specific listing and you already know its name, simply go to the back of the book and find the listing you're looking for in our alphabetical list of resources.

Other helpful tools:

INFORMATION BOXES...

Throughout the book, you'll find information boxes, such as this one, that offer useful insights, interesting facts, or tips on how to find additional information.

HIGHLIGHTED LISTINGS...

Because resources come with varying degrees of reliability, we've highlighted several listings in the following manner to let you know that prisoners have found these listings to be especially reliable resources. If you know of resources that you would recommend, please let us know by telling how they were especially useful to you so that we can highlight them in our next edition.

PRISON LIVES
PO Box 842, Exeter, CA 93221
www.prisonlives.com

Prison Lives is the nation's largest provider of prisoner resources and information. Through up-to-date and reliable publications, we provide prisoners with the most useful tools to make the best use of their time despite their confines.

Thank you for letting *Prison Lives* help you discover your path to productivity!

If you find something particularly enjoyable, or if you would like to suggest an edit or change, please feel free to contact us.

In the meantime, enjoy your *Prison Lives Almanac,* and check out our other products, including:

Prison Lives Almanac: 2017 Prisoner Entertainment Guide – Spring Edition

(Available mid-February! New editions are available every three months)

Prison Lives Almanac: 2016/2017 Prisoner Education Guide

(Available now!)

Remember to order your completely updated:

Prison Lives Almanac: 2018 Prisoner Resource Guide

(Available by the end of November!)

Resource Center

One of our goals is to provide you with the ultimate treasure trove of resources to help you live the most satisfying life possible, despite your confines. Before you can find the treasure though, you need the lay of the land and a detailed treasure map.

In the **Resource Center**, you will find an annually updated and detailed guide of the prisoner resources landscape, the outside world of advocacy, and exactly where to go to find the information you need to be able to navigate it all.

RESOURCE CENTER

National Resources

National Resources

Look at the following resource listings as a treasure map.

Many of the resources will lead you right to the treasure you seek. Others will require more digging. When you contact a listing, always be sure to ask about other organizations that may provide something more in line with what you are seeking.

Don't get discouraged. The treasure you seek is out there!

These are not the only resources!

You can find numerous additional listings in specifically themed chapters throughout this guide.

NOTE: The following resources represent the majority of organizations that exist for the purpose of assisting prisoners. While *Prison Lives Almanac* maintains the most complete, current and relevant information available, new resources crop up every day and older ones change without notice. With thousands of contacts, there are bound to be some whose information has changed.

If you know that one of our listings is wrong, or if you discover a new helpful organization or resource that we don't have listed, let us know! We will verify the resource and include it in our next edition. If you find a verifiably bad address, or provide us with a particularly valuable new listing, we will reward you with discounts on our upcoming publications.

Advocacy Organizations

ADOPT AN INMATE

PO Box 1543, Veneta, OR 97487
(971) 236-7897
www.adoptaninmate.org info@adoptaninmate.org

Adopt an Inmate works to provide family-like support to prisoners by connecting them with "adopters." They encourage prisoners and others to submit a prisoner's name for possible "adoption", as well as writings, artwork, and book reviews, which they post on their website and blog. Their website provides a wide variety of resources for those who would like to advocate for prisoners.

ALLIANCE OF CONCERNED MEN

3227 Dubois Place SE, Washington, DC 20019
(202) 903-1002
www.allianceofconcernedmen.com
allianceofconcernedmen@gmail.com

The Alliance of Concerned Men...

AMERICAN-ARAB ANTI-DISCRIMINATION COMMITTEE

1990 M. St. NW, #610, Washington, DC 20036
(202) 244-2990
www.adc.org

AADC provides advocacy and assistance to Arab-Americans offenders, as well as promotes Arab culture. They assist in filing complaints to the DOJ and Federal BOP on national origin or religious discrimination cases, and can assist with filing testimony with the federal

Privacy & Civil Liberties Oversight Board in private contracted facilities.

AMERICAN CIVIL LIBERTIES UNION (ACLU)

125 Broad Street, New York, NY 10004
(212) 549-2500
www.aclu.org

ACLU is a civil rights organization that defends and provides advocacy for U.S. citizens whose rights have been violated. See their listings under each state for an office in your region.

AMERICAN CIVIL LIBERTIES UNION – NATIONAL PRISON PROJECT

915 15th St., NW, 7th Floor, Washington, DC 20005
(202) 393-3930
www.aclu.org/prisoners-rights npp@npp-aclu.org

ACLU's NPP handles class action lawsuits involving civil rights violations against prisoners. They do not typically handle individual prisoner cases, but focus more towards issues that will affect prison conditions more broadly. NPP has recently discontinued publication of their print resources, including the **NPP Journal,** the *Prisoners' Assistance Directory*, and *Play It Safe*.

AMERICAN FRIENDS SERVICE COMMITTEE – PRISON WATCH PROJECT

89 Market St., 6th Floor, Newark, NJ 07102
(973) 643-3192
www.afsc.org

ASFC Prison Watch Project is an advocacy organization that raises awareness of prison conditions, with a focus on solitary confinement. They provide various resources and publications, including *The Survivor's Manual: Surviving in Solitary*, a 94-page booklet FREE to prisoners ($3 to non-prisoners).

AMNESTY INTERNATIONAL

5 Penn Plaza, New York, NY 10001
(212) 807-8400
www.amnestyusa.org

Amnesty International is a clearinghouse for information on crimes against prisoners and prisoner rights violations, including prison torture, beatings, rape, and death penalty issues.

AN END TO SILENCE – PROJECT ON ADDRESSING PRISON RAPE

Washington College of Law, 4801 Massachusetts Ave., NW, Washington, DC 20016
(202) 274-4385
www.wcl.american.edu/endsilence

An End to Silence provides information on prisoner rights and specific laws against prison rape. No direct legal services offered, but they may refer you to legal or mental health services. Letters can be marked "Legal Mail" to better ensure confidentiality.

ASSOCIATION OF STATE CORRECTIONAL ADMINISTRATORS (ASCA)

213 Court St., Middletown, VT 06547
(860) 704-6403
www.asca.net

ASCA is a membership organization comprised of directors of state correctional agencies. They are dedicated to the improvement of correctional services and practices through research in correctional practices and the development and application of correctional standards and accreditation.

CENTER FOR CONSTITUTIONAL RIGHTS

666 Broadway, New York, NY 10012
(212) 614-6481
www.ccrjustice.org

CCR is an advocacy group established to advance and protect the rights guaranteed by the U.S. Constitution. They co-publish the *Jailhouse Lawyer's Handbook.: How to Bring a Lawsuit to Challenge Violations of Your Rights in Prison*, FREE to prisoners.

CENTER ON JUVENILE & CRIMINAL JUSTICE

440 9th St., San Francisco, CA 94103
(415) 621-5661
www.cjcj.org ssp@cjcj.org

CJCJ advocates and studies issues involving minors in the criminal justice system. While they mainly focus on youths in the California prison system, they publish a wide variety of publications on prison conditions and the criminal justice system. Write for more info. (See separate California listing.)

CENTER ON WRONGFUL CONVICTIONS OF YOUTH

Northwestern University School of Law, 375 E. Chicago Ave., Chicago, IL 60611-3069
(312) 503-8576
www.cwcy.org

CWCY is an innocence project that focuses solely on individuals who were wrongfully accused or convicted of crimes as minors. They provide investigative service and representation to youths who are innocent. (Find additional 'innocence" organizations in our Legal Center.)

CENTURION MINISTRIES

1000 Herrontown Rd., Princeton, NJ 08540
(609) 921-0334
www.centurionministries.org

CM is an innocence project that focuses on wrongfully convicted prisoners who are either sentenced to death, life in prison without the possibility of parole, or those who have completely exhausted all appeal options. They will not assist in accidental or self-defense cases.

CITIZENS UNITED FOR REHABILITATION OF ERRANTS (CURE) - NATIONAL

Capital Station, PO Box 2310, Washington, DC 20013
(202) 789-2126
www.curenational.org

CURE is an advocacy organization that informs and fights for the rights of prisoners and seeks to reform the criminal justice system. See listings in each state for the CURE office in your region.

COALITION FOR PRISONERS' RIGHTS

PO Box 1911, Santa Fe, NM 87504
www.realcostofprisoners.org
info@realcostofprisoners.org

CPR provides information and resources for prisoners upon request. They publish a 2-page monthly newsletter of national prison news. Send SASE for every month you would like to receive a copy. Back issues are available from their website.

CRITICAL RESISTANCE

1904 Franklin St., Suite 504, Oakland, CA 94612
(510) 444-0484
www.criticalresistance.org
crnational@criticalresistance.org

CR is an advocacy group that seeks to build an international movement to end mass incarceration. They publish *The Abolitionist*, a tri-annual newspaper FREE to prisoners.

DIRECT ACTION FOR RIGHTS AND EQUALITY (DARE)

340 Lockwood St., Providence, RI 02907
(401) 351-6960
www.daretowin.org

DARE advocates and provides services for low-income minorities who are affected by the criminal justice system.

DISABILITY RIGHTS EDUCATION & DEFENSE FUND

3075 Adeline St., Suite 210, Berkeley, CA 94703
(510) 644-2555

DRDF Provides legal aid to those whose civil rights have been violated that are related to disabilities.

EQUAL JUSTICE INITIATIVE

122 Commerce St., Montgomery, AL 36104
(334) 269-1803
www.eji.org

EJI provides advocacy and representation for prisoners who have been wrongfully convicted of mistreated by the criminal justice system. They focus on death penalty, juvenile, or wrongfully convicted cases, especially where the defendant was biased based on race or indigence.

EXONERATION PROJECT, THE

311 N. Aberdeen St., Suite 2E, Chicago, IL 60607
(312) 789-4955
www.exonerationproject.org

EP provides legal assistance representation, and support for wrongfully convicted prisoners. Typical cases accepted involve DNA testing, coerced confessions, official misconduct, faulty eyewitness testimony and evidence, ineffective assistance of counsel claims, and convictions attained through junk science. Cases of self-defense will not be considered. Eligible clients must be innocent of the crime, already convicted, and in the U.S. You can find many additional innocence organizations in our *Legal Center*. (Find additional "innocence" organizations in our Legal Center.)

FAMILIES AGAINST MANDATORY MINIMUMS (FAMM)

1100 H St. NW, Suite 1000, Washington, DC 20005
(202) 822-6700
www.famm.org famm@famm.org (CorrLinks registered)

FAMM advocates for a change in mandatory minimum sentencing practices. They work with the American Legislative Exchange Council (ALEC) on sentencing reform. Federal prisoners can receive updates through Corrlinks. Other may receive limited information through the mail or more detailed information on current reforms from their website. Published newsletter *FAMM-Gram*, FREE to prisoners. Contributions appreciated.

FAMILIES FOR JUSTICE AS HEALING

197 Humboldt Ave., Boston, MA 02121
www.justiceashealing.org

FJH advocates to end mass incarceration.

FEDERAL BUREAU OF PRISONS

320 First St. NW, Washington, DC 20534
(202) 307-3198
www.bop.gov

FORTUNE SOCIETY

29-76 Northern Blvd., Long Island City, NY 11101
(212) 691-7554 ext. 501
www.fortunesociety.org

The Fortune Society is a reentry organization that assists ex-offenders in the New York City area. However, their website contains useful information or anyone reentering society, under the '*Resources & Publications*' tab. See separate New York listing.

HELPING EDUCATE TO ADVANCE THE RIGHTS OF THE DEAF (HEARD)

PO Box 1160, Washington, DC 20013
(202) 455-8076, TTY/Videophone: (202) 436-9278
www.beheardd c.org www.facebook.com/hearddc

HEARD provides advocacy for the deaf, hard of hearing, and deaf-blind prisoners to ensure that they receive equal justice and rights. Maintains a database of all deaf prisoners in the U.S., and trains prison systems on deaf prisoner rights and standards.

HUMAN RIGHTS COALITION

4134 Lancaster Ave., Philadelphia, PA 19104
(267) 293-9109
www.hrcoalition.org info@hrcoalition.com

HRC advocates against mass incarceration and for prisoner rights, giving voice to families of prisoners. They publish a bimonthly newsletter, *The Movement*, ($12 for prisoners) as well as the HRC Legal Pamphlet series and other pamphlets available online. They focus mainly on Pennsylvania, but can lend some support to other states. See separate Pennsylvania listing.

HUMAN RIGHTS DEFENSE CENTER

PO Box 1151, Lake Worth, FL 33460
(561) 360-2523
www.humanrightsdefensecenter.org

HRDC is a prisoner rights defense organization that litigates for free speech, public records, wrongful death cases. They also advocate on behalf of prisoners and their families in various forums, such as legislatures, news media, protest events, administrative agencies, conferences and more. HRDC publishes *Prison Legal News* (see separate listing.) They appreciate donations to help defray the costs of the considerable litigation they do on behalf of prisoners.

HUMAN RIGHTS WATCH

350 Fifth Ave., 34th Floor, New York, NY 10118-3299
(212) 290-4700
www.hrw.org

HRW advocates against human rights abuses. They conduct investigations into violations and publish their findings in local and international media.

INNOCENCE PROJECT - NATIONAL

40 Worth St., Suite 701, New York, NY 10013
(212) 364-5340
www.innocenceproject.org

The *Innocence Project* advocates and represents those who have been wrongfully convicted in cases where physical evidence, such as DNA, can prove their innocence. Those who have been wrongfully convicted can send for an application, but be aware that most of the offices are overwhelmed with submissions. See separate listings under each state for the office in your region. You can find **many** more innocence organizations in our *Legal Center* chapter later in this book!

U.S. GOVERNMENT PUBLISHING OFFICE (GPO)

Below are selected FREE and low-cost publications currently available from the GPO. To order, send a request with the appropriate item number and fee, and the once-per-order $2 service fee to the address in our listing. (You can order as many as you want for one $2 service fee, plus any other fees, if ordered in one request.) Most publications are also available in espanol.

Publication	Item #	Fee
Education		
Catch the Spirit: A Student's Guide to Community Service	5483	FREE
Civil War at a Glance (full-color civil war map)	1256	$2
Smart Saving for College: Better Buy Degrees	5823	FREE
Employment		
Resumes, Applications and Cover Letters	1207	$2.75
Federal Programs		
Federal benefits for Veterans, Dependents & Survivors	1050	$5
Food		
4 Basic Steps to Food Safety	5954	FREE
Food Safety for Pregnant Women	6177	FREE
Health		
Health Scams	6071	FREE
Mammograms	5874	FREE
Sunscreens & Tanning	5969	FREE
Tattoos & Permanent Make-Up	5861	FREE
Drugs & Health Aids		
Contact Lens Care	5872	FREE
Dietary Supplements	5801	FREE
Medicine & Pregnancy	5877	FREE
Menopause & Hormones	5794	FREE
Menopause & Hormones: Questions to Ask Your Doctor	5792	FREE
My Medicines (questions to ask the doctors)	6708	FREE
Use Medicines Wisely	5878	FREE
Your Glucose Meter	6084	FREE
Medical Problems		
HPV (human papillomavirus)	6002	FREE
Health Heart for Women	5800	FREE
Osteoporosis	5968	FREE
Sleep Problems	5955	FREE
Women & HIV	6003	FREE
Housing		
Beware of Foreclosure Rescue & Loan Modification Scams	6073	FREE
Considering a Reverse Mortgage	6107	FREE
Need Help with Your Mortgage? Don't Get Scammed	6143	FREE
Ready to Buy a Home?	6183	FREE
Money		
*Consumer Action Handbook (144 pages)	5131	FREE
Are Your Finances Ready for a Stressful Life Event?	6179	FREE
Financial Tips for Seniors	6154	FREE
Getting the Most From Your Bank Account	6104	FREE
Guide to Disability Income Insurance	6042	FREE
Guide to Long-Term Care Insurance	5879	FREE
How to Submit a Complaint	6137	FREE
Is it Time for a Financial Checkup	6180	FREE
Credit		
Act Fast if You Can't Pay Your Credit Cards	6115	FREE
Be in Charge of Your Credit Cards: Tips for Choosing & Using Them	6169	FREE
Check Your Credit Report	6106	FREE
How to Find the Best Credit Card for You	6138	FREE
How to Fix Mistakes in Your Credit Card Bill	6187	FREE
How to Stop Mystery Credit Card Fees	6136	FREE
Know Your Rights When a Debt Collector Calls	6184	FREE
Understand Your Credit Score	6185	FREE
You Have a Right to See Specialty Credit Reports	6139	FREE
Investing & Saving		
A Guide for Seniors: Protect Yourself Against Investment Fraud	6014	FREE
Questions You Should Ask About Your Investments	5790	FREE
Banking in a High-Tech World	6147	FREE
Travel		
Gettysburg National Military Park (maps, pix & history)	1333	$13
National Park System: Map & Guide	1116	$3
National Trails System: Map & Guide	1262	$3
Washington: The Nation's Capital (map)	1211	$2

FEDERAL CITIZEN INFORMATION CENTER

c/o Superintendent of Documents, FCIC – 16A, PO Box 100, Puebla, CO 81002
(719) 295-2675
www.publications.usa.gov

FCIC provides a wide variety of U.S. government information through publications, including the *Consumers Information Catalog*, which lists the majority of the FREE and low-cost publications available. Write for a FREE copy.

NOTE: Because using online resources has become more prevalent in recent years, the FCIC will discontinue printing the *Consumers Information Catalog* after this year.

INSTITUTE FOR CRIMINAL POLICY RESEARCH (ICPR) | UNIVERSITY OF LONDON

42 Store St., London WC1E 7DB UK

(44 90) 7824-999028

www.icpr.org.uk

ICPR is a world organization that focuses on prison systems around the globe. They release a bimonthly report, the International Prison News Digest, which brings the latest news items from around the world on prison and the use of imprisonment. This is a FREE online resource.

JUST DETENTION INTERNATIONAL

3325 Wilshire Blvd., Suite 340, Los Angeles, CA 90010
(213) 384-1400
www.justdetention.org info@justdetention.org

JDI advocates to end sexual abuse in prisons. Anyone who has experienced any form of sexual abuse while in prison, including sexual harassment, sex-for-protection, sexual assault, etc., is encouraged to contact them for information and guidance. Prisoners can do so through "Confidential Legal Mail" is addressed to their attorney, Cynthia Totten, CA Atty. Reg. 199266, at the above address.

JUSTICE DENIED

PO Box 66291, Seattle, WA 98166
www.justicedenied.org

JD advocates for the wrongfully convicted by publishing their stories. Currently they only publish online. They do have some publications and resources available to prisoner. Write for current offerings.

LAW OFFICES OF ALAN ELLIS

1120 Nye St., Suite 300, San Rafael, CA 94901
(415) 256-9775
www.alanellis.com aelaw1@alaneliss.com

Legal firm specializing in federal criminal appeals and information pertaining to the appellate processes. Publishes the *Federal Prison Guidebook, Federal Sentencing Guidebook,* and *Federal Post-Conviction Guidebook.*

LAW OFFICE OF MARCIA SHEIN

2392 N. Decatur Rd., Decatur, GA 30033
(404) 633-3797
www.msheinlaw.com

Legal firm specializing in appellate services, some of which are available to prisoners who are representing themselves *pro se*. Distributes the newsletter *Federal Criminal Law News.*

LEWISBURG PRISON PROJECT

PO Box 128, Lewisburg, PA 17837
(570) 523-1104
www.lewisburgprisonproject.org

LPP is a prisoner legal assistance organization that primarily assists prisoners in the Pennsylvania region. However, they distribute legal bulletins and prisoner rights publications for a nominal fee. Write for current list of publications. See separate Pennsylvania listing.

LIFE AFTER INNOCENCE | PHILIP H. CORBOY LAW CENTER

25 E. Pearson St., Chicago, IL 60611
www.luc.edu lifeafterinnocence@luc.edu

Life After Innocence advocates for innocence people who are being released from prison by helping them reenter society and enabling them to reclaim their rights as citizens. They do so by providing individualized legal and support services and wider reaching public policy initiatives.

MAOIST INTERNATIONAL MINISTRY OF PRISONS

PO Box 40799, San Francisco, CA 94140
www.prisoncensorship.info

MIM is a "revolutionary anti-imperialist" organization that works to fight injustices in the criminal system and educate those trapped within. Publishes a monthly magazine *Under Lock & Key*, FREE to prisoners, and sends other related publications upon request.

NATIONAL ASSOCIATION FOR THE ADVANCEMENT OF COLORED PEOPLE (NAACP) - NATIONAL

4805 Mt. Hope Dr., Baltimore, MD 21215
(800) NAACP-98 (622-2798), (410) 580-5777 (local)
www.naacp.org

NAACP is an advocacy group that fights for the rights and against the unequal treatment of minorities, in the criminal justice system and free society. They are active in fighting against the death penalty and unfair sentencing practices, and offer some reentry resources. They have offices in all 50 states and many countries. See their website for an office in region.

NAACP – LEGAL DEFENSE & EDUCATION FUND

Headquarters: 99 Hudson St., Suite 1600, New York, NY 10013
(212) 965-2200
Washington DC office: 1444 I St. NW, Washington, DC 20005
(202) 682-1300
www.naacpldf.org

NAACP's Legal Defense & Education Fund provides legal aid and representation to those involved in racial injustices. They also handle a small number of death penalty and life without the possibility of parole cases. They typically will not respond to letters unless they are interested in your case.

NATIONAL ASSOCIATION OF CRIMINAL DEFENSE LAWYERS (NACDL)

1600 L St., NW, 12th Floor, Washington, DC 20036
(202) 876-8600
www.nacdl.org

NACDL is a national membership organization of criminal defense lawyers. They will not consider your case, but they can provide attorney referrals and general information on professional legal representation standards. Publishes the monthly magazine *Champion*, as subscription-based publication focusing on the needs of attorneys.

NATIONAL CENTER ON INSTITUTIONS AND ALTERNATIVES (NCIA)

7205 Rutherford Rd., Baltimore, MD 21244
(443) 780-1300
www.ncianet.org info@ncianet.org

NCIA, in partnership with the *National Institute of Corrections*, acts as the coordinator of the Jail Suicide Prevention Task Force. They conduct annual jail suicide prevention seminars, technical assistance to state officials and correctional facilities, and publish a quarterly newsletter, *Jail Suicide/Mental Health Update*.

NATIONAL CRIME INFORMATION CENTER

1000 Custer Hollow Rd., Clarksburg, WV 26306
(304) 625-2000
www.fbi.gov

The National Crime Information Center provides copies of a subjects FBI Identification Record. Individuals can request their own records for purposes of review, to challenge information on the record, or to satisfy various requirements.

NATIONAL INSTITUTE OF CORRECTIONS

791 N. Chambers Rd., Aurora, CO 80011
(800) 877-1461, (303) 682-0213

The National Institute of Corrections offers information and resources to assist families of offenders, including a FREE booklet, Directory of Programs Serving Families of Adult Offenders. send SASE for booklet and more information.

NATIONAL LAWYERS GUILD – PRISON LAW PROJECT

132c Nassau St., Room 922, New York, NY 10038
(212) 679-5100
www.nlg.org

NLG assists supports prison lawyers through resources and information. Co-publishes the *Jailhouse Lawyer's Handbook* and other publications focused on prisoner rights issues. See separate listing in our *Legal Center*.

NATIONAL RELIGIOUS CAMPAIGN AGAINST TORTURE

110 Maryland Ave., NE Suite 502, Washington, DC 20002
(202) 547-1920
www.nrcat.org

NRCAT is an advocacy group which has a focus against solitary confinement.

NATIONAL COMMISSION ON CORRECTIONAL HEALTH

1145 W. Diversey Pkwy., Chicago, IL 60614
(773) 880-1460
www.ncchc.org

NCCHC provides information and advocacy focused on improving the quality of health care in prisons. Publishes a quarterly newspaper, *Correct Care*, available FREE to prison libraries, amongst other publications. Write for a current list of publications.

NATIONAL CRIMINAL JUSTICE REFERENCE CENTER

PO Box 6000, Rockville, MD 20849-6000
(800) 851-3420
www.ncjrs.gov

NCJRS is an information clearinghouse for criminal justice reports. They distribute publications and information from the *Institute of Justice* (NIJ), the *Bureau of Justice Statistics* (BJS), the *Office for Victims of Crime* (OVC), and the *Office of Juvenile Justice and Delinquency Protection* (OJJDP).

PARTNERSHIP FOR SAFETY & JUSTICE

825 NE 20th Ave., Suite 250, Portland, OR 97232
(503) 335-8449
www.safetyandjustice.org

PSJ is a prisoner advocacy group that focuses on actively making changes through legislative efforts and policy initiatives, balancing the interest of victims, prisoners, and their families. While they primarily focus on prison issues in Oregon, they do offer some prisoner rights and resource information to others. See separate Oregon listing.

PEOPLE'S LAW OFFICE

1180 N. Milwaukee Ave., Chicago, IL 60642-4019
(773) 235-0070
www.peopleslawoffice.com

PLO is an advocacy group that fights against social injustice where people have been physically abused or tortured, wrongfully arrested or convicted, sentenced to death, and who have received injustices based on political beliefs or activism.

PRISON ACTIVIST RESOURCE CENTER (PARC)

PO Box 70477, Oakland, CA 94612
(510) 893-4648
www.prisonactivist.org info@prisonactivist.org

PARC raises awareness for the challenges of racism and classism within the criminal justice system. Provides a resource directory FREE to prisoners upon request.

PRISONER EXPRESS

Cornell University, 127 Anabel Taylor Hall, Ithaca, NY 14853
(607) 255-6486
www.prisonerexpress.org

Prisoner Express actively promotes rehabilitation through opportunities for prisoners to participate in creative projects of self-expression. Prisoners are encouraged to subscribe to their biannual publication, FREE of charge, which contains regular programs for prisoner involvement, including writing, art, poetry, education, book clubs, and several other options.

PRISONERS' RIGHTS RESEARCH PROJECT

University of Illinois College of Law, 332 Law Building, m/c 594, 504 E. Pennsylvania Ave., Champlain, IL 61820

PRRP provides legal research support for prisoners. Answers specific legal questions, but does not provide legal advice or representation. Will copy no more than 10 pages of info.

PRISONER VISITATION & SUPPORT

1501 Cherry St., Philadelphia, PA 19012
(215) 241-7117
www.prisonervisitation.org pvs@afsc.org

PVS is an organization that provides visitation to prisoners in the U.S. Volunteers primarily visit federal and military facilities, with priority to those on death row, in solitary confinement, those serving long sentences, and those who receive frequent transfers between federal facilities.

PRISON LEGAL NEWS

PO Box 1511, Lake Worth, FL 33460
(561) 360-2523
www.prisonlegalnews.org

PLN is a monthly magazine covering prison related news and issues affecting prisoners, including recent case law summaries and analysis. They also publish and sell several publications related to prisoner rights and legal assistance. Write for a FREE publications list. See their ads in this publication and go to our *Legal Center* for more info.

PRISON POLICY INITIATIVE

PO Box 127, Northampton, MA 01061
www.prisonpolicy.org

PPI provides information and resources on issues affecting prisoners and the criminal justice system, including listings of legal resources for prisoners by state. Most resources are only available online.

PROJECT ON ADDRESSING PRISON RAPE | WASHINGTON COLLEGE OF LAW

4801 Massachusetts Ave. NW, Washington, DC 20016
(202) 274-4385
www.wcl.american.edu/endsilence

POPR provides information on addressing prison rape issues through publications, including *an End to Silence: Inmates' Handbook on Identifying and Addressing Sexual Abuse.* They have an online directory to U.S. crisis centers.

PROJECT FOR OLDER PRISONERS

Jonathan Turley National Law Center, 2000 H St., NW, Washington, DC 20052

(202) 994-7001
www.law.gwu/academics/el/clinic/pages/pops.aspx

POP assists prisoners over the age of 55 with alternative means of incarceration through parole and pardon filing assistance.

SAFER SOCIETY FOUNDATION

PO Box 340, Brandon, VT 05733
(802) 247-3132
www.safersociety.org info@safersociety.org

SSF is an advocacy organization that fights for sexual abuse prevention. Offers FREE and confidential services to prisoners, their families, social workers, courts, and corrections personnel seeking treatment information on sexually offending behaviors.

SENTENCING PROJECT

1705 DeSales St. NW, 8th Floor, Washington, DC 20036
(202) 628-0871
www.sentencingproject.org
staff@sentencingproject.org

SP provides technical assistance and support services to criminal justice reform initiatives, including developing alternative sentencing programs and conducting research on criminal justice issues. They do not offer any direct services to prisoners.

SOLITARY WATCH

PO Box 11374, Washington, DC 20008
www.solitarywatch.com

Solitary Watch is an activism group that works against the use of solitary confinement in prison. The encourage writing submissions by prisoners who are currently in solitary confinement and those who have been in the past, which they may publish in their quarterly newsletter, FREE to prisoners.

STUDENT INSURGENT

1228 University St., Eugene, OR 97403
(541) 346-3716

SI is a tri-annual publication that provide a forum for students to freely express themselves. They encourage prisoners to submit art, and writings to be included. FREE to prisoners.

UNICOR BONDING PROGRAM

320 First St. NW, Washington, DC 20534
(202) 305-3972
www.unicor.gov

The UNICOR Bonding Program provides a $5,000 fidelity bond for employed ex-federal prisoners who worked in the UNICOR program for at least six months during their incarceration.

URBAN INSTITUTE

2100 M St. NW, Washington, DC 20037
(202) 833-7200
www.urban.org

The Urban Institute provides information and analysis to public and private decision makers to help them address challenges within the criminal justice system and other challenging areas of our nation. They help individuals understand the issues and tradeoffs in policymaking that affects change.

U.S. DEPARTMENT OF JUSTICE – SPECIAL LITIGATION, CIVIL RIGHTS DIVISION

950 Pennsylvania Ave., NW, Washington, DC 20530
(202) 514-6255, (877) 218-5228
www.usdoj.gov/crt/split

USDOJ's Special Litigation section works to protect the civil rights of U.S. citizens, including the rights of prisoners. They act on behalf of prisoners at risk of harm. Send a detailed explanation of your issue, including a chronology and description of any incidents, especially if you are in danger of harm. They typically will not respond unless interested in assisting you, but their assistance can be substantial if they do choose to get involved.

U.S. DEPARTMENT OF LABOR | EMPLOYMENT AND TRAINING ADMINISTRATION

20 Constitution Ave. NW, Washington, DC 20210
(202) 693-2796
www.dol.gov

The U.S. Department of Labor oversees many of the programs that affects prisoners and ex-offenders, including programs for people with disabilities, occupational safety and health, seniors, veterans, and adult training.

U.S. DEPARTMENT OF STATE

Washington, DC 20520
(877) 487-2778
www.state.gov

U.S. Department of State provides information and applications for passports and visas.

U.S. SOCIAL SECURITY ADMINISTRATION (SSA)

Office of Public inquiry, 6401 Security Blvd., Baltimore, MD 21235
(800) 772-1213
www.socialsecurity.gov

SSA provides information on application processes and requirements for obtaining social security insurance and documentation.

VERA INSTITUTE OF JUSTICE

233 Broadway, 12th Floor, New York, NY 10279
(212) 334-1300
www.vij.org

VIJ supports and sponsors various programs that work for the overall benefit of prisoners throughout the U.S., such as the *Pathways* educational programs (in Michigan, New Jersey, and North Carolina.) Contact them for current programs around the country.

Art & Writing Resources

Looking for more art and writing resources?

For a more comprehensive listing of our Art & Writing Resources, please go to the *Prisoner Services* section of this book.

AMERICAN PRISON WRITING ARCHIVE

198 College Hill Rd., Clinton, NY 13323-1218
www.dhinitiative.org/projects/apwa

American Prison Writing Archive accepts non-fiction prisoner written essays focusing on prison conditions for publishing on their website, 5,000-word max. Write for guidelines.

BEAT WITHIN, THE

P.O. Box 34310, San Francisco, CA 94134
Phone: 415-890-5641 (415) 503-4170
www.thebeatwithin.org

The Beat Within is a prison-focused publication that accepts prisoner written essays, commentary, and poetry directed towards teaching, inspiring, and giving hope. If they publish you, they will send you the issue you are published in. Write for submission guidelines. They are unable to provide free subscriptions. Donations are appreciated.

CAPTIVE IMAGERY

Out of Business

3300 NW 185th St. #129, Portland, OR 97229
www.captiveimagery.com,
captiveimagery@captiveimagery.com

Captive Imagery I is a large online displayer of prisoner art. Their goal is to only display the best prison artists from around the world. Potential prisoner clients can send up to five samples in the form of originals, photos or scans, which they will evaluate. WARNING: They will typically not return samples. If they like what they see, they will send you an agreement to sign. Send SASE for more info.

JOURNAL OF PRISONERS ON PRISONERS

School of Criminology, Simon Fraser University, Burnaby, B.C. Canada V5A 1S6
www.jpp.org

Journal of Prisoners on Prisoners is an annual publication that seeks submissions from prisoner writers, including papers, collaborative essays, interviews, book reviews, and photo or graphic essays. No fiction or poetry. Write for more info. Publishes articles in French and English.

PEN PRISON WRITING PROGRAM

PEN American Center, 588 Broadway, Suite 303,
New York, NY 10012
(212) 334-1660 ext. 117
www.pen.org *prisonwriting@pen.org*

PEN Prison Writing Program encourages prisoner writers through information and an annual writing contest. Write for a FREE copy of their *Handbook for Writers in* Prison. See our *Prisoner Service Center* for more information.

POET'S WORKSHOP | ST. LOUIS COUNTY JAIL

4334 Haines Rd., Duluth, MN 55811

The *Poet's Workshop* publishes a monthly magazine. They encourage poetry submissions from prisoners. If you are published in their pages, they will provide the magazine to you FREE of charge.

PRISONS FOUNDATION

2512 Virginia Ave., NW #58043, Washington, DC 20037
(202) 393-1511
www.prisonsfoundation.org
staff@prisonsfoundation.org

Prisons Foundation seeks prisoner writings for publication on their website, any subject, uncensored. A good source for attracting agents or drawing attention to others interested in prisoner writings. Will scan your handwritten or types pages in and post as-is. Write for more info.

SAFE STREETS ART FOUNDATION

2512 Virginia Ave. NW, #58043, Washington, DC 20037
www.safestreetarts.org sales@safestreetarts.org

Safe Streets Arts Foundation accepts prisoner art for display and sale at various art galleries. Send SASE for more info. General submission guidelines: Simply send your art to them, which they will prepare for display at no cost to you. Include name and address on the back of your art, and description of your piece, and any background info or additional info you'd like to include. They pay you 50% of the selling price, less any matting/framing expenses incurred.

DO YOU HAVE IDEAS THAT MAY IMPROVE THIS BOOK?

We Want to Hear Them!

Send thoughts to:

PRISON LIVES
PO Box 842, Exeter, CA 93221
info@prisonlives.com (Corrlinks-friendly)

Consumer Affairs Organizations

The following resources are useful when seeking to resolve concerns or conflicts related to companies you are doing business with.

Many agencies will require you to voice your complaints through your state consumer protection agency. You will find these in the *State-by-State* section.

COUNCIL OF BETTER BUSINESS BUREAUS

3033 Wilson Blvd., Suite 600, Arlington, VA 22201
(703) 276-0100
www.bbb.org

The *Council of Better Business Bureaus* is the umbrella organization of the Better Business Bureau (BBB) They can assist with complaints of truthfulness and accuracy of national advertising claims and other conflicts between you and businesses. They maintain lists of national local BBBs, which you can obtain by writing.

CONSUMER ACTION

221 Main St., Suite 480, San Francisco, CA 94105
(415) 777-9635
www.consumer-action.org

Consumer Action is an advocacy organization that specializes in credit, finance, and telecommunications conflicts. They offer education materials on consumer issues in eight languages, FREE upon request.

CONSUMER FEDERATION OF AMERICA

1620 I St. NW, Washington, DC 20006
(202) 387-6121
www.consumerfed.org

CFA represents consumer interests on issues such as telecommunications, insurance, financial services, product safety, indoor air pollution, health care, product liability, and utility rates. They develop and distribute studies, consumer guides and educational materials, FREE upon request.

CONSUMER PROTECTION OFFICES - NATIONAL

General Services Administration, 1800 F St. NW, 2nd Floor, Washington, DC 20405
www.usa.gov/consumer

CPOs mediate complaints, conduct investigations, license and regulate professionals, provide educational materials, and advocate for consumer interests. They offer a FREE *Consumer Action Handbook*, as well as other materials upon request. See individual state listings in our *State-by-State* section.

FEDERAL TRADE COMMISSION

Bureau of Consumer Protection, 600 Pennsylvania Ave. NW, Washington, DC 20580
(877) 382-4357
www.ftc.org

The *FTC* works for consumers to prevent fraudulent, deceptive, and unfair business practices and provides materials to help consumers spot, stop, and avoid becoming prey to them.

CONSUMER CREDIT REPORTING AGENCIES

EQUIFAX

Office of Consumer Affairs, PO Box 740241, Atlanta, GA 30374 (800) 685-1111

EXPERIAN

National Consumer Assistance Center, PO Box 2002, Allen, TX 75013 (888) 397-3742

TRANSUNION

Consumer Solutions, PO Box 2000, Chester, PA 19022 (800) 888-4213

ANNUAL CREDIT REPORT REQUEST SERVICE

PO Box 105281, Atlanta, GA 30348 (877) 322-8228

Death Penalty Organizations

Looking for more death penalty resources?

You can find additional death row resources and a complete listing of death row locations in our *Prison Center.*

ACLU CAPITAL PUNISHMENT PROJECT

201 W. Main St., #402, Durham, NC 27701
(919) 682-5959
www.aclu.org/capital

The *ACLU's Capital Punishment Project* is an advocacy initiative that is working to raise awareness for death penalty issues and is working to abolish capital punishment.

AMNESTY INTERNATIONAL – USA DEATH PENALTY ABOLISHMENT CAMPAIGN

600 Pennsylvania Ave. SE, 5th Floor, Washington DC 20003
(202) 509-8135
www.amnestyusa.org

Amnesty International's Death Penalty Abolishment Campaign actively advocates for the abolishment of capital punishment in the U.S. They keep track of death penalty trends and publish a variety of reports. They will not provide legal services.

CAMPAIGN TO END THE DEATH PENALTY

PO Box 25730, Chicago, IL 60625
(773) 955-4841
www.nodeathpenalty.org

CEDP is a national grassroots organization that advocates for the end of capital punishment in the U.S. Write for FREE newsletter, *The New Abolitionist*, featuring writings by prisoners and their families.

CANADIAN COALITION AGAINST THE DEATH PENALTY

80 Lillington Ave., Toronto, Ontario M1N 3K7, Canada
www.ccadp.org

CCADP provides pen pal services for death row prisoners. Send a maximum of 3 paragraphs, which they will post on their website. Letters require international postage.

CAPITAL PUNISHMENT RESEARCH INITIATIVE

135 Western Ave., 245 Draper Hall, Albany, NY 12222
(518) 442-5231

CPRI provides research on issues involving capital punishment issues. Write for a listing of research available to prisoners.

CENTURION MINISTRIES

1000 Herrontown Rd., Princeton, NJ 08540
(608) 921-0334
www.centurionministries.org

Centurion Ministries is a non-legal investigative agency that provides services to death row and LWOP prisoners. Focuses on cases where innocence of murder or rape is shown by facts. Send up to 4-page letter containing facts. (Do not send transcripts of original documents.) They have stringent qualifying criteria and a long waiting list.

COMPASSION

140 W. South Boundary St., Perrysburg, OH 43551

Compassion is a bimonthly newsletter by and for death row prisoners, FREE to death row prisoners. Death row prisoners are encouraged to send writing, art and poetry submissions. They offer scholarships to immediate family members of victims.

DEATH PENALTY FOCUS

5 Third St., Suite 725, San Francisco, CA 94103
(414) 243-0143
www.deathpenalty.org

DPF is a national grassroots organization that advocates for the end of capital punishment in the U.S. Through media outreach, education of lawmakers, political and civic leaders, and the public, they advocate for alternatives to death penalty. They do not offer legal services or become involved in individual cases.

DEATH PENALTY INFORMATION CENTER

1015 18th St. NW, Washington, DC 20036
(202) 289-2275
www.deathpenaltyinfo.org

DPIC is a clearinghouse for death penalty information. They provide comprehensive reports on capital punishment related stats and facts in the U.S., available largely through their website. You can send requests for information, but they will not provide legal assistance.

DEATH ROW SUPPORT PROJECT

PO Box 600, Department P, Liberty Mills, IN 46946
www.brethren.org/drsp

DRSP is a faith-based company that provides pen pal services for death row prisoners ONLY.

EQUAL JUSTICE USA

20 Jay St., Suite 808, Brooklyn, NY 11201
act.ejusa.org

EJ USA advocates to end the death penalty through policy initiatives. Publications can be downloaded from their website, including the *Capital Defense Handbook for Defendants and their Families.*

GRASSROOTS INVESTIGATION PROJECT (GRIP) | QUIXOTE CENTER

PO Box 5206, Hyattsville, MD 20782
(301) 699-0042
www.quixote.org

GRIP works to empower family members of those on death row and anti-death penalty advocates to create partnerships with journalists, attorneys, and academicians to find avenues for conducting proper investigations of death penalty cases. Write for more information.

HIDDEN VOICES

9602 Art Rd., Cedar Grove, NC 27231
www.hiddenvoices.org

Hidden Voices encourages expression from death row prisoners, letting their voices be heard by those on the outside through interactive touring exhibits and other methods. Prisoners are encouraged to end their personal "prayers" in an effort to show outsiders the humanity that exists on death row.

LIFELINES

63 Forest Road, Garston, Watford, WD25 7QP, United Kingdom.
www.Lifelines-uk.org.uk

Lifelines is an organization that supports and befriends prisoners on death row in the United States through letter writing. It was founded in 1988 in Cambridge Great Britain and it is the longest established UK organization of its kind. Our Patron is Clive Stafford Smith. We have a dedicated team of Coordinators who look after all the states and we have a conference twice a year for members. It is not a religious, political or campaigning organization, though respectful of the varied individual beliefs and values of its members. It is not associated with other groups who find pen friends for people on death row. Remember to use international postage when corresponding.

MURDER VICTIM'S FAMILIES' FOR RECONCILIATION

PO Box 27764., Raleigh, NC 27611-7764
www.mvfr.org

MVRF is a coalition of the families of murder victims and the executed that advocates for the repeal of the death penalty and alternatives to capital punishment. NOTE: Resources are currently only online.

NATIONAL COALITION TO ABOLISH THE DEATH PENALTY

1620 L St. NW, Suite 250, Washington, DC 20036
(202) 331-4090
www.ncadp.org info@ncadp.org

NCADP advocates for the abolishment of capital punishment on the state level. They do not provide legal assistance, but they do publish the bimonthly newsletter *Lifelines*. Contact for more information.

NATIONAL CAPITAL CRIME ASSISTANCE NETWORK (NCCAN)

October – May: 14985 Road 40.2, Mancos, CO 81328
June – September: 6 Tolman Rd., Peaks Island, ME 04108
www.nccan.org

NCCAN provides training and assistance to death row prisoners to help them develop the skills advocate for themselves, including how to understand and summarize case issues identify tasks, and finding appropriate resources.

NATIONAL DEATH ROW ASSISTANCE NETWORK

6 Tolman Rd. Peaks Island, ME 04108
or
12200 Road 41.9, Mancos, CO 81328
(207) 766-2418, (970) 533-7383
www.ndran.org

NDRAN is a division of CURE, which was established to assist death row prisoners in gaining access to legal resources, community support, and financial tools. Write for more information.

OTHER DEATH PENALTY PROJECT, THE

PO Box 1486, Lancaster, CA 93584
www.theotherdeathpenalty.org

ODPP is not actually an anti-death penalty organization, but rather an advocacy group that fights against life without the possibility of parole (LWOP). They hope to join the death penalty abolition movement to end all forms of the death penalty, including death by incarceration. Write for their *Prisoner Organizing Kit*, containing detailed information on how to get involved.

SOUTHERN CENTER FOR HUMAN RIGHTS

83 Poplar St. NW, Atlanta, GA 30303-2122
(404) 688-1202
www.schr.org tganzy@schr.org

SCHR advocates and provides representation to death row prisoners (Alabama/Georgia only) challenging conditions of confinement and human rights violations in prisons. They also advocate for criminal justice reform.

Education Organizations

AMERICAN COUNCIL ON EDUCATION

One Dupont Cir. NW, Suite 250, Washington, DC 20036-1193
(800) 626-9433
www.aenet.edu www.gedtest.org

ACE regulates and provides information on GED testing and ACE credits, credit hours earned through supervised exams used as transfer credits to various colleges. Write for more information.

COLLEGE LEVEL EXAM BOARDS

45 Columbus Ave., New York, NY 10023
(212) 713-8000
www.collegeboard.org

Regulates and provides information on *CLEPs* (College Level Exam Programs), online testing to assess potential student's knowledge for placement in college or transfer credits.

CORRECTIONAL EDUCATION ASSOCIATION

8182 Lark Brown Rd., Suite 202, Elkridge, MD 21075
(800) 783-1232
www.ceanational.org

CEA is a professional organization of educators and administrators who provide legislative support and awareness for prison education efforts around the U.S. They typically will not work directly with prisoners, but they will work with those who support prisoner education efforts. They publish *The Journal of Correctional Education.*

DISTANCE EDUCATION AND TRAINING COUNCIL (DEAC)

1601 18th St. NW, Washington, DC 20009
(202) 234-5100
www.deac.org

Formerly the Distance Education and Training Council, the Distance Education Accrediting Commission (DEAC) accredits correspondence schools across the U.S. They provide prisoners with a FREE listing of current DEAC accredited schools. NOTE: There are many schools that offer correspondence education to prisoners that are not listed with DEAC.

For a complete listing of schools that provide education options to prisoners, purchase Prison Lives Almanac: Prisoner Education Edition.

EXCELSIOR

7 Columbia Cir., Albany, NY 12203

Provides information on Excelsior exams, formerly Regents exams, an entrance exam service used to provide schools an accurate assessment of a potential student's knowledge for placement or transfer credit.

FEDERAL STUDENT AID INFORMATION CENTER

PO Box 84, Washington, DC 20044
(800) 433-3243
www.studentaid.ed.gov

FSAIC provides information on federal student aid and recent Pell grant considerations.

NATIONAL COLLEGE STUDIES

675 Blue Mountain Rd., Saugerties, NY 12477

NCS provides information on Experiential Credits, college credits granted for life experience. Write for a copy of the *Experiential Learning Guidebook.*

PRISON ENTREPRENEURSHIP PROGRAM

PO Box 926274, Houston, TX 77292-6274
www.prisonentrepreneurship.org

PEP is an education program that connects prisoners with successful business people to teach them professional and entrepreneurial skills, including a 5-month business concepts and theory, and presentation and networking course. Through a thorough application process and intensive study requirements, they ensure that those involved in the program are determined and willing to improve their circumstances. You must be within three years of release, have a clean disciplinary record, and have no gang affiliations or history of sexual convictions.

PRISON SCHOLAR FUND

1752 NW Market St., #953, Seattle, WA 98107
www.prisonscholars.org

The Prison Scholar Fund works to build partnerships and find investors to supply assistance and funds for educational grants for prisoners. Prisoners are funded for a single class, with consideration for further education upon successful completion of that class. Write with a summary of your education goals and the classes you are interested in.

U.S. DEPARTMENT OF EDUCATION

400 Maryland Ave., Washington, DC 20002
www.ed.gov

DoE provides general information on education options in the U.S., including accreditation, current financial aid information and more.

Go to School!

If you would like to get an education during your stay in prison, or to learn more about opportunities available to you now, including current schools, tuition rates, courses offered to prisoners, financing and much more, purchase *'Prison Lives Almanac: Prisoner Education Guide'.* Updated before every fall term (released in July), it is the most current and reliable resource for prisoner education. See our ad in this book.

Family Organizations

ALLIANCE FOR CHILDREN AND FAMILIES

1100 W. Lake Park Dr., Milwaukee, WI 53224
(800) 221-3726
www.alliance1.org info@alliance1.org

The Alliance for Children and Families provides services to nonprofit organizations that serve families of the incarcerated. They can provide information and resources that are available in your area.

AMACHI

2000 Market St., Suite 600, Philadelphia, PA 19103
(215) 557-4418
www.amachimentoring.org

Amachi provides support services and technical assistance to programs that focus on mentoring children affected by the criminal justice system.

BIG BROTHER/BIG SISTERS | NATIONAL OFFICE

230 N. 13th St., Philadelphia, PA 19107
(215) 567-7000
www.bbbs.org actioncenter@bbbs.org

The Big Brothers/Big Sisters organization offers one-on-one mentoring to children affected by incarceration and other unfortunate life circumstances. Contact them for information on services in your area. (look for state listings in our state-by-state section.)

CHILDREN OF INCARCERATED PARENTS MENTORING (CHIP) | NOTRE DAME MISSION VOLUNTEERS-AMERICORPS (NDVMA)

403 Markland Ave., Baltimore, MD 21212
(410) 532-6864
www.ndmva.org natloffice@ndmva.org

NDVMA's CHIP program provides one-on-one mentoring for children affected by incarceration. They also build partnerships with local schools and social service agencies to provide educational support.

CENTER FOR CHILDREN OF INCARCERATED PARENTS (CPIP)

PO Box 41-286, Eagle Rock, CA 90041
(626) 449-2470
www.e-ccip.org ccip@earthlink.net

CCIP offers education opportunities for incarcerated parents to provide better parenting skills for their children and families. Write for the *Incarcerated Parents* catalog containing more than 200 FREE resources for prisoner's families.

CHILDREN'S LAW CENTER

1325 S. Colorado Blvd., Suite 701, Denver, CO 80222
(303) 692-1165
www.childlawcenter.org info@childlawcenter.org

Children's Law Center works with troubled families to resolve complex issues for the benefit of their children's safety, stability and success through legal advocacy. education, and public policy reform.

FAMILIES AGAINST MANDATORY MINIMUMS

1100 H St. NW, #1000, Washington, DC 20005
(202) 822-6700
www.famm.org famm@famm.org
(Corrlinks registered)

FAMM is a coalition of prisoners' families that advocates against mandatory minimum sentencing and gathers data from prisoners under mandatory minimums. To submit a case for profiling, send a written summary of your circumstances. They receive many, but only use a few. They provide an email newsletter to friends and family. Look for regional offices by state.

FAMILY & CORRECTIONS NETWORK

93 Old York Rd., Suite 1 #510, Jenkintown, PA 19046
(215) 576-1110
www.fcnetwork.org

F & CN provides a variety of online resources for families of prisoners, including information on parenting, prison visitation, mothers and fathers in prison, and more. Limited resources are available through the mail.

GIRL SCOUTS BEYOND BARS | HEADQUARTERS

420 5th Ave., New York, NY 10018
(800) 478-7248 (212) 852-8000
www.girlscouts.org

Girl Scouts Beyond Bars provides daughters of those incarcerated with the opportunity to participate in the Girl Scout Leadership Experience. Part of the program includes facilitated discussions about family life, conflict resolution, and the prevention of drug abuse and violence. Write for services in your area.

HOPE HOUSE

PO Box 60682, Washington, DC 20039
(301) 408-1452
www.hopehousedc.org

Hope House assists families of the incarcerated by strengthening the bonds between prison and home, helping reduce the stigma associated with having family member behind bars, and by raising public awareness about this at-risk population. They focus on the Washington DC area, but can provide information and resources to any location.

LEGAL SERVICES FOR PRISONERS WITH CHILDREN

1540 Market St., Suite 490, San Francisco, CA 94102
(415) 255-7036
www.prisonerswithchildren.org

LSPC organizes communities affected by the criminal justice system and advocates for incarcerated parents and their children to reunify families and communities. They cannot provide individual legal assistance to prisoners, but they will provide referrals and information on family matters, reentry services, and prison conditions.

MOTHERS AND FATHERS FOR THE ADVANCEMENT OF SOCIAL REFORM

3737 Atlanta St., Dallas, TX 75215
(214) 421-0303
www.massjab.org

MASS assists families of prisoners at high-risk for substance abuse, medical or emotional disorders, and poverty. They also assist ex-offenders to readjust to society. Write for more information.

NATIONAL BILL OF RIGHTS PARTNERSHIP FOR CHILDREN OF THE INCARCERATED

5414 Edgewood Rd., Little Rock, AR 72207
(501) 366-3647
www.nationalBORpartnership.net
borpartnershi@yahoo.com

The BOR Partnership for Children of the Incarcerated is a coalition of 14 state groups that advocates to seek changes in policies that harm the innocent loved ones of the incarcerated. They may be able to provide access to children support and advocacy resources in your area.

NATIONAL FATHERHOOD INITIATIVE

PO Box 126157, Harrisburg, PA 17112-6157
www.fatherhood.org

NFI develops and distributes resources to help men become better fathers in their children's lives. Write for further information.

NATIONAL PARENTS AND FAMILIES NETWORK (NIPFN)

PO Box 6745, Harrisburg, PA 17112
(717) 943-2492
www.incarceratedparents.org

NIPFN provides consulting and mentoring services for families that are affected by incarceration through workshops surrounding all aspects of life surrounding incarceration as well as assistance through reentry services.

NATIONAL ORGANIZATION OF PARENTS OF MURDERED CHILDREN (POMC)

4960 Ridge Ave., Suite 2, Cincinnati, OH 45209
www.pomc.org

POMC provides support and assistance to all survivors of homicide victims while working to create a world free of murder.

NATIONAL RESOURCE CENTER ON CHILD & FAMILY OF THE INCARCERATED

Rutgers University Camden, 405-7 Cooper St., #103, Camden, NJ 08102-1521
(856) 225-2718
www.nrccfi.camden.rutgers.edu

NRCCFI is an information resource for prisoners and their families who are affected by prison visitation, communication, reentry, and prison marriage issues. They do not provide any legal assistance.

OFFICE OF CHILD SUPPORT ENFORCEMENT

370 L'Enfant Promenade SW, Washington, DC 20447
www.acf.hhs.gov

The Office of Child Support Enforcement provides information to parents who face child custody issues, including application for child support services, modification of orders, incarceration-specific concerns, location of local state child support offices and more. (See more information on child support orders while behind bars in our Reference Center.)

POPS THE CLUB

4160 Lyceum Ave., Los Angeles, CA 90066
(310) 709-2484

www.popstheclup.com popsvenice@gmail.com

POPS the Club creates and supports clubs for students who are affected by the incarceration of a loved one. Through in-school (generally high school) clubs, they offer camaraderie, compassion, and community. POPs publishes the expressed writings and art of those affected in annual anthologies as a means of advocacy. Write for opportunities in your area.

PRISONMAIL.ORG

PO Box 1602, Altoona, PA 16603
(814) 742-7500
www.prisonmail.org

PrisonMail.org simplifies communication between imprisoned loved ones and their families to facilitate regular contact. Write for current services.

PRISONERS WITH CHILDREN

1540 Market St., Suite 490, San Francisco, CA 94102
(415) 255-7036
www.prisonerswithchildren.org

Prisoners With Children is part of the California Coalition for women Prisoners (see separate listing under California.) They provide legal materials based on California law, but will also provide some national information that may be helpful if not housed in California, including copies of the Jailhouse Lawyer's Manual. Send SASE for current listing of services.

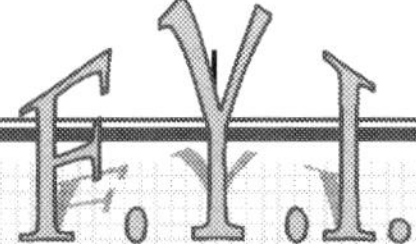

Child Support Orders While Behind Bars

Do you need to change your child support order due to your incarceration? The following in some vital information you'll want to know.

If I'm incarcerated, can I change my order?

States and counties have varied procedures to seek a three-year review to modify or suspend your order. Federal law requires states to review an order if the parent makes a request and shows that there has been a "substantial change in circumstances." In most states, you can ask to change your order if you are incarcerated. In only a few places, state law won't allow it. Unfortunately, some states consider incarceration as "voluntary unemployment." Contact your state or local child support agency to see what rules apply in your area. (If you do not have your local agencies address, write the Office of Child Support Enforcement)

Why is changing my child support order important? Can't I just wait until I am released?

Generally, child support orders can be changed when your ability to pay changes substantially. Child support programs rely on one of the parents to request the change in amount. Orders are not automatically reduced when you enter prison, even if you no longer have the ability to pay. Therefore, it is important that you contact your local child support office and ask for a change in the order. If you wait until you leave prison, you will owe the entire amount that built up while you were inside. You cannot change your order after the fact!

Federal prisoners: The Bureau of Prisons Program Statement, Inmate Financial Responsibility program, outlines procedures for Bureau staff to help you develop a financial plan and monitor progress in meeting obligations, including child support payments. To determine the amount owed, Bureau staff must have documentation such as a court order or judgment, or a letter with your obligation from a state child support enforcement unit.

What if I'm incarcerated in one state, but my child support order was issued in another state, or my children (or caregivers) live in another state?

If this is so, your case is called an "interstate' or "intergovernmental" case. Certain laws apply. All state, territorial, and trial child support agencies must address child support issues, including location and establishment of support obligations for children who live outside their borders. Contact the office where your child support order was established.

I live in a federal Residential Reentry Center (RRc0 -- what do I need to know about child support?

as a resident of an RRC, you are expected to pay both subsistence and child support. You are also expected to address your debts, including child support. When you arrive at RRC, inform the staff r counselor of your child support obligation, and inform the child support agency of your release and location.

You can request a change in the amount of subsistence to enable you to make your child support payments. The BOP must approve modification of the subsistence amount collected by the RRC. If the state garnishes your paycheck while you reside at an RRC, you and your case manager can request a modification in the amount of subsistence collected at any time during your designation to the RRC or Home Confinement.

Health Organizations

GENERAL HEALTH INFORMATION

CDC – NATIONAL PREVENTION INFORMATION NETWORK

PO Box 6003, Rockville, MD 20849-6003
(800) 458-5231, International: (404) 679-3860
www.cdcnpin.org info@cdcnpin.org

CDCNPIN is an information clearinghouse for reports, stats and other information pertaining to HIV/AIDS, STDs, and tuberculosis. They also maintain a database of up-to-date resources and services, educational materials, funding opportunities, and media releases on these issues. Write for listing of current publications available to prisoners.

CENTERS FOR MEDICARE AND MEDICAID SERVICES

7500 Security Blvd., Baltimore, MD 21244
(800) 633-4227
www.medicare.gov www.medicaid.gov

Government-sponsored health care for low-income families and individuals (Medicaid) and people 65 years of age and older, some younger people with disabilities, and those with permanent kidney failure (Medicare). Provides literature on services offered.

JUST DETENTION INTERNATIONAL

3325 Wilshire Blvd., Suite 340, Los Angeles, CA 90010
(213) 384-1400 (collect calls accepted)
www.justdetention.org

JDI is a health and human rights organization that seeks to end sexual abuse behind bars. They publish the *Resource Guide for Survivors of Sexual Abuse Behind Bars*, a state-by-state guide to legal and psychological counseling services for survivors who are incarcerated and their loved ones.

MEDICARE RIGHTS CENTER

520 8th Ave., North Wing, 3rd Floor, New York, NY 10018
(800) 333-4114
www.medicarerights.org

MRC works to access to affordable health care for older persons and individuals with disabilities. Provides a wide variety of education materials to those looking for accurate and reliable information on Medicare related issues.

NATIONAL COMMISSION ON CORRECTIONAL HEALTH CARE

1300 W. Belmont Ave., Chicago, IL 60657-3240

NCCHC publishes standards for health care in prisons. They train correctional staff and act as a clearinghouse for correctional health care information. Their newsletter, *Correctional Care*, is available for FREE to prison libraries.

NATIONAL HEALTH INFORMATION CENTER

PO Box 1133, Washington, DC 20013
(800) 336-4797
www.health.gov/nhic

NHIC provides the public and professionals locate health information through a comprehensive health resources database. Provides publications and directories on health and disease prevention topics.

PRISON HEALTH NEWS
c/o Philadelphia Fight, 1233 Locust St. 5th Floor, Philadelphia, PA 19107
www.fight.org
PHN is a quarterly newsletter for prisoners covering health news and information specific to prisoners, FREE to prisoners.

PRISON YOGA PROJECT

PO Box 415, Bolinas, CA 94924
www.givebackyoga.org/shop/prison-yoga-project-a-path-for-healing-and-recovery

Prison Yoga Project: A Path for Healing & Recovery is a 100-page yoga manual for prisoners, which focuses on self-reflection and personal discipline. It provides physical practice (asana), breathing (pranayama), and meditation (dyhana) techniques.

ALLERGIES/ ASTHMA

ASTHMA & ALLERGY FOUNDATION OF AMERICA

1233 20th St NW, Suite 402, Washington, DC 20036
(800) 727-8462
www.aafa.org

National clearinghouse for asthma and allergy information. Write for answers to any related questions.

ASTHMA & ALLERGY NETWORK

8229 Boone Blvd., #260, Vienna, VA 22182
(800) 878-4403
www.allergyasthmanetwork.org

Provides FREE information fact sheets ad pamphlets on asthma. Send for information and a FREE copy of *Allergy & Asthma Today* magazine.

ARTHRITIS

ARTHRITIS FOUNDATION

ATTN: CIC, 1330 W. Peachtree St. NW, #100, Atlanta, GA 30309
(404) 872-7100
www.arthritis.org

Provides FREE publications on arthritis, including *Coping with Arthritis, Managing Your Pain, Exercise & Arthritis,* (all available in English and Spanish), and *Back Pain, Drug Guide,* and *Walking Guide* (available in English only. Limit four pamphlets per request.

NATIONAL INSTITUTE OF ARTHRITIS & MUSCULOSKELETAL & SKIN DISEASES

National Institute of Health, 1 AMS Cir., Bethesda, MD 20892-3675
(877) 226-4267
www.naims.nih.gov

National clearinghouse for arthritis and skin disorder information. Write for FREE answers to any related questions.

CANCER

AMERICAN CANCER SOCIETY

250 Williams St. NW, Atlanta, GA 30303
(800) 227-2345
www.cancer.org

Provides FREE information and literature on specific cancers, treatments and support.

CANCERCARE

275 Seventh Ave., New York, NY 10001
(800) 813-HOPE (4673)
www.cancercare.org

Provides FREE literature on specific cancers and care. Write for more information.

CANCER SUPPORT COMMUNITY

1050 17th St. NW, #500, Washington, DC 20036
(888) 793-9355
www.cancersupportcommunity.org

Provides FREE fact sheets on specific cancers, treatments, side effects, and patient support.

NATIONAL CANCER INSTITUTE

6116 Executive Blvd., Room 3036A, Bethesda, MD 20892-8322
(800) 422-6327
www.cancer.gov

National clearinghouse for cancer information. Write for FREE answers to any related questions.

DIABETES

AMERICAN DIABETES ASSOCIATION

Attn: Center for Information, 1701 N. Beauregard St., Alexandria, VA 22311
(800) 342-2382
www.diabetes.org

Provides FREE literature on diabetes management, nutrition, exercise, medication and legal rights to diabetes care for prisoners.

JOSLIN DIABETES FOUNDATION

One Joslin Place, Boston, MA 02215
www.joslin.harvard.edu

JDF provides various research on diabetes in America and guides to assist those who have diabetes, including *The Joslin Guide to Diabetes: A Program for Managing your Treatment.*

NATIONAL DIABETES INFORMATION CLEARINGHOUSE

1 Information Way, Bethesda, MD 20892-3560
(800) 860-8747
www.diabetes.niddk.nih.gov

National clearinghouse for diabetes information. Write for FREE answers to related questions.

PRISONER DIABETES HANDBOOK

c/o Prison Legal News, PO Box 1151, Ft. Worth, FL 33460

37-page handbook about diabetes information and care. Free for prisoners.

HEPATITIS

HCV ADVOCATE

PO Box 15144, Sacramento, CA 95813
www.hcvadvocate.org

HCV Advocate offers information and fact sheets on Hepatitis C, including a monthly newsletter. Write for a FREE sample of the newsletter, (subscription is $12 per year.)

NATIONAL HEPATITIS PRISON COALITION

911 Western Ave., #302, Seattle, WA 98104
www.hcvinprison.org contact1@hcvinprison.org

NHPC is a coalition formed to educate prisoners of the dangers of hepatitis, treatment of the virus, the latest medical advancements and how prisoners can obtain cures. They distribute fact sheets and a biannual newsletter, FREE to prisoners upon request.

HIV / AIDS ORGANIZATIONS

Each year, 150,000 prisoners living with HIV/AIDS are released from prison. 1.25% of prisoners live with HIV/AIDS. Comparatively, 0.4% of free Americans live with it.

AIDS INFONET

PO Box 810, Arroyo Seco, NM 87514
www.aidsinfonet.org

Provides information fact sheets on HIV prevention and treatment (in English and 10 other languages). Write for FREE information. Request *Fact Sheet 1000* for a listing of all their available fact sheets, 802 in all.

CDC NATIONAL STD/HIV HOTLINE

(800) 232-4636, TTY: (888) 232-6348
www.cdc.gov/std cdinfo@cdc.gov

Hotline for information STDs and referrals to STD clinics.

CENTER FOR HEALTH JUSTICE

900 Avila St., #102, Los Angeles, CA 90012
(213) 229-0979 (prisoner hotline), (213) 229-0985
www.centerforhealthjustice.org

CHJ provides assistance to prisoners who have HIV/AIDS. They offer a FREE treatment hotline service that accepts collect calls from prisoners Mon-Fri 8AM – 3PM (PST).

NATIONAL MINORITY AIDS COUNCIL – PRISON INITIATIVE

1931 13th St. NW, Washington, DC 20009

MNAD – Prison Initiative provides HIV/AIDS education, technical assistance, and nationally advocacy programs. They publish materials for prisoners, case managers, and care providers. Write for HIV, prison resource guide, and other information.

POSITIVELY AWARE

5050 N. Broadway St., Chicago, IL 60640
(773) 989-9400
www.positivelyaware.com

PA is a national magazine containing current information on HIV/AIDS, including treatment, social issues, and financial and legal matters. FREE subscriptions to HIV+ prisoners. Complete issues can be downloaded from their website.

POZ MAGAZINE

462 Seventh Ave., 19th Floor, New York, NY 10018
(212) 242-2163
www.poz.com

POX is an advocacy magazine for people living with or affected by HIV/AIDS. 8 issues per year with an annual guide to HIV drugs. FREE to prisoners with HIV.

SERO PROJECT

PO Box 1233, Milford, PA 18337

The SERO Project against the criminal prosecution of those with HIV/AIDS for non-disclosure of HIV status, potential, or perceived exposure or HIV transmission. Write to join their network of prisoners with HIV or for information about HIV criminalization.

MENTAL HEALTH

> **FYI**
> **YOU CAN FIND MANY MORE MENTAL HEALTH RESOURCES IN OUR PRISON TRENDING CENTER**

MIND FREEDOM INTERNATIONAL

454 Willamette, Suite 216, PO Box 11284, Eugene, OR 97440-3484
(877) 623-7743
www.mindfreedom.org

MFI is an advocacy group that raises awareness for the rights of those with mental disabilities. There is no direct legal or medical aid offered, but they will send you advocacy and education material for FREE.

NATIONAL ALLIANCE ON MENTAL ILLNESS

3803 N. Fairfax Dr., Suite 100, Arlington, VA 22203
(703) 524-7600
www.nami.org

NAMI is the nation's largest mental health advocacy organization, which is dedicated to building better lives for the millions of Americans who have mental illness. Write for publications and other resources available to prisoners

NATIONAL INSTITUTE OF MENTAL HEALTH

6001 Executive Blvd., Room 8184, MSC93, Bethesda, MD 20892-9663
(866) 615-6464
www.nimh.nih.gov

NIMH is the national clearinghouse for mental health information. They can provide FREE answers to most mental health related questions, or provide referrals to where you can find additional information, services, or support.

WINGS BEYOND WALLS

PO Box 7019, Richmond, VA 23221
www.wingsbeyondwalls.wordpress.com

WBW matches prisoners with mental health concerns to non-judgmental pen pals. FREE to prisoners, but patience is appreciated, as it may take months to get a response.

ORGAN & TISSUE DONATION

> **GAVE**
> (971) 208-3879
> *www.gavelife.org* *info@gavelife.org*
> GAVE is an organization dedicated to advocating for prisoner's rights to donate healthy organs and tissues to those in need while incarcerated. They publish the book *Lethal Rejection: The Fight to Give Life from Prison & Other Pointlessly Forbidden Places*. b See more information in our *Health Center* under *Organ Donation*.

UNOS

UNOS, which stands for the United Network for Organ Sharing is the national database and organization that set the standards for organ matching and donation. Write for FREE information.

WOMEN'S HEALTH

ACLU – REPRODUCTIVE FREEDOM PROJECT

125 Broad St., 17th Floor, New York, NY 10004
(212) 549-2633
www.aclu.org/reproductiverights

The ACLU RFP provides support for issues related to reproductive rights and abortion. Contact should be made first through state affiliates. See our *State-by-State Resources* for an ACLU in your region.

> **LIVING & WELLNESS PROJECT**
> c/o Justice Now, 1322 Webster St., #210, Oakland, CA 94612
> *www.jnow.org*
> The LW Project provides literature on women's health concerns, including *Reproductive Health*, a 53-page manual, and *Navigating the Medical System*, a guide to prison health care in CA prisons. Write for FREE information.

NATIONAL ADVOCATES FOR PREGNANT WOMEN

15 W. 36th St., Suite 901, New York, NY 10018-7910
(212) 255-9252
www.advocatesforpregnantwomen.org

NAPW provides advocacy and support for pregnant incarcerated women, including legal support in civil and criminal cases, especially in cases related to medical issues related to pregnant women.

NATIONAL WOMEN'S HEALTH NETWORK

1413 K St., NW, 4th Floor, Washington, DC

(202) 682-2646
www.nwhb.org

NWHN provides literature on women's health concerns, including fibroids, osteoporosis, mammograms, hysterectomies, and others. Write for FREE information, or call Mon-Fri, 9 AM – 5 PM (EST)

WOMEN ORGANIZED TO RESPOND TO LIFE-THREATENING DISEASES

449 15th St., Suite 303, Oakland, CA 94612
(510) 986-0340
www.womenhiv.org

WORLTD provides information support to women living with HIV and other life-threatening diseases, including treatment information, advocacy tips, referrals, and a newsletter addressing these topics. Write with questions or their FREE quarterly newsletter.

Immigration Organizations

ADVOCATES FOR HUMAN RIGHTS

330 Second Ave. South, Suite 800, Minneapolis, MN 55401
(612) 341-9845 (Immigrant clients), (612) 746-4674 (Asylum hotline)
www.theadvocatesforhumanrights.org

AHR provides FREE legal assistance and services to immigrants seeking asylum who have been detained, trafficked, or abused in detention. Call for assistance, or encourage outside advocates to visit their website (available in Spanish, French, and English.)

ALLIANCE OF INCARCERATED CANADIANS/FOREIGNERS IN AMERICAN PRISONS

c/o NMB, 131 Bloor St. W, Suite 200, Toronto, Canada M5S 1R8

AICAP/AIFAP advocates for the rights of and provides assistance to foreigners who are incarcerated in U.S. prisons. Send an international SASE with a request for more information. Provide your country of origin, whether you have been denied a treaty transfer, and if you have an international detainer.

AMERICAN CIVIL LIBERTIES UNION | NATIONAL IMMIGRANTS RIGHTS PROGRAM

405 14th St., Suite 300, Oakland, CA 94612
(510) 625-2010
www.aclu.org

The National Immigrants Rights Program defends the civil rights of immigrants through litigation and education. They can provide specific resources in your area if you are facing immigration concerns.

END ISOLATION | COMMUNITY INITIATIVE FOR VISITING IMMIGRANTS IN CONFINEMENT

PO Box 40677, San Francisco, CA 94140
(385) 212-4842
www.endisolation.org/resources/for-families

End Isolation provides advocacy and assistance to immigrants through visitation, independent monitoring, storytelling, and more. Their website offers answers to basic immigration and detainee questions, detainer locator services, and family resource directories.

IMMIGRATION DETENTION JUSTICE CENTER

www.imigrationdetention.org

IDJC provides legal information and resources to immigrants facing deportation and incarceration. They also provide basic information to friends and family on the process of getting a loved one released from immigration detention, including immigration bonds, the removal process, the immigration court system, and finding an immigration attorney.

IMMIGRATION EQUALITY

40 Exchange Place, 17th Floor, New York, NY 10005
(212) 714-2904
www.immigrationequality.org

Immigration Equality provides information and support for LGBT and HIV-Positive immigrants.

NATIONAL IMMIGRANT JUSTICE CENTER

208 S. LaSalle St., Suite 1300, Chicago, IL 60604
(312) 660-1331
www.immigrantjustice.org

NIJC advocates for the rights of immigrants and promotes those rights through political reform and public education. Write for publications and information.

NATIONAL IMMIGRATION LAW CENTER

3435 Wilshire Blvd., #2850, Los Angeles, CA 90010
(213) 639-3900

NILW advocates for the rights of immigrants by providing information on immigration law and employment benefit rights. Request information on your specific issue, and ask for *Dream Act* information for your state.

NATIONAL IMMIGRATION PROJECT

National Lawyers Guild, 14 Beacon St., Suite 602, Boston, MA 02108
(617) 227-9727
www.nationalimmigrationproject.org

NIP provides immigration advocacy in five areas: criminal and deportation defense, victims of crimes and intimate partner violence, raids and immigration enforcement, non-citizens living with HIV/AIDS, and defending political rights. Write for more information if your need fits into one of these categories.

NATIONAL NETWORK FOR IMMIGRANT AND REFUGEE RIGHTS (NNIRR)

310 8th St., Suite 303, Oakland, CA 94609
www.nnirr.org

NNIRR works to defend the rights of immigrants. They provide a variety of information and support.

Legal Resources

F.Y.I.

Looking for legal resources?

There were too many to list here. You can find a wealth of legal resources and much more legal information in our *Legal Center* later in this book.

LGBTQ Organizations

ACLU – GET EQUAL

125 Broad Street, 18th Floor, New York, NY 10004-2400
(212) 549-2627
www.aclu.org/getequal

ACLU Get Equal is an LGBT and AIDS project established to advocate for the rights of those affected by these issues. They typically will only provide representation in class actions, but they may be able to provide you with information and referrals.

AMERICAN VETERANS FOR EQUAL RIGHTS (AVER)

PO Box 150160, Kew Gardens, NY 11415
(718) 849-5665
www.averny.tripod.com

AVER provides services for veterans who are members of the LGBT community, including assistance with benefits, advocacy, and political action.

BLACK & PINK

614 Columbia Rd., Dorchester, MA 02125
(617) 519-4387
www.blackandpink.org members@blackandpink.org

Black & Pink provides LGBT support and resources to prisoners, including pen pals, art programs, a FREE monthly newsletter, religious and erotic publications, and direct advocacy where possible

CENTER, THE | LGBT COMMUNITY CENTER

208 W. 13th St., New York, NY 10011
(212) 620-7310
www.gaycenter.org

The Center offers a number of connections to enable LGBT prisoners to find the assistance they need, including cultural, advocacy, recovery and mental health services.

CLAGS | CENTER FOR LGBT STUDIES

365 Fifth Ave., Room 7115, New York, NY 10016
(212) 817-9555
www.clags.org info@clags.org

CLAGS is a university-based LGBTQ research center committed to nurturing scholarship opportunities and networking among academics, artists, activists, policy makers, and community members with a focus on the LGBTQ community.

EQUALITY MATTERS

c/o Media Matters for America, PMB 512, Washington, DC 20001
www.equalitymatters.org

Equality Matters is a campaign for full gender and lifestyle equality nationwide.

FAMILY EQUALITY COUNCIL

PO Box 960510, Boston, MA 02196
(617) 502-8700
www.familyequality.org

Family Equality provides advocacy and services to LGBT parents and their families.

GAY & LESBIAN ADVOCATES & DEFENDERS (GLAD)

30 Winter St., #800, Boston, MA 02108
(800) 455-GLAD, (617) 426-1350
www.glad.org gladlaw@glad.org

GLAD provides advocacy and support of those in the LGBT community, including litigation, information, resources, and a hotline. Prisoners can call for legal information Mon-Fri 1:30-4:30 (EST).

GAY & LESBIAN ALLIANCE AGAINST DEFAMATION (GLAAD)

104 w. 29th St., 4th Floor, New York, NY 10001
(212) 629-3322
www.glaad.org glaad@glaad.org

GLAAD promotes fair and accurate representation of LGBT individuals to prevent discrimination.

GAY & LESBIAN MEDICAL ASSOCIATION (GLMA)

1326 18th St. NW, Suite 22, Washington, DC 20036
(202) 600-8037
www.glma.org info@glma.org

GLMA works to ensure healthcare equality for LGBT individuals.

GENDER IDENTITY CENTER OF COLORADO

1151 S. Huron St., Denver, CO 80223
(303) 202-6466
www.gic-colorado.org

GICC provides information on gender variant and

transgender issues. They publish a quarterly newsletter *T.I.P.*, FREE to prisoners.

GMHC

446 W. 33rd St., New York, NY 10001
(212) 367-1000
www.gmhc.org

GMHC is the world's leading provider of HIV/AIDS prevention advocacy and information. They host several projects for the rights of those living with HIV, including the Lesbians with AIDS project. Write for more information or resources.

HIV LAW PROJECT

15 Maiden Lane., New York, NY 10038
(212) 557-3001
www.hivlawproject.org info@hivlawproject.org

HIV Law Project provides civil legal services for HIV-positive individuals in the New York area, as well as some support nationally.

HUMAN RIGHTS CAMPAIGN

1640 Rhode Island Ave. NW, Washington, DC 20036-3278
(800) 777-4723, (202) 628-4160
www.hrc.org

HRC is the nation's largest LBGTQ civil rights organization. They provide advocacy for the rights of the LGBTQ community. Write for more information.

IMMIGRATION EQUALITY

40 Exchange Place, 17th Floor, New York, NY 10005
(212) 714-2904
www.immigrationequality.org
info@immigrationequality.org

Immigration Equality represents LGBT asylum seekers, detainees, and bi-national couples who are fighting for safety, fair treatment, and freedom.

INTERNATIONAL FOUNDATION FOR GENDER EDUCATION

PO Box 540229, Waltham, MA 02454-0229
(781) 894,8340, (781) 899-2212
www.ifge.org info@ifge.org

IFGE provides resources to educate and promote acceptance of all sexual orientations.

INTERNATIONAL GAY & LESBIAN HUMAN RIGHTS COMMISSION (IGLHRC)

80 Maiden Lane, Suite 1505, New York, NY 10038
(212) 430-6054
www.iglhrc.org iglhrc@iglhrc.org

IGLHRC advocates for the advancement of human rights to end discrimination based on sexual orientation, gender identity, or gender expression.

LAMBDA LEGAL

120 Wall St., 19th Floor, New York, NY 10005
(866) 542-8336
www.lambdalegal.org

LL provides legal services for those discriminated against based on sexual orientation, gender identity/expression, and HIV, which could significantly advance the rights of LGBT people and those with HIV. Other cases may be discussed or referred to other assistance providers. Write for FREE information on transgender rights, including *Transgender Prisoners in Crisis,* available in English and Spanish.

LAGAI-QUEER INSURRECTION

3543 18th St., Suite 26, San Francisco, CA 94110
(510) 434-1304
www.lagai.org

LAGAI provides advocacy and education for radical social change for LGBT rights. Publishes and distributes *Ultraviolet*, a bi-monthly newsletter, FREE for prisoners.

MATTHEW SHEPARD FOUNDATION

800 18th St., Suite 101, Denver, CO 80202
(303) 830-7400
www.matthewshepard.org

The Matthew Shepard Foundation advocates against hatred by replacing it with understanding, compassion and acceptance. Through national outreach, they assist by addressing the bias in challenging communities.

MARRIAGE EQUALITY USA (MEUSA)

PO Box 121, Old Chelsea Station, New York, NY 10113
(347) 913-6369
www.marriageequality.org

MEUSA is a national organization that fights for marriage equality for all couples and their families through education and organizing.

MIDWEST TRANS PRISONER PEN PAL PROJECT

c/o Boneshaker Books, 2022 23rd Ave. South, Minneapolis, MN 55404

MTPPP reaches out to LGBT prisoners and provides correspondence and support opportunities.

NATIONAL CENTER FOR LESBIAN RIGHTS

870 Market St., #370, San Francisco, CA 94102
(415) 392-6257
www.nclrights.org/legal-help-resources

NCLR provides information on laws the affect LGBT people and ways to protect them against rights abuses.

NATIONAL CENTER FOR TRANSGENDER EQUALITY

1400 16th St. NW, Suite 510, Washington, DC 20036
(202) 642-4542
www.transequality.org ncte@transequality.org

NCTE provides information for all transgender people.

NATIONAL COALITION FOR LGBT HEALTH

2000 S St. NW, Washington, DC 20009
(202) 507-4727
www.healthlgbt.org coalition@lgbthealth.net

The National Coalition for LGBT Health advocates for the health rights of LGBT individuals through research, education, policy and training.

NATIONAL GAY & LESBIAN TASK FORCE

1325 Massachusetts Ave. NW, Suite 600, Washington, DC 20005
(202) 393-5177
www.thetaskforce.org thetaskforce@thetaskforce.org

The National Gay & Lesbian Task Force fights to improve the rights of LGBT individuals to bring about lasting change and opportunity for all.

PARENTS FAMILY AND FRIENDS OF LESBIANS & GAYS (PFLAG)

1828 L St. NW, Suite 660, Washington, DC 20036
(202) 467-8180
www.pflag.org

PFLAG advocates and promotes acceptance for the LGBT community, including legislative and educational initiatives, and support for family and friends of LGBT people. They have chapters across the U.S. Write for a list of a branch in your region.

POINT FOUNDATION | NATIONAL LGBTQ SCHOLARSHIP FUND

Los Angeles: 5055 Wilshire Blvd., Suite 501, Los Angeles, CA 90036
New York: 1357 Broadway, Suite 401, New York, NY 10018
(323) 933-1234, (866) 33-POINT
www.pointfoundation.org

The Point Foundation assists those within the LGBTQ community with higher education opportunities including scholarships, mentoring, leadership development, and community service training.

PRISONER CORRESPONDENCE PROJECT

QPIRG Concordia, Concordia University, 1455 de Maisonneuve O, Montreal, QC H3G 1M8 Canada
www.prisonercorrespondenceproject.com
info@prisonercorrespondenceproject.com

PCP provides pen pals and correspondence opportunities for LGBT prisoners in the U.S. write for more information. Requires international postage.

QUEER DETAINEE EMPOWERMENT PROJECT

252 Java St. #237, Brooklyn, NY 11222
(347) 645-9339
www.qdep.org info@qdep.org

QDEP is an alternative to detention program for LGBT and HIV-positive detainees who are currently seeking status in the U.S. and who are in or are being released from immigration detention centers.

SAGEWORKS

305 7th Ave., 15th Floor, New York, NY 10001
(212) 741-2247 ext. 224
www.sageusa.org/programs/sageworks.cfm

SAGEWorks provides national employment support for those in the LGBT community who are 40 or older including technology training, job placement and workshops at various centers around the country.

SINISTER WISDOM

PO Box 3252, Berkeley, CA 94703
www.sinisterwisdom.org

SW provides information and a literary journal FREE to women prisoners.

SYLVIA RIVERA LAW PROJECT

147 W. 24th St., 5th Floor, New York, NY 10011
(212) 337-8550
www.srlp.org info@srlp.org

SRLP provides direct legal representation for low-income transgender people, including a *Prisoner Rights Project* that assists in the following areas: Name changes, obtaining trans-affirming health care, assistance with safety issues, advocacy for gender-affirming placement and conditions, reentry assistance, and criminal history checks.

TRANSFORMATIVE JUSTICE LAW PROJECT OF ILLINOIS

4707 N. Broadway, Suite 307, Chicago, IL 60640
(773) 272-1822
www.tjlp.org info@tjlp.org

TJLP is a coalition of activist including radical attorneys, social workers and community organizers who are committed to prison abolishment, gender-determination and other issues pertaining to the LGBT community. Provides FREE legal services to transgender and gen non-conforming people targeted by the criminal justice system. They also offer a FREE bimonthly magazine, *Hidden Expressions,* which encourage trans prisoners to express themselves through stories, art, recipes, and other sendings.

TRANSGENDER, GENDER-VARIANT & INTERSEX JUSTICE PROJECT

370 Turk St., Suite 370, San Francisco, CA 94102
(415) 252-1444
www.tgijp.org info@tgijp.org

TGIJP supports transgender people through information and advice, including a newsletter, resource guide, and survival guide FREE to Transgender prisoners. They publish the *Stiletto Prison Newsletter* and the 72-page *Still We Rise: Prison Resource Guide,* FREE to all TGI prisoners. *TGIJP* offers some reentry services to TGI ex-offenders in the San Francisco Bay area.

TRANSGENDER LAW CENTER – LEGAL INFORMATION HELPLINE

1629 Telegraph Ave., #400, Oakland, CA 94612
(510) 380-8229 (collect calls accepted)
www.transgenderlawcenter.org

TLC provides basic information on laws that affect transgender people, including health care, civil rights, family law, and ID changes. They not offer legal advice, but may review your case and refer to TLC.

TRANSGENDER LEGAL DEFENSE & EDUCATION FUND

20 W. 20th St., Suite 705, New York, NY 10011
(646) 862-9396
www.tldef.org info@transgenderlegal.org

TLDEF advocates for transgender civil rights and provides legal assistance to transgender people who have been discriminated against because of their gender identity or expression.

TRANZMISSION PRISON BOOKS

PO Box 1874, Asheville, NC 28801

TPB offers FREE books and other resources to LGBTQIA prisoners.

VICTORY FUND

1133 15th St. NW, Suite 350, Washington, DC 20005
(202) 842-8679
www.victoryfund.org

Prison Publications

Looking for more prisoner publications?

You can find additional listings offering prisoner newsletters and other publications related to more specific topics throughout the book.

Anti-Establishment

4STRUGGLE MAGAZINE

PO Box 97048, RPO Roncesvalles Ave., Toronto, Ontario, M6R 3B3 Canada
www.4strugglemag.org

4Struggle is a "anti-imperialist" publication that supports "progressive national liberation." Each issue, published three times annually, typically contains a few main articles as well as essays, poems, and art, featuring articles by political prisoners in the U.S. concerning improvement of prison conditions and system injustice. FREE subscriptions, but stamps are appreciated.

NEWS & LETTERS

228 S. Wabash Ave., Suite 230, Chicago, IL 60604
(312) 431-8242
www.newsandletters.org

News & Letters is a bimonthly "Marxist-Humanist" newspaper that features articles by prisoners who sympathize with the newspaper's ideals of the abolition of capitalism. FREE to prisoners.

RESIST NEWSLETTER | RESIST

259 Elm St., Suite 201, Somerville, MA 02144
(617) 623-5110
www.resistinc.org

Resist Newsletter is a bi-monthly newsletter focused on social justice issues. They have a suggested donation price of $25/year, but they will send copies FREE of charge to indigent prisoners.

SLINGSHOT MAGAZINE

3124 Shattuck Ave., Berkeley, CA 94705
(510) 540-0751 ext. 3
www.slingshot.tao.ca

Slingshot is a quarterly newspaper that contains radical ideals on a variety of topics. FREE to prisoners.

UNDER LOCK & KEY | MIM

PO Box 40799, San Francisco, CA 94140
www.prisoncensorship.info

Under Lock & Key is a monthly newspaper produced by MIM, a "revolutionary anti-imperialist" group that fights the criminal justice system, and especially the censorship within. They help organize prisoners through its pages and through other publications. FREE to prisoners.

Education

EDUCATION BEHIND BARS

www.prisoneducation.com news@prisonlawblog.com (Corrlinks)

Education behind Bars is a FREE bimonthly online/email newsletter for prisoner-students and prison educators. Publishes writings on prisoner rights and education. CorrLinks registered users and receive a three-times weekly education news update.

PRISONER EXPRESS

127 Anabel Taylor Hall, Cornell University, Ithaca, NY 14853
(607) 255-6486
www.prisonerexpress.org alt-lib@cornell.edu

Prisoner Express is a biannual newsletter designed to promote prisoner rehabilitation through education and engaging programs that prisoners can actively participate in, including art, writing, poetry, journaling and much more. They also offer a used book program. Send $4, or 8 stamps, to receive a package of 4-6 books in your chosen genre.

General/Prisoner Publications

BEAT WITHIN

275 Ninth St., San Francisco, CA 94103
(415) 503-4170
www.thebeatwithin.org

The Beat Within is a monthly magazine that presents writings and art from juvenile prisoners, with editorial commentary on each piece. FREE to prisoners.

CELL DOOR MAGAZINE

Mid-September to June: 12200 Road 41.9, Mancos, CO 81328
July to mid-September: 6 Tolman Rd., Peaks Island, ME 04108
www.celldoor.com publisher@celldoor.com

Cell Door is a bi-monthly magazine written mostly for prisoners. They display prisoner works, such as art and writings and includes news, essays, humor, fiction and case information.

CRY JUSTICE NEWS

PO Box 2525, New Bloomfield, MO 65063

Cry Justice News publishes serious articles on issues affecting prisoners, as well as prisoner poetry and art.

FAMM-GRAM

1612 K St. NW, Suite 700, Washington, DC 20006
www.famm.org famm@famm.org

FAMM-gram is a 3-times annually e-newsletter published for families of those incarcerated, which advocates for fair sentencing practices in the criminal justice system. [Not a print publication.]

GRATERFRIENDS | PENNSYLVANIA PRISON SOCIETY

245 N. Broad St., Suite 300, Philadelphia, PA 19107

Graterfriends is a monthly newsletter that provides a platform for prisoners and the community to voice their opinions and concerns about the criminal justice system. Focuses on PA prisons. Subscriptions are $5 per year for prisoners.

JOURNAL OF PRISONERS ON PRISONERS

542 King Edward Ave., Ottawa, Ontario, Canada K1N 6N2
www.jpp.org jpp@uottawa.ca

Journal of Prisoners on Prisoners is an annual publication, FREE to prisoners. They seek submissions from prisoner writers, including papers, collaborative essays, interviews, book reviews, and photo or graphic essays. No fiction or poetry. Write for more info. Publishes articles in French and English.

PRISON FOCUS NEWSLETTER | CALIFORNIA PRISON FOCUS

1904 Franklin St., Suite 507, Oakland, CA 94612
www.prisons.org

Prison Focus Newsletter is a quarterly newsletter by and for prisoners and their families, covering various aspects of prison life. Donations of $20 per year are recommended to help cover publishing/shipping costs. Issues are available online.

PRISON INFORMATION NETWORK

PO Box 165171, Salt Lake City, UT 84165

Prison Information Network is a bimonthly newsletter that covers a broad range of topics affecting prisoners. FREE to prisoners.

UNSTOPPABLE!

PO Box 11032, Pueblo, CO 81001

Unstoppable is a newsletter that covers life in prison, including surviving, self-care, building community and more. They encourage prisoner art and writing submissions for possible publication. Write for a FREE subscription.

Health

PRISON HEALTH NEWS | PHILADELPHIA FIGHT

1233 Locust St., 5th Floor, Philadelphia, PA 19107
(215) 985- 4448
www.fight.org

PHN is an informative quarterly 12-page newsletter that focuses on prisoner health information. FREE to prisoners upon request.

Legal/Innocence

CORRECTIONAL LAW REPORTER | CIVIC RESEARCH INSTITUTE

PO Box 585, Kingston, NJ 08528
(609) 683-4450
www.civicresearchinstitute.com

Correctional Law Reporter is a comprehensive bimonthly legal publication that covers developments in correctional law and recent court developments. $179.95 per year.

FLORIDA PRISON LEGAL PERSPECTIVES

PO Box 1151, Christmas, FL 32709

Florida Prison Legal Perspectives is a bimonthly newsletter that covers prison legal news for the Florida region, FREE to prisoners.

GEORGETOWN LAW JOURNAL | ANNUAL REVIEW OF CRIMINAL PROCEDURE (ARCP)

600 New Jersey Ave. NW, Washington, DC 20001-2075
(202) 662-9457
www.law.georgetown.edu
criminalprocedure@law.georgetown.edu

The ARCP is a comprehensive annual summary of criminal justice-related legal actions. Each year's edition is published in the summer of the following year and cost $25. Older editions are available at the same price. For prisoners who are indigent, and can provide proof of indigency through prison account statement, they will send a complimentary copy of an older edition, pending availability (currently the 2010 edition).

JUSTICE QUARTERLY | ROUTLEDGE

325 Chestnut St., 8th Floor, Philadelphia, PA 19106
(800) 354-1420
www.tnfonline.com support@tnfonline.com

Justice Quarterly is a quarterly academic journal featuring articles approved by the Academy of Criminal Justice Services (ACJS). $75 per year and includes a membership to the ACJS.

PRISON JOURNAL | SAGE PUBLICATIONS

2455 Teller Rd., Thousand Oaks, CA 91320
(800) 818-7243

The Prison Journal is an international publication that features in-depth articles on issues affecting prisoners and criminal justice, as well as features on emerging trends and developments in the world of corrections.

RAZOR WIRE | NOVEMBER COALITION

282 W. Astor, Colville, WA 99114

Razor Wire is a quarterly newsletter that reports on the drug war in America and its effect on prisoners in this country. $6 per year for prisoners ($25 for others.)

Lifers/Death Row

CALIFORNIA LIFER NEWSLETTER

PO Box 277, Rancho Cordova, CA 95741
(916) 402-3750
www.lifesupportalliance.org

California Lifer Newsletter is a comprehensive bi-monthly newsletter containing information specific to prisoners in CA and around the nation. It contains reviews of the latest published and unpublished state and federal cases concerning parole issues, legislation, statistics, and information on correctional issues around the nation. Each issue is 50-70 pages. Subscriptions are $35 to prisoners, or 60 stamps. $99/ for others.

COMPASSION

140 West South Boundary St., Perrysburg, OH 43551

Compassion is a bi-monthly newsletter written for and by death row prisoners. FREE to death row prisoners.

CURE LIFE-LONG

665 W. Willis St., Suite B-1, Detroit, MI 48201
(313) 442-3629

CURE Life-Long publishes a quarterly "lifer's" newspaper that covers topics of interest to prisoners with sentences of more than 25 years. $5 per year for prisoners.

LIFER-LINE | LIFE SUPPORT ALLIANCE

PO Box 277, Rancho Cordova, CA 95741
(916) 402-3750
www.lifesupportalliance.org'

Lifer-Line is a FREE monthly online newsletter with a focus towards issues affecting life-term prisoners. Copies may be mailed in to prisoners based on the availability of funds. Donations are appreciated.

LIFELINES | NATIONAL COALITION TO ABOLISH THE DEATH PENALTY

1750 DeSales St. NW, Fifth Floor, Washington, DC 20036
(202) 331-4090

Lifelines is a sporadic newsletter published by the NCADP addressing issues concerning the death penalty. It is not regular, but it is FREE to prisoners upon request.

VOICES.CON

PO Box 361, King City, CA 93930
www.voicedotcon.org

Voices is a monthly newsletter written by lifers for lifers. Send SASE for more information.

Newspapers

ANGOLITE

Louisiana State Penitentiary, Angola, LA 70712
www.corrections.state.state.la.us/lsp/angolite.htm
support@prisontalk.com

The Angolite is a monthly newspaper that is published and edited for and by prisoners in the Louisiana State Penitentiary in Angola. $20 per year.

SAN QUENTIN NEWS

1 Main St., San Quentin, CA 94964
www.sanquentinnews.com

The *San Quentin News* is a monthly 20-page newspaper written, edited, and produced by San Quentin prisoners. They encourage prisoners and others outside to send articles, art and poetry for possible inclusion in the newspaper. $1.61 per issue, but they request $4 a donation of $40 or more per year to help cover the costs of publishing/mailing. Stamps are accepted as payment.

Prison Reform

COALITION FOR PRISONERS' RIGHTS

PO Box 1911, Santa Fe, NM 85704
www.realcostofprisoners.org
info@realcostofprisoners.org

Coalition for Prisoners' Rights provides information and resources for prisoners upon request. They publish a 2-page monthly newsletter of national prison news. Send SASE for every month you would like to receive a copy. Back issues are available from their website.

COMMUNITY, THE

PO Box 100392, Milwaukee, WI 87504
thecommunitywis.wix.com/home
thecommunitywis@gmail.com

The Community is a nonprofit bimonthly newsletter written for and by prisoners and is devoted to anti-mass incarceration advocacy and finding better criminal justice alternatives through community. Currently focuses mostly on Wisconsin. Write to be included on their mailing list. Subscriptions are FREE, but donations are appreciated.

PRISON LEGAL NEWS

PO Box 1151, Lake Worth, FL 33460
(561) 360-2523
www.prisonlegalnews.org,
info@prisonlegalnews.org

Prison Legal News is a comprehensive monthly publication that focuses on prisoner rights and provides prisoner-related news, summaries of recent court decisions affecting prisoners and analysis of prison issues across the country. $30/yr for prisoners. Also distributes many prisoner-focused publications. Write for a complete list or see ads in this issue.

Reentry

FORTUNE NEWS | THE FORTUNE SOCIETY

29-76 Northern Blvd., Long Island City, NY 11101
(212) 691-7554
www.fortunesociety.org info@fortunesociety.org

Fortune News is a quarterly publication dedicated to prisoner advocacy, education, and successful reentry. FREE to prisoners.

Religious

(The following are religious publications specifically designed for prisoners. You can find many more general religious publication's listings in our Religion Center)

CROSSROAD JOURNAL OF THE ARTS | CROSSROAD BIBLE INSTITUTE

PO Box 900, Grand Rapids, MI 49509

Crossroad Journal of the Arts is a FREE bimonthly newsletter published by prisoners for prisoners, which contains articles art and poetry. Submissions are encouraged.

DHARMA GARDEN

1 Fairtown Lane, Taneytown, MD 21787
dharmagardensangha@gmail.com

Dharma Garden is a FREE quarterly Buddhism-based newsletter. Submissions of articles, artwork, poetry and fiction are encouraged.

FISHERS OF MEN PRISON MINISTRIES

5403 N. Second St., Loves Park, IL 61111
(815) 633-7508

www.prisonministry.net.fompm

Fishers of Men Prison Ministries publishes a FREE monthly Christian-based newsletter for prisoners. hey encourage prisoners to submit stories -- fiction and nonfiction -- personal essays and poetry about God.

INSIDE JOURNAL | PRISON FELLOWSHIP

44180 Riverside pkwy., Lansdowne, VA 20176
(800) 251-7411
www.pfm.org insidejournal@pfm.org

Inside Journal is a FREE Christian-based newspaper published by Prison Fellowship that teaches the Gospel in a way that prisoners can relate. It includes inspirational stories and practical guidance

GOOD-NEWS LETTER | JOY WRITER'S MINISTRY

2001 Liberty Square Dr., Cartersville, GA 30121

Good-News Letter is a FREE Christian-based newsletter. Submissions of poetry and articles are encouraged.

PRISON JOURNAL

6041 Watch Chain Way, Columbia, MD 21044-4107
theprisonjournal@gmail.com

[Not to be confused with the Sage Publications magazine of the same title!] *The Prison Journal* is a faith-based publication that published prisoner works in their pages, including art, poetry and other writings, without restrictions on professional standards.

PRISONWORLD MAGAZINE | DAWAH INTERNATIONAL LLC

PO Box 380, Powder Springs, GA 30127
(678) 233-8286
dawahinternationalllc@gmail.com

Prisonworld Magazine is a bimonthly Muslim-based entertainment magazine with a format similar to the National Inquirer. $5 per year. All proceeds go towards prison outreach programs.

YARD OUT | PRISONERS FOR CHRIST OUTREACH MINISTRIES

PO Box 1530, Woodinville, WA 98072
www.pfcom.org

Yard Out is a FREE three-times annually released Christian-based newsletter that contains prison-related articles and stories. Submissions of poetry and articles are encouraged.

Veterans

VETERANS ADVOCATE | NATIONAL VETERANS LEGAL SERVICES

PO Box 65762, Washington, DC 20035
(202) 265-8305

Veterans Advocate is a newsletter focused on veteran's issues, including advocacy, law, and lifestyle. $80 per year ($120/2 years.)

Women

FIRE INSIDE | CALIFORNIA COALITION FOR WOMEN PRISONERS

1540 Market St., Suite 490, San Francisco, CA 94102
(415) 255-7036 ext. 4
www.womenprisoners.org info@womenprisoners.org

The Fire Inside is a biannual newsletter giving women prisoners a platform to discuss issues specific to them, FREE to prisoners. They encourage writings and art from women prisoners.

Prison Reform Organizations

Anti-Mass Incarceration

The following organizations seek to end mass-incarceration through advocacy for changes in criminal justice policy and by informing the public and prisoners in the system.

BRENNAN CENTER FOR JUSTICE | NEW YORK UNIVERSITY SCHOOL OF LAW

New York office: 161 Avenue of the Americas, 12th Floor, New York, NY 10013
Washington, DC office: 1140 Connecticut Ave NW, 11th Floor, Suite 1150, Washington, DC 20036
(606) 292-8310
www.brennancenter.org brennancenter@nyu.edu

The *Brennan Center for Justice* Program seeks to secure the nation's promise of "equal justice for all' by creating a rational, effective, and fair justice system. Its primary focus is to reduce mass incarceration while keeping down crime by conducting research and analysis, crafting policies, and advocating for reform.

CENTER FOR CRIMINAL JUSTICE REFORM | AMERICAN CONSERVATIVE UNION FOUNDATION

1331 H Street NW, Suite 500, Washington, DC 20005
(202) 347-9388
www.acufoundation.conservative.org

CCJR advocates for criminal justice policy change. Their website provides a variety of links to other anti-mass incarceration organizations and projects.

CENTER FOR NULEADERSHIP ON URBAN SOLUTIONS

510 Gates Ave., First Floor, Brooklyn, NY 11216
(718) 484-5879
www.centerfornuleadership.org
info@centerfornuleadership.org

The Center for Nuleadership provides research, advocacy and leadership training to prisoners, ex-offenders, their families and criminal justice professionals to promote active participation in reforms and criminal justice policy.

COMMUNITY, THE

PO Box 100392, Milwaukee, WI 87504
thecommunitywis.wix.com/home
thecommunitywis@gmail.com

The Community is a nonprofit bimonthly newsletter written for and by prisoners and is devoted to anti-mass incarceration advocacy and finding better criminal justice alternatives through community. Currently focuses mostly on Wisconsin. Write to be included on their mailing list. Subscriptions are FREE, but donations are appreciated.

CRITICAL RESISTANCE

1904 Franklin St., Suite 504, Oakland, CA 94612
(510) 444-0484
www.criticalresistance.org

CR is an advocacy group that seeks to build an international movement to end mass incarceration. They publish *The Abolitionist*, a tri-annual newspaper FREE to prisoners.

FAMILIES AGAINST MANDATORY MINIMUMS (FAMM)

1612 K St., NW #700, Washington, DC 20006
(202) 822-6700
www.famm.org famm@famm.org

FAMM advocates changing mandatory minimum sentencing laws. They can provide information about mandatory minimum laws and how to fight against them. Published newsletter *FAMM-Gram*, FREE to prisoners. Contributions appreciated.

HUMAN RIGHTS COALITION

1213 Race St., Philadelphia, PA 19107
(215) 496-9661
www.hrcoalition.org info@hrcoalition.com

HRC advocates against mass incarceration and for prisoner rights, giving voice to families of prisoners. They publish a bimonthly newsletter, *The Movement*, ($12 for prisoners) as well as the HRC Legal Pamphlet series and other pamphlets available online. They focus mainly on Pennsylvania, but can lend some support to other states. See separate Pennsylvania listing.

HUMAN RIGHTS DEFENSE CENTER

PO Box 1151, Lake Worth, FL 33460
(561) 360-2523
www.humanrightsdefensecenter.org
www.prisonlegalnews.org

HRDC is a prisoner rights defense organization that litigates for free speech, public records, wrongful death cases. They also advocate on behalf of prisoners and their families in various forums, such as legislatures, news media, protest events, administrative agencies, conferences and more. HRDC publishes *Prison Legal News* (see separate listing.) They appreciate donations to help defray the costs of the considerable litigation they do on behalf of prisoners.

JUSTICE & MERCY

PO Box 223, Shillington, PA 19607
(610) 208-0406
www.justicemercy.org

Justice & Mercy advocates for cost-effective and practical reforms within the criminal justice system, as well as supports and encourages wise public policy.

JUSTICE POLICY INSTITUTE

1012 14th St. NW, Suite 600, Washington, DC 20005
(202) 558-7974
www.justicepolicy.org

UI's *Justice Policy Center* publishes materials showing the effect of mass-incarceration on cities in the U.S. and advocates to change criminal-justice policy. They provide a comprehensive online resource containing other criminal justice reform efforts.

MARSHALL PROJECT, THE

156 W. 56th St., Suite 701, New York, NY 10019
(212) 803-5200
www.themarshallproject.com
info@themarshallproject.com

The Marshall Project is a nonpartisan online journalism organization that focuses on criminal justice issues in the U.S. Prisoner editorial/opinion writings can be submitted for possible publication on their site. Generally no more than 800 words.

NATIONAL CENTER ON INSTITUTIONS & ALTERNATIVES (NCIA)

7222 Ambassador Rd., Baltimore, MD 21244
(410) 265-1490
www.nciante.org

NCIA works to reduce the reliance on incarceration by utilizing alternatives to imprisonment such as community service, addressing substance abuse problems, and by using third-party monitors. They offer presentence investigative services, parole release advocacy, and public information on criminal justice matters.

PRISON ACTIVIST RESOURCE CENTER (PARC)

PO Box 70477, Oakland, CA 94612
(510) 893-4648
www.prisonactivist.org info@prisonactivist.org

PARC raises awareness for the challenges of racism and classism within the criminal justice system. Provides a resource directory FREE to upon request.

PRISON POLICY INITIATIVE

PO Box 127, Northampton, MA 01061
www.prisonpolicy.org

PPI provides information and resources on issues affecting prisoners and the criminal justice system, including listings of legal resources for prisoners by state. Most resources are only available online.

SENTENCING AND JUSTICE REFORM ADVOCACY (SJRA)

Box 71, Olivehurst, CA 95961
(530) 329-8566
www.sjra1.com yeswecanchange3x@aol.com

SJRA produces a sentencing reform advocacy newsletter, available on their website. Send SASE for more information.

SENTENCING PROJECT, THE

1705 DeSales St. NW, 8th Floor, Washington, DC 20036
(202) 628-0871
www.sentencingproject.org
staff@sentencingproject.org

SP provides technical assistance and support services to criminal justice reform initiatives, including developing alternative sentencing programs and conducting research on criminal justice issues. They have a huge online resource list of other criminal justice reform sites and services. They do not offer any direct services to prisoners.

TURN2YOU | THE LAST MILE

717 Market St., Suite 100, San Francisco, CA 94103
www.thelastmile.org info@thelastmile.org

The Last Mile works inside prisons to offer prisoners entrepreneurial training and on-the-job instruction. They currently operate programs in six California prisons, such as the Code.7370 web/app development school where participants are paid real wages (currently $16.77 an hour) to learn and code computer programs. In 2017, they will offer programs in prisons outside of California.

URBAN INSTITUTE

2100 M St. NW, Washington, DC 20037
(202) 833-7200
www.urban.org

The Urban Institute provides information and analysis to public and private decision makers to help them address challenges within the criminal justice system and other challenging areas of our nation. They help individuals understand the issues and tradeoffs in policymaking that affects change.

Phone Reform

ETC | CAMPAIGN TO PROMOTE EQUITABLE TELEPHONE CHARGES

c/o Michigan CURE, PO Box 2736, Kalamazoo, MI 49003

eTc campaigns nationally for prison phone system reform and provides comprehensive information on current reform efforts.

PRISON LEGAL NEWS

PO Box 1151, Lake Worth, FL 33460
www.prisonlegalnews.org
ptsolskas@prisonlegalnews.org

PLN regularly publishes information about phone reform and other prison profiteering information, such as on the high rates for money transfer services and fees. They fund their fight for reform through subscription sales of the *Prison Legal News*. Subscribe today. $30 per year for prisoners.

WASHINGTON PHONE JUSTICE CAMPAIGN

c/o HRDC, PO Box 1151, Lake Worth, FL 33460
(877) 410-4863
www.wappj.org

WAPPJ focuses primarily on Washington state prison phone system reforms and video visitation issues. But they can provide information on other state reform efforts.

Your Phone Calls Will Get Cheaper Soon... Maybe

If you are housed in Ohio, New Jersey, or Pennsylvania, consider yourselves very fortunate, at least as far as prison phone rates are concerned. Thanks to the efforts of the Human Rights Defense Center (HRDC) and others, the Federal Communications Commission (FCC) has finally gotten involved to begin ordering caps on the amount that these phone companies charge for phone call from prison.

Some states, such as the ones mentioned above, have proactively reduced their rates. Others, such as Alabama and Louisiana, are currently undergoing regulation by their state's utility commissions. But the rest are stubbornly waiting until they are forced to change by FCC requirements.

The first of the FCC regulations occurred in February 2014. Out-of-state collect calls were capped at $0.25, while debit and prepaid calls could cost no more than $0.21. A year later, in October, the FCC announced rate caps on in-state calls of $0.11 per minute. This time, however, the prison phone companies, backed by several state and corrections officials, revolted by filing an appeal with the federal government to prevent the rate reduction from happening.

In September, 2016, the FCC entered a revised order for $0.13 per minute in an effort to compromise so that price reductions would not remain stalled in court. The prison phone companies renewed their appeal and have refused to budge.

It is expected that the court will acknowledge the right of the FCC to protect citizens from excessive phone rates. What's more, U.S. Senator Bernie Sanders has introduced legislation to regulate rates once and for all.

CURRENT PRISON PHONE COSTS (& KICKBACKS)

State	Kickback to prison system	Current rate	Rank (from cheapest)
Federal	NA	$3.75	42nd
Alabama	3,000,000	$3.75	42nd
Alaska	85,000	$3.75	42nd
Arizona	4,300,00	$3.60	38th
Arkansas	2,000,000	$4.80	47th
California	NA	$2.03	24th
Colorado	2,000,000	$1.80	22nd
Connecticut	4,200,000	$4.87	48th
Delaware	1,000,000	$3.20	36th
Florida	5,100.000	$2.10	26th
Georgia	5,300,000	$2.55	31st
Hawaii	100,000	$3.55	37th
Idaho	1,400,00	$1.65	15th
Illinois	13,000,000	$3.63	40th
Indiana	1,700,000	$3.60	38th
Iowa	700,000	$1.65	15th
Kansas	1,800,00	$2.70	32nd
Kentucky	2,800,000	$5.70	50th
Louisiana	3,000,000	$2.44	30th
Maine	370,000	$4.50	46th
Maryland	5,000,000	$5.15	49th
Massachusetts	1,700,000	$1.50	13th
Michigan	NA	$3.00	34th
Minnesota	3,700,000	$0.75	8th
Mississippi	1,700,000	$1.65	15th
Missouri	NA	$1.75	20th
Montana	220,000	$2.04	25th
Nebraska	NA	$1.45	12th
New	300,000	$0.68	5th
New Jersey	NA	$0.66	4th
New Mexico	NA	$0.65	3rd
New York	NA	$0.72	7th
North Carolina	6,800,000	$1.50	13th
North Dakota	98,000	$6.06	51st
Ohio	NA	$0.75	8th
Oklahoma	1,000,000	$3.00	34th
Oregon	3,000,000	$2.40	28th
Pennsylvania	7,600,000	$0.89	10th
Rhode Island	NA	$0.70	6th
South Carolina	NA	$1.65	15th
South Dakota	500,000	$1.20	11th
Tennessee	2,600,000	$2.40	28th
Texas	7,000,000	$3.90	45th
Utah	800,000	$2.85	33rd
Vermont	400,000	$1.76	21st
Virginia	3,400,000	$0.62	2nd
Washington	5,000,000	$1.65	15th
West Virginia	1,000,000	$0.48	1st
Wisconsin	2,300,000	$1.80	22nd
Wyoming	600,000	$3.72	41st
Wyoming	600,000	$3.72	41st

It's only a matter of time before rates finally come down.

Of course, the phone companies won't just accept the rate caps. They've already begun securing their positions in the money transfer and video visitation businesses. They'll try to get their money somehow. But efforts are being made to prevent them from doing so.

You can join in these efforts. Here's how:

If you or your loved ones are forced to pay extreme fees to use the phone, to deposit money on your prison account, or fees to use pre-paid debit cards upon release, tell the ones who are working to stop this practice all about it.

Write in detail how this is affecting you and your loved ones and send it to the address below. They want to hear from you.

PRISON LEGAL NEWS

Attn: Panagioti Tsolkas
PO Box 1151
Lake Worth, Florida 33460
Or have friends and family email, call, or go to the websites below:
ptsolkas@PrisonLegalNews.org
(561) 360-2523
www.StopPrisonProfiteers.org
www.PrisonPhoneJustice.org
www.PhoneJustice.org

SEE CURRENT PRISON PHONE RATES IN OUR PRISON CENTER!

Prison Service Providers

The following companies provide services directly to prisons, such as phone service, tablets, canteen and more.

For a listing of services provided to prisoners, visit the *Prisoner Service Center* section of this book.

ACCESS CATALOG COMPANY

10880 Lin Page Place, St. Louis, MO 63132
(866) 754-2812
www.keefegroup.com

Access Catalog Company sells a variety of prison-friendly products to prisons and through prison-approved packages for family and friends to purchase for loved ones.

ACCESS CORRECTIONS

St. Louis, MO
(866) 345-1884
Idaho Customer Service: (855) 745-3414
www.accesscorrections.com
customerservice@accesscorrections.com

AC provides email communication solutions for prisoners through a kiosk system and in-cell MP3 players. Also provides payment solutions. Subsidiary of Keefe Group.

AMERICAN PRISON DATA SYSTEMS

601 W. 26th St., Suite 325, New York, NY 10001
(646) 592-1072
www.apdscorporate.com
information@apdscorporate.com

APDS provides communication services to prisons around the country. They specialize in the development of tablets that prisoners use for education and entertainment purposes.

CORRLINKS | INMATE EMAIL SYSTEM

www.corrlinks.com

Corrlinks provides FREE email communication solutions for federal prisoners and some states. States serviced: parts of Arizona, Texas, and the entire federal system.

EMMA'S PREMIUM SERVICES

162 Washington Ave., Edison, NJ 08817
(888) 638-9994
www.emmaspremiumservices.com

Emma's Premium Services provides commissary package options for New York area prisons, specializing in fresh fruits and vegetables, steak, turkey and lobster. They hope to expand to surrounding states in the near future.

GLOBAL TELLINK (GTL) | TOUCHPAY HOLDINGS, LLC

www.gtl.net

GTL is the largest provider of communication services to prisons for prisoners. Services include phone and video visitation systems and in-cell tablet options.

HOMEWAV

(877) 241-7559
www.homewav.com info@homewav.com

Provides communication services to prisons for prisoners.

JPAY

12864 Biscayne Blvd., Suite 214, Miami, FL 33181
(800) 574-5729
www.jpay.com

JPay provides communication and payment services for prisoner's family and friends. Services include email services, tablets, email, and direct payment methods. *JPay* was just acquired by *Securus*, one of the nation's largest prison phone service providers.

KEEFE COMMISSARY NETWORK

Box 17490, St. Louis, MO 63178-7490

(866) 754-2812
www.keefegroup.com

Keefe Commissary Network is the subdivision of Keefe Group that works directly with prison administration for the orderly operation of prison canteens.

KEEFE GROUP

10880 Lin Page Place, St. Louis, MO 63132
(800) 325-8998
www.keefegroup.com

Keefe Group is the nation's leader in prisoner products and services. Most prison canteens use them as a wholesaler for everything from deodorant to shoes. They also provide communications services through *Access Corrections, ATG* and ICSolutions, including email, tablets, money deposits, phone systems, and more. They offer the *Access Catalog*, containing prison canteen-friendly products, FREE upon request.

SECURE ELECTRONICS

5569 Route 9 West, Building 1, Marlboro, NY 12542
(570) 704-3451
www.s-celectronics.com

Secure Electronics produces and supplies clear electronics and accessories to prisons and prisoners. Send SASE for a catalog and more information.

SECURUS

Securus is one of the nation's largest prison phone service providers. They recently acquired JPay.

SHIP A PACKAGE

33 William St., Suite 8A, Auburn, NY 13021
(800) 918-9352
www.shipapackage.net

Ship A Package supplies care packages to the New York area. Write for a FREE catalog.

TELMATE

PO Box 1137, Fruitland, ID 83619
www.gettingout.com

Telmate provides communication services to prisons for prisoners. Services include phone systems, kiosk systems (VIP) for video visitation, commissary ordering and messaging, tablet systems for in-cell communication and entertainment, and trust deposits.

WALKENHORSTS

540 Technology Way, Napa, CA 94558
(800) 660-9255
www.walkenhorsts.com

Walkenhorsts is the nation's largest catalog service that supplies prison-approved food and products. Many prison systems use them as outsourced commissary system. It is a good source to learn what products are available to prisoners around the country. Catalog is FREE.

Reentry Organizations

Looking for more reentry organizations?

You can find additional reentry organizations and listings located in your area in the *State-by-State Resources* section of this book.

AID TO INMATE MOTHERS

PO Box 986, Montgomery, AL 36101-0986
(800) 679-0246, (334) 262-2245
www.inmatemoms.org

AIM provides reentry services for ex-offending moms who are between 18 and 24 months of their release date, including release planning, educational programs, monthly visitation arrangements with their children, family outreach, and case management for up to a year after release.

ALL OF US OR NONE OF US

Legal Services for Prisoners with Children, 1540 Market St., #490, San Francisco, CA 94102
(415) 255-7036 ext. 337
www.allofusornone.org

AUNU is a coalition of prisoners and ex-offenders established to combat the discrimination many ex-offenders face when reentering society. They will typically not answer prisoner's letters, but family and friends can learn more about involvement in local or national campaigns through their website.

AMERICAN PROBATION & PAROLE ASSOCIATION (APPA)

PO Box 11910, Lexington, KY 40578
(859) 244-8203
www.appa-net.org

APPA acts as a clearinghouse for information, ideas, training, standards and models for post-prison supervision.

CIRCLES OF SUPPORT

www.circlesofsupport.org

Circles of Support provides ex-offenders with a support network of volunteers to provide guidance in all areas of their reentry.

CORPORATION FOR SUPPORTIVE HOUSING (CSH)

50 Broadway, 17th Floor, New York, NY 10004
(212) 986-2966
www.csh.org

CSH assists organizations that provide transitional housing by providing high-quality advice and development expertise, facilitating financial support for housing sponsors, and reforming public policy to create and operate supportive housing.

EDPUBS

PO Box 22207, Alexandria, VA 22304
(877) 433-7827
www.edpubs.gov edpubs@edpubs.gov

EDPUBS is a U.S. government information and referral service that provides resource information on community reentry programs, including education, drug and alcohol support services, employment assistance, housing, counseling and more.

FAIRSHAKE REENTRY RESOURCE CENTER

PO Box 63, Westby, WI 54667
(608) 634-6363
www.fairshake.net sue@fairshake.net

Fairshake is a web-based national reentry resource center that provides comprehensive reentry information to prisoners and their families. If you are releasing soon, they will provide you with helpful reentry documents to assist in your transition.

FEDERAL BONDING PROGRAM

c/o The McGlaughlin Co., 9210 Corporate Blvd., Suite 250, Rockville, MD 20850
(202) 293-5566

FBP is a business insurance policy that protects employers in case of losses due to employee dishonesty, which is provided for any at-risk applicant, such as ex-offenders, whose background may otherwise discourage employers to hire them.

FEDERAL BUREAU OF PRISONS – INMATE TRANSITION BRANCH

320 First St. NW, Washington, DC 20534
(202) 353-3598
www.bop.gov

The *FBP's Inmate Transition Branch* administers several reentry related programs and services designed to enhance a successful transition into society, including UNICOR. They publish the *Employment Information Handbook*, FREE to prisoners, which contains information on how to prepare for release, what kinds of employers will hire ex-offenders, where to get financial assistance, training programs, and other basics needed for life outside of prison.

GOODWILL INDUSTRIES - NATIONAL

15810 Indianola Dr., Rockville, MD 20855
(800) 644-3945
www.goodwill.org

Goodwill Industries has hundreds of locations nationwide that provide reentry services, including job training, housing assistance, and shelter services. Write for listings of services in your area.

GRADUATE GROUP, THE

PO Box 370351, West Hartford, CT 06137-0351
(860) 233-2330
www.graduategroup.com, graduategroup@hotmail.com

GG publishes and distributes prisoner reentry focused publications, including *Opportunities for Newly Released Offenders*, an in-depth guide for prisoners about to reenter society ($22). Write for current list of publication. Stamps accepted as payment.

HABITAT FOR HUMANITY

Habitat & Church Streets, Americus, GA 31709
www.habitatforhumanity.org

HFH builds homes for the poor in 400 communities across the country. They accept applications for both volunteering and assistance. If you volunteer for them, you may qualify for housing and living assistance.

IMPACT PUBLICATIONS

9104-N Manassas Dr., Manassas Park, VA 20111
(703) 361-7300

IP publishes a series of handbooks for ex-offenders, including *Best Jobs for Ex-Offenders, Ex-Offender's 30/30 Job Solution, Ex-Offender's Job Interview Guides, Ex-Offender's Job Interview Guide, Ex-Offender's Quick Job Hunting Guide, Ex-Offender's Reentry Success Guide, and the Reentry Employment* and *Life Skills Pocket Guide.* Write for a listing of more current titles and an order form.

In 2016, IMPACT released updated versions of their titles: The Ex-Offender's New Job Finding & Survival Guide (240 pages, $19.95), 99 Days to Reentry Success Journal, 2nd Edition (64 pages, $4.95), and The Ex-Offender's Reentry Assistance Directory (227 pages, $29.95)

JOB ACCOMMODATION NETWORK (JAN) | WEST VIRGINIA UNIVERSITY

PO Box 6080, Morgantown, WV 26506-6080
(800) 526-7232 TTY: (877) 718-9403
www.askJAN.org

JAN is a program by the U.S. Department of Labor that provides employment resources for those with disabilities, including information, counseling, and referral services, as well as information on small business development and self-employment.

LEGAL ACTION CENTER

www.lac.org/roadblocks-to-reentry

LAC offers an online state-by-state database of resources for reentering prisoners who face reentry barriers due to criminal records.

MILES OF FREEDOM

milesoffreedom.org

Miles of Freedom offers a comprehensive system of support to ex-offenders based on spiritual, mental, physical, and emotional mechanics, including temporary employment in house construction and lawn care.

NATIONAL HIRE NETWORK

Legal Action Center, 225 Varick St., New York, NY 10014
(212) 243-1313
www.hirenetwork.org

National HIRE network stands for *National Helping Individuals with Criminal Records Re-enter through Employment Network.* It is a clearinghouse for information and advocacy for policy change to increase the number of jobs available to ex-offenders. Write for services available in your region.

NATIONAL REENTRY RESOURCE CENTER

100 Wall St., 20th Floor, New York, NY 10005
(877) 332-1719
www.cjsnationaljusticecenter.org/nrrc

NRRC is a comprehensive online reentry resource center. They offer a variety of both national and state-by-state resources accessible through their website.

NONPROFIT CAREER NETWORK

PO Box 912, Essex, CT 06426-0912
(860) 767-1424
www.nonprofitcareer.com nonprofitcareer@comcast.net

The Nonprofit Career Center is a one-stop resource center for nonprofit organizations as well as employment and volunteer opportunities available within these organizations.

OPEN, INC. (OFFENDER PREPARATION & EDUCATION NETWORK)

PO Box 472223, Garland, TX 75047-2223
(800) 966-1966, (972) 271-1971
www.openinc.org info@openinc.org

OPEN offers FREE self-help handbooks and educational materials to help ex-offenders make the best transition into society and family life. Distributes *99 Days and Get*

Up, a reentry guide covering the 6-month pre- and post-release plan.

NATIONAL EMPLOYMENT LAW PROJECT (NELP)

75 Maiden Lane, Suite 601, New York, NY 10038
(212) 285-3025
www.nelp.org nelp@nelp.org

NELP advocates for and promotes policies and programs that create job opportunities, worker's rights, and improved benefits and services. They work on the broad scale issue and do not assist individuals.

PRISON ENTREPRENEURSHIP PROGRAM

PO Box 926274, Houston, TX 77292-6274
www.prisonentrepreneurship.org

PEP is an education and reentry program that connects prisoners with successful business people to teach them professional and entrepreneurial skills, including a 5-month business concepts, theory, and a presentation & networking course. Graduates receive extensive reentry support, including job skills training, career counseling, transportation, professional clothing, referrals and introductions to professional business executives, and more. For those participants who take an entrepreneurial path, they receive extensive consultation support and networking assistance. Must be within 3 years of release, have a clean disciplinary record, and have no gang affiliations or history of sexual convictions.

PRISONER REENTRY INSTITUTE | JOHN JAY COLLEGE OF CRIMINAL LAW

524 W. 59th St., Room 600BMW, New York, NY 10019
(212) 621-3792
www.johnjaypri.org/category/research-and-publications

The Prisoner Reentry Institute provides the prisoner reentry guide, Back to School: A Guide to Continuing Your Education After Prison (2015, 63 pages), FREE to prisoners. Other publications are available. write for a current listing.

SALVATION ARMY – NATIONAL

615 Slaters Lane, PO Box 269, Alexandria, VA 22313
(800) 728-7725
www.salvationarmyusa.org

The *Salvation Army* has hundreds of locations nationwide that provide reentry services, including housing vouchers, shelter services, meals, clothing, and other essential reentry needs. Write for a listing of services in your area.

SEVENTH STEP FOUNDATION – INTERNATIONAL HQ

101-1009 7th Ave., SW, Calgary, Alberta Canada T2P 1AB

The *7th Step Foundation* provides reentry services and assistance in becoming a productive member of society through various support services. Write to locate a local chapter and services in your region.

STEP-UP, INC.

983 Ingleside Rd., Norfolk, VA 23502

Step-Up provides parole preparation and pre-release services to offenders and those reentering society from any prison system or local jail. Write for more information and services available in your region.

STRIVE

715 I St. NE, Washington, DC 20002
(202) 484-1262

STRIVE is a program that provides job training and job retention skills, and assists program participants in their job search. Write for program listings in your region.

TEMPORARY EMPLOYMENT AGENCIES

Temporary employment agencies provide a means of employment immediately upon release. The following national offices of temporary employment agencies can be contacted in advance of reentry to learn the requirements and offices in your area.

KELLY SERVICES

999 W. Big Beaver Rd., Troy, MI 48084
(248) 362-4444
www.kellyservices.com

LABOR FINDERS INTERNATIONAL

11426 N. Jog Rd., Palm Beach Gardens, FL 33418
(561) 627-6502
www.laborfinders.com

MANPOWER GROUP

100 manpower Place, Milwaukee, WI 53212
(414) 961-1000

www.manpower.com

USAJOBS

(478) 757-3000
www.usajobs.opm.gov

USAJOBS is the federal government's one-stop source of federal employment information. They offer several downloadable resources such as how to apply for jobs, resume building, and job location.

U.S. DEPARTMENT OF LABOR

Francis Perkins Building, 200 Constitution Ave. NW, Washington, DC 20210
(866) 487-2365
www.dol.gov

DOL is the U.S. governments clearinghouse for all employment related data and statistics. They will provide information on employment and training programs available for ex-offenders, people with disabilities, veterans and others.

U.S. GOVERNMENT PRINTING OFFICE

PO Box 100, Pueblo, CO 81002
(202) 512-1800

The *U.S. GPO* is the printing source for all U.S. government information to the public. For reentry services, they offer the *Occupational Outlook Handbook* and the *Career Guide to Industries*, as well as the *Occupational Outlook Quarterly*, a quarterly publication designed to keep job-seekers apprised of employment developments. (See separate listing containing details of other publications at the end or the National Resource Listings at the front of this section.)

VOLUNTEERS OF AMERICA

1660 Duke St., Alexandria, VA 22314
(202) 512-1800
www.volunteersofamerica.org

VA provides emergency services and resources to ex-offenders and their families, including employment training, technical assistance, clothing, tools, food and more. Write for a listing of services in your region.

WELCOME HOME MINISTRIES

1701 Mission Ave., Trailer A, Oceanside, CA 92054
(760) 439-1136
www.welcomehomeint.org

WH Ministries is a national faith-based program that provides reentry support for women ex-offenders, including reunification with children, education, job support, and more.

Felon-Friendly Employers

Below is a list of over 150 employers who have made it known that they will hire felons. This does not necessarily mean that they will hire YOU, the need for qualifications still apply. This is simply a resource that you can comfortably seek employment from, despite your criminal record.

Felon-friendly employers come and go. Just because you do not see a company you'd like to work at on this list, do not assume that they will not hire felons.

Aamco
Ace Hardware
Advance Auto Parts
Albertsons
Allied Van Lines
American Greetings
Anderson Windows
Apple
Applebees
Aramark
AT&T
Avon Products
Bahama Breeze
Baskin-Robbins
Bed, Bath & Beyond
Best Western
Black & Decker
Blue Cross & Shield
Braums
Bridgestone
Buffalo Wild Wings
Campbell's Soup
Canon
Carl's Jr.
Carrier Corporation
Caterpillar
CEFCO
CDW
Chick-fil-A
Chili's
Chipotle
Chrysler
Cintas
Colgate-Palmolive
Community Education Centers
ConAgra Foods
Copart
Costco
Dairy queen
Dart Containers
Deer Park Spring Water
Delta Faucets
Denny's
Dillards
Dole Food Company
Dollar Rent-a-Car
Dollar Tree
Divizio Industries
Dr. Pepper
Dunlop Tires
Dunkin' Donuts
DuPont
Duracell
Eddie V's Prime Seafood
Einstein Bros. Bagels
Embassy Suites
Epson
ERMCO
Family Dollar
Firestone Auto Care
Flyng J (Pilot)
Food Service of America
Foot Locker
Frito-Lay
Fruit of the Loom
Fujifilm
Genetech
General Electric
General Mills
General Motors
Georgia-Pacific
Golden Corral
Goodman
Goodwill
Grainger
Great Clips
Greyhound
Hanes
Harris Teeter
HH Gregg
Holiday Inn
Home Depot
IBM
IHOP
Ikea
In-N-Out Burger
International Paper
Interstate Batteries
Jack in the Box
J. B. Hunt Transport
Jiffy Lube
Jimmy Johns
K-Mart
Kelly Moore Paints
KFC
Kohl's
Kraft Foods
Kroger
Labatt Food Services
Longhorn Steakhouse
Lowes
LSG Sky Chefs
McDonald's
Men's Warehouse
Metal's USA
Michaels
Miller Brewing Company
Motorola
New York Times
NFI
Nordstrom
O'Charleys
Olive Garden
Pactiv
Papa John's
Pappadeaux
PepsiCo
PetSmart
PFS
Phillip Morris
Pilgrim's
Praxair
Preferred Freezer Services
Radisson
Ralph's
RC Willey
Red Lobster
Red Robin
REI
Republic Services
Restaurant Depot
Reyes Beverage Group
Rubbermaid
Ruby Tuesday
Rumpke
Safeway
Safelite
Salvation Army
Sara Lee
Sears
Seasons 52
Shell Oil
Shoprite
Smash Burger
Sonic Drive-In
Sony
Subway
Sysco
Teleperformance
Tesla
Toys "R" Us
Trader Joes
Tyson Foods
United Healthcare
US Foods
US Military
US Steel Corporation
Volunteers of America
Walgreens
Waste Connections
Wendy's
WinCo Foods
Wyndham Hotels
Xerox

Rehabilitation Organizations

AL-ANON FAMILY GROUP

1600 Corporate Landing Pkwy., Virginia Beach, VA 23454
(757) 563-1600
www.al-anon.org

Al-Anon Family Group provides support to family and friends who are recovering from the effects of someone else's drinking.

ALCOHOLICS ANONYMOUS

PO Box 459, New York, NY 10163
(212) 870-3400
www.aa.org

AA provides recovery support and FREE information and publications to prisoners suffering from alcohol addiction. They offer meetings in most prison communities. Write for a listing of services in your region.

ASSOCIATION FOR THE TREATMENT OF SEXUAL ABUSERS (ATSA)

4900 SW Griffith Dr., Suite 274, Beaverton, OR 97005
(503) 643-1023
www.asta.com

ASTA provides advocacy and research for the prevention and treatment of sexual abuse. They maintain a comprehensive database of treatment providers and organizations that assist individuals with the treatment of sexually abusive behaviors.

CURE-SORT

PO Box 1022, Norman, OK 73070-1022
(405) 639-7262
www.cure-sort.org

CURE-SORT provides support services to individuals affected by sexual abuse and helps those who are recovering from related addictions. They offer FREE information on registry and residency laws. *The Neighborhood Guide,* provides information on conducting meeting and addressing concerns of residents as a part of a positive reentry process, $5 for those on the sex offender registry.

NARCOTICS ANONYMOUS

PO Box 9999, Van Nuys, CA 91409
(818) 773-9999
www.na.org

NA provides rehab support services for those suffering from narcotics addictions, including FREE publications concerning addiction and recovery, such as the monthly newsletter, *Reaching Out*. They offer meetings in most prison communities. Write for a list of publications and services in your region.

NATIONAL ASSOCIATION OF SHOPLIFTING PREVENTION

225 Broadhollow Rd., Suite 400E, Melville, NY 11747
(631) 923-2737
www.shopliftingprevention.org

NASP provides information to offenders to educate them on the effects of shoplifting on the economy, community, and local businesses.

NATIONAL SUICIDE PREVENTION LIFELINE

(800) 273-8255

REFORM SEX OFFENDER LAWS

PO Box 400838, Cambridge, MA 02140
www.nationalrsol.org

RSOL advocates for evidence-based laws, a law-enforcement-only offender registry, rehabilitation, and the successful reintegration of law-abiding offenders into society. Publishes a monthly newsletter, *The Digest*, for $9 per year.

SAFER SOCIETY FOUNDATION, THE

PO Box 340, Brandon, VT 05733-0340
(802) 247-3132
www.safersociety.org

SSF advocates and supports efforts for the prevention of sexual abuses through treatment referrals for sex-offenders, education and literature. They publish adult sex-offender workbooks and related titles for purchase.

SEX ADDICTS ANONYMOUS

PO Box 70949, Houston, TX 77270
(800) 477-8191
www.saa-recovery.org info@saa-recovery.org

SAA provides a spiritual-based recovery program for sex addicts, based on the principles and traditions of Alcoholics Anonymous.

Religion Resources

Looking for religion resources?

There are too many to print here, so visit our *Religion Center* later in the book.

Veteran's Organizations

Looking for more veteran's resources?

Additional veteran's listings can be found under each state in the *State-by-State Resources* section of this book.

AMERICAN LEGION

1608 K St. NW, Washington, DC 20006
(202) 861-2700
www.legion.org

The *AL* provides support services to veterans, including assisting veterans in obtaining benefits through Veteran's Affairs, job placement and education opportunities. Write for services available in your region.

DEPARTMENT OF VETERAN'S AFFAIRS

810 Vermont Ave. NW, Washington, DC 20420
(800) 827-1000 (VA benefits)
(888) 442-4551 (GI Bill)
(877) 222-8387 (Health care benefits)
(888) 492-7844 (Mammography helpline)
(800) 749-8387 (Toxic issues, such as Agent Orange and Gulf War Syndrome)
www.va.gov

The *VA* is the national support and information clearinghouse for veteran's affairs related materials and services.

DISABLED AMERICAN VETERANS

National HQ: 3725 Alexandria Pike, Cold Spring, KY 41076
(877) 426-2838
Legislative HQ: 807 Maine Ave. SW, Washington, DC 20024
(202) 554-3501
www.dav.org

DAV offers support and resources to disabled veterans, including information and other services. Write for listing of services and programs in your region.

NATIONAL ARCHIVES AND RECORDS ADMINISTRATION

Military Personnel Records, 1 Archives Dr., St. Louis, MO 63138
(314) 801-0800
www.nara.gov

NARA supplies military service records upon requests of veterans. FREE to vets. Write for records, providing military ID# and last duty station.

NATIONAL ASSOCIATION OF BLACK VETS (NABVETS)

Appeal Office, 1612 K St. NW, Suite 202, Washington, DC 20006
(866) 548-7303, (202) 547-0000
www.nabvets.org

NABVETS provides support service for African American veterans. Write for list of services available in your region.

NATIONAL COALITION FOR HOMELESS VETS

333½ Pennsylvania Ave. SE, Washington, DC 20003
(800) 838-4357, (877) 424-3838
www.nchv.org nchv@nchv.org

NCHV provides information and support for homeless veterans and ex-offenders, including community based service providers and literature, such as *Planning for Your Release: A Guide for Incarcerated Vets*, FREE upon written request.

NATIONAL GULF WAR RESOURCE CENTER

1725 SW Gage Blvd., Topeka, KS 66604
(866) 531-7193
www.ngwrc.org www.ngwrc.net

NGWRC provides advocacy, education, and support for veterans suffering from Gulf War Illness, traumatic brain injury, and PTSD. Write for support guide and other FREE information. 'Forgotten Warriors' of *Desert Shield through Operation Southern Watch* are encouraged to share experiences through their website.

NATIONAL VETERANS FOUNDATION

5777 Century Blvd., Suite 350, Los Angeles, CA 90045
(888) 777-4443 (9 AM to 5 PM (PST))
www.nvf.org/veterans

National Veterans Foundation is a non-governmental resource that provides advice and assistance to veterans. Their *Lifeline for Vets* toll-free service assists veterans in finding resources in their area or nationally on a wide variety of veterans' issues, including mental health, benefits, health care, financial problems, housing, employment, family counseling, and many others.

NATIONAL VETERANS LEGAL SERVICES PROGRAM (NVLSP)

2001 S Street NW, Suite 610, Washington, DC 20009
(202) 265-8305
www.nvlsp.org

NVLSP publishes a comprehensive Veteran's Benefits Manual (updated annually, 1,900 pages). $158.

TRILOGY INTEGRATED RESOURCES

1101 Fifth Ave., Suite 250, San Rafael, CA 94801
(415) 458-5900
www.networkofcare.org
nocinformation@networkofcare.org

TIR is a data provider for information affecting veterans. Write with questions on any topic affecting veterans.

VETERAN'S ADMINISTRATION

Eastern Region: PO Box 4616, Buffalo, NY 14240-4616
(Services: DE, DC, ME, NH, NY, OH, PA, VT, and WV)
Southern Region: PO Box 100022, Decatur, GA 30031-7022 (Services: AL, FL, GA, MS, NC, SC, and Puerto Rico)
Central Region: PO Box 66830, St. Louis, MO 63166-6830 (Services: CO, IA, IL, IN, KS, KY, MI, MN, MO, MT, NE, ND, SD, TN. WI, and WY)
Western Region: PO Box 88, Muskogee, OK 74402-8888 (Services: AL, AZ, CA, HI, ID, LA, NM, NV, OK, TX, UT, and WA)

VETERAN'S BENEFITS CLAIMS ASSISTANCE

East of Mississippi River: PO Box 11432, Milwaukee, WI 53211
West of Mississippi River: 5515 Steilacoom Blvd. SW, Suite 105, Lakewood, WA 98499

VBCA addresses the benefits needs of minority and economically disadvantaged veterans.

VETERAN'S CONSORTIUM | PRO BONO PROGRAM

2101 L St. NW, Suite 420 Washington, DC 20037
(888) 838-7727, (202) 265-8305
www.vetsprobono.org www.nvlsp.org

Veteran's Consortium Pro Bono Project assist veteran's whose benefits have been denied by the Board of Veterans' Appeals. If case is being appealed to the U.S. Court of Appeals, they will review the case for FREE representation. A "Request Representation" form can be downloaded from their website. They also offer a newsletter, *The Veteran's Advocate.* ($90/year or $120 for two years.)

VETJOBS.COM

PO Box 71445, Marietta, GA 30007-1445
(877) 838-5627, (770) 903-5117
www.vetjobs.net

VETjobs hosts the largest database of employees who want to hire vets. They also offer career advice. Write for a list of services available in your region.

Women's Resources

ACLU – REPRODUCTIVE FREEDOM PROJECT

125 Broad St., 17th Floor, New York, NY 10004
(212) 549-2633
www.aclu.org/reproductiverights

The *ACLU RFP* provides support for issues related to reproductive rights and abortion. Contact should be made first through state affiliates. See our *State-by-State Resources* for an ACLU in your region.

ACLU – NATIONAL WOMEN'S RIGHTS PROJECT

125 Broad St., 17th Floor, New York, NY 10004
(212) 549-2633
www.aclu.org/womensrights

ACLU NWR provides advocacy and representation for women through education, representation, and community outreach. They focus on poor women, women of color, and women who have been victimized by gender bias and who have to fight for equality.

BATTERED WOMEN'S JUSTICE PROJECT – NATIONAL CLEARINGHOUSE

125 S. 9th St., Suite 302, Philadelphia, PA 19107
(800) 903-0111 ext. 3, (215) 351-0010
www.bwjp.org www.ncdbw.org

BWJP provides support services to battered women who have been charged with crimes, including, assisting legal defenses and supplying information. They assist advocates for women who have injured or killed their batterers in self-defense, battered women who have been coerced into criminal activity, and women charged with failing to protect their children for the batterers' violence. They do not offer direct representation. They have a FREE newsletter.

CENTER ON WRONGFUL CONVICTIONS – WOMEN'S PROJECT

Northwestern University School of Law, 375 E. Chicago Ave., Chicago, IL 60611-3069
(312) 503-2391
www.law.northwestern.edu/wrongfulconvictions/women

CWC provides advocacy and representation for wrongfully convicted women prisoners. They also raise public awareness to ensure similar injustices are not repeated.

CHICAGO BOOKS TO WOMEN IN PRISON | RFUMC

4511 N. Hermitage Ave., Chicago, IL 06040
www.chicagobwp.org chicagobwp@gmail.com

Chicago BWP provides FREE paperback books to women in prison nationwide (except Texas). Write with your genre preference. See for additional FREE books to prisoners in our *Service Center* later in this book.

ESSIE JUSTICE GROUP

340 Pine St., Suite 302, San Francisco, CA 64104
(415) 321-2046
www.essiejusticegroup.org

EJG advocates for the end of mass incarceration through a community of women with incarcerated loved ones. Write for current programs, including their *Healing to Advocacy* curriculum.

FAMILIES UNITED FOR RADICAL & ECONOMIC EQUALITY

81 Willoughby St., #701, Brooklyn, NY 11201
(718) 852-2960
www.furee.org

FUREE organizes low-income families to make changes in the economic system so that everyone is equal, regardless of social status or race. They are comprised almost exclusively by women of color.

FUERZA UNIDA

710 New Laredo Hwy., San Antonio, TX 78211
www.lafuerzaunida.org

FU is a women's group that assists families find justice through advocacy, organization, and education.

LIVING & WELLNESS PROJECT

c/o Justice Now, 1322 Webster St., #210, Oakland, CA 94612
www.jnow.org

The *LW Project* provides literature on women's health concerns, including *Reproductive Health*, a 53-page manual, and *Navigating the Medical System*, a guide to prison health care in CA prisons. Write for FREE information.

HASTING'S WOMEN'S LAW JOURNAL

U.C. Hastings College of Law, 200 McAllister St., San Francisco, CA 94102-4707 www.hastingswomenslj.org

HWLJ is a publication that focuses on the legal landscape and criminal justice system as they pertain to women. They seek written submissions from women for possible inclusion in the journal. Write for details.

JUSTICE NOW

1322 Webster St., Suite 210, Oakland, CA 94612
www.jnow.org

JN is a law clinic that focuses exclusively on the needs of women prisoners. They provide legal services and representation to women prisoners on the following issues: Compassionate release, access to health care, defense of parental rights, sentencing mitigation, and placement into community-based programs.

MS. MAGAZINE | MS. IN PRISON PROGRAM

1600 Wilson Blvd., Suite 801, Arlington, VA 22209

Ms. Magazine is a feminist publication that covers culture, politics, and current events. Women prisoners can write for a FREE subscription

NATIONAL ADVOCATES FOR PREGNANT WOMEN

875 6th Ave., Suite 1807, New York, NY 10001
(212) 255-9252
www.advocatesforpregnantwomen.org

NAPW provides advocacy and support for pregnant incarcerated women, including legal support in civil and criminal cases, especially in cases related to medical issues related to pregnant women.

NATIONAL ORGANIZATION FOR WOMEN (NOW)

1100 H St NW, Suite 300, Washington, DC 20005
(202) 628-8669
www.now.org now@now.org

NOW is the largest organization of feminists' activists in the U.S. They work to eliminate discrimination in the justice system and all other sectors of society, secure women's rights, end all forms of violence against women, and promote equality.

NATIONAL WOMEN'S HEALTH NETWORK

1413 K St., NW, 4th Floor, Washington, DC
(202) 682-2646
www.nwhb.org

NWHN provides literature on women's health concerns, including fibroids, osteoporosis, mammograms, hysterectomies, and others. Write for FREE information, or CALL Mon-Fri, 9 AM – 5 PM (EST)

OFF OUR BACKS

2337B 18th St. NW, Washington, DC 2009
(202) 234-8072
offourbacks@cs.com

Off Our Backs is a bimonthly women's news journal by and for women. Subscriptions are FREE to women prisoners. They accept writing and art submissions for possible inclusion in their publication.

TENACIOUS – ART & WRITING BY WOMEN IN PRISON

c/o V. Law – Black Star Publishing, PO Box 20388, Tompkins Square Station, New York, NY 10009

Tenacious is a bimonthly publication written by female prisoners for female prisoners. They encourage writing and art submissions from incarcerated women for possible inclusion in the magazine. $3 per magazine.

WOMEN & PRISON

Beyond Media Education, 4001 N. Ravenswood Ave., Suite 204-B, Chicago, IL 60613
www.womenandprison.org

Women & Prison is an online e-zine that covers women in prison. They encourage writing and art submissions from incarcerated women for possible online publication. Write for submission guidelines.

WOMEN ORGANIZED TO RESPOND TO LIFE-THREATENING DISEASES

449 15th St., Suite 303, Oakland, CA 94612
(510) 986-0340
www.womenhiv.org

WORLTD provides information support to women living with HIV and other life-threatening diseases, including treatment information, advocacy tips, referrals, and a newsletter addressing these topics. Write with questions or their FREE quarterly newsletter.

WOMEN'S PRISON BOOK PROJECT

c/o Boneshaker Books, 2002 23rd Ave. S., Minneapolis, MN 55404
www.wpbp.org

WPBP provides FREE books to women and transgender prisoners nationwide, except in the following states: CA, CT, FL, IL, IN, MA, MI, MS, OH, OR, and PA.

Women's Resources

ACLU – REPRODUCTIVE FREEDOM PROJECT

125 Broad St., 17th Floor, New York, NY 10004
(212) 549-2633
www.aclu.org/reproductiverights

The *ACLU RFP* provides support for issues related to reproductive rights and abortion. Contact should be made first through state affiliates. See our *State-by-State Resources* for an ACLU in your region.

ACLU – NATIONAL WOMEN'S RIGHTS PROJECT

125 Broad St., 17th Floor, New York, NY 10004
(212) 549-2633
www.aclu.org/womensrights

ACLU NWR provides advocacy and representation for women through education, representation, and community outreach. They focus on poor women, women of color, and women who have been victimized by gender bias and who have to fight for equality.

BATTERED WOMEN'S JUSTICE PROJECT – NATIONAL CLEARINGHOUSE

125 S. 9th St., Suite 302, Philadelphia, PA 19107
(800) 903-0111 ext. 3, (215) 351-0010
www.bwjp.org www.ncdbw.org

BWJP provides support services to battered women who have been charged with crimes, including, assisting legal defenses and supplying information. They assist advocates for women who have injured or killed their batterers in self-defense, battered women who have been coerced into criminal activity, and women charged with failing to protect their children for the batterers' violence. They do not offer direct representation. They have a FREE newsletter.

CENTER ON WRONGFUL CONVICTIONS – WOMEN'S PROJECT

Northwestern University School of Law, 375 E. Chicago Ave., Chicago, IL 60611-3069
(312) 503-2391
www.law.northwestern.edu/wrongfulconvictions/women

CWC provides advocacy and representation for wrongfully convicted women prisoners. They also raise public awareness to ensure similar injustices are not repeated.

CHICAGO BOOKS TO WOMEN IN PRISON | RFUMC

4511 N. Hermitage Ave., Chicago, IL 06040
www.chicagobwp.org chicagobwp@gmail.com

Chicago BWP provides FREE paperback books to women in prison nationwide (except Texas). Write with your genre preference. See for additional FREE books to prisoners in our *Service Center* later in this book.

ESSIE JUSTICE GROUP

340 Pine St., Suite 302, San Francisco, CA 64104
(415) 321-2046
www.essiejusticegroup.org

EJG advocates for the end of mass incarceration through a community of women with incarcerated loved ones. Write for current programs, including their *Healing to Advocacy* curriculum.

FAMILIES UNITED FOR RADICAL & ECONOMIC EQUALITY

81 Willoughby St., #701, Brooklyn, NY 11201
(718) 852-2960
www.furee.org

FUREE organizes low-income families to make changes in the economic system so that everyone is equal, regardless of social status or race. They are comprised almost exclusively by women of color.

FUERZA UNIDA

710 New Laredo Hwy., San Antonio, TX 78211
www.lafuerzaunida.org

FU is a women's group that assists families find justice through advocacy, organization, and education.

LIVING & WELLNESS PROJECT

c/o Justice Now, 1322 Webster St., #210, Oakland, CA 94612
www.jnow.org

The *LW Project* provides literature on women's health concerns, including *Reproductive Health*, a 53-page manual, and *Navigating the Medical System*, a guide to prison health care in CA prisons. Write for FREE information.

HASTING'S WOMEN'S LAW JOURNAL

U.C. Hastings College of Law, 200 McAllister St., San Francisco, CA 94102-4707 www.hastingswomenslj.org

HWLJ is a publication that focuses on the legal landscape and criminal justice system as they pertain to women. They seek written submissions from women for possible inclusion in the journal. Write for details.

JUSTICE NOW

1322 Webster St., Suite 210, Oakland, CA 94612
www.jnow.org

JN is a law clinic that focuses exclusively on the needs of women prisoners. They provide legal services and representation to women prisoners on the following issues: Compassionate release, access to health care, defense of parental rights, sentencing mitigation, and placement into community-based programs.

MS. MAGAZINE | MS. IN PRISON PROGRAM

1600 Wilson Blvd., Suite 801, Arlington, VA 22209

Ms. Magazine is a feminist publication that covers culture, politics, and current events. Women prisoners can write for a FREE subscription

NATIONAL ADVOCATES FOR PREGNANT WOMEN

15 W. 36th St., Suite 901, New York, NY 10018-7910
(212) 255-9252
www.advocatesforpregnantwomen.org

NAPW provides advocacy and support for pregnant incarcerated women, including legal support in civil and criminal cases, especially in cases related to medical issues related to pregnant women.

NATIONAL ORGANIZATION FOR WOMEN (NOW)

1100 H St NW, Suite 300, Washington, DC 20005
(202) 628-8669
www.now.org now@now.org

NOW is the largest organization of feminists' activists in the U.S. They work to eliminate discrimination in the justice system and all other sectors of society, secure women's rights, end all forms of violence against women, and promote equality.

NATIONAL WOMEN'S HEALTH NETWORK

1413 K St., NW, 4th Floor, Washington, DC
(202) 682-2646
www.nwhb.org

NWHN provides literature on women's health concerns, including fibroids, osteoporosis, mammograms, hysterectomies, and others. Write for FREE information, or CALL Mon-Fri, 9 AM – 5 PM (EST)

OFF OUR BACKS

2337B 18th St. NW, Washington, DC 2009
(202) 234-8072
offourbacks@cs.com

Off Our Backs is a bimonthly women's news journal by and for women. Subscriptions are FREE to women prisoners. They accept writing and art submissions for possible inclusion in their publication.

PRISON BIRTH PROJECT

Northampton, MA

PBP provides advocacy, education, and support to pregnant women who are incarcerated.

TENACIOUS – ART & WRITING BY WOMEN IN PRISON

c/o V. Law – Black Star Publishing, PO Box 20388, Tompkins Square Station, New York, NY 10009

Tenacious is a bimonthly publication written by female prisoners for female prisoners. They encourage writing and art submissions from incarcerated women for possible inclusion in the magazine. $3 per magazine.

WOMEN & PRISON

Beyond Media Education, 4110 N. Ravenswood Ave., Suite 204-B, Chicago, IL 60613
www.womenandprison.org

Women & Prison is an online e-zine that covers women in prison. They encourage writing and art submissions from incarcerated women for possible online publication. Write for submission guidelines.

WOMEN ORGANIZED TO RESPOND TO LIFE-THREATENING DISEASES

449 15th St., Suite 303, Oakland, CA 94612
(510) 986-0340
www.womenhiv.org

WORLTD provides information support to women living with HIV and other life-threatening diseases, including treatment information, advocacy tips, referrals, and a newsletter addressing these topics. Write with questions or their FREE quarterly newsletter.

WOMEN'S PRISON BOOK PROJECT

c/o Boneshaker Books, 2002 23rd Ave. S., Minneapolis, MN 55404
www.wpbp.org

WPBP provides FREE books to women and transgender prisoners nationwide, except in the following states: CA, CT, FL, IL, IN, MA, MI, MS, OH, OR, and PA.

More women are incarcerated in the U.S. than anywhere else in the world!

Even though the U.S. only contains 5% of the world's population, this country imprisons nearly one-third of all incarcerated women and girls.
West Virginia holds the world record, where 1 in 366 women in the state are behind bars.

State-By-State Resources

The following represents the majority of current resources available specific to prisoners in each state. However, there are many organizations that were not specifically established to assist prisoners but that may be willing to help you find what you're seeking. When you contact a group, always be sure to ask about other services or organizations that may be able to assist you in your region. Many of the following resources maintain their own local resource lists and may be able to provide you with the exact services you need.

NOTE: The organizations listed under our *Reentry Resources* headings all provide post-release services to the recently incarcerated and often to those about to get out. We will continually update the programs offered under each listing and add more with each new edition of this resource guide.

You can find numerous additional state-by-state listings of organizations, and courts in specifically themed chapters throughout this guide.

State-by-State Directory

Alabama (AL) | Heart of Dixie

State Capital: Montgomery

Time Zone: CST

Population: 4,849,377

(69.7% white; 26.7% black; 1.3% Asian; 0.7% American Indian (4.1% Hispanic)

Name Origin: Alabama is a Choctaw word for a Chickasaw tribe. First noted in accounts of Hernando de Soto expedition.

Motto: Audemus Jura Nostra Defendre (We Dare Defend our Rights)

Famous Alabamians: Hank Aaron, Charles Barkley, George Washington Carver, Nat King Cole, Courtney Cox, Bo Jackson, Helen Keller, Joe Louis, Jesse Owens, Rosa Parks, Condoleezza Rice, Lionel Richie, Octavia Spencer, Channing Tatum, Booker T. Washington, Hank Williams.

State Agencies

CONSUMER PROTECTION

Office of the Attorney General, 11 S. Union St., Montgomery, AL 36130
(334) 242-7335

DRIVER RECORDS

Department of Public Safety, PO Box 1471, Montgomery, AL 36102-1471
(334) 242-4400
www.dps.state.al.us

SECRETARY OF STATE

PO Box 5616, Montgomery, AL 36103-5616
(334) 242-5324
www.sos.state.al.us

VITAL RECORDS

Center for Health Statistics, PO Box 5625, Montgomery, AL 36103-5625
(334) 206-5418
www.ph.state.al.us/chs/vitalrecords

Prisoner Support

ACLU | ALABAMA

207 Montgomery St., Suite 910, Montgomery, AL 36104
(334) 262-0304
www.aclualabama.org info@aclualabama.org

ACLU advocates for the civil rights of prisoners, generally through class actions. They typically will not accept individual prisoner cases, but may provide referrals.

AID TO INMATE MOTHERS (AIM)

PO Box 986, Montgomery, AL 36101-0986
(334) 262-2245
www.inmatemoms.org

AIM offers support to incarcerated Alabama mothers with a focus towards building and maintaining bonds with their children.

ALABAMA COALITION ON BLACK CIVIC PARTICIPATION

423 S. Hull, Montgomery, AL 36701
(770) 778-4889

ACBCP advocates for the rights of African Americans, including those incarcerated. Contact for current programs.

ALABAMA CURE

PO Box 190504, Birmingham, AL 35219-0504
(800) 665-3602, (205) 481-3781

CURE provides advocacy and organization through prisoners and their supporters to achieve reforms in the prison system.

ALABAMA NON-VIOLENT OFFENDERS ORGANIZATION

701 Andrew Jackson Way, Suite 118, Huntsville, AL 35801
(256) 288-3175
www.anvoo.org

ALABAMA PRISON ARTS & EDUCATION PROJECT

203 Spidle Hall, Auburn, AL 36849
(334) 844-8946
www.humsci.auburn.edu/apaep

The *APA&EP Project* assists Alabama prisoners through education opportunities hosted by Auburn University.

Note: to find additional education opportunities throughout the country, order the *Prison Lives Almanac: Prisoner Education Guide*. See ad in this book.

ALABAMA WOMEN'S RESOURCE NETWORK

401 Beacon Parkway, West Birmingham, AL 35209
(205) 916-0135 ext. 501
www.awrn.org awrn.org@gmail.com

AWRN provides Alabama with a variety of support resources, including to those incarcerated. Write for current list of programs.

ARK DOTHAN

475 W. Main St., Dothan, AL 36301
(334) 794-7223
www.thearkdothan.org

CATHOLIC SOCIAL SERVICES

4455 Narrow Lane, Montgomery, AL 36116
(334) 28-8890
www.cssalabama.org

EQUAL JUSTICE INITIATIVE OF ALABAMA

122 Commerce St., Montgomery, AL 36104
(334) 269-1803
www.eji.org contact_us@eji.org

EJI provides representation for LA death row prisoners in direct appeal and post-conviction challenges.

GEORGIA INNOCENCE PROJECT | ALABAMA INITIATIVE

2645 N. Decatur Rd., Decatur, GA 30033
(404) 373-4433

See Georgia listing.

SOUTHERN CENTER FOR HUMAN RIGHTS

83 Poplar St. NW, Atlanta, GA 30303-2122
(404) 688-1202
www.schr.org

SCHR provides legal representation for to Alabama (and Georgia) prisoners who are facing the death penalty and prisoners whose civil rights have been violated in a way that affects broad numbers of prisoners. They will respond to complaints that include capital convictions, physical or sexual assault.

Reentry Resources

DAY OF NEW BEGINNINGS

114 Brown Ave., suite B, Rainbow City, AL 35906
(256) 399-6908

Day of beginnings offers reentry services for women ex-offenders.

FOUNDRY MINISTRIES | THE REENTRY MINISTRIES

PO Box 824, 1800 4th Ave. N, Bessemer, AL 35020
(205) 424-HOPE (4673)
www.foundryministries.com

FOUNTAIN HOUSE

116 N. McDonough St., Montgomery, AL 36104
(334) 391-7508
www.thefountainhouse.net

Fountain House offer transitional housing services for women ex-offenders.

LOVELADY CENTER

7916 2nd Ave. S, Birmingham, AL 36206
(205) 836-3121
www.loveladycenter.org

Lovelady Center provides reentry services for women ex-offenders.

REENTRY MINISTRIES

PO Box 100461, Birmingham, AL 35219
(206) 320-2101

Reentry Ministries provides faith-based reentry service for AL ex-offenders, including spiritual services, job readiness and placement assistance, and AA meetings.

ORDINARY PEOPLE SOCIETY (TOPS)

403 W. Powell St., Dothan, AL 36303
(334) 671-2882

www.weartops.org

TOPS provides faith-based reentry assistance and some support to Alabama prisoners and those soon to release. Contact for current programs.

RENASCENCE

215 Clayton St., Montgomery, AL 36104
(334) 832-1402
www.halfway-home.net

Renascence provides reentry support for AL ex-offenders, including interpersonal and life skills training, health services, education, employment opportunities, housing, and more.

WINNERS

8800 Three Mile Rd., Irvington, AL 36544
(251) 824-1585

Winners (Women in Need of Nurturing, Education and Recovery Services)

FIND ANY ERRORS?

We want to know!

Please let us know if you find any mistakes or if you have additional organizations that you would like to see added to our resource guide. Thank you.

PRISON LIVES
PO Box 842, Exeter, CA 93221
info@prisonlives.com (Corrlinks-friendly)

Alaska (AK) | The Last Frontier State

State Capital: Juneau

Time Zone: AK (Alaska Standard Time)

Population: 736,732

(66.9% white; 14.8% American Indian, 6.1% Asian, 3.9% black, (6.1% Hispanic))

Name Origin: "Alaska" is the Russian version of the Aleutian (Eskimo) word *alakshak*, for 'peninsula', 'great lands', or 'land that is not an island.'

Motto: North to the Future

Famous Alaskans: Tom Bodett, Jewel (Kitcher), Sarah Palin, and Curt Schilling.

State Agencies

CONSUMER PROTECTION

Office of the Attorney General, 1031 W. 4th Ave., Suite 200, Anchorage, AK 99501-5903
(888) 576-2529, (907) 269-5100

DRIVER RECORDS

Division of Motor Vehicles, 2760 Sherwood Lane, #B, Juneau, AK 99801
(907) 465-4363
www.state.ak.us/dmv

VITAL RECORDS

Department of Health & Social Services, PO Box 110675, Juneau, AK 99811-0675
(907) 564-3391
www.hss.state.ak.us/ph/bvs

Prisoner Support

ACLU | ALASKA

1057 W. Fireweed Lane, Suite 207, Anchorage, AK 99503
(907) 276-2258
www.akclu.org akclu.org@akclu.org

ACLU advocates for the civil rights of AK prisoners, generally through class actions. They typically will not accept individual prisoner cases, but they may provide referrals.

ALASKA AIDS ASSISTANCE ASSOCIATION

Anchorage: 1057 W. Fireweed Lane, #102, Anchorage, AK 99503
(800) 478-AIDS, (907) 263-2050
Juneau: PO Box 21481, Juneau, AK 99802
(888) 660-AIDS, (907) 586-6089
www.alaskanaids.org aaaa@alaskanaids.org

AAAA provides support services to AK prisoners with HIV/AIDS and their families, including emotional support, support groups, a helpline, advocacy and practical support. They also offer a FREE tri-annual newsletter.

ALASKA CORRECTIONAL MINISTRIES

6901 DeBarr Rd., Suite 204, Anchorage, AK 99504
(907) 339-0432
www.godinprison.org alaskacorrectionalministries.org

ALASKA CURE

PO Box 84, Willow, AK 99688
(907) 481-1686
www.alaskacure.org

CURE provides advocacy and organization through prisoners and their supporters to achieve reforms in the prison system.

ALASKA FAMILY SERVICES

1825 S. Chugach St., Palmer, AK 99645
(907) 746-4080
www.akafs.org

ALASKA HUMAN RIGHTS COMMISSION

800 A St., #204, Anchorage, AK 99520-1844
(800) 479-4692, (907) 274-4692
www.gov.state.ak.us/aschr

ASCHR provides assistance to AK prisoners by investigating human rights abuses and discrimination complaints around the state.

Alaska Innocence Project

PO Box 201656, Anchorage, AK 99520-1656
(907) 279-0454
www.alaskainnocence.org

AIP provides advocacy and representation for wrongfully convicted AK prisoners, including education, legal, and charitable assistance. They also work to implement reforms for the prevention, identification, and release of the innocent.

Alaska Legal Services Corporation

Anchorage: 1016 W. 6th Ave., #200, Anchorage, AK 99501
(888) 478-2572, (907) 272-9431
anchorage@alsc-law.org
Bethel: PO Box 248, Bethel, AK 99559-0248
(800) 478-2230, (907) 543-2237
bethel@alsc-law.org
Fairbanks: 1648 Cushman, #300, Fairbanks, AK 99701-6202
(800) 478-5401, (907) 452-5181
fairbanks@alsc-law.org
Juneau: 419 6th St., #322, Juneau, AK 99801-1096
(800) 789-6426, (907) 586-6425
juneau@alsc-law.org
www.alskalawhelp.org
www.alsc-law.org

ALSC provides FREE legal assistance to low-income people in AK, including ex-offenders They will not provide assistance to prisoners currently incarcerated. Their focus is on civil matters, and will not help on criminal issues.

Alaska Native Justice Center

3600 San Jeronimo Dr., Suite 264, Anchorage, AK 99508
(907) 793-3550
www.anjc.org

Catholic Social Services

3710 E. 20th Ave., Anchorage, AK 99508
(907) 222-7300
www.cssalaska.org

Reentry Resources

New Life Development

3016 E. 9th Ave., Anchorage, AK 99508
(907) 646-2200
www.newlifeak.org

NLD provides reentry assistance to AK ex-offenders, including transitional housing, job skills training, chemical dependency education, and job placement assistance.

No Limits | South Side Reentry Center

253 Romans Way, Fairbanks, AK 99701
(907) 451-9650
www.nolimitinc.org

Partners for Progress | Reentry Center

417 Barrow St., Anchorage, AK 99501
(907) 258-1192
www.partnersforprogressak.org/focus-on-re-entry

Prisoner Reentry Task Force

550 W. 7th Ave., Suite 601, Anchorage, AK 99501
(907) 269-7405

The *Prisoner Reentry Task Force* is an effort run by the Alaska Department of Corrections to assist prisoners in making a positive transition back into society. They provide several resources and listings upon request.

Arizona | Grand Canyon State

State Capital: Phoenix

Time Zone: MST (Mountain Standard Time)

Population: 6,731,484

(83.7% white; 5.3% American Indian, 4.7% Black, 3.3% Asian, (30.2% Hispanic))

Name Origin: Arizona is the Spanish version of the Pima Indian word for "little spring place" or Aztec 'arizuma', meaning "silver bearing."

Motto: Dilat Deus (God Enriches)

Famous Arizonans: Alice Cooper, Geronimo, John McCain, Linda Ronstadt, Emma Stone, and Frank Lloyd Wright.

State Agencies

CONSUMER PROTECTION

Office of Attorney General, 400 W. Congress South Building, Suite 315, Tucson, AZ 85701
(520) 628-6504
www.azag.org

DRIVER RECORDS

Motor Vehicles Division, PO Box 2100, Mail Drop 539M, Phoenix, AZ 85001-2100
(602)712-8420
www.azdot.gov/mvd

SECRETARY OF STATE

1700 W. Washington, 7th Floor, Phoenix, AZ 85007
(602) 542-6187
www.azsos.gov

VITAL RECORDS

Department of Health Services, PO Box 6018, Phoenix, AZ 85005
(602) 255-3260
www.azdhs.gov

Prisoner Support

ACLU | ARIZONA

PO Box 17148, Phoenix, AZ 85011-0148
(602) 650-1854
www.acluaz.org/az *intake@acluaz.org*

ACLU advocates for the civil rights of prisoners in Arizona, generally through class actions. They typically will not accept individual prisoner cases, but they may provide referrals.

AMERICAN FRIENDS SERVICE COMMITTEE

103 N. Park Ave., Suite 111, Tucson, AZ 85719
(520) 623-9141
www.afsc.org/az *afscaz@afsc.org*

AFSC provides general information and resources to prisoners, their families, and ex-offenders, and offers some individual prisoner advocacy. They will act as a liaison to bring prison issues to government officials.

ARIZONA DEPARTMENT OF CORRECTIONS | PAROLE OFFICE

4600 S. Park, #8, Tucson, AZ 85714
(520) 889-3100

ARIZONA JUSTICE PROJECT | ARIZONA STATE UNIVERSITY

MC4420, 411 N. Central Ave., Suite 600, Phoenix, AZ 85004-2139
(602) 496-0286
www.azjusticeproject.org

AJP provides assistance to the innocent, those who have been wrongfully convicted, and cases where severe justice has occurred. They well consider DNA and non-DNA cases where actual innocence can be proven, and can provide post-conviction DNA testing in cases where testing may demonstrate actual innocence.

BEHAVIORAL HEALTH SERVICES COURT-ORDERED PROGRAMS (CPES)

4825 N. Sabino Canyon Rd., Tucson, AZ 85750
(520) 884-7954
www.CPES.com

CPES directs court-ordered programs administered to Arizona sexual offenders.

MIDDLE GROUND PRISON REFORM | CURE

139 E. Encanto Dr., Tempe, AZ 85281
(480) 966-8116
www.middlegroundprisonreform.org
middleground@msn.com

MGPR is a division of CURE that provides advocacy and education services, including legislative advocacy for prison reform, litigation on policies and procedures affecting visitation, education/training/speaking on criminal justice issues, and informal counseling. They provide some referrals to social service agencies. Donations are appreciated.

NAVAJO NATION CORRECTIONS PROJECT

PO Drawer 709, Window Rock, AZ 86815
(928) 871-7555

NNCP advocates for prisoner's right to religion, native and non-native alike. They also provide native-specific religious rites support to Native American prisoners.

NORTHERN ARIZONA JUSTICE PROJECT | NORTHERN ARIZONA UNIVERSITY

PO Box 15005, Flagstaff, AZ 86011-5005
(928) 523-7028
jan.ucc.nau/d-najp

NAJP provides legal support services for wrongfully convicted AZ prisoners. DNA and non-DNA cases are accepted if they have actual innocence evidence. Must have 8 or more years left on sentence. They specialize in arson, shaken baby syndrome, and child abuse cases.

READ BETWEEN THE BARS | DAILY PLANET PUBLISHING

PO Box 1509, Tucson, AZ 85702
www.readbetweenthebars.com

RBB provides FREE books to prisoners in Arizona. For more free-books-to-prisoners' programs, see our *Service Center* later in this book.

SOUTHERN ARIZONA AIDS FOUNDATION

375 S. Euclid Ave., Tucson, AZ 85719
(520) 638-7223
www.saaf.org info@saaf.org

SAAF provides services to prisoners with AIDS, including limited legal representation for guardianship arrangements and referrals for assistance with wills, power of attorneys, and other legal matters.

Reentry Resources

ARIZONA 2-1-1

www.211arizona.org/reentry

ARIZONA COMMON GROUND

2406 S. 24th St., Suite E-114, Phoenix, AZ 85034-6822
(602) 914-9000
www.azcommonground.org

BUCKEYE OUTREACH FOR SOCIAL SERVICES (BOSS) | EX-OFFENDER SERVICES

501 E. Mahoney Ave., Buckeye, AZ 85326-3223
(623) 386-6365
www.bosssite.org

CATHOLIC CHARITIES

4747 North 7th Ave., Phoenix, AZ 85013
(602) 285-1999
www.catholiccharitiesaz.org

CENTER FOR LIFESKILLS DEVELOPMENT

2001 W. Orange Grove Rd., Suite 604, Tucson, AZ 85704-1141
(520) 229-6220
www.lifeskillstucson.com

Center for Life Skills Development offers reentry services for ex-offenders with sexual crime convictions.

DEPARTMENT OF ECONOMIC SECURITY | JOB SERVICE

PO Box 28880, Tucson, AZ 85726-8880
www.azdes.gov

DES provides job search assistance and some training to ex-offenders. They also supply government benefits, including SNAP, cash assistance, and health care (AHCCCS).

FAMILY SERVICE AGENCY | COMMUNITY RE-INTEGRATION PROGRAM

2400 N. Central Ave., Suite 101, Phoenix, AZ 85004-1315
(602) 264-9891
fsaphoenix.org

FATHER MATTERS | REENTRY PROGRAM

PO Box 13575, Tempe, AZ 85284
(602) 774-3298
www.fathermatters.org

GALIVANS

9511 E. 5th St., Tucson, AZ 85730

Galivans provides housing to AZ ex-offenders. Contact them prior to release to apply. No violent or sex offenders.

GOODWILL INDUSTRIES OF NORTHERN ARIZONA | FRESH START

4308 E. Route 66, Flagstaff, AZ 86004
(928) 526-9188
www.goodwillna.org

HOPE HAVEN TRANSITIONAL HOUSING

1645 W. 150 Valencia Rd., #109-404, Tucson, AZ
(520) 409-8869

Hope Haven is a faith-based discipleship program that provides coed transitional housing and reentry services to ex-offenders, including food, transportation, and some employment referral assistance. No violent or sex offenders.

HOPE'S CROSSING

830 N. 1st Ave., Suite 212, Phoenix, AZ 85003-1402
(602) 795-8098
www.hopescrossing.org

Hope's Crossing provides reentry services for women ex-offenders.

JOBPATH

924 N. Alueron Way, Tucson, AZ 85711
(520) 324-0402
www.jobpath.net

JobPath provides employment training for ex-offenders, including resume prep, interview techniques, education, and counseling.

MASTER'S HOUSE

44 E. 23rd St., Tucson, AZ 84713
(512) 312-1977

Master's House is a faith-based transitional housing provider. No sex offenders.

VETERAN'S AFFAIRS | HEALTH CARE FOR REENTERING VETERANS

355 E. Germann Rd., Suite 201, Gilbert, AZ 85297
(480) 397-2700

VIVRE

2719 W. Maryland Ave., Phoenix, AZ 85017
(602) 421-8066
www.vivrehousing.org

VIVRE housing offers transitional housing for Arizona ex-offenders.

WOMEN LIVING FREE

9220 W. Coolidge St., Phoenix, AZ 85037
(623) 206-2823

Women Living Free provides education and support services to Arizona women ex-offenders, including job readiness, job search and placement.

Arkansas | Razorback State

State Capital: Little Rock

Time Zone: CST

Population: 2,966,369

(79.7% white; 15.6% Black, 1.5% Asian, 1.0% American Indian (6.8% Hispanic))

Name Origin: Algonquin name for the Quapaw Indians, meaning "south wind."

Famous Arkansans: Al Green, John Grisham, Scottie Pippin, Winthrop Rockefeller, Billy Ray Thornton, Sam Walton.

State Agencies

CONSUMER PROTECTION

Office of the Attorney General, 323 Center St., Suite 200, Little Rock, AR 72201
(501) 682-2007
www.ag.state.ar.us consumer@ag.state.ar.us

DRIVER RECORDS

Department of Driver's Services, PO Box 1272, Room 1130, Little Rock, AR 72203-1272
(501) 682-7207
www.accessarkansas.org/dfa/driverservices

SECRETARY OF STATE

State Capitol Building, Little Rock, AR 72201
(501) 682-3409
www.sos.arkanasas.org

VITAL RECORDS

Arkansas Department of Health, 4815 W. Markham St., Slot 44, Little Rock, AR 72205
(800) 637-9314
www.healthyarkansas.com

Prisoner Support

ACLU | ARKANSAS

904 W. Second St., #1, Little Rock, AR 72201
(501) 374-2660, (501) 374-2842
www.acluarkansas.org

ACLU advocates for the civil rights of Arkansas prisoners, generally through class actions. They will typically not accept individual prisoner cases, but they may provide referrals.

ARKANSAS JUSTICE PROJECT | UNIVERSITY OF ARKANSAS SCHOOL OF LAW

1045 W. Maple St., Fayetteville, AR 72701
www.law.uark.edu

AJP provides advocacy and representation for wrongfully convicted Arkansas prisoners. Write for current requirements and guidelines.

ARKANSAS VOICES FOR CHILDREN LEFT BEHIND

2715 Marchfield Ct., Wrightsville, AR 72206
(501) 897-0809
www.arkansasvoices.com

AVCLB provides advocacy and assistance to families and children affected by the criminal justice system. Write for current programs.

CENTRAL ARKANSAS LEGAL SERVICES

303 W. Capitol Ave., Little Rock, AR
(501) 376-3423
lawyers.justia.com/legalservice/central-arkansas-legal-services

CURE | ARKANSAS

PO Box 56001, Little Rock, AR 72215
(501) 223-2620
www.curenational.org

CURE provides advocacy and organization through Arkansas prisoners and their supporters to achieve reforms in the prison system.

MIDWEST INNOCENCE PROJECT

605 W. 47th St., Kansas City, MO 64113
(816) 221-2166
www.themip.org

MIP provides advocacy and representation for wrongfully convicted prisoners in Kansas, Arkansas, Missouri, Iowa and Nebraska. They will accept cases of actual innocence where the convicted had nothing to do with the crime, has more than 10 years left on their sentence or has to register as a sex offender, and who is not currently represented by counsel. They will not accept death penalty or self-defense cases.

Reentry Resources

CENTER FOR YOUTH AND FAMILY PRISON PROJECT

5905 Forest Place, Suite 202, Little Rock, AR 72207
(501) 660-6886

CYFPP provides reentry services for AR prisoners, including mental health and substance abuse counseling, family crisis intervention, literacy, housing and employment assistance.

CENTRAL ARKANSAS REENTRY (CARE) COALITION

Willie E. Horton Center, 3805 W. 12th St., Little Rock, AR 72204
(501) 444-2273
www.arkansasreentry.com

CARE offers a reentry service directory for Arkansas offenders. Address above is a monthly meeting place and may not result in a quick response.

CENTER FOR WOMEN IN TRANSITION

1116 Garland St., Little rock, AR 72201
(501) 372-5522
www.cwitlr.org

CWIT provides reentry services for women ex-offenders.

CITY OF LITTLE ROCK REENTRY SERVICES

500 W. Markham St., Little Rock, AR 72201
(501) 371-4510
www.littlerock.org/citydepartments/communityprograms/reentry.aspx

GOODWILL INDUSTRIES OF ARKANSAS

1110 W. 7th St., Little Rock, AR 72201
(501) 372-5151
www.goodwillar.org/career_training/reentry-services.htm

GYST HOUSE

8101 Frenchmans Lane, Little Rock, AR 72209
(501) 568-1682
www.gysthouseinc.com

Gyst house offers transitional housing to ex-offenders.

OUR HOUSE

302 E. Roosevelt Rd., Little Rock, AR 72206
(501) 374-7383
www.ourhouseshelter.org

Our House offers transitional housing to ex-offenders.

PATHWAY TO FREEDOM

PO Box 1010, 22522 Asher Rd., Wrightsville, AR 72183
(501) 897-9764
www.ptfprison.org

RAMOTH

PO Box 4934, Little Rock, AR 72214
(501) 615-1090

Ramoth provides AR ex-offenders with job search and employment services.

California | Golden State

State Capital: Sacramento

Time Zone: PST

Population: 38,802,500

(73.2% white; 14.4% Asian, 6.5% Black, 1.7% American Indian (36.1% Hispanic))

Name Origin: It was the name given by Spanish conquistadors (possible Cortez) for an imaginary island in the 1510 novel *Las Sergas de Esplandian*, by Garcia Rodriguez de Montalvo.

Motto: Eureka! (I have found it!)

Famous Californians: Tom Brady, Julia Child, Cameron Diaz, Leonardo DiCaprio, Joe DiMaggio, Clint Eastwood, Diane Feinstein, Tom Hanks, Steve Jobs, Angelina Jolie, Jason Kidd, George Lucas, Marilyn Monroe, Ronald Reagan, John Steinbeck, Tiger Woods.

State Agencies

CONSUMER AFFAIRS

1625 N. Market Blvd., Sacramento, CA 95834
(916) 445-1254
www.dca.ca.gov *dca@dca.ca.gov*

DEPARTMENT OF BUSINESS OVERSIGHT

1515 K St., Suite 200, Sacramento, CA 95814
(800) 622-0620
consumer.services@dbo.ca.gov

DRIVER RECORDS

Department of Motor Vehicles, PO Box 944247, MS-G199, Sacramento, CA 94244-2470
(916) 657-8098
www.dmv.ca.gov

SECRETARY OF STATE

1500 11th St., 3rd Floor, Sacramento, CA 95814
(916) 657-5448
www.ss.ca.gov

VITAL RECORDS

Department of Public Health, PO Box 997410, MS 5103, Sacramento, CA 95899-7410
(916) 445-2684
www.dhs.ca.gov/chs

Prisoner Support

ACLU | NORTHERN CALIFORNIA

39 Drumm St., San Francisco, CA 94111
(415) 621-2488
www.aclunc.org

ACLU | SAN DIEGO AND IMPERIAL CITIES

PO Box 87131, San Diego, CA 92198
(619) 232-2121
www.aclusandiego.org

ACLU | SOUTHERN CALIFORNIA

1313 W. Eighth St., Los Angeles, CA 90026
(213) 977-9500
www.aclu-sc.org *acluinfo@aclu-sc.org*

ACLU advocates for the civil rights of California prisoners, generally through class actions. They typically will not accept individual prisoner cases, but they may provide referrals.

CALIFORNIA AIDS HOTLINE

995 Market St., #200, San Francisco, CA 94103
(800) 367-AIDS (2437), TTY: (888) 225-AIDS (2437)
www.aidshotline.org *contact-us@aidshotline.org*

CA AIDS Hotline answers questions from prisoners about HIV/AIDS and STDs. English and Spanish.

CALIFORNIA COALITION FOR WOMEN PRISONERS

1540 Market St., #490, San Francisco, CA 94102
(415) 255-7036

www.womenprisoners.org info@womenprisoners.org

CCWP advocates for women prisoners by giving them a voice to express concerns over issues specific to women behind bars and inhumane prison conditions. The publish and distribute a newsletter, *The Fire Inside*, FREE for prisoners.

CALIFORNIA FAMILIES TO ABOLISH SOLITARY CONFINEMENT | CHICO'S JUSTICE CENTER

1137 E. Redondo Blvd., Inglewood, CA 90302
(714) 290-9077
www.solitarywatch.com/cfasc

CFASC advocates to stop the inhumane treatment of California prisoners, especially those held in solitary confinement.

CALIFORNIA INNOCENCE PROJECT | CALIFORNIA WESTERN SCHOOL OF LAW

225 Cedar St., San Diego, CA 92101
(619) 525-1485
www.californiainnocenceproject.org

CIP advocates and provides representation for cases of actual innocence in Southern California. DNA and non-DNA cases are accepted, with a focus on police and prosecutorial misconduct, firearm and fingerprint analysis, shaken baby syndrome, and death penalty cases. Must have 3 or more years left on sentence.

CALIFORNIA LIFER NEWSLETTER

PO Box 277, Rancho Cordova, CA 95741
(916) 402-9450
www.lifesupportalliance.org

California Lifer Newsletter is a comprehensive newsletter for prisoners, which contains state and federal legal cases, parole board news, statistics, legislation, and other issues affecting California lifers and their supporters. $30 per year (or 100 stamps) for prisoners. $90 per year for others. Make checks out to LSAEF.

CALIFORNIA PRISON FOCUS

1904 Franklin St., Suite 507, Oakland, CA 94612
(510) 836-7222
www.prisons.org contact@prisons.org

CPF actively ensures conditions at several California security housing units (SHUs) through regular on-site visits, housing, and education. They publish a quarterly magazine, *Prison Focus*, which focuses on CA prison conditions, policies, and legislation. FREE to prisoners with CA SHU addresses. $6 per year to all others.

CALIFORNIA PRISON RECEIVERSHIP

PO Box 588500, Elk Grove, CA 95758
(916) 691-3000
www.cphcs.ca.gov

CPR actively oversees medical care in the CA prison system to ensure that it complies with recent reforms. They will investigate prison medical injustices, excluding mental, dental, or substance abuse treatment issues.

CENTER FOR CHILDREN OF INCARCERATED PARENTS

PO Box 41-286, Eagle Rock, CA 90031
(626) 449-2470
www.e-ccip.org

CCIP provides research and resource information on family reunification, therapeutic services, education and other topics specific to prisoners and their families.

CENTER FOR HEALTH JUSTICE

900 Avila St., Suite 301, Los Angeles, CA 90012
(213) 229-0985 (HIV hotline, Mon-Fri 8 to 3pm pst)
www.centerforhealthjustice.org

The Center for Health Justice provides health information and services to California prisoners through information and advocacy. HIV, HepC and other medical and treatment issues are addressed directly through their FREE hotline, giving ill and newly diagnosed prisoners instant support. Write for more information and publications, including HepC Inside and HIV Inside.

CENTERFORCE

2955 Kerner Blvd., 2nd Floor, San Rafael, CA 94901
(415) 456-9980
www.centerforce.org

Centerforce advocates and supports anyone affected by incarceration. They do so through a variety of services during incarceration, reentry, and after release through active programs at several CA prisons. Current programs include educating prisoners on HIV reduction and parenting. Write for a listing of new programs and resources.

CRITICAL RESISTANCE

1904 Franklin St., #504, Oakland, CA 94612
(510) 444-0484

www.criticalresistance.org
crnational@criticalresistance.org

Critical Resistance is an advocacy group that seeks to build an international movement to end mass incarceration, but they also focus on issues specific to California prisoners. They publish *The Abolitionist*, a tri-annual newspaper FREE to prisoners.

DIOCESE OF OAKLAND PRISON MINISTRY

2121 Harrison St., Oakland, CA 94612
(510) 267-8378
www.oakdiocese.org

DOPM provides religious services in the jails and juvenile halls of Alameda and Contra Costa Counties, as well as counseling and emergency assistance services.

DISABILITY RIGHTS EDUCATION AND DEFENSE FUND

3075 Adeline St., Suite 210, Berkeley, CA 94703
(510) 644-2555
www.dredf.org

DREDF provides civil rights information and resources pertaining to disability issues, with a focus on CA prisoners. They do not provide individual benefits assistance. Do not send original documents.

FRIENDS COMMITTEE ON LEGISLATION IN CALIFORNIA

1225 8th St., Suite 220, Sacramento, CA 95814-4809
(916) 443-3734
www.fclca.org

FCLCA is a Quaker-based group that lobbies for CA law changes that are for the common good of the people, including prisoners. They publish a quarterly newsletter, *FCLCA*, which tracks pending litigation, available FREE to prisoners.

FRIENDS OUTSIDE

620 N. Aurora St., Stockton, CA 95202
(209) 955-0701
www.friendsoutside.org

FO provides social services to prisoners and their families, including family services, reentry assistance, and visitor centers throughout the CA prison system. Visitor Centers provide childcare, transportation, information and resources for those visiting CA prisoners. Write for more information.

GED RECORDS CENTER

PO Box 4005, Concord, CA 94524-4005
(866) 370-4720

Write for a copy of your GED.

INNOCENCE MATTERS

PO Box 1098, Torrance, CA 90505
(310) 755-2518
www.innocencematters.us

IM advocates and represents prisoners who are innocent of the crime they've been convicted of, and who meet the following criteria: Must have been convicted in LA County, be factually innocent and willing to submit to and pass a polygraph test, have already been rejected by the California Innocence Project, and have no conflict of interest with IM.

INSIGHT PRISON PROJECT

PO Box 151642, San Rafael, CA 94915
(415) 459-9800
www.insightproject.org

IPP provides rehabilitative tools and programs to CA prisoners, which are often conducted by crime victims, volunteers, and prisoners. They also offer some reentry services and provide unique programs, including the Victim/Offender Education Group (VOEG). an 18-month curriculum designed to aid the healing processes for all involved.

JUSTICE NOW

1322 Webster St., #210, Oakland, CA 94612
(510) 839-7654
www.now.org

Justice Now provides legal services for women prisoners concerning issues of compassionate release, health care access, parental rights defense, and sentencing mitigation. They provide a FREE 50+ page manual about incarcerated women's reproductive health, *Navigating the California Medical System*. They also work with women prisoners to documents prisoner rights abuses. CA women prisoners can call collect Tue. – Fri. 10 AM to 6 PM (PST).

LEGAL SERVICES FOR PRISONERS WITH CHILDREN

1540 Market St., Suite 490, San Francisco, CA 94102
(415) 255-7036
www.prisonerswithchildren.org

LSPC organizes communities affected by the criminal justice system and advocates for incarcerated parents and their children to reunify families and communities.

They cannot provide individual legal assistance to prisoners, but they will provide referrals and information on family matters, reentry services, and prison conditions. They publish a manual on SSI/SSDI for Prisoners & Their Advocates, FREE for prisoners as well as several publications covering prison condition, family matters, reentry services, and government aid for prisoners and their advocates..

MOTHERS RECLAIMING OUR CHILDREN

13 Peter Behr Dr., San Rafael, CA 94903
(415) 499-3203

MROC provides support to prisoners' families to attend court hearings and trials. They will work with prisoner's attorneys to help facilitate family support.

NORTHERN CALIFORNIA INNOCENCE PROJECT | SANTA CLARA UNIVERSITY OF LAW

900 Lafayette St., Suite 105, Santa Clara, CA 95053-0422
(408) 554-1945
www.law.scu.edu/ncip

NCIP provides advocacy and representation for prisoners in Central and Northern California who have been wrongfully convicted. They accept DNA and non-DNA cases that originated in CA resulting in a serious felony conviction or a felony involving 3-strikes sentencing in any of the following matters: official misconduct, shaken baby syndrome, arson, firearms or fingerprint analysis, ineffective assistance, false confessions, or death penalty issues.

NORTHERN CALIFORNIA SERVICE LEAGUE

40 Boardman Place, San Francisco, CA 94103
(415) 863-2323
www.norcalserviceleague.org

NCSL provides counseling and referral services to CA prisoners and their families. They also offer some reentry services, including job and life-skills training. NOTE: Their website is currently offline. They may not be an active organization.

PENAL LAW PROJECT | CHICO STATE UNIVERSITY

25 Main St., Suite 102, Chico, CA 95929
(530) 898-4911
www.ascho.com/clic/programsandadvocacy

PLP students provide legal research and information to CA prisoners about prisoner rights, record expunging, sentencing, parole, pardons, and more. They will not provide legal advice or counseling.

POST-CONVICTION ADVOCACY PROJECT | UC BERKELEY SCHOOL OF LAW

215 Boalt Hall, Berkeley, CA 94720-7200
(510) 642-1741
www.law.berkeley.edu

P-CAP provides assistance to CA lifers in navigating the parole process and to prisoners who have been denied parole.

PRISON LAW CLINIC | UC DAVIS SCHOOL OF LAW

One Shields Ave., Building TB30, Davis, CA 95616
(530) 752-0822
www.law.ucdavis.edu

PLC provides legal services to CA prisoners on matters of constitutional and state law, rules of professional conduct, and prison regulations.

PRISON LAW OFFICE

General Delivery, San Quentin, CA 94964
(510) 280-2621
www.prisonlaw.com

The Prison Law Office provides legal representation to CA prisoners in civil rights matters, including prison medical care, mental health, disability access, and more. They also distribute self-help literature on a range of legal topics. Write for a list of current publications.

PRISON UNIVERSITY PROJECT

(415) 450-8088
www.prisonuniversityproject.org

PUP is a program designed to educate prisoners in San Quentin with the intention of becoming a model and public awareness for higher education in prisons.

PROJECT AVARY

PO Box 150088, San Rafael, CA 94915-0088
(415) 382-8799
www.projectavary.org

Project AVARY provides support to children of prisoners, including summer camp, monthly outings, family support, and leadership training. Write for more information.

PUBLIC INTEREST LAW FIRM

152 N. Third St., 3rd Floor, San Jose, CA 95112
(408) 280-2417

PILF advocates and represents those incarcerated in the Santa Clara County Jail in class actions and matters that have a broad impact on civil rights. They do not provide representation in criminal or personal injury cases.

SOLANO VISION NEWSPAPER

c/o CSP Solano, PO Box 4000, Vacaville, CA 95696-4000
(707) 451-0182

The Solano Vision is a quarterly newspaper produced inside the Solano (CSP) prison by prisoners covering all areas of interest. Subscriptions are available nationwide.

SANTA CRUZ BARRIOS UNIDOS

1817 Soquel Ave., Santa Cruz CA 95062
(831) 457-8208
www.barriosunidos.net

SCBO advocates for prison reform and supports reentry and family reunification efforts while providing cultural and spiritual education.

SENTENCING AND JUSTICE REFORM ADVOCACY ADVOCATE

PO Box 71, Olivehurst, CA 95961
(530) 329-8566
www.sjra1.com

SJRA Advocate is a monthly magazine designed to educate, inspire, and motivate CA prisoners, their families and those who care about CA prisons, prisoners, and their unique issues. $18 per year for prisoners (or 40 stamps/year, 3 stamps/issue). $20 per year for all others.

STANFORD THREE STRIKES PROJECT | STANFORD LAW SCHOOL

559 Nathan Abbot Way, Stanford, CA 94305-8610
(650) 736-7757
www.law.stanford.edu

STSP advocates against the CA Three Strikes law. They represent prisoners currently incarcerated under the Three Strikes law while working to affect reform.

STATE OF CALIFORNIA PRISON INDUSTRY AUTHORITY (CALPIA)

560 E. Natoma St., Folsom, CA 95630
pia.ca.gov

STATE PUBLIC DEFENDER

221 Main St., 10th Floor, San Francisco, CA 94105
(415) 904-5600

Represents CA capital appellate cases.

U.S. FEDERAL PROBATION OFFICE | NORTHERN CALIFORNIA DISTRICT

450 Golden Gate Ave., Suite 17-6884
(415) 436-1540
canp.uscourts.gov

U.S. Federal PO supervises federal offenders on probation and parole. They require a check-in within 72 hours of release. Write for supervision guidelines and requirements.

VETERAN'S JUSTICE OUTREACH | SAN FRANCISCO VA MEDICAL CENTER

401 3rd St., San Francisco, CA 94107
(415) 281-5116
www.va.gov

VJO is an outreach program for veterans, which collaborates with the CA justice system to assist CA prisoners who are veterans in obtaining services and treatment.

Reentry Resources

211 SAN DIEGO

PO Box 420039, San Diego, CA 92142
(858) 300-1211
www.211sandiego.org/re-entry

ALLIED FELLOWSHIP SERVICES

1524 29th Ave., Oakland, CA 94601
(510) 535-1236

AFS provides employment training, workshops, health education and drug counseling services in the Bay area to CA ex-offenders. They also operate a 30-bed residential program. Write for requirements prior to release.

AMITY FOUNDATION

2202 S. Figueroa St., Suite 717, Los Angeles, CA 90007
(213) 743-9075
www.amityfdn.org/california

ANTI-RECIDIVISM COALITION

448 South Hill St., Suite 908, Los Angeles, CA 90013
www.anntirecidivism.org

ARRIBA JUNTOS

1850 Mission St., San Francisco, CA 94103

(415) 487-3240
www.arribajuntos.org

AJ provides employment services, including skills training in computer technologies, certified nursing assistance, and MUNI driver, as well as interview techniques, resume writing, and job placement assistance for CA ex-offenders. They also offer hiring incentives for employers by subsidizing them to offer on-the-job training to ex-offenders.

BEIL T'SHUVAH | HOUSE OF RETURN

8831 Venice Blvd., Las Angeles, CA 90034
(310) 204-5200
www.beiltshuvahia.org

House of Return provides reentry services to CA Jewish ex-offenders, including employment services, education, and drug counseling.

BERKELEY-OAKLAND SUPPORT SERVICES

PO Box 1996, Berkeley, CA 94701
(510) 649-1930
www.self-sufficiency.org

BOSS provides pre-release and parole planning to prisoners about to be released. Write for current services.

BETHESDA FAMILY MINISTRIES INTERNATIONAL

3882 Stillman Park Cir., Suite 19A, Sacramento, CA 95824
(877) 492-0115
www.bethesdafamily.org

BFMI provides spiritual support and services to CA ex-offenders and their families in the Sacramento area.

CALIFORNIA FOOD POLICY ADVOCATES

116 New Montgomery St., Suite 633, San Francisco, CA 94105
(415) 777-4422
www.cfpa.net

CFPA provides pre-release and parole planning to CA prisoners releasing into the Bay area. They also provide information and general services, such as welfare, social security, and financial aid.

CALIFORNIA REENTRY INSTITUTE

PO Box 51, Clayton, CA 94517
(925) 549-1416
californiareentryinstitute.org

CENTERFORCE

PO Box 415, San Quentin, CA 94964
(415) 456-9980
www.centerforce1.org

Centerforce, based in San Quentin, provides a variety of reentry services to ex-offenders in the San Francisco Bay area, as well as Fresno and Madera Counties.

COMMUNITY CONNECTION RESOURCE CENTER

4080 Centre St., Suite 104, San Diego, CA 92103
(619) 294-3900
www.community-connection.org

CCRC provides comprehensive statewide reentry resources, including housing, job development and placement, social services, counseling, and more.

COMMUNITY RESOURCES AND SELF-HELP (CRASH)

927 24th St., San Diego, CA 92102
(619) 233-8054
www.crash.org

CRASH provides recovery planning and release preparation, as well as long-term residential programs. Write them for current reentry programs.

DELANCEY STREET FOUNDATION

Los Angeles: 400 N. Vermont Ave., Los Angeles, CA 90004
(323) 644-4122
San Francisco: 600 Embarcadero, San Francisco, CA 94107
(415) 957-9800
www.eisenhowerfoundation.org

DSF provides a variety of reentry support options, including housing, job training, and employment services. They own and operate several businesses that train and employ CA ex-offenders in a variety of fields, including restaurants and catering, retail and wholesale sales, advertising, automotive, moving and trucking, as well as managerial opportunities.

EAST LOS ANGELES SKILLS CENTER

3921 Selig Place, Los Angeles, CA 90031
(323) 227-0018
www.elasc.adultinstruction.org

ELASC provides a unique reentry program the incorporates academic study and employment training for CA prisoners about to be released.

INMATE FAMILY COUNCIL CSP SOLANO

2100 Peabody Rd., Vacaville, CA 95687

www.ifc-solano.org/reentry

JOBTRAIN

1200 O'Brien Dr., Menlo Park, CA 94025
(650) 330-6429
www.jobtrainworks,org

Job Train is a one-stop career center and vocational training school that provides no-cost entry level training in a variety of fields. Training classes run from six weeks to six months, depending on the field of interest.

KICKSTART REENTRY EMPLOYMENT SERVICES

730 La Guardia St., Room 102, Salinas, CA 93905
(800) 870-4750
www.kickstart-employment.com

LOS ANGELES REGIONAL REENTRY PARTNERSHIP (LARP)

2202 S. Figueroa, 717, Los Angeles, CA 90007
www.lareentry.org info@lareentry.org

NORTHERN CALIFORNIA SERVICE LEAGUE

San Francisco: 28 Boardman Place, San Francisco, CA 94103
(415) 863-2323
San Jose: 598 N. First St., Suite 202, San Jose, CA 95112
(408) 297-9601

NCSL provides reentry services to county ex-offender, including life skills training, social services, and a 30-day shelter program. They also offer assistance to prisoners' families, including counseling, GED tutoring, and parenting skills.

PARTNERSHIP FOR REENTRY PROGRAM (PREP)

c/o Sister Mary Sean Hodges, PO Box 77850, Los Angeles, CA 90007
(213) 438-4820
www.la-archdiocese.org

PLAYA VISTA JOB OPPORTUNITIES & BUSINESS SERVICES

4112 S. Main St., Los Angeles, CA 90037
(323) 432-3955
www.pvjobs.org

PRISONER REENTRY NETWORK

1201 Martin Luther King Jr. Way, Suite 200, PO Box 7152, Oakland, CA 94612
www.prisonerreentrynetwork.org

The Prisoner Reentry Network provides a variety of reentry services for ex-offenders in the Oakland area. write for a current resource listing, or a FREE copy of the VA Guidebook for Incarcerated California Veterans.

PROJECT REBOUND

1650 Holloway Ave., T-138, San Francisco, CA 94132
(415) 405-0954
www.ssu.edu/-rebound

Project Rebound is a program of the San Francisco State University, which offers admission and tutoring services to CA ex-offenders who would like to continue their education after release.

REENTRY COUNCIL OF THE CITY AND COUNTY OF SAN FRANCISCO

880 Bryant St., Room 200, San Francisco, CA 94103
(415) 241-4252
www.sfgov.org/reentry

The Reentry Council of SF publishes a comprehensive reentry directory, Getting Out and Staying Out, for ex-offenders in the San Francisco Bay area, FREE for prisoners.

ROOT & REBOUND

1730 Franklin St., Suite 300, Oakland, CA 94612
www.rootandrobound.org
info@rootandrebound.org
R&R offers a comprehensive reentry guide, *Roadmap to Reentry: A California Legal Guide,* which provides information on the major barriers to reentry in California. They also conduct statewide community training and legal assistance to reentry organizations to better equip reentry organizations to assist ex-offenders.

RUBICON PROGRAMS | REENTRY SUCCESS CENTER

2500 Bissell Ave., Richmond, CA 94804
(510) 235-1516
www.rubiconprograms.org

SANTA CLARA COUNTY REENTRY SERVICES

151 W. Mission St., San Jose, CA 95110
(408) 535-4280
www.sccgov.org/sites/reentry

SECOND CHANCE | STRIVE

6145 Imperial Ave., San Diego, CA 92114
(619) 234-8888
www.secondchanceprogram.org

Second Chance provides CA ex-offenders with job readiness skills. Using the STRIVE model, they offer a 3-week training program, which includes resume writing, interview and clothing techniques, and personal skills. STRIVE graduates have an 80% employment success rate.

SENIOR EX-OFFENDER PROGRAM

1706 Yosemite Ave., San Francisco, CA 94124
(415) 593-8235
www.seopsf.org

SEOP provides reentry services to CA ex-offenders who are over the age of 50 (45 for women), including benefits assistance (SSI, GA, TANF, etc.), clothing, counseling, food, phone services, and referrals.

SEVENTH STEP FOUNDATION | EAST BAY CHAPTER

474 Medford Ave., Hayward, CA 04541
(510) 278-8031

The 7th Step Foundation – East Bay Chapter provides reentry services to Bay area ex-offenders, including housing through the Freedom House, meals, clothing, and employment services.

SWORDS TO PLOWSHARES

1060 Howard St., San Francisco, CA 94103
(415) 252-4788
www.swords-to-plowshares.org

Swords to Plowshares provides reentry assistance to ex-offender veterans reentering into the San Francisco Bay area.

TIME FOR CHANGE FOUNDATION

PO Box 25040, San Bernardino, CA 92406
(909) 886-2994
www.timeforchangefoundation.org

VOA REENTRY

Bay Area | Northern California/Northern Nevada
3434 Marconi Ave., Sacramento, CA 95821
(916) 265-3400
www.voa-ncnn.org

Los Angeles | Greater LA
543 Crocker St., Los Angeles, CA 90013
(213) 228-1911
www.voala.org

WORKPLACE CA, THE

3407 W. 6th St., Suite 705, Los Angeles, CA 90020
(714) 392-4231
www.theworkplace.com

The Workplace CA is a for-profit agency that provides reentry services to ex-offenders in Orange County, San Fernando Valley, and LA County, including employment skills training and enrollment into vocational training. Schedule an appointment upon release.

WELCOME HOME MINISTRIES

1701 Mission Ave., Trailer A, Oceanside, CA 92054
(760) 439-1136
www.welcomehomeint.org

WH Ministries is a national faith-based program that provides reentry support for women ex-offenders, including reunification with children, education, job support, and more.

YOUTH OPPORTUNITIES FOR SAN FRANCISCO

1850 Mission St., San Francisco, CA 94103
(415) 487-3912

YOSF provides reentry support to CA youth ex-offenders, ages 14-21, including employment and development resources.

Colorado | Centennial State

State Capital: Denver

Time Zone: MST

Population: 5,355,866

(87.7% white, 4.5% Black, 3.1% Asian, 1.6% American Indian (19.4% Hispanic))

Name Origin: From the Spanish word for red. First applied to the Colorado River

Motto: Nil Sine Numine (Nothing without providence)

Famous Californians: Tim Allen, Chauncey Billups, Lon Chaney, Jack Dempsey, Trey Parker.

State Agencies

CONSUMER PROTECTION

Colorado Attorney General, 1525 Sherman St., 5th Floor, Denver, CO 80203-1760
(800) 222-4444, (303) 866-5079

DRIVER RECORDS

Motor Vehicle, Business Group Driver Control, Denver CO 80246-1530
(303) 205-5613
www.revenue.state.co.us/mv-dir

SECRETARY OF STATE

1700 Broadway, Suite 200, Denver, CO 80290
(303) 894-2200
www.sos.state.co.us

VITAL RECORDS

Department of Public Health, 4300 Cherry Creek Dr. S., Denver, CO 80246-1530
(303) 692-2234
www.cdphe.state.co.us/hs

Prisoner Support

72 HOUR FUND

2015 Glenarm Place, Denver, CO
(303) 292-2304
www.doinghistime.org

ACLU OF COLORADO

400 Corona St., Denver, CO 80218
(303) 777-5482
www.aclu-co.org info@aclu-co.org

Advocates for the civil tonight of Colorado prisoners, generally through class actions. They typically will not accept individual prisoner cases, but they may provide referrals.

CENTER FOR SPIRITUALITY AT WORK

PO Box 102168, Denver, CO 80250
www.cfsaw.org

CSAW provides counseling, mentoring and life-skills services to CO prisoners and ex-offenders.

COLORADO CORRECTIONAL INDUSTRIES

2862 S. Circle Dr., Colorado Springs, CO 80906
(719) 226-4208
www.coloradoci.com

COLORADO CRIMINAL JUSTICE REFORM

1212 Mariposa St., Suite 6, Denver, Co 80204
(303) 825-0122
www.ccjrc.org

CCJRC is a coalition of organizations and individuals who are fighting against mass-incarceration in Colorado. They publish and distribute information guides and a newsletter, FREE for prisoners, as well as a 200-page reentry guide, *Go Guide*, for $10.

CURE | COLORADO

3470 Poplar St., Suite 406, Denver, CO 80204
(303) 758-3390
www.coloradocure.org

CURE provides advocacy and organization through prisoners and their supporters to affect reforms in the CO prison system.

DRUG POLICY ALLIANCE | COLORADO

1839 York St., #100, Denver, CO 80206
www.drugpolicy.org co@drugpolicy.org

DPA is a national organization that focuses on laws and punishments related to drug convictions and abuses. Their Colorado office can provide information specific to Colorado prisoners and state drug policies.

KOREY WISE INNOCENCE PROJECT | UNIVERSITY OF COLORADO LAW SCHOOL

Wolf Law Building, 404 UCB, Boulder, CO 80309-0404
(303) 492-8126
www.colorado.edu/law/academics/experiential-learning/clinics/innocence

CO Innocence Project provides advocacy and representation to CO prisoners with provable claims of innocence. Cases must have originated in CO and have already gone through the appellate process. Write for a copy of their evaluation criteria.

UNCHAINED BOOKS

PO Box 784, Fort Collins, CO 80522
www.unchainedbooks.wordpress.com

UB supports prisoners through fundraising, outreach, and community awareness for prisoner-related legal issues. They also send books, FREE to prisoners, and corresponds with political prisoners.

UNIVERSITY OF DENVER | STURM COLLEGE OF LAW

2255 E. Evans Ave., Denver, CO 80208
(303) 871-6140
www.law.du.edu

The Sturm College of Law provides student advocacy and representation to prisoners in the Colorado prison system. Typically, they accept both individual cases and issues that affect a large group of prisoners through class actions.

Reentry Resources

COLORADO PRISON ASSOCIATION | VOLUNTEERS OF AMERICA

2660 Larimer St., Denver, CO 80205
(303) 297-0400

CPA provides reentry support to CO ex-offenders through referrals for emergency financial assistance.

COMMUNITY REENTRY PROJECT

391 Delaware St., Denver, CO 80204
(720) 865-2330
www.communityreentryproject.org

E-COLORADO REENTRY SERVICES | COLORADO DEPARTMENT OF LABOR & EMPLOYMENT

633 17th St., Suite 700, Denver, CO 80202--3660
(303) 318-8822
e-colorado.coworkforce.com

EMPOWERMENT PROGRAM, THE

1600 York St., Denver, CO 80206
(303) 320-1989
www.empowermentprogram.org

EP provides reentry support for CO women ex-offenders in the Denver area, including housing, job training and placement assistance, health and education services, case management, and transportation

FOCUS REENTRY

4705 Baseline Rd., Boulder, CO 80303
(720) 304-6446
www.focusreentry.org

REDEEMED ONES JAIL AND PRISON MINISTRY

PO Box 31105, Aurora, CO 80041
(720) 290-0721
www.redeemedonesoutreachministries.org

THE ROAD CALLED STRATE

1532 Galena St., Suite 395, Aurora, CO 80010
(303) 520-5118
www.theroadcalledstrate.com

ST. FRANCIS CENTER EMPLOYMENT SERVICES

1630 E. 14th Ave., Denver, CO 80218
(303) 813-0005
www.turnaboutprogram.org

TURNABOUT

1630 E. 14th Ave., Denver, CO 80218
(303) 813-0005
www.turnaboutprogram.org

Turnabout provides reentry services to CO ex-offenders in the Denver Metro area, including job training and placement assistance, access to computers, and transportation assistance.

Connecticut | Nutmeg State

State Capital: Hartford

Time Zone: EST

Population: 3,596,677

(81.2% white, 11.5% Black, 4.5% Asian, 0.5% American Indian (13.3% Hispanic))

Name Origin: From Mohican and other Algonquin words meaning 'long river place.'

Motto: Qui Transtulit Sustinet (He who transplanted still sustains.)

Famous "Nutmeggers": Ethan Allen, P.T. Barnum, Glen Close, Ann Coulter, Katherine Hepburn, Seth MacFarlane, John Mayer, J.P. Morgan, Mark Twain.

State Agencies

CONSUMER PROTECTION

165 Capitol Ave., Hartford, CT 46106
(860) 713-6050
www.ct.gov/dcp

DRIVER RECORDS

Department of Motor Vehicles, 60 State St., Wethersfield, CT 06161-0503
www.ct.gov/dmv

SECRETARY OF STATE

30 Trinity St., Hartford, CT 06106
(860) 509-6003
www.sos.ct.gov

VITAL RECORDS

Department of Public Health, 410 Capitol Ave., MS #11 VRS, Hartford, CT 06134

Prisoner Support

ACLU | CONNECTICUT

330 Main St., First Floor, Hartford, CT 06106
(860) 523-9146
www.acluct.org info@acluct.org

Advocates for the civil rights of CT prisoners through class actions. They typically will not accept individual prisoner cases, but may provide referrals. Prisoners can call between 9AM-10AM on Fridays to voice prison concerns.

A BETTER WAY FOUNDATION | CONNECTICUT

PO Box 942, Hartford, CT 06143
(860) 270-9585
www.awbf-ct.org

A Better Way Foundation provides advocacy to affect lower rates of recidivism. Write for current programs.

CENTER FOR PRISON EDUCATION

222 Church St., Middletown, CT 06459
(860) 685-2247

CPE provides education opportunities for prisoners at the following correctional institutions: Cheshire, MacDougall-Walker and York.

CONNECTICUT CORRECTIONS OMBUDSMAN

110 Bartholomew Ave., Suite 4010, Hartford, CT 06106
(866) 951-8867 (collect calls accepted)

CCO fields and investigates complaints made by CT prisoners about conditions of confinement. They encourage going through the prison counselor first.

COMMUNITY PARTNERS IN ACTION

Parkville Business Center, 110 Bartholomew Ave., #3010, Hartford, CT 06143
(860) 566-2030
www.cpa-ct.org

CPA works to provide concepts and advocacy for policy changes that affect community through community support. Some advocacy reaches into the Connecticut prison system. Write for current programs.

CONNECTICUT INNOCENCE PROJECT

82275 Silas Deane Highway, Rocky Hill, CT 06067
(860) 509-6400
www.ct.gov/ocpd

CIP provides advocacy and representation to wrongfully convicted CT prisoners, DNA and non-DNA cases are accepted. Must have at least 5 years left on prisoner sentence of 10 years of more, be indigent, and there must be some new evidence.

FAMILIES IN CRISIS

Hartford: 60 Popielusko Ct., Hartford, CT 06106
(860) 727-5800
New Haven: 45 Court St., New Haven, CT 06511
(203) 498-7790
Waterbury: 232 N. Elm St., Waterbury, CT 06702
(203) 573-8656
www.familiesincrisis.org
administration@familiesincrisis.org

FIC provides a wide range of services for CT prisoners and their families, including counseling, childcare, transportation, group support, training programs, domestic violence intervention, and more. They also offer some reentry programs.

INMATES LEGAL ASSISTANCE PROGRAM

78 Oak St., PO Box 260237, Hartford, CT 06126-0237
(860) 246-1118

ILAP provides legal assistance to CT prisoners who are representing themselves on civil matters, including identifying and researching legal claims, advice, preparation for filings, and more. They will NOT represent you or appear on your behalf in court.

JEROME N. FRANK LEGAL SERVICES ORGANIZATION

PO Box 209090, New Haven, CT 06520
(203) 432-4800
www.law.yale.edu

JF Legal Services Organization provides legal assistance and legal referrals on a variety of legal issues.

PEOPLE EMPOWERING PEOPLE | UCONN COOPERATIVE EXTENSION SERVICE

UConn Pox 70, Haddam, CT 06438

PEP provides support to CT prisoners and their families by teaching life skills, mentoring, and other services. Write for a current list of programs.

Reentry Resources

CAREER RESOURCES

350 Fairfield Ave., Bridgeport, CT 06604
(203) 333-5129
www.careerresources.org

CR provides ex-offenders in CT with career training and job skills development. Prisoners can receive a FREE local directory of job development organizations in the Bridgeport area.

CITY OF NEW HAVEN | FRESH START

Office of the Mayor, 165 Church St., New Haven, CT 06510
(203) 946-6721
www.cityofnewhaven.com/mayor/prisonreentry.asp

COMMUNITY PARTNERS IN ACTION

110 Bartholomew Ave., Suite 3010, Hartford, CT 06106
(860) 566-2030
www.cpa-ct.org

CPA provides a variety of reentry services to ex-offenders in CT. Write for a current listing of services.

COMMUNITY RENEWAL TEAM

303 Market St., Hartford, Ct 06120-2901
(860) 761-7900
www.crtct.org

CRT provides a variety of reentry services to ex-offenders in CT. Write for a current listing of services.

CONNECTICUT WORKS CENTERS | CONNECTICUT DEPARTMENT OF LABOR

200 Folly brook Blvd., Wethersfield, CT 06109
(860) 263-6000
www.ctdol.state.ct.us

FAMILY REENTRY (FRE)

9 Mott Ave., suite 104, Norwalk, CT 06850
(203) 838-0496
www.familyreentry.org

ISAIAH 61:1, INC.

PO Box 1399, Bridgeport, CT 06601
(203) 368-6116

Isaiah 61:1 provides reentry support to prisoners and ex-offenders in CT, including pre-release programs, work release, career guidance, counseling and education, life-skills training, and family therapy. Programs typically last 3-4 months for men and 6-9 months for women.

PERCEPTION PROGRAMS

54 North St., Box 407, Willimantic, CT 06226
(860) 450-7122

PP provides CT prisoners with alternatives to incarceration, including work release programs, substance abuse treatment and education.

STRIVE

New Haven: 904 Howard Ave., 2nd Floor, New Haven, CT 06511
(203) 777-1720
www.strivenewhaven.com
South Arsenal Neighborhood Development: 1500 Main St., Hartford, CT 06120
(860) 278-8460
www.sandcorporation.com

The STRIVE program assists ex-offenders with job skills and with employment opportunities for program participants.

Delaware | Diamond State (also, First State)

State Capital: Dover

Time Zone: EST

Population: 935,614

(70.8% white, 22.2% Black, 3.8% Asian, 0.7% American Indian (7.8% Hispanic))

Name Origin: Named for Lord De La War, the early governor of Virginia.

Motto: Liberty and Independence

Famous Delawareans: Joe Biden, Howard Pyle, Caesar Rodney

State Agencies

CONSUMER PROTECTION

Office of Attorney General, Carvel State Office Building, 820 N. French St., Wilmington, DE 19801
(800) 220-5424, (302) 577-8600, TTY: (302) 577-6499
www.state.de.us/attgen

DRIVER RECORDS

Division of Motor Vehicles, PO Box 698, Dover, DE 19801
(302) 744-2511
www.dmv.de.gov

SECRETARY OF STATE

PO Box 898, Dover, DE 19903
(302) 739-3073
www.state.de.us

VITAL RECORDS

Department of Health, 417 Federal St., Dover, DE 19901
(302) 744-4549
www.dhss.delaware.gov

Prisoner Support

ACLU | DELAWARE

100 W. 10th St., Suite 603, Wilmington, DE 19801
(302) 654-3966
www.aclu-de.org

Advocates for the civil rights of DE prisoners, generally through class actions. They will typically not accept individual cases, but may provide referrals.

AIDS DELAWARE

Wilmington: 100 W. 10th St., Suite 315, Wilmington, DE 19801
(302) 652-6776
Kent and Sussex County: 706 Rehobeth Ave., Rehobeth, DE 19971
(302) 226-5350
www.aidsdelaware.org contact@aidsdelaware.org

AIDS DE provides FREE HIV/AIDS services to prisoners, including testing and counseling, case management, prevention and educational programs, support groups and an anonymous hotline. They also provide safe-sex literature and newsletters FREE to prisoners.

CURE | DELAWARE

PO Box 542, New Castle, DE 19720

CURE provides advocacy and organization through prisoners and their supporters to achieve reforms in the DE prison system.

DELAWARE CENTER FOR JUSTICE

100 W. 10th St., Suite 905, Wilmington, DE 19801
(302) 658-7174
www.dcjustice.org center@dcjustice.org

DCJ provides advocacy for prisoners and their families, including assistance with prison grievances, legislative advocacy, AIDS education and counseling, and more. They have a quarterly newsletter, *Delaware Center for Justice Commentary,* FREE to Delaware prisoners.

MENTORING CHILDREN OF PRISONERS

2500 w. 4th St., Suite 5B, Wilmington, DE 19805

(302) 656-7737

The Mentoring Children of Prisoners Program provides weekly one-on-one mentoring of youth who are adversely affected by life circumstances, including a parent's incarceration.

OFFICE OF PUBLIC DEFENDER

Carvel State Office Building, 820 N. French St., 3rd Floor, Wilmington, DE 19801
(302) 577-5160

ODP provides representation to DE prisoners with actual innocence claims with DNA evidence only.

Reentry Resources

CENTER FOR RELATIONAL LIVING | SECOND CHANCES PROGRAM

100 W. 10th St., Suite 614, Wilmington, DE 19801
(302) 428-3850
www.relationalliving.org

DELAWARE CENTER FOR JUSTICE

100 W. 10th St., Suite 905, Wilmington, DE 19801
(302) 658-7174
www.dcjustice.org

ONE-STOP CAREER CENTERS | DEPARTMENT OF LABOR

4425 N. Market St., Wilmington, DE 19802
(302) 761-8085
www.joblink.delaware.gov/ada

WAY HOME, THE

PO Box 1103, Georgetown, DE 19947
(302) 856-9870
www.thewayhomeprogram.org

The Way Home program provides reentry services to DE ex-offenders, including housing, case management, job search assistance, transportation, support groups, and more.

District of Columbia

Time Zone: EST

Population: 658,893

(43.6% black; 49% White, 4% Asian, 0.6% American Indian (8.3% Hispanic))

Name Origin: Named for Christopher Columbus

District Agencies

CONSUMER PROTECTION

941 N. Capitol St. NE, Washington, DC 20002
(202) 442-4400
www.dcra.dc.gov

DRIVER RECORDS

Department of Motor Vehicles, 65 K St. NE, Washington, DC 20002
(202) 727-1530
www.dmc.dc.gov

VITAL RECORDS

Department of Health, 899 N. Capitol St. NE, First Floor, Washington, DC 20002
(202) 442-9009
www.dchealth.dc.gov

Prisoner Support

ACLU | NATIONAL CAPITOL AREA

4301 Connecticut Ave., Suite 434, Washington, DC 20008-2368
(202) 457-0800
www.aclu-nca.org

Advocates for the civil rights of DC prisoners, generally through class actions. They typically will not accept individual prisoner cases, but they may provide referrals.

ALLIANCE OF CONCERNED MEN

3227 Dubois Place SE, Washington DC 20019
(202) 575-7544
www.acmdc.org info@acmdc.org

ACMDC provides programs designed to prevent the mistreatment of prisoners, decrease recidivism, and promote a better understanding of justice in our society.

COURT SERVICES AND OFFENDER SUPERVISION AGENCY FOR THE DISTRICT OF COLUMBIA (CSOSA)

633 Indiana Ave. NW, Washington, DC 20004-2902
(202) 220-5300
www.csosa.gov/reentry

CURE | NATIONAL

PO Box 2310, Washington, DC 20013
(202) 789-2126
www.curenational.org cure@curenational.org

CURE provides advocacy and organization through prisoners and supporters to achieve reforms in the prison system.

DC PRISONERS' PROJECT

11 Dupont Cir. NW, Suite 400, Washington, DC 20036
(202) 319-1000, (202) 775-0323 (prisoner helpline, collect calls accepted.)
www.washlaw.org/projects/dc-prisoners-rights

DCPP provides representation to DC Code offenders in prison-related civil matters, and for some parole grant hearings. They also provide information to prisoners and their families on prisoner rights issues related to DC, health services, HIV/AIDS education, and referrals.

MID-ATLANTIC INNOCENCE PROJECT

200 H St. NW, Washington, DC 20052
(202) 994-4586
www.exonerate.org

MAIP provides DC, Virginia, and Maryland prisoners that they have determined to be innocent with legal representation and investigative services.

PRISONS FOUNDATION

2512 Virginia Ave. NW, Suite 58034, Washington, DC 20037
(202) 393-1511
www.prisonsfoundation.org

PF sponsors prison art and craft shows around the U.S. with the support of the National Endowment of the Arts.

They also sell prisoner art through various galleries in the DC area and put on shows at the Kennedy Center to showcase prisoner talents in acting and music performance. Write for information on how you can participate.

PRISONERS' RIGHTS PROGRAM

633 Indiana Ave. NW, Washington, DC 20004
(202) 628-1200

PRP provides legal advocacy to prisoners in the DC area on conditions of confinement issues. (See the Legal Center in this book for rights in this area.) They will not represent prisoners in criminal matters or reduction of sentence issues. Write for more information and fact sheets and various prison law topics.

VISITORS' SERVICE CENTER

1422 Massachusetts Ave. SE, Washington, DC 20003
(202) 544-2131
www.vscdcjails.net

VSC provides volunteers to those incarcerated in DC jails and assists various needs, including housing and job assistance, referrals to drug treatment, and third-party custodianship support.

Reentry Resources

CATHOLIC CHARITIES | WELCOME HOME REENTRY PROGRAM

924 G St. NW, Washington, DC 20001
(202) 772-4300
www.catholiccharitiesdc.org

JUBILEE HOUSING

1640 Columbia Rd. NW, 2nd Floor, Washington, DC 20009
(202) 299-1240
www.jubileehousing.org

Jubilee Housing is a faith-based organization that provides housing assistance to disadvantaged residents of DC

JUBILEE JOBS

2712 Ontario Rd. NW, Washington, DC 20009
(202) 667-8970
www.jubileejobs.org

Jubilee Jobs is a faith-based organization that provides job training and placement assistance to DC area residents in need.

OFFICE OF RETURNING CITIZEN AFFAIRS

2100 MLK Jr. Ave. SE, Washington, DC 20020
(202) 715-7670
www.orca.dc.org

ORCA provides support assistance to DC ex-offenders though counseling, guidance and referrals.

OUR PLACE DC

801 Pennsylvania Ave. SE, Suite 301, Washington, DC 20003
(202) 548-2400
www.ourplacedc.org

Our Place DC provides reentry services for ex-offenders in the DC area, including housing and employment resources, and referrals to other services for a positive reentry.

REENTRY NETWORK FOR RETURNING CITIZENS, THE

4322 Sheriff Rd. NE, Washington, DC 20019
(202) 450-1401
thereentrynetworkdc.wordpress.com

STRIVE | DC

715 I St. NE, Washington, DC 20002
(202) 484-1264

The STRIVE program assists ex-offenders with job skills and with employment opportunities for program participants.

VOICES FOR A SECOND CHANCE

1422 Massachusetts Ave. SE, Washington, DC 20003
(202) 544-2131
www.vscdc.org

Florida | Sunshine State

State Capital: Tallahassee

Time Zone: EST

Population: 19,893,297

(77.8% white, 16.8% Black, 2.8% Asian, 0.5% American Indian (21.2% Hispanic))

Name Origin: Named by Juan Ponce de Leon Pasqua Florida, meaning 'flowery Easter', on Easter Sunday, 1513.

Motto: In God We Trust

Famous Floridians: Jeb Bush, Perez Hilton, Tom Petty, Janet Reno, Marco Rubio, Deion Sanders, Emmit Smith, Amar'e Stoudemire.

State Agencies

CONSUMER PROTECTION

Economic Crimes Division, Office or the Attorney General, PL-01, The Capitol, Tallahassee, FL 32399-1050
(866) 966-7226, (850) 444-3600, TTY: (800) 955-9771
www.myfloridalegal.com

DRIVER RECORDS

Division of Driver's Licenses, PO Box 5775, Tallahassee, FL 32314-5775
(850) 488-0250
www.hsmv.state.fl.us

SECRETARY OF STATE

PO Box 6327, Tallahassee, FL 32314
(800) 755-5111
www.sunbix.org

VITAL RECORDS

Department of Health, PO Box 210, Jacksonville, FL 32231-0042
(904) 359-6900

Prisoner Support

ACLU | FLORIDA

4500 Biscayne Blvd., Suite 340, Miami, FL 33137
(786) 363-2700
www.aclufl.org aclufl@aclufl.org

Advocates for the civil rights of FL prisoners, generally through class actions. They typically will not accept individual prisoner cases, but they may provide referrals.

COMMUNITY LEGAL SERVICES OF MID-FLORIDA

128 Orange Ave., Suite 300, Daytona Beach, FL 32114
(386) 255-6573
www.clsmf.org

CURE | FLORIDA

PO Box 40934, Jacksonville, FL 32203
(904) 861-7659
www.flcure.org

CURE provides advocacy and organization through prisoners and their supporters to achieve reforms in the Florida prison system.

INNOCENCE PROJECT OF FLORIDA

1100 E. Park Avenue Blvd., Suite 340, Miami, FL 33137-3227
(786) 363-2700
www.floridainnocence.org

IP of Florida provides advocacy and representation for wrongfully convicted Florida prisoners. They only accept cases with DNA evidence, but have no sentencing requirements. They also provide transitional services for those who have been exonerated.

FAMILIES AGAINST MANDATORY MINIMUMS | FLORIDA PROJECT

PO Box 142933, Gainesville, FL 32614
(352) 682-2542
www.famm.org/florida famm@famm.org
(Corrlinks registered)

FAMM is a coalition of Florida prisoner's families that advocates against mandatory minimum sentencing and gathers data from prisoners under mandatory minimums. To submit a case for profiling, send a written summary of your circumstances. They receive many, but only use a few. They provide an email newsletter to friends and family.

FLORIDA INSTITUTIONAL LEGAL SERVICES

14260 W. Newberry Rd., Suite 412, Newberry, FL 32669
(352) 375-2494
www.floridalawhelp.org

FILS provides comprehensive advocacy for FL prisoners through class actions and individual prisoner litigation that has a broad impact on the prison system. They also work with other advocacy groups to increase and improve assistance for prisoners to promote alternatives to incarceration and successful reentry. They publish *Florida Parental Rights Manual for Incarcerated Parents* (2008, 106 pages), FREE for prisoners.

FLORIDA JUSTICE INSTITUTE

100 SE Second St., Suite 3750, Miami, FL 33131
(305) 358-2081
www.floridajusticeinstitute.org

FJI advocates for Florida prisoners who have conditions of confinement issues through legal actions and lobbying with legislators, including damage suites and civil rights actions. They do not accept post-conviction or criminal cases.

OPEN BOOKS PRISON BOOK PROJECT

1040 N. Guillemard St., Pensacola, FL 32501
(850) 453-6774
www.openbookspcola.org

Open Books provides FREE books to indigent Florida prisoners.

RISE

413 W. Imogene St., Arcadia, FL 34266
www.riseflorida.org *generalquestions@riseflorida.org*

RISE offers support to families of the incarcerated by providing summer programs for children, carpool arrangements for visiting family retreats, a quarterly newsletter, and more.

UNIVERSITY OF MIAMI LAW INNOCENCE CLINIC

1311 Miller Dr., Coral Gable, FL 33146
(305) 284-2339
www.law.miami.edu/clinics/innocence

MU UL Innocence Clinic provides legal representation to wrongfully convicted Florida prisoners who are serving at least 10 years. Case must be provable through new evidence.

Reentry Resources

2ND CHANCE MENTAL HEALTH CENTER

1541 SE Port St. Lucie Blvd., Suite F, Port St. Lucie, FL 34952
(772) 335-0166
www.2ndchancemhc.com

CENTER FOR MEN & WOMEN | FRESH START PROGRAM

1200 W. International Speedway Blvd., Daytona Beach, FL 32114
(386) 506-3059
www.daytonastate.edu/centerforwomenandmen/freshstart

DISMAS CHARITIES

6860 Edgewater Dr., Orlando, FL 32810
(407) 285-1989
www.dismas.com

FAITH REENTRY ENTERPRISE

4851 S. Apopka-Vineland Rd., Orlando, FL 32819
(407) 876-4991, ext. 298
www.freelifelines.org

FDOC REENTRY RESOURCES DIRECTORY

www.doc.state.fl.us/resourcedirectory

The FDOC reentry resource directory is searchable database of reentry programs and services in the Florida area, listed by county, city, and zip code.

GOODWILL INDUSTRIES | GULFSTREAM

1715 Tiffany Dr. E., West Palm Beach, FL 33407
(561) 848-7200
www.gulfstreamgoodwill.com

HOUSE OF HOPE

29 SE 21st St., Gainesville, FL 32641
(352) 672-5082
www.houseofhopegnv.org

HOH is a faith-based organization that provides reentry services to Florida ex-offenders, including housing and job placement. Must apply through prison chaplain six months prior to release.

OPERATION NEW HOPE COMMUNITY DEVELOPMENT CORPORATION

1830 N. Main St., Jacksonville, FL 32206
(904) 354-4673
www.operationnewhope.com

ONH provides reentry support to Florida ex-offenders, including on-the-job training and employment in the construction field.

PINELLAS EX-OFFENDER REENTRY COALITION

PO Box 15936, St. Petersburg, FL 33733
(727) 538-4191
6160 Ulmerton Rd., Unit 10, Clearwater, FL 33760
(855) 505-7372
1601 16th St., St. Petersburg, FL 33705
(727) 954-3993
1200 S. Pinellas Ave., Suite 8, Tarpon Springs, FL 34689
(855) 505-7372
www.exoffender.org

PEORC is a coalition of more than 40 churches and other organizations that promote reentry services for ex-offenders in the Pinellas region, including housing, clothing, food, job training, and employment services.

PROJECT 180: REENTRY

PO Box 25684, Sarasota, FL 34277-2684
(941) 677-2281
www.project180reentry.org

RESTORATION MINISTRIES

1732 NW 2nd Ave., Ocala, FL 34478
(352) 369-6364

RESTORATION MINISTRIES FOR WOMEN

302 Buchanon Ave., Orlando, FL 32809
(407) 438-0943
www.rmwchanginglives.org

TAMPA CROSSROADS

5120 N. Nebraska Ave., Tampa, FL 33603
(812) 238-8557
www.tampacrossroads.com

TC provides reentry services to Tampa area ex-offenders, including housing, job skills training, case management, and therapy.

TIME FOR FREEDOM

2006 NE 8th Rd., Ocala, FL 34470
(352) 351-1280
www.thefreedomhouse.org

TFF is a faith-based reentry service provider for Ocala area ex-offenders. Services include transitional housing and general support. Residents are required to attend group meetings, bible studies, and life skills courses.

WEAVER FOUNDATION, THE

5904 Lemos Ct., Orlando, FL 32808
(407) 325-8225
www.weaverforwomen.com

The Weaver Foundation provides reentry services for Florida women ex-offenders.

Georgia | Empire State of the South

State Capital: Atlanta

Time Zone: EST

Population: 10,097,343

(62.1% white, 31.5% Black, 3.8% Asian, 0.5% American Indian (8.5% Hispanic))

Name Origin: Named by Colonial Administrator James Oglethorpe for King George II of England.

Motto: Wisdom, Justice, and Moderation

Famous Georgians: James Brown, Jimmy Carter, Ray Charles, Ty Cobb, Newt Gingrich, Nancy Grace, Larry Holmes, Martin Luther King, Jr., Gladys Knight, Julia Roberts, Ted Turner.

State Agencies

DRIVER RECORDS

Department of Driver Services, PO Box 80447, Conyers, GA 30013
(678) 413-8441
www.dds.ga.gov

SECRETARY OF STATE

315 W. Tower 2, MLK Dr., Atlanta, GA 30034
(404) 656-2817
www.sos.state.ga.us

VITAL RECORDS

Department of Human Resources, 2600 Skyland Dr. NE, Atlanta, GA 30319-3640
(404) 679-4701
www.health.state.ga.us

Prisoner Support

ACLU | GEORGIA

1900 The Exchange, Suite 425, Atlanta, GA 30339
(707) 303-9966
www.acluga.org info@acluga.org

Advocates for the civil rights of Georgia prisoners, generally through class actions. They typically will not accept individual prisoner cases, but may provide referrals.

BIG BROTHERS/BIG SISTERS OF THE HEART OF GEORGIA | MENTORING CHILDREN OF PROMISE IN CENTRAL GEORGIA

777 Walnut St., Macon, GA 31201
(478) 745-3984
www.bbbsheaatga.org

Big Brothers/Big Sisters of the Heart of Georgia provides one-on-one mentoring to children of the incarcerated in Central Georgia.

CURE | GEORGIA

2173 Waterway Lane, Snellville, GA 30078
(678) 252-8256

GA CURE provides advocacy and organization through GA prisoners and their supporters to achieve reforms in the GA prisoner system. Write to see how you can get involved.

FOREVER FAMILY

765 McDaniel St. SW, Suite 3104, Atlanta, GA 30310
(404) 658-9606
www.foreverfam.org

FF advocates and provides services for incarcerated parents, including information and guidance support. They also provide social services to prisoners in the Atlanta area.

FRIENDS OF PRISON FAMILIES

1020 DeKalb Ave. NE, Atlanta, GA 30306
(404) 523-7110

FPF provides support services for prisoner and their families, including arranging monthly visits and phone calls, educational programs in social and family responsibility, and pre-release planning in which family members are enlisted to help develop job and housing opportunities.

GEORGIA INNOCENCE PROJECT

2645 N. Decatur Rd., Decatur, GA 30033
(404) 373-4433

www.ga-innocenceproject.org

GIP advocates and provides representation for wrongfully convicted prisoners in GA and AL. They help secure DNA testing where adequate testing was not available at trial and where it may provide innocence, as well as other legal assistance.

GIDEON'S PROMISE

34 Peachtree St. NW, PO Box 2460, Atlanta, GA 30303

GP provides assistance to GA public defenders to better ensure that prisoners receive quality legal representation.

SOUTHERN CENTER FOR HUMAN RIGHTS

83 Poplar St. NW, Atlanta, GA 30303-2122
(404) 688-1202
www.schr.org rights@schr.org

SCHR provides legal representation to Georgia (and Alabama) prisoners who are facing the death penalty and prisoners whose civil rights have been violated in a way that affects broad numbers of prisoners. They will respond to complaints that include capital convictions, physical or sexual assault.

SOUTHERN PRISON MINISTRY

910 Ponce de Leon Ave. NE, Atlanta, GA 30306-4212
(404) 874-9652
www.opendoorcommunity.org

SPM provides advocacy and support for prisoners and their families, including visitation, correspondence, transport, and hospitality for visiting family members. They primarily focus on death row prisoners and their families, but some service may be available to others.

Reentry Resources

ATLANTA CENTER FOR SELF-SUFFICIENCY

100 Edgewood Ave NE, Suite 700, Atlanta, GA 30303
(404) 874-8001
www.atlantacss.org

CRISON MINISTRIES WITH WOMEN

465 Boulevard SE, Suite 205, Atlanta, GA 30312
(404) 622-4314

CMW provides reentry support to GA ex-offenders, including transitional housing, job training, and other services.

DEKALB WORKFORCE DEVELOPMENT | THE REENTRY PROGRAM

774 Jordan Lane, Building 4, Decatur, GA 30033
(404) 687-3400
www.workdev.dekalbcountyga.gov

GEORGIA DEPARTMENT OF CORRECTIONS | POST-RELEASE TRANSITIONAL PROGRAM

2 Martin Luther King Jr. Dr. SE, Twin Towers East, Room 756, Atlanta, GA 30334
(404) 656-4593
www.dcor.state.ga.us

GEORGIA JUSTICE PROJECT

438 Edgewood Ave., Atlanta, GA 30312
(404) 827-0027
www.gjp.org

GJP provides pre- and post-release support for prisoners, including advocacy and visitation by staff attorneys and social workers who assist with planning and transition after release, as well as employment in landscaping upon successful reentry.

GEORGIA PRISONER REENTRY INITIATIVE | DEPARTMENT OF COMMUNITY SUPERVISION

Governor's Office of Transition, Support and Reentry, 2 Martin Luther King Jr. Dr. SE, Suite 458, East Tower, Atlanta, GA 30334-4909
(404) 656-9770
des.georgia.gov/georgia-prisoner-reentry-initiative

GEORGIA REENTRY PARTNERSHIP HOUSING (RPH)

Georgia's Office of Transition, Support and Reentry, 270 Washington St., Suite 1198, Atlanta, GA 30334
(770) 639-8517
www.dca.state.ga.us/housing

GOODWILL OF NORTH GEORGIA

235 Peachtree St., North Tower, Suite 2300, Atlanta, GA 30303
(404) 420-9900
www.ging.org

GOODWILL INDUSTRIES OF THE COASTAL EMPIRE

7220 Sallie Mood Dr., Savannah, GA 31406-3921
(912) 354-6611

Gwinnett Reentry Intervention Program (GRIP) | United Way of Greater Atlanta
(404) 527-3511
www.unitedwayofatlanta.org/the-challenge/homelessness/grip

NATIONAL ASSOCIATION OF PREVIOUS PRISONERS

PO Box 82, Stone Mountain, GA 30086

NAPP provides reentry services to GA prisoners by coordinating with the community and faith-based organizations to make quality and helpful referrals to those reentering.

REENTRY COALITION

135 West Center St., Carrollton, GA 30117
(770) 834-6093
www.cfwg.net/re-entry-coalition-inc

TOPSTEP

GA Department of Labor, 148 Andrew Young International Blvd. NE, Suite 426, Atlanta, GA 30303
(404) 232-3540

TOPSTEP is a state government program that works with GA corrections to provide vocational training, provide gainful employment, and offer counseling and treatment services for ex-offenders.

TRANSITIONAL HOUSING FOR OFFENDER REENTRY DIRECTORY

pap.georgia.gov/transitional-hosing-offender-reentry

UNITED WAY ATLANTA

100 Edgewood Ave. NE, Atlanta, GA 30303
(404) 527-7200
www.unitedwayatlanta.org/get-help-2-1-1

Hawai'i | Aloha State

State Capital: Honolulu

Time Zone: HT

Population: 1,419,561

(37.5% Asian, 26.7% white, 2.5% Black, 0.4% American Indian (8.5% Hispanic))

Name Origin: Possibly derived from 'Hawaiki' or 'Owhyhee', Polynesian word for 'Homeland'.

Motto: Ua mau ke ea o ka aina I ka pono (The life of the land is perpetuated in righteousness.)

Famous Hawaiians: Tia Carrere, Don Ho, Nicole Kidman, Jason Scott Lee, Bruno Mars, Barack Obama, Michelle Wie.

State Agencies

DRIVER RECORDS

Traffic Violations Bureau, 1111 Alakea St., 2nd Floor, Honolulu, HI 96813
(808) 538-5530
www.hawaii.gov/dot

SECRETARY OF STATE

PO Box 40, Honolulu, HI 96810
(808) 586-2727
www.hawaii.gov/dcca

VITAL RECORDS

State Department of Health, PO Box 3378, Honolulu, HI 96801
(808) 586-4533
www.hawaii.gov/health/vital-records

Prisoner Support

ACLU | HAWAI'I

PO Box 3410, Honolulu, HI 96801
(808) 522-5900
www.acluhawaii.org office@acluhawaii.org

Advocates for the civil rights of Hawaii prisoners, generally through class actions. They typically will not accept individual prisoner cases, but they may provide referrals.

COMMUNITY ALLIANCE ON PRISONS

76 N. King St., Suite 203, Honolulu, HI 96817
(808) 927-1214

CAP advocates for prisoner rights through an initiative that works to improve prison conditions, the quality of justice, and smarter justice policies.

GOOD NEWS JAIL AND PRISON MINISTRY HAWAII

PO Box 31006, Honolulu, HI 96820
(808) 677-6665
www.goodnewshawaii.org

HAWAII FRIENDS OF RESTORATIVE JUSTICE

PO Box 489, Waialua, HI 96791
(808) 218-3712
www.hawaiifriends.org

HAWAI'I INNOCENCE PROJECT

2515 Dole St., Honolulu, HI 96822
(808) 956-6547
www.innocenceprojecthawaii.org

HIP provides advocacy and representation for wrongfully convicted HI prisoners who have a credible claim of innocence. Must have been convicted in HI, have considerable time left on sentence, and have evidence that can support a claim of actual innocence.

NEW HOPE PRISON MINISTRY

290 Sand Island Access Rd., Honolulu, HI 96819
(808) 842-4242 ext. 417
www.newhope.org.ministries

OFFICE OF THE OMBUDSMAN

465 S. King St., 4th Floor, Honolulu, HI 96813
(808) 587-0770, TTY: (808) 587-0773
www.ombudsman.hawaii.gov
complaints@ombudsman.hawaii.gov

Receives and attempts to resolve complaints from prisoners regarding conditions of confinement in state prison facilities (no federal or private facilities.) They will not provide legal assistance, case management, or advocacy services.

Reentry Resources

COMMUNITY ASSISTANCE CENTER | JOHN HOWARD ASSOCIATION

200 N. Vineyard Blvd., Suite 330, Honolulu, HI 96817
(808) 537-2917
www.cahawaii.org

CAP provides a variety of reentry and transition services for HI ex-offenders, including transitional housing for women and youths, counseling, and other services. They also educate the public on criminal justice and crime prevention.

GOING HOME HAWAII

296 Kilauea Ave., Hilo, HI 96720
(808) 935-3050
www.goinghomehawaii.org

GOODWILL INDUSTRIES OF HAWAII

2610 Kilihua St., Honolulu, HI 96819-2020
(808) 836-0313
www.higoodwill.org

HAWAII DEPARTMENT OF PUBLIC SAFETY REENTRY GUIDES

dps.hawaii.gov/about/divisions/corrections/about-corrections/

HOPE SERVICES

296 Kilauea Ave., Hilo, HI 96720
(808) 935-3050
www.hopeserviceshawaii.org

KA HALE HO'ALA HOU NO HA WAHINE

c/o T.J. Mahoney & Associates, 524 Kaahi St., Honolulu, HI 96817
(808) 748-4300
www.reawakeningforwomen.org

Ka Hale Ho'ala Hou No Ha Wahine provides reentry services for Hawaiian women ex-offenders.

NETWORK ENTERPRISES

1505 Dillingham Blvd., Suite 303 Honolulu. HI 96817
(808) 521-7774
www.networkenterprises.org
mail@networkenterprises.org

NE provides job support, including counseling, training, and job placement to anyone in need.

SALVATION ARMY ADULT REHABILITATION CENTER

322 Summer St., Honolulu, HI 96817
(808) 522-8400
www.hawaii.salvationarmy.org/hawaii/arc

WORKHAWAII PRISONER REENTRY PROGRAM

Oahu WorkLinks, 1505 Dillingham Blvd., Suite 110, Honolulu, HI 96817
(808) 768-5600
www.honolulu.gov/dcs/workforce.html

WORKNET | RESTORING LIVES, STRENGTHENING COMMUNITIES

c/o The Nimitz Business Center, 1130 N. Nimitz Hwy., Suite B-224, Honolulu, HI 96817
(808) 521-7770
www.worknetinc.org

Idaho | Gem State

State Capital: Boise

Time Zone: MST

Population: 1,634,464

(93.5% white, 1.7% American Indian, 1.4% Asian, 0.8% Black (10.8% Hispanic))

Name Origin: Said to coined with the invented meaning "gem of the mountains." Another theory suggests 'Idaho' may be Kiowa Apache term for the Comanche.

Motto: Esto Perpetua (It is Perpetual)

Famous Idahoans: Lou Dobbs, Fred Dubois, Sacagewea, Picabo Street, Lana Turner.

State Agencies

DRIVER RECORDS

Idaho Transportation Department, PO Box 34, Boise, ID 83731-0034
(208) 334-8736
www.itd.idaho.gov/dmv

SECRETARY OF STATE

PO Box 91720, Boise, ID 83720
(208) 224-2301
www.idsos.state.id.us

VITAL RECORDS

PO Box 83720, Boise, ID 87220-0036
(208) 334-5988
www.healthandwelfare.idaho,gov

Prisoner Support

ACLU | IDAHO

PO Box 1897, Boise, ID 83701
(208) 344-9750
www.acluidaho.gov admin@acluidaho.org

Advocates for the civil rights of Idaho prisoners, generally through class actions. They typically will not accept individual prisoner cases, but they may provide referrals.

IDAHO INNOCENCE PROJECT

1910 University Dr., Boise, ID 83725
(208) 426-4207
www.innocenceproject/boisestate.edu

IIP provides advocacy and legal representation for wrongfully convicted Idaho and Eastern Oregon prisoners. DNA and non-DNA cases accepted, with no minimum sentencing requirement.

ROMAN CATHOLIC DIOCESE OF BOISE PRISON MINISTRY

1501 S. Federal Way, Suite 400, Boise, ID 83705
(208) 342-1311
www.catholicidaho.org

WELLBRIETY FOR PRISONS

912 12th Ave. S, Suite 204, Nampa, ID 83686
(208) 484-0231
wellbrietyforprisons.wordpress.com

Wellbriety provides rehabilitation services for tribal communities and associated prisoners.

Reentry Resources

EASTER SEALS GOODWILL REENTRY CENTER

8620 W. Emerald St., Suite 100, Boise, ID 83704
(208) 672-2900
www.esgw.org

GOOD SAMARITAN REHABILITATION

901 E. Best Ave., Coeur d'Alene, ID 83814
(208) 664-1453
www.goodsamrehabilitation.org

IDAHO DEPARTMENT OF LABOR REENTRY SERVICES

219 W. Main St., Boise, ID 83735
(208) 332-3575

Provides reentry information for prisoners about to be released from the Idaho prison system.

IDAHO REENTRY SERVICES

1299 N. Orchard St., Suite 110, Boise, ID 83706
www.idoc.idaho.gov/content/probation_and_parole/reentry_services

OFFENDER RESOURCES IDAHO

www.offenderresourcesidaho.org

Illinois | Prairie State

State Capital: Springfield

Time Zone: CST

Population: 12,880,580

(77.5% white, 14.7% Black, 5.3% Asian, 0.6% American Indian (15.7% Hispanic))

Name Origin: French for 'Illini' of 'Land of Illini' after the Algonquin word for "men" or "warriors."

Motto: State Sovereignty, National Union

Famous Illinoisans: John Belushi, Jack Benny, Al Capone, Hillary Clinton, John Deere, Wyatt Earp, Harrison Ford, Hugh Hefner, Ernest Hemingway, Charlton Heston, Oscar Meyer, Eliot Ness, Michelle Obama, Ronald Reagan, Shel Silverstein.

State Agencies

DRIVER RECORDS

Driver Services Department, 2701 S. Dirksen Pkwy, Springfield, IL 62723
(217) 782-2720
www.sos.state.il.us

SECRETARY OF STATE

330 Howlett Building, 3rd Floor, Springfield, IL 62756
(217) 782-7880
www.ilsos.net

VITAL RECORDS

Department of Public Health, 925 E. Ridgely Ave., Springfield, IL 62702
(217) 782-6553
www.idph.state.il.us

Prisoner Support

ACLU | ILLINOIS

180 N. Michigan Ave., Suite 2300, Chicago, IL 60601-1287
(312) 201-9740
www.aclu-il.org complaint@aclu-il.org

Advocates for the civil rights of Illinois prisoners, generally through class actions. They typically will not accept individual prisoner cases, but they may provide referrals.

CENTER ON WRONGFUL CONVICTIONS

357 E. Chicago Ave., Chicago, IL 60611-3069
www.law.northwestern.edu/cwc

CWC provides advocacy and legal representation for wrongfully convicted Illinois prisoners who are in no way responsible for the crimes they are convicted of. They focus on various factors, including erroneous witness testimony, false of coerced confessions, official misconduct, inadequate legal defense, false or misleading forensic evidence, and jailhouse informant testimony.

CHICAGO INNOCENCE PROJECT

205 W. Monroe St., Suite 315, Chicago, IL 60606
(312) 263-6213
www.chicagoinnocenceproject.org

CIP provides advocacy for wrongfully convicted Illinois prisoners who are serving death sentences or LWOP. They investigate innocence claims and work with members of the press and community to bring legitimately innocent cases to light, and may seek legal representation to bring new evidence to the courts.

CHICAGO LEGAL ADVOCATES FOR INCARCERATED MOTHERS(CLAIM)

c/o Cabrini Green, 740 N. Milwaukee Ave., Chicago, IL 60642
(312) 738-2451 ext. 451, (312) 675-0911 (collect calls)
www.cgla.net

CLAIM provides advice and some legal representation for incarcerated parents and their family members for family issues, including guardianship, visitation, and child custody. They publish an Illinois-focused resource guide for parents, which is FREE to prisoners. Women write to CLAIM. Men write to Cabrini Green at the same address.

CURE | ILLINOIS

1911 S. Clark, Unit D, Chicago, IL 60616
(312) 600-7455

CURE provides advocacy and organization through prisoners and their supporters to achieve reforms in the Illinois prison system.

EDUCATION JUSTICE PROJECT

805 Pennsylvania Ave., MC-057, Urbana, IL 61801
(217) 244-3344
www.educationjustice.net

EJP offers education programs to student prisoners at the Danville Correctional Center.

Note: Any prisoner can receive an education while behind bars. Order the *Prison Lives Almanac: Prisoner Education Guide*. See ad in this book.

ILLINOIS INNOCENCE PROJECT

One University Plaza, MS PAC 451, Springfield, IL 62703-5407
(217) 206-6569
www.uis.edu/innocenceproject

IIP provides advocacy and legal representation for wrongfully convicted Illinois prisoners in both DNA and non-DNA cases. They look for various factors that can help establish innocence, including absence of physical evidence, reliability of eye witnesses, identification of alternative suspects, official misconduct, and inconsistency in the nature of the crime with the background of the prisoner. Must have four or more years left on sentence.

ILLINOIS VOICES FOR REFORM

PO Box 95114, Hoffman Estates, IL 60195
www.ilvoices.com info@ilvoices.com

INCARCERATED VETERANS | ILLINOIS GUIDEBOOK

www.va.gov/homeless/docs/reentry/09_il.pdf

INSTITUTE OF WOMEN TODAY

7315 S. Yale Ave., Chicago, IL 60621
(773) 651-8372
instituteofwomen@sbcglobal.net

IWT provides advocacy for Illinois women prisoners, including legal representation for civil rights actions, prison health care, reentry services, and counseling and advocacy for children of incarcerated parents. They also have two transitional shelters. Write for a listing of current programs.

JEWISH PRISONERS ASSISTANCE FOUNDATION

9401 N. Margail, Suite 529, Chicago, IL 60016
(847) 296-1770
www.chabadandfree.com

JPAF advocates for the rights of Jewish prisoners.

JOHN HOWARD ASSOCIATION

PO Box 10042, Chicago, IL 60610-0042
(312) 291-9183
www.thejha.org info@john-howard.org

JHA is an independent prison monitor and advocates for prison reform and the civil rights of Illinois prisoners. They visit Illinois prisons and write reports on conditions, which are then provided to the public and to prisoners upon request. Write for current reports, or for copies of statutes, court decisions, forms, IDOC rules, and more.

LUTHERAN SOCIAL SERVICES OF ILLINOIS (LSSI) | PRISONER & FAMILY MINISTRY

1001 E. Touhy Ave., Suite 50, Des Plaines, IL 60018
(847) 635-4600
www.lssi.org

MACARTHUR JUSTICE CENTER | NORTHWESTERN UNIVERSITY LAW SCHOOL

375 E. Chicago Ave., Chicago, IL 60611
(312) 503-1271
www.law.northwestern.edu/macarthur

MJC advocates and litigates on Illinois justice matters, especially conditions of confinement. They typically will not accept individual prisoner cases unless it has a broad impact on prison issues.

MEDILL JUSTICE PROJECT | NORTHWESTERN UNIVERSITY

1845 Sheridan Ave., Evanston, IL 60208
(847) 491-5840
www.medilljusticeproject.org

MJP provides investigation services for Illinois prisoners who have been wrongfully convicted of murder. The case must have already been affirmed by the appellate courts and the crime must have been committed within 250 miles of Evanston, Illinois.

PEOPLE'S LAW OFFICE

1180 N. Milwaukee Ave., Chicago, IL 60642-4019
(773) 235-0070
www.peopleslawoffice.com

The People's Law Office advocates for those in the Illinois justice system who have been abused, unfairly sentenced to death, wrongfully convicted, or targeted for their religious beliefs.

PRISONER'S RIGHTS RESEARCH PROJECT

504 E. Pennsylvania Ave., Champaign, IL 61820
(217) 333-0930
www.law.illinois.edu

PRRP provides research and information services to anyone requesting answers to questions pertaining to Illinois state and federal prison law.

TRANSFORMATIVE JUSTICE LAW PROJECT OF ILLINOIS

4707 N. Broadway, Suite 307, Chicago, IL 60640
(773) 272-1822
www.tjlp.org

TJLP is a collective of activists, including radical attorneys, social workers, and community organizers who provides legal assistance and advocacy to transgender and gender non-conforming prisoners in Illinois.

UPTOWN PEOPLE'S LAW CENTER

4413 N. Sheridan, Chicago, IL 60640
(773) 769-1411
www.uplcchicago.org

UPLC Chicago advocates for the civil rights of prisoners in Illinois by helping find pro bono (FREE) attorneys for prisoners challenging denial of medical care, excessive force, denial of religious rights, access to courts, discrimination, and cruel and unusual punishment claims. No criminal law cases or habeas corpus petitions.

URBANA-CHAMPAIGN BOOKS-TO-PRISONERS PROJECT

PO Box 515, Urbana, IL 61803
(708) 782-4608
www.books2prisoners.org

UC Books-to-Prisoners provides FREE books to Illinois prisoners.

Note: You can find many more FREE books-to-prisoners programs and guidelines in our *Service Center* section.

Reentry Resources

7-70 REENTRY SERVICES

9146 Lincoln Ave., Brookfield, IL 60513
(706) 680-7075
www.ilreentryresources.com

BREAKTHROUGH URBAN MINISTRIES

PO Box 47200., Chicago, IL 60647
(773) 989-8353
www.breakthroughministries.com
info@breakthroughministries.com

BTM offers some reentry assistance to Illinois ex-offenders, including job training and placement, addiction recovery programs, food, and clothing. They also have limited overnight accommodations. Contact them prior to release.

CITY OF CHICAGO EX-OFFENDER REENTRY INITIATIVES

Office of the Mayor, 121 N. LaSalle St., Chicago, IL 60602
(312) 744-5500
www.cityofchicago.org/city/en/depts/mayor/supp_info/ex-offender_reentryintiatives.html

CORPORATION FOR SUPPORTIVE HOUSING | REENTRY ILLINOIS

205 W. Randolph, Chicago, IL 60606
(312) 332-6690 ext. 21
www.reentryillinois.net

INNER-CITY MUSLIM ACTION NETWORK (IMAN) | GREEN REENTRY

2744 W. 63rd St., Chicago, IL 60629
(773) 434-4626
www.imancentral.org/project-green-reentry

IMAN provides reentry services to Muslim ex-offenders in the Chicago area.

LIFE SKILLS CENTER | ROOSEVELT UNIVERSITY

100 Northwestern Ave., Chicago, IL
(312) 633-1670, (773) 881-2958
www.roosevelt.edu

LSC provides Illinois ex-offenders and others with life skills training, resume services, employment readiness, shelter, transportation, and counseling.

MEN AND WOMEN IN PRISON MINISTRIES

10 W. 35th St., Suite 9C5-2, Chicago, IL 60616

Men and Women in Prison Ministries provides reentry information to ex-offenders in the Chicago area, including health, faith, and other helpful resources.

PHALANX FAMILY SERVICES

4628 W. Washington, Chicago, IL 60644
(773) 261-5100
www.phalanxgrpservices.org

PFS assists ex-offenders in the Chicago area attain life skills, job readiness, and marketable skills through on-the-job training.

PRISON ACTION COMMITTEE | COMMUNITY REENTRY PROJECT

661 E. 79th St., Chicago, IL 60619
(773) 874-7390

PAC-CRP provides job readiness and opportunities for ex-offenders in the Chicago area based on their knowledge and skills.

PRISONER RELEASE MINISTRY

PO Box 69, Joliet, IL 60434-0069
(815) 730-8541
www.prisonerreleraseministyr.com
prministry@sbcglobal.net

PRM is a faith-based organization that provides reentry services in the Kane and Will County regions for ex-offenders, including counseling and job preparation and placement.

RICK'S MINISTRY

PO Box 248, Aurora, IL 60507
(630) 966-0252
www.ricksministry.org

RM is a faith-based organization that provides a variety of reentry services to ex-offenders in the Aurora area.

SAFER FOUNDATION

571 W. Jackson Blvd., Chicago, IL 60661-5701
(312) 922-2200
www.saferfoundation.org

SF provides reentry services to ex-offenders releasing to the Chicago and Quad Cities areas, including job readiness, basic education, substance abuse counseling, food, clothing, and shelter. They also distribute materials on the "Safer" programs as well as a quarterly newsletter, FREE to prisoners.

SOUTHERN ILLINOIS REENTRY GROUP

1616 W. Main St., Marion, IL
(618) 997-9166
www.lssi.org

SIRG provide information on reentry organizations in the Southern Illinois region.

SPOTLIGHT/GEO REENTRY CENTERS

Aurora: 32 E. Galena Blvd., Aurora, IL
(630) 801-0790
Chatham: 007 S. Cottage Grove Ave., Suite A, Chicago, IL 60619
(773) 846-6260
Chicago Heights: 1010 Dixie Highway, Lower Level, Chicago Heights, IL
(708) 709-0284
Decatur: 876 W. Grand Ave., East Side, Decatur, IL
(217) 428-5043
East St. Louis: 10 Collinsville Ave., Suite 201, East St. Louis, IL
(618) 482-5608
Rockford: 119 N Church St., Suite 213, Rockford, IL
(815) 961-0281
Southside: 1758 W. 57th St., Chicago, IL
(773) 918-1740
West Fulton: 2650 West Fulton, Suite 5, Chicago, IL 60612
(773) 638-5702
West Grand: 3490 W. Grand Ave., Chicago, IL
(773) 918-1740
www.bi.com *www.georeentry.com*

Spotlight/GEO Reentry Centers provide a variety of reentry services to ex-offenders around the state of Illinois, including job readiness and training, education, treatment, mental health services, housing assistance, ID attainment, family reunification, and more.

ST. LEONARD'S MINISTRIES | MICHAEL BARLOW CENTER

2120 W. Warren Blvd., Chicago, IL 60612
(312) 738-1414
www.slministries.org

SLM is a faith-based organization that provides reentry services to ex-offenders in the Chicago area, including education, training, and job placement.

TOWER OF REFUGE

329 S. New St., Springfield, IL
(217) 492-9497
www.towerofrefugeinc.com

TR provides in-prison reentry readiness programs, including interview skills, housing assistance, employment referrals, support groups, and more. Write for services in your area.

Indiana | Hoosier State

State Capital: Indianapolis

Time Zone: EST

Population: 6,596,855

(86.1% white, 9.6% Black, 2.0% Asians, 0.4% American Indian (5.9% Hispanic))

Name Origin: Means "Land of the Indians"

Motto: Crossroads of America

Famous Hoosiers: Larry Bird, James Dean, John Dillinger, Jeff Gordon, Michael Jackson, David Letterman, John Mellencamp, Cole Porter, Red Skelton, Tony Stewart, Kurt Vonnegut, Wilbur Wright.

State Agencies

CONSUMER PROTECTION

Government Center South, 5th Floor, 302 W. Washington St., Indianapolis, IN 46204
(317) 232-6220

DRIVER RECORDS

Bureau of Motor Vehicles, 100 N. Senate Ave., Indiana Government Center N., Room N405, Indianapolis, IN 46204
(317) 232-6000
www.in.gov/bmv

SECRETARY OF STATE

302 W. Washington St., Room E-108, Indianapolis, IN 46204
(317) 232-6576
www.in.gov/sos

VITAL RECORDS

State Department of Health, PO Box 7125, Indianapolis, IN 45206-7125
(317) 233-2700
www.in.gov/isdh

Prisoner Support

ACLU | INDIANA

1031 E. Washington St., Indianapolis, IN 46202
(317) 635-4059 ext. 102
www.aclu-in.org

Advocates for the civil rights of Indiana prisoners, generally through class actions. They typically will not accept individual prisoner cases, but they may provide referrals.

BROTHER'S KEEPER | PRISON MINISTRY OF TRI-STATE MEN'S CENTER

PO Box 6164, Evansville, IN 47719
(812) 453-1747
www.tristatemenscenter.org

CHURCHES EMBRACING OFFENDERS (CEO)

119 N. Mortnona Ave., Suite 200C, Evansville, IN 47711
(812) 422-2226
www.ceoevv.org

CORRECTIONAL EDUCATION PROGRAM | BALL STATE UNIVERSITY

Distance Education, Carmichael Hall, Room 200, Muncie, IN 47306
(765) 285-1593
www.bsu.edu

BSU's Correctional Education Program offers Associate's and Bachelor's degrees to prisoners in the Pendleton Correctional Facility.

Note: If you would like to learn about education opportunities available to you, regardless of the prison you live in, order the *Prison Lives Almanac: Prisoner Education Guide*. See ad in this book.

CURE | INDIANA

PO Box 61, Camby, IN 46113
(317) 831-0765

www.incure.org director@incure.org

CURE provides advocacy and organization through prisoners and their supporters to achieve reforms in the Indiana prison system.

CORRECTIONS EDUCATION PROGRAM | INDIANA STATE UNIVERSITY

200 N. Seventh St., Terre Haute, IN 47809-1902
(812) 237-2951
www.indstate.edu/cep

ISU's Corrections Education Program offers Associate's and Bachelor's degrees in Liberal Arts to prisoners in the following Indiana correctional facilities: Putnamville, Plainfield, Rockville, Wabash Valley, and the Terre Haute Federal Correctional Complex.

Note: If your prison s not listed here, and you want a quality education while behind bars, purchase *Prison Lives Almanac: Prisoner Education Guide.* Education is possible at ANY facility.

GRACE COLLEGE | PRISON EXTENSION PROGRAM

200 Seminary Dr., Winona Lake, IN 46590
(800) 544-7223
www.grace.edu

GC's Prison Extension Program offers Associate's and Bachelor's degrees in Religious Studies to prisoners in the following maximum security correctional facilities: Indiana State Prison, Wabash Valley, Miami, and Pendleton.

Note: You can earn degrees in religious fields from over 30 colleges around the country. Order the *Prison Lives Almanac: Prisoner Education Guide* today. See ad in this book.

GUIDANCE MINISTRIES

216 N. 2nd St., Elkhart, IN 46516
(574) 296-7192
www.guidanceministries.org

KAIROS PRISON MINISTRY OF INDIANA

PO Box 681515, Indianapolis, IN 46268-1515
www.kairosofindiana.org

PRISON MINISTRY PROJECTS | OAKLAND CITY UNIVERSITY

138 N. Lucretia St., Oakland City, IN 47660
(812) 749-1224
www.oak.edu/about-ocu/prison-ministries.php

OCU's Prison Ministry Projects offers various Associate's and Bachelor's degree programs to prisoners in the following Indiana correctional facilities: Branchville, Madison, Miami, Rockville, Newcastle, and the Indiana Women's Prison.

PUBLIC DEFENDER OF INDIANA

1 N. Capitol, Suite 800, Indianapolis, IN 46204
(317) 232-2475

The public defender of Indiana provides legal representation for indigent prisoners in state post-conviction proceedings. They will also represent juvenile offenders in parole revocation proceedings and accept trail or appeal county-paid appointments.

WRONGFUL CONVICTION CLINIC | INDIANA UNIVERSITY SCHOOL OF LAW

530 W. New York St., Room 111, Indianapolis, IN 46202-3225
(317) 274-5551
www.indylaw.indiana.edu

WCC provides advocacy and legal representation for wrongfully convicted Indiana prisoners where actual innocence can be proven. DNA and non-DNA cases are accepted. They will consider cases that involve child abuse, shaken baby syndrome, and arson.

Reentry Resources

AFTERCARE FOR INDIANA THROUGH MENTORING (AIM)

4155 Boulevard Place, Indianapolis, IN 46208
(318) 874-8470
www.aimmentoring.org

AIM provides Indiana ex-offenders with consultation and support services through mentoring.

BLUE JACKET, INC.

2826 South Calhoun St., Ft. Wayne, IN 46807
(260) 744-1900
www.bluejacketinc.org

BJ provides employment opportunities for Indiana ex-offenders in the Fort Wayne area, including vocational training and job placement.

COMMUNITY ACTION PROGRAM | PUBLIC ACTION IN CORRECTIONAL EFFORT

Offender Aid Restoration, 3214 Hovey St., Indianapolis, IN 46218

(317) 283-5979

CAP provides numerous reentry services for ex-offenders in the Indianapolis area, including housing, direct job placement, clothing, transportation, and more.

COMPANIONS ON THE JOURNEY | CENTRAL UNITED METHODIST CHURCH

1920 S. Michigan St., South Bend, IN 46613
(574) 289-9130
www.in.gov/idoc

CJ is a faith-based organization that provides pre-release services for prisoners, including "faith teams" who are matched with prisoner 4-6 months prior to release to help develop an action plan and provide spiritual; and emotional development.

DISMAS HOUSE OF SOUTH BEND

521 S. St. Joseph St., South Bend, IN 46601
(574) 233-8522
www.dismas.org/about/south-bend

DH provides reentry services to ex-offenders in the South Bend area, including housing, job referrals, transportation, life skills, and counseling.

GILEAD HOUSE

406 E. Sycamore St., Kokomo, IN 46901
(765) 865-9427
www.gileadhousekokomo.org

Gilead House provides transitional housing for ex-offenders in the Kokomo area.

OFFENDER AID AND RESTORATION

1426 W. 29th St., Suite 101, Indianapolis, IN 46208
(317) 612-6804

OARI provides reentry support to ex-offenders in the Indianapolis region, including substance abuse therapy information and referrals, as well as job training and placement assistance.

PRISON MINISTRIES OF INDIANA

1205 E. New York St., Indianapolis, IN 46202
(317) 612-6804

PMI provides reentry services to ex-offenders in the Indianapolis area, including assistance in securing housing, job training and placement assistance, food, clothing, and referrals for other needs.

PUBLIC ACTION IN CORRECTIONAL EFFORT

1426 W. 29th St., Suite 204, Indianapolis, IN 46208
(317) 612-6800

PACE assists ex-offenders transition into society by acting as counselors who assist with personal problems and in finding services such as housing, food, clothing, and employment. They teach job search and retention services and provide referrals.

PUBLIC ADVOCATES IN COMMUNITY REENTRY

2855 N. Keystone Ave., Suite 110, Indianapolis, IN 46218
(317) 612-6800
www.paceindy.org

PACR is a collaborative effort of PACE and Offender Aid and Restoration, which was established to identify resources within the community for ex-offenders. Their goal is to maximize resources offered by community and faith-based organizations and to identify businesses that will hire ex-offenders. They will also assist in obtaining housing, clothing, food, training, and transportation.

SALVATION ARMY REHABILITATION CENTER

711 Washington St., Indianapolis, IN 46202
(317) 638-6585

SAARC provides personal support services to ex-offenders, including counseling and work therapy. Must be 21 or older.

SPA WOMEN'S MINISTRY HOMES

512 1/2 S. Main, Elkhart, IN 46516
(574) 333-3150
www.spaministryhomes.org

SPA provides transitional housing opportunities for Indiana women ex-offenders.

VOA INDIANA

927 N. Pennsylvania St., Indianapolis, IN 46204
(317) 686-5800
www.voain.org/corrections

VOA provides transitional assistance for ex-offenders across Indiana, including mentoring, health and housing assistance.

Iowa | Hawkeye State

State Capital: Des Moines

Time Zone: CST

Population: 3,107,126

(92.1% white, 3.4% Black, 2.2% Asian, 0.5% American Indian (4.9% Hispanic))

Name Origin: Named for the Iowa Indians. Indian word variously translated to mean "here I rest" or "beautiful land."

Motto: Our Liberties We Prize and Our Rights We Will Maintain

Famous Iowans: Tom Arnold, Johnny Carson, Herbert Hoover, Ashton Kutcher, Chloris Leachman, Kurt Warner, John Wayne, Elijah Wood.

State Agencies

CONSUMER AGENCIES

1305 E. Walnut St., Des Moines, IA 50319
(515) 281-5926

DRIVER RECORDS

Department of Transportation, PO Box 9204, Des Moines, IA 50306-9204
(515) 537-3253
www.iowadot.gov/mvd

SECRETARY OF STATE

321 E. 12th St., 1st Floor, Lucas Building, Des Moines, IA 50319
(515) 281-5204
www.sos.state.ia.us

VETERAN'S AFFAIRS

210 Walnut St., Room 1063, Des Moines, IA 50309
(800) 827-1000

VITAL RECORDS

Department of Public Health, Lucas Office Building, 1st Floor, 321 E. 12th St., Des Moines, IA 50319-0075

Prisoner Support

ACLU | IOWA

505 Fifth Ave., Suite 901, Des Moines, IA 50309
(515) 992-0150
www.aclu-ia.org info@aclu-ia.org

Advocates for the civil rights of Iowa prisoners, generally through class actions. They typically will not accept individual prisoner cases, but they may provide referrals.

CATHOLIC CHARITIES

1229 Mt. Loretta Ave., Dubuque, IA 52003
(563) 588-0558
www.catholiccharitiesdubuque.org

CURE | IOWA

PO Box 41005, Des Moines, IA 50311
(515) 277-6296
www.iowacure.org

CURE Iowa is part of a 17-member coalition that works to pass legislation that will bring about positive change in the Iowa criminal justice system and prison conditions.

IOWA CITIZENS' AIDE OMBUDSMAN

1112 E. Grand Ave., Des Moines, IA 50319
(515) 281-3592
www.legis.iowa.gov/ombudman
ombudsman@legis.iowa.gov

The Ombudsman fields complaints from prisoners and others concerning Iowa correctional facilities and works to resolve them.

INNOCENCE PROJECT OF IOWA

19 S. 17th St., Estherville, IA 51334
www.iowainnocence.org

IP of Iowa provides advocacy and legal representation of wrongfully convicted Iowa prisoners whose actual innocence claims can be proven. DNA and non-DNA cases accepted, with no sentencing requirements.

MIDWEST INNOCENCE PROJECT

605 W. 47th St., Kansas City, MO 64113
(816) 221-2166
www.themip.org

MIP provides advocacy and representation for wrongfully convicted prisoners in Kansas, Arkansas, Missouri, Iowa and Nebraska. They will accept cases of actual innocence where the convicted had nothing to do with the crime, has more than 10 years left on their sentence or has to register as a sex offender, and who is not currently represented by counsel. They will not accept death penalty or self-defense cases.

Reentry Resources

CREATIVE VISIONS EX-OFFENDER & FAMILY REUNIFICATION PROGRAM

1343 13th St., Des Moines, IA 50314
(515) 244-4003
creativevisionsia.org

MICROENTERPRISE TRAINING FOR WOMEN IN CORRECTIONS | INSTITUTE OF SOCIAL AND ECONOMIC DEVELOPMENT

910 23rd Ave., Coralville, IA 52241
(319) 338-2331
www.ised.org/economicdevelopment.asp

MTWC is a program that provides pre-release entrepreneurial training to Iowa female prisoners. Their goal is to train offenders to start small businesses or obtain quality employment upon release.

REENTRY AFTERCARE

PO Box 562, Altoona, IA 50009
(515) 230-8815
www.reentryaftercare.org

REENTRY REINTEGRATION MINISTRY OF "THE INMATES' CONGREGATION" | THE CHURCH OF THE DAMASCUS ROAD

239 N. 11th St., Fort Dodge, IA 50501
(515) 955-3579
www.frontiernet.net

SAFER FOUNDATION | IOWA

1411 Brady St., Davenport, IA 52803
(563) 322-7002
www.saferfoundation.org

SF of Iowa provides reentry resources to Iowa ex-offenders in the Davenport area, including education, substance abuse treatment, case management, and job support services.

Kansas | Sunflower State

State Capital: Topeka

Time Zone: CST (although westernmost counties are MST)

Population: 2,904,021

(86.8% white, 6.3% Black, 2.8% Asian, 1.2% American Indian (10.3% Hispanic))

Name Origin: Sioux word meaning "south wind people."

Motto: Ad Astra per Aspera (To the stars through difficulties)

Famous Kansans: Kirstie Alley, Ed Asner, Bob Dole, Amelia Earhart, Dwight D. Eisenhower, Melissa Etheridge, Dennis Hopper. Don Johnson, Buster Keaton, Barry Sanders.

State Agencies

CONSUMER PROTECTION

120 SW 10th St. Suite 430, Topeka, KS 66612
(785) 296-3751

DRIVER RECORDS

Division of Vehicles, 915 Harrison, Room 155, Topeka, KS 66626-0001
(785) 296-3621
www.ksrevenue.org

SECRETARY OF STATE

Memorial Hall, 1st Floor, 120 SW 10th, Topeka, KS 66612-1594
(785) 296-4564
www.kssos.org

VETERAN'S AFFAIRS

PO Box 21318, Wichita, KS 67208
(800) 827-1000

VITAL RECORDS

Kansas Department of Health & Environment, 1000 SW Jackson, Suite 120, Topeka, KS 66612-2221
(785) 296-3253
www.kdheks.org

Prisoner Support

ACLU | KANSAS & WESTERN MISSOURI

3601 Main St., Kansas City, MO 64111
(816) 756-3113
www.acluksmo.org

Advocates for the civil rights of Kansas and Western Missouri prisoners, generally through class actions. They typically will not accept individual prisoner cases, but they may provide referrals.

CURE | KANSAS

2137 N. Battin St., Wichita, KS 67208
(316) 618-8652

CURE provides advocacy and organization through prisoners and their supporters to achieve reforms in the Kansas prison system.

LANSING CORRECTIONAL FACILITY PROGRAM | DONNELLY COLLEGE

8 N. 18th St., Kansas City, MO 66102
(913) 621-8700
www.donnelly.edu/htdocs/lansing.html

Donnelly College is a Catholic college that offers education opportunities to prisoners in the Lansing Correctional Facility in Lansing, KS, including an Associate's degree track.

Educational opportunities are available to prisoners in ever facility in the country from a wide variety of schools.

To learn more, order the *Prison Lives Almanac: Prisoner Education Guide.* See ad in this book.

KANSAS LEGAL SERVICES

712 S. Kansas Ave., Suite 200, Topeka, KS 66603
(785) 296-3317
www.kansaslegalservices.org

LS of Kansas provides legal assistance to no or low-income Kansans. They also provide some reentry assistance, including case management, farm training and employment, computer and office training, and job placement.

MIDWEST INNOCENCE PROJECT

605 W. 47th St., Kansas City, MO 64113
(816) 221-2166
www.themip.org

MIP provides advocacy and representation for wrongfully convicted prisoners in Arkansas, Missouri, Iowa and Nebraska. They will accept cases of actual innocence where the convicted had nothing to do with the crime, has more than 10 years left on their sentence or has to register as a sex offender, and who is not currently represented by counsel. They will not accept death penalty or self-defense cases.

PAUL E. WILSON PROJECT FOR INNOCENCE & POST-CONVICTION REMEDIES

409 Green Hall, Lawrence, KS 66045
(785) 864-5572

PWP provides assistance and legal representation to prisoners in Kansas state prisons and Leavenworth on habeas corpus and post-conviction cases. They will only give advice on civil matters and will not sue for damages.

Reentry Resources

BROTHERS IN BLUE REENTRY

301 E. Kansas Ave., PO Box 2, Lansing, KS 66043
(913) 727-3235
brotherinbluereentry.org

FOREVER CROWNED OUTREACH MINISTRIES

2046 E. 9th St., North Wichita, KS 67214
(316) 267-1244
www.forevercrowned.org

Forever Crowned is a faith-based organization that provides reentry services to Kansas ex-offenders, including job skills training, employment placement, counseling, mentoring, and more.

GRACIOUS PROMISE FOUNDATION | ADULT REENTRY MENTORING

PO Box 642, Shawnee Mission, KS 66202
(913) 342-1707
www.graciouspromise.org

KANSAS OFFENDER RISK REDUCTION AND REENTRY

714 SW Jackson, Suite 300, Topeka, KS 66603-
(785) 233-2068
www.doc.ks.gov/reentry

KANSAS WORKS | KANSAS DEPARTMENT OF COMMERCE

1000 SW Jackson St., Suite 100, Topeka, KS 66612-1354
(785) 296-0607
www.kansascommerce.com
workforcedev@kansascommerce.com

KansasWorks works with the Department of Corrections to help find employment solutions for Kansas ex-offenders.

ONE-STOP CAREER CENTER SYSTEM | COMMUNITY & FIELD SERVICES KANSAS DOC

900 SW Jackson St., 4th Floor, Topeka, KS 66612
(785) 296-3317
www.doc.state.ks.us

SECOND CHANCE RISK REDUCTION CENTER

2700 E. 18th St., Suite 150, Kansas City, MO 64127
(816) 231-0450
www.secondchancekc.org

SHAWNEE COUNTY REENTRY PROGRAM | SHAWNEE COUNTY DOC

501 SE Ave., Topeka, KS 66607
(785) 291-5000
www.snco.org/doc/programs_work_release.asp

SUBSTANCE ABUSE CENTER OF KANSAS'S REENTRY PROGRAM

731 N. Water, Suite 2, Wichita, KS 67203
(316) 267-3825
www.saack.org/re-entry-program.php

Kentucky | Bluegrass State

State Capital: Frankfort

Time Zone: EST

Population: 4,413,457

(88.3% white, 8.2% Black, 1.4% Asian, 0.3% American Indian (3.0% Hispanic))

Name Origin: Indian word variously translated to mean "dark and bloody ground," "meadowland," and "land of tomorrow."

Motto: United We Stand, Divided We Fall

Famous Kentuckians: Muhammad Ali, Ned Beatty, George Clooney, "Casey Jones," Jennifer Lawrence, Diane Sawyer, Hunter S. Thompson.

State Agencies

CONSUMER PROTECTION

1024 Capitol Center Dr., Frankfort. KY 40601
(502) 696-5389

DRIVER RECORDS

Department of Motor Vehicles, PO Box 2014, Frankfort, KY 40622
(502) 564-3298
www.kytc.state.ky.us

SECRETARY OF STATE

PO Box 718, Frankfort, KY 40602-0718
(502) 564-2848
www.sos.ky.gov

VETERAN'S AFFAIRS

321 W. Main St., Suite 390, Louisville, KY 40202
(800) 827-1000

VITAL RECORDS

Department of Health, 275 E. Main St., IE-A, Frankfort, KY 40621-0001
(502) 564-4212
www.chfs.ky.gov/dph/vital

Prisoner Support

ACLU | KENTUCKY

315 Guthrie St., Suite 300, Louisville, KY 40202
(502) 581-1181
www.aclu-ky.org info@aclu-ky.org

Advocates for the civil rights of Kentucky prisoners, generally through class actions. They typically will not accept individual prisoner cases, but they may provide referrals.

CURE | KENTUCKY

PO Box 221481, Louisville, KY 40252

CURE provides advocacy and organization through prisoners and their supporters to affect reforms in the Kentucky prison system.

JAIL AND PRISON MINISTRY AT THE CATHOLIC CHARITIES DIOCESE OF COVINGTON

3629 Church St., Covington, KY 41015
(859) 581-8975, ext. 117
www.covingtoncharities.org

KENTUCKY DEPARTMENT OF PUBLIC ADVOCACY | CAPITAL POST-CONVICTION BRANCH

100 Fair Oaks Lane, Suite 302, Frankfort, KY 40601
(502) 564-8006
www.dpa.ky.gov

Kentucky DPA handles prisoner post-conviction cases at the state and federal levels. They also provide training and referrals for other attorneys.

KENTUCKY INNOCENCE PROJECT

Department of Public Advocacy, 100 Fair Oaks Lane, Suite 302, Frankfort, KY 40601
(502) 564-3948
www.dpa.gov/kip

KIP provides advocacy and legal representation to wrongfully convicted Kentucky prisoners. DNA and non-DNA cases accepted, with a minimum of ten years left on the sentence.

PRISON LIFE MAGAZINE | GOOD ACRES SANCTUARIES

PO Box 4845, Frankfort, KY 40517
(502) 353-4138

Prison Life Magazine is quarterly produced and distributed for all Kentucky offenders, FREE of charge. It contains entertainment, news and articles specific to Kentucky prisons and reentry.

Reentry Resources

CENTRAL KENTUCKY CAREER CENTER RE-ENTRY | BLUEGRASS AREA DEVELOPMENT DISTRICT

699 Perimeter Dr., Lexington, KY 40517
(859) 269-8021
www.bgadd.org

GOOD ACRES SANCTUARIES

PO Box 4845, Frankfort, KY 40604
(502) 353-4138
www.goodacres.org

Good Acres Sanctuaries provides transitional assistance to Kentucky ex-offenders, including a halfway farm for job skills development and transitional living. They also provide emergency housing for displaced children and wives of the incarcerated.

GOODWILL INDUSTRIES OF KENTUCKY

909 E. Broadway, Louisville, KY 40204
(502) 584-5221
www.goodwillky.org/programs/reentry-by-design

KENTUCKY REENTRY ONLINE

www.kentuckyreentry.org

KENTUCKIANA WORKS REENTRY BY DESIGN

401 W. Chestnut St., Suite 200, Louisville, KY 40202
(502) 574-2500
www.kentuckianaworks.org

LOUISVILLE REENTRY TASK FORCE | ST. STEPHEN FAMILY LIFE CENTER

1508 W. Kentucky St., Louisville, KY 40210
www.louisvillereentry.org

MENTAL HEALTH AMERICA OF NORTHERN KENTUCKY & SOUTHWEST OHIO OFFENDER REENTRY

912 Scott St., Covington, KY 41011
(859) 431-1077
www.mhankyswoh.org

MOUNTAIN COMPREHENSIVE CARE CENTER | OFFENDER REENTRY PROGRAM

104 S. Front Ave., Prestonsburg, KY 41653
(806) 886-8572
www.mtcomp.org

NEW BEGINNINGS TRANSITION HOMES

PO Box 1736, Murray, KY 42071
(270) 753-0156
www.nbth.org

Louisiana | Pelican State

State Capital: Baton Rouge

Time Zone: CST

Population: 4,649,676

(63.4% white, 32.5% Black, 1.8% Asian, 0.8% American Indian (4.1% Hispanic))

Name Origin: Part of the territory called Louisiana by Rene-Robert Cavalier Sieur de la Salle, for French King Louis XIV.

Motto: Union, Justice, and Confidence

Famous Louisianans: Louis Armstrong, Harry Connick Jr., Ellen DeGeneres, Fats Domino, "Buddy" Guy, Jerry Lee Lewis, Peyton and Eli Manning, Wynton Marsalis, Tim McGraw, Anne Rice, Britney Spear.

State Agencies

CONSUMER PROTECTION

1885 N. 3rd St., Baton Rouge, LA 70802
(225) 326-6485

DRIVER RECORDS

Office of Motor Vehicles, PO Box 64886, Baton Rouge, LA 70896
(977) 368-5463
www.expresslane.org

SECRETARY OF STATE

PO Box 92145, Baton Rouge, LA 70804-9125
(225) 925-4704
www.sos.louisiana.gov

VETERAN'S AFFAIRS

1250 Poydras St., Suite 200, New Orleans, LA 70113

VITAL RECORDS

PO Box 60630, New Orleans, LA 70160
(504) 568-5152
www.dhh.lousiana.gov

Prisoner Support

ACLU | LOUISIANA

PO Box 56157, New Orleans, LA 70156
www.laaclu.org *admin@laaclu.org*

Advocates for the civil rights of Louisiana prisoners, generally through class actions. They typically will not accept individual prisoner cases, but may provide referrals.

CATHOLIC CHARITIES ARCHDIOCESE OF NEW ORLEANS

1000 Howard Ave., Suite 1200, New Orleans, LA 70113
(504) 523-3755 ext. 2223
www.ccano.org

CURE | LOUISIANA

PO Box 181, Baton Rouge, LA 70821
(225) 270-5245
www.curelouisiana.org

CURE provides advocacy and organization through prisoners and their supporters to achieve reforms in the Louisiana prison system.

FRIENDS AND FAMILY OF LOUISIANA INCARCERATED CHILDREN

1600 Oretha Castle Haley Blvd., New Orleans, LA 70113
(504) 522-5437
www.fflic.org *www.jjpl.org*

FFLIC advocates for a better life for Louisiana youth, especially those involved in the criminal justice system. They provide legal representation for youths through the 'Juvenile Justice Program of Louisiana', at the same address.

INNOCENCE PROJECT OF NEW ORLEANS

4051 Ulloa St., New Orleans, LA 70119
(504) 943-1902
www.ip-no.org

IP of New Orleans provides advocacy and representation for wrongfully convicted Louisiana and Southern Mississippi prisoners. Must be factually innocent, have at least 10 years left on the sentence, and be beyond review of all appeals. They take several factors into account, including official misconduct, false testimony, mistaken identity, faulty forensic evidence, and ineffective assistance of counsel.

INNOCENCE PROJECT OF NORTHWEST LOUISIANA

PO Box 400, Shreveport, LA 71162
www.notguilty.ws

IP of NW Louisiana provides advocacy and representation for wrongfully convicted Louisiana prisoners. Contact for current criteria.

JUVENILE JUSTICE PROJECT OF LOUISIANA

1600 Oretha Castle Haley Blvd., New Orleans, LA 70113
(504) 522-5437
www.jjpl.org

JJPL provides advocacy and information on juvenile justice issues in Louisiana.

LOUISIANA BOOKS TO PRISONERS

1631 Elysian Fields, Suite 117, New Orleans, LA 70117
www.lab2.wordpress.com

LBP sends FREE books to prisoners in Louisiana, Alabama, Mississippi, and Arkansas.

Note: You can find many more listings of FREE books to prisoner companies in our *Service Center.*

PROMISE OF JUSTICE INITIATIVE

636 Barrone St., New Orleans, LA 70113
www.justicepromises.org

PJI provides group representation for conditions of confinement cases in Louisiana prisons. Their goal is to affect change, not to seek monetary damages.

TULANE UNIVERSITY LAW LIBRARY

6329 Freret St., New Orleans, LA 70118

TULL provides copies of legal materials to Louisiana state prisoners (no federal prisoners), including case-law citations, law review articles, criminal procedures, and more. Request specific case cites, docket numbers or article titles. Limit: one per month, maximum of pages.

Reentry Resources

CAPITAL AREA REENTRY

429 Winbourne Ave., Baton Rouge, LA 70805
(225) 771-8715
www.caparadmin.org/louisiana-resources.html

COMMUNITY SERVICE CENTER

4000 Magazine St., New Orleans, LA 70115.
(504) 897-6277
cnouw@aol.com

CSC provides post-release reentry services to LA prisoners, including counseling, case management, support groups, substance abuse referrals, family reunification and parenting classes.

ENHANCED JOB SKILLS PROGRAM | LAFAYETTE PARISH CORRECTIONAL CENTER

PO Box 3508, Lafayette, LA 70502
(337) 236-5494

EJSP provides reentry services to LA prisoners with drug convictions, including employment assistance. They do so through a four-phase program, including assessment, computer skills training, job search, interview and placement.

GOODWILL INDUSTRIES

Acadiana: 2435 W. Congress St., Lafayette, LA 70506
(337) 261-5811
www.lagoodwill.com

Baton Rouge Workforce training Center: 647 Main St., Baton Rouge, LA 70801
(225) 308-0220
www.goodwillno.org

North Louisiana Rehabilitation Center: 800 W. 70th St., Shreveport, LA 71106
(318) 869-2575 ext.2223
www.goodwillnla.org

LOUISIANA REENTRY INITIATIVE (LRI)

1515 Poydras St., Suite 1200, New Orleans, LA 70112
(504) 301-9800
lphi.org

PROJECT RETURN

51 Yosemite Dr., New Orleans, LA 70131
(504) 452-5585
www.projectreturn.org

PR provides reentry services to ex-offenders in the New Orleans area, including case management, referrals, education, life skills training, and job placement assistances.

REENTRY BENEFITING FAMILIES | REFINED BY FIRE INDUSTRIES

5635 Main St., Suite A, Zachary, LA 70791
(225) 963-2074

REENTRY SOLUTIONS

1617 Branch St., Suite 500, Alexandria, LA 71031
(318) 443-0189
re-entrysolutions4la.com

TOTAL COMMUNITY ACTION

1420 S. Jefferson Davis Pkwy., New Orleans, LA 70125
(504) 827-2200
www.tca-nola.org

TCA is a community based organization that was established to provide services to the disadvantaged, including job counseling, transportation, and job skills training.

VOA | GREATER NEW ORLEANS RESIDENTIAL REENTRY PROGRAM

4152 Canal St., New Orleans, LA 70119
(504) 482-2130
www.voagno.org

Maine | Pine Tree State

State Capital: Augusta

Time Zone: EST

Population: 1,330,089

(95% white, 1.4% Black, 1.2% Asian, <0.05% American Indian (1.3% Hispanic))

Name Origin: From the ancient French province of Maine

Motto: Diringo (I direct)

Famous "Down Easters": Patrick Dempsey, Stephen King, Henry Wadsworth Longfellow, Judd Nelson, Liv Tyler

State Agencies

CONSUMER PROTECTION

35 State House Station, Augusta, ME 04333
(297) 624-8849

DRIVER RECORDS

Bureau of Motor Vehicles, 101 Hospital St., 29 State House Station, Augusta, ME 04333-0029
(207) 624-9000
www.state.me.us/sos/bmv

SECRETARY OF STATE

101 State House Station, Augusta, ME 04333-0101
(207) 624-7736
www.maine.gov/sos

VETERAN'S AFFAIRS

1 VA Center, Togus, ME 04330
(207) 623-8411

VITAL RECORDS

Maine Department of Human Services, 11 State House Station, 220 Capitol St., Augusta, ME 04333-0011
(207) 287-3181
www.maine.gov/dhhs

Prisoner Support

ACLU | MAINE

121 Middle St., Suite 301, Portland, ME 04101
(207) 774-5444
www.aclumaine.org *info@aclumaine.org*

Advocates for the civil rights of prisoners in Maine, generally through class actions. They typically will not accept individual prisoner cases, but may provide referrals.

COASTAL AIDS NETWORK | PRISON PROJECT

9 Field St., Suite 434, Belfast, ME 04915
(207) 338-6330 (collect calls accepted)

CAN provides HIV classes, case management, peer education groups and family referrals to Maine prisoners.

CUMBERLAND LEGAL AID CLINIC | UNIVERSITY OF MAINE SCHOOL OF LAW

246 Deering Ave., Portland, ME 04102
(877) 780-2522, (207) 780-4370

CLAC provides legal representation for prisoners in the Maine Correctional Center, including civil rights and other civil matters in state and federal court.

CURE | MAINE

23 Washington St., Sanford, ME 04073
kaymaine@yahoo.com

CURE provides advocacy and organization through prisoners and their supporters to achieve reforms in the Maine prison system.

MAINE STATE PRISON COLLEGE PROGRAM | UNIVERSITY COLLEGE AT ROCKLAND

807 Cushing Rd., Warren, ME 04073
(207) 273-5300
www.prisonstudiesproject.org
MSPCP offers education to Maine prisoners that could lead to Associate's and Bachelor's degrees.

Note: For comprehensive information on a wealth of education opportunities for prisoners, request information about *Prison Lives Almanac: Prisoner Education Guide* – Available Now!

NEW ENGLAND INNOCENCE PROJECT

120 Tremont St., Suite 735, Boston, MA 02108
(617) 830-7655
www.newenglandinnocence.org

See Massachusetts listing.

RESTORATIVE JUSTICE INSTITUTE OF MAINE

14 Maine St., Box 24, Brunswick, ME 04011
(207) 619-3630
rjimaine.org

SUCCESS WITH THE COURT'S HELP (SWITCH) | U.S. PROBATION & PRETRIAL SERVICES

400 Congress St., 5th Floor, Portland, ME 04101
(207) 780-3358
www.mep.uscourts.gov/switch-success-court's-help

Reentry Resources

KENNEBEC REGIONAL REENTRY PROGRAM (KERRP)

9 Green St., Suite 3-A, Augusta, ME
(207) 623-9677
www.mainepretrial.org/resources

ONE-STOP CAREER CENTERS | MAINE DEPARTMENT OF LABOR

55 State House Station, Augusta, ME 04333
(207) 624-6390
www.mainecareercenter.com

PORTLAND RECOVERY COMMUNITY CENTER | REENTRY GROUP

468 Forest Ave., Portland, ME 04101
(207) 553-2575
www.portlandrecovery.org

SET FREE IN MAINE

Rural Route 1, 674 Riverside Rd., Augusta, ME 04330
(207) 622-4709

SF is a faith-based organization that provides reentry services to Maine ex-offenders, including mentoring, life skills training, and employment services.

SOUTHERN MAINE REENTRY CENTER

2 Layman Way, Alfred, ME 040002
(207) 490-5205
www.maine.gov/corrections

Southern Maine Reentry Center provides transitional services for Maine women ex-offenders.

VOA | NORTHERN MAINE REGIONAL REENTRY CENTER

14 Maine St., Suite 301, Brunswick, ME 04011
(207) 373-1140
www.voanne.org

Maryland | Old Line State -- Free State

State Capital: Annapolis

Time Zone: EST

Population: 5,976,407

(60.1% white, 30.3% Black, 6.4% Asian, 0.6% American Indian (7.9% Hispanic))

Name Origin: For Queen Henrietta Maria, wife of Charles I of England.

Motto: Fatti Maschii, Parole Femini (Manly deeds, womanly words)

Famous Marylanders: Tom Clancy, Francis Scott Key, Michael Phelps, Edgar Allen Poe, Cal Ripkin Jr., Babe Rust, Harriet Tubman, John Waters.

State Agencies

CONSUMER PROTECTION

200 Saint Paul Place, Baltimore, MD 21202
(410) 576-6550

DRIVER RECORDS

MVA, Room 145, 6601 Ritchie Highway NE, Glen Burnie, MD 21062
(410) 787-7758
www.mva.state.md.us

SECRETARY OF STATE

State House, Annapolis, MD 21401
(410) 974-5521
www.marylandsos.gov

VITAL RECORDS

Department of Health, PO Box 68760, Baltimore, MD 21215-0036
(410) 764-3038
www.dhmh.state.md.us

VETERAN'S AFFAIRS

Federal Building, 31 Hopkins Plaza, Baltimore, MD 21201

Prisoner Support

ACLU | MARYLAND

3600 Clipper Mill Rd., Suite 350, Baltimore, MD 21211
(443) 524-2558 (collect calls accepted Tue & Fri, 1-3 PM (EST)
www.aclu-md.org aclu@aclu-md.org

Advocates for the civil rights of prisoners in Maryland, generally through class actions. They typically will not accept individual prisoner cases, but they may provide referrals. The Maryland office also handles all prisoner cases in Eastern shore jails.

ALTERNATIVE DIRECTIONS

2505 N. Charles St., Baltimore, MD 21218
(410) 889-5072
www.alternativedirectionsinc.org

AD provides legal assistance to prisoners in Maryland, generally for domestic matters. They also provide regular workshops to prisoners covering legal rights and responsibilities, and a mentoring program for children of incarcerated parents.

CURE | MARYLAND

PO Box 23, Simpsonville, MD 21150
www.marylandcure.webs.com
marylandcure@comcast.net

CURE provides advocacy and organization through prisoners and their supporters to achieve reforms in the Maryland prison system. They have a quarterly newsletter, *Maryland CURE*, $2 for prisoner members, $10 for others.

GOUCHER PRISON EDUCATION PARTNERSHIP

1021 Dulaney Valley Rd., Baltimore, MD 21204
(410) 337-6000
www.goucher.edu

GPEP provides education opportunities to prisoners currently housed in the Maryland Correctional Institution – Jessup and the Maryland Correctional Institution for Women. Write for current programs.

JUSTICE MARYLAND

22 E. 25th St., Suite 423, Baltimore, MD 21218
(443) 759-4159
www.justicemaryland.org

JM provides advocacy on a variety of legal issues that affect Maryland prisoners.

MARYLAND RESTORATIVE JUSTICE INITIATIVE

PO Box 33313, Baltimore, MD 21218
(443) 413-6076
www.mandelaenterprise.org

MID-ATLANTIC INNOCENCE PROJECT

200 H St. NW, Washington, DC 20052
(202) 994-4586
www.exonerate.org

MAIP provides DC, Virginia, and Maryland prisoners that they have determined to be innocent with legal representation and investigative services.

OFFICE OF PUBLIC DEFENDER | COLLATERAL REVIEW DIVISION

300 W. Preston St., Suite 213, Baltimore, MD 21201
(410) 767-8460
www.ops.state.md.us

OPD-CRD provides legal service to Maryland prisoners, including post-convictions, parole revocations and extradition matters.

PRISONER RIGHTS INFORMATION CENTER OF MARYLAND

PO Box 929, Chestertown, MD 21620

PRIS provides legal assistance to Maryland prisoners, including direct referrals, representation for select grievance hearings, sentencing reviews, and conditions of confinement matters.

UNIVERSITY OF BALTIMORE INNOCENCE PROJECT CLINIC

1420 N. Charles St., Baltimore, MD 21201
(410) 837-4200

UB-IPC provides legal representation for wrongfully convicted Maryland prisoners. DNA and non-DNA cases accepted for actual innocence claims.

Reentry Resources

CATHOLIC CHARITIES WELCOME HOME PROGRAM | CORRECTIONAL SUPPORT SPECIALIST

22-A Irongate Dr., Waldorf, MD 20602
(301) 367-0599
www.catholiccharitiesdc.org/welcomehome

DHCDC | REENTRY PROGRAM

2140 McCulloh St., Baltimore, MD 21217
(410) 523-1350
www.druidheights.com

FREEDOM ADVOCATES CELEBRATING EX-OFFENDERS (FACE)

1564 Sheffield Rd., Baltimore, MD 21218
(410) 522-3223
www.facebaltimore.org

HOMELESS PERSON REPRESENTATION PROJECT (HPRP)

201 N. Charles St., Suite 1104, Baltimore, MD 21201
(410) 685-6589
www.hprplaw.org

JERICHO REENTRY PROGRAM

901 N. Milton Ave., Baltimore, MD 21213
(410) 522-3293
www.ecsm.org

JOB OPPORTUNITIES TASK FORCE

111 Water St., Suite 201, Baltimore, MD 21202
(410) 234-8040
www.jotf.org

JOTF provides job opportunities for ex-offenders in Maryland.

MARYLAND DEPARTMENT OF PUBLIC SAFETY & CORRECTIONAL SERVICES REENTRY PROGRAM | PATUXENT INSTITUTION

7555 Waterloo Rd., Jessup, MD 20794
(410) 799-3400
www.dpscs.state.md.us/rehabservs/patx/reentry.shtml

MARYLAND JOB SERVICE | MARYLAND DEPARTMENT OF LABOR

110 N. Eutaw St., Baltimore, MD 21201
(866) 247-6034
www.dllr.state.md.us/ce

MEN & FAMILIES CENTER REENTRY PROGRAM

222 Jefferson St., Baltimore, MD 21205
(410) 614-5353
www.menandfamiliescenter.org

NATIONAL WOMEN'S PRISON PROJECT

1701 Madison Ave., Suite 505, Baltimore, MD 21217

(410) 233-3385
www.nwpp-inc.com

NWPP provides reentry support for female ex-offenders in Maryland, including housing, job training, clothing, mentoring, and support groups.

NORTHWEST ONE-STOP CAREER CENTER | THE REENTRY CENTER

Mondawmin Mall, 2401 Liberty Heights Ave., Suite 302, Baltimore, MD 21215
(410) 396-7873
www.oedworks.com

POWER INSIDE | REENTRY & AFTERCARE

PO Box 4796, Baltimore, MD 21211
(410) 889-8333
www.powerinside.org

HPRP works to reduce barriers to housing and employment imposed on those with criminal records.

SUPPORTING EX-OFFENDERS IN EMPLOYMENT TRAINING AND TRANSITIONAL SERVICES | GOODWILL INDUSTRIES OF CHESAPEAKE

222 E. Redwood St., Baltimore, MD 21202
(410) 827-1800
www.goodwillches.org

SEETTS provides reentry services to Maryland ex-offenders, including 7-week job readiness training courses and job placement services.

VOA CHESAPEAKE | RESIDENTIAL REENTRY CENTER

5000 E. Monument St., Baltimore, MD 21205
(410) 276--5880
www.voachesapeake.org/rrc

WOMEN ACCEPTING RESPONSIBILITY | OPENING DOORS

2200 Garrison Blvd., 2nd Floor, Baltimore, MD 21216
(410) 878-0357
www.womenacceptingresponsibility.org

Massachusetts | Bay State -- Old Colony

State Capital: Boston

Time Zone: EST

Population: 6,745,408

(82.6% white, 8.3% Black, 6.3% Asian, 0.5% American Indian (9.3% Hispanic))

Name Origin: From Indian tribe whose name meant "at or about the great hill" in Blue Hills region in the south of Boston.

Motto: Ense Petit Placidam Sub Libertate Quietem (By the sword we seek peace, but peace only under liberty)

Famous "Bay Staters": John Quincy Adams, Samuel Adams, Susan B. Anthony, George H.W. Bush, Steve Carell, Betty Davis, Emily Dickinson, John F. Kennedy, Jack Kerouac, Emeril Lagasse, Jack Lemmon, Conan O'Brien, Paul Revere, Norman Rockwell, Barbara Walters.

State Agencies

CONSUMER PROTECTION

One Ashburton Place, Boston, MA 02108
(617) 727-8400

DRIVER RECORDS

Registry of Motor Vehicles, PO Box 199150, Boston, MA 02119-1950
(617) 351-9213
www.mass.gov.rmv

SECRETARY OF THE COMMONWEALTH

One Ashburton Place, 17tgh Floor, Boston, MA 02108
(617) 727-2850
www.sec.state.ma.us

VETERAN'S AFFAIRS

JFK Building, Room 1625, Boston, MA 02203-0393

VITAL RECORDS

150 Mt. Vernon St., 1st Floor, Dorchester, MA 02125
(617) 740-3600
www.mass.gov/dph

Prisoner Support

ACLU | MASSACHUSETTS

211 Congress St., Boston, MA 02110
(617) 482-3170
www.aclu-mass.org info@aclu-mass.org

Advocates for the civil rights of Massachusetts prisoners, generally through class actions. They typically will not accept individual prisoner cases, but they may provide referrals.

AMERICAN FRIENDS SERVICE COMMITTEE | CRIMINAL JUSTICE PROGRAM

2161 Massachusetts Ave, Cambridge, MA 02140
(617) 661-6130
www.afsc.org

AFSC-CJP provides prisoners with referrals for available legal assistance and community organizations working on prisoner-related matters.

BOSTON UNIVERSITY | PRISON EDUCATION PROGRAM

808 Commonwealth Ave., Room 234, Boston, MA 02215
(617) 353-3025
www.bu.edu/pep

BU – Prison Education Program provides education opportunities for prisoners in Norfolk, Framingham, and Bay State facilities. Prisoners can earn a Bachelor's in Liberal Studies in Interdisciplinary Studies, including programs in English Composition, Latin, Biology, Sociology, Marketing, Acting, a variety of language offerings, and more.

COMMITTEE FOR PUBLIC COUNSEL SERVICES INNOCENCE PROGRAM

21 McGrath Highway, 2nd Floor, Somerville, MA 02143
(617) 623-0591
www.publiccounsel.net

CPCS provides advocacy and representation to wrongfully convicted Massachusetts prisoners. DNA and non-DNA cases accepted. Highest priority is given to cases that involve serious felonies and where the convicted is currently serving a substantial sentence.

CURE | MASSACHUSETTS

670 Washington St., Dorchester, MA 02124
(617) 697-4149

CURE provides advocacy and organization through prisoners and their supporters to achieve reforms in the Massachusetts prison system.

FAMILIES AGAINST MANDATORY MINIMUMS | MASSACHUSETTS PROJECT

PO Box 54, Arlington, MA 02474
(617) 546-0878
www.famm.org/massachusetts famm@famm.org
(Corrlinks registered)

FAMM is a coalition of Massachusetts prisoner's families that advocates against mandatory minimum sentencing and gathers data from prisoners under mandatory minimums. To submit a case for profiling, send a written summary of your circumstances. They receive many, but only use a few. They provide an email newsletter to friends and family.

HARVARD PRISON LEGAL ASSISTANCE PROJECT

Gannett House 100, Harvard Law School, Cambridge, MA 02138
(617) 495-3969, (617) 495-2137 (in-state collect calls accepted.)

Harvard PLAP provides legal representation for Massachusetts prisoners at disciplinary and parole hearings, as well as assistance on other prison-related matters via their hotline. They will NOT provide legal materials or manuals through the mail.

JUSTICE BRANDEIS INNOCENCE PROJECT | BRANDEIS UNIVERSITY SCHUSTER INSTITUTE FOR INVESTIGATIVE JOURNALISM

415 South St., MS 043, Waltham, MA 02454
(681) 736-4953
www.brandeis.edu/investigate/innocence-project

JBIP assists Massachusetts prisoners who were wrongfully convicted. They use investigative journalism techniques to probe cases of actual innocence. DNA and non-DNA cases accepted.

MASSACHUSETTS CORRECTIONAL LEGAL SERVICES

8 Winter St., 11th Floor, Boston, MA 02108
(617) 482-2773
www.mcls.net

Provides legal assistance on a variety of legal issues related to Massachusetts prisoners.

PRISONERS' LEGAL SERVICES

10 Winthrop Square, 3rd Floor, Boston, MA 02110-1264
(617) 482-2773
Collect calls are accepted at the following numbers:
(800) 882-1413 (Mon. 9-11 AM and 1-4 PM (EST) for prisoners in seg and with an emergency.)
(617) 482-4124 (prisoners in county jail.)
(877) 249-1342 (prisoners in other DOC facilities.)

www.plsma.org

PLSMA provides direct legal assistance to Massachusetts prisoners in the following areas: Denial of medical care, brutality, recovery of property, sentence calculation, parole application and revocation, disciplinary hearings, visitation, and other civil rights matters. They also provide indirect assistance in post-conviction proceedings. They publish a quarterly newsletter, *MCLS Notes*, FREE to prisoners.

NEW ENGLAND INNOCENCE PROJECT

St., Boston, MA 02116
(857) 277-7858
www.newenglandinnocence.org

HEIP provides advocacy and legal representation for wrongfully convicted prisoners in Massachusetts, Vermont, Rhode Island, Maine, New Hampshire, and Connecticut. The convicted must be factually innocent, currently in custody, and the case must involve one of the following elements: invalidated forensic science, false confession, jailhouse informant testimony, official misconduct, or poor defense lawyering. Cases of arson, shaken baby syndrome, and child abuse are given priority. DNA and non-DNA cases accepted.

SUFFOLK COUNTY HOUSE OF CORRECTION | INMATE LEGAL SERVICES

20 Bradston St., Boston, MA 02118
(617) 635-1000 ext. 2178

SCHC – Inmate Legal Services provides legal services for indigent prisoners in the Suffolk County House of Corrections in Boston, including sentencing, habeas corpus matters, claims for bail money and personal property, post-conviction motions, parole and disciplinary hearings, pro se civil matters, and referrals to outside attorneys.

Reentry Resources

AFTER INCARCERATION SUPPORT SYSTEMS (AISS) | WW JOHNSON LIFE CENTER

736 State St., Springfield, MA 01160
(413) 781-2050 ext. 8328
www.hcsdmass.org/aiss.htm

AID TO INCARCERATED MOTHERS

434 Massachusetts Ave., Suite 503, Boston, MA 02118
(617) 536-0058

AIM provides reentry services to Massachusetts ex-offending mothers and their children.

COMING HOME DIRECTORY

www.cominghomedirectory.org

The Coming Home Directory is an annual guide to reentry resources in the Greater Boston area.

COMMUNITY RESOURCES FOR JUSTICE

355 Boylston St., Boston, MA 02116
(617) 482-0520
www.crjustice.org

CRJ provides reentry services to Massachusetts ex-offenders, including education, counseling, job assistance, housing, and substance abuse treatment.

DISMAS HOUSE

PO Box 30125, Worchester, MA 01603
(508) 799-9389
www.dismashouse.org

DH provides transitional housing support services to ex-offenders in Massachusetts. Programs are designed to assist in developing and achieving employment, education, and housing goals.

EX-PRISONERS AND PRISONERS ORGANIZING FOR COMMUNITY ADVANCEMENT (EPOCA)

4 King St., Worchester, MA 01610
(774) 420-2722
www.exprisoners.org

FIRST INCORPORATED

37 Intervale St., Roxbury, MA 02119
(617) 445-2291

FI provides reentry services to Massachusetts ex-offenders with mental health or substance abuse concerns. The program provides counseling services with the intention of building structured living conditions.

FRANKLIN HAMPSHIRE CAREER CENTER | EX-OFFENDER SERVICES

One Arch Place, Greenfield, MA 01301
(413) 774-4361
fhcc-onestop.com

FRIENDS OF PRISONERS | GUINDON HOUSE

84 Bearses Way, Hyannis, MA 02601
(508) 790-8004
www.friendsofprisoners.org

IMPACT | THE FRIENDS OF SHATTUCK SHELTER

105 Chauncey St., Boston, MA 02111
(617) 542-3388
www.shattuckshelter.org

IMPACT is an employment service for Boston residents, including ex-offenders. They provide counselors who work with prisoners before and after release to provide job search planning, referrals, assistance in finding education and job skills opportunities.

MASS COMMUNITY RESOURCE CENTERS

Boston: 110 Arlington St., Boston, MA 02116
(617) 423-0750
Fall River: 186 S. Main St., Fall River, MA 02721
(508) 676-3729
Lowell: 45 Merrimack St., Suite 500, Lowell, MA 08152
(978) 458-4286
Springfield: 136 Williams St., Springfield, MA 01105
(413) 737-8544
Worchester: 324 Grove St., Worchester, MA 01605
(508) 831-0050

MASS are state-funded multi-service centers for prisoners and ex-offenders. They provide transitional intervention, including counseling, work readiness, sex offender referrals, support, and more.

NEIL J. HOUSTON HOUSE

9 Notre Dame St., Roxbury, MA 02119
(617) 445-3066

NJHH provides pre-release substance abuse treatment programs for Massachusetts prisoners about to be released. They also provide pregnant offenders alternatives to incarceration, pre- and post-natal care and intervention services for infants.

SALVATION ARMY | HARBOR LIGHT CENTER

83 Brookline St., Boston, MA 02118
(617) 536-7469

SA Harbor Light Center provides reentry services to Massachusetts ex-offenders, including residential substance abuse treatment, daily meals, counseling, life skills classes, referrals, and more.

SPAN

105 Chauncey St., 6th Floor, Boston, MA 02111
(617) 423-0750
www.spaninc.org

SPAN provides reentry services to Massachusetts ex-offenders, including counseling, housing, employment skills assistance, and health services.

STRIVE | BOSTON

651 Washington St., Boston, MA 021124
(617) 825-1800
www.bostonstrive.org

STRIVE offers an employment service program for ex-offenders in the Boston area.

TIP HEALTH AND EDUCATION SERVICES

60 Merrimack St., Haverhill, MA 01830

TIP programs assist HIV-positive prisoners with transition needs by providing advocacy, counseling, crisis intervention, and transportation services, as well as referrals for medical care, housing, benefits.

Michigan | Great Lakes State -- Wolverine State

State Capital: Lansing

Time Zone: EST (except the four northwestern-most counties, which are CST)

Population: 9,909,877

(79.9% white, 14.2% Black, 2.9% Asian, 0.7% American Indian (4.4% Hispanic))

Name Origin: From Chippewa 'mici gama', meaning "great water" from lake of the same name.

Motto: Si Quaeris Peninsulam Amoenam Circumspice (If you seek a pleasant peninsula, look about you)

Famous Michiganders: Thomas Edison, Eminem, Gerald Ford, Henry Ford, Aretha Franklin, Magic Johnson, Kasey Kasem, Elmore Leonard, Joe Louis, Madonna, Malcomb X, Diana Ross, Tom Selleck, Sinbad.

State Agencies

CONSUMER PROTECTION

PO Box 30213, Lansing, MI 48909
(517) 373-1140

SECRETARY OF STATE (ALSO DRIVER RECORDS)

764 Crowther Dr., Lansing, MI 48198
(517) 322-1624
www.michigan.gov/sos

VETERAN'S AFFAIRS

477 Michigan Ave., Room 1280 Detroit, MI 48226

VITAL RECORDS

Department of Health, PO Box 30721, Lansing, MI 48909
(517) 335-8666
www.michigan.gov/mdch

Prisoner Support

ACLU | MICHIGAN

2966 Woodward Ave., Detroit, MI 48201
(313) 577-6800
www.aclumich.org

Advocates for the civil rights of Michigan prisoners, generally through class actions. They typically will not accept individual prisoner cases, but they may provide referrals.

AMERICAN FRIENDS SERVICE COMMITTEE

124 Pearl St., Suite 607, Ypsilanti, MI 48197
(734) 761-8283
www.afsc.org

AFSC provides general information and resources to prisoners, their families, and ex-offenders, and offers some individual prisoner advocacy. They will act as a liaison to bring prison issues to government officials.

CURE | MICHIGAN

PO Box 2736, Kalamazoo, MI 49003-2736
(269) 383-0028

Cure provides advocacy and organization through prisoners and their supporters to achieve reforms in the Michigan prison system. They have a quarterly newsletter, *Michigan CURE*, FREE to prisoners.

FIND | CURE

PO Box 51334, Kalamazoo, MI 49005
(269) 384-5755

FIND (Furnish Imprisoned Non-Citizens with Direction) provides support and information for non-U.S. citizens who are incarcerated or detained in the U.S. to better enable them to advocate for themselves.

MCM MINISTRIES

1260 28th St. SE, Grand Rapids, MI 49508
(616) 475-5787
www.newcreationsmin.ne

MCM provides spiritual support for Michigan prisoners. Write for services in your area.

MICHIGAN COUNCIL ON CRIME AND DELINQUENCY

1000 West St., St. Joseph, Suite 400, Lansing, MI 48915
(517) 482-4161
www.miccd.org

MICHIGAN INNOCENCE CLINIC

710 S. State St., Ann Arbor, MI 48109
(734) 763-9353
www.las.mich.edu/clinical/innocenceclinic

MIC provides advocacy and legal representation for wrongfully convicted Michigan prisoners, for non-DNA cases only. Crime must have occurred in Michigan and contain one of the following elements: eyewitness misidentification, false confession, junk science, official misconduct, jailhouse informant testimony, and bad lawyering. Must be currently serving time for the case.

PRISON CREATIVE ARTS PROJECT

435 S. State St., 3187 Angell Hall, Ann Arbor, MI 48109
(734) 647-7673
ww.lsa.mich.edu/englis/pcap

PCAP hosts art, writing, and theater workshops in Michigan prisons and juvenile facilities, as well as annual art exhibits, with all income going to the prisoner artists.

PRISON LEGAL SERVICES OF MICHIGAN

209 E. Washington Ave., Jackson, MI 49201
(517) 780-6639
www.prisoneradvocacy.org

PLSM provides Michigan prisoners with legal advice and materials on a variety of prison-related issues.

THOMAS M. COOLEY LAW SCHOOL INNOCENCE PROJECT | WESTERN MICHIGAN UNIVERSITY

300 S. Capitol Ave., PO Box 13138, Lansing, MI 48901
(517) 371-5140
www.cooley.edu/clinincs/ionnocence_project.html

TM Cooley Law School Innocence Project provides legal representation for wrongfully convicted Michigan prisoners. They only accept actual innocence cases proved by DNA evidence. Prisoner must currently be in custody.

Reentry Resources

ADVOCACY, REENTRY, RESOURCES, OUTREACH (ARRO) | NORTH WEST INITIATIVE

510 Ottawa St., 2nd Floor, Lansing, MI 48933
(517) 999-2894
www.nwlansing.org/programs/a-r-r-o

DETROIT CENTRAL CITY COMMUNITY MENTAL HEALTH | COMMUNITY REENTRY SERVICES

10 Petersboro St., Detroit, MI 48201
(313) 831-3160
www.dcccmh.org

DETROIT EMPLOYMENT SOLUTIONS CORP. | RETURNING CITIZENS

440 E. Congress St., Detroit, MI 48226
(313) 876-0674
www.descmiworks.com/jobseekers/intensive-programs/returning-citizens

GOODWILL INDUSTRIES

Greater Detroit Work Readiness Program: 3111 Grand River Ave., Detroit, MI 48208
(313) 964-3900 ext. 406
www.goodwilldetroit.org

Western Michigan Career Center: 271 E. Apple Ave., Muskegon, MI 49442
www.goodwillwm.org

Michigan Council on Crime & Delinquency | Prisoner Reentry Initiative
1000 W. St. Joseph, Suite 400, Lansing, MI 48915
(517) 371-1100
www.miccd.org

MICHIGAN WORKS! | ONE-STOP CENTERS

2500 Kerry St., Suite 210, Lansing, MI 48912
(517) 371-1100
www.michiganworks.org

OAK COUNTY LIFE EMPLOYMENT AND SKILLS PROGRAM FOR FELONS (LESP)

1201 N. Telegraph Rd., Building 10E, Pontiac, MI 48341
(248) 858-5093
www.oakgov.com/commcor/pages/program-service/lesp_felony

PROJECT TRANSITION | MATRIX HUMAN SERVICES

16260 Dexter, Detroit, MI 48221
(313) 862-3400

PT offers a court-mandated residential treatment program for Michigan ex-offenders. They provide counseling, housing, and job readiness.

TRANSITION OF PRISONERS

PO Box 02938, Detroit, MI 48244
(313) 875-3883
www.topinc.net

TOP provides faith-based reentry services for Michigan ex-offenders through churches and community groups. A case manager develops a reentry plan and an assigned mentor assists with implementing it. Referrals are given for essential needs and assistance is given for job development skills.

VOLUNTEERS IN PREVENTION, PROBATION & PRISON

163 Madison Ave., Detroit, MI 48226
(313) 964-1110

VPPP provides a variety of reentry services and programs for Michigan ex-offenders in the Detroit area. Write for current list of programs.

WOMEN RISE | PROVE PROJECT

13100 Averhill Court, Detroit, MI 48215
(313) 331-1800

WA PROVE Project provides reentry services for female ex-offenders in the Detroit area, including education and vocational assistance, counseling, parenting classes, tutoring and employment services.

Minnesota | North Star State -- Gopher State

State Capital: St. Paul

Time Zone: CST

Population: 5,457,173

(85.7% white, 5.9% Black, 4.7% Asian, 1.3% American Indian (4.6% Hispanic))

Name Origin: From a Dakota Sioux word, meaning "cloudy water" or "sky-tinted water" from the Minnesota River.

Motto: L'Etoile du Nord (The star of the North)

Famous Minnesotans: Coen Brothers, Bob Dylan, F. Scott Fitzgerald, Judy Garland, Jessica Lange, Prince, Charles Schultz, Lindsey Vonn.

State Agencies

CONSUMER PROTECTION

1400 Bremer Tower, 445 Minnesota St., St. Paul, MN 55101
(651) 296-3353

DRIVER RECORDS

445 Minnesota St., Suite 161, St. Paul, MN 55101
(651) 215-1335
www.mndriveinfo.org

SECRETARY OF STATE

180 State Office Building, 100 MLK Blvd., St. Paul, MN 55108
(651) 342-5120
www.corr.state.mn.us

VETERAN'S AFFAIRS

1 Federal Dr., Fort Snelling, MN 55111

VITAL RECORDS

Department of Health, PO Box 64499, St. Paul, MN 55164
(612) 676-5120
www.health.state.mn.us

Prisoner Support

ACLU | MINNESOTA

2300 Myrtle Ave., Suite 180, St. Paul, MN 55114
www.aclu-mn.org

Advocates for the civil rights of Minnesota prisoners, generally through class actions. They typically will not accept individual prisoner cases, but they may provide referrals.

ALPHA HUMAN SERVICES

2712 Fremont Ave. S, Minneapolis, MN 55408
(612) 872-8218
www.alphaservices.org

Alpha Human Services provides resources and support to sexual offenders.

COUNCIL ON CRIME AND JUSTICE

822 S. 3rd St., Suite 100, Minneapolis, MN 55415
(612) 353-3000
www.crimeandjustice.org

INNOCENCE PROJECT OF MINNESOTA

1536 Hewitt Ave., MSC 1973, St. Paul, MN 55104
(651) 523-3152
www.ipmn.org

IPMN provides legal representation to wrongfully convicted prisoners in Minnesota, North Dakota, and South Dakota. Non-DNA cases are accepted in ND and SD. There are no minimum sentencing requirements. They look for cases that involve junk science, false confessions, informant testimony, eyewitness misidentification, official misconduct, bad lawyering, and other factors.

LEGAL ASSISTANCE TO MINNESOTA PRISONERS | WILLIAM MITCHELL COLLEGE OF LAW

875 Summit Ave., Room 254, St. Paul, MN 55105
(651) 290-6413

LAMP provides a variety of civil and family law services, including representation to Minnesota prisoners who cannot afford an attorney. State prisoners only, no federal prisoners. They also have a reentry clinic for female Minnesota ex-offenders. Write for more information.

LEGAL RIGHTS CENTER

1611 Park Ave. South, Minneapolis, MN 55404
(612) 337-0030
www.legalrightscenter.org
office@legalrightscenter.org

LRC provides legal services, including representation, to Minnesota prisoners. They handle post-convictions, direct referrals, and criminal defense cases only. No appeals.

PRISON MIRROR

970 Pickett St. N, Bayport, MN 55003-1490
(651) 779-2700

The *Prison Mirror* is the oldest continuously published prison newsletter of specific interest to prisoner in the Stillwater Correctional Facility. Monthly newsletter, $12 per year.

Reentry Services

ACCESSABILITY, INC.

360 Hoover St. NE, Minneapolis, MN 55413
(612) 852-1805
www.AccessAbility.org cep@AccessAbility.org

AccessAbility has an 80-year history of assisting Minnesota ex-offenders with overcoming barriers to employment and community inclusion. They do so through a pre-release transition employment program, *Project Connect*, which includes job readiness, mentoring, introduction to post-secondary education, career assessment, vocational training, social services assistance, and post-placement follow-up.

AMICUS | THE RECONNECT PROGRAM

3041 4th Ave. S, Minneapolis, MN 55408
(612) 877-4250
www.amicususa.org

AMICUS provides reentry support to Minnesota area ex-offenders that are designed to assist them in finding the resources they need upon reentry, including housing, family services, clothing, food jobs, and more.

CENTRAL MINNESOTA REENTRY PROJECT (CMNRP)

1121 Lincoln Ave., Sauk Rapids, MN 56379
(320) 656-9004
www.cmnrp.org

DAMASCUS WAY REENTRY CENTER

1449 4th Ave. SE, Rochester, MN 55904
(507) 292-1700

FAMILIES AND OFFENDERS UNITED PROJECT| COUNCIL OF CRIME & JUSTICE

822 S. 3rd St., Suite 100, Minneapolis, MN 55415
(612) 348-7874
www.criminaljustice.org

FOUP is a reentry program for Minneapolis area ex-offenders that includes supervision, life skills and job skills training, support, and janitorial/maintenance employment. Referrals are made for counseling and housing needs.

GOODWILL INDUSTRIES | PRISONER REENTRY INITIATIVE

Minnesota St. Paul Campus, 553 Fairview Ave, N, St. Paul, MN 55104
(651) 379-5867
www.goodwilleasterseals.org

PROJECT FOR PRIDE IN LIVING

2516 Chicago Ave., Minneapolis, MN 55404
(612) 874-8511
www.ppl-inc.org

PPL assists low income people with job skills training and affordable housing through work readiness programs, paid training, and other services.

PROJECT REENTRY | GREATER MINNEAPOLIS COUNCIL OF CHURCHES

1001 E. Lake St., Minneapolis, MN 55407
(612) 721-8687
www.gmcc.org

GMCC's Project Reentry recruits and assists congregations in developing faith-based reentry services for ex-offenders in Hennepin County, Minnesota, including housing and employment programs, mentoring, and support groups.

SECOND CHANCE COALITION

(612) 813-5071
www.mnsecondchancecoalition.org

SCC provides a variety of reentry advocacy to Minnesota prisoners. Write for current programs.

SECOND CHANCE RANCH GROUP HOME

25167 Highway 248, Minnesota City, MN 55959
(507) 410-2080
www.secondchanceranch.info

ST. STEPHEN'S EX-OFFENDER HOUSING SERVICES

2211 Clinton Ave. S, Minneapolis, MN 55404
(612) 874-0311
www.endhomelessness.org

STEP AHEAD | MINNESOTA DOC REENTRY SERVICES UNIT

Career Planning for People with Criminal Convictions

(651) 361-7200
www.iseek.org/exoffenders

Step Ahead is an online reentry workbook to assist prisoners with career planning.

WILDER FOUNDATION

919 Lafond Ave., St. Paul, MN 55104
(651) 917-6225
www.wilder.org
WF provides reentry services to ex-offenders in the Ramsey County, Minnesota area. They assist with education, a range of job readiness and placement services, and cognitive skills training.

Mississippi | Magnolia State

State Capital: Jackson

Time Zone: CST

Population: 2,994,079

(59.7% white, 37.5% Black, 1.0% Asian, 0.6% American Indian (2.7% Hispanic))

Name Origin: Likely Chippewa 'mici zibi', meaning "great river" or "gathering in all waters." Also an Algonquin word, 'messipi'.

Motto: Virtute et Armis (By valor and arms)

Famous Mississippians: Jimmy Buffet, Bo Diddley, William Faulkner, Brett Favre, Morgan Freeman, Jim Henson, Faith Hill, James Earl Jones, B.B. King, Elvis Presley, LeAnn Rimes, Robin Roberts, Oprah Winfrey.

State Agencies

DRIVER RECORDS

Department of Public Safety, PO Box 958, Jackson, MS 39205
(601) 987-1274
www.dps.state.ms.us

SECRETARY OF STATE

PO Box 136, Jackson, MS 39205-0136
(601) 395-1633
www.sos.state.ms.us

VETERAN'S AFFAIRS

1600 E. Woodrow Wilson Ave., Jackson, MS 39216

VITAL STATISTICS

Department of Health, PO Box 1700, Jackson, MS 39215-1700
(601) 576-7960
www.msdh.state.ms.us

Prisoner Support

ACLU | MISSISSIPPI

PO Box 2242, Jackson, MS 39225-2242
(601) 355-6464
www.msaclu.org msacluoffice@msaclu.org

Advocates for the civil rights of Mississippi prisoners, generally through class actions. They typically will not accept individual prisoner cases, but they may provide referrals.

CURE | MISSISSIPPI

PO Box 97175, Pearl, MS 39288-7175
(888) 247-8177, (601) 914-5658
www.mississippicure.org

CURE provides advocacy and organization through prisoners and their supporters to achieve reforms in the Mississippi prison system.

INNOCENCE PROJECT | NEW ORLEANS

4051 Ulloa St., New Orleans, LA 70119
(504) 943-1902
www.ip-no.org

The Innocence Project | New Orleans provides representation for wrongfully convicted prisoners in the southern Mississippi counties. Potential clients must be serving life or near-life sentences, with at least 10 years remaining on sentence, not serving a double sentence, has completed the direct appeal phase, and cannot afford an attorney.

MISSISSIPPI INNOCENCE PROJECT | UNIVERSITY OF MISSISSIPPI SCHOOL OF LAW

PO Box 1848, University, MS 38677
(662) 915-5207
www.mississippiinnocence.org

MIP provides legal representation for wrongfully convicted prisoners in Mississippi and North Louisiana. DNA and non-DNA cases accepted, with no sentencing requirements.

MISSISSIPPI STATE CONFERENCE NAACP

1072 West J.R. Lynch St., Jackson, MS 39203
(601) 353-6906
www.naacpms.org

Reentry Resources

BURIED TREASURES HOME

PO Box 720672, Byram, MS 39272
(601) 371-9835
www.buriedtreasures.com

Buried Treasures Home provides Mississippi women ex-offenders with transitional services.

DAYLIGHT MINISTRIES HOME | OUR PROGRAM

PO Box 325, Tougaloo, MS 39174
(601) 454-3843
www.daylightministrieshome.org

Daylight Ministries Home offers Mississippi women prisoners religious-based transitional information and services.

DISMAS CHARITIES

5209 Highway 42 Bypass, Hattiesburg, MS 39401
(601) 582-0843
www.dismascharities.org

Dismas Charities provides ex-offenders with education, employment and support opportunities.

FOUNDATION FOR THE MID-SOUTH | MISSISSIPPI REENTRY GUIDE

www.msreentryfuide.com www.fndmidsouth.org

Foundation for mid-South offers an essential guide to county-sorted Mississippi reentry programs and services for ex-offenders.

GOODWILL INDUSTRIES | SOUTH MISSISSIPPI

Gulf Port: 2407 31st St., Gulfport, MS 39501
(228) 863-2323
Ridgeland: 104 E. State St., Ridgeland, MS 39157
(610) 853-8110
www.goodwillms.org

GI provides training, skills development, and work opportunities to ex-offenders in Mississippi.

SUE'S HOME FOR WOMEN & CHILDREN | COMMUNITY CARE NETWORK

7400 Fontainebleau Rd., Oceana Springs, MS 39564
(228) 215-2662
www.ccnms.org

Sue's Home for Women & Children assists ex-offending women and their children through housing and services.

Missouri | Show Me State

State Capital: Jefferson City

Time Zone: CST

Population: 6,063,589

(83.5% white, 11.8% Black, 1.9% Asians, 0.5% American Indian (3.5% Hispanic))

Name Origin: Algonquin Indian name, meaning "river of the big canoes."

Motto: Salus Populi Suprema Les Esto (Let the welfare of the people be the supreme law)

Famous Missourians: Maya Angelou, Yogi Berra, Chuck Berry, Daniel Boone, Cheryl Crow, Walt Disney, T.S. Eliot, John Hamm, Jesse James, Rush Limbaugh, Brad Pitt, Ginger Rogers.

State Agencies

DRIVER RECORDS

Driver License Bureau, PO Box 200, Jefferson City, MO 65105-0100
(573) 751-4300
www.dor.mo.gov/mvdll

SECRETARY OF STATE

PO Box 778, Jefferson City, MO 65102
(573) 751-4153
www.sos.mo.gov

VETERAN'S AFFAIRS

400 S. 18th St., St. Louis, MO 63103

VITAL RECORDS

Department of Health, 930 Wildwood, PO Box 570, Jefferson City, MO 65102-0570
(573) 751-4300
www.dhss.mo.gov

Prisoner Support

4-H FOR LIFE | MISSOURI DEPARTMENT OF CORRECTIONS

Institutional Activities Coordinator, 11593 State Highway O, Mineral Point, MO 63660
(573) 438-6000 ext. 1534

4-H for Life provides enhanced opportunities for prisoners in the Potosi Correctional Center, including parenting education and group activities for prisoners and their families.

ACLU | EASTERN MISSOURI

454 Whittier St., St. Louis, MO 63108
(314) 652-3111
www.aclu-em.org

Advocates for the civil rights of Missouri prisoners, generally through class actions. They typically ill not accept individual prisoner cases, but they may provide referrals.

AGAPE HOUSE

810 High, Jefferson City, MO 65101
(573) 636-5737
agapehousejc@earthlink.net

AH provides overnight accommodations and family reunification support for visiting friends and families of prisoners.

CRIMINAL JUSTICE MINISTRY

PO Box 15160, St. Louis, MO 63110
(314) 652-8062
www.cjmstloius.org

CLM is a faith-based organization that provides general advocacy, information, mentoring, and referrals for Missouri prisoners.

CRIMINAL JUSTICE MINISTRY | ST. VINCENT DE PAUL

1310 Papin St., Suite 104, St. Louis, MO 63105-3132
(314) 881-6000
www.svdpstloius.org

CURE | MISSOURI

PO Box 1245, Cape Girardeau, MO 63702
(877) 525-CURE (2873)

www.www.missouricure.org
missouricure@hotmail.com

CURE provides advocacy and organization through prisoners and their supporters to achieve reforms in the Missouri prison system.

GIRL SCOUT COUNCIL OF GREATER ST. LOUIS

2300 Ball Dr., St. Louis, MO 63146
(314) 592-2300
www.girlscoutsem.org

GSC provides Girl Scout support services for Girl Scouts Beyond Bars, including transportation, expenses, troop meetings, and activities with moms and their daughters at Missouri correctional facilities.

GOOD SAMARITAN PROJECT

3030 Walnut St., Kansas City, MO 64108-3811
(618) 561-8784
www.gsp-kc.org

GSP provides support to prisoners affected by HIV/AIDS through education and advocacy.

MESSAGES PROJECT

PO Box 8325, Norfolk, VA 23503
www.themessagesproject.org

The Messages Project works with incarcerated parents to make expressions to their children and other loved ones through recorded videos of the prisoner sending a message to the ones they left behind. The service is offered in Virginia, Nebraska, and Missouri.

MIDWEST INNOCENCE PROJECT

605 W. 47th St., Kansas City, MO 64113
(816) 221-2166
www.themip.org

MIP provides advocacy and representation for wrongfully convicted prisoners in Kansas, Arkansas, Missouri, Iowa and Nebraska. They will accept cases of actual innocence where the convicted had nothing to do with the crime, has more than 10 years left on their sentence or has to register as a sex offender, and who is not currently represented by counsel. They will not accept death penalty or self-defense cases.

MISSOURI ASSOCIATION FOR SOCIAL WELFARE

606 E. Capitol Ave., Jefferson City, MO 65101
(573) 634-2901
www.masw.org

MASW provides information and support services for positive living in Missouri. Write for current programs the affect prisoners and those reentering.

PARENTS AS TEACHERS | MEXICO EDUCATION CENTER

905 N. Wade, Mexico, MO 65265
(573) 581-3773 ext. 2416

PT provides family support to prisoners in Audrain County, Missouri, including parental education, counseling information, referrals, gifts for children, and family reunification.

PATCH | CHILLICOTHE

PO Box 871, Chillicothe, MO 64601
(800) 284-0145
www.chillicothepatch.org
director@chillicothepatch.org

PATCH provides family support for prisoners in the Chillicothe Correctional Center, including mother-child visits in a private setting, pre- and post-visit counseling, parental education and support groups, and some transportation services.

REGENERATION COURAGE-2-CHANGE

PO Box 300573, St. Louis, MO 63130
(314) 368-2426
regeneration2chg@aol.com

RG2C provides family services to prisoners in Missouri, including mentoring and life skills programs for children of incarcerated parents, parental education, self-help support groups, religious ministry, family reunification, education, advocacy, treatment, and reentry services.

Reentry Resources

CENTER FOR WOMEN IN TRANSITION

7529 S. Broadway, St. Louis, MO 63111
(314) 771-5207
www.cwitstl.org

CWT provides reentry and alternative sentencing options for female ex-offenders in Missouri, including mentoring, referrals, information, and child needs.

CONNECTION TO SUCCESS

109 Archibald, Kansas City, MO 64111
(816) 561-5115
www.connectiontosuccess.org

CTS coordinates efforts between community groups and faith-based organizations to provide Kansas City ex-offenders positive employment opportunities.

EMPLOYMENT CONNECTION

2838 Market St., St. Louis, MO 63103
(314) 333-5627
www.employmentstl.org

EC provides employment services to ex-offenders in the St. Louis area, including readiness training, career development, and placement assistance. Get a referral to EC from parole/probation officer.

JAIL MINISTRY OUTREACH

8631 Delmar, Suite 306, St. Louis, MO 63124
(314) 754-2821

JMO provides faith-based group support services to ex-offenders in the St. Louis area.

JEFFERSON COUNTY COMMUNITY PARTNERSHIP

1671 Marriott Lane, Barnhart, MO 63012
(634) 464-5144
www.jccp.org mrp@jccp.org

JCCP provides reentry guides, FREE to Missouri prisoners.

JOB POINT REENTRY SERVICES

2116 Nelwood Dr., Suite 200, Columbia, MO 65202
(573) 474-8560
www.jobpointmo.org

LET'S START

1408 S. 10th St., St. Louis, MO 63104
(314) 541-2324
www.letsstart.org

Let's Start provides support for female Missouri ex-offenders, their children, and their children's caregivers, in addition to education and advocacy.

LUTHERAN MINISTRIES

1120 S. 6th St., St. Louis, MO 63107
(314) 772-7720

LM runs the *Next Steps Home Program*, which assists Missouri ex-offenders who have a job with housing support, transportation, support groups, mentoring, religious ministry and referrals.

MISSION GATE MINISTRY | AFTER CARE PROGRAM

PO Box 6644, Chesterfield, MO 63006
(636) 391-8560
www.missiongateministry.org

MISSOURI DEPARTMENT OF CORRECTIONS | REENTRY SERVICES

2729 Plaza Dr., PO Box 236, Jefferson City, MO 65102
(573) 751-2389
www.doc.mo.gov/od/do/mrp.php

NEXT STEPS HOME

1120 S. 6th St., Suite 120, St. Louis, MO 63104
(314) 772-7720
humanitri.org

OUR SAVIOR LUTHERAN PRISON MINISTRY SERVICE GROUP

1500 San Simeon Way, Fenton, MO 63026
(636) 343-2192

OSLPM is a faith-based groups that networks with other community providers to offer reentry services to Missouri ex-offenders, including food, clothing, jobs, and housing.

PROJECT COPE | CONGREGATION OFFENDER PARTNERSHIP ENTERPRISE

3529 Marcus Ave., St. Louis, MO 63115
(314) 389-4804
www.projcope.org

Project COPE is a faith-based organization that pairs Missouri ex-offenders with community reentry service providers, including health care, job search, housing, counseling, and treatment options.

ST. PATRICK CENTER | PROJECT REACH

800 N. Tucker Blvd., St. Louis, MO 63101
(314) 802-0700
www.stpatrickcenter.org

ST. LOUIS ALLIANCE FOR REENTRY (STAR)

539 N. Grand Blvd., 6th Floor, St. Louis, MO 63103
(314) 534-0022
www.stlreentry.org

STAR is an alliance of 38 organizations that offer a variety of reentry resources for ex-offenders in the St. Louis area.

START HERE | INSIDE DHARMA

PO Box 220721, St. Louis, MO 63122
(314) 726-2982
www.startherestl.org

Inside Dharma offers a FREE reentry resource directory for ex-offenders returning to the St. Louis area.

Montana | Treasure State

State Capital: Helena

Time Zone: MST

Population: 1,023,579

(89.4% White, 6.6% American Indian, 0.8% Asians, 0.6% Black (2.8% Hispanic))

Name Origin: Latin or Spanish for "mountainous."

Motto: Oro y Plata (Gold & Silver)

Famous Montanans: Dana Carvey, Gary Cooper, Phil Jackson, David Lynch, Brett Musberger.

State Agencies

DRIVER RECORDS

PO Box 201430, Helena, MT 59620-1430
(406) 444-4292
www.doj.mt.gov

SECRETARY OF STATE

PO Box 202801, Helena, MT 59620-2801
(406) 444-3665
www.sos.state.mt.us

VETERAN'S AFFAIRS

3633 Veterans Dr., PO Box 188, Fort Harrison, MT 59636-0188

VITAL RECORDS

Montana Department of Health, 111 N. Sanders, Room 6, PO Box 4210, Helena, MT 59604
(406) 444-2685
www.vhsp.dphhs.mt.gov

Prisoner Support

ACLU | MONTANA

PO Box 1317, Helena, MT 59624
(406) 443-8590
www.aclumontana.org aclu@aclumontanana.org

Advocates for the civil rights of Montana prisoners, generally through class actions. They typically will not accept individual prisoner cases, but they may provide referrals.

MONTANA CORRECTIONAL ENTERPRISES | MONTANA DOC

350 Conley Lake Rd., Deer Lodge, MT 59722
(406) 846-1320
www.cor.mt.gov/adult/mce

MONTANA INNOCENCE PROJECT

PO Box 7607, Missoula, MT 59807
(406) 544-6698
www.mtinnocenceproject.org

MT IP provides advocacy and legal representation for wrongfully convicted Montana prisoners. DAN and non-DNA cases accepted. Must have been convicted in Montana, have completed direct appeals and not be currently represented by counsel. Priority is given to cases with clear and convincing proof of innocence. They are unlikely to take cases without independent and verifiable evidence to support the prisoner's claim.

Reentry Resources

CENTER FOR FAMILIES & CHILDREN | FAMILY MATTERS

3021 3rd Ave. N, Billings, MT 59101
(406) 294-5090
www.forfamilies.org

The Center for Families & children provide support services to families in the Montana area, including some services to ex-offenders. Write for more information.

GREAT FALLS WEED & SEED TRANSITION COALITION | NEIGHBORWORKS GREAT FALLS

509 1st Ave. S, Great Falls, MN 59401
(406) 761-5861
www.gfweedandseed.org

MONTANA REENTRY INITIATIVE | MONTANA DOC

5 S. Last Chance Gulch, Helena, MT 59620-1301
(406) 444-0340
www.cor.mt.gov/reentry

The Montana Reentry Initiative provides information and resources to prisoners who will soon be reentering society.

MONTANA WOMEN'S PRISON & PASSAGES

701 S. 27th St., Billings, MT 59404
(406) 247-5160
www.montana.networkofcare.org

Montana Women's Prison & Passages provides pre-release reentry information and services to women prisoners in Montana.

THE PARENTING PLACE

1644 S. 8th St. W, Missoula, MT 59801
(406) 728-5437
www.parentingplace.net

The Parenting Place provides support for families of those touched by incarceration.

VETERAN'S REENTRY PROGRAM

3678 Veterans Dr., Ft. Harrison, MT 56636
(406) 442-6410
www.va.gov/homeless/reentry.asp

Nebraska | Cornhusker State

State Capital: Lincoln

Time Zone: CST/MST (19 westernmost counties are MST)

Population: 1,881,503

(89.4% White, 4.9% Black, 2.2% Asians, 1.4% American Indian (8.9% Hispanic))

Name Origin: From the Omaha and Otos Indian word meaning "broad water" or "flat river," describing the Platte River.

Motto: Equality Before the Law

Famous Cornhuskers: Grover Cleveland, Fred Astaire, Marlon Brando, Warren Buffet, Dick Cheney, Henry Fonda, Nick Nolte.

State Agencies

CONSUMER PROTECTION

2115 State Capitol Building, Lincoln, NE 68509
(402) 471-2682

DRIVER RECORDS

Department of Motor Vehicles, PO Box 94789, Lincoln, NE 68509-4789
(402) 471-3918
www.wcc.ne.gov

SECRETARY OF STATE

1301 State Capitol Building, Lincoln, NE 68509
(402) 472-4079
www.sos.state.ne.gov

VETERAN'S AFFAIRS

3800 Village Dr., PO Box 85816, Lincoln, NE 68501

VITAL RECORDS

Health & Human Services, PO Box 95065, Lincoln, NE 68509-5065
(402) 471-2871
www.hhs.state.ne.us

Prisoner Support

ACLU | NEBRASKA

941 O St., Suite 706, Lincoln, NE 68508
(402) 476-8091
www.aclunebraska.org info@aclunebraska.org

Advocates for the civil rights of Nebraska prisoners, generally through class actions. They typically will not accept individual prisoner cases, but they may provide referrals.

MESSAGES PROJECT

PO Box 8325, Norfolk, VA 23503
www.themessagesproject.org

The Messages Project works with incarcerated parents to make expressions to their children and other loved ones through recorded videos of the prisoner sending a message to the ones they left behind. The service is offered in Virginia, Nebraska, and Missouri.

MIDWEST INNOCENCE PROJECT

605 W. 47th St., Kansas City, MO 64113
(816) 221-2166
www.themip.org

MIP provides advocacy and representation for wrongfully convicted prisoners in Kansas, Arkansas, Missouri, Iowa and Nebraska. They will accept cases of actual innocence where the convicted had nothing to do with the crime, has more than 10 years left on their sentence or has to register as a sex offender, and who is not currently represented by counsel. They will not accept death penalty or self-defense cases.

NEBRASKA AIDS PROJECT

250 S. 77th St., Suite A, Omaha, NE 68114
(800) 782-2437, (402) 552-9260
www.nap.org

NAP provides support services to Nebraska prisoners and others living with HIV/AIDS, including case management, support groups, emergency assistance, prevention strategies, and more. Services are also available to family members of those living with HIV/AIDS.

NEBRASKA APPLESEED

941 O St., Suite 105, Lincoln, NE 68508
(402) 438-8853
www.neappleseed.org

Appleseed provides a variety of support services for Nebraska residents and limited opportunities for prisoners. Write for current programs.

NEBRASKA INNOCENCE PROJECT

PO Box 24183, Omaha, NE 68124
(412) 241-7194
www.nebraskainnocenceproject.org

NIP provides advocacy and legal representation to wrongfully convicted Nebraska prisoners. Must claim actual innocence, not currently have representation, and there must be DNA-testable evidence to verify (although non-DNA cases may be considered where there is new evidence.)

Reentry Resources

CEGA SERVICES | OFFENDER REFERRAL

PO Box 81826, Lincoln, NE 68501
(402) 464-0602

CEGA provides reentry services to Lincoln area ex-offenders, including pre-release for housing, employment, and substance abuse treatment.

CROSSOVER PRISON MINISTRIES

18616 Anne St., Omaha, NE 68114
(402) 871-7904
www.facebook.com/CrossOver-Prison-Ministries

DEPARTMENT OF CORRECTIONAL SERVICES | REENTRY

PO Box 94661, Lincoln, NE 68509-4661
(402) 471-2654
www.corrections.nebraska.gov/reentry.html

GOOD NEWS JAIL & PRISON MINISTRY

702 S. 17th St., Omaha, NE 68102
(402) 599-2293
local.goodnewsjail.org/omaha

GOODWILL INDUSTRIES

Central Nebraska: 1804 S. Eddy St., Grand Island, ME 68802
(308) 384-7896
Lincoln: 22100 Judson St., Lincoln, NE 68521
(402) 438-2002
www.lincolngoodwill.org

Omaha: 4805 N. 72nd St., Omaha, NE 68134
(402) 341-4609
www.goodwillomaha.org

Eastern and Southwest Nebraska: 1111 S. 41st St., Omaha, NE 68105
(402) 341-4609
www.goodwillomaha.org

GI assists Nebraska ex-offenders with job skills training, career counseling, and transportation services. Additional services vary by location.

OMAHA CON-NECTIONS

4140 N. 42nd St., Omaha, NE 68111
(402) 451-1100
www.omahacon-nections.org

OC offers reentry services for Omaha area ex-offenders who are veterans, including pre-release materials, job development skills, and referrals.

NEBRASKA PEN | FRIENDS & FAMILY OF INMATE

PO Box 84424, Lincoln, NE 68501
(402) 477-8568

NEBRASKA AFTERCARE IN ACTION (NAIA)

PO Box 6757, Lincoln, NE 68506
(308) 991-2310
www.aftercareinaction.org

REENTRY ALLIANCE OF NEBRASKA (RAN) | CALVARY UNITED METHODIST

1610 S. 11th St., Lincoln, NE 69502
(402) 476-7353
www.re-entrynebraska.org

RELEASED AND RESTORED

PO Box 22962, Lincoln, NE 68452
(402) 806-0565
www.releasedandrestored.com

Nevada | Sagebrush State -- Battle Born State -- Silver State

State Capital: Carson City

Time Zone: PST

Population: 2,839,099

(76.2% White, 9.1% Black, 8.3% Asians, 1.6% American Indian (25.2% Hispanic))

Name Origin: Spanish, meaning "snow-clad."

Motto: All For Our Country

Famous Nevadans: Andre Agassi, Kyle Busch, John Mackay, Pat McMarran.

State Agencies

DRIVER RECORDS

Department of Motor Vehicles, 555 Wright Way, Carson City, NV 89711-0250
(775) 684-4950
www.dmvsat.com

SECRETARY OF STATE

202 N. Carson City, NV 89701-4707
(800) 486-2880
www.sos.state.nv.us

VETERAN'S AFFAIRS

5460 Reno Corporate Dr., Reno, NV 89511
Benefits Office: 4800 Alpine Place, Las Vegas, NV 89107

VITAL RECORDS

Nevada Department of Health, 4150 Technology Way, Suite 104, Carson City, NV 89706
(775) 684-4242
www.health2k.state.nv.us

Prisoner Support

ACLU | NEVADA

601 S. Rancho Dr., #B-11, Las Vegas, NV 89106
(702) 366-1226
www.aclunv.org aclunv@aclunv.org

Advocates for the civil rights of Nevada prisoners, generally through class actions. They typically will not accept individual prisoner cases, but they may provide referrals.

BROKEN CHAINS OUTREACH MINISTRY OF LAS VEGAS

2559 E. Desert Inn Rd.., Suite 585, Las Vegas, NV 89121
(844) 772-5623
www.brokenchains outreach.com

Broken Chain Outreach provides spiritual support to Las Vegas are jails and prisons.

CURE | NEVADA

540 E. St. Louis Ave., Las Vegas, NV 89104
(702) 347-1731
www.aclunv.org aclunv@aclunv.org

CURE provides advocacy and organization through prisoners and their supporters to achieve reforms in the Nevada prison system.

FRIENDS AND FAMILY OF INCARCERATED PERSONS

PO Box 27708, Las Vegas, NV 89126
(702) 870-5577
www.ffipnv.org

FFIP provides support services for friends and family members of prisoners, including group support meetings and more.

HOPE FOR PRISONERS

3430 E. Flamingo Rd., Suite 350, Las Vegas, NV 89121
(702) 586-1371
www.hopeforprisoners.org

Southern Nevada Prison Ministries
(702) 277-9315
www.prisonministry.net/snvpm

LAS VEGAS URBAN LEAGUE | REENTRY INITIATIVES SUPPORTING EX-OFFENDERS (RISE)

3575 W. Cheyenne Ave., Suite 101, North Las Vegas, NV 89032
(702) 636-3949
www.lvul.org/re-rentry-initiatives-supporting-ex-offenders

ROCKY MOUNTAIN INNOCENCE CENTER

385 S. 700 East, Suite B235, Salt Lake City, UT 84102
(801) 355-1888
www.rminnocence.org

See Utah listing.

Reentry Resources

EVOLVE

1971 Stella Lake Dr., Las Vegas, NV 89106
(702) 638-6371

EVOLVE provides reentry services for Nevada ex-offenders, including counseling, case management, vocational education, job skills training, and placement services.

LAS VEGAS REENTRY PROGRAM

930 W. Owens Ave., Las Vegas, NV 89106

LVRP provides pre-release services for Nevada ex-offenders about to be released. Services are offered 3-6 months prior to release and include psychological assessment, life skills training, transitional assistance, and referrals from criminal justice agencies.

NEVADA AIDS FOUNDATION

900 W. 1st, Suite 200, Reno, NV 89503
(775) 348-9888

NAF provides HIV-positive ex-offenders with housing and other support.

RIDGE HOUSE

900 West 1st St., Suite 20, Reno, NV 89503
www.ridgehouse.org

RH offers reentry services to Nevada ex-offenders, including a 3-month residential treatment program, career counseling, and job referrals from seven locations around the state.

TRANSITIONAL LIVING COMMUNITIES

210 N. 10th St., Las Vegas, NV 89101
(702) 387-3131

TLC serves as a halfway house for Nevada ex-offenders. They also offer a 3-month residential substance abuse treatment and job search assistance.

WALTER HOVING HOME

3353 Red Rock St., Las Vegas, NV 89146
(702) 386-1965
www.walterrovinghome.com

Walter Roving Home provides transitional housing for women ex-offenders in the Las Vegas area.

WESTCARE NEVADA REENTRY PROGRAMS OF LAS VEGAS | COMMUNITY INVOLVEMENT CENTER

401 S. Martin Luther King Blvd., Las Vegas, NV 89106
(702) 385-3330
www.westcare.com

WELLNESS, REDEMPTION, AND REHABILITATION PROGRAM (WRRP)

1555 E. Flamingo Rd., Suite 158, Las Vegas, NV 89119
(702) 385-9097
www.wrrp.org

New Hampshire | Granite State

State Capital: Concord

Time Zone: EST

Population: 1,326,813

(94% white, 2.5% Asians, 1.5% Black, 0.3% American Indian (2.8% Hispanic))

Name Origin: Named by Captain John Mason of the Plymouth Council, in 1629, for his home country in England.

Motto: Live Free or Die

Famous New Hampshirites: Dan Brown, Robert Frost, John Irving, Seth Meyers, Bode Miller, Adam Sandler, Sarah Silverman.

State Agencies

CONSUMER PROTECTION

33 Capitol St., Concord, NH 03301
(603) 271-3641

DRIVER RECORDS

Department of Motor Vehicles, 23 Hazen Dr., Concord, NH 03305
(603) 271-2322
www.nh.gov/safety/dmv

SECRETARY OF STATE

107 N. Main St., Concord, NH 03301
(603) 271-3246
www.sos.nh.gov

VETERAN'S AFFAIRS

Norris Cotton Federal Building, 275 Chestnut St., Manchester, NH 03101

VITAL RECORDS

Archives Building, 71 S. Fruit St., Concord, NH 03301-2410
(603) 271-4650
www.sos.nh.giv/vitalrecords

Prisoner Support

ACLU | NEW HAMPSHIRE

18 Low Ave., Concord, NH 03301
(603) 225-3080
www.nhaclu.org

Advocates for the civil rights of New Hampshire prisoners, generally through class actions. They typically will not accept individual prisoner cases, but they may provide referrals.

MATTANOKIT OUTREACH

Attention: Medicine Story, 173 Merriam Hill Rd., Greenville, NH 03048
(603) 878-4005
www.circleway.org

MO offers Native American education and traditions information, as well as services to various New Hampshire prisons, including Native circles. Write for more information and a list of publications.

NEW ENGLAND INNOCENCE PROJECT

St., Boston, MA 02116
(857) 277-7858
www.newenglandinnocence.org

See Massachusetts listing.

Reentry Resources

CHRISTIAN AFTERCARE MINISTRIES

50 Lowell St., Manchester, NH 03101
(603) 669-5090
www.christianaftercare.com

CRJ HAMPSHIRE HOUSE

1490-1492 Elm St., Manchester, NH 03101
(603) 518-5128
www.crj.org/sjs

NEW HAMPSHIRE WORKS | OFFICE OF WORKFORCE OPPORTUNITY

172 Pembroke Rd., Concord, NH 03301
(603) 271-7275
www.nhworks.org

New Hampshire Works assists ex-offenders in the New Hampshire area with employment opportunities

RISE AGAIN OUTREACH

34 Staniels Rd. , Suite 5, Loudon, NH 03307
(800) 266-5017
www.riseagainoutreach.org

TRANSFORMATION PROGRAM | NEW HAMPSHIRE COMMUNITY TECHNICAL COLLEGE

879 Belmont Rd., Laconia, NH 03246
(603) 524-3207
www.laconia.tec.nh.us

TP assists New Hampshire ex-offenders with life and employment skills, as well as job placement.

New Jersey | Garden State

State Capital: Trenton

Time Zone: EST

Population: 8,938,175

(73% White, 14.8% Black, 9.4% Asians, 0.6% American Indian (17.4% Hispanic))

Name Origin: The Duke of New York gave a patent to Lord John Berkeley and Sir George Carteret for 'Nova Caesari', or New Jersey, after England's Isle of Jersey.

Motto: Liberty and Prosperity.

Famous New Jerseyans: Buzz Aldrin, John Bon Jovi, Danny DeVito, Thomas Edison, Albert Einstein, James Gandolfini, Whitney Houston, Jack Nicholson, Bill Parcells, Kelly Ripa, Bruce Springsteen, Martha Stewart, Meryl Streep, John Travolta.

State Agencies

CONSUMER AFFAIRS

124 Halsey St., Newark, NJ 07102
(973) 504-6200

DRIVER RECORDS

Motor Vehicle Commission, PO Box 142, Trenton, NJ 08666
(609) 984-7771
www.state.nj.us/mvc

SECRETARY OF STATE

PO Box 40, Trenton, NJ 08646
(609) 292-9292
www.state.nj.us/treasury

VETERAN'S AFFAIRS

20 Washington Place, Newark, NJ 07102

VITAL RECORDS

Bureau of Vital Statistics, PO Box 370, Trenton, NJ 08625-0370
(609) 292-4087
www.state.nj.us/health/vital

Prisoner Support

ACLU | NEW JERSEY

PO Box 32159, Newark, NJ 07102
(973) 642-2084
www.aclu-nj.org info@aclu-nj.org

Advocates for the civil rights of New Jersey prisoners, generally through class actions. They typically will not accept individual prisoner cases, but they may provide referrals.

AMERICAN FRIENDS SERVICE COMMITTEE

89 Market St., 6th Floor, Trenton, NJ 07102
(973) 643-2205
www.afsc.org

AFSC provides support to New Jersey prisoners and community groups who are working on prison issues, including referrals and other assistance.

CURE | NEW JERSEY

PO Box 1215, Willow Grove, PA 19090
(215) 892-8796
gardenstatecure@yahoogroups.com

CURE provides advocacy and organization through prisoners and their supporters to affect reforms in the New Jersey prison system.

DRUG POLICY ALLIANCE | NEW JERSEY

16 W. Front St., Suite 101A, Trenton, NJ 08608
(609) 396-8613
www.drugpolicy.org nj@drugpolicy.org

HYACINTH AIDS FOUNDATION

317 George St., Suite 203, New Brunswick, NJ 08901
(800) 833-0254, (732) 246-0204
www.hyacinth.org info@hyacinth.org

HAF offers support to New Jersey prisoners living with HIV/AIDS and their families, including support groups, information to both staff and prisoners, as well as reentry assistance, including rental assistance programs in Essex County.

LAST RESORT INNOCENCE PROJECT | SETON HALL UNIVERSITY SCHOOL OF LAW

One Newark Center, 1109 Raymond Blvd., Newark, NJ 07102
(973) 642-8500
www.law.shu.edu/programscenters

LRIP provides advocacy and legal representation for wrongfully convicted New Jersey Prisoners. DNA and non-DNA cases accepted. Must claim actual innocence and have been convicted in New Jersey.

NEW JERSEY INSTITUTE FOR SOCIAL JUSTICE

60 Park Place, Suite 511, Newark, NJ 07102
(973) 624-9400
www.njisj.org

NEW JERSEY PARENTS' CAUCUS

275 Route 10 East, Suite 220-114, Succasunna, NJ 07869
(908) 994-9471, (973) 989-8870
www.newjerseyparentscaucus.org

NJPC provides representation and support services to parents, family members, and youth offenders serving time in the juvenile justice system, including peer support, education, and legislative advocacy.

OMBUDSMAN'S OFFICE | NEW JERSEY DEPARTMENT OF CORRECTIONS

PO Box 855, Trenton, NJ 08625
(555) 555-5555 (toll-free for prisoners), (609) 292-8020 (prisoner line, no collect calls), (609) 633-2596 (friends/family line.)
www.state.nj.us/correctionsombudsman/

The DOC Ombudsman provides New Jersey prisoners with a mechanism to resolve problems encountered while in custody. Ombudsman are required to follow through on any prisoner complaints regarding safety and security of prisoners and prison conditions.

PRISON TEACHING INITIATIVE

www.teacherprep.princeton.edu
ssusman@princeton.edu

PTI provides post-secondary education opportunities in math, natural sciences, humanities, and social sciences for prisoners in New Jersey. They currently have programs at the following facilities: A.C. Wagner Youth Correctional Facility in Bordentown, Garden State Youth Correctional Facility in Yardville, East Jersey State in Rahway, and Mountainview Youth Correctional Facility in Annandale.

Reentry Resources

CITY OF NEWARK | OFFICE OF REENTRY

1008 Broad St., Newark, NJ 07102
(973) 733-3747
www.ci.newark.nj.us

GEO COMMUNITY REENTRY CENTERS

Atlantic City: 26 S. Pennsylvania Ave., 4th Floor, Atlantic City, NJ 08401
(609) 344-6785
Elizabeth: 208 Commerce Place, 2nd Floor, Elizabeth, NJ 07201-2320
(908) 282-1001
Neptune City: 2040 6th Ave., Suite A, Neptune City, NJ 07753
(732) 774-0777
Perth Amboy: 207 New Brunswick Ave., Perth Amboy, NJ 08861
(732) 826-4200
Vineland: 1338 N. Delsea Dr., Suite 4, Vineland, NJ 08360
(856) 696-4579
www.georentry.com

HOPE FOR EX-OFFENDERS

259 Passaic St., Hackensack, NJ 07601
(201) 646-1995 (for prisoners), (201) 646-0103 (others)

HOPE provides advocacy and reentry services for New Jersey ex-offenders in Bergen, Passaic, Essex, Hudson, and Morris counties, including housing, clothing, transportation, identity replacement, family services, medication, and job referrals.

NEW JERSEY ASSOCIATION ON CORRECTIONS

986 S. Broad St., Trenton, NJ 08611
(609) 396-8900

NJAC provides residential facilities and resource centers for a variety of special needs ex-offenders, including family services and assistance for those living with HIV/AIDS.

NJAC'S CLINTON HOUSE

21 N. Clinton Ave., Trenton, NJ 08609
(609) 369-9186

CH provides a work release 42-bed transitional housing facility for New Jersey ex-offenders. Must be within 18 months of parole eligibility and be on full minimum status. Most residents are A304 (violent offenders.)

NJAC'S SANFORD BATES HOUSE

33 Remsen Ave., New Brunswick, NJ 08901
(732) 846-7220

SBH is a transitional housing program for New Brunswick area ex-offenders, with services including family, financial, and substance abuse counseling, as well as employment assistance.

NEW JERSEY EMPLOYMENT AND TRAINING PROGRAM (JCETP) | REENTRY PROGRAM

Martin's Place, 398 Martin Luther King Jr. Dr., Jersey City, NJ 07305
(551) 222-4323
www.jcetp.org

NEW JERSEY STATE PAROLE BOARD | STEP

PO Box 862, Trenton, NJ 08625
(609) 292-4257
www.state.nj.us/parole

STEP (Stages to Enhance Parolee Success) is offered by the New Jersey Parole Board as a training program for all New Jersey ex-offenders.

OFFENDER AID & RESTORATION | ESSEX COUNTY

1064 Clinton Ave., Suite 170, Irvington, NJ 07111
(973) 373-0100

OAR provides reentry services to New Jersey ex-offenders releasing to Essex County, including job development and placement assistance, substance abuse treatment, and more.

VOA | REENTRY SERVICES DIVISION

235 White Horse Pike, Collingswood, NJ 08107
(856) 854-4660
www.voa.org/correctional-re-entry-services

VOA provides a variety of reentry services through a number of centers throughout New Jersey, including transitional housing, mental health treatment, and other assistance. Write for a list of current services.

New Mexico | Land of Enchantment

State Capital: Santa Fe

Time Zone: MST

Population: 2,085,572

(82.8% White, 10.4% American Indian, 2.5% Black, 1.7% Asian (45.7% Hispanic))

Name Origin: Spaniards in Mexico applied the term to the north and the west of the Rio Grande River.

Motto: Crescit Eundo (It grows as it goes)

Famous New Mexicans: Jeff Bezos, Billy the Kid, Kit Carson, Neil Patrick Harris, Al and Bob Unser.

State Agencies

DRIVER RECORDS

Motor Vehicles Division, PO Box 1028, Santa Fe, NM 87504-1028
(505) 827-4636
www.state.nm.us/tax/mvd

SECRETARY OF STATE

325 Don Gaspar, Suite 301, Santa Fe, NM 85703
(505) 827-3615
www.secure.sos.state.nm.us

VETERAN'S AFFAIRS

500 Gold Ave. SW, Albuquerque, NM 87102

VITAL RECORDS

PO Box 25767. Albuquerque, NM 87125
(505) 827-2338
www.health.state.nm.us

Prisoner Support

ACLU | NEW MEXICO

PO Box 566, Albuquerque, NM 87103
(505) 266-59153
www.aclu-nm.org

Advocates for the civil rights of New Mexico prisoners, generally through class actions. They typically will not accept individual prisoner cases, but may provide referrals. Prisoners looking for research assistance or statutes should contact the prison research staff at UNM Library (Albuquerque, NM 87131-2039)

CURE | NEW MEXICO

PO Box 543, Deming, NM 88031
(575) 546-9003
nmcure@yahoo.com

CURE provides advocacy and organization through prisoners and their supporters to affect reforms in the New Mexico prison system.

DISABILITY RIGHTS OF NEW MEXICO

1720 Louisiana Blvd. NE, Suite 204, Albuquerque, NM 87110
(800) 432-4682

DRNM provides legal assistance for prisoners with disability issues, including advocacy, information, referrals, representation, training for prison staff, and more.

DRUG POLICY ALLIANCE | NEW MEXICO

343 E. Alameda, Santa Fe, NM 87501-2229
(505) 983-3277
www.drugpolicy.org nm@drugpolicy.org

INNOCENCE & JUSTICE PROJECT | UNIVERSITY OF NEW MEXICO SCHOOL OF LAW

1117 Stanford NE, Albuquerque, NM 87131-0001
(505) 277-2671
www.lawschool.unm.edu

IJP provides legal representation for wrongfully convicted New Mexico prisoners. DNA and non-DNA cases accepted, with no minimum sentencing requirement.

NEW MEXICO WOMEN'S JUSTICE PROJECT (NMWJP)

PO Box 25501, Albuquerque, NM 87125
(505) 999-1935
www.nmwjp.org

NMWJP provides assistance to women who have been adversely affected by the justice system.

PB & J FAMILY SERVICES

1101 Lopez Rd. SW, Albuquerque, NM 87105
(505) 291-6412
www.pbjfamilyservices.org info@pbjfamilyservices.org

PBJ provides parenting education to incarcerated parents, as well as some assistance with release preparation and family reunification.

WINGS MINISTRY

2770 D Wyoming Blvd. NE, Suite 130, Albuquerque, NM 87112
(505) 291-6412
www.wingsministy.org

WM provides support to spouses and children of New Mexico prisoners by connecting them with local church members.

Reentry Resources

CROSSROADS FOR WOMEN

805 Tijeras Ave. NW, Albuquerque, NM 87102 (505) 242-1010
www.crossroadsabq.org

Crossroads for women provides transitional services for New Mexico women ex-offenders.

DELANCEY STREET FOUNDATION

PO Box 1240, San Juan Pueblo, NM 87566
(505) 852-4291

DSF provides comprehensive on-the-job training and employment assistance to New Mexico ex-offenders. They operate several businesses that they use to assist those reentering society.

DISMAS HOUSE | ST. MARTIN'S HOSPITALITY CENTER

PO Box 27258, Albuquerque, NM 87125
(505) 343-0746
www.dismashousenewmexico.org

DH provides transitional housing to New Mexico ex-offenders, which is contracted with NMDOC.

KAIROS OUTSIDE OF NEW MEXICO

PO Box 4226, Roswell, NM 88201
(505) 304-5578
www.kairosoutsideofnm.org

LA ENTRADA OFFENDER REENTRY PROGRAM | AMITY FOUNDATION

609 Gold Ave. SW, Albuquerque, NM 87102
(505) 246-9300
www.amityfdn.org/newmexico

PEACEFUL HABITATION | POST-PRISON A& AFTERCARE MINISTRY

PO Box 53516, Albuquerque, NM 87153
(505) 440-5937
www.apeacefulhabitation.org

PROJECT IMPACT | PB & J FAMILY SERVICES

1101 Lopez Rd. SW, Albuquerque, NM 87105
(505) 877-7060
www.pbjfamilyservices.org info@pbjfamilyservices.org

Project IMPACT is a project of PB & J Family Services that assists New Mexico ex-offenders with reentry planning and family services, including counseling, reentry, and more.

WOMEN'S HOUSING COALITION

3005 San Pedro NE, Albuquerque, NM 87110
(505) 884-8856
www.womenshousingcoalition.org

The Women's Housing Coalition provides housing solutions for women ex-offenders in the Albuquerque area.

New York | Empire State

State Capital: Albany

Time Zone: EST

Population: 19,746,227

(70.4% White, 17.6% Black, 8.5% Asians, 1% American Indian (17.3% Hispanic))

Name Origin: For James, Duke of New York and Albany, who received a patent for New Netherland from his brother Charles II and sent an expedition to capture it, in 1664.

Motto: Excelsior (Ever Upward)

Famous New Yorkers: Woody Allen, Lucille Ball, Francis Ford Coppola, Tom Cruise, Robert DeNiro, Jimmy Fallon, Nancy Reagan, Jerry Seinfeld, Barbara Streisand, Donald Trump, Luther Vandross, Denzel Washington, Mark Zuckerberg.

State Agencies

DRIVER RECORDS

Department of Motor Vehicles, MV-15, Room 430, Albany, NY 12228
(518) 473-5595
www.nydmv.state.ny.us

SECRETARY OF STATE

Department of State, 41 State St., Albany, NY 12231-0001
(518) 473-2492
www.dos.state.ny.us

VETERAN'S AFFAIRS

Niagara Center, 130 E. Elmwood Ave., Buffalo, NY 14202

VETERAN'S AFFAIRS | NYC

245 W. Houston St., New York City, NY 10014

VITAL RECORDS

800 N. Pearl St., Menands, NY 12204-1842
(518) 474-3038
www.health.state.ny.us/vital-records

All New York state records, except for NYC.

VITAL RECORDS | NYC

125 Worth St., CN4, Room 133, New York, NY 10013
(212) 788-4520
www.nyc.gov

Birth and death records only.

Prisoner Support

ACCESS | ARGUS COMMUNITY

760 E. 160th St., Bronx, NY 10456
(718) 401-5741
www.arguscommunity.org

ACCESS provides support services to prisoners living with HIV/AIDS, including ex-offenders and their families. Most services are for those reentering society, but they can assist with information and planning.

AIDS-RELATED COMMUNITY SERVICE

235 Main St., Poughkeepsie, NY 12601
(800) 992-1442, (845) 471-0707
www.arcs.org

ARCS provides support and services to New York prisoners with HIV/AIDS including case management, counseling, crisis intervention, referrals for medical, legal, funeral and other needs. They also provide printed materials.

BARD PRISON INITIATIVE | BARD COLLEGE

PO Box 5000, Annandale-on-Hudson, NY 12504-5000
(845) 758-7300
www.bpi.bard.edu

BPI offers college degree courses to New York prisoners in the following correctional facilities: Bayview, Eastern, Elmira, Green Haven, and Woodbourne.

BRONX DEFENDERS, THE

360 E. 161st St., Bronx, NY 10451
(718) 838-7878
www.bronxdefenders.org

CHILDREN'S CENTER | BEDFORD HILLS CORRECTIONAL FACILITY

237 Harris Rd., Bedford Hills, NY 10507
(914) 241-3100 ext. 4050

CC provides programs and services for incarcerated mothers and their children, including parenting classes, foster care workshop, nursery, children's advocacy, family literacy, holiday activities, transportation, the Infant Development Center, and more. They will also provide the *Foster Care Handbook for Incarcerated Parents*, and *Parenting from Inside/Out: The Voices of Mothers in Prison.*

CORRECTIONAL ASSOCIATION OF NEW YORK

2090 Adam Clayton Powell, New York, NY 10027
(212) 254-5700
www.correctionalassociation.org

CA of NY advocates for the humane treatment of prisoners and a more effective criminal justice system in New York. Current projects include *Women in Prison Project*, *Prison Visiting Project*, and the *Juvenile Justice Program.*

CURE | NEW YORK

207 Riverside Ave., Scotia, NY 12302
(518) 346-6949
www.curenewyork.wordpress.com
curenewyork@aol.com

CURE provides advocacy and organization through prisoners and their supporters to achieve reforms ion the New York prison system.

CIVIL RIGHTS CLINIC | NYU CLINICAL LAW CENTER

245 Sullivan St., 5th Floor, New York, NY 10012
(212) 998-6430

CRC provides limited legal support services to New York prisoners on civil rights issues.

CORNELL PRISON EDUCATION PROGRAM

115 Day Hall, Ithaca, NY 14853
(607) 255-9091
ccep.cornell.edu

The Cornell Prison Education Program brings FREE Cornell college-level liberal arts education into the Auburn and Cayuga Correctional Facilities.

DEVELOPING JUSTICE PROJECT | FIFTH AVENUE COMMITTEE

141 Fifth Ave., Brooklyn, NY 11217
(718) 237-2017
www.fifthave.org

DRUG POLICY ALLIANCE | NEW YORK

131 W. 33rd St., 15th Floor, New York, NY 10001
www.nyc@drugpolicy.org

EDWIN GOULD SERVICES FOR CHILDREN | INCARCERATED MOTHERS PROGRAM

151 Lawrence St., Suite 5, Brooklyn, NY 11201
(212) 437-3500
www.egscf.org

EGSC works with incarcerated mothers to prevent foster care placement of children. They provide advocacy, counseling, vocational training, and parenting groups.

EMMA'S PREMIUM SERVICES

162 Washington Ave., Edison, NJ 08817
(888) 638-9994
www.emmaspremiumservices.com

Emma's Premium Services provides commissary package options for New York area prisons, specializing in fresh fruits and vegetables, steak, turkey and lobster. They hope to expand to surrounding states in the near future.

EXONERATION INITIATIVE

233 Broadway, Suite 2370, New York, NY 10279
(212) 965-9335
www.exonerationinitiative.org

EI provides legal representation to wrongfully convicted New York prisoners who have actual innocence claims. DNA and non-DNA cases accepted, with no sentencing minimums.

FAMILIES RALLY FOR EMANCIPATION AND EMPOWERMENT (FREE!)

29-76 Northern Blvd., Long Island City, NY 11101
(718) 706-0195
www.freefamilies.us

FREE! is a coalition of women who have loved one behind bars who strive to impact policy and fight for social justice. Write them for current programs.

HARLEM JUSTICE CORPS | CENTER FOR COURT INNOVATION

127 W. 127th St., New York, NY 10027
(646) 593-8520
www.nycjusticecorps.org/justice-corp/harlem-corp

HOUR CHILDREN

36-11 12th St., Long Island, NY 11106
(718) 433-4724
www.hourchildren.org

HC supports incarcerated New York mothers and their children. They provide services in English and Spanish.

HUDSON LINK FOR HIGHER EDUCATION IN PRISON

PO Box 862, Ossining, NY 10562
(914) 941-0794
www.hudsonlink.org

HL provides college degree opportunities to prisoners in the following facilities: Fishkill, Sing Sing, Sullivan CF, and Taconic CF. GED or high school equivalency diploma required.

LEGAL ACTION CENTER

225 Varick St., 4th Floor, New York, NY 10014
(800) 223-4044, (212) 243-1313
www.lac.org lacinfo@lac.org

LAC provides assistance to HIV-positive prisoners and their families. Services include advocacy for discrimination matters, helping secure government benefits, assistance with health care proxies, wills, etc., as well as reentry assistance and more.

LEGAL AID SOCIETY

199 Water St., Suite 400, New York, NY 10038
(212) 577-3530
www.legal-aid.org

LAS offers legal counsel and advice to New York residents who cannot afford a private lawyer, including prisoners on matters such as parole revocation defense. Representation typically comes in the form of class actions.

NEW YORK BOARD OF CORRECTION

51 Chamber St., Room 923, New York, NY 10007
(212) 788-7840
www.nyc.gov/boc

NYC Board of Correction ensures that the Department of Corrections meets minimum compliance standards in matters such as prisoner health care, mental health care, and conditions of confinement. They review prisoner and employee complaints and grievances, investigate serious incidents, and assist in corrections planning to ensure the rights of all involved.

NEW YORK CITY COMPTROLLER | NYC LGBTQ GUIDE

One Centre St., New York, NY 10007
(212) 669-3500
comptroller.nyc.gov

The New York City Comptroller provides a comprehensive LGBTQ guide for all of the services and resources for ex-offenders in the NYC area.

NEW YORK CLU | LEGAL INTAKE COMMITTEE

125 Broad St., 19th Floor, New York, NY 10004
(212) 607-3300
www.nyclu.org

NY CLU legal representation and referrals to New York residents with violations of civil liberties. New York prison issues are generally referred to the Prisoners' Rights Project of Legal Aid Society of Prisoners Legal Services of New York. Collect calls can be placed Mon-Thu 11AM – 1PM.

NEW YORK INITIATIVE CHILDREN FOR INCARCERATED PARENTS

809 Westchester Ave., Bronx, NY 10455
(800) 344-3314, (718) 637-6560
www.osborneny.org nyinitiative@osbornent.org

NYI for Children of Incarcerated Parents is a special project of the Osborne Association focused on visitation for children of incarcerated parents in NY. They advocate for family visitation by educating the public, legislators, and prison administration on the benefits of such visits and works towards improving visitation opportunities.

NEW YORK STATE PRISONER JUSTICE COALITION | NYS PRISONER JUNETWORK

33 Central Ave., Albany, NY 12210
(518) 434-4037
www.nysprisonerjustice.org

The NY Prisoner Justice Coalition publishes the New York State Prisoner Justice Network Directory, a FREE directory of over 100 NY prisoner support organizations.

OSBOURNE ASSOCIATION, THE

809 Westchester Ave., Bronx, NY 10455
(718) 707-2600
www.osbourne.org info@osbourneny.org

OA provides a variety of services to prisoners on Riker's Island and 8 prisons around the NYC and

Duchess County to ex-offenders and their families – especially children. Most programs require participants to meet eligibility requirements related to education, addiction, and supervision status. Write for publications and services available.

OSSINING PRISON MINISTRY

34 S. Highland Ave., Ossining, NY 10562
(914) 641-0540

OPM provides support for families visiting prisoners at Sing Sing, including breakfast supervised childcare on weekends, as well as some counseling and other hospitality services.

PACE POST-CONVICTION PROJECT

78 N. Broadway, White Plains, NY 10603
(914) 422-4230
ww.law.pace.edu/criminal-justice-clinic-post-conviction-project

PPCP provides legal services for unlawfully convicted New York prisoners that claim actual innocence. DNA and non-DNA cases accepted with no sentencing requirement. They will consider shaken baby syndrome, arson, and child abuse cases.

PRISONERS' LEGAL SERVICES | NEW YORK

Albany: 41 State St., Suite M112, Albany, NY 12207
(Serves Bedford Hill, Camp Mt. McGregor, Camp Summit, CNYPC, Coxsackie, Downstate, Great Meadow, Eastern Fishkill, Green Haven, Greene, Hale Creek, Hudson, Johnstown, Marcy, Mid-State, Mohawk, Oneida, Sing Sing, Sullivan, Walsh, and Washington.)
(518) 445-6053

Ithaca: 102 Prospect St., Ithaca, NY 14850
(Serves Auburn, Butler, Camp Georgetown, Camp Monterrey, Camp Pharsalia, Cape Vincent, Cayuga, Elmira, Five Points, Southport, Watertown, and Willard.)
(607) 273-2283

Plattsburgh: 212 Bridge St., Suite 292, Plattsburgh, NY 21901
(Serves: Adirondack, Altoona, Bare Hill, Camp Gabriels, Chateauguay, Clinton, Franklin, Gouvernour, Moriah, Ogdensburg, Riverview, and Upstate.)
(518) 561-3088

Buffalo: 237 Main St., Suite 1535, Buffalo, NY 14203

(Serves: Albion, Attica, Buffalo, Collins, Gowanda, Groveland, Lakeview, Livingston, Orleans, Rochester, Wende, and Wyoming.)
(716) 854-1007

www.plsny.org

PLS provides legal services for civil matters to New York prisoners where no other counsel is available. They typically handle conditions of confinement cases involving disciplinary procedures, medical/mental health care, excessive force, sentence commutation, parole matters. Contact the PLS branch that serves your prison area.

PRISON FAMILIES OF NEW YORK

40 N. Main Ave., Albany, NY 12203
(518) 453-6659
www.prisonfamiliesofnewyork.org

Prison families of New York provides support groups for families of the incarcerated, training to those who work with families of prisoners, as well as policy development and advocacy.

PRISONERS' RIGHTS PROJECT OF THE LEGAL AID SOCIETY

199 Water St., New York, NY 10038
(212) 577-3530
www.legal-aid.org

PRP provides legal aid and referrals to New York prisoners on conditions of confinement complaints, typically through habeas proceedings in federal court. They can also provide printed material on prisoner's rights and remedies.

REINVESTIGATION PROJECT | OFFICE OF THE APPELLATE DEFENDER

11 Park Place, Suite 160, New York, NY 10007
(212) 402-4100
www.appellatedefender.org/reinvestigation.html

RP provides legal representation for wrongfully convicted prisoners in Manhattan and the Bronx areas. DNA and non-DNA cases accepted, with no sentencing requirements.

RISING HOPE

PO Box 906, Croton Falls, NY 10519
(914) 276-7948
www.risinhopeinc.org risinghopeinc@optonline.net

Rising Hope offers FREE college-level education opportunities, including a Certificate in Ministry and Human Services, to prisoners in the following institutions: Sing Sing, Green Haven, Arthurkill, Fishkill, Mod-Orange, and Woodbourne.

SECOND LOOK PROGRAM | BROOKLYN LAW SCHOOL

250 Joralemon St., Brooklyn, NY 11201
www.brooklaw.edu/academics/clinic

VERA INSTITUTE OF JUSTICE

233 Broadway, 12th Floor, New York, NY 10279
(212) 334-1300
www.vera.org

The Vera Institute of justice offers a variety of programs throughout the U.S., including New York. Write for local programs in your area.

Reentry Resources

ARGUS COMMUNITY REENTRY INITIATIVE (ACRI)

760 e. 160th St., Bronx, NY 10456
(718) 401-5726
www.arguscommunity.org

BLACK VETERAN'S FOR SOCIAL JUSTICE

665 Willoughby Ave., Brooklyn, NY 11206
(718) 852-6004

BVSJ assists veterans reentering the NYC area with VA benefits, employment, and housing.

CENTER FOR COMMUNITY ALTERNATIVES

115 E. Jefferson St., Suite 333, Syracuse, NY 13202
(315) 422-5638
www.communityalternatives.org

Provides prisoner-specific reentry planning. Reentry services include education, HIV-positive support, and referrals for housing needs. Spanish spoken.

CENTER FOR COMPREHENSIVE CARE | MORNINGSIDE CLINIC ST. LUKE'S

309 W. 114th St., 3rd Floor, New York, NY 10025
(212) 523-6500
www.centerforcare.org

CCC provides comprehensive health care options for New York ex-offenders who have chronic illnesses. No medical insurance required.

CENTER FOR COURT INNOVATIONS | REENTRY

520 8th Ave., 18th Floor, New York, NY 10018
(646) 386-3100
www.courtinnovation.org

CENTER FOR EMPLOYMENT OPPORTUNITIES

50 Broadway, Suite 1604, New York, NY 10004
(212) 422-4430
www.ceoworks.org

CEO assists ex-offenders find employment throughout the greater New York area.

CEPHAS ATTICA

660 Smith St., Buffalo, NY 14210
(716) 856-6131
www.peaceprintspm.org

CA provides reentry services to ex-offenders reentering the Buffalo and Rochester areas, including housing, education and job opportunities, substance abuse and group counseling, and more. Must commit to a 90-day program.

CMO NETWORK

East New York: 653 Schenck Ave., Brooklyn, NY 11207
Bronx: 283 St. Ann's Ave., Floor 1, Bronx, NY 10454
Calvary Church: 61 Gramercy Park North, New York, NY 10010
(646) 597-8433
www.cmo-network.org

Provides group support services in anger management, substance abuse prevention, job readiness, legal empowerment, money management, housing, education, and parole mediation assistance.

COLLEGE AND COMMUNITY FELLOWSHIP

365 5th Ave., Suite 5113, New York, NY 10016
212) 817-8906
www.collegaandcommunity.org
info@collegeandcommunity.org

CCF works with released prisoners, mostly women, who want to continue their education after release from prison.

COMALERT

210 Joralemon St., 3rd Floor, Brooklyn, NY 11201
(708) 250-3281
www.brooklynnda.org/barrier_free_justice/ca/comalert.htm

Reentry group for Brooklyn residents. Services include job training, literacy instruction, education, and counseling. Referrals for housing and job placement.

CORRECTIONAL LIBRARY SERVICES
NEW YORK PUBLIC LIBRARY

455 Fifth Ave., 6th Floor, New York, NY 10016
(212) 592-7553
www.nypl.org

CLS publishes and distributes a comprehensive NYC reentry guide, called Connections, FREE to prisoners reentering the area. Spanish speakers may request up to 40 pages of their Conexiones 2015 resource directory.

CROWN HEIGHT COMMUNITY MEDIATION CENTER

265 Kingston Ave., Brooklyn, NY 11213
(718) 773-6886
www.crownheights.org

CH publishes a comprehensive local reentry resource directory covering Brooklyn, Manhattan, and the Bronx. FREE to prisoners.

DELANCEY STREET FOUNDATION

100 Turk Hill Rd., Brewster, NY 10609
(845) 278-6181

DSF provides reintegration programs for NY ex-offenders through comprehensive on-the-job training programs at facilities and businesses run by the organization.

EXODUS TRANSITIONAL COMMUNITY

2271 Third Ave., 2nd Floor, New York, NY 10035
(914) 492-0990
www.etcny.org

ETCNY provides reentry services to New York area ex-offenders, including career consultation, mental health and substance abuse counseling and treatment, and housing and job referrals.

EXPONENTS | CASE MANAGEMENT CONNECTION

151 W. 26th St., 3rd Floor, New York, NY 10001
(212) 243-6424
www.exponents.org

Exponents provides long-term case management services for NYC area HIV-positive ex-offenders.

FAST FORWARD

500 8th Ave., Suite 1207, New York, NY 10018
(212) 714-0600

FF provides reentry services to NYC-area ex-offenders, including vocational and educational assessments, job placement, and counseling.

FATHERS COUNT: REENTRY PLUS | FAMILY SERVICES OF WESTCHESTER

One Gateway Plaza, 4th Floor, Port Chester, NY 10573
(914) 937-2320
www.fsw.org

Fathers Count provides employment and parenting skills training to ex-offender fathers in the Port Chester and Yonkers areas.

FORGING AHEAD FOR COMMUNITY EMPOWERMENT AND SUPPORT (FACES)

317 Lenox Ave., 10th Floor, New York, NY 10027
(212) 663-7772
www.facesny.org

FACES provides pre-release planning and reentry services for HIV-positive ex-offenders, including housing, legal education, and services. Applicants must be NYC residents, HIV-positive, and have an M11Q form.

FORTUNE SOCIETY

29-76 Northern Blvd., Long Island City, NY 11101
(212) 691-7554 ext. 501
www.fortunesociety.org
info@fortunesociety.org

FS provides a variety of comprehensive reentry support services for ex-offenders releasing to the NYC area, including educational programs, HIV/AIDS counseling, employment services, counseling, court advocacy, and much more.

FRIENDS OF ISLAND ACADEMY

127 West 127th St., Suite 127, New York, NY 10027
(212) 760-0755
www.friendsny.org

Provides reentry services for New York ex-offenders between the ages of 16 and 24, including counseling, education, job readiness, and placement.

GANG DIVERSION, REENTRY AND ABSENT FATHERS INTERVENTION CENTERS (GRAAFICS)

116 Nassau St., 7th Floor, Brooklyn, NY 11201
(718) 694-8357
www.graficss.org

GRAAFICS provides current and former gang members, both ex-offenders and those currently incarcerated, with alternatives to gang life. Contact them for current programs.

GETTING OUT AND STAYING OUT (GOSO)

91 East 116th St., New York, NY 10029
(212) 831-5020
www.gosonyc.org

GOSO works with offenders transitioning back into society through pre-release interviews to determine housing, counseling, and treatment needs, then makes referrals to appropriate agencies. They mostly work with offenders aged 18-24.

GREENHOPE SERVICES FOR WOMEN

435 East 119th St., New York, NY 10035
(212) 996-8633 ext. 1100
www.greenhope.org

GSW provides reentry services to predominantly African American and Latina New York ex-offender women, including comprehensive residential treatment, housing, and outpatient programs.

HARLEM RESTORATION PROJECT

461 W. 124th St., New York, NY 10027
(212) 622-8186

HRP provides NYC ex-offenders with job opportunities in construction, as well as provides some housing assistance.

HEALING COMMUNITIES NETWORK | FUND FOR THE CITY

121 Avenue of the Americas, 6th Floor, New York, NY 10013
(212) 925-6675 ext. 293
www.healingcommunities.org

HCN provides support services for ex-offenders in the NYC area, including family adjustment, mentoring, counseling, employment search, and more. They also offer group support services within the prison setting.

NETWORK SUPPORT SERVICES

5 Bergen Ave., 3rd Floor, Bronx, NY 10455
(347) 821-9225
www.networkssi.org contact@networkssi.org

NSS provides reentry services for ex-offenders in the Five Burroughs area, including treatment, job readiness and placement services, and therapy.

OSBORNE ASSOCIATION | NEW YORK

809 Westchester Ave., Bronx, NY 10455
(718) 707-2600
www.osborneny.org

PRISONER REENTRY INSTITUTE | JOHN JAY COLLEGE OF CRIMINAL JUSTICE

524 W. 59th St., Room 609b-BMW, New York, NY 10019
(646) 558-4532
www.johnjayresearch.oorg/pri

PROVIDENCE HOUSE

703 Lexington Ave., Brooklyn, NY 11221
(718) 455-0197
www.providencehouse.org info@providencehouse.org

PH provides transitional housing and services to ex-offenders in Brooklyn, Queens, and New Rochelle. They assist their residents with obtaining education, training, and gainful employment.

REALITY HOUSE

637 W. 125th St., New York, NY 10027
(212) 666-8000

RH provides New York ex-offenders with therapies and counseling for drug addiction and HIV concerns.

REDEMPTION CENTER, THE

1186 Herkimer St., Brooklyn, NY 11233
(718) 922-1627
www.theredemptioncntr.com

RC is a faith-based organization that provides reentry services to ex-offenders in the Brooklyn area, including transitional housing, skills training, education, support groups, and referral services.

REENTRY NET

860 Courtland Ave., Bronx, NY 10451
(718) 838-7869
www.reentry.net/ny

Reentry.net provides a number of reentry resource materials and guides for those releasing into New York. Write for current options.

REENTRY RESOURCE CENTER

www.reentry.net/ny

The Reentry Resource Center is an online resource that provides comprehensive reentry resources for the New York state region.

ST. PATRICK FRIARY

102 Seymour St., Buffalo, NY, 14210
(716) 856-6131

St. Patrick Friary is a faith-based group that provides ex-offenders in the Buffalo area with transitional housing, education, transportation, job training and placement assistance.

SOCIETY OF ST. VINCENT DE PAUL

249 Broadway, Bethpage, NY 11714
(516) 623-5710
www.svdprvc.org

SVDP provides Long Island ex-offenders with emergency support services, including bail assistance, transportation, housing, and clothing.

SOUTHERN TIER AIDS PROGRAM

122 Baldwin St., Johnson City, NY 13790
(800) 333-0892, (607) 798-1706
www.stapinc.org

STAP provides HIV-positive ex-offenders with transitional services, including education programs, counseling, support, and case management. They will also provide prison officials and parole officers with educational materials.

STAND UP! | HARLEM

145 W. 130th St., New York, NY 10027
(212) 926-4072

Stand Up! Provides HIV-positive ex-offenders in the NYC area with transitional housing and support.

SUPPORTIVE HOUSING NETWORK OF NEW YORK | REENTRY

247 W. 37th St., 18th Floor, New York, NY 10018
(646) 619-9640
www.shnny.org

SYLVIA RIVERA LAW PROJECT

146 W. 24th St., 5th Floor, New York, NY 10011
(212) 337-8550
www.srlp.org

SRLP provides legal services to NY ex-offenders who are transgender, intersex, or gender non-conforming, including name changes, identity documents, public benefits, immigration, and more.

THINK OUTSIDE THE CELL FOUNDATION

511 Avenue of the Americas, Suite 525, New York, NY 10011
(877) 267-2303
www.thinkoutsidethecell.org

VOA | GREATER NEW YORK

340 W. 85th St., New York, NY 10024
(212) 873-2600
www.voa-gny.org

WOMEN CARE

105 Chambers St., 2nd Floor, New York, NY 10007
(212) 463-9500

WC provides reentry services to female ex-offenders, including housing, employment, and parenting support.

WOMEN'S PRISON ASSOCIATION AND HOME

110 Second Ave., New York, NY 10003
(646) 292-7742
www.wpa.org info@wpaonline.org

WPA provides reentry services to female ex-offenders, including family reunifications, employment, health care, housing, and more.

Best state for prison visitation award?

Did you know that New York's visitation policies are the most liberal in the nation, including allowing visitation to prisoners 365 days per year? They are also one of the few states that still have active conjugal visitation programs.

North Carolina | Tar Heel State -- Old North State

State Capital: Raleigh

Time Zone: EST

Population: 9,943,964

(71.5% White, 22.1% Black, 2.7% Asians, 1.6% American Indian (8% Hispanic))

Name Origin: In 1626, Charles I gave a patent to Sir Robert Heath for the Province of Carolana, from *Carolus,* Latin name for Charles. It was divided into North and South in 1710.

Motto: Esse Quam Videra (To be rather than to seem)

Famous Carolinians: John Coltrane, Rick Dees, Dale Earnhardt Sr., Ava Gardner, Billy Graham, Michal Jordan, Dolly Madison, Richard Petty.

State Agencies

CONSUMER PROTECTION

MSC 9001, Raleigh, NC 27699
(919) 716-6000

DRIVER RECORDS

Department of Motor Vehicles, 3101 MSC, Raleigh, NC 27699
(919) 715-7000
www.ncdot.org/dmv

SECRETARY OF STATE

PO Box 29622, Raleigh, NC 27626-0622
(888) 246-7636
www.sosnc.com

VETERAN'S AFFAIRS

Federal Building, 251 Main St., Winston-Salem, NC 27155

VETERAN'S AFFAIRS | QUICK START OFFICE

100 N. Main St., Suite 1900, Winston-Salem, NC 27101

VITAL RECORDS

Center for Health Statistics, 1903 MSC, Raleigh, NC 27699-1903
(919) 733-3526
www.vitalrecords/dhhs/state.nc.us

Prisoner Support

ACLU | NORTH CAROLINA

PO Box 28004, Raleigh, NC 28202
(919) 834-3390
www.acluofnorthcarolina.org contact@acluofnc.org

Advocates for the civil of prisoners in North Carolina, generally through class action. They typically will not accept individual prisoner cases, but they may provide referrals.

CAROLINA JUSTICE POLICY CENTER

PO Box 309, Durham, NC 27707
(919) 682-1149
www.justicepolicycenter.org

CJPC provides information on criminal justice matters affecting prisoners in the Carolinas. They can provide stats, policy information, and information on reform efforts.

CURE | NORTH CAROLINA

PO Box 49572, Charlotte, NC 28277
(252) 722-3414

CURE provides advocacy and organization through prisoners and their supporters to achieve reforms in the North Carolina prison system.

INNOCENCE AND JUSTICE CLINIC | WAKE FOREST UNIVERSITY LAW SCHOOL

1834 Wake Forest Rd., Winston-Salem, NC 27109
(336) 757-5430
www.innocence-clinic.law.wfu.edu

IJC provides legal representation for wrongfully convicted prisoners in North Carolina. DNA and non-DNA cases accepted, with no sentencing minimum.

MATCH

PO Box 14469, Raleigh, NC 27620
(919) 828-4767
www.prisonmatch.org director@prisonmatch.org

MATCH provides parenting education and ongoing visitation support to incarcerated North Carolina women.

NORTH CAROLINA CENTER ON ACTUAL INNOCENCE

PO Box 52446, Durham, NC 27717-2446
(919) 489-3268
www.ncaai.org

NCCAI provides legal representation for wrongfully convicted North Carolina prisoners. Prisoner must have been convicted in NC, have an actual claim of innocence with no involvement in the crime, have no more appeal rights and are currently unrepresented, and have the possibility of new evidence that was presented at trial or during appeals.

NORTH CAROLINA DOC | OFFENDER FAMILY SERVICES

40 W. Morgan St., 4280 MSC, Raleigh, NC 27610
(919) 838-3629
www.doc.state.nc.us/familyservices

Offender Family Services of the NC DOC provides family liaison services between family and offender, psychological support, crisis intervention, education of the criminal justice system, referrals and transition services to benefit families.

NORTH CAROLINA DIVISION OF PRISONS | EDUCATION SERVICES

831 W. Morgan St., 4264 MSC, Raleigh, NC 27699-4264
(919) 838-4000

North Carolina is the second largest provider of secondary education for prisoners in the country (after Texas). Throughout more than 70 prisons, they provide extensive vocational training and other programs through partnerships with in-state colleges.

NORTH CAROLINA INNOCENCE INQUIRY COMMISSION

ADMINISTRATION OFFICE OF THE COURTS

PO Box 2448, Raleigh, NC 27602
(919) 890-1580
www.innocencecommission-nc.org

NCIIC reviews actual innocence claims of North Carolina prisoners through an independent and balanced forum established by the NC General Assembly. Someone found to be innocent by the forum is declared innocent and cannot be tried again, regardless of the appellate process.

NORTH CAROLINA JUSTICE CENTER

224 S. Dawson St., Raleigh, NC 27601
(919) 856-2570
www.ncjustice.org

NORTH CAROLINA PRISONER LEGAL SERVICES

PO Box 25397, Raleigh, NC 27611
(919) 856-2200
www.ncpls.org ncpls@ncpls.org

NCPLS provides legal assistance to North Carolina prisoners, typically on conditions of confinement issues. They may provide referrals for other legal matters.

OUR CHILDREN'S PLACE

PO Box 1086, Chapel Hill, NC 27514
(919) 843-2670
www.ourchildrensplace.org
ourchildrensplace@gmail.com

Our Children's Place provides alternative sentencing opportunities to women offenders. Through a planned residential facility, women can serve their time with their infant/pre-school-aged children. During their stay, women receive counseling, treatment and services, while children receive quality care and developmental services.

PRISON BOOKS COLLECTIVE

PO Box 625, Carrboro, NC 27510
(919) 443-9238
www.prisonbooks.info

Prison Books Collective is an anti-mass-incarceration group that sends FREE books to prisoners. They also offer a radical magazine directory and publish prisoner writings and art.

SOUTHERN COALITION FOR SOCIAL JUSTICE

1415 West Highway 54, Durham, NC 27707
(919) 323-3380
www.southerncoalition.org

SUPPORT FOR KIDS OF INCARCERATED PARENTS (SKIP)

115-A S. Walnut Cir., Greensboro, NC 27409
(336) 547-7461
www.tristansquest.com

SKIP provides in-school support for children of incarcerated parents, which includes counseling and relationship strengthening through weekly letter-writing and guidance.

Reentry Resources

CENTER FOR COMMUNITY TRANSITIONS

PO Box 33533, Charlotte, NC 28223
(704) 374-0762
www.centerforcommunitytransitions.org

CCT provides various reentry programs to assist North Carolina ex-offenders, including case management, employment readiness, family reunification, referrals, transportation, and more.

COMMUNITY SUCCESS INITIATIVE | RESOURCE CENTER WITHOUT WALLS

1830-B Tillery Place, Raleigh, NC 27604
(919) 715-0111
www.communitysuccess.org

CSI provides reentry preparation assistance for North Carolina ex-offenders, including life and employment skills training, mentoring, community advocacy for system reforms for better transition to society, and more.

CROSSROADS REENTRY MINISTRIES (CRM)

PO Box 861, Huntersville, NC 28070
(704) 499-1332
www.crossroadsreentry.org

DELANCEY STREET FOUNDATION

811 N. Elm St., Greensboro, NC 27401
(336) 379-8477

DSF provides employment assistance to North Carolina ex-offenders through comprehensive on-the-job training at various businesses the organization owns and operates.

DURHAM REENTRY PROGRAM | DURHAM COUNTY CRIMINAL JUSTICE RESOURCE CENTER

326 E. Main St., Durham, NC 27701
(919) 560-0500

www.dcone.gov/government/departments-a-e/criminal-justice-resource-center

ENERGY COMMITTED TO OFFENDERS

PO Box 33533. Charlotte, NC 28233
(704) 374-0762
www.ecocharlotte.org

ECO provides pre- and post-release reentry services for prisoners reentering North Carolina society, including pre-release planning, job search, transportation, housing and clothing referrals, and family reunification programs.

GOING HOME INITIATIVE | NC DOC

2020 Yonkers Rd., 4221 MSC, Raleigh, NC 27699
(919) 716-3080
www.doc.state.nc.us/rap/goinghome.htm

GOODWILL INDUSTRIES OF NORTHWEST NORTH CAROLINA

2701 University Parkway, Winston-Salem, NC 27115
(336) 724-3621
www.goodwillnwnc.org/work

HARRIET'S HOUSE

PO Box 10347, 712 W. Johnson St., Raleigh, NC 27605
(919) 834-0666 ext. 235
www.passagehome.org

Harriet's House provides transitional housing for North Carolina women ex-offenders as well as reunification services for those mothers and their children. Referrals are made by prison social workers.

LINC | RESIDENTIAL REENTRY PROGRAM

222 Division Dr., Wilmington, NC 28401
(910) 332-1132
www.lincnc.org

PASSAGE HOME

513 Branch St., Raleigh, NC 27601
(919) 834-0666
www.passagehome.org

North Dakota | Peace Garden State

State Capital: Bismarck

Time Zone: EST

Population: 739,482

(89.1% White, 5.4% American Indian, 2.1% Black, 1.3% Asians (1.8% Hispanic))

Name Origin: Sioux word for *Dakota* meaning "friend" or "ally."

Motto: Liberty and Union, Now and Forever, One and Inseparable.

Famous North Dakotans: Angie Dickenson, Josh Duhamel, Phil Jackson, Louis L'Amour, Lawrence Welk.

State Agencies

DRIVER RECORDS

Department of Transportation, 608 E. Boulevard Ave., Department 301, Bismarck, ND 58505-0500
(710) 328-2603
www.state.nd.us/dot

SECRETARY OF STATE

600 E. Boulevard Ave., Department 108, Bismarck, ND 58505-4284
(701) 328-4284
www.nd.gov/sos

VETERAN'S AFFAIRS

2101 Elm St., Fargo, ND 58102

VITAL RECORDS

Department of Health, 600 E. Boulevard Ave., Department 301, Bismarck, ND 58505-0200
(701) 328-2360
www.ndhealth.gov/vital

Prisoner Support

CURE | NORTH DAKOTA

(701) 255-0352

CURE provides advocacy and organization through prisoners and their supporters to achieve reforms in the North Dakota prison system.

INNOCENCE PROJECT OF MINNESOTA

1536 Hewitt Ave., MSC 1973, St. Paul, MN 55104
(651) 523-3152
www.ipmn.org

IPMN provides legal representation to wrongfully convicted prisoners in Minnesota, North Dakota, and South Dakota. Non-DNA cases are accepted in ND and SD. There are no minimum sentencing requirements. They look for cases that involve junk science, false confessions, informant testimony, eyewitness misidentification, official misconduct, bad lawyering, and other factors.

Reentry Resources

BISMARCK TRANSITION CENTER

2001 Lee Ave., Bismarck, ND 58504
(701) 222-3440 ext. 101
www.cccscorp.com/btc.htm

CENTRE INC. | RESIDENTIAL TRANSITION PROGRAMS

Fargo: 123 15th St. N, Fargo, ND 58102
(701) 237-9340
Grand Forks: 201 S. 4th St., Grand Forks, ND 58201
(701) 775-2681
Mandan: 100 6th Ave. SE, Mandan 58554
(701) 663-8120
www.centreinc.org

JOB SERVICE | NORTH DAKOTA

PO Box 5507, Bismarck, ND 58506
(701) 328-2825
www.jobsnd.com

LAKE REGION RESIDENTIAL REENTRY CENTER

225 Walnut St. W, Devils Lake, ND 58301
(701) 662-0735

Ohio | Buckeye State

State Capital: Columbus

Time Zone: EST

Population: 11,594,163

(83% White, 12.6% Black, 2% Asians, 0.3% American Indian (3.1% Hispanic))

Name Origin: Iroquois word for "fine" or "good river."

Motto: With God, All Things are Possible

Famous Ohioans: Neil Armstrong, Halle Berry, Drew Carey, Clark Gable, Bob Hope, Lebron James, Jack Nicklaus, Jess Owens, Pete Rose, Steven Spielberg, Gloria Steinem, Ted Turner, Wright Brothers.

State Agencies

CONSUMER AFFAIRS

30 E. Broad St., 14th Floor, Columbus, OH 43215
(614) 466-4320

DRIVER RECORDS

Bureau of Motor Vehicles, 1970 W. Broad St., Columbus, OH 43223-1102
(614) 752-7600
www.ohiobmv.org

SECRETARY OF STATE

PO Box 2795, Columbus, OH 43216
(877) 767-3453
www.sos.state.oh.us

VITAL STATISTICS

PO Box 15098, Columbus, OH 43215-0098
(614) 466-2531
www.odh.ohio.gov

Prisoner Support

ACLU | OHIO

4506 Chester Ave., Cleveland, OH 44103
(216) 472-2200
www.acluohio.org contact@acluohio.org

Advocates for the civil rights of Ohio prisoners, generally through class actions. They typically will not accept individual prisoner cases, but they may provide referrals.

ATHENS BOOKS-TO-PRISONERS

30 First St., Athens, OH 45701

Athens Books-to-Prisoners program provides FREE books to Ohio prisoners.

CURE | OHIO

PO Box 4080, Columbus, OH 43214
(877) 826-8504
www.cure-ohio.org cure-ohio1@cure-ohio.org

CURE provides advocacy and organization through prisoners and their supporters to achieve reforms in the Ohio prison system. They publish a bi-monthly newsletter, *Against All Odds,* FREE to prisoners.

INNOCENT INMATES ASSOCIATION OF OHIO

PO Box 38100, Olmsted Falls, OH 44138
www.innocentinmates.org

OHIO INNOCENCE PROJECT | UNIVERSITY OF CINCINNATI COLLEGE OF LAW

PO Box 210040, Cincinnati, OH 45221-0040
(513) 556-0752
www.law.uc.edu/o-i-p

OIP provides legal representation to wrongfully convicted Ohio prisoners. DNA and non-DNA cases accepted, with no sentencing requirements.

OHIO JUSTICE AND POLICY CENTER

215 E. 9th St., 6th Floor, Cincinnati, OH 45202
(513) 421-1108
www.ohiojpc.org contact@ohiojpc.org

Ohio JPC helps prisoners and their families to better understand their rights, as well as assists them to use the appropriate methods to address claims against the prison. They will represent significant rights violation cases.

OHIO UNIVERSITY COLLEGE PROGRAM FOR THE INCARCERATED

222 Haning Hall, Athens, OH 45701
(800) 444-2420
www.ohio.edu/ecampus/print/correctional

Ohio University offers a variety of education opportunities for prisoners in Ohio and across the U.S. Prisoners can earn Associate's and Bachelor's degrees in a variety of disciplines. Write for a complete listing of current course offerings.

NOTE: If you'd like to see ALL the education options offered to prisoners, order *Prison Lives Almanac: Prisoner Education Guide*, updated every summer. See ad in this book.

REDBIRD BOOKS-TO-PRISONERS

c/o Ohio University, PO Box 10599, Columbus, OH 43201
www.redbirdbooks.blogspot.com

Redbird Books-to Prisoners program is a volunteer driven program that works with Ohio University to provide FREE books to Ohio prisoners.

WRONGFUL CONVICTION PROJECT | OFFICE OF OHIO PUBLIC DEFENDER

250 E. Broad St., Suite 1400, Columbus, OH 43215
(614) 477-4931
www.odp.ohio.gov/dp_wrongfulconviction

WCP provides legal representation for wrongfully convicted Ohio prisoners. Only non-DNA cases with no history of violence or lengthy criminal records accepted. Must have exhausted all appeals and have a considerable amount of time left on sentence.

Reentry Resources

AGAPE COMMUNITY REENTRY PROGRAM

1368 Loretta Ave., Columbus, OH 43211
(614) 477-4931

AGAP is a faith-based organization that offers a transitional planning program for Ohio ex-offenders, including needs assessment, employment resources, education opportunities, and group counseling.

AIDS RESOURCE CENTER | OHIO

4400 N. High St., Suite 300, Columbus, OH 43214
(800) 332-2437
www.arcohio.org

ARC provides a variety of services to Ohio ex-offenders living with AIDS, including a hotline, medical/legal referrals, and other support.

AKRON URBAN LEAGUE | TRANSITIONS PROGRAM

250 E. Market St., Akron, OH 44308
(330) 434-3101
www.akronul.org

AUL provides Akron area ex-offenders with job placement opportunities, including job readiness training.

BUTLER COUNTY REENTRY INITIATIVE

1105 Fourteenth Ave., Middletown, OH 450044
(513) 424-8284
3rdevelopment@sbcglobal.net

The Butler County Reentry Initiative provides case management to ex-offenders in the Butler County area as well as referrals to needed services and peer counseling.

CLEVELAND EASTSIDE EX-OFFENDER COALITION

8003 Broadway Ave., Cleveland, OH 44105
(216) 641-9012
www.clevelandeastside.info

COLUMBUS AREA INTEGRATED HEALTH SERVICES | REENTRY PROGRAMS

1515 Broad St., Columbus, OH 43205
(614) 252-0711

COMMUNITY CONNECTIONS

993 E. Main St., Columbus, OH 43205
(614) 252-0660
www.communityconnectionohio.org

CC assists Ohio ex-offenders with a variety of reentry services designed to establish positive employment, including assessment, the addressing of basic needs such as housing, food, and clothing, and necessary training prior to job placement.

COMMUNITY REENTRY

1468 W. 25th St., Cleveland, OH 44113
(216) 696-2717

CR provides a number of programs designed to assist Ohio ex-offenders to find and maintain employment, including job readiness, case management, and placement assistance. Referrals are also given for housing and treatment needs.

CARACOLE

1821 Summit Rd., Suite 001, Cincinnati, OH 45237
(513) 761-14803
www.caracole.org orgacle@caracole.org

Caracole provides housing services for Ohio ex-offenders and their families who are living with HIV/AIDS.

EXIT PROGRAM

897 Oakwood Ave., Columbus, OH 43206
(614) 253-8969
www.theexitprogram.com

GOODWILL INDUSTRIES OF GREATER CLEVELAND & EAST CENTRAL OHIO

408 Ninth St. SW, Canton, OH 44707
(800) 942-3577
www.goodwillgoodskills.org

IMPACT COMMUNITY ACTION | REENTRY PROGRAM

700 Bryden Rd., Columbus, OH 43215
(614) 252-2799
www.impactca.org

NEW ISLAMIC REENTRY SOCIETY

2302 Putnam Ave., Toledo, OH 43620
(419) 283-2290
www.newhomeislamicreentry.weebly.com

NORTH STAR NEIGHBORHOOD REENTRY RESOURCE CENTER

1834 East 55th St., Cleveland, OH 44103
(216) 881-5440
www.northstarreentry.org

OHIO EX-OFFENDER REENTRY COALITION | ODRC

770 W. Broad St., Columbus, OH 43222
(614) 752-0627
www.reentrycoalition.ohio.gov

OHIO REENTRY COLLABORATIVE

1133 S. Edwin C. Moses Blvd., Room 370, Dayton, OH 45408
(937) 496-7047
www.mcohio.org/dpartments/ex-offender_reentry/reentry_collaborative.php

PROES | EMPLOYMENT CONNECTION

1020 Bolivar Rd., Cleveland, OH 44115
(216) 664-4673

PROES (Providing Real Opportunities for Ex-Offenders to Succeed) provides a variety of resources to ex-offenders, including employment opportunities.

REENTRY BRIDGE NETWORK

PO Box 9491, Canton, OH 44711
(530) 209-7683
www.reentrybridgenetwork.org

REENTRY CIRCLES OF DAYTON | THINK TANK

20 S. Limestone St., Springfield, OH 45502
(937) 322-4970
www.thinktank-inc.org

2ND CHANCES 4 FELONS RESOURCE LISTING

(214) 900-4265
www.2ndchances4felons.com/ohio.php

TOWARDS EMPLOYMENT

125 Euclid Ave., Suite 300, Cleveland, OH 44115
(216) 696-5750
www.towardsemployment.org

UNLOCKING FAMILY FUTURES

PO Box 25, Brice, OH 43109
(859) 654-0284
www.unlockingfamilyfutures.com

Unlocking Family Futures offers mentoring to children of incarcerated parents, financial and food assistance to caregivers, transportation to the prison and referral services for reentry.

WOMEN'S REENTRY NETWORK

4515 Superior Ave., Cleveland, OH 44103
(216) 696-2715
www.lutheranmetro.org/womens-re-entry.html

Oklahoma | Sooner State

State Capital: Oklahoma City

Time Zone: CST

Population: 3,878,051

(75.1% White, 7.7% Black, 2.1% Asians, 9% American Indian (8.6% Hispanic))

Name Origin: Choctaw word meaning "red man," proposed by Rev. Allen Wright, a Choctaw-speaking Indian.

Motto: Labor Omnia Vincit (Labor conquers all things)

Famous Oklahomans: Troy Aikman, Vince Gill, Ron Howard, Mickey Mantle, Reba McIntire, Carrie Underwood.

State Agencies

CONSUMER PROTECTION

313 E. 21st St., Oklahoma City, OK 73105

DRIVER RECORDS

MVR
Desk, PO Box 11415, Oklahoma City, OK 73136-0415
(405) 425-2262
www.dps.state.ok.us

SECRETARY OF STATE

2300 N. Lincoln Blvd., Room 101, Oklahoma City, OK 73105
(405) 522-4582
www.sos.state.ok.us

VETERAN'S AFFAIRS

125 S. Main St., Muskogee, OK 74401

VETERAN'S AFFAIRS | BENEFITS

301 NW 6th St., Suite 113, Oklahoma City, OK 73102

VITAL RECORDS

State Department of Health, 1000 NE 10th St., Oklahoma City, OK 73117
(405) 271-4040
http://vr.health.ok.gov

Prisoner Support

ACLU | OKLAHOMA

3000 Paseo Dr., Oklahoma City, OK 73103
(405) 524-8511
www.acluok.org acluok@acluok.org

Advocates for the civil rights of Oklahoma prisoners, generally through class actions. They typically will not accept individual prisoner cases, but they may provide referrals.

CURE | OKLAHOMA

PO Box 9741, Tulsa, OK 74157-0741
(918) 744-9857
www.okcure.org okcure@okcure.org

CURE provides advocacy and organization through prisoners and their supporters to achieve reforms in the Oklahoma prison system.

NEW STARTS PRISON MINISTRY

PO Box 19353, Oklahoma City, OK 73144
(405) 387-3052
www.prisonministry.net

OKLAHOMA INNOCENCE PROJECT | OKLAHOMA CITY UNIVERSITY SCHOOL OF LAW

800 N. Harvey Ave., Oklahoma City, OK 73102
(405) 208-6161
www.innocence.okcu.org

OIP provides legal representation to wrongfully convicted Oklahoma prisoners. DNA and non-DNA cases accepted, with no sentencing requirements. Only cases of actual innocence allowed.

PASSPORT TO THE FUTURE | LITTLE DIXIE COMMUNITY ACTION AGENCY

603 SW B St., Antlers, OK 74523
(580) 298-2921
www.littledixie.org

Passport to the Future provides mentoring to children of those incarcerated by the Oklahoma prison system.

Reentry Resources

CENTER FOR EMPLOYMENT OPPORTUNITIES

228 Robert S. Kerr, Suite 600, Oklahoma City, OK 73102
(405) 448-8200
www.ceoworks.org

CRIMINAL JUSTICE AND MERCY MINISTRY | OKLAHOMA METHODIST CONFERENCE

1501 NW 24th St., Oklahoma City, OK 73106
(405) 530-2015

CJMM is a faith-based organization that provides a number of basic reentry services to ex-offenders in the Oklahoma City area.

EDUCATION AND EMPLOYMENT MINISTRY

14 NE 13th St., Oklahoma City, OK 73104
(405) 235-5671
www.teem.org

TEEM is a faith-based organization that provides reentry services to ex-offenders in the Oklahoma City area. Services include education, job placement, and social services.

EXODUS HOUSE

Oklahoma City: 433 NW 26th St., Oklahoma City, OK 73103
(405) 525-2300

Tulsa: 2624 E. Newton St., Tulsa, OK 74110
(918) 382-0905

EH provides transitional housing for ex-offenders releasing to the Oklahoma City or Tulsa areas. Additional services include treatment, counseling, referrals, and computer instruction. Sex offenders and recent violent offenders are not eligible.

FEMALE OFFENDERS COMMIT TO ULTIMATE SUCCESS | RESONANCE WOMEN'S CENTER

1608 S. Elwood Ave., Tulsa, OK 74119
(918) 587-3888

FOCUS provides non-violent ex-offenders transitional and other services in the Tulsa area. Other services include case management, counseling, treatment, job skills, housing, and more.

GEORGE KAISER FAMILY FOUNDATION | REENTRY

www.gkff.org/

George Kaiser Family Foundation focuses on reentry issues related to ex-offending women, with various online resources.

HOPE FOR HOPELESS | PRISONER REENTRY ORIENTATION CLASS

PO Box 1112, Bethany, OK 73008
(405) 615-6648
www.proclass.h4hweb.org

HH provides orientation services for ex-offenders reentering into the Oklahoma City area. They provide information on social services, legal services, employment, basic needs, and more.

NEW START PRISON MINISTRY

PO Box 19532, Oklahoma City, OK 73144
(405) 420-3192

NSPM is a faith-based organization that provides a variety of reentry services to ex-offenders in the Oklahoma City area.

OKLAHOMA HOPE PRISON MINISTRY

1839 N. Boston Ave., Tulsa, OK 74106
(918) 599-0663
www.ohpm.org operationhope@ohpm.org

OHPM is a faith-based organization that provides reentry services to Tulsa area ex-offenders, including ID cards, birth certificates and other papers, bus tokens, work passes, and more. Ex-offenders released within the last year can drop in Mon – Wed. 9AM-2PM.

OKLAHOMA PARTNERSHIP FOR SUCCESSFUL REENTRY

PO Box 60433, Oklahoma City, OK 73146-0433
(405) 202-4930
www.okreentry.org

OKLAHOMA REENTRY | TRANSITIONAL SERVICES AND RESOURCES

2901 Classen Blvd., Suite 200, Oklahoma City, OK 73118
(405) 962-6135
www.ok.gov/re-entry

TULSA REENTRY ONE-STOP CENTER

533 E. 36th St. N, Tulsa, OK 74106
(918) 938-6141
www.cstulsa.org

TURNING POINT JOB READINESS | COMMUNITY ACTION AGENCY OF OKC

319 SW 25th St., Oklahoma City, OK 73109
(405) 232-0199
www.caaofokc.org

UPWARD TRANSITIONS

1134 W. Main St., Oklahoma City, OK 73106
(405) 232-5507

WORKFORCE OKLAHOMA

1120 Frisco Ave., Clinton, OK 73601
(580) 323-1341
www.oklahomaworks.gov

WORK READY OKLAHOMA REENTRY SERVICES

3 E. Main St., Oklahoma City, OK 73194
(405) 418-3923
www.workreadyoklahoma.org

Strangest prison visit policy?

Did you know that Oklahoma is the only state that prohibits married couples from receiving visits from anyone else of the opposite gender?

Oregon | Beaver State

State Capital: Salem

Time Zone: PST

Population: 3,970,239

(87.9% White, 4.3% Asian, 2% Black, 1.8% American Indian (11.3% Hispanic))

Name Origin: Origin unknown. A prevailing theory is that the name is derived for *wauregan*, meaning "beautiful," a term used by Indians in New England.

Motto: She Flies with Her Own Wings

Famous Oregonians: Ty Burrell, Matt Groening, Phil Knight, Steve Prefontaine, Alberto Salazar.

State Agencies

CONSUMER PROTECTION

1162 Court St. NE, Salem, OR 97301
(503) 378-4320

DRIVER RECORDS

Department of Motor Vehicles, 1902 Lana Ave. NE. Salem, OR 97314
(503) 945-5000 (Salem), (503) 299-9999 (Portland)
www.oregon.gov/odot/dmv

SECRETARY OF STATE

255 Capitol St NE, Suite 151, Salem, OR 97301
(503) 986-2317
www.filinginoregon.com www.sos.state.or.us

VETERAN'S AFFAIRS

100 SW Main St., 2nd Floor, Portland, OR 97204

VITAL RECORDS

Department of Human Services, PO Box 14050, Portland, OR 97293-0050
(503) 731-4108
www.oregon.gov/dhs

Prisoner Support

ACLU | OREGON

PO Box 40858, Portland, OR 97204-0585
(503) 227-3186
www.aclu-or.org

ACLU advocates for the civil rights of Oregon prisoners, generally through class actions. They typically will not accept individual prisoner cases, but they may provide referrals.

CENTER FOR FAMILY SUCCESS | PATHFINDERS OF OREGON

17805 SE Stark St., Portland, OR 97233
(503) 286-0600
www.pathfindersoforegon.org

The Center for Family Success program provides assistance to families of the incarcerated, including education, clothes, food, mentoring and employment.

CENTER FOR HOPE & SAFETY

605 Center St. NE, Salem, OR 97301
(866) 399-7722
CHS is a community based advocacy center that provides assistance to those who have been sexually assaulted in prison. Services include options, resources, and support. They will not report back to the institution unless prisoner requests it and signs a release. MCCF, OSCI, OSP, and SCI prisoners can dial 711 on prison phones. Correspondence is confidential.

CURE | OREGON

1631 NE Broadway, Suite 460, Portland, OR 97232
(866) 357-2873
www.oregoncure.org

CURE provides advocacy and organization through prisoners and their supporters to achieve reforms in the Oregon prison system.

INSIDE-OUT PRISON EXCHANGE PROGRAM | UNIVERSITY OF OREGON

1501 E. 13th St., Eugene, OR 97403
(541) 346-1000
www.honors.uoregon.edu/story/inside-out-exchange

INOEP teaches classes through exchange programs with the Oregon State Penitentiary, where college students are taught in a classroom with student prisoners at the prison. They regularly change course offerings. Write for current offerings, or contact your education coordinator.

INSPECTOR GENERAL HOTLINE

(503) 555-1234 (in-prison prisoner hotline), (877) 678-4222 (public/staff hotline)

Oregon DOC hotline for prisoners to report abuses, prohibited conduct, staff misconduct, extortion, fraud, and other correctional matters.

OREGON INNOCENCE PROJECT

PO Box 40588, Portland, OR 97240
www.oregoninnocence.org info@oregoninnocence.org

Oregon Innocence Project provides advocacy and representation to wrongfully convicted Oregon prisoners. Write for current criteria.

OREGON OFFICE OF THE GOVERNOR

900 Court St. NE, Salem, OR 97301
(503) 378-4582
www.governor.oregon.org

The *Office of the Governor* responds to issues dealing with corrections and other law enforcement areas.

OREGON STATE PUBLIC DEFENDER

1175 State St. NE, Salem, OR 97301
(503) 378-3349
www.opds.state.or.us

OPDS provides legal representation to Oregon prisoners on direct appeal in criminal cases, parole and post-prison supervision matters, and parents in juvenile dependency appeals.

OREGONIANS FOR ALTERNATIVES TO THE DEATH PENALTY

PO Box 361, Portland, OR 97207-7060
(503) 990-7060
www.oadp.org info@oadp.org

OADP advocates for the end of the death penalty in Oregon through legislative reform, education, the promotion of research, and other efforts. They also provide pen pals to Oregon death row prisoners.

PARENTING INSIDE OUT | OREGON

7800 SW Barbur Blvd., Suite 2, Portland, OR 97219
(503) 977-6399
www.childrensjusticealliance.org
info@childrensjusticealliance.org

Parenting Inside Out is a population-specific parenting curriculum for incarcerated Oregon parents and ex-offenders. Write for current programs in your area.

PARTNERSHIP FOR SAFETY & JUSTICE

825 NE 20th Ave., Suite 250, Portland, OR 97232
(503) 335-8449
www.safetyandjustice.org
info@safetyandjustice.org

PSJ advocates for reforms in the Oregon criminal justice system, including supporting more treatment options, alternatives to mandatory minimums and prison, and many other efforts to make public safety more effective and just. Write for prisoner support packets, a transitional directory, fact sheets on prisoner rights, and their newsletter, *Justice Matters*, all FREE to Oregon prisoners.

PATHFINDERS

PO Box 3257, Gresham, OR 97030
(503) 286-0600
www.pathfindersoforegon.org

Pathfinders provides several family-related programs for Oregon prisoners and their families, including *Center for Family Success, Children's Justice Alliance, Parenting Inside/Out, Pathfinder Academy,* and *Living in Freedom Today.* Write for information packets and current programs in your area.

PORTIA PROJECT, THE

86399 N. Modesto Dr., Eugene, OR 97402
www.theportiaproject.org

Portia Project provides family resources to women at the Oregon Women's Prison, Coffee Creek, including parental rights information, divorce resources, and legal assistance.

TRUE FRIENDS | COMMITTED PARTNERS FOR YOUTH

1840 Willamette St., Suite 100, Eugene, OR 97481

(541) 344-0833
www.committedpartners.org
cpyadmin@committedpartners.org

TRUE Friends provides mentoring, group activities, and some family/caregiver services to children (6-17) of Oregon incarcerated parents.

Reentry Resources

ARCHES PROJECT

3950 Aumsville Highway SE, Salem, OR 97301
(503) 566-6927
www.committed.com/arches

ARCHES is located on the Marion County Jail property complex. They provide social services to prisoners entering society based on their unique needs, including counseling, substance abuse treatment, a one-stop job service center, and housing assistance.

BETTER PEOPLE

4310 NE Martin Luther King Jr. Blvd., Portland, OR 97211
(503) 281-2663
www.betterpeople.org

Better People provides employment placement services to Oregon ex-offenders, including counseling and employment guidance.

BRIDGES TO CHANGE

207 7th Ave., Oregon City, OR 97045
(503) 465-2749
www.bridgestochange.com

Bridges to Change provides statewide reentry services to Oregon ex-offenders, including housing, employment, and mentoring.

COMMUNITY ACTION PARTNERSHIP (CAP) OF OREGON

PO Box 7964, Salem, OR 97303
(503) 316-3951
www.caporegon.org

CAP of Oregon assists low-income people through the Oregon's Poverty Fighting Network -- a coalition of several in-state organizations that provide resources such as housing, childcare, and financial assistance.

DEPARTMENT OF HUMAN SERVICES

500 Summer St. NE, Salam, OR 97301
(503) 945-5944
www.oregon.gov/dhs

DHS administers Oregon state programs such as food stamps, TANF, and job resources.

GOODWILL JOB CONNECTION

(877) 676-5872
www.meetgoodwill.org/job-connection

Goodwill Job Connection offers employment opportunities including a FREE 30-day job search and referral program for ex-offenders.

HELPING HANDS REENTRY

1010 3rd Ave., Suite A, Seaside, OR 97138
(503) 738-4321
www.helpinghandsreentry.org

HUMAN SOLUTIONS

12350 SE Powell, Portland, OR 97236
(503) 548-0200
www.humansolutions.org

Human Solutions provides reentry services to Oregon ex-offenders, including housing, family advocacy, employment, and economic development.

IMPACT NW

10055 E. Burnside St., Portland, OR 97216
(503) 988-6887
www.impactnw.org *info@impactnw.org*

IMPACT NW provides various reentry service to Oregon and Southern Washington ex-offenders returning to the Portland area, including housing assistance, health care referrals, clothing, food, and much more.

NORTHWEST REGIONAL REENTRY CENTER (NERCC)

6000 NE 80th Ave., Portland, Or 97218
(503) 546-0470
www.nw-rrc.org

OREGON EMPLOYMENT DEPARTMENT

875 Union St. NE, Salem, OR 97311
(800) 237-3710, (503) 947-1394
www.oregon.gov/employ

OED administers unemployment benefits, workforce information, and job search opportunities.

OXFORD HOUSE | OREGON

PO Box 66699, Portland, OR 97290-6699
(503) 247-0777

www.oxfordhouse.org

Oxford House provides transitional housing to Oregon ex-offenders.

PHOENIX RISING TRANSITIONS

PO Box 723, Gresham, OR 97030
(503) 866-1554
www.phoenix-rising-transitions.org

Phoenix Rising Transitions offers reentry transition projects both inside and out of prison through over 40 organizations that provide comprehensive reentry services.

PRISONER REENTRY EMPLOYMENT PROGRAM (PREP)

7916 SE Foster Rd., Suite 104, Portland, OR 97206
(503) 772-2300
www.seworks.org/job-seekers/resources-for-ex-offenders

REENTRY TRANSITION CENTER | MERCY CORPS NW

1818 NE Martin Luther King Jr. Blvd., Suite C, Portland, OR 97212
(971) 255-0547
www.mercycorpsnw.org/what-we-do/transition-center

RTC provides one-stop reentry services to ex-offenders in the Portland area, including email, internet, phones, and referrals for education, mentoring, substance abuse programs, and much more.

TEMPORARY ASSISTANCE FOR NEEDY FAMILY (TANF)F | OREGON DEPARTMENT OF HUMAN SERVICES

500 Summer St. NE, Salem, OR 97301
www.oregon.gov/dhs/assistance

TANF provides financial assistance to low-income families with children who are attempting to become self-sufficient.

TRANSITION PROJECTS

655 NW Hoyt St., Portland, OR 97209
(503) 280-4700
www.tprojects.org

Transition Projects provides transitional services to ex-offenders in the Portland area, including referrals, to transitional programs, housing assistance, basic necessities, ID assistance, health services, transportation, and more.

UNITED COMMUNITY ACTION NETWORK (UCAN)

(541) 672-3241, (800) 301-8226
www.ucanap.org

UCAN provides resources to low-income individuals, including housing assistance, food, childcare and transportation.

VOA | OREGON

3910 SE Stark St., Portland, OR 97214
(503) 235-8655
www.voaor.org

WORKSOURCE OREGON

www.worksourceoregon.org

WorkSource Oregon offers numerous in-state resource centers that provide comprehensive job search resources, workshops, referrals, hiring events, and free internet usage.

Pennsylvania | Keystone State

State Capital: Harrisburg

Time Zone: EST

Population: 12,787,209

(82.9% White, 11.6% Black, 3.3% Asians, 0.3% American Indian (5.6% Hispanic))

Name Origin: William Penn suggested "Sylvania" or "woodland" for the name of his tract of land given to him by King Charles II in 1681. The king added "Penn" to "Sylvania" in honor of Penn's father.

Motto: Virtue, Liberty, and Independence

Famous Pennsylvanians: Kobe Bryant, Wilt Chamberlain, Bill Cosby, Tina Fey, Benjamin Franklin, Milton Hershey, Dan Marino, Joe Montana, Joe Namath, Arnold Palmer, Taylor Swift, John Updike, Andy Warhol.

State Agencies

CONSUMER PROTECTION

Strawberry Square, 14th Floor, Harrisburg, PA 17120
(717) 787-9707

DRIVER RECORDS

Department of Transportation, PO Box 68695, Harrisburg, PA 17106-8695
(717) 391-6190
www.dmv.state.pa.us

VETERAN'S AFFAIRS

PO Box 8079, 5000 Wissahickon Ave., Philadelphia, PA 19101

VITAL RECORDS

Pennsylvania Department of Health, 101 S. Mercer St., Room 401, PO Box 1528, New Castle, PA 16103
(724) 656-3100
www.dsf.health.state.pa.us

Prisoner Support

ACLU | PENNSYLVANIA

Statewide: PO Box 40008, Philadelphia, PA 19106
(877) 745-2258, (215) 592-1513
www.aclupa.org info@aclupa.org
Greater Pittsburgh Area: 313 Atwood St., Pittsburgh, PA 15213
(877) 744-2258, (412) 681-7736
www.pgh.aclu.org pgh@aclu.org

ACLU advocates for the civil rights of Pennsylvania prisoners, generally through class actions. They typically will not accept individual prisoner cases, but they may provide referrals.

AIDS LAW PROJECT OF PENNSYLVANIA

1211 Chestnut St., Suite 600, Philadelphia, PA 19107
(215) 587-9377
www.aidslawpa.org

ALPP provides assistance and services to Pennsylvania prisoners living with HIV/AIDS including legal assistance, information on compassionate release, referrals to community-based organization, and various rights related materials. They publish and distribute *AIDS & the Law: Your Rights in Pennsylvania*, FREE for prisoners.

BOOK'EM | THOMAS MORTON CENTER

5129 Penn Ave., Pittsburgh, PA 15224
(412) 361-3022 ext. 4
www.bookempgh.org

Book'Em provides FREE books to Pennsylvania prisoners. Request by subject.

You can find many more FREE books-to-prisoners programs in our Service Center section.

CENTER FOR ALTERNATIVES IN COMMUNITY JUSTICE

411 S. Burrowes St., State College, PA 16801
(814) 234-1059
www.cacj.org

CENTRE PLACE

3013 Banner Pike, Bellefonte, PA 16823-8303
(814) 353-9081
www.centerpeace.org

Centre Place is a faith-based organization that provides various services to Pennsylvania prisoners, including life skills (SCI-Rockview) and conflict resolution training, vocational skills training, and release services (Centre County Correctional Facility), as well as Christmas card programs, and distribution of the *Criminal Justice Advocacy and Support Directory,* FREE to prisoners.

CONCERNED CITIZENS / GRAY PANTHERS OF GRATERFORD | DREXEL UNIVERSITY

Philadelphia, PA 19104
(215) 895-2472

CC/GP advocacy and services for elderly SCI-Graterford prisoners, including information, external contacts, group functions with expert guest speakers in medical, legal, financial, and family fields.

CURE | PENNSYLVANIA

PO Box 8601, Philadelphia, PA 19101
(215) 820- 7001
www.pacure.org

CURE provides advocacy and organization through prisoners and their supporters to achieve reforms in the Pennsylvania prison system.

DECARCERATE PA

PO Box 40764, Philadelphia, PA 19107
www.decarceratepa.info decarceratepa@gmail.com

Decarcerate is an anti-mass incarceration campaign that seeks to reform the Pennsylvania criminal justice system.

DEFENDER ASSOCIATION OF PENNSYLVANIA

1441 Samson St., Philadelphia, PA 19102
(215) 568-3190

DAP acts as appointed counsel for adults and juveniles in the Philadelphia area.

DUQUESNE UNIVERSITY SCHOOL OF LAW INNOCENCE PROJECT

900 Locust St., Pittsburgh, PA 15282
(412) 396-4704
www.law.duq.edu/contact.html

DUSLIW provides legal support for wrongfully convicted prisoners in Pennsylvania and West Virginia. Write for current criteria.

FAMILIES OUTSIDE | FAMILY SERVICES OF WESTERN PENNSYLVANIA

3230 William Pitt Way, Pittsburgh, PA 15238
(412) 820-2050
www.fswp.org fswp@fswp.org

Families Outside provides visitation and transportation support to families of those incarcerated in Pennsylvania.

FIGHT FOR LIFERS WEST

PO Box 455, Meadowlands, PA 15347
fightforliferswest@yahoo.com

Fight for Lifers West is a support group for Pennsylvania prisoners serving life sentences and their families.

GIRL SCOUTS BEYOND BARS | PENNSYLVANIA

PO Box 27540, Philadelphia, PA 19118
(888) 564-2030
www.girlscouts.org

HUMAN RIGHTS COALITION

4134 Lancaster Ave., Philadelphia, PA 19104
(267) 293-9169
www.hrcoalition.com

Human Rights Coalition is a coalition of prisoners, their families, and other supporters who advocate for the end of solitary confinement in Pennsylvania prisons and around the U.S. They publish a bimonthly newsletter, *The Movement* ($12 per year for prisoners), the HRC pamphlet series (FREE for prisoners), and the *Pennsylvania Prison Directory Action Guide* (available online.)

INNOCENCE INSTITUTE OF POINT PARK

201 Wood St., Pittsburgh, PA 15222
www.pointpark.edu/innocence

IIPP provides advocacy for wrongfully convicted Western Pennsylvania and West Virginia prisoners through journalism. Write for current criteria.

LEWISBURG PRISON PROJECT

PO Box 128, Lewisburg, PA 17837

(570) 523-1104
www.lewisburgprisonproject.org
prisonproject@windstream.net

Lewisburg Prison Project provides information and legal representation to Pennsylvania prisoners whose rights have been violated due to conditions of confinement. They will NOT provide legal services for civil family or criminal matters, provide copies, find citations, or review briefs. They offer a number of legal information publications to prisoners nationwide. Write for current list of publications.

PENNSYLVANIA INNOCENCE PROJECT | TEMPLE UNIVERSITY

1515 Market St., 3rd Floor, Philadelphia, PA 19102
(215) 204-4255
www.innocenceprojectpa.org

PIP provides legal representation for wrongfully convicted Pennsylvania prisoners. DNA and non-DNA cases accepted, with no sentencing requirements. They will consider cases involving arson, shaken baby syndrome, and child abuse.

PENNSYLVANIA INSTITUTIONAL LAW PROJECT

718 Arch St., Suite 304 South, Philadelphia, PA 19106
(215) 925-2966
www.pailp.org

PAILP provides legal assistance to Pennsylvania prisoners on conditions of confinement issues and other civil right violations. They also distribute a variety of prisoners' self-help publications on topics such as disciplinary actions, name change, and political asylum, as well as other publications of interest to Pennsylvania prisoners, such as the *Criminal Justice Advocacy and Support Directory, The Grandparents Guide to Custody and Visitation in PA, The Prisoners' Rights Handbook,* a local referral guide and more.

PENNSYLVANIA PRISON SOCIETY

245 N. Broad St., Suite 300, Philadelphia, PA 19107-1518
(215) 564-6051
www.prisonsociety.org geninfo@prisonsociety.org

PPS provides a variety of services to Pennsylvania prisoners and ex-offenders, including parenting skills, the *Support of Kids Program* (SKIP), video teleconferencing services, skills training, and more. They operate a family resource center at SCI-Graterford and publishes two monthly newsletters, *Graterfords* ($3 for PA prisoners, and *Correctional Forum* ($5 for both.)

PROJECT IMPACT | MUNCY PARENTING & CHILDREN TOGETHER

PO Box 180, Muncy, PA 17756
(570) 546-3171 ext. 419 or 521

Project Impact operates a children's center at SCI-Muncy, which allows prisoners a family-friendly setting to spend time with their children. They also offer activity workshops, prenatal classes, and parenting support groups. Children up to age 17 can join.

WWW.PRISONER.COM

PO Box 5251, Harrisburg, PA 17110
(717) 236-6045
www.prisoners.com

Prisoners.com is an online platform to display prison-related issues to the public and to Pennsylvania legislators. They will not provide legal assistance.

Reentry Resources

BEBASHI

1217 Spring Garden St., 1st Floor, Philadelphia, PA 19123
(215) 769-3561 ext. 143
www.bebashi.org

Bebashi provides a variety of reentry services to Philadelphia County ex-offenders who are HIV-positive, including discharge planning, case management, housing, medical and behavioral health care, public benefits, and more.

CAPITAL REGION EX-OFFENDER SUPPORT ALLIANCE | CAREERLINK

100 N. Cameron St., Harrisburg, PA
www.reentrynow.org

CENTER FOR RETURNING CITIZENS | THE FRIENDS CENTER

1501 Cherry St., Philadelphia, PA 19102
(215) 305-8793
www.tcrcphilly.org

CHRISTIAN RECOVERY AFTERCARE MINISTRY (CRAM)

509 Division St., Harrisburg, PA 17710
(717) 234-3664
www.crminc.org

CRAM is a faith-based organization that provides a

variety of direct post-release services to Harrisburg ex-offenders.

GEO Reentry Service Centers

Allegheny County: 357 N. Craig St., Pittsburgh, PA 15217
(412) 578-0513
Cambria County: 499 Manor Dr., Edensburg, PA 15931
(814) 471-1801
Dauphin County: 2151 Greenwood St., Harrisburg, PA 17104
(717) 561-9600
Franklin County: 550 W. Loudon St., Chambersburg, PA 17201
(717) 263-0450
Lancaster County: 439 E. King St., Lancaster, PA 17601
(717) 391-8202
Luzerne County: 125 N. Wilkes Barre Blvd., Suite 4, Wilkes Barre, PA 18702
(570) 208-4858
Lycoming County: 330 Pine St., Williamsport, PA 17702
(570) 323-1274
Philadelphia County: 1 Reed St., Suite 10, Philadelphia, PA 19147
(215) 463-1260
York County: 1 E. Market St., Suite 204/301, York, PA 17401
(717) 848-4448
www.geoentry.com www.reentrypa.com

Goldring Reentry Initiative (GRI) | University of Pennsylvania

3701 Locust Walk, Philadelphia, PA 19104
(215) 898-5512
www.sp2.upenn.edu/degree-programs/certificate-programs-specializations/goldring-reentry-initiative-gri

Goodwill Industries of Southwestern Pennsylvania

Robert S. Foltz Building, 118 52nd St., Pittsburgh, PA 15201
(412) 481-9005
www.goodwillswpa.org

Higher Ground Foundation

PO Box 1602, Altoona, PA 16603
(814) 742-7500

HGF provides support for Pennsylvania ex-offenders through seminars and workshops. Write for current options in your area.

Impact Services Corp. | Reentry One-Stop Satellite Center

1952 Allegheny Ave., Philadelphia, PA 19134
(215) 423-2944 ext. 193
www.impactservices.org

It's About Change Program

1515 Derry St., Harrisburg, PA 17104
(717) 238-9950

IAC is a program that supports Pennsylvania mothers who are ex-offenders through various reentry services, including residential programming, transportation, job and skills training, education, case management, counseling, and more.

Mayor's Office of Reintegration Services (RISE)

900 Spring Garden St., 7th Floor, Philadelphia, PA 19123
(215) 683-3370
rise.phila.gov

New Person Ministries | Community Renewal for Sex Offenders (CR-SO)

PO Box 223, Reading, PA 19607
(610) 777-2222
www.newpersonministries.org

New Person Ministries assists sex offenders transition back into society through faith-based initiatives.

Pennsylvania Board of Probation & Parole | Offender Reentry

1101 S. Front St., Suite 5400, Harrisburg, PA 17104
(717) 787-5699
www.pbpp.state.pa.us

People For People | Project Fresh Start

800 N. Broad St., Philadelphia, PA 19130
(215) 235-2340
www.peopleforpeople.org

Philadelphia Workforce Development Corporation | Connection Training Services (CTS)

1617 John F. Kennedy Blvd., 13th Floor, Philadelphia, PA 19103-1813
(215) 557-2625
www.philaworks.org

Program for Ex-Offenders

564 Forbes Ave., Suite 930, Pittsburgh, PA 15219
(412) 281-7380
www.tpfo.org

TPFO provides reentry services to Pittsburgh area ex-offenders, including intensive inpatient drug and alcohol programs, employment and family services, life skills, and education.

PROGRAM FOR FEMALE OFFENDERS

1515 Derry St., Harrisburg, PA 17104
(717) 238-9950

PROGRAM FOR WOMEN AND FAMILIES

927 Hamilton St., Allentown, PA 18101
(601) 433-6556
www.thepwf.org contactus@thepwf.org

PWF provides reentry services to Pennsylvania women who are ex-offenders, including housing and employment counseling, case management, parenting classes, and HIV/AIDS prevention. They also offer a small transitional housing residence.

SOUTHWESTERN PENNSYLVANIA REENTRY PROJECT | MON VALLEY INITIATIVE

303 E. 8th Ave., Homestead, PA 15120
(412) 464-4000

SRSP provides a variety of reentry services for Pennsylvania ex-offenders, including housing, transportation, treatment, mental health services, childcare, and referrals.

STAR REENTRY COURTS

Eastern District of Pennsylvania Federal Building, 504 W. Hamilton St. Allentown, PA 18101
(610) 434-4062
William J. Green Federal Building, 600 Arch St., Philadelphia, PA 19106
(215) 597-7950
The Madison Building, 400 Washington St., Reading, PA 19601
(610) 320-5253
www.paep.uscourts.gov/re-rentry-court

STRIVE PHILADELPHIA | METROPOLITAN CAREER CENTER

100 S. Broad St., Suite 830, Philadelphia, PA 19110
(215) 568-9215
www.theworkforce-institute.org striveinternational.org

X-OFFENDERS FOR COMMUNITY EMPOWERMENT

2227 N. Broad St., Philadelphia, PA 19132
(215) 668-8477
x-offenders.org

Rhode Island | Little Rhody -- Ocean State

State Capital: Providence

Time Zone: EST

Population: 1,055,173

(85.1% White, 7.7% Black, 3.5% Asians, 0.9% American Indian (12.4% Hispanic))

Name Origin: Unknown. Theory has it that Giovanni de Verrazano recorded observing an island the size of the Greek Island of Rhodes.

Motto: Hope

Famous Rhode Islanders: George Cohan, Elisabeth Hasselbeck, Cormac McCarthy, Meredith Veira.

State Agencies

CONSUMER PROTECTION

150 S. Main St., Providence, RI 02903
(401) 247-4400

DRIVER RECORDS

Department of Motor Vehicles, 268 Main St., Pawtucket, RI 02860
(410) 271-2650
www.dmv.state.ri.us

SECRETARY OF STATE

100 N. Main St., Providence, RI 02903-1335
(401) 222-3040
www.corps.state.ri.us

VETERAN'S AFFAIRS

380 Westminster St., Providence, RI 02903

VITAL RECORDS

Department of Health, Room 101, 2 Capitol Hill, Providence, RI 02908-5097
(401) 222-2811
www.health.ri.gov/chic/vital/clearks.php

Prisoner Support

ACLU | RHODE ISLAND

128 Dorrance St., Suite 220, Providence, RI 02903
(401) 831-7171
www.riaclu.org riaclu@riaclu.org

Advocates for the civil right of Rhode Island prisoners, generally through class actions. They Typically will not accept individual prisoner cases, but they may provide referrals.

AMACHI PROGRAM | BIG SISTERS OF RHODE ISLAND

1540 Pontiac Ave., Cranston, RI 02920
(401) 921-2434
www.amachimentoring.org

Amachi provides mentoring for daughters of those incarcerated in Rhode Island. Girls are paired with a female mentor for at least a year through weekly or biweekly visits to the community.

DIRECT ACTION FOR RIGHTS AND EQUALITY

340 Lockwood St., Providence, RI 02907
(401) 351-6960
www.daretowin.org info@daretowin.org

Provides advocacy and support for human rights issues in Rhode Island, with some support for prisoners. Write for current programs.

NEW ENGLAND INNOCENCE PROJECT

120 Tremont St., Suite 735, Boston, MA 02108
(617) 830-7655
www.newenglandinnocence.org

See Massachusetts listing.

RHODE ISLANDERS SPONSORING EDUCATION (RISE)

17 Gordon Ave., Suite 4, Providence, RI 02905
(401) 421-2010
www.riseonline.org

RISE provides mentoring and scholarship opportunities to children of those incarcerated in Rhode Island.

Reentry Resources

CARITAS EASTMAN HOUSE | WOMEN'S PROGRAM

166 Pawtucket Ave., Pawtucket, RI 02860
(401) 722-4644
www.caritasri.org

COMMUNITY CARE ALLIANCE | NORTHERN WESTERN COMMUNITY REENTRY

PO Box 1700, Woonsocket, RI 02895
(401) 235-7000
www.communitycareri.org

CROSSROAD.S

106 Broad St., Providence, RI 02903
(410) 521-2255
www.crossroadsri.org

CrossRoad.s provides reentry services to ex-offenders in the Providence area, including case management, job development, counseling, information, and referrals.

NETWORKRI CENTER | ONE-STOP CAREER CENTER SYSTEM

1511 Pontiac Ave., Cranston, RI 02920
(401) 462-8000
www.networkri.org

OPENDOORS | RHODE ISLAND

485 Plainfield St., Providence, RI 02909
(401) 781-5208
www.opendoorsri.org admin@opendoorsri.org

OpenDoors provides pre- and post-release services to Rhode Island ex-offenders, including discharge planning, one-stop resource center, employment programs, job skills, and more.

PROJECT BRIDGE

360 Broad St., Providence, RI 02907

PB provides reentry services for Rhode Island ex-offenders who are living with HIV/AIDS, including and 18-month discharge planning program, FREE medical care, referrals, and more.

RI NETWORK CENTERS

Pawtucket: 175 Main St., Pawtucket, RI 02860
(401) 721-1800
Providence: 1 Reservoir Ave., Providence, RI 02907
(401) 462-8900

West Warwick: 1330 Main St., West Warwick, RI 02895
(401) 828-8382

Woonsocket: 219 Pond St., Woonsocket, RI 02895
(401) 235-1201

RI Network Centers provide educational training and employment assistance to ex-offenders throughout Rhode Island.

RHODE ISLAND DEPARTMENT OF CORRECTIONS | STATEWIDE REENTRY INITIATIVE

Dix Building, Cranston, RI 02920
(401) 462-1129
www.doc.ri.gov/reentry

TRAVELER'S AID SOCIETY OF RHODE ISLAND | JUSTICE SERVICES PROGRAM

177 Union St., Providence, RI 02903
(401) 521-2255

TAS provides reentry support to Rhode Island ex-offenders, including job development training both pre- and post-release.

WESTBAY COMMUNITY ACTION PARTNERSHIP | WESTBAY PROBATION PROJECT

224 Buttonwoods Ave., Warwick, RI 02886
(401) 732-4660 ext. 124
www.westbaycap.org

WOMEN IN TRANSITION

PO Box 20135, Cranston, RI 02920
(401) 452-1767

WIT provides Rhode Island women who are ex-offenders with transition services, including case management, counseling, life skills training, parenting, job skills assessment, housing, and more.

South Carolina | Palmetto State

State Capital:

Time Zone: EST

Population: 4,832,482

(68.3% White, 27.8% Black, 1.5% Asians, 0.5% American Indian (4.9% Hispanic))

Name Origin: In 1626, Charles I gave a patent to Sir Robert Heath for the Province of Carolana, from *Carolus,* Latin name for Charles. It was divided into North and South in 1710.

Motto: Dum Spiro Sparo (While I breathe I hope)

Famous South Carolinians: Stephen Colbert, Joe Frasier, Jesse Jackson, "Shoeless" Joe Jackson.

State Agencies

CONSUMER AFFAIRS

PO Box 5757, Columbia, SC 29250
(803) 734-4200

DRIVER RECORDS

Department of Motor Vehicles, PO Box 1498, Blythewood, SC 29106-0028
www.scdmvonline.com

SECRETARY OF STATE

PO Box 11350, Columbia, SC 29211
(803) 734-1961
www.scsos.com

VETERAN'S AFFAIRS

7437 Garners Ferry Rd., Columbia, SC 29209

VITAL RECORDS

DHEC, 2600 Bull St., Columbia, SC 29201-1797
(803) 898-3630
www.aschec.net/vr

Prisoner Support

ACLU | SOUTH CAROLINA

PO Box 20998, Charleston, SC 29403
(843) 720-1423
www.aclusouthcarolina.org info@aclusouthcarolina.org

Advocates for the civil rights of South Carolina prisoners, generally through class actions. They typically will not accept individual prisoners cases, but they may provide referrals.

AIKEN CENTER | OFFENDER-BASED INTERVENTION PROGRAMS

1105 Gregg Highway, Aiken, SC 29801
(803) 649-1900
www.aikencenter.org

The Aiken Center provides alcohol and drug treatment services to South Carolina prisoners.

ANGELS CHARGE MINISTRY

95 Ashley St., Spartanburg, SC 29307
(864) 529-5472
www.angelschargeministry.org

Angels Charge Ministry provides spiritual support for women prisoners through their 'A Way Out to a New Life' program.

CURE | SOUTH CAROLINA

PO Box 421, Green Pond, SC 29446

CURE provides advocacy and organization through prisoners and their supporters to achieve reforms in the South Carolina prison system.

PALMETTO INNOCENCE PROJECT | J.M. MCCULLUCH INSTITUTE

PO Box 11623, Columbia, SC 23211
(803) 779-0005

PIP provides pro bone legal representation to wrongfully or unfairly convicted prisoners in SC.

PROTECTION AND ADVOCACY FOR PEOPLE WITH DISABILITIES

3710 Landmark Dr., Suite 208, Columbia, SC 29204
(866) 275-7273, (803) 782-0639
www.pandasc.org

PANDASC provides legal assistance and information to South Carolina prisoners with disabilities. They do not provide assistance on criminal matters.

SOUTH CAROLINA CORRECTIONAL ASSOCIATION

PO Box 210603, Columbia, SC 29221
(803) 896-3301
www.myscca.org

Reentry Resources

ALSTON WILKES SOCIETY

3519 Medical Dr., Columbia, SC 29203
(803) 799-2490
www.alstonwilkessociety.org

AWS provides a variety of pre/post-release services to SC prisoners, including pre-release planning, housing, and counseling. Accepts out-of-state referral.

DEBORAH'S HOUSE

418 E. River St., Anderson, SC 29624
(864) 260-0062

Deborah's House provides transitional housing to South Carolina women ex-offenders.

SOUTH CAROLINA DEPARTMENT OF PROBATION, PAROLE, & PARDON SERVICES | REENTRY PROGRAMS

2221 Devine St., Suite 600, Columbia, SC 29250
(803) 734-9220
www.dppps.sc.gov/Offender-Supervision/Supervision-Strategies/Reentry-Programs

FIND ANY ERRORS?

We want to know!

Please let us know if you find any mistakes or if you have additional organizations that you would like to see added to our resource guide. Thank you.

PRISON LIVES
PO Box 842, Exeter, CA 93221
info@prisonlives.com (Corrlinks-friendly)

South Dakota | Coyote State

State Capital: Pierre

Time Zone: CST

Population: 853,175

(85.7% White, 8.9% American Indian, 1.9% Black, 1.3% Asian (2.6% Hispanic))

Name Origin: Sioux word for *Dakota* meaning "friend" or "ally."

Motto: Under God the People Rule

Famous South Dakotans: Sparky Anderson, Bob Barker, Tom Brokaw, Crazy Horse, Cheryl Ladd, Sitting Bull.

State Agencies

DRIVER RECORDS

Department of Public Safety, 118 W. Capitol Ave., Pierre, SD 57501-5070
(605) 773-6883
www.state.sd.us/dps/sl

SECRETARY OF STATE

500 E. Capitol Ave., Suite B-05, Pierre, SD 57501-5070
(605) 773-4845
www.sdsos.gov

VETERAN'S AFFAIRS

3501 W. 22nd. St., Sioux Falls, SD 57105

VITAL RECORDS

Department of Health, 207 E. Missouri Ave., Suite 1-A, Pierre, SD 57501
(605) 773-4961
www.state.sd.us/doh/vitalrec

Prisoner Support

ACLU | SOUTH DAKOTA

401 E. 8th St., Suite 203A, Sioux Falls, SD 57502-4661
(605) 332-2508
www.aclusd.org southdakota@aclu.org

Advocates for the civil rights of South Dakota prisoners, generally through class actions. They typically will not accept individual prisoner cases, but they may provide referrals.

CURE | SOUTH DAKOTA

804 Nunda Place, Sioux Falls, SD 57107
(605) 334-5472

CURE provides advocacy and organization through prisoners and their supporters to achieve reforms in the South Dakota prison system.

FAMILY CONNECTION | SOUTH DAKOTA

PO Box 100, Sioux Falls, SD 57101
(605) 357-0777
www.sdfamilyconnection.org

Family Connection provides over-night housing to those visiting incarcerated loved ones in the Sioux Falls area, as well as education programs to children of South Dakota prisoners.

INNOCENCE PROJECT OF MINNESOTA

1536 Hewitt Ave., MSC-1937, St. Paul, MN 55104
(651) 523-3152
www.ipmn.org

IPMN provides legal representation to wrongfully convicted prisoners in South Dakota, Minnesota, and North Dakota. Non-DNA cases are accepted in ND and SD. There are no minimum sentencing requirements. They look for cases that involve junk science, false confessions, informant testimony, eyewitness misidentification, official misconduct, bad lawyering, and other factors.

SOUTH DAKOTA PRISONER SUPPORT GROUP

PO Box 3285, Rapid City, SD 57709
groups.yahoo.com/group.SouthDakotaPrisonerSupportGroup

SDPSG provides general support to South Dakota prisoners and their families, including information and news related to prisoners, an online community for friends and family, and referrals for specific prisoner needs. No legal advice is given.

Reentry Resources

COMMUNITY ALTERNATIVES OF THE BLACK HILLS (CABH) | REENTRY PROGRAM

5031 Highway 79, Rapid City, SD 57701
(605) 341-4240
www.cecintl.com

GOODWILL OF THE GREAT PLAINS

3100 W. Fourth St., Sioux City, IA 51103
(712) 258-4511
www.goodwillgreatpains.org

HOPE CENTER REENTRY PROGRAM

615 Kansas City St., Rapid City, SD 57701
(605) 716-4673
www.hopecenterrapidcity.org

U.S. PROBATION & PRETRIAL SERVICES | SOUTH DAKOTA REENTRY

314 S. Main Ave., Room 100, Sioux Falls, SD 57104
(605) 977-8900
www.sdp.uscourts.gov/offender-re-entry

RAPID CITY OFFENDER REENTRY PROGRAM

333 Sixth St, Rapid City, SD 57701
(605) 716-4005
www.rcgov.org

SOUTH DAKOTA DEPARTMENT OF CORRECTIONS | REENTRY

3200 East Highway 34, c/o 500 e. Capitol Ave., Pierre, SD 57501
(605) 773-3478
www.doc.sd.gov/about/reentry

SOUTH DAKOTA DEPARTMENT OF LABOR | ONE-STOP CAREER CENTERS KNELP BUILDING, 700 GOVERNOR'S DR., PIERRE, SD 57501

(605) 773-3101
www.www.state.sd.us/dol/sdjob

VOA DAKOTAS

PO Box 89306, Sioux Falls, SD 57109
(605) 334-1414
www.voa-dakotas.org

Tennessee | Volunteer State

State Capital: Nashville

Time Zone: CST (west), EST (east)

Population: 6,549,352

(78.9% White, 17.1% Black, 1.7% Asians, 0.4% American Indian (4.4% Hispanic))

Name Origin: *Tanasi* was the name of the Cherokee villages on the Little Tennessee River.

Motto: Agriculture and Commerce

Famous Tennesseans: Kenny Chesney, Aretha Franklin, Andrew Jackson, Andrew Johnson, Casey Jones, Dolly Parton, Elvis Presley (claimed, but actually born in Tupelo, MS), Justin Timberlake, Tina Turner, Hank Williams Jr.

State Agencies

DRIVER RECORDS

Department of Safety, 1150 Foster Ave., Nashville, TN 37210
(615) 741-3954
www.tennessee.gov/safety

SECRETARY OF STATE

312 Eighth Ave. N., 6th Floor, Nashville, TN 32743
(615) 741-2286
www.state.tn.us/sos

VETERAN'S AFFAIRS

110 9th Ave. S., Nashville, TN 37203

VITAL RECORDS

Department of Health, 421 5th Ave. N., 1st Floor, Nashville, TN 37243
(615) 741-0778
www.state.tn.us/health/vr

Prisoner Support

ACLU | TENNESSEE

PO Box 120160, Nashville, TN 37212
(615) 320-7142
www.aclu-tn.org

Advocates for the civil rights of Tennessee prisoners, generally through class actions. They typically will not accept individual prisoner cases, but they may provide referrals.

AMACHI | KNOXVILLE

901 e. Summit Hill Dr., Suite 300, Knoxville, TN 37915
(865) 524-2774
www.klf.org questions@klf.org

Amachi faith-based mentoring to children of those incarcerated who live in the Knoxville area.

BIG BROTHERS/BIG SISTERS OF MIDDLE TENNESSEE | AMACHI

1704 Charlotte Ave., Suite 130, Nashville, TN 37203
(615) 329-9191
www.mentorakid.org

Big Brother/Big Sisters provides mentoring services to children of single parents, as well as those with an incarcerated parent.

CURE | TENNESSEE

3850 Dunbar Dr., Nashville, TN 37207

CURE provides advocacy and organization through prisoners and their supporters to achieve reforms in the Tennessee prison system.

FAMILIES OF INCARCERATED | PROJECT AWARE MENTORING PROGRAM (PAMP)

1380 Poplar Ave., Memphis, TN 38125
(901) 726-6191
www.familiesofincarcerated.org
info@familiesofincarcerated.org

Families of Incarcerated support and advocacy for families affected by the incarceration of a loved one in an effort to deter future incarcerations.

FAMILY RECONCILIATION CENTER | YOUTH & FAMILY OUTREACH

PO Box 90827, Nashville, TN 37209
(615) 292-6371

www.familyreconciliationcenter.com

The Family Reconciliation Center provides support services to those affected by incarceration through family reunification programs, youth outreach, resources, referrals, and their Guesthouse.

RECONCILIATION MINISTRIES

702 51st Ave. N., Nashville, TN 37209
(615) 292-6371
www.reconciliation84.org

RM provides support for family and friends of Tennessee prisoners, including overnight accommodations for visitors, responses to questions related to prisoners, FREE information and publications, such as *The Separate Prisoners'* newsletter, and the *Handbook for Family and Friends of Tennessee Prisoners.* They also offer parole information packets to Tennessee prisoners for $8.

TENNESSEAN'S ALTERNATIVES TO THE DEATH PENALTY

PO Box 120552, Nashville, TN 37212
(615) 256-3906
www.tennesseedeathpenalty.org
info@tennesseedeathpenalty.org

TADP advocates for sentencing reforms that abolish the death penalty through legislative and community outreach. They publish a quarterly newsletter, *Tennessee Lifelines,* FREE to Tennessee death row prisoners.

Reentry Resources

CHATTANOOGA ENDEAVORS

2007 E. 27th St., Chattanooga, TN 37407
(423) 266-1888
www.chattanoogendeavors.com

CE provides employment services to Tennessee ex-offenders, including case management, computer-assisted job skills training, group sessions, and more.

DISMAS HOUSE

Nashville: 1513 16th Ave., Nashville, TN 37212
(615) 297-9287

Cookeville: 1226 Byrne Ave., Cookeville, TN 38502
(931) 520-8448

Knoxville: 1316 Forrest Ave., Knoxville, TN 37923
(931) 520-8448

Memphis: 320 East St., Memphis, TN 37212
(931) 526-3701
www.dismas.org

Dismas Houses provides transitional housing for Tennessee ex-offenders statewide. They typically allow 4-6 month stays.

FAMILIES OF INCARCERATED | DOORWAYS REENTRY PROGRAM

915 E. McLeMore Ave., Suite 201, Memphis, TN 38106
(901) 726-6191
www.familiesofincarcerated.org

FREE ENTERPRISE PROGRAM | TRICOR INDUSTRIES

240 Great Circle Rd., Suite 310, Nashville, TN 37228
(615) 741-5705
www.tricor.org

FEP provides incentives for businesses to hire Tennessee ex-offenders. Ex-offenders must qualify by participating in a one-year Tricor program within three years of release, complete the Tricor life-skills courses prior to release, be approved by the board of parole, have a high school diploma or GED, and agree to communicate regularly with Tricor staff.

KARAT PLACE

PO Box 9092, Memphis, TN 38190
(901) 525-4055
www.karatplace.org

KP provides transitional housing for Tennessee women ex-offenders and their children for up to 2 years. Some employment services are also offered.

MEN OF VALOR AFTERCARE | REENTRY PROGRAM

1410 Donelson Pike, Suite B-1, Nashville, TN 37217
(615) 399-9111
www.men-of-valor.org

PROJECT RETURN

806 4th Ave. S., Nashville, TN 37210-4000
(615) 327-9654
www.projectreturninc.org

Project Return provides pre- and post-release services for Tennessee ex-offenders, including pre-release planning, education, and job readiness.

SECOND CHANCE | YO! MEMPHIS

444 N. Main St., Memphis, TN 38103

(901) 545-0343
www.yomemphis.org

SCYM is a program that connects Tennessee ex-offenders with gainful employment through local business partnerships.

TENNESSEE DEPARTMENT OF CORRECTIONS | REHABILITATION SERVICES

Rachel Jackson Building, 6th Floor, Nashville, TN, 37243-0465
(615) 741-1000
www.tngov/correction/section/tdoc-rehabilitation

No thong zone!

Did you know that Tennessee is the only state with a visitor dress code that specifically requires visitors to wear undergarments but prohibits "thongs and water brassieres?"

Texas | Lone Star State

State Capital: Austin

Time Zone: CST (except for El Paso, and Hudspeth Counties, which are MST)

Population: 26,956,958

(80% White, 12.5% Black, 4.5% Asians, 1% American Indian (35.1% Hispanic))

Name Origin: It's the variant of a word by Caddo and the other are Indians, meaning "friend" or "allies," applied to them by the Spanish in Eastern Texas.

Motto: Friendship

Famous Texans: Lance Armstrong, Drew Brees, Carol Burnett, George H.W. and W. Bush, Joan Crawford, Morgan Fairchild, Farah Fawcett, Howard Hughes, Tommy Lee Jones, Janis Joplin, Beyonce Knowles, Miranda Lambert, Matthew McConaughey, George Strait.

State Agencies

CONSUMER PROTECTION

PO Box 12548, Austin, TX 78711
(800) 621-0508

DRIVER RECORDS

Department of Public Safety, PO Box 149246, Austin, TX 78714-9246
(512) 424-2032
www.txdps.state.tx.us

SECRETARY OF STATE

PO Box 136967, Austin, TX 78711-3697
(512) 463-5555
www.sos.state.tx.us

VETERAN'S AFFAIRS

6900 Alameda Rd., Houston, TX 77030
701 Clay Ave., Waco, TX 76799
(800) 827-1000, (713) 383-1999

VITAL RECORDS

Department of State Health Services, PO Box 12040, Austin, TX 78711-2040
(512) 758-7366
www.dshs.state.tx.us/vs

Prisoner Support

ACLU | TEXAS

PO Box 8306, Houston, TX 77288
(713) 942-8146
www.aclutx.org info@aclutx.org

Advocates for the civil rights of Texas prisoners, generally through class actions. They typically will not accept individual prisoner cases, but they may provide referrals.

AGAINST THE ODDS (ATO) MENTORING | SOUTHFAIR COMMUNITY DEVELOPMENT CORP.

2610 Martin Luther King Jr. Blvd., Dallas, TX 75215
(214) 421-1373
www.southfairdc.org atomentoring@sbcglobal.net

ATO provide mentoring to children of the incarcerated in an effort to strengthen family ties and enhance the community.

BIG BROTHERS/BIG SISTERS | LONESTAR

450 E. John Carpenter Freeway, Irving, TX 75062
(888) 887-2447
www.bbbstx.org bbbstx@bbbstx.org

Big Brothers/Big Sisters Lonestar provides one-on-one mentoring to children of single parents and of those who are incarcerated.

CENTRAL TEXAS COALITION AGAINST HUMAN TRAFFICKING

(888) 373-7888
www.ctcaht.org/services_for_victims.html

CTCAHT provides assistance to trafficking victims to become eligible for government services including Medicaid, food stamps, and more, as well as provide assistance in legal, employment, housing, and other life necessities.

CHANGED PEOPLE TODAY

3839 Gannon Lane, Suite 1206, Dallas, TX 75237
kaseystudios@gmail.com

Changed People Today provides transportation to families of those incarcerated in TCDJ.

CURE | TEXAS

PO Box 38381, Dallas, TX 75238-0381
(214) 348-0293

CURE provides advocacy and organization through prisoners and their supporters to achieve reforms in the Texas prison system. They publish and distribute a quarterly newsletter, *News & Notes,* FREE to Texas prisoners.

DALLAS COUNTY JAILS | PROGRAMS DIVISION

133 N. Riverfront Blvd., LB31, Dallas, TX 75207
(214) 653-3474

DCJ's Programs Division provides education, recreation, a library, and substance abuse programs for prisoners within the Dallas County jail system. They also provide referrals to those releasing.

DISABILITY RIGHTS | TEXAS

222 W. Braker Lane, Austin, TX 78758
(512) 454-4816
www.drtx.org

DR Texas provides advocacy and support for disabled prisoners in Texas County jail. They will not provide services to state prisoners.

EXODUS MINISTRIES

46630 Munger Ave., No. 10, Dallas, TX 75204
(214) 827-3772
www.exodusministries.org

FRIENDS OF JUSTICE

4275 Little Rd., Suite 205-3, Arlington, TX 76016
www.friendsofjustice.wordpress.com

FJ provides some support services to Texas prisoners. Write for current options.

GIRL SCOUTS BEYOND BARS | CENTRAL TEXAS

12012 Par Thirty-Five Cir., Austin, TX 78753
(512) 453-7391
www.gsctx.org

GRASSROOTS LEADERSHIP

607 W. 14th St., Austin, TX 78701
(512) 499-8111
www.grassrootsleadership.org

Grassroots Leadership provides advocacy for an end to family detention and organizes a visitation program at the T. Don Hutto Immigrant Detention Center for woman in Taylor, Texas.

HOPE PRISON MINISTRIES

3515 Sycamore School Rd., Suite 125, PMB 172, Ft. Worth, TX 76133
(817) 323-7686
www.hopeprisonministries.org

INNOCENCE PROJECT OF TEXAS

300 Burnett St., Suite 160, Ft. Worth, TX 76102
(806) 744-6525
www.ipoftexas.org

IP of Texas provides legal representation for wrongfully convicted Texas prisoners. Must claim actual innocence. DNA and non-DNA cases accepted, with no sentencing requirements. Appeals must be exhausted. No federal cases.

INNOCENCE PROJECT | THURGOOD MARSHALL SCHOOL OF LAW

3100 Cleburne St., Houston, TX 77004
(713) 313-1139
www.earlcarlinstitute.org/centers/criminal_justice/innocence_project.html

Provides legal representation for wrongfully convicted Texas prisoners. They will only accept cases where it can be proven that a crime never happened, mistaken identity, or where DNA proves innocence.

INNOCENCE PROJECT | TEXAS A&M UNIVERSITY

1515 Commerce St., Fort Worth, TX 76102

IP investigates claims of actual innocence involving Texas prisoners. They primarily focus on Northern Texas.

INSIDE BOOKS PROJECT | 12TH STREET BOOKS

827 W. 12th St., Austin, TX 78701
(512) 655-3121
www.insidebooksproject.org
contact@insidebooksproject.org

IBP sends FREE books and educational materials to Texas prisoners, including the *IBP Resource Guide.* Book requests can be made once every three months. Stamp donations are appreciated. They also accept essays, articles, book reviews, poetry, and artwork for inclusion in their newsletter or to sell for fundraisers.

NATIONAL PRISONER'S FAMILY CONFERENCE | COMMUNITY SOLUTIONS OF EL PASO

2200 N. Yarborough, Suite B245, El Paso, TX 79925
(915) 861-7733
www.prisonersfamilycoonference.org
info@prisonersfamilyconference.org

Prisoner's Family Conference is an annual forum that works to find solutions to problems encountered by families due to incarceration.

PAPERBACK SWAP'N'SHOP

1115 FM 517 Road East, Dickinson, TX 77539
(281) 534-3370
imailtoprison.com

Paperback Swap'n'Shop provides a way for friends and family of Texas prisoners to purchase large quantities of books for prisoners cheaply. They can purchase a "grab bag" of books – a 3-foot stack of books – for $30-$54. They also mail books and offer magazine subscription services to prisoners nationwide.

RESTORATIVE JUSTICE MINISTRIES OF TEXAS

1229 Avenue J, Huntsville, TX 77340
(936) 291-2156
www.rjmntexas.net

RJ provides information, training and services to prevent recidivism in the Texas justice system. They operate hospitality houses for visiting family members in Huntsville and Gatesville. Write for current programs.

SEEDLING'S PROMISE

280 S. 1H 35, Suite 170, Austin, TX 78704
(512) 323-6371
www.seedlingfoundation.org

Seedling's Promise provides school-based mentoring to children of the who are incarcerated in TDCJ

STATE BAR OF TEXAS | LAWYER REFERRAL INFORMATION SERVICE

PO Box 12487, Austin, TX 78711-2487
(800) 252-9640

Provides referrals to paid attorneys. Typically, attorneys charge a consultation fee of $20 for the first 30 minutes to discuss the case.

TEXAS ADVOCACY PROJECT

PO Box 833, Austin, TX 78767-0833
(800) 777-3247, (512) 476-5377
www,texasadvocacyproject.org
info@texasadvocacyproject.org

TAP provides legal representation for any victim of domestic violence or sexual assault in Texas.

TEXAS ASSOCIATION AGAINST SEXUAL ASSAULT (TAASA)

6200 La Calma Dr., Suite 110, Austin, TX 78752
(888) 343-4414
www.taasa.org

TAASA assists sexual assault victims to local rape crisis centers.

TEXAS CENTER FOR ACTUAL INNOCENCE | UNIVERSITY OF TEXAS SCHOOL OF LAW

727 E. Dean Keeton St., Austin, TX 78705
(512) 471-1317
www.utexas.edu/law/clinincs/innocence/tcai

TCAI provides legal representation for wrongfully convicted Texas prisoners. DNA and non-DNA cases accepted, with no sentencing requirements.

TEXAS CIVIL RIGHTS PROJECT | PRISONER RIGHTS PROGRAM

4920 North IH-35, Austin, TX 78751
(512) 474-5073
www.texascivilrightsproject.org
questions@texascivilrightsproject.org

TCRP provides advocacy and legal representation to Texas prisoners on conditions of confinement cases in Texas. They accept cases that will have a broad impact on Texas prisoners.

TEXAS COMMISSION FOR LAWYER DISCIPLINE

ATTN: CAAP, PO Box 12487, Austin, TX 78711-2487
(800) 932-1900

Investigates complaints against attorneys. Write to request a grievance form.

TEXAS COMMISSION ON JAIL STANDARDS

300 W. 155th St., Suite 503, Austin, TX 78701
(512) 463-5505

The Texas Commission on Jail Standards fields complaints against county jails (NOT TCDJ).

TEXAS COUNCIL ON FAMILY VIOLENCE (TCFV)

PO Box 163865, Austin, TX 78716
(800) 799-7933
www.tcfv.org

TCFV provides resources for those who have suffered violence, including statewide resources and a hotline.

TEXAS CRIMINAL JUSTICE COALITION

1714 Fortview Rd., Suite 104, Austin, TX 78704
(512) 441-8123 ext. 109
www.texasjc.org info@texasjc.org

TCJC advocates for changes in the Texas criminal justice policy. They will not provide legal assistance to prisoners.

TEXAS DEFENDER SERVICE

1927 Blodgett St., Houston, TX 77004
(713) 222-7788
www.texasdefender.org

TDS is an advocacy group that works to expose the systemic flaws in Texas death penalty representation. They provide only limited direct representation.

TEXAS FAIR DEFENSE PROJECT

510 S. Congress Ave., Austin, TX 78704
(512) 637-5220
www.texasfairdefenseproject.org

TFDP is an advocacy project to ensure that criminal defendants are provided with adequate legal representation. They can provide assistance or referrals.

TEXAS INMATE FAMILIES ASSOCIATION

PO Box 300220, Austin, TX 78703-0004
(512) 371-0900
www.tifa.org tifa@tifa.org

TIFA provides advocacy and support to the families of Texas prisoners, including education, legislative efforts to effect reforms and public awareness, and other services.

TEXAS JAIL PROJECT

1712 E. Riverside Dr., Box 190, Austin, TX 78741
(512) 597-8746
www.texasjailproject.org info@texasjailproject.org

The Texas Jail Project is a watchdog group that helps protect against abuses within the Texas jail system. They do not cover TCDJ.

TEXAS MEDICAL BOARD

PO Box 2018, Austin , TX 78768-2018
(512) 305-7100
www.tmb.state.tx.us

The Texas Medical Board fields complaints against physicians and investigates medical malpractice claims.

TEXAS MORATORIUM NETWORK

3616 Far West Blvd., Suite 117, Box 251, Austin, TX 78731
(512) 961-6389
www.texasmoratorium.org

TMN actively works to advance legislation that will cause a temporary halt on executions, with the overall goal of overturning the death penalty in Texas.

TEXAS PRISON MINISTRY

7520 Hillcroft St., Houston, TX 77081
(713) 972-5789
www.texasprisonministry.com

US CITIZENSHIP AND IMMIGRATION SERVICE

126 Northpoint Dr., Houston, TX 77060
(800) 375-5283
www.uscis.gov

USIS is the government agency that oversees U.S. immigration. Write with questions on immigration policy.

WINDHAM SCHOOL DISTRICT

PO Box 40, 804 Building B., FM 2821, Huntsville, Texas 77320

The Windham School District provides college level education in over 20 fields to Texas prisoners in 90 Texas facilities. They work with several in-state colleges to provide education assistance. Contact for more information, or see your prisons education coordinator.

Reentry Resources

2000 ROSES FOUNDATION

PO Box 227015, Dallas, TX 75222-7015
(214) 941-1333
www.2000roses.org

2000 Roses provides reentry assistance to Texas women ex-offenders, including transitional housing, education, job training, and more.

BRIDGING THE GAP MINISTRIES

PO Box 131747, Tyler, TX 75713
(903) 539-6797
www.bridgingthegap.com

BGM is a faith-based organization that provides reentry services for ex-offenders in the Tyler area.

CRIME PREVENTION INSTITUTE | TARGETED PROJECT RE-ENTERPRISE

8401 Shoal Creek Blvd., Austin, TX 78763
(512) 502-9704

CPI provides reentry services to ex-offenders in the Austin area, including job placement, employment monitoring, counseling follow-ups, and referrals.

DIOCESE OF BEAUMONT CRIMINAL JUSTICE MINISTRY

PO Box 3948, Beaumont, TX 77704
(409) 838-0451
www.dioceseofbmt.org

Diocese of BMT is a faith-based group that assists Texas ex-offenders and their families. They do so through a variety of programs. Write for current programs.

EXODUS MINISTRIES

4630 Munger Ave., Suite 110, Dallas, TX 75214
(214) 827-3772
www.exodusministry.4t.com
EM provides transitional services for Dallas area ex-offenders, including a 20-unit apartment building for reentering mothers and their children, employment training and placement, life skills, and transportation.

GALAXY COUNSELING CENTERS

1025 S. Jupiter Rd., Garland, TX 75042
(972) 272-4429

GCC provides post-release services for ex-offenders in the Garland, Dallas, Plano, and Richardson, Texas areas, including group therapy, family counseling, and anger management services.

GOODWILL INDUSTRIES

Dallas: 3020 N. Westmoreland Rd., Dallas, TX 75212
(214) 638-2800
www.goodwilldallas.org
Houston: 1140 West Loop North, Houston, TX 77055
(713) 692-6221
www.goodwillhouston.org
Southeast Texas/Beaumont: 460 Wall St., Beaumont, TX 77701
(409) 838-9911
www.goodwillbmt.org

Goodwill Industries provides reentry services to ex-offenders who are referred to them by the Texas Rehabilitation Commission and the Texas Workforce Commission. They provide work skills training, including computer classes, basic accounting and finance techniques, and some job placement assistance.

HELP FOR FELONS

PO Box 8008, Plano, TX 75023
www.helpforfelons.org

Help for Felons offers a comprehensive and current online Texas reentry resource directory and practical reentry information.

MASS | MOTHERS [FATHERS] FOR THE ADVANCEMENT OF SOCIAL SYSTEMS

3737 Atlanta St., Dallas, TX 75212
(212) 421-0303
www.massjab.org

MASS provides a variety of reentry services to Texas ex-offenders, including housing, employment, counseling, and any necessary support that eases reentry transition.

MERCY HEART

4805 NE Loop 820, Fort Worth, TX 76137
(817) 514-0290
www.mercyheart.org

MH is a faith-based organization that assists ex-offenders and their families through mental, emotional, and spiritual transition success.

MILES OF FREEDOM

PO Box 151342, Dallas, TX 75214
(214) 290-2337
www.milesoffreedom.org miles@milesoffreedom.org

Miles of Freedom provides reentry assistance, including a 3-month job-readiness course for Texas ex-offenders.

MINISTRY OF CHALLENGE MEN'S HOME

1500 E. 12th St., Austin, TX 78702

Ministry of Challenge Men's Home provides faith-based reentry assistance for Austin-area ex-offenders. Requires a 6-month commitment to their program.

SALVATION ARMY

6500 Harry Hines Blvd., Dallas, TX 75235
(214) 956-0600
www.salvationarmytexas.org

SA provides a variety of reentry services to Texas ex-offenders, including a regularly updated list of transitional housing, a residential rehab center, and bible correspondence courses.

TEXAS DEPARTMENT OF CRIMINAL JUSTICE | REENTRY & INTEGRATION

4616 W. Howard Lane, Suite 200, Austin, TX 78728
(512) 671-2134
www.tdcj.state.tx.us/divisions/rid

TEXAS OFFENDERS REENTRY INITIATIVE (TORI) OF BISHOP T.D. JAKES

PO Box 4386, Dallas, TX 75208
(214) 941-1325 ext. 300
PO Box 2645, Ft. Worth, TX 76113
(817) 632-7437
1703 Gray, Houston, TX 77003
(713) 650-0595
2803 E. Commerce St., San Antonio, TX 78205
www.medc-tori.org

TEXAS REENTRY SERVICES

1408 St. Louis Ave., Fort Worth, TX 76104
www.txrs.org

TXRS provides Tarrant County ex-offenders with a variety of reentry services to assist in a successful transition. Write for a current list of offerings.

UNLOCKING DOORS TEXAS REENTRY NETWORK | REENTRY BROKERAGE CENTER

1402 Corinth St., Suite 235, Dallas, TX 75215
(214) 296-9258
www.unlockingdoors.org

WELCOME HOUSE

921 N. Peak St., Dallas, TX 75204
(214) 887-0696

WH provides reentry services for Texas male ex-offenders in the Dallas area, including housing, food, clothing, counseling, mentoring, education, advocacy, and more.

VOA TEXAS

300 E. Midway Dr., Euless, TX 76039
(817) 529-7300
www.voatx.org

Utah | Beehive State

State Capital: Salt Lake City

Time Zone: MST

Population: 2,942,902

(91.4% White, 2.4% Asian, 1.5% American Indian, 1.3% Black (12.2% Hispanic))

Name Origin: From the Navajo word meaning "upper" or "higher up," as applied to the Shoshone tribe called "Ute." Proposed name "Deseret," or 'Land of honeybees', from the Book of Mormon, was rejected by Congress.

Motto: Industry

Famous Utahans: Roseanne Barr, Butch Cassidy, the Osmonds, Brigham Young.

State Agencies

CONSUMER PROTECTION

PO Box 146704, 160 E. 300 S., 2nd Floor, Salt Lake City, UT 84114
(801) 530-6601

DRIVER RECORDS

Department of Public Safety, PO Box 60560, Salt Lake City, UT 84130-0560
(801) 965-4437
www.driverlicense.utah.gov

VETERAN'S AFFAIRS

PO Box 581900, 550 Foothill Dr., Salt Lake City, UT 84158

VITAL RECORDS

PO Box 141012, Salt Lake City, UT 84114-0112
(801) 538-6105
www.healthutah.gov/vitalrecords

Prisoner Support

ACLU | UTAH

355 N. 300 West, Salt Lake City, UT 84103
(801) 521-9289
www.acluutah.org aclu@acluutah.org

Advocates for the civil rights of Utah prisoners, generally through class actions. They typically will not accept individual prisoner cases, but may provide referrals. They meet with Utah prison officials monthly to resolve ongoing problems and to discuss reforms.

CURE | UTAH

235 W. 100 South, Salt Lake City, UT 84101
(801) 335-0234

CURE provides advocacy and organization through prisoners and their supporters to achieve reforms in the Utah prison system. Through their *Behind the Wire Prisoner Information Network,* prisoners and their families can get answers to questions and concerns related to prisoner rights.

PRISONER INFORMATION NETWORK (PIN)

PO Box 165171, Salt Lake City, UT 84116
(801) 359-3589

PIN provides a variety of services to Utah prisoners and ex-offenders, including a Utah Prisoner Resource Guide ($4 for prisoners, $10 for others), and hygiene supplies for those reentering.

PRISON FELLOWSHIP UTAH

PO Box 1976, Orem, UT 84057
(801) 691-0414

Prison Fellowship provides several faith-based services to Utah prisoners, including religious services and reentry support.

ROCKY MOUNTAIN INNOCENCE CENTER

358 South 700 East, B235, Salt Lake City, UT 84102
(801) 355-1888
www.rminnocence.org

RMIC provides advocacy and legal representation for wrongfully convicted prisoners in Utah, Nevada and Wyoming. Must be completely innocent, provable through significant new evidence, have no remaining appeals options, and have more than seven years left on sentence.

SALT LAKE COUNTY CRIMINAL JUSTICE SERVICES

145 East 1300 South, Suite 501, Salt Lake City, UT 84115
(385) 468-3500
www.slco.org/criminal-justice

UTAH PRISONER ADVOCATE NETWORK

PO Box 464, Draper, UT 84020
www.utahprisoneradvocate.org
utahprisoneradvocate@gmail.com

UPAN advocates for prisoners in the Utah prison system, assisting prisoners resolve issues related to housing, medical, and other issues, and helping families understand and navigate the prison system. They also publish a monthly newsletter, FREE to Utah prisoners.

Reentry Resources

ACTIVE REENTRY

10 S. Fairgrounds Rd., Price, UT 84501
(435) 637-4950
www.arecil.org

DEPARTMENT OF WORKFORCE SERVICES

PO Box 45249, Salt Lake City, UT 84145
(801) 526-9675
jobs.utah.gov

PAPILLON HOUSE

341 North 1100 East, American Fork, UT 84003
(801) 473-3963
www.papillonhouse.com

Papillon House provides transitional housing for Utah women ex-offenders.

UTAH COUNTY REENTRY RESOURCE

www.ucreentry.wordpress.com

Vermont | Green Mountain State

State Capital: Montpelier

Time Zone: EST

Population: 626,562

(95.% White, 1.6% Asians, 1.2% Black, 0.4% American Indian (1.5% Hispanic))

Name Origin: From the French word *vert,* meaning "green," and *mont*, meaning "mountain," as suggested by Dr. Thomas Young in 1777.

Motto: Freedom and Unity

Famous Vermonters: Ethan Allen, Calvin Coolidge, Howard Dean, John Deere.

State Agencies

CONSUMER PROTECTION

146 University Place, Burlington, VT 05405
(802) 656-3183

DRIVER RECORDS

Department of Motor Vehicles, 120 State St., Montpelier, VT 05603-0001
www.aot.state.vt.us/dmv

SECRETARY OF STATE

81 River St., Montpelier, VT 05609-1104
(810) 828-2386
www.sec.state.vt.us

VETERAN'S AFFAIRS

215 W. Main St., White River Junction, VT 05009

VITAL RECORDS

Department of Health, PO Box 70, 108 Cherry St., Burlington, VT 05402-0070
(802) 863-7275
www.sec.state.vt.us/archives-records

Prisoner Support

ACLU | VERMONT

137 Elm St., Montpelier, VT 05602
(802) 223-6304
www.acluvt.org info@acluvt.org

Advocates for the civil rights of Vermont prisoners, generally through class actions. They typically will not accept individual prisoner cases, but they may provide referrals.

CENTER FOR RESTORATIVE JUSTICE

439 Main St., Suite 2, Bennington, VT 05201
(802) 447-1595
www.bcrj.org

CURE | VERMONT

PO Box 484, Montpelier, VT 05601-0484
(802) 271-9932
curevermont@gmail.com

CURE provides advocacy and organization through prisoners and their supporters to achieve reforms in the Vermont prison system.

KIDS-A-PART

79 Weaver St., PO Box 127, Winooski, VT 05404
(802) 859-3227
www.lundvt.org/kids-a-part.html

Kids-A-Part provides parenting services to prisoners and services to their children, including advocacy and education.

NEW ENGLAND INNOCENCE PROJECT

120 Tremont St., Suite 735, Boston, MA 02108
(617) 830-7655
www.newenglandinnocence.org

See Massachusetts listing.

PRISONER RIGHTS OFFICE | OFFICE OF DEFENDER GENERAL

8 Baldwin St., 4th Floor, Montpelier, VT 05633
(802) 828-3194
www.defgen.state.vt.us

PRO provides limited legal representation services for Vermont prisoners on civil right matters, post-conviction relief, habeas proceedings, conditions of confinement, parole revocation, and disciplinary matters.

VERMONT CATHOLIC CHARITIES

55 Joy Dr., South Burlington, VT 05403
(802) 658-6111 ext. 1402
www.vermontcatholic.org

VCC is a faith-based organization that provides support services for Vermont prisoners and their families, including pastoral counseling, family visitation, referrals, and reentry assistance.

Reentry Resources

BRATTLEBORO COMMUNITY JUSTICE CENTER

230 Main St., Suite 302, Brattleboro, VT 05301
(802) 251-8142
www.bcrj.org

BURLINGTON COMMUNITY JUSTICE CENTER

200 Church St., Burlington, VT 05401
(802) 865-7155
www.burlingtonvt.gov/cjc/offender-support-services

BURLINGTON OFFENDER REENTRY PROGRAM

179 W. Winooski Ave., Burlington, VT 05401
www.vabir.org

DISMAS HOUSE | VERMONT

103 E. Allen E. St., Winooski, VT 05404
(603) 795-2770
www.dismasofvermont.org

DH provides housing assistance to ex-offenders in the Burlington, Winooski, Rutland, and Hartford areas. Must apply through a case worker.

FRANKLIN GRAND ISLE RESTORATIVE JUSTICE CENTER

120 N. Main St., St. Albans, VT 05478
www.cjnvt.org/center/st-albans-community-justice-center

NEKCA COMMUNITY & JUSTICE PROGRAMS | JUDD REENTRY TRANSITIONAL HOUSING

70 Main St., Newport, VT 05855
(802) 334-7318
www.nekcavt.org

VERMONT WORKS FOR WOMEN

51 Park St., Essex Junction, VT 05401
(802) 655-8900

VWW provides transitional services for Vermont female ex-offenders, including job readiness, short-term job placement, and housing assistance.

Virginia | Old Dominion State

State Capital: Richmond

Time Zone: EST

Population: 8,326,289

(70.5% White, 19.7% Black, 6.3% Asians, 0.5% American Indian (7.6% Hispanic))

Name Origin: Named by Sir Walter Raleigh, who outfitted an expedition in 1584, in honor of Queen Elizabeth, the Virgin Queen.

Motto: Sic Semper Tyrannis (Thus always to tyrants)

Famous Virginians: Arthur Ashe, Sandra Bullock, Katie Couric, Jerry Falwell, Robert E. Lee, Lewis & Clark, Booker T. Washington, George Washington.

State Agencies

CONSUMER PROTECTION

900 E. Main St., Richmond, VA 23219
(804) 486-2042

DRIVER RECORDS

Department of Motor Vehicles, PO Box 27412, Richmond, VT 23269
(804) 367-0538
www.dmv.state.va.us

SECRETARY OF STATE

State Corporation Commission, PO Box 1197, Richmond, VA 23218-1197
(804) 371-9733
www.scc.virginia.gov

VETERAN'S AFFAIRS

116 N. Jefferson St., Roanoke, VA 24016-1928

VITAL RECORDS

PO Box 1000, Richmond, VA 23218-1000
(804) 662-6200
www.vdh.virginia.gov

Prisoner Support

ACLU | VIRGINIA

701 E. Franklin St., Suite 1412, Richmond, VA 23219
(804) 644-8022
www.acluva.org intake@acluva.org

Advocates for the civil rights of Virginia prisoners, generally through class actions. They typically will not accept individual prisoner cases, but they may provide referrals.

ADVANCEMENT PROJECT

1220 L St. NW, Suite 850, Washington, DC 20005
(202) 728-9557
www.advancementproject.org

AP is a project that works to reduce recidivism in the Virginia criminal justice system and provide better alternatives to incarceration.

AIDS/HIV SERVICES GROUP

953 2nd St. SE, Charlottesville, VA 22902
(434) 979-7714
www.asgva.org

ASGVA provides a variety of services for Virginia prisoners living with HIV/AIDS including testing, education, case management, release readiness, post-release reentry services, and more.

ASSISTING FAMILIES OF INMATES

1 N. 5th St., Suite 416, Richmond, VA 23219
(804) 643-2401
www.afoi.org family@afoi.org

AFOI provides support and assistance for Virginia prisoner's families, including visitation transportation, information, referrals for community resources, chaperones for children visiting mothers, counseling for children, video visitation, and more.

BIG BROTHERS/BIG SISTERS | HARRISONBURG-ROCKINGHAM COUNTY

225 N. High St., Harrisonburg, VA 22802

(540) 433-8886
www.bbbshr.org

CAREGIVERS CHOICE

1600 Duke St., Suite 300, Alexandria, VA 22313
(703) 224-2200
www.mentoring.org

CC provides quality mentoring services for the children of Virginia prisoners.

CURE | VIRGINIA

PO Box 2310, Vienna, VA 22183
(703) 272-3524
www.vacure.org vacure1@cox.net

CURE provides advocacy and organization through prisoners and their supporters to achieve reforms in the Virginia prison system. They infrequently publish a newsletter, *Inside Out,* concerning Virginia prison issues $2 (or 6 stamps) for VA prisoners, $15 for others.

INNOCENCE PROJECT | UNIVERSITY OF VIRGINIA

580 Massie Rd., Charlottesville, VA 22901
(434) 924-7354
www.law.virginia.edu/html/academics/practical/innocenceclinic.html

IP provides legal assistance to wrongfully convicted Virginia prisoners. DNA and non-DNA cases accepted, with no sentencing requirements.

MENTORING CHILDREN OF PRISONERS | SETON YOUTH SHELTERS

3333 Virginia Beach Blvd., Suite 28, Virginia Beach, VA 23452
(757) 963-5795
www.setonyouthshelters.org

The Mentoring Children of Prisoners Program provides weekly mentoring services for children of prisoners.

MESSAGES PROJECT

PO Box 8325, Norfolk, VA 23503
www.themessagesproject.org

The Messages Project works with incarcerated parents to make expressions to their children and other loved ones through recorded videos of the prisoner sending a message to the ones they left behind. The service is offered in Virginia, Nebraska, and Missouri.

MID-ATLANTIC INNOCENCE PROJECT

200 H St. NW, Washington, DC 20052
(202) 994-4586
www.exonerate.org

MAIP provides DC, Virginia, and Maryland prisoners that they have determined to be innocent with legal representation and investigative services.

VIRGINIA CAPITAL REPRESENTATION RESOURCE CENTER

2421 Ivy Rd., Suite 301, Charlottesville, VA 22903
(434) 817-2970
www.vcrrc.org

VCRRC provides legal consultation services to attorneys representing death penalty-sentenced Virginia prisoners.

VIRGINIA CENTER FOR RESTORATIVE JUSTICE

3420 Pump Rd., Suite 188, Richmond, VA 23233
(804) 313-9596
www.vcrj.org

Reentry Resources

COMMUNITY ACTION PROGRAM

141 Campbell Ave. SW, TAP Room, Roanoke, VA 24022
(540) 342-9344
www.tapintohope.org

CAP provides basic reentry services to Virginia ex-offenders, including assessment, employment counseling, transportation, and referrals.

HELPING HANDS WOMEN'S OUTREACH MINISTRIES (HHWOM)

PO Box 13292, Richmond, VA 23225
(804) 276-3139
www.hhwom.org

HHWOM provides psychological and spiritual counseling to Virginia women ex-offenders who have or are presently experiencing substance abuse problems.

NORFOLK PRISONER REENTRY PROGRAM | CITY OF NORFOLK

741 Monticello Ave., Norfolk, VA 23510
(757) 664-6000
www.norfolk.gov

OFFENDER AID AND RESTORATION

Arlington area: 1400 N. Uhle St., Suite 704, Arlington, VA 22201
(703) 228-7030
www.oaronline.org info@oaronline.org
Charlottesville area: 750 Harris St., Suite 207, Charlottesville, VA 22903
(434) 296-5441
www.oar-jacc.org
Richmond area: 1N. Third St., Suite 200, Richmond, VA 23219
(804) 643-2746
www.oarric.org info@oarric.org

OAR provides a variety of reentry services for Virginia ex-offenders, including emergency assistance, job skills training, supervision of community service, job placement assistance, and more.

OPPORTUNITIES, ALTERNATIVES, AND RESOURCES OF FAIRFAX COUNTY

10640 Page Ave., Suite 250, Fairfax, VA 22030-4000
(703) 246-3033
www.oarfairfax.org info@oarfairfax.org

OAR provides reentry services to ex-offenders in Fairfax County, including emergency assistance, employment guidance, family support, counseling, and more. Some resources are available to ex-offenders in Loudon and Prince Williams Counties.

OPPORTUNITY, ALLIANCE, REENTRY (OAR) OF RICHMOND

1 North 3rd St., Suite 200, Richmond, VA 23219
(804) 43-2746
www.oarric.org

RESOURCE INFORMATION HELP FOR THE DISADVANTAGED (RIHD)

PO Box 55, Highland Springs, VA 23075
(804) 426-4426
www.rihd.org

VIRGINIA CARES | DEPARTMENT OF COMMUNITY & HUMANS SERVICES

2355-A Mill Rd., Alexandria, 22314
(703) 746-5919
www.vacares.org
Virginia CARES (Community Action Reentry System) operates 12 reentry sites around Virginia.

VIRGINIA COMMUNITY CORRECTIONS | REENTRY PROGRAM

PO Box 26963, Richmond, VA 23261-6963
(804) 674-3000
vadoc.virginia.gov/community

VIRGINIA DEPARTMENT OF SOCIAL SERVICES | PRISONER REENTRY

801 E. Main St., Richmond, VA 23219-2901
(800) 777-8293
www.dss.virginia.gov/community/prisoner_reentry

VIRGINIA EMPLOYMENT COMMISSION | CAREER CONNECT

703 E. Main St., Richmond, VA 23219
(804) 786-1484
www.vec.state.va.us

Washington | Evergreen State

State Capital: Raleigh

Time Zone: EST

Population: 7,036,530

(80.7% White, 8.2% Asians, 4.1% Blacks, 1.9% American Indian (10.7% Hispanic))

Name Origin: Named after George Washington

Motto: Alki (By and by)

Famous Washingtonians: Paul Allen, Glenn Beck, Raymond Carver, Kurt Cobain, Bing Crosby, Bill Gates, Jimi Hendrix, Apolo Ohno, Hilary Swank, Adam West.

State Agencies

CONSUMER PROTECTION

PO Box 40100, 1125 Washington St. NE, Olympia, WA 98504
(206) 464-7744

DRIVER RECORDS

Department of Licensing, PO Box 9048, Olympia, WA 98507-9030
(360) 902-3913

SECRETARY OF STATE

PO Box 40234, Olympia, WA 98504-0234
(360) 753-7115
www.secstate.wa.gov

VETERAN'S AFFAIRS

Federal Building, 915 2nd Ave., Seattle, WA 98174

VITAL RECORDS

Department of Health, PO Box 47814, Olympia, WA 98504-7814
(360) 236-4300
www.doh.wa.gov

Prisoner Support

ACLU | WASHINGTON

909 Fifth Ave., Suite 630, Seattle, WA 98164
(206) 624-2180
www.aclu-wa.org administration@aclu-wa.org

Advocates for the civil rights of Washington prisoners, generally the class actions. They typically will not accept individual prisoner cases, but they may provide referrals. Prisoners can call between 10AM and 2PM, Mon-Fri

BIG BROTHERS/BIG SISTERS | PUGET SOUND

1600 S. Graham St., Seattle, WA 98108
(206) 763-9060
www.bbbsps.org

Big Brothers/Big Sisters of the Puget Sound provides (COPY FROM NTL)

COLUMBIA LEGAL SERVICES | INSTITUTIONS PROJECT

101 Yesler Way, Suite 300, Seattle, WA 98104
(206) 382-3399 (collect), (800) 542-0794, (206) 464-1518 (TDD)
www.columbialegal.org

CLS provides legal representation to Washington prisoners on a variety of issues, including conditions of confinement, discrimination, sentencing and placement, access to courts, alternatives to incarceration, rehab issues, and more.

CURE | WASHINGTON

PO Box 515, Longview, WA 98632

CURE provides advocacy and organization through prisoners and their supporters to achieve reforms in the Washington prison system.

FAMILIES ON THE OUTSIDE

9208 NE Highway 99, Suite 107, Vancouver, WA 98665
(360) 904-7302
www.familiesontheoutside.org

Families on the Outside assists families of the incarcerated through faith-based counseling, support groups, seminars, and events.

FREEDOM EDUCATION PROJECT | TACOMA COMMUNITY COLLEGE

6501 S. 19th St., Tacoma, WA 98466
(253) 566-5000
www.prisonstudiesproject.org/category/washington

FEP provides education opportunities to Washington women prisoners, including pre-college and college courses towards an Associates of Arts and Science degree. Must have a GED or high school diploma.

INNOCENCE PROJECT | NORTHWEST CLINIC

PO Box 85110, Seattle, WA 89145-1110
(206) 543-5780
www.law.washington.edu/clinics/ipnw

IPNW provides legal representation to wrongfully convicted Washington prisoners. Must have an actual innocence claim that can be proven through DNA testing or new evidence, have at least three years left on sentence, have completed direct appeals, and have no right to appointed counsel.

KEEPING THE FAITH | THE PRISON PROJECT

The Pat Graney Company, 606 Maynard Ave., Suite 201, Seattle, WA 98104
(206) 329-3705
www.patgraney.org/education.html

KTFPP provides programs to encourage women prisoners in Washington through novel methods such as dance, performance, visual arts, expository writing, and more.

SECOND MENTAL HEALTH | MENTALLY ILL OFFENDER SERVICES PROGRAM

1600 E. Olive St., Seattle, WA 98122
(206) 302-2300
www.smh.org

SPOKANE COUNTY PUBLIC DEFENDER

1033 W. Gardner, Spokane, WA 99260-0280
(509) 477-4246

SCPD provides legal representation by court appointment on a variety of criminal cases, as well as civil commitment and juvenile dependency cases.

UNIVERSITY BEYOND BARS

PO Box 31525, Seattle, WA 98103
www.universitybeyondbars.org

UBB offers education opportunities to Monroe CC and Washington CC for Women, including certificate and college credit courses. They also offer college prep courses in English and Math.

Reentry Resources

CENTRAL AREA MOTIVATION PROGRAM REENTRY SERVICES

722 18th Ave., Seattle, WA 98122
(206) 812-4940
www.campseattle.org

CAMP offers transitional employment readiness and services for Washington ex-offenders in the Seattle area.

CONVICTION CAREERS

PO Box 432, Lynnwood, WA 98046
(866) 436-1960
www.convictioncareers.org

FRESH START HOUSING OF WASHINGTON | JAIL & PRISON PROGRAMS

10924 Mukilteo Speedway, Suite 230, Mukilteo, WA 98275
(206) 486-4493
www.freshstarthousingwa.org

INTERACTION TRANSITION PROGRAM

935 16th Ave., Seattle, WA 98122
(206) 324-3932

ITP offers low-cost transitional housing and other support services to Seattle area ex-offenders.

M-2 JOB THERAPY

205 Avenue C, Snohomish, WA 96291
(877) 625-6214

M-2JT provides transitional employment services to Washington ex-offenders.

PIONEER HUMAN SERVICES

7440 W. Marginal Way South, Seattle, WA 98108
(206) 768-1990
www.pioneerhumanserv.com

PHS provides a variety of reentry services for Washington ex-offenders in the Seattle area, including training, employment, housing, and rehabilitation services.

POST-PRISON EDUCATION PROGRAM

Central Building, Suite 180, 810 Third Ave., Seattle, WA 98104-1606
www.postprison.edu

PPEP provides access to higher education for Washington ex-offenders upon release. Write for list of programs.

SEATTLE GOODWILL | STRIVE SEATTLE

700 Dearborn Place S., Seattle, WA 98144
(206) 329-1000
www.seattlegoodwill.org

SG STRIVE is an employment and training program, which includes basic education, life skills, language classes for non-English speakers, job skills training and placement opportunities, and ongoing support.

UNIVERSITY OF WASHINGTON WOMEN'S CENTER | WOMEN'S REENTRY PROGRAM

Cunningham Hall, Box 353070, Seattle, WA 98185
(206) 685-1090
www.depts.washington.edu/womenctr/programs/re-entry-program

WASHINGTON DEPARTMENT OF CORRECTIONS | OFFENDER REENTRY

801 88th Ave. SE, Tumwater, WA 98501
(360) 725-9100
www.washingtonci.com/offender-reentry.html

No illegal aliens allowed!

Did you know that Washington is the only state that explicitly requires non-citizens who wish to visit prisoners proof of their legal status in the U.S.?

West Virginia | Mountain State

State Capital: Charleston

Time Zone: EST

Population: 1,850,326

(93.7% White, 3.6% Black, 0.8% Asians, 0.2% American Indian (1.2% Hispanic))

Name Origin: So named when the Western counties of Virginia seceded from the U.S. in 1863.

Motto: Montani Semper Liberi (Mountaineers are always free)

Famous West Virginians: Stonewall Jackson, Don Knotts, Brad Paisley, Mary Lou Retton, "Chuck" Yeager.

State Agencies

CONSUMER PROTECTION

PO Box 1789, Charleston, WV 24236
(403) 558-8986

DRIVER RECORDS

Department of Motor Vehicles, 1800 Kanawha Blvd., Building 3, Room 124, Charleston, WV 25317
(304) 558-3915
www.wvdot.com

SECRETARY OF STATE

Tate Capitol Building, Room W151, Charleston, WV 25305-0776
(304) 558-8000
www.wvsos.com

VETERAN'S AFFAIRS

640 Fourth Ave., Huntington, WV 25701

VITAL RECORDS

Vital Registration Office, Room 165, 350 Capitol St., Charleston, WV 25301-3701
(304) 558-2931
www.dhhr.wv.gov

Prisoner Support

ACLU | WEST VIRGINIA

PO Box 3952, Charleston, WV 25339-3952
(304) 345-9246
www.acluwv.org mail@acluwv.org

Advocates for the civil rights of West Virginia prisoners, generally through class actions. They typically will not accept individual prisoner cases, but they may provide referrals.

ALDERSON HOSPITALITY HOUSE

PO Box 579, Alderson, WV 24910
(304) 445-2980
www.aldersonhospitalityhouse.org

AHH provides support to visitors of women housed in the Alderson Federal Prison Camp, including FREE lodging, meals, and transportation. They also distribute a FREE quarterly newsletter, *The Trumpet*. Donations are appreciated.

CURE | WEST VIRGINIA

PO Box 42, Linn, WV 26384

CURE provides advocacy and organization through prisoners and their supporters to achieve reforms in the West Virginia prison system.

WEST VIRGINIA INNOCENCE PROJECT

PO Box 6130, Morgantown, WV 26506-6130
(304) 293-7294
www.innocenceproject.wvu.edu

WVIP provides legal representation to wrongfully convicted West Virginia prisoners. DNA and non-DNA cases involving arson or shaken baby syndrome are accepted. Must have at least three years left on sentence.

Reentry Resources

NORTHERN PANHANDLE REENTRY PROGRAM

Capitol Complex, 1900 Kanawha Blvd. East, Building One, Room E-100, Charleston, WV 25305-0830
(304) 558-0145
www.courtswv.gov/lower-courts/re-entry.html

SECOND CHANCE MENTORING PROGRAM | KISRA

131 Perkins Ave., Dunbar. WI 25064
(304) 768-8924
www.kisra.org

WEST VIRGINIA REENTRY INITIATIVE

1409 Greenbrier St., Charleston, WV 25311
(304) 558-2036
www.wvdoc.com/wvdoc/offenderreentry/

Wisconsin | Badger State

State Capital: Madison

Time Zone: CST

Population: 5,757,564

(87.8% White, 6.6% Black, 2.6% Asians, 1.1% American Indian (5.8% Hispanic))

Name Origin: Chippewa Indian name *Ouisconsin* or *Mesconsing* by early chroniclers, believed to mean "grassy place."

Motto: Forward

Famous Wisconsinites: Willem Dafoe, Harry Houdini, Liberace, Danika Patrick, Les Paul, Spencer Tracy, Laura Engells Wilder.

State Agencies

CONSUMER PROTECTION

PO Box 8911, 2811 Agriculture Dr., Madison, WI 53708
(608) 224-4953

DRIVER RECORDS

Department of Motor Vehicles, PO Box 7995, Madison, WI 53707-7995
(608) 266-2353
www.dot.wisconsin.gov/drivers

SECRETARY OF STATE

Division of Consumer Affairs, PO Box 7846, Madison, WI 53707-7646
(608) 261-7577
www.wdfi.org

VITAL RECORDS

Bureau of Health Information, PO Box 309, Madison, WI 53701-0309
(608) 266-1373

Prisoner Support

ACLU | WISCONSIN

207 E. Buffalo St., Suite 325, Milwaukee, WI 53202
(414) 272-4032 ext. 216
www.aclu-wi.org inquiries@aclu-wi.org

Advocates for the civil right of Wisconsin prisoners, generally through class actions. They typically will not accept individual prisoner cases, but may provide referrals.

AIDS NETWORK

600 Williamson St., Madison, WI 53703
(800) 486-6276, (608) 252-3540
www.aidsnetwork.org info@aidsnetwork.org

AIDS Network provides a variety of services to South Central Wisconsin prisoners with HIV/AIDS, including information, referrals, and advocacy through mail, phone and visits. They also educate prisoners' attorneys on the possible effect of AIDS on their client's cases.

ASHA FAMILY SERVICES | ASHA'S CORRECTIONS CARE CONTINUUM (CCC)

3719 W. Center St., Milwaukee, WI 53210
(414) 875-1511
www.ashafamilyservices.org

ASHA provides support to families of the incarcerated through a variety of programs.

BROTHER BOB'S OUTREACH

Box 12, Mukwonago, WI 53149-0012

Brother Bob's Outreach offers correspondence opportunities to Wisconsin prisoners. They also organize annual sport events inside Wisconsin prisons.

COMMUNITY, THE | WISCONSIN

PO Box 100392, Milwaukee, WI 53210
www.thecommunitywis.wix.com
thecommunitywis@gmail.com

The Community is a non-profit bi-monthly newsletter devoted to fostering a productive, motivating sense of community among those interested in the Wisconsin prison system, and those sympathetic to the need for smarter criminal justice policies. Write to be included on mailing list. FREE to prisoners, but donations are appreciated.

CURE | WISCONSIN

PO Box 183, Greendale, WI 53129
(414) 409-7028

CURE provides advocacy and organization through prisoners and their supporters to achieve reforms in the Wisconsin prison system.

FORUM FOR UNDERSTANDING PRISONS

29631 Wild Rose Dr., Blue river, WI 53518
(608) 536-3993
www.forumforunderstandingprisons.net
pgswan@aol.com

Provides general advocacy and services for Wisconsin prisoners as well as a FREE newsletter, Bridges of Voices, to Wisconsin prisoners.

WISCONSIN BOOKS-TO-PRISONERS PROJECT | RAINBOW BOOKSTORE

426 W. Gilman St., Madison, WI 53703
(608) 257-6050
www.rainbowbookstore.org/b2p

WI B2P Project sends FREE books to Wisconsin prisoners. Place your request by subject.

WISCONSIN INNOCENCE PROJECT

975 Bascom Mall, Madison, WI 53706-1399
(608) 265-1160
www.law.wisc.edu/fjr/clinical.ip

WIP provides legal representation to wrongfully convicted Wisconsin prisoners. They accept DNA and non-DNA cases where actual innocence is claimed. Must have at least three years left on sentence.

Reentry Resources

AMOS | CIRCLES OF SUPPORT REENTRY PROGRAM

PO Box 1211, La Crosse, WI 54602
(608) 606-9419
www.amosadvocates.org

GENESIS IN MILWAUKEE

2454 W. Lisbon Ave., Milwaukee, WI 53216
(414) 344-9880
www.genesisinmke.org

Genesis in Milwaukee is a Christian organization that provides pre- and post-release services to ex-offenders.

GOODWILL INDUSTRIES NCW | CIRCLES OF SUPPORT

1800 Appleton Rd., Menasha, WI 54952
(920) 68-6832
www.circles-of-support.org

Circles of Support provides reentry transitional assistance to Wisconsin ex-offenders through counseling and support groups for the first 6 to 12 months after release.

HORIZON HOUSE

2511 W. Vine St., Milwaukee, WI 53205
(414) 342-3237
www.horizonhouse.org

HH provides transitional housing for Wisconsin women ex-offenders.

JDK MINISTRY

Box 100171, Milwaukee, WI 53210
(414) 349-4680
www.jdkm.org jim@jdkm.org

JDKM is a faith-based reentry organization that provides reentry services to Christian ex-offenders.

JOSHUA GLOVER HOUSE | FEDERAL RESIDENTIAL REENTRY CENTER

c/o Wisconsin Community Services, 2404 N. 50th St., Milwaukee, WI 53210
(414) 442-3700
www.wiscs.org/programs/reentry

JUSTICEWORKS | TEAM REENTRY PROGRAM

1578 Strongs Ave., Stevens Point, WI 54481
(715) 344-3677
www.justiceworksltd.org/team-reentry-program

MADISON AREA URBAN MINISTRY

2300 S. Park St., Suite 2022, Madison, WI 53713
(608) 256-0906
www.emum.org *mum@emum.org*

MUM is a faith-based organization that provides reentry services to Madison area ex-offenders, including finding solutions to reentry challenges such housing, employment, counseling, substance and alcohol treatment, family reunification and child support issues.

PROJECT RETURN | MILWAUKEE TRANSITIONAL JOBS REENTRY PROJECT

2821 North 4th St., Suite 211, Milwaukee, WI 53212

MTJRP works with Milwaukee area businesses to hire Wisconsin ex-offenders as part of a study on the effectiveness of transitional jobs as a bridge to permanent employment.

ROC WISCONSIN: RESTORING OUR COMMUNITIES

3195 S. Superior St., Suite 313, Milwaukee, WI 53207
(414) 831-2070
www.prayforjusticeinwi.org
wisdomforjustice@gmail.com

ROC Wisconsin is committed to reforming the Wisconsin criminal justice system through initiatives to increase state funding for alternatives to incarceration and reduce crimeless revocations, solitary confinement, and senseless parole denials.

VOICES BEYOND BARS

2300 S. Park St., Madison, WI 53713
(608) 256-0906
voicesbeyaondbars@yahoo.com

Voices Beyond Bars provides pre-and post-release reentry services for Wisconsin ex-offenders including transition strategies and preparation, support groups and education.

WISCONSIN COMMUNITY SERVICES

3732 W. Wisconsin Ave., Suite 200, Milwaukee, WI 53208
(414) 290-0418
www.wiscs.org

WISCS provides a variety of reentry services to Wisconsin ex-offenders, including employment and training, transitional housing, counseling, mediation services, and educational services.

WISCONSIN DOC | REENTRY PROGRAM

PO Box 7925, Madison, WI 53707-7925
(608) 240-5000
doc.wi.gov/about/sdoc-overview/office-of-the-secretary/reentry-unit

WORD OF HOPE MINISTRIES

2677 N. 40th St., Milwaukee, WI 53210
(414) 447-1965
www.holycathedral.org

Word of Hope Ministries provides faith-based reentry services to Wisconsin ex-offenders including health care, mentoring, job training and placement, computer skills and social services.

DO YOU HAVE IDEAS THAT MAY IMPROVE THIS BOOK?

We Want to Hear Them!

Send thoughts to:

PRISON LIVES
PO Box 842, Exeter, CA 93221
info@prisonlives.com (Corrlinks-friendly)

Wyoming | Equality State

State Capital: Cheyenne

Time Zone: MST

Population: 584,153

(92.7% White, 2.7% American Indian, 1.6% Black, 1.0% Asian (8.6% Hispanic))

Name Origin: From Algonquin words for "large prairie place," "at the big plains," and "on the bigger plain."

Motto: Equal Rights

Famous Wyomingites: Dick Cheney, "Buffalo Bill" Cody.

State Agencies

CONSUMER PROTECTION

123 State Capitol, 200 W. 24th St., Cheyenne, WY 82002
(307) 777-5833

DRIVER RECORDS

Department of Transportation, 5300 Bishop Blvd., Cheyenne, WY 82009-3340
(307) 777-4800
www.dot.state.wy.us

SECRETARY OF STATE

200 W. 24th St., Suite 110, Cheyenne, WY 82002-0020
(307) 777-5372
www.soswy.state.wy.us

VETERAN'S AFFAIRS

2360 E. Pershing Blvd., Cheyenne, WY 82001

VITAL RECORDS

Hathaway Building, Cheyenne, WY 82002
(307) 777-7826
www.health.wyo.gov

Prisoner Support

ACLU | WYOMING

PO Box 20706, Cheyenne, WY 82003
(307) 637-4565
www.aclu-wy.org wyoaclu@aol.org

Advocates for the civil rights of Wyoming prisoners, generally through class actions. They typically will not accept individual prisoner cases, but they may provide referrals.

ROCKY MOUNTAIN INNOCENCE CENTER

358 S. 700 East, Suite B235, Salt Lake City, UT 84102
(801) 355-1888
www.rminnocence.org

RMIC provides advocacy and legal representation for wrongfully convicted prisoners in Utah, Nevada and Wyoming. Must be completely innocent, provable through significant new evidence, have no remaining appeals options, and have more than seven years left on sentence.

UNIVERSITY OF WYOMING LEGAL INNOCENCE PROJECT

1000 E. University Ave., Department 3010, Laramie, WY 82071
(307) 766-2104, (307) 766-3474
www.uwyo.edu uwlsp@uwyo.edu

UW provides legal assistance for a variety of civil matters, including to victims of domestic violence, sexual assault and stalking (through their *Domestic Violence Legal Assistance Project* – dvlap@uwyo.edu) and other civil matters.

Reentry Resources

CASPER REENTRY CENTER (CRC)

10007 Land Mark Lane, PO Box 2380, Casper, WY 82604
(307) 268-4840
www.cecintl.com

GOODWILL INDUSTRIES OF WYOMING

612 W. 17th St., Cheyenne, WY 82001
(307) 634-0823
www.goodwillwy.org

SETON HOUSE | FAMILY TRANSITIONAL HOUSING

919 N. Durbin St., PO Box 1557, Casper, WY 82601
(307) 577-8026
www.setonhousecasper.org

VOA NORTHERN ROCKIES | BOOTH HALL ADULT REENTRY

1299 Raymond St., PO Box 1346, Gillette, WY 82717
(307) 682-8505
www.voanr.org

WYOMING OFFENDER REENTRY & COMMUNITY RESOURCES

1934 Wyott Dr., Suite 100, Cheyenne, WY 82002
(307) 777-3775
corrections.wy.gov/services/transition.html

Prison Trending Center

Prison Trending Center

Every prison system around the globe and across the nation is different. Yet, just like in the real world, there are trends that hit this society like a wave. Being secluded from the world around us, even if something in our own backyard, can make it difficult to know what's going on, or how it might affect us.

The *Prison Trending Center* brings you thorough **breakdowns of the most talked-about prison-related topics** from the year before. More than just a relating of the news, however, we bring you the information the news is based on and its current impact on prison society.

2016, for example, brought much awareness to the issues of the use *solitary confinement*, *mental health issues behind bars*, and comparisons between our nation's *incarceration rates* and the rest of the worlds. Several studies were done that shed light on each. We bring pour through those and bring the meat of each to you so you can see what all the fuss is about and check how it may pertain to your circumstances.

With awareness of the issues affecting prisoners comes the need for more resources to address these concerns. This wouldn't be the world's most comprehensive prisoner resource guide if we didn't bring you those as well.

Prison scene trends will keep changing. It's a good thing, then, that we update this guide every year. If you can't always rely on what happens to arrive in your cell to bring you the information on the tides sweeping across our prison systems, you can depend on Prison Lives to bring you what it was all about.

PRISON TRENDING CENTER

MENTAL HEALTH BEHIND BARS

More than half of America's incarcerated population are estimated to have a mental health problem

– 1.2 million prisoners, according to the U.S. Department of Justice Bureau of Statistics.

This is not a new phenomenon. In fact, over a decade ago, in 2006, the then Surgeon General of the United States, Richard Carmona, offered a warning on the mental health crisis that was rapidly swamping the nation's prison systems. In his 49-page report, he urged government and community leaders to formulate strategies to quickly resolve this problem by assisting prisoners both during incarceration and during their transition back into society. He emphasized how vital this move was to ensure that their mental issues did not spill into the public, further taxing the already burdened health care system.

But this report never saw the light of day. It was blocked from publication by the George W. Bush administration because, according to a 2016 USA Today exposé, officials feared that such a reveal from a Surgeon General would require the U.S. to make a financial commitment to prisons that they were not then willing to make.

Ten years after the authoring of the buried report later, the mental health crisis in America's prisons has become an epidemic, now affecting most prisoners in this country.

This chapter explores this epidemic, discusses how it may affect you as a prisoner, and what is being done to address this still growing concern.

And of course, it is full of current resources to assist you in gaining more information, knowledge and help on the mental health conditions affecting you.

Why Should You Care?

Prisoners experience mental illness at a rate 2 to 4 times higher than non-prisoners.

It is currently estimated that 56 percent of state prisoners and 45 percent of federal prisoners are experiencing mental health issues now. This means that roughly every other incarcerated person is currently suffering from a mental health condition.

These illnesses range anywhere from mild depression and social anxiety to serious disorders that require a substantial amount of care.

If you are not personally experiencing any form of mental illness, you likely know several people around you who are. Prison life is challenging enough for someone with a clear mind. Adding mental health issues to an already difficult existence without at least a base of knowledge on the potential issues affecting you puts you at a serious disadvantage at life both while on the inside and once freed. To learn all that you can about these issues and to address them will help you to better prepare you for a successful life now and, most importantly, in the future.

How Big Is This Problem?

More than half of all prisoners have a mental health disorder. The following statistics are the most recently released numbers from the Bureau of Justice Statistics Report: Mental Health Problems of Prison and Jail Inmates.

Prevalence of Mental Health Problems Among Prisoners

Around 4 in 10 jail inmates and 3 in 10 State and Federal prisoners were found to have symptoms of a mental disorder without a recent history. A smaller proportion had both a recent history and symptoms of mental disorder. 17% in State prisons and local jails, and 9% in Federal prisons.

	State Prisoners		Federal Prisoners		Local Jail inmates	
Mental Health Problem	Number	Percent	Number	Percent	Number	Percent
Any Mental Health Problem	705,600	56.2%	70,200	44.6%	479,900	64.2%
History & symptoms	219,700	17.5	13,900	8.9	127,800	17.1
History only	85,400	6.8	7,500	4.8	26,200	3.5
Symptoms only	396,700	31.6	48,100	30.7	322,900	43.2
No Mental Health Problems	549,900	43.8%	86,500	55.2%	267,600	35.6%

Characteristics of Prisoners with Mental Health Disorders

Female prisoners have much higher rates of mental health problems than male prisoners. They varied by racial groups and the age of the prisoner.

Characteristic	State Prisoners	Federal Prisoners	Jail Inmates
All Prisoners	56.2%	44.8%	64.6%
Gender			
Male	55%	43.6%	62.8%
Female	73.1	61.2	75.4
Race			
White	62.2%	49.6%	71.2%
Black	54.7	45.9	63.4
Hispanic	46.3	36.8	50.7
Other	61.9	50.3	69.5
Age			
24 or younger	62.6%	57.8%	70.3%
25-34	57.9	48.2	64.8
35-44	55.9	40.1	62
45-54	51.3	41.6	52.5
55 or older	39.6	36.1	52.4

Symptoms of Prisoners' Mental Health Disorders

Symptoms in past 12 months or since admission	State Prisoners	Federal Prisoners	Jail Inmates
Major Depressive or Mania Symptoms			
Persistently sad or numb	32.9%	23.7%	39.6%
Loss of interest in activities	35.4	30.8	36.4
Increased or decreased appetite	32.4	25.1	42.8
Insomnia or hypersomnia	39.8	32.8	49.2
Psychomotor agitation/retardation	39.6	31.4	46.2
Feelings of worthlessness/guilt	35	25.3	43
Lack of concentration	28.4	21.3	34.1
Attempted suicide	13	6	12.9
Persistent anger/irritability	37.8	30.5	49.4
Increased/decreased sexual desire	34.4	29	29.5
Psychotic Disorder Symptoms			
Delusions	11.8%	7.8%	17.5%
Hallucinations	7.9	4.8	13.7

Why Such a Big Problem?

"We've, frankly, criminalized the mentally ill and used jails as de facto mental institutions."

- Alex Briscoe (Alameda County (Northern California) Health Director)

There are now three times more people with serious mental illnesses in prisons across the U.S. than in mental institutions. Public health officials and researchers point to several factors as the cause of this, including:

- *the closure of state psychiatric hospitals in the late 1960s – closures meant to allow patients to return to their families and live independently;*
- *the poverty and transient lifestyles of many of those who suffer from mental illness, which police are often called on to deal with;*
- *the high correlation rates between substance abuse and serious mental illness;*
- *the lack of adequate community support programs for those with serious mental health disorders, and;*
- *the lack of widespread utilization of diversion programs, such as mental health and drug courts at the beginning of the criminal justice process.*

Psychiatric Facilities and Their Role in Criminal Justice

Out of necessity, the mental health institutions are used to house a fraction of the country's prisoners who have mental illnesses.

In 2016, the Treatment Advocacy Center surveyed all 50 states to determine how many state hospital beds remain and how many of them are set aside for criminal patients.

Total State Hospital Beds:	37,679
Beds Reserved for the Public:	20,078
Beds Reserved for Prisoners:	17,601

State Hospital Beds | Public Beds versus Criminal Beds

State	Beds Available	Beds reserved for criminals
Alabama	383	115
Alaska	80	10
Arizona	303	143
Arkansas	222	126
California	5,905	4,412
Colorado	543	184
Connecticut	615	232
Delaware	122	42
District of Columbia	282	0
Florida	2,648	1,124
Georgia	954	641
Hawaii	202	198
Idaho	174	55
Illinois	1,141	802
Indiana	818	88
Iowa	64	0
Kansas	451	200
Kentucky	499	0
Louisiana	616	70
Maine	144	44
Maryland	950	853
Massachusetts	608	0
Michigan	725	210
Minnesota	194	0
Mississippi	486	35
Missouri	874	874
Montana	174	59
Nebraska	289	67
Nevada	296	76
New Hampshire	158	0
New Jersey	1,543	200
New Mexico	229	44
New York	3,217	720
North Carolina	892	84
North Dakota	140	65
Ohio	1,121	0
Oklahoma	431	200
Oregon	653	416
Pennsylvania	1,334	236
Rhode Island	130	28
South Carolina	493	215

State Hospital Beds | Public Beds versus Criminal Beds		
South Dakota	128	0
Tennessee	562	0
Texas	2,236	1,047
Utah	252	100
Vermont	25	0
Virginia	1,526	356
Washington	729	138
West Virginia	260	0
Wisconsin	458	349
Wyoming	201	28

Challenges in Fixing the Mental Health Crisis in Prisons

The extreme number of prisoners who experience mental health problems present significant challenges for both prisoners and those charges with holding them. Prisoners with serious mental health conditions often require housing and services that are different from those offered to other prisoners. They may need extra medical attention, medication, treatment, added security to prevent additional dangers or even suicide, special programs, rehabilitation services, case management and transitional assistance. Prison officials often find themselves balancing the needs of mentally ill prisoners against the costs of these special services.

Mentally ill prisoners often have difficulties adapting to the routine, structure, and social aspects of prison. Prison workers oftentimes have difficulties understanding these challenges and dealing with them adequately.

Suicide Behind Bars

Suicide remains a leading cause of death for prisoners, ranking third amongst all deaths that occur in prison (after heart disease and cancer.)

Suicides in prison occur at a rate of 16 to 21 per 100,000 prisoners annually (1 in 4,800 to 6,250).

The number of male prisoners who successfully commit suicide greatly outnumber women.

Risk factors for prison suicide:

the presence of significant mental illness

a prior history of suicide attempts

having a lengthy prison sentence (20-plus years)

being 31 to 40 years of age

being housed in segregation or other isolated housing units

being male

Determining Who Needs Help

For a variety of reasons, many prisoners with mental illnesses go to great lengths to hide their condition from staff and others. Some may not even be aware that they have a mental condition or know how to adequately convey what they are experiencing to staff or others.

Prison staff often lacks the proper training to recognize serious mental disorders, much less be able to adequately monitor the entire prison population for signs of emerging problems or distinguish the serious conditions from the less serious ones.

Managing Behaviors and Symptoms

Many mental illnesses, such as schizophrenia and major depressions, may severely affect a prisoner's ability to care for themselves, much less comply with certain orders or procedures.

Other conditions tend to cause prisoners to exhibit aggression, irritability, or paranoia, which may result in a failure to relate to others or get along with them.

Mental illness can evoke fears, hostile reactions, and negative responses from other prisoners, or even staff. Bureau of Justice Statistics have shown that prisoners with mental conditions were twice as likely to as other prisoners to be involved in fights.

All of these lead prison officials to maintain order through any means at their disposal. Much too often, this leads to the use of segregation and solitary confinement (See special report: Locked Up & Locked Down – Segregation of Inmates with Mental Illness later in this chapter.)

Just as often, prison officials lean very heavily on the use of medications to control prisoners, which tend to come with serious challenges of their own, such as side effects and over-prescribing.

Recognizing the Effects of the Prison Environment on Mental Health

Everything about the prison environment negatively impacts someone with a mental illness. The lack of privacy, noise levels, victimization, overcrowding, poor living conditions, lack of meaningful work, violence, forced inactivity, and other environmental conditions often exacerbate mental illness.

For those reasons and more, mentally ill prisoners are one of the greatest risk groups for suicide.

Mental Health and Reentry

More than 90 percent of prisoners will get out of prison. Most of them will come back. Prisoners who experience mental health issues are even more likely to return.
Several factors contribute to this reality.

MENTAL HEALTH TREATMENT DECLINES

Mental health treatment rates decline to roughly 50 percent immediately after release from prison. The use of proper medication likewise dropped substantially after reentry.

	Male prisoners	Medicated	Female prisoners	Medicated
During prison	60.5%	100%	56.8%	100%
2-3 months after release	46.3	74	55	60
8-10 months after release	52.8	59	42.4	40

HOUSING PROBLEMS INCREASE

Returning men and women with mental health conditions have more housing difficulties. Although rates of homelessness were lower post-release than they had been prior to entering prison, those with mental health conditions are more likely than others to have trouble keeping housing.

	Male prisoners with mental illness	Male prisoners w/o mental illness	Female prisoners with mental illness	Female prisoners w/o mental illness
Before prison	20%	16%	27%	27%
1st night post-release	6	6	7	7
2-3 months post-release	7	7	14	3
8-10 months post-release	12	5	13	13

Staying Employed is More Difficult

Ex-offenders with mental health conditions had poorer employment outcomes after release than those without mental illness. From the moment of release, employment opportunities declined more rapidly and never reached the same level experienced by healthier ex-prisoners. Where most returning prisoners report employment rates in line with, or greater than their pre-prison employment levels, those with mental health conditions do not catch up to their pre-prison levels.

	Male prisoners with mental illness	Male prisoners w/o mental illness	Female prisoners with mental illness	Female prisoners w/o mental illness
Before prison	77%	77%	59%	59%
2-3 months post-release	36	60	26	57
8-10 months post-release	59	81	49	67

Supporting Themselves is More Difficult

Men and women with mental disorders are less likely to be able to support themselves financially without depending on others.

	Male prisoners with mental illness	Male prisoners w/o mental illness	Female prisoners with mental illness	Female prisoners w/o mental illness
Legal employment	28%	53%	18%	35%
"Under the table" work	32	32	18	24
Family/friends	57	41	53	65
SSI/SSDI disability	15	4	31	6
Public assistance	30	16	18	20
Illegal activities	6	6	18	14

More Return to Criminal Activity

Men and women with mental conditions are more likely to return to criminal activity then other returning prisoners.

	Male prisoners with mental illness	Male prisoners w/o mental illness	Female prisoners with mental illness	Female prisoners w/o mental illness
Post-release substance abuse	35%	34%	36%	35%
Criminal behavior	45	36	53	45
Re-incarcerated w/in 1 year	17	17	20	21

What Can Be Done?

The following are guidelines laid out by the International Community of the Red Cross' WHO MIND Project, a project for addressing the mental health needs of prisoners. These are meant to assist prisons in improving the probability of successful transitions for those with mental health conditions so that offenders and ex-offenders can more adequately adjust to the community in which they will be living.

Divert people with mental disorders towards the mental health system

Prisons are the wrong place for many people in need of mental health treatment, since the criminal justice system emphasizes deterrence and punishment rather than treatment and care. Legislation can be introduced which allows for the transfer of prisoners to general hospital psychiatric facilities at all stages of the criminal proceedings [arrest, prosecution, trial, imprisonment]. For people with mental disorders who have been charged with committing minor offences, the introduction of mechanisms to divert them towards mental health services before they reach prison will help to ensure that they receive the treatment they need and also contribute to reducing the prison population. The imprisonment of people with mental disorders due to lack of public mental health service alternatives should be strictly prohibited by law

Provide prisoners with access to appropriate mental health treatment and care

Access to assessment, treatment, and [when necessary] referral of people with mental disorders, including substance abuse, should be an integral part of general health services available to all prisoners. The health services provided to prisoners should, as a minimum, be of an equivalent level to those in the community. This may be achieved by providing mental health training to prison health workers, establishing regular visits of a community mental health team to prisons, or enabling prisoners to access health services outside the prison setting. Those requiring more specialist care for example, can be referred to specialist mental health providers where inpatient assessment and treatment can be provided. Primary health care providers in prisons should be provided with basic training in the recognition and basic management of common mental health disorders.

Provide access to acute mental health care in psychiatric wards of general hospitals

When prisoners require acute care, they should be temporarily transferred to psychiatric wards of general hospitals with appropriate security levels. In accordance with the principles of de-institutionalization, special psychiatric prison hospitals are strongly discouraged.

Ensure the availability of psychosocial support and rationally prescribed psychotropic medication

Prisoners-through appropriately trained health care providers-should have the same access to psychotropic medication and psychosocial support for the treatment of mental disorders as people in the general community.

Provide training to staff

Training on mental health issues should be provided to all people involved in prisons including prison administrators, prison guards and mental health workers. Training should enhance staff understanding of mental disorders, raise awareness on human rights, challenge stigmatizing attitudes and encourage mental health promotion for both staff and prisoners. An important element of training for all levels of prison staff should be the recognition and prevention of suicides. In addition, prison health workers need to have more specialized skills in identifying and managing mental disorders.

Provide information/education to prisoners and their families on mental health issues

Prisoners and their families should receive information and education on the nature of mental disorders, with a view to reducing stigma and discrimination, preventing mental disorders and promoting mental health. Information can help prisoners and their families better understand their emotional responses to imprisonment and provide practical strategies on how to minimize the negative effects on their mental health and inform them as to when and how to seek help for a mental disorder.

Promote high standards in prison management

The mental health of all prisoners, including those with mental disorders, will be enhanced by appropriate prison management that promotes and protects human rights. Attention to areas such as sanitation, food, meaningful occupation, physical activity, prevention of discrimination and violence, and promotion of social networks are essential.

Ensure that the needs of prisoners are included in national mental health policies and plans

National mental health policies and/or plans should encompass the mental health needs of the prison population. Where policies and plans fail to do so it may be necessary to advocate for their inclusion. Whenever a mental health policy or plan is being developed, prisons [staff and prisoners] should be included as stakeholders in the development process.

Promote the adoption of mental health legislation that protects human rights

All prisoners, including those with mental disorders, have the right to be treated humanely and with respect for their inherent dignity as human beings. Furthermore, conditions of confinement in prisons must conform to international human rights standards. Mental health legislation can be a powerful tool to protect the rights of people with mental disorders, including prisoners, yet in many countries mental health laws are outdated and fail to address the mental health needs of the prison population. The development of legal provisions that address these needs can help to promote the rights of prisoners, including the right to quality treatment, to confidentiality, to protection from discrimination and violence, and to protection from torture and other cruel, inhumane and degrading treatment [including abusive use of experimentation], among others. Legislation should provide prisoners with mental disorders with procedural protection s within the criminal justice system equivalent to those granted other prisoners. The protection, through legislation, of other basic rights of prisoners such as acceptable living conditions, adequate food, access to open air, meaningful activity, and contact with the family are also important and can further contribute to promotion of good mental health. Independent inspection mechanism such as mental health visiting boards can also be established through legislation, to inspect prisons as well as other mental health facilities in order to monitor conditions for people with mental disorders.

Encourage inter-sectional collaboration

Many problems and issues can be solved by bringing relevant Ministries and other actors together to discuss the needs of prisoners with mental health disorders. Different stakeholders should meet to discuss mental health in prisons and to plan an inter-sectoral response.

NATIONAL INSTITUTE OF MENTAL HEALTH (NIMH)

6001 Executive Blvd., Bethesda, MD 20892-9663

(866) 615-NIMH (6464), (301) 443-4513

www.nimh.nih.gov *nimhinfo@nih.gov*

The National Institute of Mental Health (NIMH) is the lead federal agency for research on mental disorders. It is their mission to transform the understanding and treatment of mental illnesses through basic and clinical research, paving the way for prevention, recovery, and cure. They can provide information on any mental health disorder.

Specific Mental Health Issues

Anxiety Disorders

Are you extremely worried about everything in your life, even if there is little of no reason to worry? Are you very anxious about just getting through the day? Are you afraid that everything will always go badly?

GENERALIZED ANXIETY DISORDER (GAD)

All of us worry about things like health, money, or family problems. But people with GAD are extremely worried about these and many other things, even when there is little of no reason to worry about them. They are very anxious about just getting through the day. They think things will always go badly. At times, worrying keeps people with GAD from doing everyday tasks.

GAD develops slowly. It often starts during the teen years or young adulthood. Symptoms may get better or worse at different times, and often are worse during stress.

People with GAD may visit a doctor many times before they find out they have this disorder. They ask their doctors to help them with headaches or trouble falling asleep, which can be symptoms of GAD, but they don't always get the help they need right away. It may take doctors some time to be sure that a person has GAD instead of something else.

What are the signs and symptoms of GAD?

A person with GAD may:

- Worry very much about everyday things
- Have trouble controlling their constant worries
- Know that they worry much more than they should
- Not be able to relax
- Have a hard time concentrating
- Be easily startled
- Have trouble falling or staying asleep
- Feel tired all the time
- Have headaches, muscle aches, stomach aches, or unexplained pains
- Have a hard time swallowing
- Tremble or twitch
- Be irritable, sweat a lot, and feel light-headed or out of breath
- Have to go to the bathroom a lot

SOCIAL ANXIETY DISORDER (SAD – SOCIAL PHOBIA)

Are you afraid of being judged by others or of being embarrassed all the time? Do you feel extremely fearful and unsure around other people most of the time? Do these worries make it hard for you to get through the day?

What is Social Anxiety Disorder (SAD)?

SAD is a strong fear of being judged by others and of being embarrassed. This fear can be so strong that it gets in the way of going to work or doing everyday things.

Everyone has felt anxious or embarrassed at some point. But people with SAD worry about these things for weeks before they happen.

People with SAD are afraid of doing common things in front of other people. For example, they may be afraid to eat or use the restroom in public. Most people who have SAD know that they shouldn't be afraid as they are, but they can't control it.

SAD usually starts during youth. A doctor can tell that a person has SAD if the person has had symptoms for at least 6 months. Without treatment, SAD can last for many years or a lifetime.

What are the signs and symptoms of SAD?

People with SAD tend to:

Be very anxious about being with other people and have a hard time talking to them, even though they wish they could

Be very self-conscious in front of other people and feel embarrassed

Be very afraid that other people will judge them

Worry for days or weeks before an event where other people will be

Stay away from place where there are other people

Have a hard time making or keeping friends

Blush, sweat, or tremble around other people

Feel nauseous or sick to their stomach when with other people

What Causes Anxiety Disorders?

Anxiety disorders sometimes run in families, but no one knows for sure why some people have it, while others don't. Researchers have found that several parts of the brain are involved in fear and anxiety.

Bipolar Disorder

Do you go through intense moods?

Do you feel very happy and energized some days, and very sad and depressed on other days?

Do these moods last for a week or more?

Do your mood changes make it hard to sleep, stay focused, or go to work?

What is Bipolar Disorder?

Bipolar disorder is a serious brain illness. It is called manic-depressive illness or manic depression. People with bipolar disorder go through unusual mood changes. Sometimes they feel very happy and "up," and are much more energetic and active than usual. This is called manic episode. Sometimes people with bipolar disorder feel very das and "down," have low energy, and are much less active. This is called depression or a depressive episode.

Bipolar disorder is not the same as the normal ups and downs everyone goes through. The mood swings are more extreme than that and are accompanied by changes in sleep, energy level, and the ability to think clearly. Bipolar symptoms are so strong that they can damage relationships and make it hard to live a normal day. They can also be dangerous. Some people with the disorder may try to hurt themselves or attempt suicide.

Anyone can develop bipolar disorder. It often starts in a person's late teen or early adult years. But children and older adults can have bipolar disorder too. The illness usually lasts a lifetime.

What Are the Symptoms of Bipolar Disorder?

Bipolar "mood episodes" include unusual mood changes along with unusual sleeping habits, activity levels, thoughts, or behavior. People may have manic episodes, depressive episodes, or "mixed" episodes. A mixed episode may have both manic and depressive symptoms.

People having a manic episode may:

Feel very "up" or "high"
Feel very "jumpy" or "wired"
Have trouble sleeping
Become more active than usual
Talk really fast about a lot of different things
Be agitated, irritable, or "touchy"
Feel like their thoughts are going very fast
Think they can do a lot of things at once
Do risky things, like spend a lot of money, or have reckless sex

People having depressive episodes may:

Feel very "down" or sad
Sleep too much or too little
Feel like they can't enjoy anything
Feel worried and empty
Have trouble concentrating
Forget things a lot
Eat too much or too little
Feel tired or "slowed down"
Think about death or suicide

How Can I Help Someone with Bipolar Disorder?

Be patient. Encourage your friend to talk, and listen to them carefully. Be understanding about their mood swings. Include them in fun activities. Remind them that getting better is possible, with the right treatment.

Depression

Do you feel tired, helpless, and hopeless? Are you sad most of the time and take no pleasure in your family, friends, or hobbies? Are you having trouble sleeping, eating, and functioning? Have you felt this way for a long time?

What is Depression?

Everyone feels low sometimes, but these feeling usually pass after a few days. When you have depression, the low feelings persist and they can be intense. These low feelings hurt your ability to do things that make up daily life for weeks on end. Depression is a serious illness that needs treatment.

What Are the Different Forms of Depression?

The most common types of depression are:

Major Depression – severe symptoms that interfere with your ability to work, sleep, study, eat, and enjoy life. An episode can only occur once in a person's lifetime, but more often, a per son has several episodes.

Persistent Depressive Disorder – depressed mood that lasts for at least 2 years. A person diagnosed with this may have episodes of major depression along with periods of severe symptoms, but symptoms must last for at least 2 years.

What Are the Signs and Symptoms of Depression?

Different people have different symptoms. Some symptoms of depression include:

Feeling sad or "empty"

- Feeling hopeless, irritable, anxious, or guilty
- Loss of interest in favorite activities
- Feeling very tired
- Not being able to concentrate or remember details
- Not being able to sleep, or sleeping too much
- Overeating, or not wanting to eat at all
- Thoughts of suicide, suicide attempts
- Aches or pains, headaches, cramps, or digestive problems

What Causes Depression?

Depression tends to run in families as a genetic trait. Some genes increase the risk of depression. Others increase resilience – the ability to rescore from hardship – and protect against depression. Experiences such as trauma or abuse during childhood and stress during adulthood can raise risk. However, the same stresses or losses may trigger depression in one person and not another. Factors such as warm family and healthy social connections can increase resilience.

Obsessive-Compulsive Disorder (OCD)

Do you feel the need to check and re-check things over and over? Do you have the same thoughts constantly? Do you feel a very strong need to perform certain rituals repeatedly and feeling like you have no control over what you are doing?

What is OCD?

Everyone double checks things sometimes. But people with OCD feel the need to check things repeatedly, or have certain thoughts or perform routines and rituals over and over. The thoughts and rituals associated with OCD cause distress and get in the way of daily life.

The frequent upsetting thoughts are called obsessions. To try to control them, a person will feel an overwhelming urge to repeat certain rituals or behaviors called compulsions. People with OCD can't controls these.

For many people, OCD starts during childhood or teen years. Most people are diagnosed by the age of 19. Symptoms may come and go and be better or worse at different times.

What Are the Signs and Symptoms of OCD?

People with OCD generally:

- Have repeated thoughts or images about many different things, such as fear of germs, dirt, or intruders; acts of violence; hurting loved ones; sexual acts; conflicts with religious beliefs; or being overly tidy
- Do the same rituals over and over such as washing hands, counting, keeping unneeded items, or repeating the same steps again and again
- Can't control the unwanted thoughts or behaviors
- Don't get pleasure when performing the behaviors or rituals, but get brief relief from the anxiety the thoughts cause
- Spend at least one hour a day on the thoughts and rituals, which cause distress and get in the way of daily life

What Causes OCD?

OCD sometimes runs in families, but no one knows for sure why some people have it, while others don't.

Post-Traumatic Stress Disorder (PTSD)

Are you afraid and upset weeks and months after something bad happens?

What is PTSD?

PTSD is a real illness. You can get PTSD after living through or seeing a dangerous event, such as war, a hurricane, or a bad accident. It makes you feel stresses and afraid after the danger is over.

What Are the Signs and Symptoms of PTSD?

- People with PTSD tend to have:
- Bad dreams
- Flashbacks, or feeling like the scary event is happening again
- Scary thoughts you can't control
- Staying away from places and things that remind you of what happened
- Feeling worried, guilty, or sad
- Feeling alone
- Trouble sleeping
- Feeling on edge
- Angry outbursts
- Thoughts of hurting yourself or others

Schizophrenia

What is Schizophrenia?

Schizophrenia is a serious mental disorder that affects how a person thinks, feels, and behaves. People with schizophrenia may seem like they have lost touch with reality. They may hear voices other people don't hear. They may think other people are trying to hurt them. Sometimes they don't make any sense when they talk.

Schizophrenia symptoms can make it hard for a person to interact with other people, go to school, keep a job, or take care of daily tasks. The symptoms can be very disabling, but with effective treatment many people experience recovery.

Symptoms usually start between the ages of 16 and 30, slightly more often in men than women.

What Are the Symptoms of Schizophrenia?

Schizophrenia symptoms fall into three categories: positive, negative, and cognitive.

"Positive symptoms" are psychotic experiences that are generally not seen in healthy people. People with these symptoms are sometimes unable to tell real from imagined. These symptoms can range from barely noticeable to severe. Positive symptoms include:

- Hallucinations
- Delusions
- Thought disorders
- Movement disorders

"Negative" symptoms refer to social withdrawal, difficulty showing emotions, or difficulty functioning normally. Negative symptoms include:

- Talking in a dull voice
- Showing no facial expression
- Having trouble experiencing happiness
- Having trouble planning or sticking with an activity
- Talking very little to other people

What Causes Schizophrenia?

Many factors may cause schizophrenia, including:

Genes, however just because a family member has schizophrenia does not mean that anyone else in the family will have it

Environment, such as exposure to viruses or nutrition problems before birth

Brain structure or brain chemistry

"Cognitive" symptoms are not easy to see, but they can make it hard for people to have a job or take care of themselves. Often, these symptoms are detected only when specific tests are performed. Cognitive symptoms include:

- Difficulty using information to make decisions
- Problems using information immediately after learning it
- Trouble paying attention

Locked Up and Locked Down

Segregation of Inmates with Mental Illness

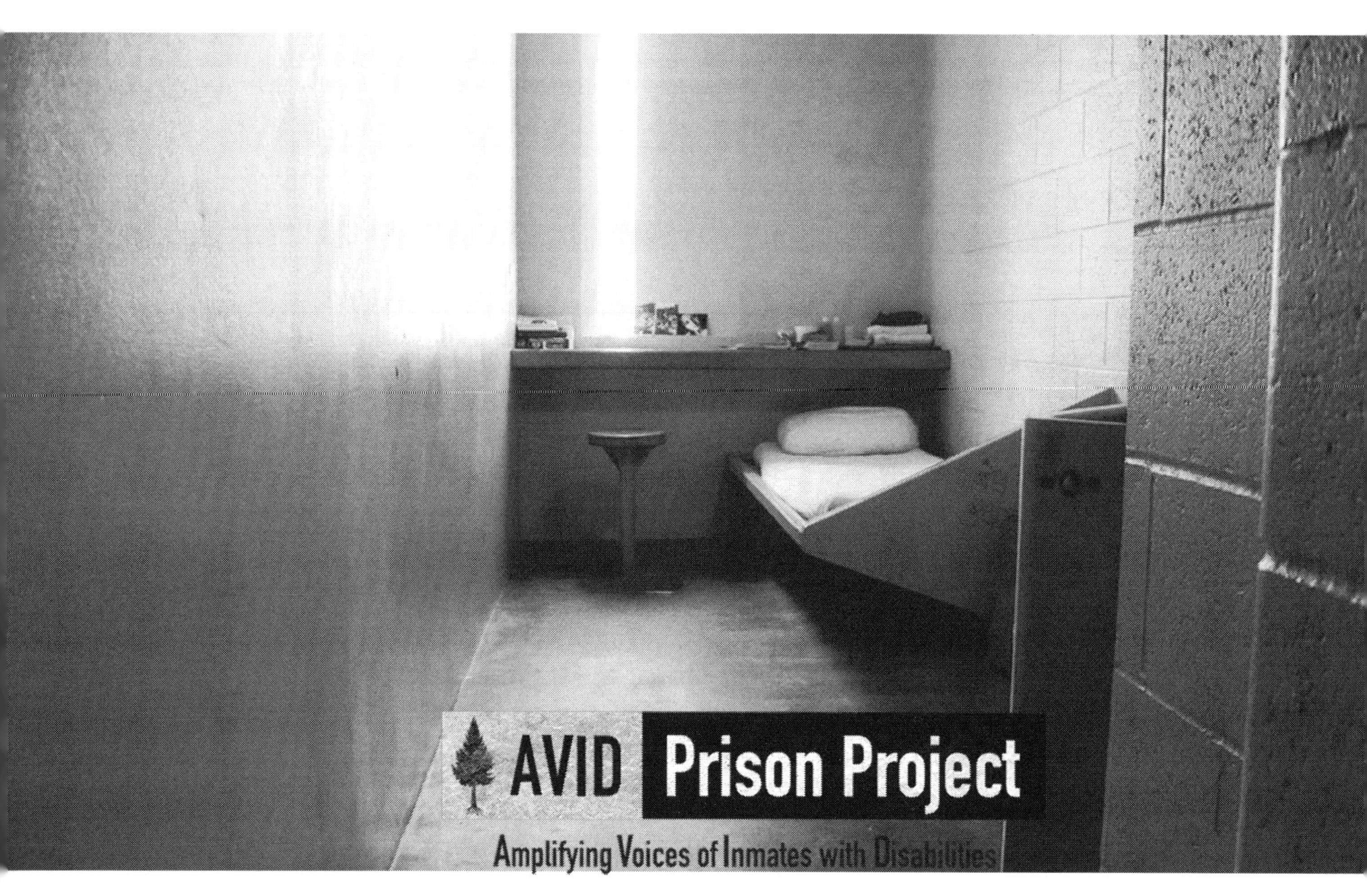

Locked Up and Locked Down

Segregation of Inmates with Mental Illness

By Anna Guy
Amplifying Voices of Inmates with Disabilities Prison Project
September 8, 2016

EXECUTIVE SUMMARY

Our nation's prison systems have been housing people in solitary confinement, or segregation,[1] for decades.[2] As inmate populations increased throughout the 1980s and 1990s, prisons turned to segregation, claiming it was a necessary intervention to curb institutional violence.[3] As a result, between 80,000 to 100,000 inmates are currently placed in small single person cells for 22 to 24 hours per day, for days, if not months or years at a time.[4] Notably, many of those housed in segregation found their way there due to behaviors associated with a mental illness,[5] or they developed symptoms of mental illness due to their prolonged isolation.[6] Many inmates with mental illness are not only locked up and serving a sentence, they are disproportionately locked down in segregation, where they remain isolated in their cells and experience severely restricted access to programs and activities, including mental health treatment.[7]

Research suggests that segregation does not in fact decrease violence or make prisons safer.[8] Moreover, experts have found that the crushing isolation of segregation has a debilitating effect on inmates, especially inmates with mental illness.[9] Even the president of the United States has recognized that a person's mental illness can worsen in segregation, and inmates with mental illness are more likely to commit suicide.[10] In response to these findings, advocates have argued that the imposition of such restrictive conditions on inmates with mental illness violates the Eighth Amendment prohibition of cruel and unusual punishment as well as the Americans with Disabilities Act (ADA) and Section 504 of the Rehabilitation Act of 1973 (Rehab Act), and have fought for an overhaul of the use of segregation in the nation's prison systems.

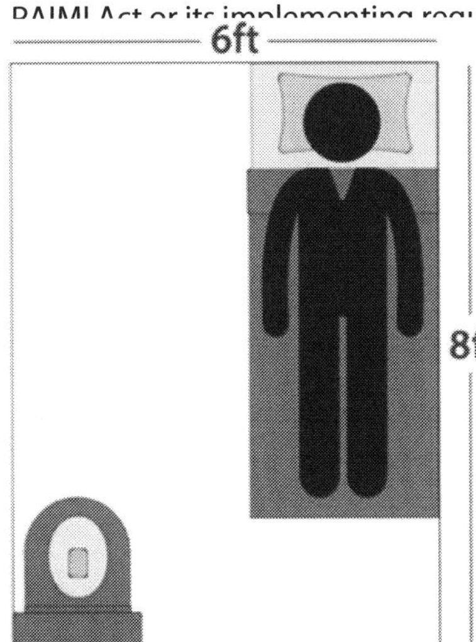

Very few outsiders are allowed into prisons, and the public rarely gets to witness the conditions in which many inmates are confined. In recent years, protection and advocacy agencies (P&As), organizations granted with the special federal authority to enter facilities that serve people with disabilities, have been going to the most segregated areas of prisons to identify issues facing people with disabilities.[11] P&As have received countless reports of abuse and neglect of inmates in segregation, including prolonged isolation, deplorable conditions, inadequate care, increased self-harm and suicide attempts, and even death.[12]

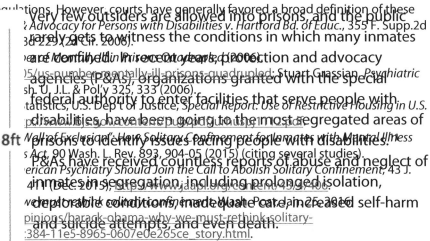

[1] Definitions of the terms "solitary confinement," "isolation," and "segregation" vary between jurisdictions and facilities. This report uses the term "segregation" to describe the general practice, described in more detail below, of isolating an inmate for 22 to 24 hours a day in a small cell.

[2] *See* Am. Civil Liberties Union, *The Dangerous Overuse of Solitary Confinement in the United States* 2 (2014), https://www.aclu.org/sites/default/files/assets/stop_solitary_briefing_paper_updated_august_2014.pdf; Peter Scharff Smith, *The Effects of Solitary Confinement on Prison Inmates: A Brief History and Review of the Literature*, 34 Crime & Just. 441, 442-43 (2006).

[3] *See* Chad S. Briggs et al., *The Effect of Supermaximum Security Prisons on Aggregate Levels of Institutional Violence*, 41 Criminology 1341, 1345 (2003).

[4] *See* Sarah Baumgartel et al., The Liman Program, Yale Law School, Association of State Correctional Administrators, *Time-in-Cell: The ASCA-Liman 2014 National Survey of Administrative Segregation in Prison* ii (2015), [illegible] liman_administrative_segregation_report_sep_2_2015.pdf.

[5] In discussing inmates with mental illness, this report uses the broad definition of "individual with a mental illness" from the Protection and Advocacy for Individuals with Mental Illness (PAIMI) Act. Under this act, an "individual with a mental illness" is an individual "who has a significant mental illness or emotional impairment, as determined by a mental health professional qualified under the laws and regulations of the State…." 42 U.S.C. § 10802(4)(A). "Significant mental illness" and "emotional impairment" are not further defined in the PAIMI Act or its implementing regulations. However, courts have generally favored a broad definition of these [illegible] & Advocacy for Persons with Disabilities v. Hartford Bd. of Educ., 355 F. Supp.2d [illegible] 3d 229 (2d Cir. 2006).

[illegible] of Mentally Ill in Prisons Quadrupled (2006) [illegible] 05/us-number-mentally-ill-prisons-quadrupled; Stuart Grassian, *Psychiatric* [illegible] sh. U. J.L. & Pol'y 325, 333 (2006).

[illegible] tatistics, U.S. Dep't of Justice, *Special Report: Use of Restrictive Housing in U.S.* [illegible]

[illegible] *Wall of Exclusion": How Solitary Confinement for Inmates with Mental Illness* [illegible] s Act, 90 Wash. L. Rev. 893, 904-05 (2015) (citing several studies).

[illegible] *erican Psychiatry Should Join the Call to Abolish Solitary Confinement*, 43 J. [illegible] 411 (Dec. 2015), [illegible]

[illegible] *we must rethink solitary confinement*, Wash. Post, Jan. 25, 2016, [illegible] pinions/barack-obama-why-we-must-rethink-solitary- [illegible] 384-11e5-8965-0607e0e265ce_story.html.

[illegible] tion of individuals with mental illness. However, some of the same concepts [illegible] and intellectual disabilities, and people with brain injuries. Therefore, much of the analysis applied throughout this report to individuals with mental illness holds for people with other cognitive disabilities as well.

[12] *See* Rebecca Vallas, Center for American Progress, *Disabled Behind Bars: The Mass Incarceration of People With Disabilities in America's Jails and Prisons* 1-2 (2016), https://www.americanprogress.org/issues/criminal-justice/report/2016/07/18/141447/disabled-behind-bars/.

t of a 6 ft. by 8 ft. cell.

In recognition of the growing population of inmates with disabilities,[12] in 2012, Disability Rights Washington, the P&A for Washington State, began focusing more attention on the state's prisons, investigating the conditions of these correctional settings and working on creative solutions to some of the most serious problems faced by inmates with mental illness, brain injuries, and physical and intellectual disabilities. In early 2014, with increased funding through a private grant, Disability Rights Washington created Amplifying Voices of Inmates with Disabilities (AVID), a project with the sole purpose of protecting and advancing the rights of inmates with disabilities and assisting those who are reentering society.[13] In September 2014, AVID brought together staff from the P&As in New York, South Carolina, Arizona, Colorado, Louisiana, and Texas, as well as from the National Disability Rights Network, to strategize about ways to increase national attention on the issues faced by inmates with disabilities.

This report, which has grown out of that collaborative national effort, examines issues related to the segregation of inmates with mental illness in our state prison systems, including the harmful effects of prolonged isolation on that population, the excessive use of force that often precedes or accompanies placement in segregation, and the restricted access to programs and services in segregation.[14] P&As from across the country provided examples of either past or ongoing advocacy, demonstrating the crucial role that P&As have played in fighting against the excessive use of segregation of people with mental illness in our nation's prisons.[15] This advocacy is multi-modal, ranging from routine monitoring, to informal and individual advocacy, to systemic litigation.

This report begins with a brief overview of the P&A system, explains the different types of advocacy P&As use, describes the effect of segregation on people with mental illness, and outlines legal protections related to segregation of inmates with mental illness. Next, this report details the work P&As across the country have done to advance the rights of inmates with mental illness in segregation, dividing the advocacy into non-litigation and litigation strategies. Finally, the report concludes with a number of federal and state recommendations to build on the momentum gained by the P&As and their partners, including:

1) Increased federal funding to the P&A network for corrections-based monitoring and advocacy;

---

[13] To fund AVID, DRW applied for *cy pres* funds that were the result of litigation against AT&T regarding prison phone charges. DRW, along with dozens of other organizations in Washington, was awarded funding from this *cy pres* pool to conduct corrections-based advocacy. DRW has since obtained additional private grant funding to expand the AVID project to encompass advocacy in specific local Washington jails as well.

[14] While many P&As engage in advocacy relating to conditions in city jails, county jails, and immigration detention or holding facilities, this report primarily focuses on the work P&As have done in state prisons, with one example from a federal correctional facility.

[15] The report includes examples from the following 21 states: Arizona, Colorado, Connecticut, Florida, Illinois, Indiana, Iowa, Kentucky, Maryland, Massachusetts, Montana, Nebraska, Nevada, New York, North Carolina, Ohio, Oregon, South Carolina, Tennessee, Vermont, and Washington.

2) Creation of independent corrections ombuds offices at the state level in order to address inmate concerns before they rise to the level of litigation;
3) Increased data collection by the U.S. Department of Justice's Bureau of Justice Statistics regarding the prevalence of people with mental illness in U.S. prisons and jails;
4) Increased monitoring and outreach in prisons by P&As across the country; and
5) Fostering of collaborative relationships between state prison systems and P&As.

Ultimately, this report is a call to action and is meant to encourage partnerships among the P&A network, prison advocacy groups, and interested stakeholders to increase focus on what has become an international conversation on the use of segregation in America's prisons.

VOICES FROM SEGREGATION

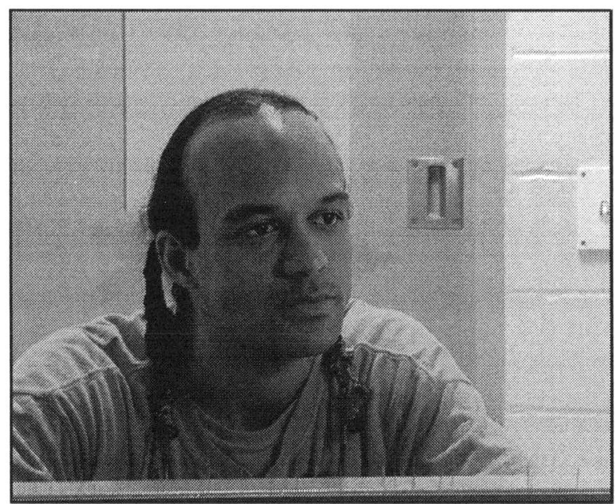

Daniel Perez,
Washington

"Segregation, for me, was pretty much hell…"

Eldorado Brown,
Washington

"They don't understand that placing me in the hole exacerbates my mental illness to a whole different degree… "

stin Rueb,
olorado

eally can't deal with other people
y well anymore…"

Five Mualimm-ak,
New York

"It's a different lens living in a world of punishment."

BACKGROUND

Overview of the P&A System

The P&A system was created in the 1970s after a series of news reports exposed the horrific institutional conditions in which people with developmental disabilities were housed.[16] This news coverage prompted federal legislation to create a national network of P&As to advocate on behalf of people with developmental disabilities. Since that time, additional legislation has been passed, expanding the scope of P&As to include advocacy on behalf of all people with disabilities, in any setting, from the community to prison.[17] This legislation also grants P&As the authority to monitor settings in which people with disabilities live, work, or receive services, as well as the power to investigate allegations of abuse and neglect of people with disabilities.[18] This unique authority allows P&As to monitor and investigate in even the most segregated settings, and gives P&As access to individuals and records as they seek to enforce and defend the rights of people with disabilities. As increasing numbers of people with disabilities have become incarcerated, the P&A network has used its access authority to conduct monitoring and advocacy in the nation's prisons.

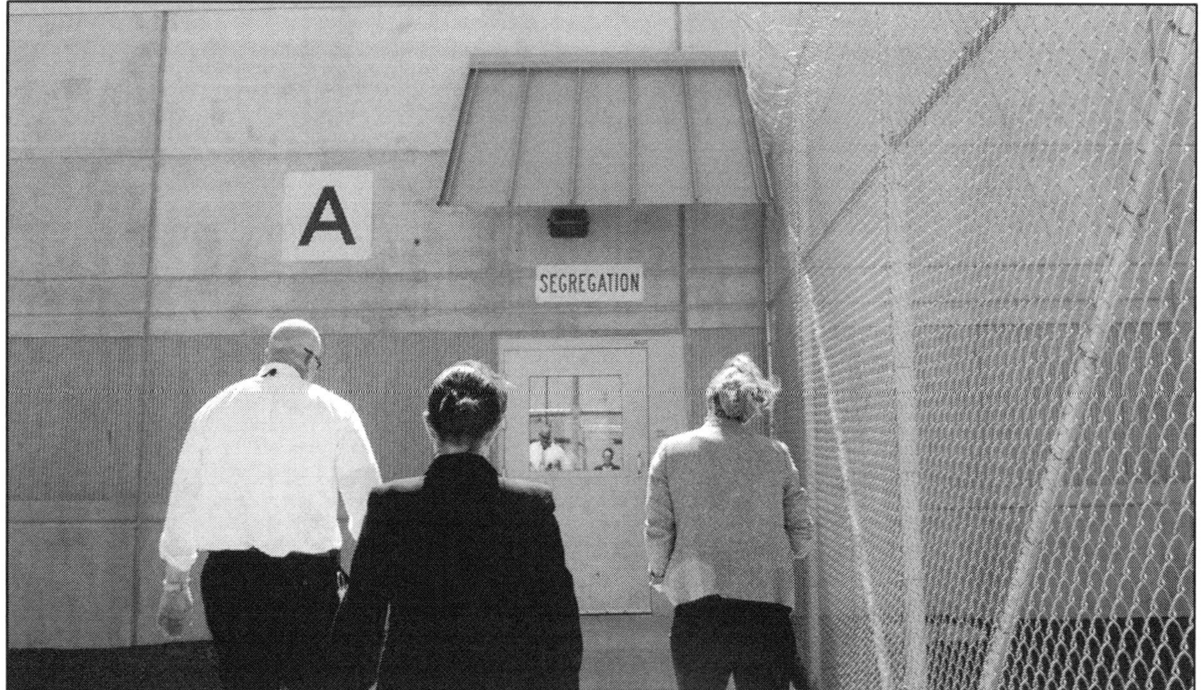

AVID Prison Project attorneys walk toward the entrance of a segregation unit.

---

[16] *See* Nat'l Disability Rights Network, *Our History*, http://www.ndrn.org/about/26-our-history.html (last visited July 22, 2016).

[17] *See, e.g.,* Developmental Disabilities Assistance and Bill of Rights Act of 1975, 42 U.S.C. § 15041-15045; Protection and Advocacy for Individuals with Mental Illnesses Act, 42 U.S.C. § 10801-10851; Protection and Advocacy of Individual Rights, 29 U.S.C. § 794e.

[18] *See* 42 C.F.R. § 51.42(b).

Methods of P&A Advocacy

In challenging the segregation of inmates with mental illness, there are numerous methods of advocacy that may be employed by the P&A network.[19] Given the statutory requirements in many of the authorizing statutes for P&As, agencies generally begin with the lowest level of intervention required, employing higher levels of advocacy as needed.[20] This advocacy may range from information and assistance to individual inmates, to systemic monitoring or large scale litigation. For the purposes of this report, these levels of advocacy, described below, are separated into two categories: non-litigation and litigation.

Non-Litigation

Non-litigation advocacy encompasses informal advocacy within a prison, systemic advocacy with corrections officials, and coordination with community stakeholders and policy makers. These advocacy strategies are described briefly below.

Informal Advocacy Within a Prison

P&As routinely provide information and assistance to inmates with mental illness over the phone or by letter. By providing prison policies, complaint forms, resources, and practical suggestions, P&As assist inmates with mental illness in navigating the prison system to access appropriate programs and services, and support them in becoming effective self-advocates. This service also allows P&As to monitor common issues occurring in the prisons, and identify any potential systemic concerns as they arise.

P&As also undertake individual representation of inmates in segregation, often beginning any such case by advocating with prison mental health staff and following through with prison administrative staff. Through working with staff within the prison, P&As have been able to secure less restrictive conditions for inmates.

Systemic Advocacy with Corrections Officials

P&As may also develop relationships with officials within a state's department of corrections. Through meeting and sharing information with prison administrations at both individual facilities and headquarters, prisons are able to take proactive steps to address issues P&As identify. P&As also often use their federal authority to monitor the conditions in prison, meeting with inmates in segregation during such visits to discuss their concerns regarding

---

[19] Given the exhaustion requirements of the Prison Litigation Reform Act, most inmates and advocates begin with advocacy via the prison's internal grievance system, moving onto other forms of advocacy, particularly litigation, only after exhausting the avenues of redress available within the prison. *See* 42 U.S.C. § 1997e(a).

[20] *See* 42 U.S.C. § 10807(a) (requiring that P&As exhaust administrative remedies where appropriate before commencing litigation).

conditions in segregation and access to mental health care in those units. When P&As raise issues to prison officials that are identified during these monitoring visits, prisons are able to resolve many problems and avoid litigation.

Coordination with Community Stakeholders and Policy Makers

P&As have also worked to create and expand the network of advocates and community stakeholders dedicated to prison-related issues. Through working with families and friends of inmates with disabilities, as well as other community organizations, P&As have built coalitions to advocate within the prison administration as well as with state and local government officials on behalf of inmates with mental illness. This work has ranged from providing training on disability-related issues to community groups and governmental agencies, to participating in workgroups and taskforces related to criminal justice and prison issues.

Similarly, P&As have worked to educate policy makers about prison-related issues, including commenting on proposed state legislation regarding prison programs, and offering information and insight related to policy and legislative reform efforts aimed at protecting the rights of inmates with mental illness in prison.

AVID Prison Project attorney, Anna Guy, speaks with an inmate in segregation through a cuff port.

Litigation

When litigation has been required, P&As have raised claims based on the Eighth and Fourteenth Amendments of the U.S. Constitution as well as the ADA and the Rehab Act. While P&As have engaged in litigation in both state and federal courts on behalf of individual inmates, these cases are most often brought as class actions. In the last decade, P&As have increasingly served as organizational plaintiffs in such cases, representing the interests of their constituents in challenging systemic conditions and practices that impact inmates with disabilities.[21]

Overall, this powerful range of advocacy tools makes the P&A network uniquely positioned to achieve a broad range of positive individual and systemic outcomes for people with mental illness in prisons and can attract partnerships with other advocacy groups and law firms to combine resources and expertise to reach common goals on behalf of the network's constituents.

The Effect of Segregation on Inmates with Mental Illness

Segregation is generally recognized as the isolated confinement of an inmate for 22 to 24 hours a day in a small cell, typically about six by eight feet, containing only a bed, a sink, and a toilet, and enclosed by a metal door with a small window and cuff port.[22] While inmates may be placed in segregation for a number of reasons, segregation can last for days, months, years, and even decades, regardless of its purpose.[23]

Designed to disconnect inmates from most forms of human contact and environmental stimulation, inmates in segregation have little access to programming, services, or treatment during the course of their confinement.[24] For inmates with mental illness, these conditions are devastating as contact with mental health clinicians typically consists of brief assessments conducted at cell-front.[25] Mental health interventions such as therapy and structured

---

[21] The requirements for an agency asserting organizational standing are set forth in *Hunt v. Wash. State Apple Adver. Comm'n*, 432 U.S. 333, 343 (1997).

[22] *See* Alison Shames et al., Vera Institute of Justice, *Solitary Confinement: Common Misconceptions and Emerging Safe Alternatives* 8 (2015), http://www.vera.org/sites/default/files/resources/downloads/solitary-confinement-misconceptions-safe-alternatives-report_1.pdf.

[23] *See* Thomas L. Hafemeister & Jeff George, *The Ninth Circle of Hell: An Eighth Amendment Analysis of Imposing Prolonged Supermax Solitary Confinement on Inmates with a Mental Illness*, 90 Denv. U. L. Rev. 1, 47-48 (2012).

[24] *See* American Bar Association, *ABA Standards for Criminal Justice: Treatment of Prisoners* 55-57, 95-99 (3d ed. 2011), http://www.americanbar.org/content/dam/aba/publications/criminal_justice_standards/Treatment_of_Prisoners.authcheckdam.pdf (recommending that inmates in segregation be provided equal access to services and mental health treatment).

[25] Grassian, 22 Wash. U. J.L. & Pol'y at 333.

activities are not usually available in these settings, and prison rules commonly preclude segregated inmates from leaving their cells; thus, the only mental health treatment for inmates in segregation is often psychotropic medication.[26] Furthermore, meaningful interaction with staff and the outside world is also restricted; food and other items are usually passed through a slot in the cell's steel door, and visitation and telephone communication may be limited or banned altogether.[27] Access to fresh air and sunlight is also limited; recreation time is spent in a cage-like enclosure up to one hour per day, three to five times a week.[28] Moreover, lights in segregation are often illuminated 24 hours per day.[29]

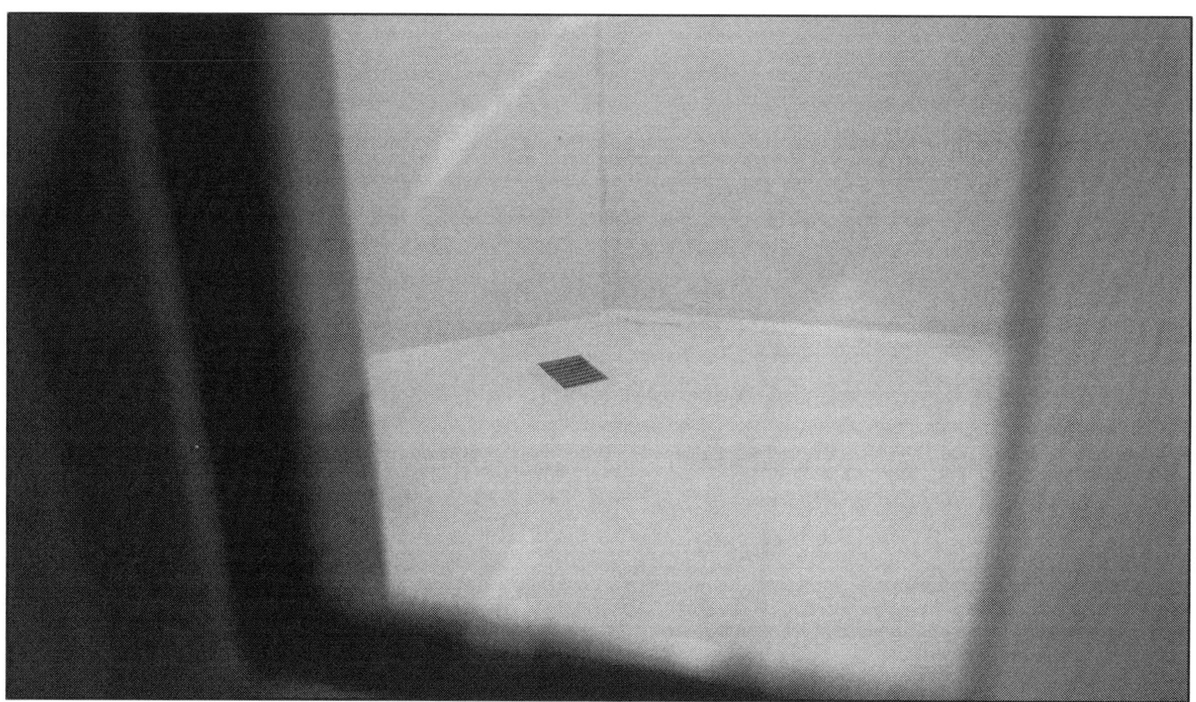

A "rubber room" used as an isolation cell for inmates at risk of self-harm. The cell has a grate in the floor where inmates relieve themselves.

Research reveals that inmates placed in these harsh conditions often experience intense mental and physical distress; for inmates with mental illness, these conditions can have a catastrophic impact. Inmates in segregation routinely report extreme sensory deprivation, sleep deprivation, psychiatric decompensation, hallucinations, and behaviors relating to self-harm and even suicide.[30] Because prison staff that work on these units often have little to no

---

[26] Jeffrey L. Metzner & Jamie Fellner, *Solitary Confinement and Mental Illness in U.S. Prisons: A Challenge for Medical Ethics*, 38 J. Am. Acad. Psychiatry & L. Online 104, 105 (2010), *http://www.jaapl.org/content/38/1/104.full*.
[27] *See* Am. Civil Liberties Union, *The Dangerous Overuse of Solitary Confinement in the United States* 3 (2014), https://www.aclu.org/sites/default/files/assets/stop_solitary_briefing_paper_updated_august_2014.pdf
[28] *See* Metzner & Fellner, *supra* note 25, at 104.
[29] *See* American Bar Association, *ABA Standards for Criminal Justice: Treatment of Prisoners* 32 (3d ed. 2011), http://www.americanbar.org/content/dam/aba/publications/criminal_justice_standards/Treatment_of_Prisoners.authcheckdam.pdf.
[30] *See* Maclyn Willigan, Solitary Watch, *What Solitary Confinement Does to the Human Brain*,

training related to working with inmates with mental illness, reports have found it is not unusual for prisons to employ chemical agents such as pepper spray or physical restraints to curtail or control the behaviors of inmates with mental illness in segregation.[31]

In addition to these harsh conditions, inmates in segregation do not have access to the same programs and activities available to inmates in other, less restricted, areas of the prison. Many systems require that inmates in solitary confinement be escorted in restraints by two or more officers.[32] This and other security restrictions often result in limited access to programs such as skill building, education, vocational training, group therapy, socialization, or other activities. These activities are important tools for helping inmates learn skills for daily living and medication compliance, including how to take care of their most basic personal hygiene and everyday needs. Thus, limiting access to programs hinders the ability of inmates to live and cope with the symptoms of their mental illnesses over time.[33]

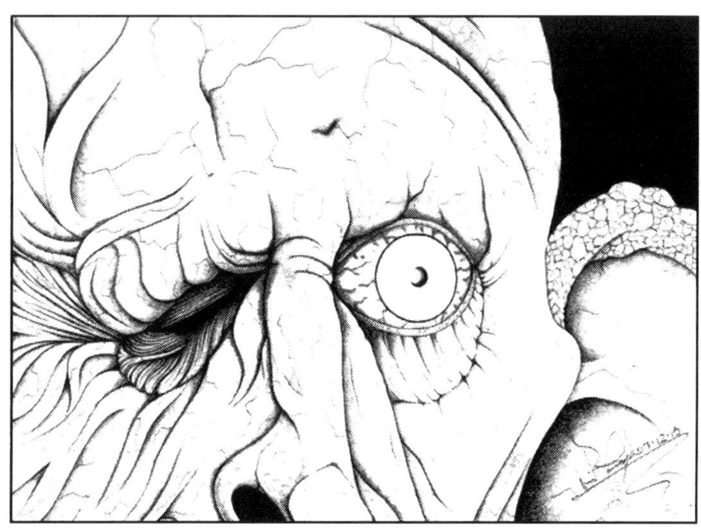

A black and white drawing of a wrinkled face with one eye, by inmate David Troupe.

Moreover, when the symptoms of a segregated inmate's mental illness escalate, the inmate may be sent to suicide watch, an even more restrictive form of segregation. While many inmates are transferred to suicide watch from another segregated setting after inflicting self-harm or attempting suicide, rather than receive therapeutic services necessary to alleviate symptoms of mental illness, inmates on suicide watch are placed under even more extreme conditions of segregation. Here, inmates are watched 24 hours a day and are generally stripped of their personal belongings, clothed in a suicide smock, and forced to urinate and defecate through a grate in the floor.[34]

---

http://solitarywatch.com/2014/08/04/what-solitary-confinement-does-to-the-human-brain/ (Aug. 2014).

[31] Am. Civil Liberties Union, *The Dangerous Overuse of Solitary Confinement in the United States* 5 (2014), https://www.aclu.org/sites/default/files/assets/stop_solitary_briefing_paper_updated_august_2014.pdf.

[32] Am. Pub. Health Ass'n, *Solitary Confinement as a Public Health Issue* (2013), https://www.apha.org/policies-and-advocacy/public-health-policy-statements/policy-database/2014/07/14/13/30/solitary-confinement-as-a-public-health-issue.

[33] *See* Sasha Abramsky & Jamie Fellner, Human Rights Watch, *Ill-Equipped: U.S. Prisons and Offenders with Mental Illness* 110 (2003), http://www.hrw.org/reports/2003/usa1003/usa1003.pdf.

[34] *See, e.g.*, Complaint, *Disability Advocates, Inc. v. N.Y. State Office of Mental Health*, No. 02 CV 4002 (S.D.N.Y. May 28, 2002), http://hrw.org/reports/2003/usa1003/NYS_Disability_Advocates_Complaint.pdf; Expert Report of Kathryn Burns & Jane Haddad for Plaintiffs at 28, *Bradley v. Hightower*, No. 92-A-70-N (N.D. Ala. June 30, 2000), http://hrw.org/reports/2003/usa1003/Alabama_Expert_Report_Hightower.pdf.

In the aggregate, while segregation is difficult for all inmates, it is particularly difficult for inmates with mental illness. While these inmates often have unique needs for specialized housing, programming, and treatment, such services are generally not available or provided. Furthermore, inmates with mental illness are often placed in the most restrictive forms of segregated housing where they receive even less mental health care and are treated more harshly than other inmates in segregation. As a result, inmates with mental illness in segregation are often subject to the most extreme conditions of confinement.

Laws Related to Segregation of Inmates with Mental Illness

In recent years, inmates and advocates have brought lawsuits challenging these excessively harsh conditions and limited access to treatment and programs, alleging that segregation violates the Eighth Amendment prohibition of "cruel and unusual punishments," particularly with respect to inmates with mental illness.[35] While the U.S. Supreme Court has held that this Eighth Amendment prohibition applies in segregation cases,[36] inmates must prove that prison staff acted with "deliberate indifference to a substantial risk of serious harm to a prisoner" to demonstrate an Eighth Amendment violation.[37] Courts have found that this "deliberate indifference" standard is equivalent to "recklessly disregarding that risk."[38] Mere negligence is not sufficient to demonstrate deliberate indifference.[39]

An Eighth Amendment challenge alleging deliberate indifference must satisfy both a subjective and objective test.[40] Under this two pronged test, the prison official must be shown to be subjectively indifferent, in that he "disregards a risk of harm of which he is aware."[41] Whether the prison official had knowledge of the risk can be demonstrated "in the usual ways, including inference from circumstantial evidence, ... and a factfinder may conclude that a prison official knew of a substantial risk from the very fact that the risk was obvious."[42] The second prong, the objective test, requires that the inmate show that the prison official's acts violated "contemporary standards of decency."[43] Such objective indifference can be manifested by prison officials in a number of ways, including intentionally delaying or denying an inmate's access to medical care, including mental health care, interfering with prescribed treatment, or in the systemic delivery of medical care.[44]

---

[35] The Eighth Amendment reads: "Excessive bail shall not be required, nor excessive fines imposed, nor cruel and unusual punishments inflicted." U.S. Const. amend. VIII.

[36] *See Hutto v. Finney*, 437 U.S. 678, 685 (1978).

[37] *Farmer v. Brennan*, 511 U.S. 825, 836 (1994).

[38] *Id.*

[39] *See Ruiz v. Johnson*, 37 F. Supp.2d 855, 887 (S.D. Tex. 1999), *rev'd and remanded sub nom. Ruiz v. United States*, 243 F.3d 941 (5th Cir. 2001).

[40] *See Helling v. McKinney*, 509 U.S. 25, 35 (1993).

[41] *Farmer*, 511 U.S. at 837.

[42] *Id.* at 842.

[43] *Estelle v. Gamble*, 429 U.S. 97, 103 (1976).

[44] *See id.* at 104-05.

Various courts have applied the two-prong deliberate indifference test to segregation claims brought by inmates with mental illness and found that segregation of this population violates the constitutional prohibition of cruel and unusual punishment. For instance, in *Madrid v. Gomez*, a California district court found that housing inmates with mental illness and inmates "at a particularly high risk" of experiencing mental illness in segregation violated the Eighth Amendment.[45] However, the court also held that conditions in segregation did not violate the Eighth Amendment for those inmates with "normal resilience."[46] In *Ruiz v. Johnson*, a Texas district court went further and held that the conditions of Texas' administrative segregation units violated the Eighth Amendment "through extreme deprivations which cause profound and obvious psychological pain and suffering."[47] With respect to inmates with mental illness, the court further reasoned that "the severe and psychologically harmful deprivations of [the] administrative segregation units are, by our evolving and maturing society's standards of humanity and decency, found to be cruel and unusual punishment."[48] The court in *Jones' El v. Berge* took the extraordinary step of removing inmates with mental illness from a super-max prison after finding the mental health screening and monitoring tools grossly inadequate and ineffective, holding deliberate indifference existed because the tools "serve as little more than band-aids to the potentially detrimental conditions to which defendants are subjecting mentally ill inmates."[49]

Along with the Eighth Amendment, advocates have argued that Title II of the ADA and Section 504 of the Rehab Act preclude prisons from discriminating against inmates with mental illness.[50] While the ADA protects inmates in state-run prisons, the Rehab Act applies to prisons that receive federal funding. Together, these statutes provide non-constitutional causes of action to challenge placement in segregation on the basis of mental illness, prolonged stays in segregation due to symptoms of mental illness, and the limitation and denial of access to services and programs to inmates in segregation with mental illness.[51]

---

[45] *Madrid v. Gomez*, 889 F. Supp. 1146, 1265 (N.D. Cal. 1995).
[46] *Id.* at 1280.
[47] *Ruiz*, 37 F. Supp.2d at 907.
[48] *Id.* at 915.
[49] *Jones' El v. Berge*, 164 F. Supp.2d 1096, 1122, 1124 (W.D. Wis. 2001).
[50] The protections of the Rehab Act are substantially the same as those afforded under Title II of the ADA in relation to inmates. *Bragdon v. Abbott*, 524 U.S. 624, 632 (1998); 42 U.S.C. § 12201(a).
[51] For more information about the ADA and prison, *see* Rachael Seevers, Disability Rights Washington, Amplifying Voices of Inmates with Disabilities Prison Project, *Making Hard Time Harder: Programmatic Accommodations for Inmates with Disabilities Under the Americans with Disabilities Act* (2016), http://www.avidprisonproject.org/. *See also* Margo Schlanger, *Memorandum Re: The ADA/Rehab Act and solitary confinement* (2015), https://www.law.umich.edu/facultyhome/margoschlanger/Documents/Schlanger_ADA-seg_memo_FINAL_12-09-2015.pdf.

PRISON ADVOCACY BY THE PROTECTION AND ADVOCACY SYSTEM

As described below, P&As and their partners have successfully advocated to limit or end the segregation of inmates with mental illness in various state and federal systems, employing advocacy methods ranging from basic information and assistance to individual inmates to large-scale systemic litigation. These examples, separated into non-litigation and litigation, demonstrate the critical role P&As have played in providing independent external monitoring and advocacy in our nation's prisons while also making clear that much still needs to be done to advance and protect the rights of inmates with mental illness in segregation.

Non-Litigation

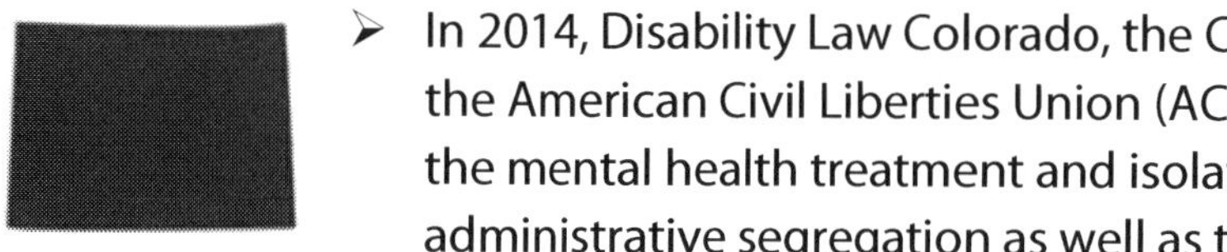

- In 2014, Disability Law Colorado, the Colorado P&A, teamed up with the American Civil Liberties Union (ACLU) of Colorado to investigate the mental health treatment and isolation of inmates in administrative segregation as well as the conditions in the residential treatment programs for inmates with mental illness within the Colorado prison system. Disability Law Colorado's concerns included the prolonged segregation of inmates with serious mental illness; the failure to provide adequate mental health care and medication management; the failure to maintain adequate numbers of appropriately trained mental health, clinical, and correctional staff; and the failure to provide meaningful out-of-cell time for recreation, therapy, and socialization. Soon after the investigation began, the prison made policy changes that instituted a minimum of 10 hours of out-of-cell therapeutic and 10 hours of out-of-cell non-therapeutic recreation per week, depending on an inmate's custody level. Monitoring and investigation are ongoing to ensure compliance with the policy changes.

- In 2015, to address concerns that inmates in segregation were routinely denied access to mental health services, including medication, Connecticut Office of Protection and Advocacy for Persons with Disabilities met with the Commissioner of the Department of Corrections and various other prison personnel, including clinical staff, to discuss inmate access to mental health treatment at the State's supermax facility. After meeting, it was agreed that inmates with mental illness and a P&A advocate would participate in treatment decisions with prison clinical staff.

- In 2015, Disability Rights Iowa selected one men's facility and one women's facility to investigate the use of segregation of inmates with mental illness as a punishment for violations of institutional rules, including the number of occurrences, duration of segregation, and consideration of mental illness in disciplinary proceedings. The Department of Corrections has been supportive of the effort, has allowed the P&A an unprecedented level of access to complete its investigation, and has requested recommendations on how to improve the Department's policies concerning segregation of inmates with mental illness. In the past, Disability Rights Iowa successfully worked with the Department to improve its restraint policies and its training about inmates with mental illness for correctional officers.

- Kentucky Protection and Advocacy made it an organizational priority to investigate reports of abuse or neglect and deaths of inmates with mental illness in segregation in 2016. To carry out this priority, the P&A plans to complete monitoring in all 14 state prisons before the end of September 2016 and has opened several individual cases involving prison inmates with serious mental illness over the last year.

Kentucky Protection and Advocacy also requested records and compiled data about the mental health treatment available to inmates in state prisons, including the reasons for placement in segregation and the length of time inmates remain in segregation. Following the P&A's records requests, the Department of Corrections implemented a new data tracking and classification system to document the number of inmates with serious mental illness, intellectual disabilities, and brain injuries in prisons throughout Kentucky.

A clock with a 23-hour awareness button in the center of the dial, above a photo of a pile of 23-hour awareness buttons.

The P&A has also provided public comments to the Department of Corrections on amendments to policies and procedures, including policies regarding special management inmates (inmates who spend 23 hours per day in a cell) and mental health services. In light of the P&A's comments, the Department decreased the duration of inmates' initial administrative segregation stay from a maximum of 60 days to a maximum of 30 days. The Department also secured an expert for consultation on further segregation reform. The P&A has also reviewed four incidents of alleged inappropriate restraint. When a review of the Department's secure restraint policies is complete, the P&A will provide additional comments to ensure inmates with mental illness are not being inappropriately restrained. The P&A will continue to monitor and review amendments to Department regulations, policies, and procedures that impact inmates with mental illness into the next legislative session.

Kentucky Protection and Advocacy also advocates for the approximately 300 inmates with serious mental illness in segregation statewide by handing out awareness buttons. The button with the number 23 signifies the number of hours per day that inmates with mental illness spend in their cell. On the 23rd day of each month, the P&A posts disability-related criminal justice reform information on its Facebook page and P&A staff wear the buttons.

- In 2014, to explore the criminalization of mental illness and the impact of segregation on mental health, Disability Rights Nebraska released a report highlighting the psychological and physical harms of segregation on inmates with mental illness, and shared its findings with the Nebraska Department of Corrections and state senators. The findings included: a connection among segregation, serious mental illness, and self-harm and suicide attempts; limited access to mental health treatment and programs in segregation and an underfunded mental health services budget for inmates in segregation; unique barriers to reentry for inmates with mental illness; and the need for systemic community mental health reform.

As a result, legislation was proposed and the P&A was consulted to provide language related to issues raised and recommendations made in its report, which included data collection on the use of segregation, developing a long-term plan to decrease the use of segregated housing, and implementing Department rules and regulations to ensure that inmates in segregation are housed under the least restrictive conditions. Disability Rights Nebraska supported these bills throughout the legislative process, and in the following session legislation was passed to limit the use of segregation and improve the treatment of inmates with mental illness. A special investigative committee was also formed to further examine prison issues, specifically inmates with mental illness and segregation. Disability Rights Nebraska has continued to educate state legislators about the need for segregation reform and participates in a workgroup with state corrections stakeholders aimed at reducing the use of segregation in Nebraska prisons. The P&A has also convened its own multi-disciplinary workgroup focused on achieving systemic improvements for inmates with mental illness. The committee and workgroups are ongoing.

---

[52] Disability Advocates, Inc., now Disability Rights New York, was a regional protection and advocacy office with the New York P&A system.

➢ In 2000, a coalition including Disability Advocates, Inc.,[52] began actively pursuing a legislative solution to the problems facing inmates with mental illness in segregation in response to New York's increased use of cell confinement sanctions and building of segregation units called Special Housing Units (SHUs). After three years of this pursuit, legislation was introduced to provide treatment to inmates with mental illness and limit the use of SHUs. Disability Advocates, Inc. remained active in this legislative advocacy until it instead focused its efforts on a lawsuit (discussed in the Litigation section of this report) against the Department of Corrections and Community Supervision, the state Office of Mental Health responsible for providing mental health services in the prison system, as well as individual superintendents and Mental Health officials to address the deliberate indifference to inmates with serious mental health needs by failing to provide adequate mental health services and imposing punishments that exacerbate mental illness. Meanwhile, the coalition continued its legislative work, but the bill was vetoed.

However, in 2007, after a litigation settlement was reached, a bill passed that incorporated and improved upon the litigation settlement's terms. With some exceptions, treatment for inmates with mental illness carrying SHU sanctions increased to four rather than two hours of out-of-cell treatment and was to take place in residential mental health treatment programs. In addition, the bill contained a presumption against added SHU sanctions for inmates in the residential mental health treatment programs. What is now known as the "SHU Exclusion Law" went into effect in 2011 following the sunset of the lawsuit's settlement agreement.

Since the law's passage, Disability Rights New York testified against a proposed delay in the bill's effective date, and twice testified by invitation before the joint Assembly and Senate hearings on mental health treatment in the state prison system. The P&A also testified in favor of expanding the law's exclusionary criteria to reach all inmates with mental illness. Disability Rights New York continues to monitor segregation in state prisons and investigate allegations of abuse and neglect of prisoners with mental illness in segregation.

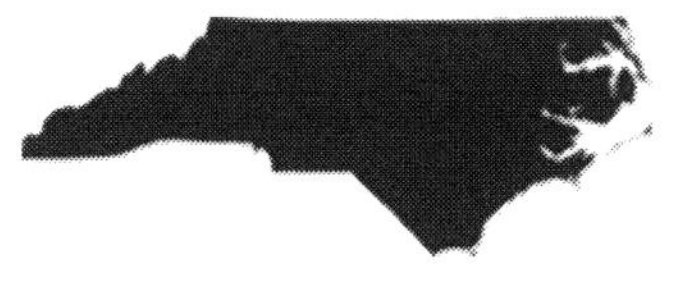

➢ Disability Rights North Carolina conducted an investigation into the segregation practices of the North Carolina Department of Corrections after learning about two inmate deaths from public reports in 2011 and 2014. The P&A's subsequent investigation revealed serious harm resulting from segregation as well as inadequate care and treatment for inmates with mental illness. In response, Disability Rights North Carolina employed a multitude of advocacy strategies to advance the rights of inmates with mental illness in segregation, including: monitoring prisons with a Centers for Medicare and Medicaid Services psychiatric nurse surveyor; conducting abuse investigations; issuing reports; making public recommendations; forming coalitions with other advocacy groups and prison leadership; and participating in forums to increase public awareness about the need for segregation reform. As a result of this advocacy, a national expert has twice provided consultation regarding the treatment of inmates with mental illness in segregation, prison Crisis Intervention Team training was initiated, and treatment chairs and tables were installed to facilitate out-of-cell treatment. In 2016, the Legislature provided funding to develop eight Therapeutic Diversion Units for inmates on control status with mental illness, and prison policies were updated to require prompt mental health screening of segregated inmates and limit the segregation of inmates with mental illness to no more than 30 days per year.

- After an inmate with mental illness died of dehydration in segregation, Disability Rights North Carolina conducted an investigation and issued a report with recommendations. In response, the North Carolina Department of Corrections convened a taskforce on mental health in prison. Disability Rights North Carolina and other advocacy groups provided input to the task force, which resulted in a 2015 report with 90 far-reaching recommendations, including improved and more frequent screening for disabilities, elimination of segregation for inmates under 21 years of age, out-of-cell treatment for inmates with a mental health designation, suicide prevention training, and clinical input in the disciplinary process.

- In March 2015, Disability Rights North Carolina conducted monitoring of the prison confining inmates under 18 years of age. The P&A discovered that as much as 38% of the youth were in segregated confinement under the same terms and conditions as segregated adults. Disability Rights North Carolina issued a report to the Director of Prisons, and continued monitoring and advocating for the elimination of segregation for youth. In June 2016, a new Youthful Offender Program was announced that eliminates the use of solitary confinement for inmates under age 18 and requires enhanced education services, behavioral health treatment, life skills development, and family and community reunification services.

- Since 2012, Disability Rights North Carolina's monitoring and advocacy has resulted in concrete improvements to the conditions of confinement for inmates with disabilities, including: removal of thick metal-mesh screens from cell door windows in segregation blocks; issuing mattresses to every inmate placed in a suicide watch cell and upon admission to the acute mental health service unit; issuing a suicide smock and blanket instead of one or the other; and enforcing the out-of-cell exercise policy.

- Disability Rights Ohio began receiving an above average number of complaints from Ohio's maximum security prisons, where most of the inmates are placed in segregation for extended periods of time. The first complaints were from inmates placed on suicide watch or crisis watch. They indicated that segregation was making their mental health symptoms worse and the prisons were offering little to no effective mental health care to address them. Some inmates even reported that prison officers were encouraging them to go ahead with their suicidal ideations, or chiding them not to commit suicide during their shift so they could avoid the paperwork. Throughout late 2015, the P&A investigated further by visiting three Ohio prisons with the largest populations in segregation. The P&A took pictures of the cells, recreation cages, and other areas used by inmates, and went cell-to-cell in selected units, speaking to over 110 individuals in segregation, over 75 of whom had a documented mental illness. These conversations revealed a number of other problems that resulted in further advocacy and follow up, including claims of excessive use of force, inadequate medical care, retaliation, and prolonged periods of 24-hour confinement. Finally, the P&A recorded extended interviews of 22 individuals who wanted to share their story with the public. Disability Rights Ohio then teamed up with the ACLU of Ohio to publish a public report in May 2016, *Shining a Light on Solitary Confinement: Why Ohio Needs Reform*. The report detailed findings from the investigation, outlined research into the problems of long-term solitary confinement, and listed specific reforms for the Department of Rehabilitation and Corrections to drastically reduce its use of solitary confinement and provide more rehabilitation, programming, and out-of-cell time to every inmate in segregation. The P&A and the ACLU of Ohio held a joint press conference and multiple interviews to publicize the report on Ohio television and radio programs. The Department of Rehabilitation and Corrections has stated that they will work to reduce solitary confinement, particularly for individuals with mental illness, and that new reforms will be announced in late 2016.

- Disability Rights Oregon conducted an investigation into the Oregon State Penitentiary's Behavioral Health Unit (BHU), an intensive behavioral management and skills training unit for inmates with serious mental illness who have committed violent acts or disruptive behavior. Disability Rights Oregon released an investigation report, which concluded that inmates in the BHU were routinely isolated in their cells for 23 hours a day without timely access to mental health care and that mental-health related behaviors were often dealt with using force. While the Oregon Department of Corrections did not agree with all of the findings and conclusions in the P&A's report, the Department agreed to improve treatment in the BHU and conducted a comprehensive review of the BHU that included consultation with a nationally-recognized expert. Following that review, the prison and the P&A entered into a Memorandum of Understanding that reflects the parties' commitment to changes that include: allowing BHU inmates an average of 20 hours per week out-of-cell time, including 10 structured programing hours and 10 unstructured hours; enhanced access to mental health services with greater consideration of individual treatment needs; quarterly reports to the P&A for four years; and to pay for ongoing guidance from the expert. The required improvements will involve architectural, operational, and staffing changes. Following a joint funding request by the P&A and the Department, the Oregon Legislature allocated more than 8 million dollars that will be used by the Department to comply with the terms of the Memorandum of Understanding.

- Disability Rights Tennessee received a report in June 2015 that an inmate with mental illness was denied medical treatment by prison staff. Upon investigation, the P&A learned that the inmate requested pain medication after an assault and engaged in self-harm when the medication was denied. As a result of the self-harm behavior, the inmate was moved to a mental health segregation unit where he continued to self-harm, was placed on 24-hour watch, and was ultimately put in six-point restraints. The P&A's investigation further revealed that the inmate remained restrained and in segregation for three months, during which time a feeding tube, and intravenous fluids and medications were required. Disability Rights Tennessee initiated discussions with the Department of Corrections medical and mental health directors who agreed to develop a treatment plan for the inmate that included regular individual therapy, clear guidelines for the inmate's personal care, incentives to refrain from self-harm, and weekly treatment team meetings with the inmate's mother and medical conservator. Though Disability Rights Tennessee continues to investigate this report, the P&A's intervention has produced a treatment plan for the inmate that has removed him from restraints and allowed him to be moved to a less restrictive setting within the prison.

- In September 2014, Disability Rights Washington opened a systemic investigation into the Washington State Department of Corrections' treatment of inmates with personality disorders. The investigation focused on the use of segregation for these inmates, the use of restraints and force in response to incidents of self-harm, and inmate access to mental health and programming while in segregation. DRW determined that additional expertise was required in order to address the issues raised by this population and presented a proposal to the prison system to jointly hire an expert. In March 2015, the expert did a tour of two prisons where inmates with personality disorders are often concentrated, reviewed policies, and interviewed inmates, staff, mental health providers, prison administrators, and P&A staff. The expert then produced a report, identifying areas of concern and making recommendations for change. The recommendations included, among other things, modifications to the prison's restraint policy, shorter time periods before inmates get privileges in segregation, more out-of-cell time, more programming, better yards, and private mental health appointments for inmates on the mental health units. In response to the report, the prison system has drafted a plan of corrective action. Disability Rights Washington is currently monitoring the implementation of that corrective action plan.

- As a result of its ongoing monitoring and advocacy related to the needs of inmates with mental illness, developmental disabilities, and traumatic brain injuries, Disability Rights Washington noted that many of these inmates were placed in segregated units for prolonged periods of time, sometimes as long as several years. In 2013, Disability Rights Washington and the Department of Corrections established an ongoing relationship in which the P&A and the prison system work collaboratively to identify and develop plans to address the needs of inmates with disabilities. As a result, the prison system developed a specialized unit for inmates with developmental disabilities and traumatic brain injuries and works closely with the P&A on individual cases where actions related to a person's disability results in the inmate being held in more restrictive settings than necessary.

- After learning that the Washington State Department of Corrections punished individuals for self-harm and attempted suicide, Disability Rights Washington sent a letter to the prison system asking for this practice to stop, citing a case based on similar facts brought by Disability Rights Vermont. In 2013, the Washington State Department of Corrections formed a workgroup comprised of prison clinical and corrections staff, as well as a Disability Rights Washington attorney. As a result of this workgroup, the prison system agreed to stop infracting people for self-harm behavior and to restore good time lost due to infractions related solely to self-harm behavior.

Litigation

- The Prison Law Office, a nonprofit public interest law firm in California, and the ACLU N[illegible]n Project investigated prison conditions in Arizona, specifically at the Ey[illegible]nce, Tucson, Lewis, and Perryville complexes. The investigation revealed that in[illegible] mental illness were impacted by significant deficiencies in diagnosis, st[illegible]cation delivery, therapeutic treatment, and protocols for inmates with suicidal ideations. Prison Law Office, through the National Disabilities Rights Network, contacted Arizona Center for Disability Law, the Arizona P&A, regarding a potential partnership. In October 2011, Prison Law Office wrote a letter to the Director of the Arizona Department of Corrections demanding that the Department remedy the conditions described above on the grounds that the conditions violated the Eighth Amendment. When the Department did not timely remedy the conditions, Prison Law Office along with the National and Arizona chapters of the ACLU, Perkins Coie, and Jones Day, filed a class action lawsuit against the Department. The Arizona Center for Disability

Law joined as an organizational plaintiff on the mental health care claim on behalf of the class of inmates with mental illness.

After two years of discovery and lengthy monitoring visits, the Department of Corrections and Plaintiffs settled the case. The settlement included provisions regarding the improvement of health care, mental health care, and conditions of isolation and confinement for inmates in maximum custody. The settlement provisions related to inmates in maximum custody included: requiring minimum levels of out-of-cell time; restrictions on length of stay in segregated housing; incentives for out-of-cell time, programs, and property; and restrictions on use of pepper spray and other chemical agents. The settlement also ensured ongoing monitoring of prison facilities by Plaintiffs, including the Department's monthly submission of inmate health care records, 20 prison monitoring days per year, substantial compliance in performance measures agreed upon by the parties, as well as attorneys' fees.

The formal monitoring process for the settlement began in March 2015. After reviewing reports produced by the Department as well as other documents, and conducting monitoring visits during the first year of implementation of the settlement, Plaintiffs found that the Department of Corrections was substantially noncompliant with many performance measures and that prisoners were still experiencing lengthy delays in receiving care. Plaintiffs provided the Department with a Notice of Substantial Noncompliance in October 2015 and, as required by the settlement, the parties attended mediation and attempted to address the matter. Following the mediation, several issues remained unresolved and Plaintiffs filed a Motion to Enforce the settlement in April 2016. In May 2016, the Court ordered the Department of Corrections to develop and submit to the Court for review a remedial plan to come into compliance with numerous performance measures in the settlement. The Department's remedial plan was submitted to the Court in June 2016 and is currently under review.

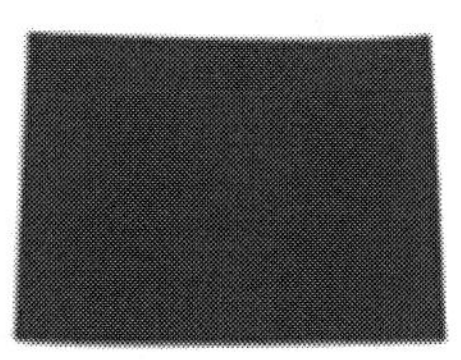

➢ In 2012, Disability Law Colorado, the Colorado P&A, joined in a class action lawsuit against the federal Bureau of Prisons to improve conditions that were alleged to violate the Eighth Amendment for confining inmates with severe mental illness for 23 hours per day, seven days per week in the United States Penitentiary, Administrative Maximum Facility (ADX).[53] The United States District Court for the District of Colorado granted Disability Law Colorado's motion for partial summary judgment on the issue of the P&A's associational standing to pursue claims for declaratory and injunctive relief for all inmates with mental illness incarcerated at the ADX. As of the date of this report, the parties are in confidential settlement negotiations. However, the

---

[53] Disability Law Colorado is not using federal grant money to fund this litigation because it involves a federal agency.

Bureau of Prisons has taken significant action to cure the alleged constitutional violations. Some of the significant actions taken by the Bureau of Prisons include: system-wide policy formulation and revisions concerning the care and treatment of inmates with serious mental illness, excluding inmates with serious mental illness from the ADX, screening inmates at the ADX for serious mental illness, and transfer of inmates from the ADX who have a serious mental illness to new programs at treatment facilities within the Bureau of Prisons system. As this case progresses to settlement or trial, Disability Law Colorado intends to monitor the Bureau of Prisons' progress in correcting the identified areas of concern.

➢ In 2003, Connecticut Office of Protection and Advocacy for Persons with Disabilities filed a lawsuit against the Department of Corrections on behalf of inmates with mental illness confined at the supermax prison in Connecticut. The action alleged that the prison system confined inmates under conditions of extreme isolation sufficient to exacerbate mental illness and failed to provide appropriate mental health treatment. The parties ultimately agreed to a settlement in 2006, which, among other things, required prison clinical staff to review an inmate's mental health records to determine whether the behavior that led to a potential sanction was a manifestation of the inmate's mental illness. If the inmate's behavior was deemed to be a symptom of mental illness, sanctions were not to be imposed if clinically determined to cause harm to the inmate.

➢ In 2014, Disability Rights Florida began investigating the scalding death of an inmate in the inpatient mental health unit of a state prison. The P&A quickly discovered that this was not an isolated incident of abuse and that the correctional officers at the unit had a pattern of abusing inmates exhibiting behaviors that were the result of untreated or undertreated mental illness. Further investigation revealed the mental health care being provided to inmates on the unit was inadequate to the point of being almost nonexistent. With Disability Rights Florida serving as an organizational plaintiff, the P&A, along with private firm co-counsel, filed a federal lawsuit against the state's department of corrections and its mental health contract provider, Wexford, for their failure to protect inmates in the unit from abusive correctional officers and to provide adequate mental health care. The lawsuit raises claims under the Eighth Amendment, the ADA, and the Rehab Act. Shortly after litigation was filed, the parties met regarding potential settlement and agreed that each side would retain a mental health expert and security expert to visit the unit, review records, and interview staff and inmates. The experts wrote reports identifying the issues that needed to be addressed in settlement, including provision of treatment interventions, individualized service plans, training of security and mental health staff, treatment team meetings, the use of restraints, and enhanced oversight to prevent inmate abuse. Based on the experts' reports, the parties negotiated a settlement and a plan of compliance, which was finalized in early 2016. Under the terms of the agreement, the prison has six months to implement the plan, at which point the experts for both sides will return to evaluate whether the plan has been adequately implemented. If not, the case will be reopened in the federal court and litigation will resume. This case remains pending.

- Equip for Equality, the Illinois P&A, investigated conditions at four Illinois prisons that contained residential treatment units for inmates with mental illness. The investigation revealed a lack of appropriate treatment and punitive approach to mental illness, including the overuse of isolation, including disciplinary segregation and "crisis" cells. The P&A subsequently joined a prisoners' rights organization, the Uptown People's Law Center, and two private law firms, Dentons and Mayer Brown, to represent all prisoners with mental illness in a class action case challenging the conditions of confinement and lack of mental health treatment in the Illinois Department of Corrections. The case included claims brought under the ADA and the Rehab Act, as well as the Eighth Amendment.

In December 2015, after years of negotiations and litigation, the parties reached a settlement. The settlement agreement requires a complete overhaul of the prison mental health system, including mechanisms and timelines for appropriate treatment, as well as the construction of a psychiatric hospital and additional residential treatment units at four facilities. Under the settlement, all prisoners with mental illness in long-term segregation (more than 60 days) will have both structured and unstructured out-of-cell time, starting with eight hours and increasing to 20 hours per week. The settlement requires other changes to the disciplinary procedures to prevent discipline for mental illness-related behaviors such as self-harm and to reduce the segregation of seriously mentally ill prisoners. Additionally, the settlement calls for increased training for all correctional and clinical staff, and contains enforcement measures that include ongoing monitoring and reporting, an independent monitor, the ability to return the case to litigation if the Department of Corrections does not substantially comply with the settlement terms, as well as attorneys' fees and costs. The court held a fairness hearing on the proposed settlement agreement in May 2016 and approved the settlement agreement.

- In 2008, Indiana Disability Rights and the ACLU of Indiana filed a lawsuit against the Indiana Department of Correction on behalf of the P&A Commission and three individuals representing a class of inmates with serious mental illness. The lawsuit alleged that the Department was housing inmates with mental illness in segregated or excessively isolated and harsh conditions where they failed to receive adequate mental health care. After four years of litigation, the court found that the Department, which had been placing inmates with serious mental illness in isolation with little or no access to treatment, violated Eighth Amendment prohibitions against cruel and unusual punishment. Inmates subjected to these conditions faced significant worsening of symptoms and illness, including hallucinations, increased paranoia and depression, self-harm, and suicide. In an effort to resolve this action, the parties worked together to come to a settlement agreement to improve conditions for inmates with serious mental illness.

The agreement prohibits, with some exceptions, the confinement of inmates with serious mental illness in restrictive status housing or protective custody (segregation). The agreement also provides for "minimum adequate treatment" for these inmates, which includes: an individualized treatment plan created by a team consisting of mental health professionals and correctional staff who are familiar with the inmate, reviewed at least every 90 days; 10 hours each week of therapeutic programming, which includes individual and group therapy; recreation and showers; and additional therapy and out-of-cell time where possible and appropriate.

The agreement also stipulates that inmates in restrictive housing will receive frequent monitoring of their mental health status and needs by mental health personnel, including daily visits by correctional and medical staff. In addition, any inmate with a mental health diagnosis will be visited at least once a week by mental health personnel and offered monthly out-of-cell monitoring by a mental health professional.

- Disability Rights Maryland settled a case in which the federal district court asked the P&A to represent an inmate who had filed a lawsuit alleging brutality in prison. Sidley Austin LLP agreed to co-counsel the matter pro bono. The inmate had a history of mental illness and multiple adjudications of incompetency to stand trial. The P&A's initial obligation, tasked by the federal court, was to determine if the inmate could proceed in person or needed a guardian. It was determined that the inmate was competent to engage counsel and the P&A began investigating the inmate's brutality claims. Unfortunately, the events leading up to the inmate's lawsuit were barred by the statute of limitation. However, while investigating, the P&A learned that the inmate had been held in segregation for over three years, which was harmful to his mental health.

Disability Rights Maryland and Sidley Austin negotiated a settlement agreement with the State Department of Public Safety and Correctional Services to address the following: the inmate's transfer from the prison where he had been seriously injured and continued to feel that he was in danger to a prison closer to his family; agreement not to discipline the inmate for self-injurious behavior, and to avoid the use of administrative segregation whenever possible; continued assessment of the inmate's mental health status if segregation is used in the future and consideration of alternatives to segregation, including recommendations for services and time out-of-cell; use of a multi-disciplinary team to address the inmate's somatic and mental health needs; and, since the inmate uses a wheelchair, specific accessibility features in his cell unless no longer medically necessary.

The case gave the P&A insight into the Department's use of segregation that will be useful as it continues to investigate use of segregation for inmates with mental illness. The P&A's PAIMI Council and Board of Directors have voted to add a provision to the P&A's Advocacy Services Plan to include advocacy work to reduce the use of segregation for prisoners with mental illness.

Subsequent to settling this case, Disability Rights Maryland has visited other Department facilities, reviewed records and state documents, and interviewed inmates with disabilities. The P&A also worked successfully with other groups to advocate for state legislation that will require the Department to collect and make available data on the use of segregation, disaggregated by various factors including "serious mental illness," and to include such information as length of stay and attempts at self-harm.

- After receiving complaints of excessive restraint and seclusion at Bridgewater State Hospital, a hospital run as a correctional facility by the Massachusetts Department of Corrections, as opposed to a mental health hospital run by the Department of Mental Health, the Disability Law Center, the Massachusetts P&A, opened an investigation in the spring of 2014. The P&A conducted an intense investigation over three months, using five attorneys and additional assistance provided by law students. The P&A conducted tours on site, interviewed correctional and mental health staff, and did in-depth interviews of 75 patients and record reviews of 64 patients. At the conclusion of its investigation, the P&A issued a 24-page letter of findings to the Governor, identifying 11 critical problems with excessive use of restraint and seclusion and providing policy recommendations, including a need to restructure agency oversight, provide greater resources for staffing, and require more rigorous training.

  After negotiations with Disability Law Center, the Commonwealth approved a series of systemic reforms at the hospital, including major improvements around restraint and seclusion practices. The P&A also contracted to monitor the hospital for a period of two years beginning at the end of 2014. Finally, the P&A also agreed to serve as court monitor to oversee an agreement reached by the Commonwealth with other parties in Superior Court litigation. Since that time, Disability Law Center attorneys have typically been on-site three full days a week. This on-site review includes meeting with patients; touring units (especially the seclusion rooms); meeting with leadership and other correctional and mental health staff; troubleshooting; and identifying areas of noncompliance and issues for policy reform. The P&A has also worked with state agency leadership, representatives from the Governor's office, legislators, families, other advocates, and representatives of the media to help explain the urgent need for restructuring and improvement at the facility.

  There have been several positive developments at the hospital. Rates of restraint and seclusion have decreased considerably. The hospital is more closely following the legal standard governing the use of its Intensive Treatment Unit, or segregation unit. The Department of Corrections also established an Executive Committee to advocate for more hospital resources. Additionally, the hospital's mental health contractor has been able to obtain some additional funds to improve staffing ratios and new leadership now administers the facility. The P&A continues to work with key stakeholders to place the hospital under the control of the Department of Mental Health, and to improve and restructure the facility. The P&A will continue intensive monitoring at least until the end of 2016.

Unfortunately, however, the modest progress at the hospital has also been accompanied by tragedy. In April 2016, a patient with mental illness committed suicide while in the isolation unit at the hospital. The Disability Law Center has opened an intensive investigation into this death due to its concerns that patients at the hospital will continue to be at risk of harm to themselves until the facility is transitioned from the Department of Corrections to the Department of Mental Health.

- The Disability Law Center, the Massachusetts P&A, in partnership with the Center for Public Representation, Prisoners' Legal Services, and the private law firms of Bingham McCutcheon and Nelson Mullins, sued the Massachusetts Department of Corrections and several of its senior administrators alleging that housing inmates with serious mental illness in segregation violated their constitutional rights against cruel and unusual punishment and violated the ADA. The P&A filed suit in 2007 after 11 inmates committed suicide in segregation within 28 months. At least seven of the inmates had serious mental illness.

  After five years of litigation, a settlement was approved and the Department of Corrections implemented significant systemic reforms, including a mental health classification system, a policy to exclude inmates with severe mental illness from long-term segregation, and the design and operation of two maximum security mental health treatment units as alternatives to segregation. These units have dramatically reduced the number of acts of self-harm and suicide attempts. They have also made the prisons safer for staff and other inmates by substantially reducing disruptive and assaultive behavior. Under the terms of the agreement, the Department must maintain the number of beds in the alternative secure treatment units and "strictly regulate" the amount of time that prisoners with severe mental illness are held in other segregation units. In addition, the Department also must provide expanded mental health services and out-of-cell time for prisoners with mental illness who are awaiting placement in treatment units or removal from segregation. Plaintiffs' attorneys closely monitored the implementation of the agreement.

- After a year-long investigation, Disability Rights Montana signed on as organizational plaintiff in 2014 in a federal lawsuit challenging the policy and practices at Montana State Prison in treating and confining inmates with mental illness. The lawsuit raised claims under the Eighth and Fourteenth Amendments of the U.S. Constitution as well as the ADA, and alleged that the prison impermissibly imposed solitary confinement or behavior modification plans on inmates with mental illness, thereby depriving them of clothing, bedding, human contact, a working toilet, and proper food as punishment for behaviors caused by mental illness. This case is ongoing.

-  The Nevada Disability Advocacy and Law Center, Nevada's P&A, was contacted by the Ninth Circuit Administrator concerning a case filed on behalf of a female inmate with borderline personality disorder, mental illness, and intellectual disability who had been housed in segregation on the mental health unit at a men's prison in excess of 13 months. The women's prison in Las Vegas was not equipped to handle the inmate's mental health condition and self-injurious behaviors.

  Nevada Disability Advocacy and Law Center was appointed as counsel for the limited purpose of investigating the inmate's claims and representation at an early settlement conference. The court also appointed a psychiatrist as guardian ad litem to assist with the investigation and early settlement. The matters at issue in this case were whether the Department of Corrections failed to protect the inmate from sexual harassment by male inmates; prolonged solitary confinement for a period in excess of 13 months; failed to provide meaningful mental health treatment; and deprived the inmate of outdoor recreation for a period in excess of 13 months, as a result of "deliberate indifference." The facts of the case also highlighted the disparity in mental health treatment options for female and male inmates. Shortly after the complaint was filed, the inmate was transferred back to the women's prison and the case was ultimately settled for a substantial sum of money. As part of the settlement, the Department of Corrections was to pay for a Dialectical Behavior Therapy specialist to consult with the inmate's treatment team to develop an appropriate treatment plan, as well as develop a safe release plan. Subsequently, an intensive forensic mental health team from the state mental health division agreed to accept the inmate to its program and coordinate with the Department.

- In 2002, Disability Advocates, Inc., now Disability Rights New York, joined as co-counsel with Prisoners' Legal Services of New York, the Legal Aid Society of New York's Prisoners' Rights Project, and Davis Polk & Wardwell in bringing systemic litigation to address what had become a cycle of misery for hundreds of prisoners housed in Special Housing Units (SHUs), or segregation. The P&A also appeared as plaintiff in the litigation on behalf of a constituency of prisoners with "significant mental illness or emotional impairment who reside in New York State prisons." The complaint for injunctive, systemic relief was brought against the Department of Corrections and Community Supervision, the state Office of Mental Health responsible for providing mental health services in the prison system, as well as individual superintendents and Office of Mental Health officials. It alleged deliberate indifference to prisoners' serious mental health needs, by failing to provide adequate mental health services and imposing punishments which aggravate mental illness, as well as violations of the ADA and the Rehab Act. The complaint described the systemic failure to provide necessary mental health care, the suffering and suicides of inmates with mental illness in SHU, and the knowledge by prison and mental health officials of these continuing harms. Finally, it outlined the remedies needed, including increased treatment resources and a prohibition against placement of prisoners with mental illness in solitary confinement.

After the complaint was filed, the parties embarked on years of discovery, culminating in a partial trial in 2006. During the trial in April 2006, following the testimony of experts and several inmate witnesses, the federal district court judge toured several prisons with the parties and informed the parties of the gravity of the conditions in solitary confinement that he had observed, particularly the withdrawal and idleness of so many inmates in isolation. Following this court conference, defendants offered to meet with the plaintiff to discuss settlement, and the trial was adjourned for purposes of these discussions.

One year later, in April 2007, settlement was finally reached in the form of a private settlement agreement.[54] As a result, SHU confinement for inmates was subject to increased levels of review and out-of-cell treatment and programming was required for inmates meeting criteria for "serious mental illness." The settlement's key components were:

1) a "heightened level of care" for inmates meeting criteria for "serious mental illness" and with SHU sanctions greater than 30 days, of two hours of out-of-cell treatment five days a week;
2) criteria for serious mental illness, including psychotic disorders, bipolar disorders, schizophrenic disorders, major depressive disorders; other mental illness, organic disorders, and personality disorders included if rising to high levels of dysfunction; and serious, recent suicide attempt;
3) suicide prevention screenings within 24 hours and Mental Health assessments within one working day of admission to SHU;
4) universal mental health screening at reception into the prison system;
5) increases in treatment bed capacity and residential mental health programming, including SHU diversion programs, with two programs offering up to four hours daily programming;

---

[54] Many of the settlement terms were incorporated into New York's "SHU Exclusion Law" which passed both houses and was signed into law in July 2007. The SHU Exclusion provisions went into effect in July 2011, following the anticipated sunset of the lawsuit's settlement agreement. (See discussion above under Non-Litigation).

6) joint facility-based Department and Office of Mental Health case management committees reviewing all Office of Mental Health caseload inmates in SHU, as well as a central office administration committee rotating through the facility committees to oversee the reviews, and a one-time central office committee review of SHU sanctions for all inmates with serious mental illness;

7) monitoring of the agreement, consisting of semi-annual tours, with periodic reporting and document production to plaintiff; and

8) required mediation before the Court for pervasive non-compliance of a material provision of the settlement, following which the Court may recommend extension of the settlement or plaintiff may move to reinstate the lawsuit.

➢ In 2005, Protection and Advocacy for People with Disabilities, Inc., the South Carolina P&A, filed a class-action lawsuit on behalf of inmates with serious mental illness under the state constitution alleging inadequate mental health treatment for inmates held by the South Carolina Department of Corrections. The suit alleged that inmates endured multiple hours of restraint with no bathroom breaks; prolonged segregation; placement naked in shower stalls, interview booths, and holding cells for hours and days with no toilets; and routine and excessive use of pepper spray. The lawsuit asked the court to require the Department to design and maintain a program that provided adequate treatment to inmates with mental illness. In 2012, a five-week trial was held, and in 2014 the trial judge ordered the Department to remedy constitutional violations by submitting a remedial plan to include: the development of a mental health screening tool and treatment program to end inappropriate segregation of inmates in mental health crisis; the employment of sufficient mental health professionals; the maintenance of treatment records and administration of psychotropic medication with appropriate supervision and periodic evaluation; and a program to identify, treat, and supervise inmates at risk for suicide. The parties subsequently engaged in mediation and in 2016 reached an agreement to implement the remedial plan. The plan provides segregated inmates access to group and individualized therapy, access to higher levels of mental health services, more out-of-cell time, and improved cleanliness and temperature of segregation cells. It also calls for staff to collect and report data on the percentage of inmates in segregation with mental illness and their average lengths of stay, timely review treatment records, and implement a formal quality management program under which segregation practices and conditions are reviewed. The settlement is currently pending approval before the State Supreme Court.

➢ The Vermont Prisoners' Rights Office referred Disability Rights Vermont to an inmate with mental illness in segregation. The inmate's mental health had deteriorated such that he had become manic, delusional, and paranoid, refused his medications, pulled his hair out, sobbed uncontrollably, banged his head, and screamed. After conducting a record review, the P&A determined that the inmate had been identified many weeks earlier as requiring inpatient psychiatric care, but because no inpatient bed was available, the inmate remained in segregation where his condition worsened. Within a week of the P&A contacting the Department with its concern that the inmate's rights to adequate treatment and freedom from unnecessary isolation were being violated, the inmate was transferred to an acute care facility where he received appropriate treatment and improved, and was furloughed directly home. Disability Rights Vermont filed a federal complaint asserting violations of the Eighth Amendment and the ADA regarding the inmate's circumstances and the case remains in litigation at this time.

CONCLUSION

For over thirty years, the P&A network has zealously advocated on behalf of individuals with mental illness in facilities nationwide. As the number of inmates with mental illness in prisons continues to grow, the P&A outreach and advocacy effort in prisons has grown in response. However, much more work needs to be done to help those inmates with mental illness who are locked up and locked down in segregation. Although prison advocates are employing a multitude of tactics to pressure departments of corrections to effect reform, it remains difficult for inmates in segregation to navigate the complex grievance and judicial process, and reach resources and organizations on the outside to assist with legal claims. This lack of access to advocates results in the continuation of inmates in segregation facing prolonged isolation in harmful conditions. Thus, this report concludes with a call to action and a series of recommendations. These recommendations encompass steps that can be taken at the local, state, and federal levels and are intended to spur action by P&As, as well as correctional systems and local lawmakers. They are also intended to add a disability perspective to the ongoing conversation about prison conditions, and inform national policymakers about the unique issues faced by inmates with mental illness.

RECOMMENDATIONS

National Recommendations

1. The U.S. Department of Justice should effectively enforce all statutes and regulations necessary to protect the rights of prisoners with disabilities. As set forth in the report above, the violations are flagrant and consistent nationwide, resulting in significant harm to prisoners with disabilities.

2. As the Bureau of Prisons (BOP) operates facilities that inappropriately use solitary confinement, it should follow the recommendations set forth in this report that are

provided for states. The federal government should reform the use of solitary confinement in all BOP facilities so that it fully conforms to U.S. and to international law and standards for humane treatment.

3. The U.S. Department of Justice should provide guidance about the need to accommodate prisoners with disabilities. Specifically, it should clarify its commitment to enforcement and state that the following or similar administrative structures and activities may assist in ensuring appropriate accommodations.

    a. ADA Coordinator

    Most prison systems have designated a specific staff person at each facility to respond to requests for accommodations for inmates. These ADA coordinators have the potential to be a valuable resource for inmates with disabilities. They should be trained in the requirements of the ADA, and familiar with the array of accommodations that may be employed in the prison setting.

    b. Corrections Ombuds Programs

    Though the foregoing case synopses make clear that there are grievance and appeals processes in place for inmates to lodge complaints regarding prison conditions and programming, in most states there is no independent entity that may conduct investigations on prison-related claims. Existing processes may lack accessibility for multiple disabilities such as people with low vision or those who are deaf or hard of hearing. Similarly, very few states have administrative bodies that will hear prison-related issues. Thus, once inmates have exhausted the internal grievance system in prison, there is little for them to do but file litigation in state or federal court.

    In addition to effective and consistent enforcement at the state and federal level by those entities that have the duty to enforce the law, creating an independent ombuds office would provide for a level of oversight not currently present in most states. This would potentially decrease the number of lawsuits filed by inmates and their advocates by resolving issues at this lower level. P&A agencies already perform similar work by virtue of their Congressional mandate. P&As should be funded to provide this ombuds function.

    States with human rights commissions or other administrative bodies that hear claims of discrimination may also consider including prison-related issues within the jurisdiction of those bodies, so that inmate claims regarding disability-based discrimination may be addressed without resorting to full litigation.

4. The U.S. Department of Justice's Bureau of Justice Statistics (BJS) should track the rate of mental illness in state and federal prisons, as well as in local jails. There is no standardized tracking of the numbers of inmates with mental illness in the nation's correctional systems. In order to address the concerns raised in this report, understanding the scope of the issue is critical, and thus better data is needed. BJS's National Prisoner Statistics Program currently tracks data points in state and federal prisons twice per year. BJS should include questions about mental illness in that survey. Similarly, BJS's Annual Survey of Jails should be amended to capture mental illness specific data as well. BJS should also issue a special report on inmates with mental illness in order to provide a comprehensive overview of the data collected on this inmate population.

5. Congress should fund a P&A program for the representation of individuals with disabilities housed in correctional settings. P&A agencies have a mandate to protect the rights of individuals with disabilities in institutional settings, including, but not limited to, the mandate to investigate allegations of abuse and neglect. P&As provide substantial and increasing levels of representation for inmates with disabilities housed in a variety of correctional settings.

   As this report documents, the reported violations of individual rights are significant in number and we surmise that many go unreported due to prison culture and in some cases, labyrinthine and inaccessible complaint procedures. These barriers result in worse conditions for prisoners with disabilities than for other prisoners. P&As can help solve these problems before they require full litigation; funding for a P&A can improve conditions, reduce recidivism, and conserve public funds.

6. Congress should ensure that sentencing reform efforts result in reductions in the number of individuals with mental health needs who are incarcerated for low-level non-violent offenses. This reform should include increasing access to criminal justice diversion programs, and increasing the availability of low cost or free voluntary community-based mental health services.

   Reducing the number of individuals with mental health needs who are incarcerated will diminish the number who are confined in settings not designed to meet their needs. These efforts will also result in an increase in the availability of correctional resources to ensure appropriate mental health treatment for those men and women who must be incarcerated for reasons of public safety.

State Recommendations

1. P&As across the country should consider increased monitoring and outreach in the prisons in their state. While many P&As are engaging in effective, wide-ranging advocacy related to inmates with disabilities, with increasing numbers of people with disabilities

entering the prison system, prisons are quickly becoming the new institutions for people with disabilities. Given the P&As' decades-long history of advocating on behalf of institutionalized people with disabilities, the P&As are encouraged to employ that expertise in the prison context.

2. State prison systems should develop relationships with the state's P&A. While the prison systems in each state are invariably distinct from one another, those systems that appear most able to respond to and accommodate inmates with disabilities share some common traits. Generally, and not surprisingly, the states with what appear to be the most progressive prison systems often have an ongoing, collaborative relationship with the state P&A. As seen in the foregoing case studies, P&As use a variety of advocacy methods to address disability-related issues in prison and those systems that routinely meet with the state P&A are often able to resolve issues through informal advocacy and negotiation. Obviously not all issues can be resolved this way, and P&As have litigated disability-related issues in the prisons, in both state and federal court. However, on balance it appears that those systems faring the best are those that are collaborators rather than adversaries with the state P&A.

3. Law firms and other advocacy groups should partner with P&As to increase capacity to help inmates with disabilities. With the congressional authority to monitor and conduct investigations and advocacy in the correctional setting, many P&As have extensive, first-hand information regarding issues facing inmates with disabilities. Moreover, as demonstrated in some of the foregoing case summaries, P&As have successfully used their agency standing to serve as organizational plaintiffs in prison-related litigation. Other advocacy partners should leverage this advantage by partnering with P&As in assessing and mounting such litigation.

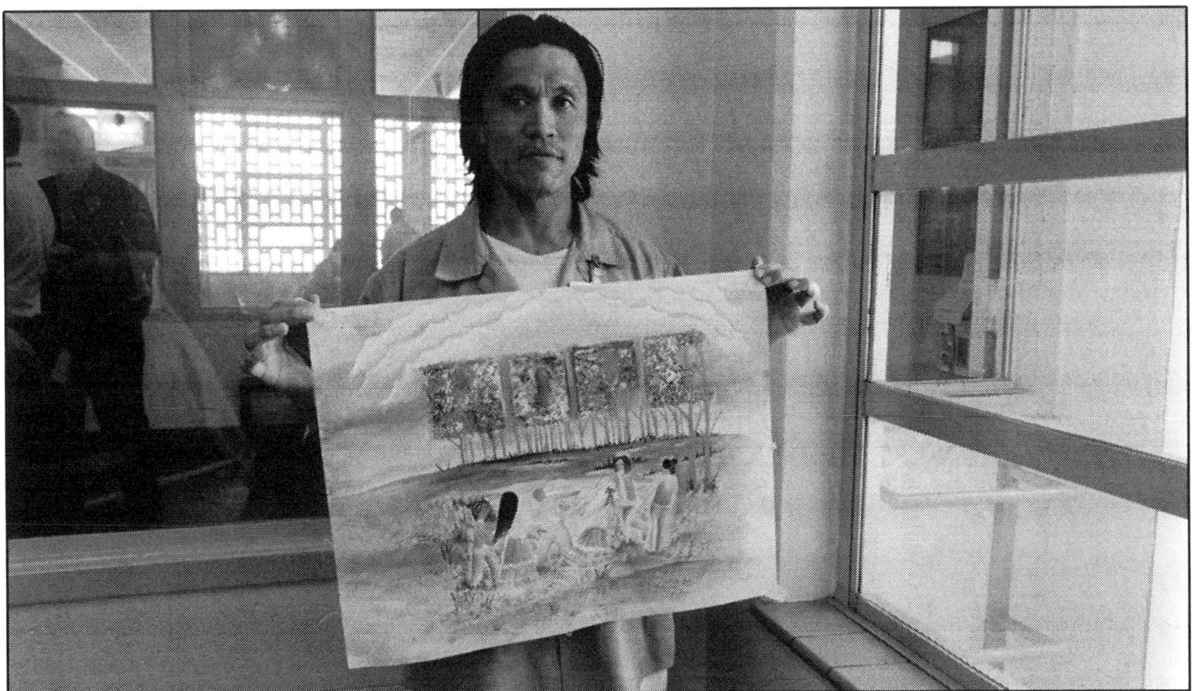

Barry Siphoy, an inmate at Washington Corrections Center in Shelton, Washington holds up a colorful painting with the word "Hope." Barry was housed in the Skill Building Unit, an example of a less-restrictive housing alternative to segregation.

ABOUT THE PROJECT

The Amplifying Voices of Inmates with Disabilities (AVID) Prison Project produced this report through a collaboration between The Arizona Center for Disability Law, Disability Law Colorado, The Advocacy Center of Louisiana, Disability Rights New York, Protection and Advocacy for People with Disabilities of South Carolina, Disability Rights Texas, Disability Rights Washington, and the National Disability Rights Network, with contributions from other protection and advocacy agencies.

ABOUT THE AUTHOR

Anna Guy is an attorney with Disability Rights Washington's AVID Prison Project, where she focuses on both individual and systemic advocacy on behalf of inmates with disabilities. Prior to coming to Disability Rights Washington, Anna protected the rights of individuals with disabilities by serving as a voting member on the Behavioral Associates of Massachusetts, Human Rights Committee. Anna graduated from Roger Williams University School of Law (RWU) where she received recognition for her commitment to public service. While at RWU, Anna participated in a medical-legal collaborative program with the Warren Alpert Medical School of Brown University. She also represented clients as a student attorney in the RWU Criminal Defense Clinic, and held various internships and externships in which she was an advocate for marginalized populations. Prior to attending law school, Anna graduated on the Dean's List from the University of Nevada, Las Vegas with a B.A. in Psychology.

This report, the multimedia report and associated videos, were designed and produced by Rooted in Rights.
Learn more at rootedinrights.org.

Published September 8, 2016

Mental Health Glossary

ADDICTION SEVERITY INDEX: Developed by the National Institute on Drug Abuse [NIDA], this is the most widely used instrument for measuring substance abuse. Its structured interview examines seven areas of functioning commonly affected by substance abuse. It is in the public domain and therefore available at no cost [McLellan et al,1980. 1992].

ADDICTION: A chronic relapsing disease characterized by compulsive drug seeking and use and by long lasting changes in the brain.

ADVANCED PRACTICED REGISTERED NURSE [APRN]: A nurse with post-graduate education in nursing. APRNs are prepared with advanced informative and clinical education, knowledge, skills, and scope of practice in nursing.

ALCOHOL DEPENDENCE SCALE: This 25-item instrument screens for symptoms of alcohol dependence and was derived from the larger 147-item Alcohol Use Inventory [AUI] via factor analysis [Skinner and Horn, 1984].

ANTISOCIAL PERSONALITY DISORDER: A disorder characterized by antisocial behaviors that involve pervasive disregard for and violation of the rights, feelings, and safety of others. These behaviors begin in early childhood [conduct disorder] or the early teenage years and continue into adulthood.

ANXIETY DISORDER: Varied disorders that involve excessive or inappropriate feelings of anxiety or worry. Examples are panic disorder, PTSD, social phobia, and others.

ATTENTION-DEFICIT HYPERACTIVITY DISORDER [ADHD]: A disorder that typically presents in early childhood, characterized by tension, hyperactivity, and impulsivity.

BIPOLAR DISORDER: A mood disorder characterized by alternating episodes of depression and mania or hypomania.

BRIEF SYMPTOM INVENTORY: This is a short form [53 items] for another instrument, the Symptom Checklist 90-Revised [SCL-90-R]. It provides both global indices of psychology and specific psychiatric symptom dimensions [Derogatis and Melisaratos, 1983].

CASE MANAGEMENT: A process which plans, coordinates and implements services required to meet an individual's needs.

CERTIFIED ALCOHOL AND DRUG COUNSELOR [CADC]: A certified individual that provides alcohol and drug counseling.

CLINICIAN-ADMINISTERED PTSD SCALE [CAPS]: This clinician-administered scale provides an accurate diagnosis of posttraumatic stress disorder [Blake et al., 1995]

COMORBIDITY: The occurrence of two disorders or illnesses in the same person, either at the same time [co-occurring comorbid conditions] or with a time difference between the initial occurrence of one and the initial occurrence of the other [sequentially comorbid conditions].

CONDUCT DISORDER: A repetitive and persistent pattern of behavior in children or adolescents in which the basic rights of others or major age-appropriate societal norms or rules are violated.

CO-OCCURRING DISORDERS: A person with substance abuse issues and mental health diagnosis.

DEPRESSION: A disorder marked by sadness, inactivity, difficulty with thinking and concentration, significant increase or decrease in appetite and time spent sleeping, feelings of dejection and hopelessness, and, sometimes, suicidal thoughts or an attempt to commit suicide.

DOPAMINE: A brain chemical, classified as a neurotransmitter, found in regions of the brain that regulate movement, emotion, motivation, and pleasure.

Dual Diagnosis Treatment: Treatment for an individual with substance abuse issues as well as mental health diagnosis.

Dual Diagnosis/Mentally Ill Chemical Abuser [MICA]: Other terms used to describe the comorbidity of a drug use disorder and another mental illness.

Evidence Based Practice [EBP]: Preferential use of mental and behavioral health interventions for which systematic empirical research has provided evidence of statistically significant effectiveness as treatments for specific problems.

Family Psycho-Education: Provides education to individuals living with mental illness and their families. The goal is to assist the individual and their family to better understand his/her present illness, avoid relapse and contribute to their own health and wellness on a long-term basis.

Intake [Interview]: Occur when a client first seeks help from a clinician. It's the first interaction that occurs between the client and the clinician.

Intensive Outpatient Program [IOP]: The highest level of outpatient treatment before inpatient care.

Licensed Alcohol and Drug Counselor [LADC]: A licensed individual who helps people suffering from alcohol and substance abuse problems. Counselors help patients overcome addiction and adopt sober lifestyles, often in residential or outpatient rehabilitation programs.

Licensed Clinical Social Worker [LCSW]: An individual that holds a Master's degree in social work [MSW] and specializes in clinical practice. They work with clients in order to help them deal with issues involving their mental and emotional health. This could be related to substance abuse, past trauma or mental illness. There are a wide variety of specializations the Licensed Clinical Social Worker can focus on. These include Specialties such as : working with mental health issues, substance abuse, public health, school social work, medical social work, marriage counseling or children and family therapy.

Licensed Marriage and Family Therapist [LMFT]: An individual educated with a Master's or Doctoral degree, trained with a minimum of two [2] years of supervised clinical experience. LMFT's are trained and licensed to independently diagnose and treat mental health and substance abuse problems.

Licensed Professional Counselor [LPC]: Licensed professional counselor [LPCs] are Master's-degreed mental health service providers, trained to work with individuals, families, and groups in treating mental, behavioral, and emotional problems and disorders.

Major Depressive Disorder: A mood disorder having a clinical course of one or more serious depression episodes that last 2 or more weeks. Episodes are characterized by a loss of interest or pleasure in almost all activities; disturbances in appetite, sleep, or psychomotor functioning; a decrease in energy; difficulties in thinking or making decisions; loss of self-esteem or feelings of guilt; and suicidal thoughts or attempts.

Mania: A mood disorder characterized by abnormally and persistently elevated, expansive, or irritable mood; mental and physical hyperactivity; and/or disorganization of behavior.

Medication Evaluation/Medical Management: A psychiatrist or nurse practitioner monitors and evaluates a client's medications to ensure that the client is on the proper medications. Medication evaluation can be done at various intervals.

Mental Disorder: A mental condition marked primarily by sufficient disorganization of personality, mind, and emotions to seriously impair the normal psychological or behavioral functioning of the individual. Addiction is a mental disorder.

Millon Clinical Multiaxial Inventory-III: This self report instrument yields scores on clinical syndromes and vitality scales [Millon, 1983 and 1992].

MINNESOTA MULTIPHASTIC PERSONALITY INVENTORY-2 [MMPI-2]: The MMPI-2 is a re-standardized version of the MMPI. This 567-item self-reported measure provides scores on 10 clinical scales, 10 supplementary scales, and 4 validity scales [Hathaway and McKinley, 1989].

NEUROTRANSMITTER: A chemical produced by neurons to carry messages from one nerve cell to another.

NURSE PSYCHOTHERAPIST: A nurse, who practices psychotherapy in a structured relationship with the client.

OUTPATIENT: Treatment that is provided in the community and not in a hospitalized setting.

PARAPROFESSIONALS: Paraprofessionals work under a trained professional in clinical settings, i.e.: Licensed Social Worker Associates [Bachelor level social workers].

PARTIAL HOSPITALIZATION PROGRAM [PHP]: A short-term day program that offers psychiatric services. PHP is less intrusive and traumatic than inpatient care. Clients are able to return to their homes at the end of the day, while still remaining under the care of mental health professionals on a daily basis.

PEER SUPPORT: Individuals or family members of those living with mental illness coming together to provide a self-directed, grassroots association that works to enhance the mental health of other local consumers. Peer support members meet as equals to give each other support on a reciprocal basis.

PERSONALITY ASSESSMENT INVENTORY: This self-report instrument contains 344 items and yields scores on 22 clinical scales [Morey, 1991].

POST-TRAUMATIC STRESS DISORDER [PTSD]: A disorder that develops After exposure to a highly stressful event [e.g., wartime combat, physical violence, or natural disaster]. Symptoms include sleeping difficulties, hyper-vigilance, avoiding reminders of the event, and re-experiencing the trauma through flashbacks or recurrent nightmares.

PSYCHIATRIC REHABILITATION PROGRAM [PRP]: A program that provides support and rehabilitation to individuals who suffer from mental illness. PRP focuses on daily living skills through the use of the community environment.

PSYCHIATRIC EVALUATION/ASSESSMENT: An evaluation performed by a psychiatrist or nurse practitioner. A psychiatric evaluation includes the history of the present illness, current symptoms the individual is experiencing, past history of illness, family history, a review of medications, mental status examinations and a physical examination.

PSYCHIATRIC MENTAL HEALTH NURSE PRACTITIONER [PMH-NP]: A registered nurse certified by the Connecticut State Board of Nursing, who is able to independently engage in mental health specialist activities.

PSYCHIATRIC NURSE PRACTITIONER: An experienced registered nurse who possess advanced training and education in the area of diagnosing and treating illness. Nurse practitioners are able to prescribe medication. Psychiatric nurse practitioners specialize in providing psychiatric care to individuals.

PSYCHIATRIST [MD/DO]: A medical doctor who possesses specialized training in the field of psychiatry. Psychiatrist must be licensed physicians in the state in which they practice and must also be certified by the American Board of Psychiatry.

PSYCHOLOGICAL TESTING: Tests which are given to individuals to assess and evaluate information. Psychological tests are administered and interpreted by a psychologist.

PSYCHOLOGIST [PHD/PSYD]: An individual who possesses a Doctoral degree in psychology. One must be licensed by the Connecticut State Board of Examiners of Psychologists. A psychologist can be a clinical or a counseling psychologist.

PSYCHOSIS: A mental disorder [e.g., schizophrenia] characterized by delusional or disordered thinking detached from reality; symptoms often include hallucinations.

REFERRAL DECISION SCALE: This self-administered, 14-item instrument specifically identifies the mental health problems of individuals entering jails [Teplin and Swartz, 1989].

RESIDENTIAL REHABILITATION PROGRAM [PRP]: Housing for individuals with a chronic mental health diagnosis, who are unable to live independently in the community.

RESPITE: Temporary shelter for a person in need of a short-term relief from a crisis they are experiencing or to provide relief to a caregiver.

SCHIZOPHRENIA: A psychotic disorder characterized by symptoms that fall into two categories: [1] positive symptoms, such as distortions in thought [delusions], perception [hallucinations], and language and thinking and [2] negative symptoms, such as flattened emotional responses and decreased goal directed behavior.

SELF-MEDICATION: The use of a substance to lessen the negative effects of stress, anxiety, or other mental disorders [or side effects of their pharmacotherapy]. Self-medication may lead to addiction and other drug-or alcohol-related problems.

SIMPLE SCREENING INSTRUMENT: This instrument examines five areas related to drug and alcohol dependence. It is in the public domain and therefore available at no cost [Center for Substance Abuse Treatment, 1994].

SLIDING SCALE: Fees are set according to the client's income [i.e., if the client has no income, the fee may be as low as $0].

STAGES OF CHANGE READINESS AND TREATMENT EAGERNESS SCALE [SOCRATES]: This instrument has two forms [one for alcohol use and one for drug use], with 19 items each. Subscale scores indicate which stage of change the individual is in. It is in the public domain and therefore available at no cost [Miller and Tonigan, 1996].

TCU DRUG DEPENDENCE SCREEN: This instrument provides diagnosable Symptoms of substance use and includes 19-items. It is in the public domain and therefore available at no cost [Simpson, 1993].

THE DISSOCIATIVE EXPERIENCE SCALE [DES]: This self-report Measure examines several areas as dissociative phenomena [e.g., amnesia, identity alterations, and spontaneous trance states] that are often signs of trauma [Bernstien and Putnam, 1986].

THE TRAUMATIC ANTECEDENT QUESTIONNAIRE [TAQ]: This widely use instrument measures life time experiences of trauma in 10 areas, e.g., amnesia, physical, sexual, witnessing trauma [Herman, Perry, and Van der Kolk, 1989].

TRAUMA SYMPTOM CHECKLIST 40: This 40-item, self- report instrument evaluates symptoms in adults that may have arisen from trauma experienced as a child or adult. The instrument contains six subscales, and items are related on a 4-point scale and cover frequency over the previous 2 months [Briere, 1996].

UNINSURED: An individual that does not have private insurance, Medicaid or Medicare.

UNIVERSITY OF RHODE ISLAND CHANGE ASSESSMENT [URICA] SCALE: This instrument does not require clinical training to administer and, like SOCRATES, subscale scores indicate which stage of change the individual is in [McConnaughy, Prochaska, and Velicer, 1983; DiClemente and Hughes, 1990].

Mental Health Resources | National

NATIONAL EMPOWERMENT CENTER

599 Canal St., 5th Floor East, Lawrence, MA, 01840
(800) 769-3728
www.power2u.org

A consumer/survivor/ex-patient-run organization that carries a message of recovery, empowerment, hope and healing to people with mental health and trauma issues; provides training, education, information, referrals and more.

NATIONAL MENTAL HEALTH CONSUMERS' SELF-HELP CLEARINGHOUSE

1211 Chestnut St., Suite 1100, Philadelphia, PA, 19107
(800) 553-4539
www.mhselfhelp.org

A peer operated national technical assistance center which has played a major role in the development of the mental health consumer/survivor/ex-patient movement. The movement strives for dignity, respect, and opportunity for those diagnosed with mental health conditions.

U.S. DEPT. OF JUSTICE – ADA UNIT/CIVIL RIGHTS DIVISION

950 Pennsylvania Avenue, NW, Civil Rights Division, Washington D.C., 20530
(800) 514-0301
www.ada.gov

The Division enforces federal statutes prohibiting discrimination on the basis of race, color, sex, disability, religion, familial status and national origin. Write to or call to obtain answers to general and technical questions regarding the American with disabilities Act: Mon, Tue, Wed and Fri 9:00am-5:30pm; Thur 12:30pm-5:30pm EST. Calls are confidential.

Suicide Prevention

AMERICAN FOUNDATION FOR SUICIDE PREVENTION (AFSP)

120 Wall St., 29th Floor, New York, NY 10005
(888) 333-2377, (212) 363-3501
www.afsp.org inquiry@afsp.org

AFSP is dedicated to understanding and preventing suicide through research, education, outreach to those with disorders, and those affected by suicide.

NATIONAL CENTER ON INSTITUTIONS AND ALTERNATIVES (NCIA)

7205 Rutherford Rd., Baltimore, MD 21244
(443) 780-1300
www.ncianet.org info@ncianet.org

NCIA, in partnership with the *National Institute of Corrections*, acts as the coordinator of the Jail Suicide Prevention Task Force. They conduct annual jail suicide prevention seminars, technical assistance to state officials and correctional facilities, and publish a quarterly newsletter, *Jail Suicide/Mental Health Update*.

TREVOR PROJECT, THE

80 Maiden Lane, New York 10038
(866) 488-7386
www.thetrevorproject.org

The Trevor Project focuses on suicide prevention efforts for those in the LGBT community. They operate a free helpline, provide educational materials and advocate for public policy.

Mental Health Resources | State-by State

Arizona

ARIZONA DIVISION OF BEHAVIORAL HEALTH SERVICES

150 North 18th Avenue, Phoenix, AZ 85007
(602) 364-4558
www.azdhs.gov/bhs

Arkansas

ARKANSAS DIVISION OF BEHAVIORAL HEALTH SERVICES

305 South Palm Street, Little Rock, AR 72205
(501) 686-9164
Humanservices.arkansas.gov/dbhs

California

CALIFORNIA DEPARTMENT OF HEALTH CARE SERVICES, MENTAL HEALTH SERVICES

1501 Capitol Avenue, MS 4000, P.O. Box 997413, Sacramento, CA, 95899
(916) 322-7445
www.dhcs.ca.gov

ALLIANCE FOR CHILDREN'S RIGHTS

3333 Wilshire Blvd Suite 550, Los Angeles, CA, 90010
(213) 368-6010
www.kids-alliance.org

Provides free legal services and advocacy. The alliance ensures children have safe, stable homes, health care, and the education they need to thrive. Write for additional information.

BOARD OF BEHAVIORAL SCIENCE EXAMINERS

1625 N. Market Blvd., Suite S-200 Sacramento, CA, 95834
(916) 574-7830
www.bbs.ca.gov/consumer/index.shtml

Protects and serves Californians by setting, communicating, and enforcing standards for safe and competent mental health practice

CENTER FOR HEALTH CARE RIGHTS

520 S. Lafayette Park Pl, Suite 214, Los Angeles, CA, 90057
(800) 824-0780

A non-profit organization dedicated to Medicare advocacy and education for Californians. Telephone Counseling available Mon-Fri 9:00am to 4:00pm.

DISABILITY RIGHTS CALIFORNIA (DRC)

1831 K St., Sacramento, CA, 95811
(800) 776-5746

Advocates, educates and litigates to advance and protect the rights of Californians with disabilities. Offers legal advice and representation to clients of the State's 21 regional centers.

LOS ANGELES COUNTY DEPARTMENT OF MENTAL HEALTH PATIENT'S RIGHTS OFFICE

550 S. Vermont Ave., 6th Floor, Los Angeles, CA, 90020
(213) 738-4888
www.lacounty.gov/patientsrights

Programs include representation at Certification Review Hearings and Riese Medication Capacity Hearings; Beneficiary Services Program: Investigates and responds to grievances/complaints against directly operated clinics and contracted agencies, assist with appeals and State Fair Hearings and provides advocacy and mediation services; Residential Advocacy Program; Jail Advocacy Program; Project Search Program; Training and Consultation.

MENTAL HEALTH ADVOCACY SERVICES, INC. (MHAS)

3255 Wilshire Blvd., Suite 902 Los Angeles, California 90010
(213) 389-2077
www.mhas-la.org

Provides free legal services to people with mental and developmental disabilities.

MENTAL HEALTH AMERICA OF LOS ANGELES

100 W. Broadway, Suite 5010, Long Beach, CA, 90802
(888) 242-2522
www.mhala.org

Promotes mental health recovery and wellness; works to ensure that individuals with mental illness reach rightful place as participating, productive members of the community.

THE MEDICAL BOARD OF CALIFORNIA

2005 Evergreen St., Suite 1200, Sacramento, CA, 95815
(800)633-2322
www.mbc.ca.gov/consumers

Responsible for investigating complaints and taking disciplinary actions against physicians, surgeons and other healthcare professionals, if a violation is confirmed.

Colorado

COLORADO DEPARTMENT OF HUMAN SERVICES

3824 West Princeton Circle, Denver, CO 80236-3111
(303) 866-7400
www.colorado.gov/cs

Connecticut

CONNECTICUT DEPARTMENT OF MENTAL HEALTH & ADDICTION SERVICES

410 Capital Avenue, Hartford, CT 06134
(860) 418-7000
www.ct.gov/dmhas

Delaware

DELAWARE HEALTH & SOCIAL SERVICES

1901 North DuPont HWY, Man Building, Room 187, New Castle, DE 19720
(302) 255-9398
www.dhss.delaware.gov/dsamh

District of Columbia

DC DEPARTMENT OF BEHAVIORAL HEALTH

64 New York Avenue, NE, 3rd floor, Washington, DC 20002
(202) 673-7440
dbh.dc.gov

Florida

FLORIDA DEPARTMENT OF CHILDREN & FAMILIES

1317 Winewood Boulevard, Building 6, Room 275, Tallahassee, FL 32399
(850) 487-2920
www.dcf.state.fl.us

Georgia

GEORGIA DEPARTMENT OF BEHAVIORAL HEALTH & DEVELOPMENTAL DISABILITIES

2 Peachtree Street, NW. 22nd floor, Atlanta, GA 30303-3171
(404) 657-2331
Dbhdd.georgia.gov/portal/site/D8HDD

Hawaii

HAWAII DEPARTMENT OF HEALTH-MENTAL HEALTH

1250 Punchbowl Street, Room 256. Honolulu, Hi 96813
(808) 586-4686
health.hawaii.gov/amhd/

Idaho

IDAHO DEPARTMENT OF HEALTH & WELFARE

450 West State Street 3rd Floor, Boise, ID 83702-0036
(208) 334-5935
www.healthand welfare.idaho.gov

Illinois

ILLINOIS DEPARTMENT OF HUMAN SERVICES-MENTAL HEALTH

401 South Clinton Street, Chicago, IL 60607
(312) 814-8755
www.dhs.state.il.us

Indiana

INDIANA FAMILY AND SOCIAL SERVICES ADMINISTRATION

402 West Washington Street, Indianapolis, IN 46207-7083
(317) 232-7800
www.in.gov/fssa/dmha

Iowa

IOWA DHS DIVISION OF MENTAL HEALTH AND DISABILITY SERVICES (MHDS)

1305 East Walnut Street 5th floor SE, Des Moines, IA 50319-0114
(515) 281-7277
dhs.iowa.gov/mhds

Kansas

KANSAS DEPARTMENT FOR AGING & DISABILITY SERVICES-MENTAL HEALTH

503 South Kansas Avenue, NE State Office Building, Topeka, KS 66603-3404
(785) 296-3471
www.kansasbehavioralhealthservices.org

Kentucky

KENTUCKY DEPARTMENT FOR BH, DEVELOPMENTAL & INTELLECTUAL DISABILITIES

275 East Main Street, 4WG, Frankfort, KY 40601
(502) 564-4527
dbhdid.ky.gov

Louisiana

LOUISIANA DEPARTMENT OF HEALTH AND HOSPITALS

628 North 4th Street, Baton Rouge, LA 70821-0629
(225) 342-2540
www.dhh.louisiana.gov

Maine

MAINE DEPARTMENT OF HEALTH & HUMAN SERVICES OFFICE OF SA & MH SERVICES

41 Anthony Avenue, State House Station #11, Augusta, ME 04333-0011
(207) 287-2595
www.maine.gov/dhhs/samhs

MARYLAND

MARYLAND DEPARTMENT OF HEALTH AND MENTAL HYGIENE

55 Wade Avenue, Catonsville, MD 21228
(410) 402-8300
bha.dhmh.maryland.gov

MASSACHUSETTS

MASSACHUSETTS DEPARTMENT OF MENTAL HEALTH

25 Staniford Street, Boston, MA 02114
(617) 626-8000
www.mass.gov/eohhs/consumer/ behavioral-health/

MICHIGAN

MICHIGAN DEPARTMENT OF COMMUNITY HEALTH

320 South Walnut, Lewis Cass Building, Lansing, MI 48913
(517) 335-0196
www.michigan.gov/mdch/

Minnesota

MINNESOTA DEPARTMENT OF HUMAN SERVICES AMHD & CMHD

PO Box 64918, Saint Paul, MN 55164-0981
(651) 431-2225
www.mn.gov/dhs/people-we-serve/people-wth-disabilities/health-care

Mississippi

MISSISSIPPI DEPARTMENT OF MENTAL HEALTH-MENTAL HEALTH

239 North Lamar Street, Robert E Lee Bldg. #1101, Jackson, MS 39201
(601) 359-1288
www.dmh.ms.gov/service-options/mental-health/

Missouri

MISSOURI DEPARTMENT OF MENTAL HEALTH-MENTAL HEALTH

1706 East Elm Street, Jefferson City, MO 65102
(573) 751-8017
dmh.mo.gov/ada/

Montana

MONTANA DEPARTMENT OF PUBLIC HEALTH & HUMAN SERVICES

100 North Park Avenue, Suite 300, Helena, MT, 59620-2905
(406) 444-3964
www.dphhs.mt.gov/amdd

Nebraska

NEBRASKA DEPARTMENT OF HEALTH & HUMAN SERVICES

301 Centennial Mall South, Lincoln, NE 68509-5026
(402) 471-8553
www.dhhs.ne.gov/behavioral-health

Nevada

NEVADA DIVISION OF PUBLIC AND BEHAVIORAL HEALTH

4150 Technology Way 2nd floor, Carson City, NV 89706-2009

(775) 684-4200
www.health.nv.gov

New Hampshire

NH DEPARTMENT OF HEALTH AND HUMAN SERVICES-MENTAL HEALTH

105 Pleasant Street, Concord, NH 03301
(603) 271-5000
www.dhhs.nh.gov/dcdcs/bbh

New Jersey

NEW JERSEY DEPARTMENT OF HUMAN SERVICES

222 South Warren Street, Trenton, NJ 08611
(609) 777-0702
www.state.nj.us/humanservices/dmhas

New Mexico

NM HUMAN SERVICES DEPARTMENT, BEHAVIORAL HEALTH SERVICES DIVISION

37 Plaza La Prenza, PO Box 2348, Santa Fe, NM 87504-1234
(505) 476-9256
www.hsd.state.nm.us/Behavioral Health Services Division

New York

NEW YORK OFFICE OF MENTAL HEALTH

44 Holland Avenue, Albany, NY 12229
(800) 597-8481
www.omh.ny.gov/omhweb

North Carolina

NC DEPARTMENT OF HEALTH AND HUMAN SERVICES

325 North Salisbury Street, Suite 679-C, Raleigh, NC 27699-3007
(919) 733-4670
www.ncdhhs.gov/mhddsas

North Dakota

NORTH DAKOTA DEPARTMENT OF HUMAN SERVICES

1237 West Divide Avenue, Suite 1-C, Bismarck, ND 58501
(701) 328-8920
www.nd.gov/dhs/services/mentalhealth/

Ohio

OHIO DEPARTMENT OF MENTAL HEALTH AND ADDICTION SERVICES

30 East Broad Street, 36th floor, Columbus, OH 43215-3430
(614) 466-2596
Mha.ohio.gov/

Oklahoma

OKLAHOMA DEPARTMENT OF MENTAL HEALTH AND SUBSTANCE ABUSE SERVICES

1200 NE 13th Street, Oklahoma City, OK 73152-3277
(405) 522-3908
www.ok.gov/odmhsas

Oregon

OREGON HEALTH AUTHORITY

500 Summer Street NE, E-86, Salem, OR 97301-1118
(503) 945-5763
www.oregon.gov/oha/amh

Pennsylvania

PENNSYLVANIA DEPARTMENT OF HUMAN SERVICES

625 Forster Street, Health and Welfare Building, Harrisburg, PA 17120
(717) 783-8200
www.dhs.state.pa.us/provider/mentalhealth

Puerto Rico

PUERTO RICO MENTAL HEALTH & ANTI ADDICTION

PO Box 607087, Bayamon, PR 00960-7087
(787) 763-7575
www.assmca.pr.gov

Rhode Island

RI DEPARTMENT OF BEHAVIORAL HEALTHCARE, DEVELOPMENTAL DISABILITIES & HOSP

14 Harrington Road, Barry Hall, Cranston, RI 02920
(401) 462-1000
www.bdhddh.ri.gov/bhservices

South Carolina

SC DEPARTMENT OF MENTAL HEALTH

2414 Bull Street, Columbus, SC 29202
(803) 898-8581
www.state.sc.us/dmh

South Dakota

SOUTH DAKOTA DEPARTMENT OF SOCIAL SERVICES

700 Governors Drive, Pierre, SD 57501
(605) 773-3123
dss.sd.gov/behavioralhealth/

Tennessee

TENNESSEE DEPARTMENT OF MENTAL HEALTH AND SUBSTANCE ABUSE SERVICES

500 Deaderick Street, Andrew Jackson Building, 5th Floor, Nashville, TN 37243
(800) 560-5767
tn.gov/mental/a&d

Texas

TEXAS DEPARTMENT OF STATE HEALTH SERVICES

PO Box 149347, M20503, Austin, TX 78714-9347
(877) 966-3784
www.dshs.state.tx.us/about-mhsa

Utah

UTAH DEPARTMENT OF HUMAN SERVICES

195 North 1950 West, 2nd floor, Salt Lake City, UT 84116
(801) 538-3939
www.dsamh.utah.gov

Vermont

VERMONT DEPARTMENT OF MENTAL HEALTH

26 Terrance Street, Redstone Building, Montpelier, VT 05609-1101
(802) 828-3824
mentalhealth.vermont.gov

Virginia

VIRGINIA DEPARTMENT OF BEHAVIORAL HEALTH & DEVELOPMENTAL SERVICES

PO Box 1797, Richmond, VA 23218-1797
(804) 786-3966
www.dbhds.virginia.gov

Washington

WASHINGTON DEPARTMENT OF SOCIAL AND HEALTH SERVICES

PO Box 45330, Lacey, WA 98504-5330
(877) 301-4557
www.dshs.wa.gov/dphr

West Virginia

WV BUREAU FOR BEHAVIORAL HEALTH & HEALTH FACILITIES

350 Capital Street, Room 350, Charleston, WV 25304
(304) 358-0627
www.dhhr.wv.gov/bhhf

Wisconsin

WISCONSIN DEPARTMENT OF HEALTH SERVICES-MENTAL HEALTH

1 West Wilson Street, Room 850, Madison, WI 53707-7851
(608) 266-2717
www.dhs.wisconsin.gov/mh-bamh

Wyoming

WYOMING DEPARTMENT OF HEALTH

6101 North Yellowstone Road, Suite 220, Cheyenne, WY 82002
(307) 777-5253
www.health.wyo.gov/behavioralhealth

2016: THE YEAR OF SOLITARY CONFINEMENT

itary Confinement:

Being held for 22 hours or more a day for longer than 15 days without meaningful human contact.

nited Nations Standard Minimum Rules for the Treatment of Prisoners

Also known as the "**Nelson Mandela Rules.**"

Solitary confinement received a lot of attention during 2016.

It began with the "**Nelson Mandela Rules**," unanimously adopted in December 2015 by the United Nations General Assembly. The rules defined solitary confinement as being held for 22 hours or more a day for longer than 15 days without "meaningful human contact," and stated that solitary confinement:

"shall be used only in exceptional cases as a last resort, for as short a time as possible and subject to independent review, and only pursuant to the authorization by a competent authority"

"shall not be imposed by virtue of a prisoner's sentence"

"should be prohibited in the case of prisoners with mental or physical disabilities when their conditions would be exacerbated by such measures"

it should not be used for indefinite and prolonged periods of time

it shall not be used on women or children

Every prisoner, prison administrator, and those with loved ones in prison knows the negative and long-term effects of those housed in solitary confinement. Medical research confirms that the denial of meaningful human contact can cause "isolation syndrome" the symptoms of which include anxiety, depression, anger, cognitive disturbances, perceptual distortions, paranoia, psychosis, self-harm and suicide, and can destroy a person's personality. The lack of contact is reduced to a point that is insufficient for most prisoners to remain mentally well functioning. (see "Mental Health Center" for more information.) While temporary use may be necessary for the orderly operation of a prison, it has clearly been overused by most state correction systems.

A November 2016 report from the *Association of State Correctional Administrators*, *Aiming to Reduce Time-In-Cell* revealed just how prevalent the use of solitary confinement is in this country, and what has been done to begin stemming the tide of its use since the release of the Nelson Mandela Report.

Recent Actions to Change the Use of Solitary Confinement

2016 was a busy year for awareness of the issues surrounding solitary confinement and the need for change. Even though there were many efforts made to make these changes, little has been solidified that will instantly change the way that solitary confinement is implemented.

Prisoners are all too aware that change is slow in the prison system. This is just the beginning.

As Leann K. Bertsch, President of the *Association of State Correctional Administrators* (ASCA) explained:

"What we are seeing is that prison systems are motivated to reduce the use of isolation in prisons and are actively putting into place policies designed to reduce the use of restricted housing. Restricted housing place substantial stress on both the staff working in those settings as well as the prisoners housed in those units. Our highest priority is to operate institutions that are safe for staff and inmates, and to keep communities to which prisoners will return safe."

Below is the timeline of steps taken towards quelling the use of solitary confinement in this country.

Presidential Action

President Barack Obama orders a review of the use of solitary confinement in the federal prison system. (July 2015)

Result:

January 2016: The review resulted in a report, U.S. Department of Justice Report and Recommendations Concerning the Use of Restrictive Housing.

Statement by President Obama:

"The Justice Department has completed its review, and I am adopting its recommendations to reform the federal prison system. These include banning solitary confinement for juveniles and as a response to low-level infractions, expanding treatment for the mentally ill and increasing the amount of time inmates in solitary can spend outside of their cells."

In addition to the restrictions the president announces, the Justice Department recommended the following changes:

Pregnant women should not be placed in restricted housing.

- Ban on the practice of using the status of LGBTI and gender non-conforming individuals as the sole basis for placement in restricted housing.

- Absent special circumstances, seriously mentally ill should not be placed in restricted housing.
- The use of disciplinary segregation should be eliminated as a sanction for "low level" offenses and the amount of should be reduced for time spent there for other offenses.
- Prisoners should be housed "in the least restrictive setting necessary" to ensure the safety of all, placement should be based on specific "clearly articulated" reasons, and should serve "a specific penological purpose." There should be a clear plan for returning the prisoner to less restrictive housing as promptly as possible, and each individual's placement in restrictive housing should be reviewed on a regular basis by a committee that includes medical and mental health professionals.

March 2016: President Obama issued a Presidential Memorandum, "Limiting the Use of Restrictive Housing by the Federal Government," directing executive departments and agencies to implement the Justice Department's recommendations.

Prison Administration Actions

American Correctional Association (ACA), an umbrella organization comprised of correctional facilities' leaders from across the U.S., created a *Restrictive Housing Ad Hoc Standards Committee* to revise its model standards. (Established in 2014)

Result: In August of 2016, the ACA approved recommendations from a revised report of its Ad Hoc Committee. The ACA's new standards called for many of the same recommendations made by the Department of Justice and enacted by presidential order. Additionally, the ACA 2016 standards included "living conditions that approximate those of the general inmate population" with "all exceptions… clearly documented."

Legislative Action

State legislative actions over solitary confinement issues increased in 2016, with limited success.

October 2016, **New Jersey** enacted a statute limiting the use of "isolated confinement" to no more than 15 consecutive days, and no more than 20 days during any 60-day period, amongst many other restrictions similar to the Justice Department's recommendations.

Result: VETOED by Governor Chris Christie.

Legislative solitary confinement reform bills under consideration for the fall 2016 session:

Federal legislation to limit solitary confinement (Senate Bill 3432, "SCRA 2016")

Known as the "***Solitary Confinement Reform Act***," the legislation seeks to mandate *that solitary confinement be limited to "the briefest term and the least restrictive conditions practicable,"* including at least four hours of out-of-cell time daily unless a prisoners "poses a substantial and immediate threat." The bill would likewise restrict the same uses as put forth by the Department of Justice (mentioned earlier.)

Further, the bill would *limit placement in administrative segregation to a maximum of 15 consecutive days*, and 20 total days in a 60-day period, unless necessary to contain a "substantial and immediate threat." It would also mandate that correctional facilities *allow prisoners in restricted housing to participate in programming "as consistent with those available in general population where practicable."* It would also *create a "Civil Rights Ombudsman"* within the Bureau of Prisons, who would be required to submit reports to Congress on problems related to civil rights violations and recommendations for change.

Finally, the bill proposed the *establishment of a national resource center* to coordinate activities among state, local, and federal prison systems to centralize data and research concerning solitary confinement.

Result: ***Pending***

Illinois (House Bill 5417) ***Result: Initial approval. Pending.***

Massachusetts (Senate Bill 2362) ***Result: Pending.***

Rhode Island (House Bill 7481) ***Result: Pending.***

Court Actions

California

Result: Limits were placed on the amount of time that prisoners may be confined in the Security Housing Unit (SHU) at Pelican Bay State Prison, providing for review of prisoners then in security housing units on the basis of gang affiliation within 12 months of the settlement agreement; and set forth a presumption that all prisoners detained in SHU for more than 10 years would be moved into the general population.

Indiana

Result: Prohibited, with some exceptions, the placement of mentally ill prisoners in restricted housing and provided standards for the minimum adequate treatment of those prisoners, including provision of recreation, showers, additional out-of-cell time, and therapeutic programming.

New York

Result: Settlement agreement included reforms to limit the frequency and duration of solitary confinement, including a detailed modification of the Department's guidelines for restrictive housing sentencing aimed at limiting the length of solitary confinement sentences, alternatives to restrictive housing programs designed to address causes of disciplinary issues, and increased opportunities for prisoners to earn sentence reductions and lesser restricted housing sanctions.

The settlement also provided for greater protections for vulnerable populations such as prisoners with special needs, juveniles, prisoners in need of substance abuse treatment. It also mandated improvements in the conditions of confinement in restrictive housing, including the abolishment of "nutra loaf," increased movement options for good behavior, improved library services, access to correspondence courses and radio programming, and increased access to mental health consultations and treatments.

The following tables and information are excerpted from this report to show you the most current activity against the use of solitary confinement and the new standards that are slowly being adopted across the nation.

Number of Prisoners in Solitary Confinement – State-by-State

Over 67,000 prisoners were housed in solitary confinement across U.S. prisons a year ago (or the 45 responding jurisdictions, as of Fall 2015).

	Total prison population	Prisoners in solitary confinement	Percentage of prison population
Federal BOP	205,508	8,942	4.7%
Alabama	25,284	1,402	5.7
Alaska	4,919	352	7.2
Arizona	42,736	2,544	6
California	128,164	1,104	0.9
Colorado	18,231	217	1.2
Connecticut	16,056	128	0.8
Delaware	5,824	381	8.8
D.C.	1,153	95	8.2
Florida	99,588	8,103	8.1
Georgia	56,656	3,880	6.8
Hawaii	4,200	23	0.5
Idaho	8,013	404	5
Illinois	46,609	2,255	4.8
Indiana	27,508	1,621	5.9
Iowa	8,302	247	3
Kansas	9,952	589	5.9
Kentucky	11,669	487	4.2
Louisiana	36,511	3,003	8.2
Maryland	19,687	1,485	7.5
Massachusetts	10,004	235	2.3
Michigan	42,826	1,339	3.1
Minnesota	9,321	622	6.7
Mississippi	18,866	185	1
Missouri	32,266	2,028	6.3
Montana	2,554	90	3.5
Nebraska	5,456	598	11
New Hampshire	2,699	125	4.6
New Jersey	20,346	1,370	6.7
New Mexico	7,389	663	9
New York	52,621	4,498	8.5
North Carolina	38,039	1,517	4
North Dakota	1,800	54	3
Ohio	50,248	1,374	2.7
Oklahoma	27,650	1,552	5.6
Oregon	14,724	630	4.3
Pennsylvania	50,349	1,716	3.4
South Carolina	20,978	1,068	5.1
South Dakota	3,526	106	3
Tennessee	20,095	1,768	8.8
Texas	148,365	5,832	3.9
Utah	6.497	915	14
Vermont	1,783	106	5.9
Virginia	30,412	854	2.8
Washington	16,308	274	1.7
Wisconsin	22,965	751	3.7
Wyoming	2,128	131	6.2
Totals	1,437,276	67,442	4.9%

Hours Per Day Spent in Solitary Confinement

The following represent the amount of prisoners who spend more than 16 hours per day in their cell, and have done so for 15 consecutive days or longer.

	Prison population	22 hours or more	20-21 hours	16-19 hours	Total 16-24 hours	Percent of prison population
Alaska	4,919	352	0	0	352	7.2%
California	117,171	1,104	6,628	597	8,329	7.1
Colorado	18,231	217	202	99	518	2.8
Connecticut	16,056	128	186	381	695	4.3
D.C.	1,153	95	0	0	95	8.2
Hawaii	4,200	23	0	0	23	0.5
Idaho	8,013	404	0	0	404	5.0
Indiana	27,508	1,621	246	640	2,507	9.1
Iowa	8,302	247	213	0	460	5.5
Kansas	9,952	589	392	0	981	9.9
Louisiana	18,515	2,689	0	0	2,689	14.5
Maryland	19,687	1,485	0	0	1,485	7.5
Massachusetts	10,004	235	0	29	264	2.6
Michigan	42,826	1,339	0	0	1,339	3.1
Mississippi	18,866	185	0	0	185	1
Missouri	32,266	2,028	0	222	2,250	7
Montana	2,554	90	6	0	96	3.8
Nebraska	5,456	598	0	0	598	11
New Hampshire	2,699	125	44	0	169	6.3
New Jersey	20,346	1,370	6	0	1,376	6.8
New Mexico	7,389	663	0	175	838	11.3
New York	52,621	4,498	347	245	5,090	9.7
North Carolina	38,039	1,517	815	0	2,332	6.1
North Dakota	1,800	54	0	0	54	3.0
Oklahoma	27,650	1,552	20	0	1,572	5.7
Oregon	14,724	630	22	34	686	4.7
Pennsylvania	50,349	1,716	226	0	1,942	3.9
South Dakota	3,526	106	0	5	111	3.1
Texas	148,365	5,832	1,063	2,183	9,078	6.1
Utah	6,497	912	122	0	1,034	15.9
Virginia	30,412	854	1,289	0	2,143	7
Washington	16,308	274	0	0	274	
Wyoming	2,128	131	0	17	148	7

Length of Time Prisoners are in Solitary Confinement

At least 3,000 U.S. prisoners have been held in solitary confinement for more than six years.

	15 days to one month	1-3 months	3-6 months	6 months to one year	1-3 years	3-6 years	6+ years
Federal BOP	1,690	3,802	1,449	929	731	183	158
Alaska	124	74	49	60	43	5	0
Arizona	140	472	530	809	488	34	71
California	23	106	177	181	270	168	154
Colorado	64	65	64	23	1	0	0
Connecticut	19	20	23	17	22	7	13
Delaware	25	99	84	76	67	12	18
D.C.	33	51	6	5	0	0	0
Florida	2,026	3,254	1,327	741	401	195	159
Hawaii	21	2	0	0	0	0	0
Idaho	55	91	49	55	21	3	1
Indiana	212	224	388	496	175	80	46
Iowa	97	80	30	24	16	0	0
Kansas	125	146	87	105	94	22	10
Kentucky	139	222	52	41	28	4	1
Louisiana	327	551	334	302	450	221	0
Maryland	201	725	357	136	56	8	2
Massachusetts	2	3	12	65	71	24	43
Minnesota	102	308	103	47	7	0	0
Mississippi	3	21	29	41	69	17	5
Montana	58	0	67	2	4	0	3
Nebraska	48	121	158	87	106	48	30
New Jersey	54	247	295	354	184	128	108
New York	1,615	1,454	671	257	101	32	0
North Carolina	461	579	460	12	4	1	0
North Dakota	8	13	12	17	4	0	0
Ohio	119	360	181	253	162	43	22
Oklahoma	169	270	206	270	490	77	70
Oregon	90	152	277	81	26	4	0
Pennsylvania	349	524	288	156	157	52	190
South Carolina	238	370	128	114	151	67	0
South Dakota	18	16	10	15	27	12	8
Tennessee	89	239	222	353	500	166	205
Texas	109	204	277	537	1,840	1,278	1,587
Utah	233	169	173	125	166	35	11
Vermont	17	3	2	0	0	0	0
Virginia	219	306	119	89	101	20	0
Washington	16	55	68	70	37	16	12
Wisconsin	278	285	88	60	36	4	0
Wyoming	8	30	24	59	9	0	1
Totals	9,638	15,725	8,891	7.087	7,132	2.976	2,933

INCARCERATION RATES

WORLD PRISON POPULATION

The following list are the total numbers of prisoners around the world and rates of incarceration, by continent and select countries. These include both pre-trial and convicted individuals.

	Prison Population	Area Population	Incarceration Rate (per 100,000)
World	**10,357,134**	**7.2 billion**	**144**

Americas	**3,780,528**	**970 million**	**387**
North America			
U.S.A.	2,217,000	318 million	698
Canada	37,864	36 million	106
Greenland	116	55,700	208

Central America			
Belize	1,545	344,000	449
Costa Rica	17,440	4.9 million	352
El Salvador	31,686	6.4 million	492
Guatemala	19,810	16.4 million	121
Honduras	16,331	8.3 million	196
Mexico	255,138	120.2 million	212
Nicaragua	10,569	6.2 million	171
Panama	15,508	3.7 million	392
Caribbean			
Bahamas	1,396	385,000	363
Cuba	57,337	11.3 million	510
Dominican Republic	24,832	10.6 million	233
Haiti	10,266	10.5 million	97
Jamaica	4,050	2.79 million	145
Trinidad & Tobago	3,481	1.4 million	258
Puerto Rico	12,327	3.5 million	350

	Prison Population	Area Population	Incarceration Rate (per 100,000)
South America			
Argentina	69,060	43.2 million	160
Bolivia	13,468	11.1 million	122
Brazil	607,731	202 million	301
Chile	44,238	17.9 million	247
Colombia	121,389	49.7 million	244
Ecuador	25,902	16.03 million	162
Guyana	1,967	758,500	259
Paraguay	10,949	6.9 million	158
Peru	75,379	31.2 million	242
Uruguay	9,996	3.4 million	291
Venezuela	55,007	30.9 million	178

Africa	1,038,735	1.1 billion	94
Northern Africa			
Algeria	60,220	37.3 million	162
Egypt	62,000	82.1 million	76
Libya.	6,187	6.24 million	99
Morocco	76,000	34.3 million	222
Sudan	19,101	38 million	50
Tunisia	23,686	11.2 million	212
Western Africa			
Benin	7,247	9.4 million	77
Ghana	14,297	26.96 million	53
Guinea	3,110	12.1 million	26
Liberia	1,719	4.4 million	39
Mali	5,209	15.8 million	33
Niger	7,424	18.87 million	39
Nigeria	56,620	180.8 million	31
Senegal	8,630	13.9 million	62
Sierra Leone	3,488	6.4 million	55
Togo	4,493	7 million	64

	Prison Population	Area Population	Incarceration Rate (per 100,000)
Central Africa			
Angola	22,826	21.45 million	106
Cameroon	25,914	4.8 million	115
Chad	4,831	12.26 million	39
Congo (Dem.)	21,722	67.8 million	32
Eastern Africa			
Ethiopia	111,050	86.47 million	128
Kenya	54,145	45.80 million	118
Madagascar	18,719	22.48 million	83
Malawi	12,156	16.73 million	73
Mozambique	15,430	25.38 million	61
Rwanda	54,297	12.5 million	434
Seychelles	735	92,000	799
Tanzania	34,196	49.72	69
Uganda	45,092	39.19 million	115
Zambia	18,560	14.82 million	125
Zimbabwe	18,857	10.01 million	145
Southern Africa			
Botswana	3,826	2.03 million	188
Lesotho	2,073	2.26 million	92
Namibia	3,560	2.48 million	144
South Africa	159,241	54.6 million	292
Swaziland	3,616	1.25 million	289

Asia	**3,897,797**	**4.2 billion**	**92**
Western Asia			
Bahrain	4,028	1.34 million	301
Iraq	42,880	34.8 million	123
Israel	20,245	7.9 million	256
Jordan	10,089	6.7 million	150
Kuwait	3,200	3.48 million	92
Lebanon	6,012	5.02 million	120
Oman	1,300	3.63 million	36
Qatar	1,150	2.17 million	53

	Prison Population	Area Population	Incarceration Rate (per 100,000)
Saudi Arabia	47,000	29.17 million	161
Syria	10,599	17.7 million	60
United Arab Emirates	11,193	4.88 million	229
Yemen	14,000	26.23	53
Central Asia			
Kazakhstan	41,333	17.68 million	234
Kyrgyzstan	9,729	5.85 million	166
Tajikistan	9,317	7.7 million	121
Turkmenistan	30,568	5.24 million	583
Uzbekistan	43,900	29.33 million	150
South Central Asia			
Afghanistan	26,519	35.6 million	74
Bangladesh	69,719	160.65 million	43
India	418,536	1.28 billion	33
Iran	225,624	78.6 million	287
Nepal	16,813	28.27 million	59
Pakistan	80,169	187.5 million	43
Sri Lanka	19,774	21.45 million	92
South Eastern Asia			
Cambodia	16,497	15.69 million	105
Indonesia	161,692	253.18 million	64
Laos	4,020	5.7 million	71
Malaysia	51,946	30.45 million	171
Myanmar	60,000	53.26 million	113
Philippines	120,076	99.17 million	121
Singapore	12,596	5.56 million	227
Thailand	311,036	67.45 million	461
Vietnam	142,636	92.55 million	154
Eastern Asia			
China	1,657,812	1.39 billion	119
Hong Kong (China)	8,284	7.29 million	114
Japan	60,486	127.02 million	48
Macau (China)	1,258	646,700	195
Mongolia	7,773	2.92 million	266

	Prison Population	Area Population	Incarceration Rate (per 100,000)
South Korea	50,800	50.1 million	101
Taiwan	63,734	23.47 million	272

Europe	**1,585,348**	**827 million**	**192**
Northern Europe			
Denmark	3,481	5.67 million	61
Estonia	2,830	1.31 million	216
Finland	3,105	5.47 million	57
Iceland	147	325,700	45
Ireland	3,733	4.64 million	80
Latvia	4,745	1.99 million	239
Lithuania	7,810	2.91 million	268
Norway	3,710	5.19	71
Sweden	5,400	9.75 million	55
UK: England & Wales	85,843	58.02 million	148
UK: N. Ireland	1,607	1.8 million	87
UK: Scotland	7,692	5.37 million	143
Southern Europe			
Albania	5,455	2.89 million	189
Andorra	55	76,250	72
Bosnia & Herzegovina			
(Federation)	1,722	2.35 million	73
(Republic)	940	1.32 million	71
Croatia	3,763	4.23 million	89
Cyprus	811	860,600 million	94
Greece	11,798	10.8 million	109
Italy.	52,434	60.8 million	86
Kosovo	1,816	1.81 million	100
Macedonia	3,034	2.07 million	147
Malta	582	429,740 million	135
Montenegro	1,083	621,900	174
Portugal	14,233	10.3 million	138
Serbia	10,500	7.1 million	148
Slovenia	1,511	2.06 million	73

	Prison Population	Area Population	Incarceration Rate (per 100,000)
Spain	63,025	46.38 million	136
Gibraltar (UK)	48	32,730	147
Western Europe			
Austria	8,188	8.58 million	95
Belgium	11,769	11.24 million	105
France	60,896	64.39 million	95
Germany	63,628	81.29 million	78
Liechtenstein	8	37,370 million	21
Luxembourg	631	562,400 million	112
Monaco	28	37,800 million	74
Netherlands	11,603	16.88 million	69
Switzerland	6,923	8.2 million	84
Central & Eastern Europe			
Belarus	29,000	9.47 million	306
Bulgaria	9,028	7.21 million	125
Czech Republic	20,628	10.56 million	195
Hungary	18,424	9.83 million	187
Moldova	7,643	3.55 million	215
Poland	72,609	37.99 million	191
Romania	28,383	19.79 million	143
Slovakia	9,991	5.43 million	184
Ukraine	71,046	36.5 million	195
Europe/Asia			
Armenia	3,880	2.99 million	130
Azerbaijan	22,526	9.54 million	236
Georgia	10,236	3.73 million	274
Russian Federation	642,470	144.4 million	445
Turkey	172,5662	78.47 million	220

Oceania			
Australia	35,949	23.75	151
Fiji	1,555	894,000	174
Kiribati	141	104,000	136
Marshall Islands	35	53,000	66

	Prison Population	Area Population	Incarceration Rate (per 100,000)
Micronesia	132	104,00	127
New Zealand	8,906	4.6 million	194
Palau	72	21,000	343
Papua New Guinea	4,580	7.53 million	61
Samoa	481	192,500	250
Solomon Islands	323	575,000	56
Tonga	176	106,000	166
Vanuatu	230	265,000	87
American Samoa	214	56,000	382
Cook Islands	25	23,000	109
French Polynesia	451	283,000	159
Guam	797	170,000	469
New Caledonia	459	263,000	175
N. Mariana Island	175	65,500	267
Institute for Criminal Policy Research (ICPR), World Prison Brief 11th Edition			

Which States Put the Most People in Prison?

The U.S. has the highest percentage of its population in prison in the world. But which states put the most in prison? The U.S. average incarceration rate is 471/100,000, or a 1 in 212 chance of incarceration (per 100,000 people). You might want to consider paroling to the bottom of the list!

RANK (WORST TO BEST)	STATE	INCARCERATION RATE (PER 100,000)	ODDS OF BEING IMPRISONED (PER 100,000)
1	Louisiana	877	1 in 114
2	Oklahoma	700	1 in 142
3	Alabama	633	1 in 158
4	Arkansas	599	1 in 167
5	Mississippi	597	1 in 168
6	Arizona	593	1 in 169
7	Texas	584	1 in 171
8	Missouri	526	1 in 190
9	Georgia	517	1 in 193
10	Florida	513	1 in 195
11	Idaho	489	1 in 204
12	Kentucky	474	1 in 211
13	Virginia	449	1 in 223
14	Ohio	444	1 in 225
15	Indiana	442	1 in 226
16	Delaware	440	1 in 227
17	Tennessee	437	1 in 229
18	Michigan	437	1 in 229
19	Nevada	434	1 in 230
20	South Carolina	429	1 in 233
21	South Dakota	421	1 in 233
22	Wyoming	408	1 in 245
23	Pennsylvania	394	1 in 254
24	Colorado	383	1 in 261
25	Oregon	378	1 in 265
26	Illinois	375	1 in 267
27	Alaska	374	1 in 267
28	West Virginia	372	1 in 269
29	Wisconsin	371	1 in 270
30	Montana	360	1 in 278
31	North Carolina	358	1 in 279
32	California	349	1 in 287
33	Maryland	346	1 in 289
34	New Mexico	329	1 in 304
35	Connecticut	326	1 in 307
36	Kansas	322	1 in 311
37	Nebraska	283	1 in 353
38	Iowa	282	1 in 355
39	New York	265	1 in 377
40	Hawaii	257	1 in 389
41	New Jersey	241	1 in 415
42	Vermont	241	1 in 415
43	Utah	237	1 in 421
44	New Hampshire	219	1 in 457
45	North Dakota	214	1 in 467
46	Minnesota	194	1 in 515
47	Massachusetts	188	1 in 532
48	Rhode Island	178	1 in 562
49	Maine	153	1 in 654

RANDOM TRENDS

Prisoner Recidivism Rates

This year, the U.S. Department of Justice's Bureau of Justice Statistics released recidivism rates of offenders over the last ten years (June 2016). As has been consistent throughout this century, among those conditionally released from federal prison, nearly half (47%) were arrested within 5 years, while more than three-quarters (77%) of state prisoners were arrested.

	FEDERAL PRISONERS		STATE PRISONERS	
Characteristic	**Arrest**	**Return to prison**	**Arrest**	**Return to prison**
All released prisoners	47.2%	31.6%	76.5%	59.4%
Sex				
Male	49.6%	33.4%	77.5%	56.4%
Female	35.4	22.1	68.1	44.9
Race				
White	39.7%	26.2%	73.1%	53.2%
Black/African American	55.1	35.7	80.6	55.6
Hispanic/Latino	48.3	33.1	75.7	57.8
Other	48.5	38.5	74.2	58.8
Age at release				
24 or younger	64.7%	45.8%	84.2%	62.2%
25-29	59.3	40.7	80.6	57.3
30-34	52.9	34.7	77	54.8
35-39	48.6	31.9	78.1	56
40-44	44.5	29.4	74.2	55
45-49	37.7	24.7	69	48.8
50+	23.5	14.7	58.8	41.9
Most serious commitment offense				
Violent	58.1%	44.3%	73.8%	51%
Property	39.5	26.1	82.2	62.5
Drug	44	27.1	76.7	53.2
Other public order	57	40.2	73	54.2
Sex offense	36.7	33.9	61	45.4

How Do Prisoners Die?

	State Prison	Local Jail	Male	Female
All causes	100%	100%	100%	100%
Illness				
Heart Disease	24.9%	23.3%	24.8%	20.3%
AIDS-related	2.8	3.4	2.9	4.7
Cancer	26.6	4.0	22.3	15
Liver Disease	9.3	3.7	8.3	4.7
Respiratory Disease	6.5	3.6	5.8	7.4
Unnatural Deaths				
Suicide	6.2%	31%	11.2%	14.1%
Homicide	1.7	2.0	1.9	0.1
Drug/alcohol related	1.4	6.5	2.4	4.7
Accident	0.9	2.1	1.1	1.3
Other/Unknown	1.0%	3.2%	1.4%	2.0%

Murder Rates in the U.S. (largest cities)

The national murder rate is projected to increase by 13.1 percent. In 2015, Baltimore, Chicago and Washington DC were responsible for half the increase. In 2016, nearly half of the increase will have occurred in Chicago alone.

City	2015 total murders	2016 total murders (projected)	Percent change
New York	352	359	+2.1%
Los Angeles	283	276	-2.6
Chicago	493	727	+47.4
Houston	303	345	+13.9
Philadelphia	273	293	+7.5
San Antonio	94	144	+52.9
San Diego	37	48	+30.4
Dallas	170	204	+20.2
San Jose	30	51	+70.6
Austin	24	52	+115.4
San Francisco	52	56	+8.3
Charlotte	60	56	-7.4
Seattle	24	26	+8.3
Denver	54	56	+3.1
Detroit	300	293	-2.5
Washington DC	162	144	-10.9
Boston	39	49	+26.7
Nashville	63	85	+34.5
Oklahoma City	74	95	+28.6
Las Vegas	134	168	+25.3
Baltimore	343	309	-9.9
Louisville	87	111	+27.3

How Much Does Prison Cost | A State-By-State Look

Recently, the Vera Institute of Justice sent out a survey to prison systems in every state to determine the total cost of prisons the previous year. Forty states responded. Here are those results:

State	Total Cost	Cost per Prisoner (avg)
Alabama	$462.5 m	$17,285
Arizona	$998.5 m	$24,805
Arkansas	288.6 m	$24,291
California	$7.9 b	$47,421
Colorado	$606.2 m	$30,374
Connecticut	$929.4 m	$50,262
Delaware	$215.2 m	$32,967
Florida	$2.08 b	$20,553
Georgia	$1.1 b	$21,039
Idaho	$144.7 m	$19,545
Illinois	$1.7 b	$38,268
Indiana	$569.5 m	$14,823
Iowa	$276 m	$32,925
Kansas	$158.2	$18,207
Kentucky	$311.7 m	$14,603
Louisiana	$698.4 m	$17,486
Maine	$100.6 m	$46,404
Maryland	$836.2 m	$38,383
Michigan	$1.3 b	$28,117
Minnesota	$395.3 m	$41,364
Missouri	$680.5 m	$22,350
Montana	$76 m	$30,227
Nebraska	$163.3 m	$35,950
Nevada	$282.9 m	$20,656
New Hampshire	$81.4 m	$34,080
New Jersey	$1.4 b	$54,865
New York	$3.6 b	$60,076
North Carolina	$1.2 b	$29,965
North Dakota	$58.1 m	$39,271
Ohio	$1.32 b	$25,814
Oklahoma	$453.4 m	$18,467
Pennsylvania	$2.1 b	$42,339
Rhode Island	$172.1 m	$49,133
Texas	$3.3 b	$21,390
Utah	$186 m	$29,349
Vermont	$111.3 m	$49,502
Virginia	$748.6	$25,129
Washington	$799.6 m	$46,897
West Virginia	$169.2 m	$26,498
Wisconsin	$874.4	37,994

The Price of Prisons: What Incarceration Costs Taxpayers, Vera Institute of Justice

Legal Center

Legal Center

There are currently over 2.3 million Americans incarcerated in the U.S.

Some within this number have been wrongly convicted. Many others were convicted unfairly. Still others, although perhaps rightfully and fairly convicted, are living under conditions that are in violation of their constitutionally given rights established to protect them while they live in prison.

The *Legal Center* is a resource designed to give you an overview of specific rights that you have as a prisoner, to help you determine if those rights have been violated, and if so, to help you to navigate the legal system so that you can fight for those rights.

This is your legal roadmap established to provide you with many of the tools, resources, and information you need to send you in the right direction to ensure that your rights are protected now, and continue to be during your prison stay.

LEGAL CENTER

Your Rights

Prisoners never used to have rights.

> *"A convicted felon has, as a consequence of his crime, not only forfeited his liberty, but all of his personal rights except those which the law in its humanity accords to him. He is for the time being the slave of the state."*
>
> ◦ ***Ruffin v. Commonwealth***, 62 Va. 790, 796 (1871)

Prisoners were once slaves of the state.

Until the 1960s, the "prisoner's rights" were rarely, if ever, enforced by the courts. The general consensus at the time was that prisoners forfeited any rights that they had by committing a crime. Others believed that even if inmates had rights, the courts had no business enforcing those rights. There was a fear that that courts may interfere with the delicate and difficult task of operating a prison. Therefore, this judicial policy of refusing to adjudicate prisoner's constitutional claims became known as the hands-off doctrine.

> *"It is well settled that it is not the function of the courts to superintend the treatment and discipline of prisoners in penitentiaries, but only to deliver from imprisonment those who are illegally confined."*
>
> o ***Stroud v. Swope***, 187 F.2d 850, 851 (9th Cir. 1951)

That time has passed.

In the 1960s and 70s, in part because of their increasing awareness of the deplorable conditions in many of the nations prisons. the lower courts began to abandon the hands-off doctrine, Disturbances and riots in those prisons, including the 1971 riot at the Attica State Prison in Attica, New York in which 43 correctional officers and inmates were killed, made it clear that courts could no longer entrust to the executive and legislative branches of the government the exclusive responsibility for protecting the rights of prisoners. The courts themselves would have to intervene to protect prisoners' rights.

Fortunately, courts and most prison directors have come to their senses and have long rejected this doctrine. Although prisoner's rights may be necessarily narrowed to some degree, due to the sentence given or the need to assure prison security, prisoners are certainly not wholly without rights. There is no razor wire lined wall between the Constitution and the prisons of this country.

Today, it is widely accepted that if you as a prisoner have a constitutional right to something, and if some harm has come to you from denying one of your rights that is sufficiently grievous and that cannot be justified by the demands of incarceration, the violation against you must be corrected.

However, in order for you to even be aware of whether one of your rights has been violated, it is vital that you know what your rights are.

The Bill of PRISONER'S Rights

The Constitution of the United States is the supreme law of the land, a law that has been doctrine since 1803. Any laws, statutes, regulations, or government policies in conflict with the Constitution are unenforceable. It is the standard by which all governmental action is measured.

Prisoners are protected under the Constitution and its amendments. The Bill of Rights, adopted at the same time as the Constitution, protects prisoners from actions of the government.

Courts have reviewed conduct by prison officials under the following specific constitutional provisions:

1st Amendment

Congress shall make no law respecting an establishment of religion, or prohibiting the free exercise thereof; or abridging the freedom of speech, or of the press; or the right of the people peaceably to assemble, and to petition the Government for a redress of grievances.

Prisoner Translation:

- ✓ You are free to practice religion.
- ✓ You have unfettered access to the courts.
- ✓ You have access to communication (telephones, mail, and media).
- ✓ You have access to specific communication equipment if you are hearing impaired.
- ✓ You have the right to complain through appropriate grievance procedures.

4th Amendment

The right of the people to be secure in their persons, houses, papers, and effects, against unreasonable searches and seizures, shall not be violated, and no Warrants shall issue, but upon probable cause, supported by Oath or affirmation, and particularly describing the place to be searched, and the persons or things to be seized.

Prisoner Translation:

- ✓ You have specific rights against unlawful search and seizure.
- ✓ You have protection against unreasonable use of force.

5th Amendment

No person shall be held to answer for a capital, or otherwise infamous crime, unless on a presentment or indictment of a Grand Jury, except in cases arising in the land or naval forces, or in the Militia, when in actual service in time of War or public danger; nor shall any person be subject for the same offence to be twice put in jeopardy of life or limb; nor shall be compelled in any criminal case to be a witness against himself, nor be deprived of life, liberty, or property, without due process of law; nor shall private property be taken for public use, without just compensation.

Prisoner Translation:

- ✓ You have a right against telling on yourself, such as in criminal appeals and in some disciplinary proceedings.
- ✓ You have a right against being tried twice for the same offense.

6th Amendment

In all criminal prosecutions, the accused shall enjoy the right to a speedy and public trial, by an impartial jury of the State and district wherein the crime shall have been committed, which district shall have been previously ascertained by law, and to be informed of the nature and cause of the accusation; to be confronted with the witnesses against him; to have compulsory process for obtaining witnesses in his favor, and to have the Assistance of Counsel for his defence.

Prisoner Translation:

- ✓ You have a right to a speedy trial, an impartial jury, to confront and obtain witnesses, and to attorney assistance in criminal matters.
- ✓ You have a right to an attorney for some civil rights matters (solely at the court's discretion.)
- ✓ You have a right to contact attorneys from prison.
- ✓ You have a right to defend yourself.

7th Amendment

In suits at common law, where the value in controversy shall exceed twenty dollars, the right of trial by jury shall be preserved, and no fact tried by a jury, shall be otherwise reexamined in any Court of the United States, than according to the rules of the common law.

8th Amendment

Excessive bail shall not be required, nor excessive fines imposed, nor cruel and unusual punishments inflicted.

Prisoner Translation:

- ✓ You have a right against unreasonable searches meant to harass.
- ✓ You have a right to clean clothing adequate for the conditions you live under.
- ✓ You have a right to nutritionally adequate and sanitarily prepared food and water.
- ✓ You have a right to special diets for medical and religious needs.
- ✓ You have a right to reasonably adequate medical care commensurate with modern medical science regardless of your ability to pay.
- ✓ You have a right to reasonable safety, including protection from assault and other abuses by prisoners and staff, hazardous living and working conditions, and unnecessary use of force.

- ✓ You have a right to reasonable amounts of exercise and recreation.

13th Amendment

SECTION 1: Neither slavery nor involuntary servitude, except as a punishment for crime whereof the party shall have been duly convicted, shall exist within the United States, or any place subject to their jurisdiction.

Prisoner Translation:

- ✓ You have a right to not be a slave.

14th Amendment

SECTION 1: All persons born or naturalized in the United States, and subject to the jurisdiction thereof, are citizens of the United States and of the State wherein they reside. No State shall make or enforce any law which shall abridge the privileges or immunities of citizens of the United States; nor shall any State deprive any person of life, liberty, or property, without due process of law; nor deny to any person within its jurisdiction the equal protection of the laws.

Prisoner Translation:

- ✓ You have a right to be protected against discrimination based on age, race, religion, sexual preference, and disabilities.
- ✓ You have a right to specific "Due Process," the right to be heard in a specific and meaningful way, including additional protections in:
- ✓ Disciplinary proceedings (such as written notice, the right to be heard, to call and cross-examine witnesses, obtain defense assistance, a prompt hearing, an impartial decision-maker, standards of proof, and appeal opportunities.)
- ✓ Administrative segregation (such as notice of reasons for placement, an opportunity to present your views, and periodic review.)
- ✓ Excessive confinement (being held beyond your release date.)

* The 14th amendment is often linked with other constitutional and statutory violations to bolster 'due process' and 'equal protection' claims.

Have you heard your neighbors mention filing a "1983" action?

Here's what they were referring to:

1983 CIVIL ACTION (LAWSUIT) FOR DEPRIVATION OF RIGHTS

"Every person who, under color of any statute, ordinance, regulation, custom, or usage, of any State or Territory or the District of Columbia, subjects, or causes to be subjected, any citizen of the United States or other person within the jurisdiction thereof to the deprivation of any rights, privileges, or immunities secured by the Constitution and laws, shall be liable to the party injured in an action at law, suit in equity, or other proper proceeding for redress, except that in any action brought against a judicial officer for an act or omission taken in such officer's judicial capacity, injunctive relief shall not be granted unless a declaratory decree was violated or declaratory relief was unavailable. For the purposes of this section, any Act of Congress applicable exclusively to the District of Columbia shall be considered to be a statute of the District of Columbia."

For more information on civil lawsuits, see 'Your Right to Sue' later in this chapter.

Your Rights Explained

NOTE: The foregoing section provides overviews explaining specific prisoner rights in further detail. We urge you to consider the following:
1) We are not attorneys, and therefore provide no specific or binding legal assistance.
2) The law does not stop evolving with our publication release dates. Before using any of the following information, check with your law library to confirm that the cases and law cited are the most current information available.

The following are, of course, not ALL of your rights. That would be a publication in itself, several of which are referenced in our resource listings. And this is by no means a definitive amount of information on any of the topics. It is meant to be used as an overview, a guide to help you better understand some of the topics that may impact you.

If you decide that your rights may have been violated, refer to the case citings to further guide you towards a deeper understanding of your topic of interest. If you are uncertain how to proceed, refer to the 'Legal Resources' portion of this chapter.

Prisoner's rights are essentially categorized under three main headings:

- Conditions of Confinement
- Civil Liberties
- Due Process

Under each heading, you'll find the constitutional provision that governs this portion of your rights, as well as several of your rights therein. We'll then give you a better idea of some of your specific rights through a thorough breakdown of that right, complete with case law so you can research the right yourself.

Again, we cannot emphasize enough the importance of doing your own research. The following is just a starting point to give you a general overview and the resources you need to both understand your rights and know where to go to better ensure that those rights are protected.

Conditions of Confinement

> *"Prisons, of course, are not Hilton hotels. And disciplinary segregation units within prisons are not like rooms at a Motel 6. But even nasty prisoners cannot be knowingly housed in ghastly conditions reminiscent of the Black Hole of Calcutta."*
>
> ◦ **Isby v. Clark, 100 F.3d 502, 505 (7th Cir. 1996)**

Most prisoners at some point complain about their *conditions of confinement*. Understandably so, in many cases. Many prisons are overcrowded, unsafe, unsanitary places to have to visit, much less live in. The reason for this is that the Constitution does not give prisoners the right to be comfortable. Rather it grants them various rights to ensure that the "basic human needs" of each prisoner are met.

This portion of the Legal Center informs you of your essential rights under the *conditions of confinement* standards. These rights fall under the Eighth Amendment, unless otherwise noted.

Conditions of Confinement Rights

Shelter	A prisoner must be provided with "shelter which does not cause his degeneration or threaten his mental well-being." *Ramos v. Lamm*, 639 F.2d 559, 568 (10th Cir. 1980)
Sanitation	"A sanitary environment is a basic human need that a penal institution must provide for all inmates." *Toussaint v. McCarthy*, 597 F.Supp 1388. 1411 (N.D.Cal. 1984)
Food	"Food is one of the basic human necessities of life protected by the Eighth Amendment." Knop v. Johnson, 667 F.Supp 512, 525 (W.D.Mich. 1987)
Clothing	Prisoners are entitled to clothing that is "at least minimally adequate for the conditions under which they are confined." Knop v. Johnson, 667 F.Supp 467, 475-77 (W.D.Mich. 1987)
Medical Care *	"Deliberate indifference to serious medical needs of prisoners constitutes the 'unnecessary and wanton infliction of pain'... proscribed by the Eighth Amendment." *Estelle v. Gamble*, 429 U.S. 97, 104, 97 S, Ct. 285 (1976)
Personal Safety *	The Constitution requires prison officials to provide "reasonable safety" for prisoners. *Farmer v. Brennan*, 511 U.S.825, 844, 114 S. Ct. 1970 (1994)
Exercise	"It is generally recognized that total or near deprivation of exercise or recreational opportunity without penological justification, violates eighth amendment guarantees." Antonelli v. Sheahan, 81 F.3d 1422, 1432 (7th Cir. 1996)

*** Discussed in further detail in this section.**

Due Process Rights

The Due Process Clauses prohibit prison officials from depriving prisoners of "life, liberty, and property without due process of law.."

° **U.S. Constitutional Amendments V, XIV**

Prisoners have limited rights when it comes to Due Process, especially as it pertains to deprivations of their liberty and property. That does not mean, however, that you are without Due Process rights. In 1995, the U.S. Supreme Court limited the Due Process protections of prisoners, holding that prisoners should only be found to have liberty interests under three circumstances: 1) when the right at issue is independently protected by the Constitution. 2) When the challenged action causes the prisoner to spend more time in prison. 3) When the action imposes "atypical and significant hardship on the inmate in relation to the ordinary incidents of prison life." (*Sandin v. Conner*, 515 U.S. 472, 115 S. Ct. 2293 (1995).)

Remember, if you are housed in a federal facility, your Due Process rights are governed by the Fifth Amendment. If you are in state or local custody, these rights are governed by the Fourteenth Amendment.

Due Process Rights	
Segregation	The placement of convicts in segregation is a deprivation of liberty requiring due process protections if they are subjected to "atypical and significant hardship... in relation to ordinary incidents of prison life," and if there is a state-created liberty interest. *Sandin v. Conner*, 515 U.S. 472, 115 S. Ct. 2293 (1995)
Disciplinary Proceedings	Generally, prison disciplinary procedures will comply with due process requirements on paper, but they may be in violation if the prison officials do not follow their procedures.
Restraints	Limited use of restraints is constitutional, but more restrictive restraints, such as restraint chairs, or four-point restraints, their constitutionality depends on the circumstances in which they are used. Therefore, they are typically only to be used in extraordinary circumstances, such as when a prisoner presents a serious risk of danger to himself or others. Officials cannot use such restraints for punishment or to inflict pain. Stewart v. Rhodes, 473 F.Supp 1185, 1193 (S.D.Ohio 1979)
Transfers *	Transfers between prisons can usually be done without due process protections. *Meachum v. Fano*, 427 U.S. 215, 224-29, 96 S. Ct. 2532, 49 L. Ed. 2d 451 (1976) There are some special transfer situations where a court will find a constitutional liberty interest and offer some protections, which are discussed in this section.
Property	Prison officials may substantially restrict the property prisoners can possess. "But when inmates are afforded the opportunity... to possess property, they enjoy a protected interest in that property that cannot be infringed without due process." *McCrae v. Hankins*, 720 F.2d 863, 869 (5th Cir. 1983) If the prison

	intentionally takes or destroys your property, you can file a state-law tort action, or if none available, a federal civil rights claim.
Excessive Confinement	Failure to obey a court order requiring a prisoner's release denies due process. But most courts hold that due process is denied only if a prisoner is not released on time as a result of deliberate indifference. *Davis v. Hall*, 375 F.3d 703, 718-19 (8th Cir. 2004)

*** Discussed in further detail in this section.**

Civil Liberty Rights

"There is no iron curtain drawn between the Constitution and the prisons of this country."

° ***Wolff v. McDonnell*, 418 U.S. 539, 555-56, 94 S. Ct 2963 (1974)**

Civil liberties are rights shared by everyone in the United States. People do not lose these rights when they go to prison. However, prison official may severely restrict civil liberty rights to further its goals, such as to maintain security or promote rehabilitation.

The Supreme Court has held that "when a prison regulation impinges on inmates' constitutional rights, the regulation is valid if it is reasonably related to legitimate penological interests." (*Turner v.* Safley, 482 U.S. 78, 107 S.Ct. 2254 (1987).) To determine whether a challenge on these limitations is constitutionally protected, courts apply what is known as a "reasonable relationship" test, or the *Turner* test. Four factors are used in applying this test:

1) Whether there is a "valid, rational connection" between the limitation and the prison officials' justification for it.
2) Whether there is a different way for prisoners to exercise their civil liberty.
3) What the effect of exercising the civil liberty has on prison operations and other prisoners.
4) Whether there is a different way for officials to achieve their goals that still allows prisoners to exercise the civil liberty.

Courts trend to apply the *Turner* test in a way that strongly favors the prison's interests. Therefore, if you choose to challenge the prison officials in court, it is wise to emphasize three key points. 1) "reasonableness" under *Turner* requires courts to strike a balance between the interests of officials and the constitutional rights of prisoners. (*Reed v. Faulkner,* 842 F.2d 960, 962 (7th Cir. 1988).) 2) While it's appropriate for courts to defer to well-supported judgments of prison officials, "deference does not mean abdication." (Walker v. Sumner, 917 F.2d 382, 385 (9th Cir. 1990).) In other words, there are situations where prison officials overstep their bounds and violate the Constitution.

Most civil liberties claims are governed by the First Amendment.

Civil Liberty Rights

Access to the Courts	Prisoners have the right to access to the courts, but laws have made it difficult for prisoners to pursue claims. (SEE Prison Litigation Reform Act in this chapter.) There are three basic kinds of access claims: 1) Right to assistance (law libraries, etc.), 2) Interference claims (when prison officials interfere with access to courts), and 3) Retaliation Claims (when prison officials retaliate for legal actions.)
Religious Freedom	Prisoners have a First Amendment right to the exercise religion; however, what you can do about it while in prison is more limited. SEE our 'Religion Center' for a full discussion on this right.
Correspondence *	Prisoners have a First Amendment right to communicate by mail. However, prison officials can restrict these rights, so long as these restrictions are reasonably related to legitimate prison interests. Outgoing mail is less restricted, in that it cannot be greater than "necessary or essential" to protect "important or substantial interests." *Thornburgh v. Abbot*, 490 U.S. 401, 413-14, 109 S. Ct. 1874 (1989)
Publications	Prisoners have a First Amendment right to read, and publishers and others have the same right to send reading material to prisoners. Censorship is governed by the *Turner* test (see Intro)
Communication with the Media	Prisoners have a First Amendment right to "be free from governmental interference with [their] contacts with the press if that interference is based on the content of [their] speech or proposed speech." *Kimberlin v. Quinlan*, 199 F.3d 496, 502 (DC Cir. 1999). However, prisons can restrict by what method you make contact with the media.
Organization	The First Amendment protects "the right of the people peaceably to assemble, and to petition the Government for a redress of grievances." However, these rights are severely restricted in prisons. There is no right to belong to a gang. Restrictions are even upheld on informal or social association of prisoners. *Burnette v. Phelps*, 621 F.Supp. 1157, 1159-60 (M.D.La 1985)
Protests/Grievances	Grievances filed through an official grievance procedure are constitutionally protected. *Hoskins v. Lenear*, 395 F.3d 372, 375 (7th Cir. 2005). Other forms of individual protest are protected so long as it does not advocate to violate prison rules. *Pilgrim v. Luther*, 571 F.3d 201, 204-5 (2nd Cir. 2009)
Visiting *	The Constitution provides very little protection for visitation in prison. While prisons generally allow visitation, restrictions against minors, on visitation with ex-offenders, and on time, place and attire, are typically upheld under the *Overton v. Bazzetta,* 539 U.S. 126, 131, 123 S. Ct. 2162 (2003).
Telephones	Prisoners have a First Amendment right to telephone access within certain limitations, such as pre-approved lists, amount of time, or further restrictions to those housed in segregation units. *Johnson v. State of California*, 207 F.3d 650, 656 (9th Cir. 2000)
Voting	States can choose whether to deny prisoners the right to vote (termed "disenfranchise") under the Fourteenth Amendment. Currently all states except for Maine and Vermont bar prisoners form voting, and 35 disallow parolees from voting, and 30 disallow probationers. *Richardson v. Ramirez*, 418 U.S. 24, 55-6,(1974)
Family Life	Prisoners have a constitutional right to marry, but not to have conjugal visitation. There is no right to conceive a child while in custody. *Zablocki v. Redhail*, 434 U.S. 374, 383-86, 98 S. Ct. 673 (1976)

*** Discussed in further detail in this section.**

Your Right to Sue

The Supreme Court has repeatedly affirmed that one of the fundamental rights within the due process clause of the Fourteenth Amendment is the right of access to the courts. Essential to the concept of due process of law is the right of an individual to have "an opportunity . . . granted at a meaningful time and in a meaningful manner," (*Armstrong v. Manzo*, 380 U.S. 545, 552 (1965)) "for [a] hearing appropriate to the nature of the case." (*Mullane v. Central Hanover Tr. Corp.*, 339 U.S. 306, 313 (1950).

During the middle of the 20th century, prisoners rarely ever filed lawsuits challenging the conditions of their confinement. For instance, through all of the 1960s only a few hundred were filed. By the late 20th, that trend had changed dramatically. For instance, by 1993, over 33,000 lawsuits had been filed by prisoners. That number rose to over 40,000 within just a few years more. Now suddenly lawsuits from prisoners absorbed more that 15 percent of the entire federal docket, requiring an inordinate amount of judicial time and energy. The government had to do something about that.

Enter the *Prison Litigation Reform Act* (PLRA)

Prison Litigation Reform Act (PLRA)

The PRLA is a federal statute designed specifically to make it harder for prisoners to pursue legal claims in federal court and to make it more difficult for prisoners to receive meaningful relief if they do pursue those claims. It was enacted in **1996** as a means of stemming the tide of lawsuits from prisoners, which is exactly what it did.

Some of the ways the government made it more difficult for prisoners...just to file a claim will cost you **$350**, ($450 for appeals.) If you can't afford it, your prison trust account will be taxed until you've completely paid it off.

If your case is dismissed by the court, you will likely incur a "strike." Three strikes will bar you from being able to use the payment plan. Therefore, if you file again, you must have the filing fee up front.

In addition to the monetary deterrents, however, there are many other hoops that you must jump through before even considering filing a lawsuit.

If you are thinking about filing a federal lawsuit against your prison, you'll need to familiarize yourself with the PLRA. Because a lawsuit is something that should be weighed very carefully, you would be wise to consider getting a book that details your legal rights in this matter. See the *Legal Resources* section ahead for some available options.

Prison Litigation Reform Act

42 USCS 1997e. Suits by prisoners

(a) Applicability of administrative remedies. No action shall be brought with respect to prison conditions under section 1979 of the Revised Statutes of the United States (42 U.S.C. 1983), or any other Federal law, by a prisoner confined in any jail, prison, or other correctional facility *until such administrative remedies as are available are exhausted.*

(b) Failure of State to adopt or adhere to administrative grievance procedure. The failure of a State to adopt or adhere to an administrative grievance procedure shall not constitute the basis for an action under section 3 or 5 of this Act [42 USCS 1997a or 1997c].

(c) Dismissal.

(1) The court shall on its own motion or on the motion of a party dismiss any action brought with respect to prison conditions under section 1979 of the Revised Statutes of the United States (42 U.S.C. 1983), or any other Federal law, by a prisoner confined in any jail, prison, or other correctional facility if the court is satisfied that the action is frivolous, malicious, fails to state a claim upon which relief can be granted, or seeks monetary relief from a defendant who is immune from such relief.

(2) In the event that a claim is, on its face, frivolous, malicious, fails to state a claim upon which relief can be granted, or seeks monetary relief from a defendant who is immune from such relief, *the court may dismiss the underlying claim without first requiring the exhaustion of administrative remedies.*

(d) Attorney's fees.

(1) In any action brought by a prisoner who is confined to any jail, prison, or other correctional facility, in which attorney's fees are authorized under section 2 of the Revised Statutes of the United States (42 U.S.C. 1988), such fees shall not be awarded, except to the extent that--

(A) the fee was directly and reasonably incurred in proving an actual violation of the plaintiff's rights protected by a statute pursuant to which a fee may be awarded under section 2 [722] of the Revised Statutes; and

(B)

(i) the amount of the fee is proportionately related to the court ordered relief for the violation; or

(ii) the fee was directly and reasonably incurred in enforcing the relief ordered for the violation.

(2) Whenever a monetary judgment is awarded in an action described in paragraph (1), a portion of the judgment (not to exceed 25 percent) shall be applied to satisfy the amount of attorney's fees awarded against the defendant. If the award of attorney's fees is not greater than 150 percent of the judgment, the excess shall be paid by the defendant.

(3) No award of attorney's fees in an action described in paragraph (1) shall be based on an hourly rate greater than 150 percent of the hourly rate established under section 3006A of title 18, United States Code, for payment of court-appointed counsel.

(4) Nothing in this subsection shall prohibit a prisoner from entering into an agreement to pay an attorney's fee in an amount greater than the amount authorized under this subsection, if the fee is paid by the individual rather than by the defendant pursuant to section 2 [722] of the Revised Statutes of the United States (42 U.S.C. 1988).

(e) Limitation on recovery. *No Federal civil action may be brought by a prisoner confined in a jail, prison, or other correctional facility, for mental or emotional injury suffered while in custody without a prior showing of physical injury or the commission of a sexual act* (as defined in section 2246 of title 18, United States Code).

(f) Hearings.
(1) To the extent practicable, in any action brought with respect to prison conditions in Federal court pursuant to section 1979 of the Revised Statutes of the United States (42 U.S.C. 1983), or any other Federal law, by a prisoner confined in any jail, prison, or other correctional facility, pretrial proceedings in which the prisoner's participation is required or permitted shall be conducted by telephone, video conference, or other telecommunications technology without removing the prisoner from the facility in which the prisoner is confined.
(2) Subject to the agreement of the official of the Federal, State, or local unit of government with custody over the prisoner, hearings may be conducted at the facility in which the prisoner is confined. To the extent practicable, the court shall allow counsel to participate by telephone, video conference, or other communications technology in any hearing held at the facility.
(g) Waiver of reply.
(1) Any defendant may waive the right to reply to any action brought by a prisoner confined in any jail, prison, or other correctional facility under section 1979 of the Revised Statutes of the United States (42 U.S.C. 1983) or any other Federal law. Notwithstanding any other law or rule of procedure, such waiver shall not constitute an admission of the allegations contained in the complaint. No relief shall be granted to the plaintiff unless a reply has been filed.
(2) The court may require any defendant to reply to a complaint brought under this section if it finds that the plaintiff has a reasonable opportunity to prevail on the merits.
(h) "Prisoner" defined. As used in this section, the term "prisoner" means any person incarcerated or detained in any facility who is accused of, convicted of, sentenced for, or adjudicated delinquent for, violations of criminal law or the terms and conditions of parole, probation, pretrial release, or diversionary program.

Federal Torts Claim Act (FTCA)

Are you a federal prisoner who has been wronged by a federal employee?

The *Federal Torts Claim Act* (FTCA) permits a federal prisoner to seek damages from the United States government for injuries caused by its employees. This is type of lawsuit is known as a "tort."

The FTCA is the ***only*** remedy for most torts committed by a federal employee within the scope of their employment. This is due to the fact that individual employees are typically protected from being sued for such offenses. In other words, ordinarily, if you are suing a federal employee (federal contractors excluded), the court will dismiss the employee from the action and the United States will be substituted as the defendant. If you filed suit in state court, your case will be moved to federal jurisdiction and be treated as a suit against the U.S. government. The only exception to this is for a constitutional claim for civil rights violations, also known as a *Bivens Claim*.

The following are some things to keep in mind when considering filing a federal tort claim under FTCA:

You *CAN* file a federal tort claim for the following offenses committed by federal law enforcement officers, including federal corrections officers:

- ✓ Assault
- ✓ Battery
- ✓ False imprisonment
- ✓ False arrest
- ✓ Abuse of process
- ✓ Malicious prosecution
- ✓ Medical malpractice
- ✓ Intention infliction of emotional distress
- ✓ Other negligent or intentional violations to the BOP's duty of providing "suitable quarters and provid[ing] for the safekeeping, care, and sustenance" and "protection, instruction, and discipline" of prisoners. [18 USCS 4042(a)

You *CANNOT* file a federal tort claim for any of the following offenses:

- ✓ Libel
- ✓ Slander
- ✓ Misrepresentation
- ✓ Deceit
- ✓ Property loss
- ✓ Interference with contract rights
- ✓ Acts discretionary in nature, which involve an element of judgment or choice.
- ✓ For constitutional violations or violations of federal statutes or regulations, UNLESS it is also combined with a federal tort claim or offense.

Other FTCA restrictions:

- ✓ Before you can file a claim under FTCA, you MUST exhaust all prison administration remedies. (See "exhaustion" under PLRA) Your claim must state the facts concerning your exhaustion of administrative remedies and administration filing/denial.
- ✓ Your claim must be filed in your federal judicial district OR in the district where the injury occurred. (See state-by-state listings for court address in your district.)
- ✓ Your claim must be filed within 2 years from when the injury occurred.
- ✓ There is no right to a jury trial under FTCA [28 USCS 2402]
- ✓ You cannot file under FTCA to receive punitive damages, an injunction, or expungement of prison records.
- ✓ You can only recover compensatory damages.
- ✓ If filing against the BOP, you must first file a claim in the regional office of where your injury occurred, which must state the amount of damages you are seeking. If the BOP denies your claim, you must file your FTCA claim within 6 months of the date in the denial, even if the 6 months expires before the two-year limitation.

TREATMENT OF PRISONERS – GENEVA CONVENTION

The following are the minimum rules for the treatment of prisoners, as agreed upon by member nations of the Geneva Convention in 1955, and as approved by the Economic and Social Council by resolution 663 C (XXIV) of July 31, 1957 and 2076 (LXII) of May 13, 1977.

Accommodations:

- Cells for individuals should not be used to accommodate two or more persons overnight; dormitory facilities are to be supervised at night.

Exercise and Sport:

- If not employed in outdoor work, every prisoner shall have at least one hour of exercise in the open air, weather permitting.
- Young prisoners and others of suitable age and physique are to receive physical and recreational training.

Medical Services:

- Pre-natal and post-natal care and treatment are to be provided by women's institutions; where nursing infants are allowed to remain with their mothers, a nursery staffed by qualified persons is needed.
- The medical officer shall see sick prisoners daily., along with those who complain of illness or are referred to his/her attention.
- The medical officer is to report to the director on prisoners whose health is jeopardized by continued imprisonment and on the quality of the food, hygiene, bedding, clothing, and physical regimen of the prisoners.

Discipline and Punishment:

- Cruel, inhuman, and/or degrading punishments, including corporal punishment and restriction to a dark cell, shall be prohibited.

Instruments of Restraint:

- Handcuffs, straightjackets, and other instruments of restraint are never to be applied as a punishment, and irons and chairs are not to be used as a means of restrain.

Information to and Complaints by Prisoners:

- Upon admission, prisoners shall be informed of the regulations they are to live by and authorized channels for seeking information and making complaints.
- Prisoners are to have the right to make complaints to the director of the institution, as well as to the central prison administration and the judicial authority, in the proper form but without censorship to substance, and they are to have the opportunity to

speak directly to the inspector of prisons outside the presence of institutional staff members.

- Unless evidently frivolous, each complaint shall be replied to promptly.

Contact with the Outside World:

- Prisoners are to be allowed regular contact with family and friends, by both correspondence and personal visits.
- Prisoners who are foreign nationals shall be allowed a communication with diplomatic and consular representatives of their state, or a state of international authority that has taken charge of their interests.
- Prisoners are to be kept informed of current events and important items of news.

Books:

- Every institution shall maintain for the use of prisoners a library with recreational and instructional books.

Guiding Principles:

- The prison system shall not aggravate unnecessarily the suffering inherent in a prisoner's loss of self-determination and liberty.
- Prisons shall utilize all remedial, educational, medical, and spiritual forms of assistance to treat prisoner's needs and facilitate his return to society as a law-abiding member.
- Government or private agencies should be available for the after care of released prisoners.

Treatment:

- Treatment of prisoners under sentence shall be directed to achieve the capacity for law-abiding and self-supporting lives, utilizing professional services whenever possible.

Education and Recreation:

- The ongoing education of prisoners is to be facilitated, and schooling of illiterates and youthful prisoners is to be considered compulsory.
- Recreational and cultural activities are to be made available.

Legal Resources

The following organizations provide useful legal resources and publications specifically designed with prisoners in mind.
Be sure to look at the Resource Center at the front of this book to find other national and state-by-state listings that may be of help to your specific needs.

Organizations

ACLU NATIONAL PRISON PROJECT

915 15th St., NW, 7th Floor, Washington, DC 20005
(202) 393-4930
www.aclu.org/prisons, npp@aclu.org

ACLU NPP provides numerous fact sheets on topics affecting prisoners. Write for list. May charge a small fee.

AMERICAN BAR ASSOCIATION (NATIONAL OFFICE)

321 N. Clark St., Chicago, IL 60654
(312) 988-5000
www.americanbar.org

ABA is a national organization that holds attorneys accountable to professionalism and ethics standards. They provide legal information, resources, bar directories, referrals, and written responses to prisoner's complaints concerning attorneys. See state-by-state listings of ABA offices later in this chapter.

ASIAN PACIFIC AMERICAN LEGAL CENTER

1145 Wilshire Blvd., 2nd Floor, Los Angeles, CA 90017
(888) 349-9695
www.apalc.org

Provides legal and education services to Asian Americans and Pacific Islanders, especially those who speak little to no English.

CENTER ON JUVENILE & CRIMINAL JUSTICE

54 Dore St., San Francisco, CA 94103
(415) 621-5661
www.cjcj.org

CJCJ publishes numerous legal articles and publications focused on prison conditions and criminal justice. Write for a current listing.

CENTER FOR CONSTITUTIONAL RIGHTS

666 Broadway, 7th Floor, New York, NY 10012

CCR provides information on the constitutional rights of prisoners. They also co-publish the *Jailhouse Lawyers Handbook ($2)*, with the National Lawyers Guild.

CIVIC RESEARCH INSTITUTE

PO Box 585, Kingston, NJ 08528
(609) 683-4450

CRI covers recent developments in corrections and criminal justice law, which they publish bi-monthly in the *Correctional Law Reporter*. Write for current information.

COALITION FOR PRISONER'S RIGHTS

PO Box 1911, Santa Fe, NM 87504-1911
(505) 982-9520
www.realcostofprisons.org/coalition.html,
info@realcostofprisons.org

CPR publishes a monthly two-page newsletter, which features a variety of topics on prisoner rights, and a new resource that may be helpful to you. Send an SASE for each month you'd like to receive a newsletter. (1 year = 12 SASEs or stamps.) Back issues available on their website.

COLUMBIA HUMAN RIGHTS LAW REVIEW

435 West 116th St., New York, NY 10027
(212) 854-1601
www3.law.columbia.edu/hrlr/jlm

CHRLR publishes several publications on prisoner's rights, including the *Jailhouse Lawyer's Manual*, and the *Columbia Human Rights Law Review*, amongst others. Write for a complete listing.

EXONERATION PROJECT, THE

312 N. May St., Suite 100, Chicago, IL 60607

(312) 789-4955
www.exonerationproject.org

EP provides legal assistance representation, and support for wrongfully convicted prisoners. Typical cases accepted involve DNA testing, coerced confessions, official misconduct, faulty eyewitness testimony and evidence, ineffective assistance of counsel claims, and convictions attained through junk science.

FASTLAW PUBLISHING ASSOCIATION

PO Box 577, Upland, CA 91785
www.fastlaw.org

FastLaw publishes several prisoner rights-related publications, including *Winning Habeas Corpus & Post-Conviction Relief.* Write for current list of publications.

FEDERAL LEGAL CENTERS

Mid-Atlantic Region (MARO): 302 Sentinel Dr., Suite 200, Annapolis Junction, MD 20701
(301) 317-3120

Northeast Region (NERO): U.S. Custom House, 7th Floor, 2nd and Chestnut Streets, Philadelphia, PA 19106
(215) 521-7375

North Central Region (NCRO): Gateway Complex Tower II, 8th Floor, 4th and State Ave., Kansas City, KS 66101
(913) 551-1004

Western Region (WXRO): 7338 Shoreline Dr., Stockton, CA 95219
(209) 956-9732

South Central Region (SCRO): U.S. Armed Forces Reserve Complex, 344 Marine Forces Dr., Grand Prairie, TX 75051
(972) 730-8920

Southeast Region (SERO): 3800 Camp Creek Pkwy. SW, Building 2000, Atlanta, GA 30331-6226
(678) 686-1260

The Federal Legal Centers are the regional legal offices of the Bureau of Prisons. Complaints can be addressed through them and attorneys can contact them for needs related to prisoner contact.

INNOCENCE PROJECT (NATIONAL OFFICE)

40 Worth St., Suite 701, New York, NY 10013
(212) 364-5340
www.innocenceproject.org

The Innocence Project provides legal assistance to those who have been wrongfully convicted and are completely innocent of their crimes. Typically, they only accept cases where DNA evidence can prove innocence. See state-by-state listings for regional branches in your area.

INNOCENT.ORG

20 W. Muskegon Ave., Muskegon, MI 49440
www.innocent.org

Innocent.org is a network that tries to locate assistance for those who have been wrongfully convicted and are innocent of their crimes. Contact them for more info.

JUSTICE DENIED

PO Box 68911, Seattle, WA 98168
(206) 335-4254
www.justicedenied.org

Justice Denied maintains an online database of innocent prisoner cases and provides limited resources to assist those who are wrongfully convicted and innocent. They are now an online only resource that primarily assists prisoners through your lawyers or friends and family. They no longer provide a newsletter.

JUSTICE STUDIES ASSOCIATION

c/o Dept. of Criminal Justice, Hudson Valley CC. 80 Vanderburgh Ave., Troy, NY 12180
(518) 629-7331
www.justicestudies.org

JSA provides various criminal justice related publications, including their bi-monthly newsletter, *Justitia.* Write for current listing of publications.

LEGAL INSIGHTS, INC.

25602 Alicia Parkway, #323, Laguna Hills, CA 92653
(714) 941-0578
www.legalinsights.org info@legalinsights.org

LI provides legal assistance to state and federal prisoners at a discount. Services include legal assistance in challenging convictions, illegal sentences, parole denials, pleas, DNA and sentencing modifications and more. Payment plans are available.

LEGAL SERVICES CORPORATION

3333 K St., NW, 3rd Floor, Washington, DC 20007-3522
(202) 295-1500
www.lsc.org

LSC provides legal assistance on a variety of issues, including social security, family matters, welfare, and worker's compensation.

LEWISBURG PRISON PROJECT

PO Box 128, Lewisburg, PA 17837
(570) 523-1104
www.lewisburgprisonproject.org

LPP distributes legal bulletins (ranging in price from $1-3), ACLU fact sheets, and other publications related to prisoner rights for a nominal fee. Send SASE for a complete list. They do NOT have lawyers on staff and therefore cannot provide any legal advice.

MUSLIM LEGAL FUND OF AMERICA

2701 W. 15th St., Suite 640, Plano, TX 75075
(972) 331-9021
www.mlfa.org

Promotes the civil rights of Muslims in the U.S. legal system. Provides legal assistance in some cases.

NATIONAL ASSOCIATION FOR THE ADVANCEMENT OF COLORED PEOPLE (NAACP) - NATIONAL

4805 Mt. Hope Dr., Baltimore, MD 21215
(800) NAACP-98 (622-2798), (410) 580-5777 (local)
www.naacp.org

NAACP is an advocacy group that fights for the rights and against the unequal treatment of minorities, in the criminal justice system and free society. They are active in fighting against the death penalty and unfair sentencing practices, and offer some reentry resources. They have offices in all 50 states and many countries. See their website for an office in region.

NAACP – LEGAL DEFENSE & EDUCATION FUND

Headquarters: 40 Rector St., 5th Floor, New York, NY 10006
(212) 965-2200
Washington DC office: 1444 I St. NW, Washington, DC 20005
(202) 682-1300
www.naacpldr.org

NAACP's Legal Defense & Education Fund provides legal aid and representation to those involved in racial injustices. They also handle a small number of death penalty and life without the possibility of parole cases. They typically will not respond to letters unless they are interested in your case.

NATIONAL ASSOCIATION OF CRIMINAL DEFENSE LAWYERS (NACDL)

1600 L St., NW, 12th Floor, Washington, DC 20036
(202) 876-8600
www.nacdl.org

NACDL is a national membership organization of criminal defense lawyers. They will not consider your case, but they can provide attorney referrals and general information on professional legal representation standards. Publishes the monthly magazine *Champion*, as subscription-based publication focusing on the needs of attorneys.

NATIONAL CLEMENCY PROJECT

3907 N. Federal Highway, #151, Pompano Beach, FL 33064
(954) 271-2304

NCP is a professional organization that assists prisoners by assembling clemency packages for sentence reduction. This is a paid service, which costs about $1,275 per package. Write for more info.

NATIONAL CRIMINAL JUSTICE

PO Box 6000, Rockville, MD 20849
(800) 851-3420
www.ncjrs.org
NCJRS is the Bureau of Justice's national data center and information clearinghouse. They will provide FREE information on all criminal justice statistics. Sign up for their information service online, or write for specific information.

NATIONAL LAWYERS GUILD

132 Nassau St., Room 922, New York, NY 10038
(212) 679-5100
www.nlg.org

NLG is a membership organization that researches and publishes information on civil rights violations in prisons. They co-publish *Jailhouse Lawyer's Handbook ($2)*, and provide FREE membership and support services to jailhouse lawyers.

NATIONAL LEGAL AID & DEFENDERS ASSOCIATION

1140 Connecticut Ave., NW, Suite 900 Washington, DC 20036

(202) 452-0620
www.nalda.org

NALDA provides referral information on obtaining legal representation in your area.

NOVEMBER COALITION

282 West Astor St., Colville, WA 99114
(509) 684-1550

NC publishes prisoner rights and criminal justice related information. They currently offer a bi-monthly newsletter *Razor Wire*, which focuses on criminal justice and the drug war, for $10/year to prisoners.

OXFORD UNIVERSITY PRESS

2001 Evans Rd., Cary, NC 27513
(800) 445-9714

Publishes a variety of legal manuals. See 'Legal Publications' list in this chapter.

PRISON ACTIVIST RESOURCE CENTER

PO Box 70447, Oakland, CA 94612
(510) 893-4648
www.prisonactivist.org, info@prisonactivist.org

PARC works on anti-mass incarceration activism and provides prisoners with a FREE resource directory upon request.

PRISON LEGAL NEWS

PO Box 1151, Lake Worth, FL 33460
(561) 360-2523
www.prisonlegalnews.org, info@prisonlegalnews.org

PLN is a comprehensive monthly publication that focuses on prisoner rights and provides prisoner-related news, summaries of recent court decisions affecting prisoners and analysis of prison issues across the country. $30/yr. for prisoners. Also distributes many prisoner-focused publications. Write for a complete list or see ads in this issue.

PSI PUBLISHING

413-B 19th St., #168, Lynden, WA 98264
(800) 557-8868
www.prisonerlaw.com

PSI publishes a variety of prisoner legal assistance information, including *The Prisoner's Guide to Survival.* ($49.95) Write for a complete list of publications.

SET MY WAY FREE MINISTRIES

221 N. Hogan St., Box 141, Jacksonville, FL 32202
Or PO Box 1655, Semmes, AL 36575
(877) 344-8035

Set My Way provides legal assistance, including legal research, manuscript proofreading, pleading revisions and attorney searches, for a fee. NOTE: They are not attorneys.

SOUTHERN POVERTY LAW CENTER

400 Washington Ave., Montgomery, AL 36104
(334) 956-8200
www.splcenter.org

SPL advocates on behalf of prisoner rights and publishes numerous reports and articles on criminal justice matters. Write for a complete list of available publication.

THOMSON/ WEST GROUP PUBLISHING

610 Oppermans Dr., Eagan, MN 55123

T/WG publishes several prison-focused self-help books, including *Criminal Law in a Nutshell, Prisoners & the Law,* and *Rights of Prisoners.* Write for a complete listing.

Innocence Organizations

The following is a worldwide listing of groups who specialize in advocacy and potential representation for the wrongfully convicted. You can request information from them directly, but the greatest response rate is to those who support you, friends, family, attorneys, and other advocates.

If you do contact any of the following organizations directly, here are a few things to keep in mind:

- Be as direct and clear as you can in explaining yourself and why you believe they can be of assistance to you and your case, but do not try to sound like an attorney.
- Do not send legal materials unless they are requested by the organization, and when you do send legal documents, be sure to only send copies. Never submit original paperwork.
- Be aware that it may take some time, even several months, before anyone can get back to you. Most of these organizations are small and flooded with requests. Please be patient.

National Organizations

AMERICA'S WRONGFULLY CONVICTED

www.americaswrongfullyconvicted.com

AMERICAN FALSE MEMORY SYNDROME

www.fmsonline.org

CENTER ON WRONGFUL CONVICTIONS OF YOUTH

Northwestern University School of Law, 375 E. Chicago Ave., Chicago, IL 60611-3069
(312) 503-8576
www.cwcy.org

CWCY is an innocence project that focuses solely on individuals who were wrongfully accused or convicted of crimes as minors. They provide investigative service and representation to youths who are innocent.

CENTURION MINISTRIES

1000 Herrontown Rd., Princeton, NJ 08540
(609) 921-0334
www.centurionministries.org

CM is an innocence project that focuses on wrongfully convicted prisoners who are either sentenced to death, life in prison without the possibility of parole, or those who have completely exhausted all appeal options. They will not assist in accidental or self-defense cases.

CITIZENS UNITED FOR ALTERNATIVES TO THE DEATH PENALTY

www.cuadp.org

DEATH PENALTY INFORMATION CENTER

1015 18th St. NW, Washington, DC 20036
(202) 289-2275
www.deathpenaltyinfo.org

DPIC is a clearinghouse for death penalty information. They provide comprehensive reports on capital punishment related stats and facts in the U.S., available largely through their website. You can send requests for information, but they will not provide legal assistance.

DUBIOUS ACCUSATIONS AND CONVICTIONS

www.freebaran.org/cases

EQUAL JUSTICE INITIATIVE

122 Commerce St., Montgomery, AL 36104
(334) 269-1803
www.eji.org

EJI provides advocacy and representation for prisoners who have been wrongfully convicted of mistreated by the criminal justice system. They focus on death penalty, juvenile, or wrongfully convicted cases, especially where the defendant was biased based on race or indigence.

EXONERATION PROJECT, THE

312 N. May St., Suite 100, Chicago, IL 60607
(312) 789-4955
www.exonerationproject.org

EP provides legal assistance representation, and support for wrongfully convicted prisoners. Typical cases accepted involve DNA testing, coerced confessions, official misconduct, faulty eyewitness testimony and evidence, ineffective assistance of counsel claims, and convictions attained through junk science.

FALSE ALLEGATIONS

c/o Law Office of Barbara C. Johnson, 6 Appletree Lane, Andover, MA 01810-4102
(925) 256-4600
www.falseallegations.com

FALSELY ACCUSED

101 Ygnacio Valley Rd., Suite 305, Walnut Creek, CA 94596
(925) 256-4600
www.accused.com

FOREJUSTICE

http://forejustice.org

HUMANITY FOR PRISONERS!

http://humanityforprisoners.blogspot.com

INJUSTICE LINE, THE

http://home.earthlink.net/~ynot/index.html

INNOCENCE DENIED

www.innocencedenied.com

INNOCENCE PROJECT - NATIONAL

40 Worth St., Suite 701, New York, NY 10013
(212) 364-5340
www.innocenceproject.org

The Innocence Project advocates and represents those who have been wrongfully convicted in cases where physical evidence, such as DNA, can prove their innocence. Those who have been wrongfully convicted can send for an application, but be aware that most of the offices are overwhelmed with submissions. See separate listings under each state for the office in your region.

JUSTICE DENIED

PO Box 66291, Seattle, WA 98166
www.justicedenied.org

Advocates for the wrongfully convicted by publishing their stories. Currently they only publish online. They do have some publications and resources available to prisoner. Write for current offerings.

LIFE AFTER EXONERATION PROGRAM

www.exonerated.org

SHAKEN BABY SYNDROME DEFENSE

www.sbsdefense.com

TRUTH IN JUSTICE

http://truthinjustice.org

VICTIMS OF THE STATE

www.victimsofthestate.org

WRONGFUL CONVICTION READING ROOM

www.law-forensic.com/wrongful_conviction_reading_room.htm

State-By-State

ALASKA

INNOCENCE PROJECT | NORTHWEST CLINIC

PO Box 85110, Seattle, WA 89145-1110
(206) 543-5780
www.law.washington.edu/clinics/ipnw

IPNW provides legal representation to wrongfully convicted Alaska, Montana, and Washington prisoners. Must have an actual innocence claim that can be proven through DNA testing or new evidence, have at least three years left on sentence, have completed direct appeals, and have no right to appointed counsel.

ARIZONA

NORTHERN ARIZONA JUSTICE PROJECT | NORTHERN ARIZONA UNIVERSITY

PO Box 15005, Flagstaff, AZ 86011-5005
(928) 523-7028
jan.ucc.nau/d-najp

NAJP provides legal support services for wrongfully convicted AZ prisoners. DNA and non-DNA cases are accepted if they have actual innocence evidence. Must have 8 or more years left on sentence. They specialize in arson, shaken baby syndrome, and child abuse cases.

ARIZONA JUSTICE PROJECT | ARIZONA STATE UNIVERSITY

MC4420, 411 N. Central Ave., Suite 600, Phoenix, AZ 85004-2139
(602) 496-0286
www.azjusticeproject.org

AJP provides assistance to the innocent, those who have been wrongfully convicted, and cases where severe justice has occurred. They well consider DNA and non-DNA cases where actual innocence can be proven, and can provide post-conviction DNA testing in cases where testing may demonstrate actual innocence.

ARKANSAS

ARKANSAS JUSTICE PROJECT | UNIVERSITY OF ARKANSAS SCHOOL OF LAW

1045 W. Maple St., Fayetteville, AR 72701
www.law.uark.edu

AJP provides advocacy and representation for wrongfully convicted Arkansas prisoners. Write for current requirements and guidelines.

MIDWEST INNOCENCE PROJECT

605 W. 47th St., Kansas City, MO 64113
(816) 221-2166
www.themip.org

MIP provides advocacy and representation for wrongfully convicted prisoners in Kansas, Missouri, Iowa and Nebraska. They will accept cases of actual innocence where the convicted had nothing to do with the crime, has more than 10 years left on their sentence or has to register as a sex offender, and who is not currently represented by counsel. They will not accept death penalty or self-defense cases.

CALIFORNIA

CALIFORNIA INNOCENCE PROJECT | CALIFORNIA WESTERN SCHOOL OF LAW

225 Cedar St., San Diego, CA 92101
(619) 525-1485
www.californiainnocenceproject.org

CIP advocates and provides representation for cases of actual innocence in Southern California. DNA and non-DNA cases are accepted, with a focus on police and prosecutorial misconduct, firearm and fingerprint analysis, shaken baby syndrome, and death penalty cases. Must have 3 or more years left on sentence.

NORTHERN CALIFORNIA INNOCENCE PROJECT | SANTA CLARA UNIVERSITY OF LAW

500 El Camino Real, Santa Clara, CA 95053-0422
(408) 554-1945
www.law.scu.edu/ncip

NCIP provides advocacy and representation for prisoners in Central and Northern California who have been wrongfully convicted. They accept DNA and non-DNA cases that originated in CA resulting in a serious felony conviction or a felony involving 3-strikes sentencing in any of the following matters: official misconduct, shaken baby syndrome, arson, firearms or fingerprint analysis, ineffective assistance, false confessions, or death penalty issues.

INNOCENCE MATTERS

PO Box 1098, Torrance, CA 90505
(310) 755-2518
www.innocencematters.us

IM advocates and represents prisoners who are innocent of the crime they've been convicted of, and who meet the following criteria: Must have been convicted in LA County, be factually innocent and willing to submit to and pass a polygraph test, have already been rejected by the California Innocence Project, and have no conflict of interest with IM.

COLORADO

COLORADO INNOCENCE PROJECT | UNIVERSITY OF COLORADO LAW SCHOOL

Wolf Law Building, 404 UCB, Boulder, CO 80309-0404
(303) 492-8126
www.colorado.edu/law/academics/experiential-learning/clinics/innocence

CO Innocence Project provides advocacy and representation to CO prisoners with provable claims of innocence. Cases must have originated in CO and have already gone through the appellate process.

CONNECTICUT

NEW ENGLAND INNOCENCE PROJECT

160 Boylston St., Boston, MA 02116
(857) 277-7858
www.newenglandinnocence.org

HEIP provides advocacy and legal representation for wrongfully convicted prisoners in Connecticut, Massachusetts, Vermont, Rhode Island, Maine, and New Hampshire. The convicted must be factually innocent, currently in custody, and the case must involve one of the following elements: invalidated forensic science, false confession, jailhouse informant testimony, official misconduct, or poor defense lawyering. Cases of arson, shaken baby syndrome, and child abuse are given priority. DNA and non-DNA cases accepted.

DISTRICT OF COLUMBIA

MID-ATLANTIC INNOCENCE PROJECT

4801 Massachusetts Ave. NW, Washington, DC 20013
(202) 895-4519
www.exonerate.org

MAIP provides DC and Maryland prisoners they have determined to be innocent with legal representation and investigative services.

FLORIDA

INNOCENCE PROJECT OF FLORIDA

1100 E. Park Avenue Blvd., Suite 340, Miami, FL 33137-3227
(786) 363-2700
www.floridainnocence.org

IP of Florida provides advocacy and representation for wrongfully convicted Florida prisoners. They only accept cases with DNA evidence, but have no sentencing requirements. They also provide transitional services for those who have been exonerated.

UNIVERSITY OF MIAMI LAW INNOCENCE CLINIC

3000 Biscayne Blvd., Suite 100, Miami, FL 33137
(305) 284-8115
www.law.miami.edu/clinics/innocence

MU UL Innocence Clinic provides legal representation to wrongfully convicted Florida prisoners who are serving at least 10 years. Case must be provable through new evidence.

FLORIDA INNOCENCE PROJECT | NOVA

www.nsulaw.nova.edu/fip/index.cfm

WRONGFUL CONVICTIONS PROJECT

www.law.miami.edu/studentorg/wc/php

GEORGIA

GEORGIA INNOCENCE PROJECT

2645 N. Decatur Rd., Decatur, GA 30033
(404) 373-4433
www.ga-innocenceproject.org

GIP advocates and provides representation for wrongfully convicted prisoners in GA and AL. They help secure DNA testing where adequate testing was not available at trial and where it may provide innocence, as well as other legal assistance.

HAWAI'I

HAWAI'I INNOCENCE PROJECT

2515 Dole St., Honolulu, HI 96822
(808) 956-6547
www.innocenceprojecthawaii.org

HIP provides advocacy and representation for wrongfully convicted HI prisoners who have a credible claim of innocence. Must have been convicted in HI, have considerable time left on sentence, and have evidence that can support a claim of actual innocence.

IDAHO

IDAHO INNOCENCE PROJECT

1910 University Dr., Boise, ID 83725
(208) 426-4207
www.innocenceproject/boisestate.edu

IIP provides advocacy and legal representation for wrongfully convicted Idaho and Eastern Oregon prisoners. DNA and non-DNA cases accepted, with no minimum sentencing requirement.

ILLINOIS

CENTER ON WRONGFUL CONVICTIONS

357 E. Chicago Ave., Chicago, IL 60611-3069
www.law.northwestern.edu/cwc

CWC provides advocacy and legal representation for wrongfully convicted Illinois prisoners who are in no way responsible for the crimes they are convicted of. They focus on various factors, including erroneous witness testimony, false of coerced confessions, official misconduct, inadequate legal defense, false or misleading forensic evidence, and jailhouse informant testimony.

CHICAGO INNOCENCE PROJECT

205 W. Monroe St., Suite 315, Chicago, IL 60606
(312) 263-6213
www.chicagoinnocenceproject.org

CIP provides advocacy for wrongfully convicted Illinois prisoners who are serving death sentences or LWOP. They investigate innocence claims and work with members of the press and community to bring legitimately innocent cases to light, and may seek legal representation to bring new evidence to the courts.

ILLINOIS INNOCENCE PROJECT

One University Plaza, MS PAC 451, Springfield, IL 62703-5407
(217) 206-6569
www.uis.edu/innocenceproject

IIP provides advocacy and legal representation for wrongfully convicted Illinois prisoners in both DNA and non-DNA cases. They look for various factors that can help establish innocence, including absence of physical evidence, reliability of eye witnesses, identification of alternative suspects, official misconduct, and inconsistency in the nature of the crime with the background of the prisoner. Must have four or more years left on sentence.

MACARTHUR JUSTICE CENTER | NORTHWESTERN UNIVERSITY LAW SCHOOL

375 E. Chicago Ave., Chicago, IL 60611
(312) 503-1271
www.law.northwestern.edu/macarthur

MJC advocates and litigates on Illinois justice matters, especially conditions of confinement. They typically will not accept individual prisoner cases unless it has a broad impact on prison issues.

INDIANA

WRONGFUL CONVICTION CLINIC | INDIANA UNIVERSITY SCHOOL OF LAW

530 W. New York St., Room 111, Indianapolis, IN 46202-3225
(317) 274-5551
www.indylaw.indiana.edu

WCC provides advocacy and legal representation for wrongfully convicted Indiana prisoners where actual innocence can be proven. DNA and non-DNA cases are accepted. They will consider cases that involve child abuse, shaken baby syndrome, and arson.

PROVING INNOCENCE

http://provinginnocence.org

IOWA (SEE ALSO MISSOURI)

INNOCENCE PROJECT OF IOWA

19 S. 17th St., Esterville, IA 51334
www.iowainnocence.org

IP of Iowa provides advocacy and legal representation of wrongfully convicted Iowa prisoners whose actual innocence claims can be proven. DNA and non-DNA cases accepted, with no sentencing requirements.

MIDWEST INNOCENCE PROJECT

605 W. 47th St., Kansas City, MO 64113
(816) 221-2166
www.themip.org

MIP provides advocacy and representation for wrongfully convicted prisoners in Kansas, Arkansas, Missouri, and Nebraska. They will accept cases of actual innocence where the convicted had nothing to do with the crime, has more than 10 years left on their sentence or has to register as a sex offender, and who is not currently represented by counsel. They will not accept death penalty or self-defense cases.

Kansas

MIDWEST INNOCENCE PROJECT

605 W. 47th St., Kansas City, MO 64113
(816) 221-2166
www.themip.org

MIP provides advocacy and representation for wrongfully convicted prisoners in Arkansas, Missouri, Iowa and Nebraska. They will accept cases of actual innocence where the convicted had nothing to do with the crime, has more than 10 years left on their sentence or has to register as a sex offender, and who is not currently represented by counsel. They will not accept death penalty or self-defense cases.

Kentucky

KENTUCKY INNOCENCE PROJECT

Department of Public Advocacy, 100 Fair Oaks Lane, Suite 302, Frankfort, KY 40601
(502) 564-3948
www.dps.gov/kip

KIP provides advocacy and legal representation to wrongfully convicted Kentucky prisoners. DNA and non-DNA cases accepted, with a minimum of ten years left on the sentence.

LOUISIANA

INNOCENCE PROJECT OF NEW ORLEANS

4051 Ulloa St., New Orleans, LA 70119
(504) 943-1902
www.ip-no.org

IP of New Orleans provides advocacy and representation for wrongfully convicted Louisiana and Southern Mississippi prisoners. Must be factually innocent, have at least 10 years left on the sentence, and be beyond review of all appeals. They take several factors into account, including official misconduct, false testimony, mistaken identity, faulty forensic evidence, and ineffective assistance of counsel.

INNOCENCE PROJECT OF NORTHWEST LOUISIANA

PO Box 400, Shreveport, LA 71162
www.notguilty.ws

IP of NW Louisiana provides advocacy and representation for wrongfully convicted Louisiana prisoners. Contact for current criteria.

MISSISSIPPI INNOCENCE PROJECT | UNIVERSITY OF MISSISSIPPI SCHOOL OF LAW

PO Box 1848, University, MS 38677
(662) 915-5207
www.mississippiinnocence.org

MIP provides legal representation for wrongfully convicted prisoners in Mississippi and Northern Louisiana. DNA and non-DNA cases accepted, with no sentencing requirements.

MAINE

NEW ENGLAND INNOCENCE PROJECT

160 Boylston St., Boston, MA 02116
(857) 277-7858
www.newenglandinnocence.org

HEIP provides advocacy and legal representation for wrongfully convicted prisoners in Maine, Massachusetts, Vermont, Rhode Island, New Hampshire, and Connecticut. The convicted must be factually innocent, currently in custody, and the case must involve one of the following elements: invalidated forensic science, false confession, jailhouse informant testimony, official misconduct, or poor defense lawyering. Cases of arson, shaken baby syndrome, and child abuse are given priority. DNA and non-DNA cases accepted.

MARYLAND

MID-ATLANTIC INNOCENCE PROJECT

4801 Massachusetts Ave. NW, Washington, DC 20013
(202) 895-4519
www.exonerate.org

MAIP provides DC and Maryland prisoners they have determined to be innocent with legal representation and investigative services.

UNIVERSITY OF BALTIMORE INNOCENCE PROJECT CLINIC

1420 N. Charles St., Baltimore, MD 21201
(410) 837-4200

UB-IPC provides legal representation for wrongfully convicted Maryland prisoners. DNA and non-DNA cases accepted for actual innocence claims.

MASSACHUSETTS

JUSTICE BRANDEIS INNOCENCE PROJECT | BRANDEIS UNIVERSITY SCHUSTER INSTITUTE FOR INVESTIGATIVE JOURNALISM

415 South St., MS 043, Waltham, MA 02454
(681) 736-4953
www.brandeis.edu/investigate/innocence-project

JBIP assists Massachusetts prisoners who were wrongfully convicted. They use investigative journalism techniques to probe cases of actual innocence. DNA and non-DNA cases accepted.

NEW ENGLAND INNOCENCE PROJECT

160 Boylston St., Boston, MA 02116
(857) 277-7858
www.newenglandinnocence.org

HEIP provides advocacy and legal representation for wrongfully convicted prisoners in Massachusetts, Vermont, Rhode Island, Maine, New Hampshire, and Connecticut. The convicted must be factually innocent, currently in custody, and the case must involve one of the following elements: invalidated forensic science, false confession, jailhouse informant testimony, official misconduct, or poor defense lawyering. Cases of arson, shaken baby syndrome, and child abuse are given priority. DNA and non-DNA cases accepted.

MICHIGAN

MICHIGAN INNOCENCE CLINIC

710 S. State St., Ann Arbor, MI 48109
(734) 763-9353
www.las.mich.edu/clinical/innocenceclinic

MIC provides advocacy and legal representation for wrongfully convicted Michigan prisoners, for non-DNA cases only. Crime must have occurred in Michigan and contain one of the following elements: eyewitness misidentification, false confession, junk science, official misconduct, jailhouse informant testimony, and bad lawyering. Must be currently serving time for the case.

PROVING INNOCENCE

http://provinginnocence.org

THOMAS M. COOLEY LAW SCHOOL INNOCENCE PROJECT

300 S. Capitol Ave., PO Box 13138, Lansing, MI 48901
(517) 371-5140
www.cooley.edu/clinincs/ionnocence_project.html

TM Cooley Law School Innocence Project provides legal representation for wrongfully convicted Michigan prisoners. They only accept actual innocence cases proved by DNA evidence. Prisoner must currently be in custody.

MINNESOTA

INNOCENCE PROJECT OF MINNESOTA

1600 Utica Ave., Suite 140, St. Louis Park, MN 55416
(651) 523-3152
www.ipmn.org

IPMN provides legal representation to wrongfully convicted prisoners in Minnesota, North Dakota, and South Dakota. Non-DNA cases are accepted in ND and SD. There are no minimum sentencing requirements. They look for cases that involve junk science, false confessions, informant testimony, eyewitness misidentification, official misconduct, bad lawyering, and other factors.

HAMLINE UNIVERSITY SCHOOL OF LAW

www.hamline.edu/law/curriculum/clinics/innocence_clinic.html

MISSISSIPPI

MISSISSIPPI INNOCENCE PROJECT | UNIVERSITY OF MISSISSIPPI SCHOOL OF LAW

PO Box 1848, University, MS 38677
(662) 915-5207
www.mississippiinnocence.org

MIP provides legal representation for wrongfully convicted prisoners in Mississippi and North Louisiana. DNA and non-DNA cases accepted, with no sentencing requirements.

MISSOURI

MIDWEST INNOCENCE PROJECT

605 W. 47th St., Kansas City, MO 64113
(816) 221-2166
www.themip.org

MIP provides advocacy and representation for wrongfully convicted prisoners in Kansas, Oklahoma, Arkansas, Iowa and Nebraska. They will accept cases of actual innocence where the convicted had nothing to do with the crime, has more than 10 years left on their sentence or has to register as a sex offender, and who is not currently represented by counsel. They will not accept death penalty or self-defense cases.

MONTANA

INNOCENCE PROJECT | NORTHWEST CLINIC

PO Box 85110, Seattle, WA 89145-1110
(206) 543-5780
www.law.washington.edu/clinics/ipnw

IPNW provides legal representation to wrongfully convicted Montana, Alaska, and Washington prisoners. Must have an actual innocence claim that can be proven through DNA testing or new evidence, have at least three years left on sentence, have completed direct appeals, and have no right to appointed counsel.

MONTANA INNOCENCE PROJECT

PO Box 7607, Missoula, MT 59807
(406) 544-6698
www.mtinnocenceproject.org

MT IP provides advocacy and legal representation for wrongfully convicted Montana prisoners. DAN and non-DNA cases accepted. Must have been convicted in Montana, have completed direct appeals and not be currently represented by counsel. Priority is given to cases with clear and convincing proof of innocence. They are unlikely to take cases without independent and verifiable evidence to support the prisoner's claim.

NEBRASKA

MIDWEST INNOCENCE PROJECT

605 W. 47th St., Kansas City, MO 64113
(816) 221-2166
www.themip.org

MIP provides advocacy and representation for wrongfully convicted prisoners in Kansas, Arkansas, Missouri, and Iowa. They will accept cases of actual innocence where the convicted had nothing to do with the crime, has more than 10 years left on their sentence or has to register as a sex offender, and who is not currently represented by counsel. They will not accept death penalty or self-defense cases.

NEBRASKA INNOCENCE PROJECT

PO Box 24183, Omaha, NE 68124
(412) 241-7194
www.nebraskainnocenceproject.org

NIP provides advocacy and legal representation to wrongfully convicted Nebraska prisoners. Must claim actual innocence, not currently have representation, and there must be DNA-testable evidence to verify (although non-DNA cases may be considered where there is new evidence.)

NEVADA

ROCKY MOUNTAIN INNOCENCE CENTER

358 South 700 East, B235, Salt Lake City, UT 84102
(801) 355-1888
www.rminnocence.org

RMIC provides advocacy and legal representation for wrongfully convicted prisoners in Nevada, Utah, and Wyoming. Must be completely innocent, provable through significant new evidence, have no remaining appeals options, and have more than seven years left on sentence.

NEW HAMPSHIRE

NEW ENGLAND INNOCENCE PROJECT

160 Boylston St., Boston, MA 02116
(857) 277-7858
www.newenglandinnocence.org

HEIP provides advocacy and legal representation for wrongfully convicted prisoners in New Hampshire, Massachusetts, Vermont, Rhode Island, Maine, and Connecticut. The convicted must be factually innocent, currently in custody, and the case must involve one of the following elements: invalidated forensic science, false confession, jailhouse informant testimony, official misconduct, or poor defense lawyering. Cases of arson, shaken baby syndrome, and child abuse are given priority. DNA and non-DNA cases accepted.

NEW JERSEY

LAST RESORT INNOCENCE PROJECT | SETON HALL UNIVERSITY SCHOOL OF LAW

One Newark Center, 1109 Raymond Blvd., Newark, NJ 07102
(973) 642-8500
www.law.shu.edu/programscenters

LRIP provides advocacy and legal representation for wrongfully convicted New Jersey Prisoners. DNA and non-DNA cases accepted. Must claim actual innocence and have been convicted in New Jersey.

NEW MEXICO

INNOCENCE & JUSTICE PROJECT | UNIVERSITY OF NEW MEXICO SCHOOL OF LAW

1117 Stanford NE, Albuquerque, NM 87131-0001
(505) 277-2671
www.lawschool.unm.edu

IJP provides legal representation for wrongfully convicted New Mexico prisoners. DNA and non-DNA cases accepted, with no minimum sentencing requirement.

NEW YORK

EXONERATION INITIATIVE

233 Broadway, Suite 2370, New York, NY 10279
(212) 965-9335
www.exonerationinitiative.org

EI provides legal representation to wrongfully convicted New York prisoners who have actual innocence claims. DNA and non-DNA cases accepted, with no sentencing minimums.

NEW YORK STATE DEFENDERS ASSOCIATION

194 Washington St., Suite 500, Albany, NY 12210
www.nysda.org

SECOND LOOK PROGRAM | BROOKLYN LAW SCHOOL

250 Joralemon St., Brooklyn, NY 11201
www.brooklaw.edu/academics/clinics/news_2ndlook.php

NORTH CAROLINA

INNOCENCE AND JUSTICE CLINIC | WAKE FOREST UNIVERSITY LAW SCHOOL

1834 Wake Forest Rd., Winston-Salem, NC 27109
(336) 757-5430
www.innocence-clinic.law.wfu.edu

IJC provides legal representation for wrongfully convicted prisoners in North Carolina. DNA and non-DNA cases accepted, with no sentencing minimum.

NORTH CAROLINA CENTER ON ACTUAL INNOCENCE

PO Box 52446, Durham, NC 27717-2446
(919) 489-3268
www.ncaai.org

NCCAI provides legal representation for wrongfully convicted North Carolina prisoners. Prisoner must have been convicted in NC, have an actual claim of innocence with no involvement in the crime, have no more appeal rights and are currently unrepresented, and have the possibility of new evidence that was presented at trial or during appeals.

NORTH CAROLINA INNOCENCE INQUIRY COMMISSION

ADMINISTRATION OFFICE OF THE COURTS

PO Box 2448, Raleigh, NC 27602
www.innocencecommission-nc.org

NCIIC reviews actual innocence claims of North Carolina prisoners through an independent and balanced forum established by the NC General Assembly. Someone found to be innocent by the forum is declared innocent and cannot be tried again, regardless of the appellate process.

NORTH DAKOTA

INNOCENCE PROJECT OF MINNESOTA

1600 Utica Ave., Suite 140, St. Louis Park, MN 55416
(651) 523-3152
www.ipmn.org

IPMN provides legal representation to wrongfully convicted prisoners in North Dakota, Minnesota, and South Dakota. Non-DNA cases are accepted in ND and SD. There are no minimum sentencing requirements. They look for cases that involve junk science, false confessions, informant testimony, eyewitness misidentification, official misconduct, bad lawyering, and other factors.

OHIO

INNOCENT INMATES ASSOCIATION OF OHIO

PO Box 38100, Olmsted Falls, OH 44138
www.innocentinmates.org

OHIO INNOCENCE PROJECT | UNIVERSITY OF CINCINNATI COLLEGE OF LAW

PO Box 210040, Cincinnati, OH 45221-0040
(513) 556-0752
www.law.uc.edu/o-i-p

OIP provides legal representation to wrongfully convicted Ohio prisoners. DNA and non-DNA cases accepted, with no sentencing requirements.

WRONGFUL CONVICTION PROJECT | OFFICE OF OHIO PUBLIC DEFENDER

250 E. Broad St., Suite 1400, Columbus, OH 43215
(614) 477-4931

www.odp.ohio.gov/dp_wrongfulconviction

WCP provides legal representation for wrongfully convicted Ohio prisoners. Only non-DNA cases with no history of violence or lengthy criminal records accepted. Must have exhausted all appeals and have a considerable amount of time left on sentence.

PROVING INNOCENCE

http://provinginnocence.org

OKLAHOMA

MIDWEST INNOCENCE PROJECT

605 W. 47th St., Kansas City, MO 64113
(816) 221-2166
www.themip.org

MIP provides advocacy and representation for wrongfully convicted prisoners in Oklahoma, Kansas, Arkansas, Iowa and Nebraska. They will accept cases of actual innocence where the convicted had nothing to do with the crime, has more than 10 years left on their sentence or has to register as a sex offender, and who is not currently represented by counsel. They will not accept death penalty or self-defense cases.

OKLAHOMA INDIGENT DEFENDERS

www.state.ok.us/~oids

OKLAHOMA INNOCENCE PROJECT | OKLAHOMA CITY UNIVERSITY SCHOOL OF LAW

2501 N. Blackwelder, Oklahoma City, OK 73106
(405) 208-6161
www.innocence.okcu.org

OIP provides legal representation to wrongfully convicted Oklahoma prisoners. DNA and non-DNA cases accepted, with no sentencing requirements. Only cases of actual innocence allowed.

OREGON

OREGON INNOCENCE PROJECT

PO Box 40588, Portland, OR 97240
www.oregoninnocence.org info@oregoninnocence.org

OIP provides advocacy and representation to wrongfully convicted Oregon prisoners. Write for current criteria.

PENNSYLVANIA

DUQUESNE UNIVERSITY SCHOOL OF LAW INNOCENCE PROJECT

900 Locust St., Pittsburgh, PA 15282
(412) 396-4704
www.law.duq.edu/contact.html

DUSLIW provides legal support for wrongfully convicted prisoners in Pennsylvania and West Virginia. Write for current criteria.

INNOCENCE INSTITUTE OF POINT PARK

201 Wood St., Pittsburgh, PA 15222
www.pointpark.edu/innocence

IIPP provides advocacy for wrongfully convicted Western Pennsylvania and West Virginia prisoners through journalism. Write for current criteria.

PENNSYLVANIA INNOCENCE PROJECT

1719 N. Broad St., Philadelphia, PA 19122
(215) 204-4255
www.innocenceprojectpa.org

PIP provides legal representation for wrongfully convicted Pennsylvania prisoners. DNA and non-DNA cases accepted, with no sentencing requirements. They will consider cases involving arson, shaken baby syndrome, and child abuse.

RHODE ISLAND

NEW ENGLAND INNOCENCE PROJECT

160 Boylston St., Boston, MA 02116
(857) 277-7858
www.newenglandinnocence.org

HEIP provides advocacy and legal representation for wrongfully convicted prisoners in Vermont, Massachusetts, Maine, New Hampshire, and Connecticut. The convicted must be factually innocent, currently in custody, and the case must involve one of the following elements: invalidated forensic science, false confession, jailhouse informant testimony, official misconduct, or poor defense lawyering. Cases of arson, shaken baby syndrome, and child abuse are given priority. DNA and non-DNA cases accepted.

SOUTH CAROLINA

PALMETTO INNOCENCE PROJECT | J.M. MCCULLUCH INSTITUTE

PO Box 11623, Columbia, SC 23211
(803) 779-0005

PIP provides pro bone legal representation to wrongfully or unfairly convicted prisoners in South Carolina.

SOUTH DAKOTA

INNOCENCE PROJECT OF MINNESOTA

1600 Utica Ave., Suite 140, St. Louis Park, MN 55416
(651) 523-3152
www.ipmn.org

IPMN provides legal representation to wrongfully convicted prisoners in South Dakota, Minnesota, and North Dakota. Non-DNA cases are accepted in ND and SD. There are no minimum sentencing requirements. They look for cases that involve junk science, false confessions, informant testimony, eyewitness misidentification, official misconduct, bad lawyering, and other factors.

TEXAS

INNOCENCE PROJECT OF TEXAS

1511 Texas Ave., Lubbock, TX 79401
(806) 744-6525
www.ipoftexas.org

IP of Texas provides legal representation for wrongfully convicted Texas prisoners. Must claim actual innocence. DNA and non-DNA cases accepted, with no sentencing requirements. Appeals must be exhausted. No federal cases.

INNOCENCE PROJECT | THURGOOD MARSHALL SCHOOL OF LAW

3100 Cleburne St., Houston, TX 77004
(713) 313-1139
www.earlcarlinstitute.org/centers/criminal_justice/innocence_project.html

Provides legal representation for wrongfully convicted Texas prisoners. They will only accept cases where it can be proven that a crime never happened, mistaken identity, or where DNA proves innocence.

INNOCENCE PROJECT | TEXAS A&M UNIVERSITY

1515 Commerce St., Fort Worth, TX 76102

IP investigates claims of actual innocence involving Texas prisoners. They primarily focus on Northern Texas.

TEXAS CENTER FOR ACTUAL INNOCENCE | UNIVERSITY OF TEXAS SCHOOL OF LAW

727 E. Dead Keeton St., Austin, TX 78705
(512) 471-1317
www.utexas.edu/law/clinincs/innocence/tcai

TCAI provides legal representation for wrongfully convicted Texas prisoners. DNA and non-DNA cases accepted, with no sentencing requirements.

UTAH

ROCKY MOUNTAIN INNOCENCE CENTER

358 South 700 East, B235, Salt Lake City, UT 84102
(801) 355-1888
www.rminnocence.org

RMIC provides advocacy and legal representation for wrongfully convicted prisoners in Utah, Nevada and Wyoming. Must be completely innocent, provable through significant new evidence, have no remaining appeals options, and have more than seven years left on sentence.

Vermont

NEW ENGLAND INNOCENCE PROJECT

160 Boylston St., Boston, MA 02116
(857) 277-7858
www.newenglandinnocence.org

HEIP provides advocacy and legal representation for wrongfully convicted prisoners in, Vermont, Massachusetts, Rhode Island, Maine, New Hampshire, and Connecticut. The convicted must be factually innocent, currently in custody, and the case must involve one of the following elements: invalidated forensic science, false confession, jailhouse informant testimony, official misconduct, or poor defense lawyering. Cases of arson, shaken baby syndrome, and child abuse are given priority. DNA and non-DNA cases accepted.

VIRGINIA

INNOCENCE PROJECT | UNIVERSITY OF VIRGINIA

580 Massie Rd., Charlottesville, VA 22901
(434) 924-7354

www.law.virginia.edu/html/academics/practical/innocenceclinic.html

IP provides legal assistance to wrongfully convicted Virginia prisoners. DNA and non-DNA cases accepted, with no sentencing requirements.

WASHINGTON

INNOCENCE PROJECT | NORTHWEST CLINIC

PO Box 85110, Seattle, WA 89145-1110
(206) 543-5780
www.law.washington.edu/clinics/ipnw

IPNW provides legal representation to wrongfully convicted Washington prisoners. Must have an actual innocence claim that can be proven through DNA testing or new evidence, have at least three years left on sentence, have completed direct appeals, and have no right to appointed counsel.

WEST VIRGINIA

DUQUESNE UNIVERSITY SCHOOL OF LAW INNOCENCE PROJECT

900 Locust St., Pittsburgh, PA 15282
(412) 396-4704
www.law.duq.edu/contact.html

DUSLIW provides legal support for wrongfully convicted prisoners in Pennsylvania and West Virginia. Write for current criteria.

INNOCENCE INSTITUTE OF POINT PARK

201 Wood St., Pittsburgh, PA 15222
www.pointpark.edu/innocence

IIPP provides advocacy for wrongfully convicted Western Pennsylvania and West Virginia prisoners through journalism. Write for current criteria.

WEST VIRGINIA INNOCENCE PROJECT

PO Box 6130, Morgantown, WV 26506-6130
(304) 293-7294
www.innocenceproject.wvu.edu

WVIP provides legal representation to wrongfully convicted West Virginia prisoners. DNA and non-DNA cases involving arson or shaken baby syndrome are accepted. Must have at least three years left on sentence.

WISCONSIN

FRANK J. REMINGTON CENTER

www.law.wisc.edu/fjr/innocence

PROVING INNOCENCE

http://provinginnocence.org

WISCONSIN INNOCENCE PROJECT

975 Bascom Mall, Madison, WI 53706-1399
(608) 265-1160
www.law.wisc.edu/fjr/clinical.ip

WIP provides legal representation to wrongfully convicted Wisconsin prisoners. They accept DNA and non-DNA cases where actual innocence is claimed. Must have at least three years left on sentence.

WYOMING

ROCKY MOUNTAIN INNOCENCE CENTER

358 South 700 East, B235, Salt Lake City, UT 84102
(801) 355-1888
www.rminnocence.org

RMIC provides advocacy and legal representation for wrongfully convicted prisoners in Wyoming, Utah, and Nevada. Must be completely innocent, provable through significant new evidence, have no remaining appeals options, and have more than seven years left on sentence.

International Innocence Organizations

CANADA

ASSOCIATION IN DEFENCE OF THE WRONGFULLY CONVICTED

111 Peter St., Suite 626, Toronto, Ontario M5V 2H1, Canada
www.aidwyc.org

INNOCENCE INTERNATIONAL

330 Runnymede Ave., Toronto, Ontario M6S 2Y6 Canada
http://rubinthehurricanecarter.com/innocence.html

UNIVERSITY OF BRITISH COLUMBIA LAW INNOCENCE PROJECT

1822 East Mall, Vancouver, BC V6T 1Z1 Canada
www.innocenceproject.law.ubc.ca

YORK UNIVERSITY INNOCENCE PROJECT | OSGOODE HALL LAW SCHOOL

4700 Keele St. Room 118A
www.yorku.ca/dmartin/innocence/innocence.htm

IMAGINARY CRIMES

http://members.shaw.ca/imaginarycrimes
imaginarycrimes@shaw.ca

INJUSTICE BUSTERS

www.injusticebusters.com

EUROPE

EUROPEAN COURT OF HUMAN RIGHTS

www.echr.coe.int

UNITED KINGDOM

ACTION AGAINST FALSE ALLEGATIONS OF ABUSE

www.aafaa.org.uk

INNOCENT.ORG

www.innocent.org.ok

INNOCENCE NETWORK UK

www.innocencenetwork.uk

INSIDE DOUBT

www.insidedoubt.co.uk

MISCARRIAGES OF JUSTICE | MOJO SCOTLAND

www.mojoscotland.com

MISCARRIAGES OF JUSTICE UK | MOJUK

www.mojuk.org.uk

PRISONERS ABROAD

www.prisonersabroad.org.uk

Provides advocacy and services for innocent British prisoners held abroad.

SCOTCHED INJUSTICE

http://scotchedinjustice.forumotion.com

UNITED AGAINST INJUSTICE

www.unitedagainstinjustice.org.uk

UNIVERSITY OF BRISTOL INNOCENCE PROJECT

www.brostolac.uk/law/aboutus/law-aractivities/innocence-project.html

UNIVERSITY OF LEEDS INNOCENCE PROJECT

20 Lyddon Terrace, Leeds, LS2 9JT United Kingdom
011-3-343-5026

AUSTRALIA

AUSTRALIAN INNOCENCE PROJECT | GRIFFITH LAW SCHOOL INNOCENCE PROJECT

Griffith University, Southport, Queensland, 4215
www.griffith.edu.au/law/innocence-project innocence-project@griffith.edu.au

INNOCENCE PROJECT WA

Council House, Level 4, 27-29 St. George's Terrace, Perth, WA 6000 Australia
www.innocenceprojectwa.org.au
info@innocenceprojectwa.org.au

Provides representation and advocacy for the wrongfully convicted in Western Australia.

SELLENGER CENTRE CRIMINAL JUSTICE REVIEW PROJECT | THE SCHOOL OF LAW AND JUSTICE

Edith Cowan University, 270 Joondalup Dr., Joondalup, WA 6027 Australia
08-6304-5414
www.ecu.edu.au

UNIVERSITY OF MELBOURNE INNOCENCE PROJECT

185 Pelham St., Carlton, Melbourne, Victoria 3040 Australia

FRANCE

INNOCENCE PROJECT OF FRANCE

3 Place des Celestins, 69002 Lyon, France
336-81-82-0292

GERMANY

INNOCENT IN PRISON PROJECT

Kasperstrasse 6a, 21647, Moisburg, Germany
www.innocenceinprison.org

JAPAN

JAPAN INNOCENCE AND DEATH INFORMATION CENTER

www.jiadep.org

NETHERLANDS

KNOOPS' INNOCENCE PROJECT

www.knoops.info/knoops-innocence-project_en

NEW ZEALAND

INNOCENCE PROJECT OF NEW ZEALAND | UNIVERSITY OF OTAGO

PO Box 56, Dunedin, 9054, New Zealand
64-3-479-4002

NORWAY

NORWEGIAN CRIMINAL CASE REVIEW COMMISSION

www.gjenopptakelse.no

SWITZERLAND

INTERNATIONAL COMMISSION OF JURISTS

www.icj.org

American Bar Association – State-by-State Directory

The following are state-by-state listings for the American Bar Association (ABA). The ABA provides oversight of attorneys and judges within each state. They have the power to discipline attorneys and judges who do not follow professional rules of conduct or who violate the law.
If you have a complaint against an attorney who has represented you or against a judge who has overseen your case, contact the ABA listing in your state to notify them of the misconduct. They will provide you with further information.

ALABAMA

415 Dexter Ave., Montgomery, AL 36104
(334) 269-1515

ALASKA

PO Box 100279, 550 W. 7th Ave., Suite 1990, Anchorage, AK 99510
(907) 272-7469

ARIZONA

111 W. Monroe, Suite 1800, Phoenix, AZ 85003
(602) 252-4804

ARKANSAS

400 W. Markham, Little Rock, AK72201
(501) 375-4606

CALIFORNIA

180 Howard St., San Francisco, CA 94105
(415) 538-2000

COLORADO

1900 Grant St., Suite 950, Denver, CO 80203
(303) 860-1115

CONNECTICUT

30 Bank St., New Britain, CT 06050
(860) 223-4400

DELAWARE

301 N. Market St., Wilmington, DE 19801
(302) 658-5279

DISTRICT OF COLUMBIA

1101 K St. NW, Suite 200, Washington, DC 20005
(202) 737-4700

FLORIDA

651 E. Jefferson St., Tallahassee, FL 32399
(850) 561-5600

GEORGIA

104 Marietta St. NW Suite 100, Atlanta, GA 30303
(404) 527-8700

HAWAII

1132 Bishop St., Suite 906, Honolulu, HI 96813
(808) 537-1868

IDAHO

PO Box 795, Boise, ID 83701
(208) 334-4500

ILLINOIS

20 S. Clark St., Suite 900, Chicago, IL 60603
(312) 726-8775

INDIANA

230 E. Ohio St., 4th Floor, Indianapolis, IN 46204
(317) 639-5465

IOWA

521 E. Locust. Suite 300, Des Moines, IA 50309
(515) 243-3179

KANSAS

1200 SW Harrison St., Topeka, KS 66612

KENTUCKY

514 W. Main St., Frankfort, KY 40601
(502) 564-3795

LOUISIANA

601 St. Charles Ave., New Orleans, LA 70130
(504) 566-1600

MAINE

PO Box 788, Augusta, ME 04322
(207) 622-7523

MARYLAND

520 W. Fayette St., Baltimore, MD 20201
(410) 685-7878

MASSACHUSETTS

20 West St., Boston, MA 02111
(617) 338-0694

MICHIGAN

306 Townsend St., Lansing, MI 48933
(800) 968-1442

MINNESOTA

600 Nicollet Mall, Suite 380, Minneapolis, MN 55402
(612) 333-1183

MISSISSIPPI

PO Box 2168, Jackson, MS 39225
(610) 948-4471

MISSOURI

326 Monroe, Jefferson City, MO 65102
(573) 638-2235

MONTANA

PO Box 577, Helena, MT 59624
(405) 442-7660

NEBRASKA

635 S. 24th St., PO Box 81809, Lincoln, NE 68501
(402) 475-7091

NEVADA

600 E. Charleston Blvd., Las Vegas, NV 89104
(792) 382-2200

NEW HAMPSHIRE

112 Pleasant St., Concord, NH 03301
(603) 224-6942

NEW JERSEY

One Constitution Square, New Brunswick, NJ 08901
(732) 249-5000

NEW MEXICO

121 Tijeras St. NE, PO Box 25883, Albuquerque, NM 87102
(505) 842-6132

NEW YORK

1 Elk St., Albany, NY 12207
(518) 463-3200

NORTH CAROLINA

PO Box 3688, Cary, NC 27519
(919) 677-0561

NORTH DAKOTA

555½ E. Broadway, Suite 101, Bismarck, ND 58501
(701) 255-1404

OHIO

1700 Lakeshore Dr., Columbus, OH 53204
(614) 487-2050

OKLAHOMA

1901 N. Lincoln Blvd., Oklahoma City, OK 73152
(405) 416-5000

OREGON

16037 Upper Boones Ferry Rd., PO Box 231935, Tigard, OR 97224
(503) 620-0222

PENNSYLVANIA

100 South St., PO Box 186, Harrisburg, PA 17108
(717) 238-6715

RHODE ISLAND

15 Cedar St., Providence, RI 02903
(401) 421-5740

SOUTH CAROLINA

950 Taylor St., Columbia, SC 29202
(803)799-6653

SOUTH DAKOTA

222 E. Capitol, Pierre, SD 57501
(605) 224-7554

TENNESSEE

221 4th Ave. N, Nashville, TN 37219
(615) 383-7421

TEXAS

1414 Colorado, Austin, TX 78701
(512) 463-1463

UTAH

645 S. 200 East, Salt Lake City, UT 84111
(801) 531-9077

VERMONT

35-37 Court St., PO Box 100, Montpelier, VT 05260
(802) 223-2020

VIRGINIA

701 E. Franklin St., Suite 1120, Richmond, VA 23219
(804) 644-0041

WASHINGTON

2101 4th Ave., Suite 400, Seattle, WA 98121
(206) 443-9722

WEST VIRGINIA

2006 Kanawha Blvd. E, Charleston, WV 25311
(304) 558-2456

WISCONSIN

5302 E. Park Blvd., Madison, WI 53718
(608) 257-3838

WYOMING

500 Randall Ave., PO Box 109, Cheyenne, WY 82003
(307) 632-9061

Court Addresses

The following are address listings for state and federal (district) courts. If you are filing a lawsuit, need information or to make filings in a pending case, or if you require information on a past case, write to the court in your state (for state court actions) or district (for federal actions).

ALABAMA

STATE COURT ADMINISTRATOR

300 Dexter Ave., Montgomery, AL 36104-3741
(334) 954-5000
www.alacourt.gov

U.S. DISTRICT COURT (FEDERAL)

Middle: PO Box 711, Montgomery, AL 36101
(334) 954-3868
www.almb.uscourts.gov

Northern: 1729 Fifth Ave. N., Birmingham, AL 35203-2000
(877) 466-0795
www.alnd.uscourts.gov

Southern: 113 St. Joseph St., Mobile, AL 36602
www.alsb.uscourts.gov

ALASKA

STATE COURT ADMINISTRATOR

820 W. 4th Ave., Anchorage, AK 99501
(907) 264-8232
www.state.ak.us/courts

U.S. DISTRICT COURT (FEDERAL)

Internal Box 4, Anchorage, AK 99513-9513
(907) 222-6940
www.akd.uscourts.gov

ARIZONA

STATE COURT ADMINISTRATOR

1501 W. Washington St., Phoenix, AZ 85007-3231
(602) 542-9310
www.supreme.state.az.us

U.S. DISTRICT COURT (FEDERAL)

401 W. Washington St., Phoenix, AZ 85003-2146
(602) 682-4001
www.azd.uscourts.gov

ARKANSAS

STATE COURT ADMINISTRATOR

625 Marshall St., 1100 Justice Building, Little Rock, AR 72201-1078
(501) 682-9400
www.courts.state/ar/us

U.S. DISTRICT COURT (FEDERAL)

600 W. Capitol Ave., Little Rock, AR 72201
(800) 891-6741
www.are.uscourts.gov

CALIFORNIA

STATE COURT ADMINISTRATOR

455 Golden Gate Ave., San Francisco, CA 94102-3660
(415) 865-4200
www.courtinfo.ca.gov

U.S. DISTRICT COURT (FEDERAL)

Central: United States Courthouse, 312 N. Spring St., Los Angeles, CA 90012-4701
(866) 522-6053
www.cacd.uscourts.gov

Eastern: United States Courthouse, 500 I St., Sacramento, CA 95814-7300
www.caed.uscourts.gov

Northern: 450 Golden Gate Ave., Box 36060, San Francisco, CA 94102-3434
(888) 457-0604
www.canb.uscourts.gov

Southern: Federal Building, Suite 4290, San Diego, CA 92101
(619) 557-6521
www.casb.uscourts.gov

COLORADO

STATE COURT ADMINISTRATOR

1301 Pennsylvania St., Suite 300, Denver, CO 80203-2416
(303) 861-1111
www.courts.state.co.us

U.S. DISTRICT COURT (FEDERAL)

United States Courthouse, 2nd Floor, 901 19th St., Denver, CO 80294
(720) 904-7419
www.co.uscourts.gov

CONNECTICUT

STATE COURT ADMINISTRATOR

31 Capitol Ave., Hartford, CT 06106
(860) 757-2100
www.jud.state.ct.us

U.S. DISTRICT COURT (FEDERAL)

United States Courthouse, 141 Church St., New Haven, CT 06510
(800) 800-5113
www.ctd.uscourts.gov

DELAWARE

STATE COURT ADMINISTRATOR

500 N. King St., #11600, Wilmington, DE 19801
(302) 255-0090
www.courts.delaware.gov

U.S. DISTRICT COURT (FEDERAL)

Federal Building, 844 N. King St., Wilmington, DE 19801-3519
(302) 252-2560
www.ded.uscourts.gov

DISTRICT OF COLUMBIA

STATE COURT ADMINISTRATOR

500 Indiana Ave. NW, Room 1500, Washington DC, 20001
(202) 879-1700
www.dcsc.gov

U.S. DISTRICT COURT (FEDERAL)

United States Courthouse, 333 Constitution Ave. NW, Washington, DC 20001
(202) 208-1365
www.dcd.uscourts.gov

FLORIDA

STATE COURT ADMINISTRATOR

Supreme Court Building, 500 S. Duval, Tallahassee, FL 32399-1900
(850) 922-5081
www.flcourts.org

U.S. DISTRICT COURT (FEDERAL)

United States Courthouse Annex, 3rd Floor, 111 N. Adams, Tallahassee, FL 32301
(850) 435-8477
www.flnd.uscourts.gov

GEORGIA

STATE COURT ADMINISTRATOR

244 Washington St. SW, Suite 550, Atlanta, GA 30334
(404) 656-5171
www.georgiacourts.org

U.S. DISTRICT COURT (FEDERAL)

Middle: PO Box 128, Macon, GA 31202
(800) 211-3015
www.gamb.uscourts.gov

Northern: 75 Spring St. SW, Atlanta, GA 30303-3309
(800) 510-8284
www.gand.uscourts.gov

Southern: PO Box 8286, Savannah, GA 31412
www.gasd.uscourts.gov

HAWAII

STATE COURT ADMINISTRATOR

417 S. King St., Honolulu, HI 96813
(808) 539-4900
www.courts.state.hi.us

U.S. DISTRICT COURT (FEDERAL)

Building 300, Ala Moana Blvd., Honolulu, HI 96850-0001
(800) 522-8122
www.hid.uscourts.gov

IDAHO

STATE COURT ADMINISTRATOR

PO Box 83720, Boise, ID 83720-0101
(208) 334-2246
www.isc.idaho.gov

U.S. DISTRICT COURT (FEDERAL)

United States Courthouse, 550 W. Fort St., Boise, ID 83724-0101
(208) 334-9386
www.id.uscourts.gov

ILLINOIS

STATE COURT ADMINISTRATOR

222 N. LaSalle, 13th Floor, Chicago, IL 60601
(312) 793-3250
www.state.il.us/court

U.S. DISTRICT COURT (FEDERAL)

Central: United States Courthouse, 600 E. Monroe St., Springfield, IL 62701
(800) 827-9005
www.ilcd.uscourts.gov

Northern: United States Courthouse, 20th Floor, 219 S. Dearborn St., Chicago, IL 60604
(888) 232-6814
www.ilnd.uscourts.gov

Southern: United States Courthouse, 750 Missouri Ave., East St. Louis, IL 62201
(800) 726-5622
www.ilsd.uscourts.gov

INDIANA

STATE COURT ADMINISTRATOR

115 W. Washington St., #1080, Indianapolis, IN 46204
(317) 232-2542
www.in.gov/judiciary

U.S. DISTRICT COURT (FEDERAL)

Northern: United States Courthouse, 204 S. Main St., South Bend, IN 46601
(800) 755-8393
www.innd.uscourts.gov

Southern: Northern: United States Courthouse, 46 E. Ohio St., Indianapolis, IN 46204
(800) 335-8003
www.insd.uscourts.gov

IOWA

STATE COURT ADMINISTRATOR

Judicial Branch Building, 111 E. Court Ave., Des Moines, IA 50319
(515) 281-5241
www.judicial.state.ia.us

U.S. DISTRICT COURT (FEDERAL)

Northern: United States Courthouse, 4200 C St. SW, Cedar Rapids, IA 52404
(800) 249-9859
www.iand.uscourts.gov

Southern: Northern: United States Courthouse, PO Box 9344, Des Moines, IA 50306-9344
(888) 219-5534
www.iasd.uscourts.gov

KANSAS

STATE COURT ADMINISTRATOR

Judicial Center, 301 SW 10th St., Topeka, KS 66612
(785) 296-3229
www.kscourts.org

U.S. DISTRICT COURT (FEDERAL)

United States Courthouse, 500 State Ave., Kansas City, KS 66101-2400

(800) 827-9028
www.ksd.uscourts.gov

KENTUCKY

STATE COURT ADMINISTRATOR

100 Mill Creek Park, Frankfort, KY 40601
(502) 573-1682
www.kycourts.net

U.S. DISTRICT COURT (FEDERAL)

Eastern: United States Courthouse, 2nd Floor, 101 Barr St., Lexington, KY 40507-1313
(800) 827-9028
www.ksd.uscourts.gov

Western: United States Courthouse, Suite 106, 601 W. Broadway, Louisville, KY 46202-2227
(800) 263-9385
www.kywd.uscourts.gov

LOUISIANA

STATE COURT ADMINISTRATOR

400 Royal St., Suite 1190, New Orleans, LA 70130
(504) 310-2550
www.lasc.org

U.S. DISTRICT COURT (FEDERAL)

Eastern: 500 Poydras St., New Orleans, LA 70130
www.laed.uscourts.gov

Middle: 777 Florida St., Suite 139, Baton Rouge, LA 70807
(225) 382-2175
www.lamd.uscourts.gov

Western: 300 Fannin St., Suite 167, Shreveport, LA 71101
(800) 326-4026
www.lawd.uscourts.gov

MAINE

STATE COURT ADMINISTRATOR

PO Box 4820, Portland, ME 04112
(207) 822-0792
www.state.me.us/courts

U.S. DISTRICT COURT (FEDERAL)

156 Federal St., Portland, ME 04101-4152
800) 650-7253
www.med.uscourts.gov

MARYLAND

STATE COURT ADMINISTRATOR

580 Taylor Ave., Annapolis, MD 21401
(401) 260-1400
www.courts.state.md.us

U.S. DISTRICT COURT (FEDERAL)

United States Courthouse, 101 W. Lombard St., Baltimore, MD 21201-2605
(800) 829-0145
www.mdd.uscourts.gov

MASSACHUSETTS

STATE COURT ADMINISTRATOR

2 Center Plaza, Room 540, Boston, MA 02108
(617) 742-8575
www.mass.gov/courts

U.S. DISTRICT COURT (FEDERAL)

One Courthouse Way, Suite 2300, Boston, MA 02210-3002
(888) 201-3572
www.mad.uscourts.gov

MICHIGAN

STATE COURT ADMINISTRATOR

PO Box 30048, Lansing, MI 48909
(517) 373-0130
www.courts.michigan.gov/scoa

U.S. DISTRICT COURT (FEDERAL)

Eastern: United States Courthouse, 231 W. Lafayette Blvd., Detroit, MI 48226
(877) 422-3056
www.mied.uscourts.gov

Western: Federal Building, 110 Michigan St. NW, Grand Rapids, MI 49503
(866) 729-9098

www.miwd.uscourts.gov

MINNESOTA

STATE COURT ADMINISTRATOR

135 Minnesota Judicial Center, 25 Constitution Ave., St. Paul, MN 55155
(651) 296-2474
www.courts.state.mn.us

U.S. DISTRICT COURT (FEDERAL)

United States Courthouse, Suite 202, 300 S. Fourth St., Minneapolis, MN 55415
(800) 959-9002
www.mnd.uscourts.gov

MISSISSIPPI

STATE COURT ADMINISTRATOR

PO Box 117, Jackson, MS 39205
(601) 354-7406
www.mssc.state.ms.us

U.S. DISTRICT COURT (FEDERAL)

Northern: 911 Jackson Ave., E, Oxford, MS 38655
(800) 392-8653
www.msnd.uscourts.gov

Southern: PO Box 23552, Jackson, MS 39225-3552
(800) 601-8859
www.mssd.uscourts.gov

MISSOURI

STATE COURT ADMINISTRATOR

2112 Industrial Dr., PO Box 104480, Jefferson City, MO 65110
(573) 751-4377
www.courts.mo.gov

U.S. DISTRICT COURT (FEDERAL)

Eastern: 111 S. Tenth St., St. Louis, MO 63102-1116
(888) 223-6431
www.moed.uscourts.gov

Western: 400 E. Ninth St., Kansas City, MO 64106
(888) 205-2527
www.mow.uscourts.gov

MONTANA

STATE COURT ADMINISTRATOR

PO Box 203002, Helena, MT 59620-3002
(406) 444-2621
www.lawlibrary.state.mt,us

U.S. DISTRICT COURT (FEDERAL)

United States Courthouse, PO Box 8537, Missoula, MT 59807-8527
(888) 879-0071
www.mtd.uscourts.gov

NEBRASKA

STATE COURT ADMINISTRATOR

PO Box 98910, Lincoln, NE 68509-8910
(402) 471-3730
www.court.nol.org

U.S. DISTRICT COURT (FEDERAL)

United States Courthouse, Suite 1152, 111 S. 18th Plaza, Omaha, NE 68102
(800) 829-0112
www.ned.uscourts.gov

NEVADA

STATE COURT ADMINISTRATOR

201 S. Carson St., #250, Carson City, NV 89701
(775) 684-1700
www.nvsupremecourt.us

U.S. DISTRICT COURT (FEDERAL)

United States Courthouse, 1st Floor, 333 Las Vegas Blvd. S, Las Vegas, NV 89101-7065
(800) 314-3436
www.nvd.uscourts.gov

NEW HAMPSHIRE

STATE COURT ADMINISTRATOR

Supreme Court Building, Noble Dr., Concord, NH 03301

(603) 271-2521
www.courts.state.nh.us

U.S. DISTRICT COURT (FEDERAL)

United States Courthouse, 55 Pleasant St., Concord, NH 03301
(800) 851-8954
www.nhd.uscourts.gov

NEW JERSEY

STATE COURT ADMINISTRATOR

RJH Justice Complex, 7th Floor, CN 37, Trenton, NJ 08625
(609) 984-0275
www.judiciary.state.nj.us

U.S. DISTRICT COURT (FEDERAL)

United States Courthouse, 50 Walnut St., Newark, NJ 08625
(877) 239-2547
www.njd.uscourts.gov

NEW MEXICO

STATE COURT ADMINISTRATOR

237 Don Gaspar, Room 25, Santa Fe, NM 87501
(505) 827-4800
www.nmcourts.com

U.S. DISTRICT COURT (FEDERAL)

United States Courthouse, Suite 270, 333 Lomas Blvd., Albuquerque, NM 87102
(888) 435-7822
www.nmcourt.fed.us

NEW YORK

STATE COURT ADMINISTRATOR

25 Beaver St., New York, NY 10004
(212) 428-2100
www.courts.state.ny.us

U.S. DISTRICT COURT (FEDERAL)

Eastern: 1185 United States Courthouse, 225 Cadman Plaza East, Brooklyn, NY 11201-1818
(800) 252-2537
www.nyed.uscourts.gov
Northern: PO Box 7367, Syracuse, NY 13261-7367
(800) 206-1952
www.nyed.uscourts.gov
Southern: 500 Pearl St., New York, NY 10007-1312
(212) 668-2772
www.nysd.uscourts.gov
Western: United States Courthouse, 68 Court St., Buffalo, NY 14202-3328
(800) 776-9578
www.nywd.uscourts.gov

NORTH CAROLINA

STATE COURT ADMINISTRATOR

PO Box 2448, Raleigh, NC 27602
(919) 733-7107
www.nccourts.org

U.S. DISTRICT COURT (FEDERAL)

Eastern: PO Box 25670, Raleigh, NC 27611
(888) 847-9138
www.nced.uscourts.gov
Middle: Federal Building, Suite 1, 324 W. Market St., Greensboro, NC 27401-7455
(888) 319-0455
www.ncmd.uscourts.gov
Western: 401 W. Trade St., Charlotte, NC 28202
(800) 884-9868
www.ncwd.uscourts.gov

NORTH DAKOTA

STATE COURT ADMINISTRATOR

600 East Boulevard, 1st Floor, Judicial Wing, Department 180, Bismarck, ND 58505
(701) 328-4216
www.ndcourts.com

U.S. DISTRICT COURT (FEDERAL)

United States Courthouse, PO Box 1193, Bismarck, ND 58502-1193
(701) 297-7166
www.ndd.uscourts.gov

OHIO

STATE COURT ADMINISTRATOR

65 S. Front St., Columbus, OH 43215-3431
(614) 387-9000
www.sconet.state.oh.us

U.S. DISTRICT COURT (FEDERAL)

Northern: United States Courthouse, 801 W. Superior Ave., Cleveland, OH 44113
(800) 898-6899
www.ohnd.uscourts.gov
Southern: United States Courthouse, 85 Marconi Blvd., Columbus, OH 43215-2835
(800) 726-1004
www.ohsd.uscourts.gov

OKLAHOMA

STATE COURT ADMINISTRATOR

1915 N. Stiles, #305, Oklahoma City, OK 73105
405) 521-2450
www.oscn.net

U.S. DISTRICT COURT (FEDERAL)

Eastern: PO Box 607, Muskogee, OK 74402
(877) 377-1221
www.oked.uscourts.gov
Northern: United States Courthouse, 333 W. Fourth St., Tulsa, OK 74103-3819
(888) 501-6977
www.oknd.uscourts.gov
Western: United States Courthouse, 200 NW Fourth, Oklahoma City, OK 73102
www.okwd.uscourts.gov

OREGON

STATE COURT ADMINISTRATOR

Supreme Court Building, 1163 State St., Salem, OR 97301-3563
(503) 986-5500
www.ojd.state.or.us/osca

U.S. DISTRICT COURT (FEDERAL)

United States Courthouse, 1000 SW Third Ave., Portland, OR 97204-2802
(800) 726-2227
www.ord.uscourts.gov

PENNSYLVANIA

STATE COURT ADMINISTRATOR

PO Box 719, Mechanicsburg, PA 17055
(717) 795-2097
www.courts.state.pa.us

U.S. DISTRICT COURT (FEDERAL)

Eastern: United States Courthouse, 601 Market St., Philadelphia, PA 19105-1797
(215) 597-2244
www.paed.uscourts.gov
Middle: PO Box 1148, Scranton, PA 18501
(877) 440-2699
www.pamd.uscourts.gov
Western: United States Courthouse, 700 Grant St., Pittsburgh, PA 15219-1906
(412) 355-3210
www.pawd.uscourts.gov

RHODE ISLAND

STATE COURT ADMINISTRATOR

250 Benefit St., Providence, RI 02903
(401) 222-3266
www.courts.ri.us

U.S. DISTRICT COURT (FEDERAL)

One Exchange Terrace, Providence, RI 02903-1270
www.rid.uscourts.gov

SOUTH CAROLINA

STATE COURT ADMINISTRATOR

1015 Sumter St., 2nd Floor, Columbia, SC 29201
(803) 734-1800
www.sccourts.org

U.S. DISTRICT COURT (FEDERAL)

United States Courthouse, 901 Richland St., Columbia, SC 29201
www.scd.uscourts.gov

SOUTH DAKOTA

STATE COURT ADMINISTRATOR

500 E. Capitol Ave., Pierre, SD 57501
(605) 773-3474
www.sdjudicial.com

U.S. DISTRICT COURT (FEDERAL)

United States Courthouse, 200 S. Phillips Ave., Sioux Falls, SD 57401-6581
(800) 768-6218
www.uscourts.gov

TENNESSEE

STATE COURT ADMINISTRATOR

511 Union St., #600, Nashville, TN 37219
(615) 741-2687
www.tsc.state.tn.us

U.S. DISTRICT COURT (FEDERAL)

Eastern: 800 Market St., Suite 130, Knoxville, TN 37902-7902
www.tned.uscourts.gov
Middle: 801 Broadway, Nashville, TN 37203-3816
(615) 736-5584
www.tnmd.uscourts.gov
Western: Federal Building, 167 N. Main St., Memphis, TN 38103
(888) 381-4961
www.tnwd.uscourts.gov

TEXAS

STATE COURT ADMINISTRATOR

PO Box 12066, Austin, TX 78711
(512) 463-1625
www.courts.state.tx.us

U.S. DISTRICT COURT (FEDERAL)

Eastern: United States Courthouse, 211 W. Ferguson St., Tyler, TX 75702
(800) 466-1694
www.txed.uscourts.gov
Northern: United States Courthouse, 1100 Commerce St., Dallas, TX 75242-1310
800) 866-9008
www.txnd.uscourts.gov
Southern: PO Box 61010, Houston, TX 77208
(800) 745-4459
www.txsd.uscourts.gov
Western: United States Courthouse, 655 E. Durango Blvd., San Antonio, TX 78206
(888) 436-7477
www.txwd.uscourts.gov

UTAH

STATE COURT ADMINISTRATOR

450 S. State St., Salt Lake City, UT 54114
(801) 578-3800
www.utcourts.gov

U.S. DISTRICT COURT (FEDERAL)

350 S. Main St., Salt Lake City, UT 84101
(800) 733-6740
www.utd.uscourts.gov

VERMONT

STATE COURT ADMINISTRATOR

109 State St., Montpelier, VT 05609-0701
(802) 828-3278
www.vermontjudiciary.org

U.S. DISTRICT COURT (FEDERAL)

PO Box 945, Burlington, VT 05402
(800) 260-9956
www.vtd.uscourts.gov

VIRGINIA

STATE COURT ADMINISTRATOR

100 N. 9th St., 3rd Floor, Richmond, VA 23219
(804) 786-6455
www.courts.state.va.us

U.S. DISTRICT COURT (FEDERAL)

Eastern: 600 Granby St., Norfolk, VA 23510-1915
(800) 326-5879
www.vaed.uscourts.gov
Western: PO Box 1234, Roanoke, VA 24006
www.vawd.uscourts.gov

WASHINGTON

STATE COURT ADMINISTRATOR

Temple of Justice, PO Box 41174, Olympia, WA 98504
(360) 753-3365
www.courts.wa.gov

U.S. DISTRICT COURT (FEDERAL)

Eastern: United States Courthouse, Suite 840, 920 W. Riverside Ave., Spokane, WA 99201-1010
(509) 353-2404
www.waed.uscourts.gov
Western: 709 Stewart St., Seattle, WA 98101-1271
(888) 409-4662
www.wawd.uscourts.gov

WEST VIRGINIA

STATE COURT ADMINISTRATOR

1900 Kanawha Blvd., 1 East 100 State Capitol, Charleston, WV 25305
(304) 558-0145
www.state.wv.us/wvsca

U.S. DISTRICT COURT (FEDERAL)

Northern: PO Box 1518, Elkins, WV 26241
(800) 809-3028
www.wnvd.uscourts.gov
Southern: United States Courthouse, 300 Virginia St. E, Charleston, WV 25301
(304) 347-5337
www.wvsd.uscourts.gov

WISCONSIN

STATE COURT ADMINISTRATOR

PO Box 1688, Madison, WI 53701
(608) 266-6828
www.wicourts.gov

U.S. DISTRICT COURT (FEDERAL)

Eastern: Federal Building, 517 E. Wisconsin Ave., Milwaukee, WI 53202
(877) 781-7277
www.wied.uscourts.gov
Western: 120 N. Henry St., Madison, WI 53703-4304
(800) 743-8247
www.wiwd.uscourts.gov

WYOMING

STATE COURT ADMINISTRATOR

2301 Capitol Ave., Cheyenne, WY 82002
(307) 777-7583
www.courts.state.wy.us

U.S. DISTRICT COURT (FEDERAL)

2130 Capitol Ave., Cheyenne, WY 82001
www.wyd.uscourts.gov

Legal Publications

The following is a listing of many of the legal publications that have proven to be useful to prisoners. This is by no means a comprehensive listing of every legal book that may be helpful to you. Ask friends and family to help you research any specific issue you are looking for info on.

Publication	Price	Details	Distributor
Advanced Criminal Procedure in a Nutshell	$43.95 (+$6 s/h)	505 pages. Designed for supplemental reading in an advanced criminal procedure course.	**PLN***
An Introduction to the Legal System in the U.S.	$37.50 (+$5.50 s/h)	A general introduction to the structure and function of the U.S. legal system, useful for those who do not already know the fundamentals.	**Oxford University Press***
Arrested: What to do When Your Loved One's in Jail	$16.95 (+$6 s/h)	240 pages. A guide for those who want to support loved ones facing criminal charges.	**PLN***
Battling the Administration: An Inmate's Guide to a Successful Lawsuit	$34.95	Guidance on getting organized to file a lawsuit. Covers court rules, evidence, exhibits, complaints, and more.	**Wynword Press** PO Box 557, Bonners Ferry, ID 83805
Beyond Bars: Rejoining Society After Prison	$14.95 (+$6 s/h)	240 pages. Guidebook on how to prepare for release from prison for successful reentry.	**PLN***
Brief Writing & Oral Argument	$47 (+$5.50 s/h)	Explains the essentials of brief writing and oral presentations, trial, and appellate advocacy techniques.	**Oxford University Press***
California State Prisoner's Handbook, 4th Edition	$40 (2015 supplement $15)	1,100 pages. Provides everything a CA prisoner needs to know about the issues pertaining to serving time in California.	**Reach 360 Fulfillment** 440 Tesconi, Cir., Santa Rosa, CA 95401
The Colossal Book of Criminal Citations, 2nd Edition (2015)	$54.95	507 pages. Comprehensive topical collection of case citations. Includes 3700 citation references, jury instruction, 100+ topics, and 500+ legal definitions.	**Barkan Research** PO Box 352, Rapid River, MI 49878 www.barkanresearch.com
The Criminal Law Handbook: Know Your Rights, Survive the System	$39.99 (+$6 s/h)	By Bergman & Berman-Barret, 608 pages. Explains your rights from the point of being charged to being sentenced.	**PLN***
Criminal Law in a Nutshell	$43.95 (+$6 s/h)	387 pages. Provides an overview of criminal law, including punishment, specific crimes,	**Thomson/West Group* / PLN***

Publication	Price	Details	Distributor
		defenses and burden of proof.	
Criminal Procedure: **Constitutional Limitations**	$43.95 (+$6 s/h)	603 pages. Intended for use by law students. Succinct analysis of constitutional standards pertaining to criminal procedure.	**PLN***
Defending a Drug Case	$59 (+$3 s/h)	Step-by-step guide on how to defend a drug case, with extensive case law references.	**Brown's Legal Research** PO Box 723, St. Charles, MO 63302
Deposition Handbook	$34.99 (+$6 s/h)	By attorneys Bergman & Moore, 352 pages. How-to handbook for anyone who is to depose or be deposed.	**PLN***
Directory of Lawyer Referral Services	$15 (+$9.95 s/h)	Lists local and state legal referral services throughout the country.	**American Bar Assn. Orders** PO Box 10892, Chicago, IL 60610
Disciplinary Self-Help Litigation Manual, 4th Edition	$49.95 (+$6 s/h)	368 pages. A comprehensive guide of your rights pertaining to prison disciplinary hearings and matters.	**PLN***
The Drug Defendant's Handbook	$30 (+$3 s/h)	Alternative look at drug offenses and how to deal with government corruption.	**Brown's Legal Research** PO Box 723, St. Charles, MO 63302
The Essential Supreme Court Cases: 200 Most important Cases for State Prisoners	$19.95	By Ivan Denison, 2015, 330 pages.	**Amazon.com**
Federal Rules of Civil Procedure **Federal Rules of Appellate Proc.** **Federal Rules of Criminal Proc.** **Federal Rules of Evidence**	$ 18.50 $ 9.99 $ 12.50 $ 9.99	These books are available for free download from the federal government at: www.federalrulesofcivilprocedure.org www.federalrulesofappellateprocedure.org www.federalrulesofcriminalprocedures.org www.rulesofevidence.org	**U.S. Government Printing Office** PO Box 979050, St. Louis, MO 63197-9000
Flipping Your Conviction: Post-Conviction Relief for State Prisoners	$49.95	By Ivan Denison, 2013, 449 pages. PCR rules, instructions, forms and examples	**Amazon.com**
Flipping Your Habeas: Overturning your State Conviction in Federal Court	$34.95	By Ivan Denison, 2014, 336 pages. Habeas rules, instructions, forms and examples.	**Amazon.com**

Publication	Price	Details	Distributor
The Georgetown Law Journal Annual Review of Criminal Procedure	$25	1,000+ pages. Topical annual summary of criminal procedure in the U.S.	**Georgetown Law Journal** 600 New Jersey, Ave, NW, Washington, DC 20001
Habeas Citebook: Ineffective Assistance of Counsel (2010)	49.95 (+$6 s/h)	224 pages. Case cites and comprehensive case information on IAC claims	**PLN***
How to Win Your Personal Injury Claim	$34.99 (+$6 s/h)	By attorney Joseph Matthews, 304 pages. Valuable knowledge on property and injury claims. Not specifically geared towards prisoners.	**PLN***
Jailhouse Lawyer's Handbook	$2	152 pages. Self-help legal guide for filing prisoner civil rights actions.	**National Lawyers Guild***
A Jailhouse Lawyer's Manual, 10th Edition (2014)	$30 ($105 for non-prisoners)	1,288 pages. Comprehensive guide for jailhouse lawyers or those who want to learn more about protecting their prisoner's rights. They also have an Immigration & Consular Access Supplement ($5), and a Texas Supplement ($20)	**Columbia Human Rights Law Review***
Jailhouse Lawyers: Prisoners Defending Prisoners v. the USA	$16.95 ($6 s/h)	By Mumia Abu Jamal, 280 pages. PLN columnist and former death row prisoner presents stories of successful jailhouse lawyering.	**PLN***
The Law of Sentencing, Corrections, and Prisoners' Rights - Seventh Edition	$30	A nutshell guide to prisoners' rights and related issues. Written for lawyers and law students.	**Thomson/West Group***
Legal Research: How to Find & Understand the Law	$49.99 (+$6 s/h)	568 pages. Comprehensive and easy to understand guide on legal research.	**PLN***
Lethal Rejection: The Fight to Give Life from Prison and Other Pointlessly Forbidden Places	$17.99	310 pages. Comprehensive debate of organ & tissue donation from healthy and willing prisoners.	**GAVE** PO Box 842, Exeter, CA 93221 (Also Available on Amazon)
Marijuana Law	$17.95 (+$6 s/h)	271 pages. Info on legal defenses, search & seizure, surveillance, asset forfeiture and drug testing related to marijuana offenses.	**PLN***
Prisoners and the Law	$986	6 volumes, 6500-page set. The most comprehensive tool available. Covers the full-range of prisoner rights.	**Thomson/West Group***

Publication	Price	Details	Distributor
The Prisoner's Guide to Survival	$49.95 (+$5 s/h)	Legal research guide covering all aspects of federal litigation common to prisoners.	**PSI Publishing***
Prisoner's Self-Help Litigation Manual, 4th Edition (2010)	$39.95 (+$6 s/h)	1,500 pages. "The must-have "bible" of prison litigation."	**PLN***
Protecting Your Health & Safety	$10 (+$6 s/h)	By Southern Poverty Law Center, 325 pages. Explains prisoner's rights, with a focus on health & safety, and litigating those rights.	**PLN***
Represent Yourself in Court: How to Prepare & Try a Winning Case	$39.99 (+$6 s/h)	By attorneys Bergman & Berman-Barret, 528 pages. Breaks down the civil trial process in steps so you can learn how to represent yourself in court.	**PLN***
Smith's Guide to Habeas Corpus Relief	$24.95 (+$6.95 s/h)	380 pages. Step-by-step guide to federal habeas filings. Example pleadings from initial petition to writ of cert.	**Roberts Company** 15412 Electronic Lane, #101, Huntington Beach, CA 92649
Sue the Doctor and Win! Victims Guide to Secrets of Malpractice Lawsuits	$39.95 (+$6 s/h)	336 pages. Written for victims of medical malpractice and neglect. Not specifically written for prisoners.	**PLN***
Understanding Mass Incarceration: A People's Guide to the Key Civil Rights Struggle of Our Time	$17.95	By James Kilgore, 272 pages. Introduces the basics of mass incarceration, it's effects, and statistics, as well as the fight to affect reform.	**The New Press** 120 Wall Street, 31st Floor, New York, NY 10005 www.thenewpress.com
Winning Habeas Corpus & Post-Conviction Relief	$58.50	A step-by-step guide through all aspects of habeas Corpus and post-conviction filings.	**Fast Law Publishing**
Win Your Lawsuit: Sue in CA Superior Court without a Lawyer	$39.99 (+$6 s/h)	By Judge Roderic Duncan, 445 pages. Shows how to prepare court filings, serve papers, negotiate settlements, and present a case in CA Superior court.	**PLN***
Writing to Win: The Legal Writer	$19.95 (+$6 s/h)	270 pages. Explains the writing of effective complaints, responses, briefs, motions, and other legal pleadings.	**PLN***

*** Find the addresses for these distributors under our 'Legal Resources – Organizations' listings.**

Legal Research Abbreviations

A2d - Atlantic Reporter, Second Series

ADC - Appeal Cases, District of Columbia Reports

AkA - Arkansas Appellate Reports

ALR - American Law Reports, Fifth Series

ALRF - American Law Reports, Federal

ALRF2d - American Law Reports Federal, Second Series

ALR6 - American Law Reports, Sixth Series

ApDC - Court of Appeals for the District of Columbia Reports

Ark - Arkansas Reports

Az - Arizona Reports

Bankr LX - United States Bankruptcy Court & United States District Court Bankruptcy Cases LEXIS

BRW - Bankruptcy Reporter

CAAF LX - U.S. Court of Appeals for the Armed Forces LEXIS

C4th - California Supreme Court Reports, Fourth Series

CA4th - California Appellate Reports, Fourth Series

CA4S - California Appellate Reports, Fourth Series, Supplement

CaL - California Law Review

CaR2d - California Reporter, Second Series

CaR3d - California Reporter, Third Series

CCA LX - U.S. Military Courts of Criminal Appeals LEXIS

ChL - University of Chicago Law Review

Cir. (number) - United States Court of Appeals, United States District Court Circuit (number)

Cir. DC - United States Court of Appeals, United States District Court, DC Circuit

Cir. Fed. - United States Court of Appeals, Federal Circuit

ClCt - United States Claims Court and United States Court of Federal Claims

CCPA - Court of Customs and Patent Appeals

CIT - United States Court of International Trade

CLA - University of California at Los Angeles Law Review

Cor - Cornell Law Review

CR - Columbia Law Review

CS - Connecticut Supplement

Ct - Connecticut Reports

CtA - Connecticut Appellate Reports

CuCt - United States Customs Court

DC4d - Pennsylvania District and County Reports, Fourth Series

DPR - Decisiones de Puerto Rico

ECA - Temporary Emergency Court of Appeals

F2d - Federal Reporter, Second Series

F3d - Federal Reporter, Third Series

FCCR - Federal Communications Commission Record

Fed Appx - Federal Appendix

FedCl - Federal Claims Reporter

FRD - Federal Rules Decisions

FS - Federal Supplement

FS2d - Federal Supplement, Second Series

Ga - Georgia Reports

GaA - Georgia Appeals Reports

Geo - Georgetown Law Journal

Haw - Hawaii Reports

HLR - Harvard Law Review

Ida - Idaho Reports

Il2d - Illinois Supreme Court Reports 2nd Series

Ilm - Illinois Appellate Court Reports, Third Series

IlCCl - Illinois Court of Claims Reports

IlLR - University of Illinois Law Review

JTS - Jurisprudencia del Tribunal Supremo de Puerto Rico

KA2d - Kansas Court of Appeals Reports, Second Series

Kan - Kansas Reports

LCP - Law and Contemporary Problems

LEd - United States Supreme Court Reports, Lawyer's Edition, Second Series

MaA - Massachusetts Appeals Court Reports

MADR - Massachusetts Appellate Division Reports

Mas - Massachusetts Reports

MC - American Maritime Cases

McA - Michigan Court of Appeals Reports

Mch - Michigan Reports

McL - Michigan Law Review

Md - Maryland Reports

MdA - Maryland Appellate Reports

MJ - Military Justice Reporter

ML - Judicial Panel on Multidistrict Litigation

MnL - Minnesota Law Review

Mt - Montana Reports

NC - North Carolina Reports

NCA - North Carolina Court of Appeals Reports

NE - Northeastern Reporter, Second Series

Neb - Nebraska Reports

NebA - Nebraska Advance Reports

Nev - Nevada Reports

NH - New Hampshire Reports

NJ - New Jersey Reports

NJS - New Jersey Superior Court Reports

NJT - New Jersey Tax Court Reports

NM - New Mexico Reports

NVAdv - Nevada Advance Reports

Nl - Northwestern Reporter, Second Series

NwL - Northwestern University Law Review

N+ - New York Ct. of Appeals Reports, 2nd Series

Nb - New York Court of Appeals Reports, Third Series

NYAq - New York Appellate Division Reports, Second Series

NYAd - New York Appellate Division Reports, Third Series

NYL - New York University Law Review

NYW - New York Miscellaneous Reports, Second Series

NYc - New York Miscellaneous Reports, Third Series

NYS2d - New York Supplement, Second Series

OA3d - Ohio Appellate Reports, Third Series

Ohm2d - Ohio Miscellaneous Reports, Second Series

OrA - Oregon Court of Appeals Reports

Ore - Oregon Reports

OS3d - Ohio State Reports, Third Series

P2d - Pacific Reporter, Second Series

P3d - Pacific Reporter, Third Series

Pa - Pennsylvania State Reports

PaC - Pennsylvania Commonwealth Court Reports

PaL - University of Pennsylvania Law Review

PaS - Pennsylvania Superior Court Reports

PQ2d - United States Patents Quarterly, Second Series

RRR - Special Court Regional Rail Reorganization Act of 1973

SC - Supreme Court Reporter

Sr - Southeastern Reporter, Second Series

So2d - Southern Reporter, Second Series

SoC - South Carolina Reports

StnL - Stanford Law Review

Sl - Southwestern Reporter, Second Series

SX - Southwestern Reporter, Third Series

TCM - Tax Court Memorandum Decisions

TCt - Tax Court of the United States Reports; United States Tax Court Reports

TPR - Official Translations of the Opinions of the Supreme Court of Puerto Rico

TxL - Texas Law Review

UCR2d - Uniform Commercial Code Reporting Service, Second Series

US - United States Reports

USApp LX - United States Court of Appeals LEXIS

USClaims LX - United States Court of Federal Claims LEXIS

USDist LX - United States District Court LEXIS

US LX - United States Supreme Court LEXIS

Va - Virginia Reports

VaA - Virginia Court of Appeals Reports

VaL - Virginia Law Review

VCO - Virginia Circuit Court Opinions

Vt - Vermont Reports

WAp - Washington Appellate Reports

Wis2d - Wisconsin Reports, Second Series

WLR - Wisconsin Law Review

Wsh2d - Washington Reports, Second Series

WV - West Virginia Reports

YLJ - Yale Law Journal

Religion Center

Religion Center

"There is only one religion, though, there are a hundred versions of it."

George Bernard Shaw

Mr. Shaw was likely off by several hundred religious factions, but the reality is that whatever religion you choose to follow, everyone, *including prisoners*, has an absolute, constitutionally granted right to do so. With so much diversity, however, so many choices, the spiritual path is one with many trailheads. How do you decide which one to take?

There is a wealth of resources out there, even at your fingertips within the prison you reside, that can help you decide which path to take. Your prison's chaplain and other religious services that are just a kite away can be great guides for your journey. The 'Religion Center', however, will give you an overview not only of the various religious options in front of you, but of the specific rights to practice religion that you retain despite your incarceration.

Remember, though, this is only intended to be a guide to get you started on your path or to help you learn more about other religions or your rights in general. While we have provided you with many resources specifically available to prisoners, there is much more out there to provide you with even more comprehensive insights into the religion of

RELIGION CENTER

Your Religious Rights

Shortly after the Constitution of the United States was drawn up, it became apparent that it was in dire need of some amendments to truly govern the rights of U.S. citizens. The very first amendment to the U.S. Constitution:

"Congress shall make no law respecting an establishment of religion, or prohibiting the free exercise thereof..."

° **First Amendment of the U.S. Constitution**

In other words, **You have an absolute right to believe whatever you want.**

However, an obvious contradiction exists within the two clauses of this Amendment. Known as the "establishment clause," or the right to establish a religion free from government involvement, and the "free exercise clause," or the right to freely practice your religious beliefs, this contradiction is particularly apparent when the amendment is applied to the prisoners of correctional systems. It's been a careful balance for the courts to weigh out the interests of both the state, in the orderly operation of prisons, with the interests of the prisoner, in practicing whatever religion they choose.

In spite of the difficulty in balancing these two fundamental and conflicting rights, courts have given increasing attention to the needs of prisoners in this area. The traditional reluctance of the courts to interfere in the management of a prison is much less apparent when it comes to religious rights of prisoners. Rather than simply dismissing an action, as in the past, the courts are now giving recognition to the existence of First Amendment rights behind prison walls.

"Reasonable opportunity must be afforded to all prisoners to exercise the religious freedom guaranteed by the First Amendment without fear of penalty."

The Supreme Court has repeatedly held the above principle. Over time, religious freedom in the prison systems has steadily become more of a guarantee. This wasn't always the case though. As one commentator has observed, "[t]he Constitution did not breach prison walls for over 170 years." In fact, during most of the history of this country, there was some question as to whether prisoners had any constitutional rights at all, including religious freedoms. Fortunately, however, the recognition of prisoner's religious freedom rights has drastically improved throughout recent history.

RFRA & RLUIPA?

Two federal acts have specifically been used to provide protection of prisoner's religious freedom rights.

- Religious Freedom Restoration Act (RFRA) – Governs federal institutions. (42 U.S.C. 2000bb-1)
- Religious Land Use and Institutionalized Persons Act (RLUIPA) – Governs state and local institutions. (42 U.S.C. 2000cc-5)
- See full text of both the RFRA and the RLUIPA at the end of this chapter.

> The RFRA used to govern both federal and state institutions.
>
> In 1993, Congress passed the RFRA, which says that a government may not "substantially burden" a person's exercise of religion unless it demonstrates that doing so "(1) is in furtherance of a compelling government interest; and (2) is the least restrictive means of furthering that compelling government interest." (42 U.S.C. 2000bb-1) However, the Supreme Court later held that RFRA was unconstitutional as applied to states, because it exceeded Congress's power under Section 5 of the Fourteenth Amendment.
>
> In 2000, Congress fixed this problem by establishing the RLUIPA. Now, the RFRA only generally governs federal prisons, while the RLUIPA governs any facility that accepts federal funding, therefore, virtually all prisons and jails.

Under RFRA and RLUIPA, as well as under the Free Exercise Clause of the First Amendment, in establishing protection for a prisoner's religious beliefs, you must meet two requirements.

1) Your beliefs must be "religious."
2) Your beliefs must be "sincerely held."

Religious?

Being "religious" doesn't just mean that you are a mainstream follower of some easily recognizable religion. It doesn't even have to mean that you have to believe in God. (*Torcaso v. Watkins*, 367 U.S. 488, 495 (1961).) You don't need to belong to an established church, or a division of one, or even be a part of any official interpretation of church doctrine.

Simply put: You have a right to believe WHATEVER you want. If that belief affects your thoughts, and you're devoted to those beliefs… religiously so, you've met the standard.

However, depending on the uniqueness of your beliefs, prisons may not be obligated to accommodate your beliefs. Courts have often disagreed with what qualifies as a religious belief or a religion, for the purposes of freedom to worship in prison. "Mainstream" religions, Christianity, Islam, Judaism, etc., are universally known, and are therefore generally protected. However, if a more nontraditional faith, especially one with no track record, is challenged in court, you will not necessarily win, regardless of whether you consider it to be a religion.

While the Supreme Court has never really defined the term "religion," in deciding whether something is a religion, lower courts have asked whether the belief system addresses "fundamental and ultimate questions," is "Comprehensive in nature," and presents "certain formal and external signs." (*Africa v. Pennsylvania*, 662 F.2d 1025, 1032 (3rd Cir. 1981).)

A good example of the difficulties courts have in deciding how to grant rights to non-traditional religious groups is comparing *Theriault v. Carlson* (495 F.2d 390 (5th Cir. 1974) and *Remmers v. Brewer* (). Both cases dealt with a prisoner-built religion based on the Eclatarian faith and organized around *The Church of the New Song of Universal Life*. In *Theriault*, the prisoner who came up with the religion, and who was self-appointed head of the newly developed church was sent to the hole for attempting to hold unauthorized religious services to promote his new religion. The district court initially ordered his return back to general population and directed prison officials to permit him to hold religious services. However, on remand, a different district court concluded that the Eclatarian faith was not a religion entitled to First Amendment protection, and was rather "a masquerade designed to obtain protection for acts which otherwise would have been unlawful and/or reasonably disallowed by various prison authorities."

Essentially, the same issue was present in *Remmers*, but the court in that case, while aware of the holdings in *Theriault*, decided that the Eclatarian faith was a religion and that members were entitled to protection under the Free Exercise Clause. However, that court declared that if it were substantially proven that the "faith" was a sham, then prison administrators and the court would deal with that appropriately.

To determine if a non-traditional belief system can be recognized as a religion, you may have a better chance at prevailing in court if you have answers to the following questions: Are my beliefs similar to another, more established, religions? Are there many members? Is there a holy book? Are there sacred artifacts or symbols? Does it believe in a higher power? Does it believe that there is a purpose to life? Does it have an explanation as to the origin of people? Can I show that my beliefs are sincerely held?

Sincerely Held?

The second requirement to establishing protection for your religious beliefs is to show that your beliefs are "sincerely held." In other words, you must really believe it. While courts have occasionally considered how long or consistently a prisoner has adhered to their beliefs, (See *Sourbeer v. Robinson*, 791 F.2d 1094, 1102 (3rd Cir. 1986)), courts are generally reluctant to determine sincerity. Just because you have not believed something your entire life, or because you have violated your beliefs in the past, does not automatically mean that a court will find that you are insincere. (See *Reed v. Faulkner*, 842 F.2d 960, 963 (7th Cir. 1988); (*Weir v. Nix*, 890 F. Supp 769, 775-76 (S.D. Iowa 1995).) If, however, you have very recently converted or if you have repeatedly acted in a manner that is not in accordance with your beliefs, you will likely have a difficult time convincing any court that you are sincere.

Restrictions on the Free Exercise of Religion

While you have a right to believe anything you want, you do not always have a constitutional right to do any and everything that your religious beliefs dictate. If your belief isn't part of an officially recognized religion somewhere in the world, you likely have an uphill battle obtaining certain rights, regardless of how strong your beliefs are. But chances are that if it is a recognized religion, the road has been paved for your right to exercise that religion and enjoy many of the activities related to those beliefs.

The only real restrictions on a prisoner's right to exercise and practice their religious beliefs are governed by the balancing of government's interests. In other words, the prison may not impose a substantial burden on your religious exercise unless that burden is 1) in furtherance of a "compelling government interest"; and 2) is the least restrictive means of furthering that interest. (Applies to federal prisoners under RFRA: *O'bryan v. BOP*, 349 F.3d 399, 401 (7th Cir. 2003); *Kikimura v. Hurley*, 242 F.3d 950, 960 (10th Cir. 2001). Applies to state prisoners under RLUIPA: *Cutter v. Wilkinson*, 125 S. Ct. 2113 (2005).

In response to demands of the courts, prison officials have provided a number of explanations for the restrictions they have placed upon prisoners' free exercise of religion. Among these are the maintenance of discipline or security, proper exercise of authority and official discretion, the fact that the regulation is reasonable, and economic considerations. Frequently, these explanations are used interchangeably by the courts, and it is sometimes difficult to determine which justification was the basis of the decision. However, in most cases, if prison officials are able to show that restrictions on religious practices are actually based upon one or more of these enumerated reasons, the courts will allow the restrictions to continue. In addition to providing explanations for the restrictions placed upon the prisoner's free exercise of religion, prison officials and the courts have attempted to define what a religion is, and what religious practices are, for purposes of First Amendment protection. Unfortunately, few precise guidelines have emerged.

Restrictions on access to religious opportunities whether group services, chapel visits, or meetings with religious advisers are reviewed in light of four factors:

(1) Whether there is a valid, rational connection between the regulation and a legitimate government interest put forward to justify it

(2) Whether there are alternative means of exercising the right that remain open to prison prisoners

(3) Whether accommodation of the asserted constitutional right would have a significant impact on guards and other prisoners

(4) Whether ready alternatives are absent, bearing on the reasonableness of the regulation.

Practically, unless your requests for religious rights are obviously frivolous or a blatant security concern, prisons tend to accommodate legitimate reasonable religious freedoms. The prison's chaplain or religious services are good places to start if you have any questions about your particular prison system's restrictions.

Specific Religious Rights

So what are the religious rights that you can expect? Some religious freedoms that prisoners are often granted today:

RELIGIOUS SERVICES

> Group worship services ***"are essential parts of the right to free exercise of religion."***
>
> ° *Freeman v. Arpaio*, 125 F.3d 732, 736-7 (9th Cir. 1997)

Group worship and religious services for many different religions are frequently held within the prison itself. Groups such as Catholics, Jehovah's Witnesses, Asatru, Wiccan, Baptist, Pentecostal, and many more hold regular weekly meeting groups.

Even if the prison administrators cannot provide clergy themselves, often allow legitimate and screened local volunteers to sponsor group worship or conduct services. Services have been prohibited when there was a legitimate concern of violence (*Murphy v. Missouri DOC*, 372, F.3d 979, 983 (8th Cir. 2004)). Other restrictions may apply, such as close supervision by prison staff, cancelation of services if there are only a few members (*Adkins v. Kaspar*, 393 F.3d 559,563-71 (5th Cir. 2004)), suspend services for emergencies, ban use of yard or other common areas, or because of unauthorized non-religious activities (*Leonard v. Norris*, 797 F. 2d, 683, 684-5 (8th Cir. 1986)).

However, courts have generally protected prisoner's ability to attend religious services. (*Mayweather v. Newland*, 258 F.3d 930, 938 (9th Cir. 2001)).

RELIGIOUS DIET

> *"A prisoner has a right to a diet consistent with his or her religious scruples."*
>
> ° *Ford v. McGinnis, 352, F.3d 582, 597 (2d. Cir. 2003)*

Courts often hold that prison officials must provide diets that are required by prisoner's religions (see *Ford v. McGinnis.*) Diets related to major religions are generally granted, such as kosher meals to those of the Jewish faith, and no-pork, halal, and Ramadan fasting-friendly diets for Muslims and other religions.

Similarly, they have found that prisoners have a right to avoid eating foods that are forbidden by their religious beliefs. (*Moorish Science Temple of America, Inc. v. Smith*, 693 F.2d 987, 990 (2nd Cir. 1982)). The RLUIPA and RFRA have helped in many of these arguments. (See *Cutter v. Wilkinson*, 544 U.S. 709 (2005)).

However, when it comes to budgetary constraints or certain complications, courts have held that denying special diets was reasonable. (*Williams v. Morton*, 343 F.3d 212, 217-8 (3rd Cir. 2002), *Martinelli v. Dugger*, 817 F.2d 1499, 1507 (11th Cir. 1987)). When it comes to highly customized meals, prisoners rarely succeed in court. (DeHart v. Lehman, 9 F.Supp 2d 539, 543 (E.D. Pa. 1998)). They have also held that denial is appropriate if it presents a security concern. (*Goff v. Graves*, 362 F.3d 543, 549-50 (8th Cir. 2004)).

Some courts have rejected efforts by prison officials to charge for religious diets. (*Beerheide v. Suthers*, 286 F.3d 1179, 1192 (10th Cir. 2002)).

RELIGIOUS LITERATURE

Just as in the First Amendment right to read anything you want to, prisoners have the right to read religious literature. Restrictions on such literature has largely been held to violate those rights, as well as the right to free exercise of religion. (Sutton v. Rasheed, 323 F.3d 236 (3rd Cir. 2003)).

RELIGIOUS OBJECTS

Many prisons allow religious objects such as medallions, bowls, prayer cloths, rugs, feathers, oils, and other important rites associated with religious worship. However, courts have often decided that prison officials can generally ban such items if they could make a reasonable claim that these present security concerns. (*Mark v. Nix*, 983 F.2d 138, 139 (8th Cir. 1993)). It's important to note, though, that prison officials have not been allowed to ban some religious objects and not others without any specific justification. (*Sasnett v. Litscher*, 197 F.3d 290, 292 (7th Cir. 1999)).

Prison officials are generally not obligated to provide any religious items themselves so long as accommodation has been made for prisoners to purchase these items themselves. (*Frank v. Terrell*, 858 F.2d 1090, 1091 (5th Cir. 1988)).

PERSONAL GROOMING (DRESS, HAIR & BEARDS)

Courts have been mixed on decisions involving hair and beard restrictions. Even under the RFRA and RLUIPA, decisions have been mixed. I.e., in *Mayweathers v. Terhune*, where prisoners sued because they were banned from wearing beards so as to be more easily identifiable, the court held that a less restrictive alternative should be implemented, such as visual inspections and photos both bearded and unbearded. (328 F.Supp. 2d 1086, 1094-96 (E.D. Cal 2004)). But in *Diaz v. Collins*, the court held that the general length restriction on hair was perfectly acceptable under RFRA. (114 F.3d 69, 72-3 (5th Cir. 1997)).

Restrictions on headgear and other religious attire have generally been upheld. (*Muhammad v. Lynaugh*, 966 F.2d 901, 902-3 (5th Cir. 1992)).

However, courts are prone to rule in the prisoners favor of the prisoner can prove that the restriction is not enforced equally against all religions. (*Sassnett v. Litcsher*, 197 F.3d 290, 292 (7th Cir. 1999)). Also, where there is little or no legitimate justification for restricting grooming, courts may rule against the prison officials. (*Burgin v. Henderson*, 536 F.2d 501, 504 (2nd Cir. 1976)).

RELIGIOUS NAMES

Courts have generally enforced that prison officials must acknowledge genuine religious name changes for purposes such as mail delivery and other services. (*Hakim v. Hicks*, 223 F.3d 1244, 1250-51 (11th Cir. 2000); *Malik v. Brown*, 71 F.3d 724, 728-30 (9th Cir. 1995)). Officials are generally not required to use the new name, or wipe it from their old records, and requirements that the prisoner continue to respond to the old name have been found to not be in violation. (*Muhammad v. Wainwright,* 839 F.2d 1422, 1424-1425 (11th Cir. 1987)).

The state may require the prisoner to go the official name change procedures before the new name is acknowledged. (*Azeez v. Fairman*, 795 F.2d 1296, 1299 (7th Cir. 1986)).

Conclusion

The primary emphasis of decisions concerning a prisoner's religious freedom has been on the fact that the prison is a closed environment. It is because of this fact that courts frequently invoke the noninterference logic so prevalent in early cases dealing with prisons. The state interest in maintaining -security within the institution, together with the need for administrative discretion in handling disciplinary problems, has been held sufficient reason for limiting a prisoners First Amendment rights.

One of the few restrictions placed upon the prison administrator in his or her dealings with the First Amendment rights of prisoners has been that of equal protection, that is, treating all classes of prisoners equally. Courts have consistently held that when one religious group is permitted to engage in a particular activity, the same right must be accorded all other religious groups within the institution. Thus, it would appear that although prison officials have a right to regulate religious activity in order to promote valid institutional interests, the regulation must, in all cases, be equally applied to all groups. Likewise, where one group is permitted to manifest its religious beliefs in a certain -manner, all other religious groups must be accorded the same privilege.

The Religious Land Use and Institutionalized Persons Act will continue to have a substantial impact on state institution management, as will the Religious Freedom Restoration Act on federal institutions.

The World of Religion

Of the 7.3 billion people on earth, 6.5 billion claim a religious affiliation. Roughly one-third of the world's population is Christian (mostly in the Americans and Europe), while one-fifth is Muslim, and one-eighth is Hindu (the vast majority of Muslims and Hindus are found in Asia.)

The majority of Christians are Roman Catholic, while the majority of Muslims are Sunnis, and of Hindus are Vaishnavites.

In addition to the practitioners of the three major religions, there are small but noticeable percentages of Chinese folk religionists, Buddhists, ethnic religionists, and new religionists. But Followers of the remaining religions, Sikhs, Spiritists, Jews, Baha'is', Confusionists, Jians, Shinto's, Daoists (Taoists), and Zoroastrians, each make up less than one-half of one percent.

Christianity

FOUNDING:

Christianity traces its origin to the 1st Century A.D., directly to Jesus of Nazareth, whom it affirms to be the chosen one (Christ) of God.

FOLLOWERS:

2.4 billion. Christianity is the most widely spread religion in the world, in 232 countries.

DIVISIONS:

Christianity hosts a variety of sects, the largest of which is the Roman Catholic Church, then the Eastern Orthodox churches, followed by the Protestant churches.

SACRED TEXT:

The *Bible*, particularly the New Testament.

BELIEFS:

Generally, Jesus is the son of God. God's love for the world is the essential component of his being. Jesus died to redeem mankind.

PRACTICES:

Varies by denomination. See the following chart.

Major Christian Denominations: Comparison Chart

DENOMINATION	ORIGINS	ORGANIZATIONAL STRUCTURE	AUTHORITY	SACRAMENTS / SPECIAL RITES	HOW THEY WORSHIP	ETHICS	BELIEFS / DOCTRINES
Anglican / Episcopalian	Henry VII separated English Catholic Church from Rome (1534) for political reasons. Church in U.S. founded in 1789.	Episcopal (Clergy in local churches presided over by Diocesan bishops, in apostolic succession, elected by parish representatives.)	Scripture as interpreted by tradition, especially *39 Articles* (1563); tri-annual convention of bishops, priests and lay people.	Infant Baptism, Eucharist, and other sacraments; sacrament taken to be symbolic, but as having real spiritual effect.	Formal, based on *Book of Common Prayer*, updates 1979, services range from austerely simple to highly liturgical.	Tolerant, sometimes permissive; some social action programs.	Scripture, the "historic creed," which include the Apostles, Nicene, and Athanasius, and the '*Book of Common Prayer*', Calvinist influences.
Church of Christ (Disciples)	Among Evangelical Presbyterians in KY (1804) and PA (1809), in distress over Protestant factionalism and decline of fervor.	Congregational	"Where the scriptures speak, we speak; where the Scriptures are silent, we are silent."	Baptism Lord's supper	Tries to avoid any rite not considered part of the 1st Century church; some congregations reject instrumental music.	Some tendency towards perfectionism; increasing interest in social action programs.	Simple New Testament faith. Avoids any elaborate, not firmly based scripture. Holds strongly with many branches of Christendom.
Baptist	In radical Reformation, John Smyth, English Separatist (1609), Roger Williams (1638) in Providence, RI.	Congregational (Local churches are self-governed.)	Scripture. Some Baptists, particularly in the South, interpret the Bible literally.	Adult Baptism, usually early teen years or after. Lord's Supper (weekly)	Varies from staid to evangelistic; extensive missionary activity.	Usually opposed to alcohol and tobacco; some tendency towards a perfectionist ethical standard	No creed. True church is of believers only, who are all equal. Strong supporters of church and state separation.
Catholic	Traditionally, founded by Jesus who named St. Peter the first vicar; developed in early Christian proselytizing, especially after the conversion of Imperial Rome in the 4th Century.	Papal Episcopal (The pope [the Bishop of Rome] is the churches leader. Local clergy presided over by regional bishop.)	The Pope, when speaking for the whole church in matters of faith and morals; and tradition (which is expressed in church councils and in part contained in Scripture.	Mass, seven sacraments, baptism, reconciliation, Eucharist, Penance, Confirmation Marriage, Anointing of the sick, Holy orders	Relatively elaborate ritual centered on the Mass, also rosary recitation, novenas, etc.	Traditionally strict, but increasingly tolerant in practice, divorce and remarriage not accepted, but annulments sometimes granted, celibate clergy.	Highly elaborated. Salvation by merit gained through grace; dogmatic; special veneration of Mary. The mother of Jesus. Trinity doctrine
Jehovah's Witnesses	Founded in 1870 in PA by Charles Taze Russell; incorporated as Watchtower Bible and Tract Society of PA (1884). Current name adopted in 1931.	A governing body, located in NY, coordinates worldwide activity. Local congregations overseen by body of elders. Each Witness considered a minister.	The Bible.	Lord's evening meal (Memorial of Christ' death)	Meetings held in "Kingdom Halls" and homes. Extensive preaching activity outside of the congregation.	High moral code; stress on marital fidelity and family values; avoidance of tobacco and blood transfusions.	God, through his son, will destroy all wickedness. 144,000 will rule from heaven over all others on a paradise earth.

DENOMINATION	ORIGINS	ORGANIZATIONAL STRUCTURE	AUTHORITY	SACRAMENTS / SPECIAL RITES	HOW THEY WORSHIP	ETHICS	BELIEFS / DOCTRINES
Latter-Day Saints (Mormons)	In a vision of the Father and Son reported by Joseph Smith (1820s) in NY; Smith also reported receiving new Scriptures on golden tablets; The Book of Mormon	Church president and two counselors) and 12 Apostles preside over worldwide church. Local congregations overseen by priesthood leaders.	Spiritual revelations to living prophet (church president). The Bible, Book of Mormon, and other revelations to Smith and others.	Baptism at age 8, laying on of hands, Lord's Supper, Temple rites, baptism for the dead, marriage for eternity, and more.	Simple service with prayers, hymns and sermon. (Temple ceremonies are more elaborate.)	Strict moral code, tithing, a strong work ethic with communal self-reliance, strong missionary activity	Jesus is God's son, the Eternal Father. Jesus atonement saves all mankind. Those obedient to God's laws become joint heirs with Christ in God's kingdom.
Lutheran	Begun by Martin Luther in Wittenberg, Germany (1517); objection of Catholic doctrine of salvation and sale of indulgences. Break complete in 1519.	Mixture of congregational, Presbyterian and Episcopal.	The Bible; the *'Book of Concord'* (1580), which includes the three Creeds, is subscribed to as a correct exposition of Scripture.	Infant baptism, Lord's supper, Christ's true body and blood present "in, with, and under the bread and wine."	Traditional style through liturgy with emphasis on the sermon; Some contemporary worship.	Conservative in personal/social ethics. Follows the doctrine of "two kingdoms" (worldly and holy) to govern secular affairs.	Salvation by grace alone through faith. Some divisions between fundamentalists and liberals.
Methodist	Rev. John Wesley began movement in 1738, within Church of England; first U.S. denomination, Baltimore (1784)	Generally, clergy in local churches presided over by administrative bishops (not priestly.)	Scripture as interpreted by tradition, reason, and experience.	Baptism Lord's supper, marriage, ordination, solemnization of commitments.	Traditional style through liturgy; Some contemporary worship. Varies.	Originally perfectionist, but have become more tolerant.	No distinctive theology Non-binding 25 articles abridged from Church of England's 39.
Orthodox	Developed in original Christian proselytizing; broke with Rome in 1054 after centuries of doctrinal disputes and diverging traditions.	Synods of bishops in autonomous churches elect a patriarch, archbishop, or metropolitan. These men, as a group, are the heads of the church.	The Bible, tradition, and the first seven church councils up to Nicaea II in 787. Bishops in council have ultimate say in doctrine development.	Often observes the seven Catholic sacraments: infant baptism, anointing, Eucharist, ordination, penance, marriage, and anointing sick.	Elaborate liturgy, very traditional. The liturgy is the essence of orthodoxy; veneration of icons is prevalent.	Tolerant. Divorce, remarriage sometimes permitted. Bishops are celibate, priests don't have to.	Emphasis on Christ's resurrection, rather than crucifixion. The Holy Spirit proceeds from God the Father only.
Pentecostal	In Topeka, KS (1901) and Los Angeles (1906), in reaction to perceived loss of evangelical fervor among Methodists and others.	Variety of organized forms and as movement	The Bible, individual leaders, and the teachings of the Holy Spirit.	Spirit baptism (especially as shown in speaking in tongues, healing, and exorcism), Lord's supper.	Loosely structured with rousing hymns and sermons.	Perfectionist, with varying degrees of tolerance.	Simple traditional beliefs, with emphasis on the immediate presence of God in the Holy Spirit (tongues.)
Presbyterian	In 16th Century, Calvinist Reformation; differed with Lutheran's over sacraments, church government; John Knox founded about 1560.	A highly structured graded system by presbyters (lay persons or "elders") in local, regional, and national bodies.	The Bible.	Infant baptism, Lord's supper, bread and wine symbolize Christ's presence.	A simple service in which the sermon is the focus.	Tendency towards strictness, with firm church- and self-discipline.	Emphasizes the sovereignty and justice of God; No longer dogmatic.
United Church of Christ	Union (1957) of Congregationalists and Evangelical & Reformed. Calvinist/Lutheran traditions.	A General Synod representative of all congregations sets general policies.	The Bible.	Infant baptism and Lord's supper	Simple service with emphasis on sermons.	Tolerant. Some emphasis on social action.	Standard Protestant; *"Statement of Faith"* (1959) is not binding.

Christian Observances Calendar 2016

Holiday Name	Date	Denomination
The Solemnity of Mary	January 1	**Catholic**
Triodion	February 5	**Greek Orthodox**
Meat Fare	February 19	**Greek Orthodox**
Ash Wednesday	March 1	**Christian**
Lent Begins	March 5	**Christian**
Sunday of Orthodoxy	March 5	**Greek Orthodox**
St. Joseph's Day	April 8	**Catholic**
Palm Sunday ("Passion")	April 9	**Christian**
Memorial of Christ's Death	April 12	**Jehovah's Witnesses**
Good Friday	April 14	**Christian (State Holiday)**
Easter Sunday	April 16	**Christian**
Orthodox Easter	April 16	**Greek Orthodox**
Ascension Day	May 25	**Catholic**
Pentecost ("Whit Sunday")	June 4	**Christian**
Trinity Sunday	June 11	**Catholic**
All Saints' Day	June 11	**Greek Orthodox**
First Sunday of Advent	December 3	**Christian**
Christmas Eve	Dec. 24	**Christian**
Christmas Day ("Nativity of Christ")	Dec. 25	**Christian**

Major Non-Christian Religions

Islam (Arabic meaning: Submission to God)

FOUNDING:

Founded in 610 C.E. by Muhammad the Prophet (c. 570-632 C.E.)

FOLLOWERS:

1.7 billion Muslims (Arabic: One who submits), making Islam the second largest world religion. Fewer than one-fifth are Arab.

DIVISIONS:

Sunnis make up the large majority of Muslims (84%), whereas Shiites makeup the remaining majority (14%)

SACRED TEXT:

The *Qur'an* (Koran) believed to be the final, perfect, and complete word of God (Allah) as revealed to Muhammad. Divided into 114 chapters, it is the ultimate source of everything Islamic – including metaphysics, theology, sacred history, ethics, law, and art. The Hadith, a second sacred text and compliment to the *Koran*, describes Muhammad's actions, attitudes, and teachings. It does not contain Allah's unadulterated voice, but it is still seen as a powerful spiritual and behavioral code.

BELIEFS:

Monotheistic. Allah is the creator of the universe, omnipotent, omniscient, just, forgiving, and merciful. God revealed the Koran to Muhammad to guide humanity to truth and justice. Those who sincerely submit to Allah attain salvation. Abandonment of prejudice and the elimination of extremes in poverty and wealth.

PRACTICE:

Muslims submit to Allah through the five 'Pillars of Islam':

Pillar One: Shahadanah. Affirmation that that there is no god but Allah, and Muhammad is his Prophet.

Pillar Two: Salah.

Pillar Three: Pay alms, or Zakat. 2.5% of one's total wealth. Only when zakat has been paid is the rest of the Muslim's property considered purified and legitimate.

Pillar Four: Fasting on the lunar month of Ramadan, where one must abstain from eating, drinking, impure thoughts, and sexual intercourse from dawn until sunset. If able, they must also feed at least one poor person.

Pillar Five: Pilgrimage to Kaaba, which must be done at least once during a Muslim's lifetime, except for reasons of poor health or poverty.

Islamic Holy Days Calendar

Holy Day	Date	1438 (2016/2017)	1439 (2017/2018)
New Year's Day	Muharram 1	Oct. 2, 2106	Sep. 21, 2017
Ashura	Muharram 10	Oct. 12, 2016	Sep. 30, 2017
Mawlid	Rabi' l 12	Dec. 12, 2016	Dec. 1, 2017
Ramadan begins	Ramadan 1	May 27, 2017	May 16, 2018
Eid al-Fitr	Shawwal 1	June 26, 2017	June 15, 2018
Eid al-Adha	Dhu'l-Hijja 10	Sept. 1, 2017	Aug. 22, 2018

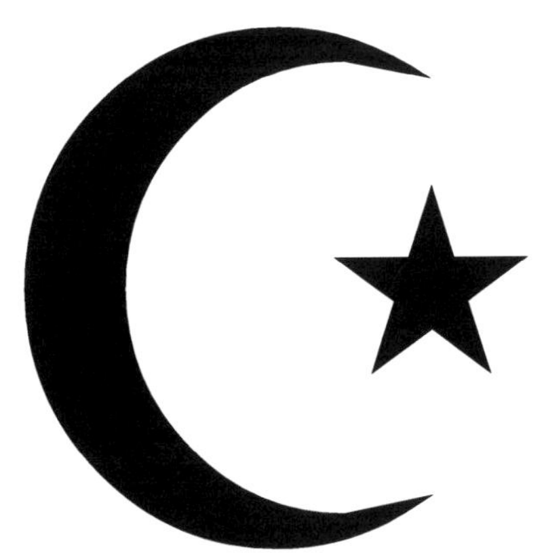

Hinduism

FOUNDING:

About 1500 B.C.E. by Aryans who migrated to India, where their Vedic religion intermixed with the practices and beliefs of the native peoples.

FOLLOWERS:

985 million – Mostly in Asia, with Africa a distant second.

DIVISIONS:

There is no concept of orthodoxy in Hinduism, which presents a variety of sects with no well-defined ecclesiastical organization. The three major living traditions are those devoted to the gods Vishnu and Shiva, and the goddess Shakti.

SACRED TEXT:

The *Veda*, including the *Upanishads*, a collection of rituals and commentaries. Other texts include a number of epic stories about gods, heroes, and saints, including the *Bhagavadgita*, a part of the *Mahabharata*, and the *Ramayana*.

BELIEFS:

There is only one divine principle: the many gods are only aspects of that unity. Life in all forms is an aspect of that divine, but it appears as a separation from the divine, a meaningless cycle of birth and rebirth (*samsara*) determined by the purity or impurity of past deeds (*karma*). To improve one's karma or escape samsara by pure acts, thought, and/or devotion is the aim of every Hindu.

PRACTICE:

Primarily passage rites, such as initiation, marriage, and death, as well as daily devotions. Of the public rites, the *puja* – ceremonial dinner for a god – is the most common.

Hindu Festival Calendar

Festival	2017	2018
Maha Shivaratri (Bight of Shiva)	February 25	February 14
Holi (Festival of Color)	March 13	March 7
Diwali (Festival of Lights)	October 19	November 7

Buddhism

FOUNDING:

About 525 B.C.E., reportedly near Benares, India, by Gautama Siddhartha (c. 563-483 B.C.E.), the Buddha. He achieved enlightenment through intense mediation.

FOLLOWERS:

520 million – Mostly in Asia, with North America a distant second.

DIVISIONS:

Three primary branches: Theravada, emphasizing the importance of thought and deed; Mahayana (includes Zen and Sokagakkai), which believes in the saving grace of higher beings or ritual practices and to practical meditative disciplines; and Vajrayana, or Tantrism, a combination of ritual magic and sophisticated philosophy.

SACRED TEXT:

The *Tripitaka*, a collection of Buddha's teachings, rules of monastic life, and philosophical commentaries on the teachings; also a vast body of Buddhist teachings and commentaries, many of them called sutras.

BELIEFS:

"Four Noble Truths":

Noble truth one: Dukkha. Existence is suffering.

Noble truth two: Trishna. Suffering has a cause, namely craving and attachment.

Noble truth three: Nirvana. There is a cessation of suffering.

Noble truth four: The eightfold path to this cessation: 1) right views, 2) right resolve, 3) right speech, 4) right action, 5) right livelihood, 6) right effort, 7) right mindfulness, 8) and right concentration.

PRACTICE:

Varies widely according to the sect, ranging from austere meditation to magical chanting and elaborate temple rights. (Buddha's birthday is observed on May 6.)

Sikhism

FOUNDING:

Late 15th Century in South Asia by Guru Nanak Dev ji, Sikhism's first guru.

FOLLOWERS:

24.7 million – Mainly in Asia.

DIVISIONS:

No divisions.

SACRED TEXT:

The *Guru Granth Sahib*, which was compiled by Sikh Gurus and contains their experiences of the Divine. It also contains writings by other saintly figures of differing faiths.

BELIEFS:

A monotheistic religion based on revelations. Sikhism preaches a message of devotion, remembrance of God at all times, truthful living, equality between all human beings, and social justice, while emphatically denouncing superstitions and blind rituals.

PRACTICE:

Prayers required are morning, evening, and before sleep. Five articles of faith are required: 1) Kesh. Uncut hair; 2) Kangha. Comb; 3) Kara. Steel bracelet; 4) Kirpan. Sword; 5) Kaccha. Short pants.

Judaism

FOUNDING:

About 2000 B.C.E. Abraham is regarded as the founding father.

FOLLOWERS:

14.6 million – primarily in Israel, Asia, and North America.

DIVISIONS:

Orthodox and Reform, otherwise known as ultraconservative and ultraliberal, largely reflecting different points of view regarding the binding character of prohibitions and duties – particularly the dietary and Sabbath observations – traditionally prescribed for the daily life of a Jew.

SACRED TEXT:

The *Torah*, the five books of Moses (Genesis, Exodus, Leviticus, Numbers, and Deuteronomy.)

BELIEFS:

Strictly monotheistic. God is the creator and ruler of the universe. He established a particular relationship with the Hebrew people: by obeying a divine law God gave them, they would be a special witness to God's mercy and justice. Judaism stresses ethical behavior (and among the traditional, careful ritual obedience) as true worship of God.

PRACTICES:

Among traditional practitioners, almost all areas of life are governed by strict discipline. Sabbath and holidays are marked by observances, and attendance at public worship in a synagogue is considered to be especially important. Orthodox Jews hold the scriptural and oral laws as authoritative and derived from God, and maintain traditional practices. Reform Jews regard the laws as binding only in their ethical sense, and they perform only those rituals that they believe can promote and enhance a Jewish, God-oriented life.

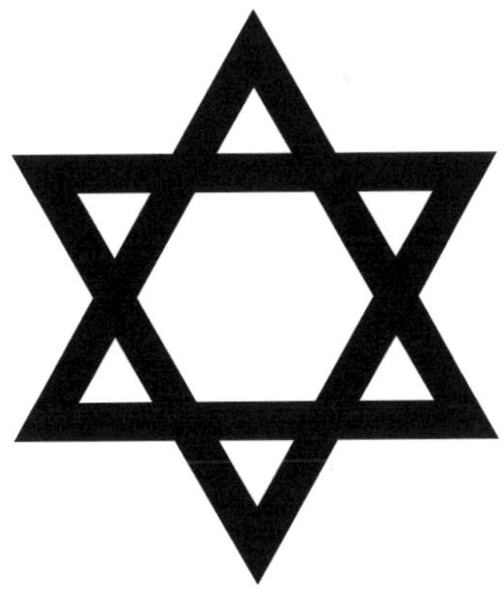

What is "Kosher"?

Kosher is a Hebrew word literally meaning 'proper', but is used in the Jewish faith to mean 'ritually correct'. It's most widely referred to when discussing food prepared in accordance with dietary laws based on Old Testament passages (Leviticus 11 and Deuteronomy 14).

Kosher Meat: Must be animals that both chew the cud and cloven hoofs, (i.e., cows and sheep). The animal must have been slaughtered by a carefully trained Jew, carefully inspected, and, unless cooked by broiling, must be salted and soaked to remove all traces of blood.

Kosher Fish: Fish that have scales and fins.

Kosher Fowl: Same rules that apply for meat preparation.

Milk Products: Cannot be cooked or consumed with or immediately after meats or meat products. The use of the same kitchen, table utensils and towels is forbidden.

*Reform Judaism does not require observance of kosher laws.

Jewish Holy Days Calendar

Holy Day	Date	(2016/2017)	(2017/2018)
Rosh Hashanah (New Year)	Tishrei 1-2		Sep. 21-22
Yom Kippur (Day of Atonement)	Tishrei 10-15		Sep. 30
Sukkot	Tishrei 15-21		Oct. 5-11
Shemini Atzeret	Tishrei 22		Oct. 12
Simchat Torah	Tishrei 23		Oct. 13
Hannukah	Kislev 25-Tevet 2 or 3	Dec. 25-Jan. 1	Dec. 13-20
Purim	Adar 14	March 24	March 1
Pesach (Passover)	Nisan 15-22	April 23-30	March 31 – April7
Shavuot (Pentecost)	Sivan 6-7	June 12-13	May 20-21
Fast of the 9th of Av	Av 9	August 14	July 22

All Jewish Holy Days begin at sunset and end at sundown on the last day.

Baha'i

FOUNDING:

Mid-19th Century by Mirza Husayn-Ali Nuri (c. 1817-1892), later known as Baha'u'llah (Arabic for "Glory of God")

FOLLOWERS:

7.8 million worldwide

DIVISIONS:

No divisions

SACRED TEXT:

The writings of Baha'u'llah and his herald, the Bab (Siyyid Al Muhammad). The primary text is *Kitabi-aqdas* ('Most Holy Book').

BELIEFS:

God has progressively revealed His purpose through a series of divine manifestations, including Jesus, Buddha, Muhammad, Zoroaster, and Baha'u'llah. Baha'u'lah's teachings include the oneness of humanity, the equality of men and women, and the harmony of science and religion.

PRACTICES:

Prayer, meditation, and fasting are key components of the Baha'i faith. Work performed in a spirit of service to humanity is considered an important form of worship. They have no clergy, limited ritual, and some congregational worship.

Religion Resources

Religion Contacts

The following is a listing of religion headquarters, in alphabetical order. These may provide direct information on the given religion. Specific prisoner-friendly religious resources follow.

ADVENTIST

SEVENTH-DAY ADVENTIST CHURCH

12501 Old Columbia Pike, Silver Spring, MD 20904
(301) 680-5600
www.adventist.org

AGNOSTICS/ ATHEISTS

AMERICAN ATHEISTS

PO Box 158, Cranford, NJ 07016
(908) 246-7300
www.atheists.org

FREEDOM FROM RELIGION

PO Box 750, Madison, WI 53701
(608) 256-8900
www.ffrf.org

ARMENIAN APOSTOLIC CHURCH OF AMERICA

EASTERN PRELACY

138 E. 39th St., New York, NY 10016
(212) 689-7810
www.armenianprelacy.org

WESTERN PRELACY

6252 Honolulu Ave., La Crescentia, CA91214
(818) 248-7737

GREEK ORTHODOX ARCHDIOCESE OF AMERICA

8 E. 79th St., New York, NY 10075
(212) 570-3500
www.goarch.org

ASATRU

ASATRU ALLIANCE

PO Box 961, Payson, AZ 85547
www.asatru.org eagle@asatru.org

BAHA'I

NATIONAL SPIRITUALITY ASSEMBLY OF THE BAHA'IS OF THE U.S.

1233 Central St., Evanston, IL 60201
(847) 733-3400
www.bahai.us

BAPTISTS

AMERICAN BAPTIST CHURCHES USA

PO Box 851, Valley Forge, PA 18482
(610) 768-2000
www.abc-usa.org

BAPTIST BIBLE FELLOWSHIP, INTERNATIONAL

720 E. Kearney St., Springfield, MO 65803
(417) 862-5001
www.bbfi.org

CONVERGE WORLDWIDE | (FORMERLY BAPTIST GENERAL CONFERENCE)

2002 S. Arlington Heights, Arlington Heights, IL 60005
(800) 323-4215
www.convergeworldwide.org

NATIONAL BAPTIST CONVENTION OF AMERICA, INTERNATIONAL

777 S.R.L. Thornton Freeway, Suite 210, Dallas, TX 75203
(214) 942-3311
www.nbcinc.com

NATIONAL BAPTIST CONVENTION, USA

1700 Baptist World Center Dr., Nashville, TN 37207

(615) 228-6292
www.nationalbaptist.com

NATIONAL MISSIONARY BAPTISTS CONVENTIONAL OF AMERICA

6925 Wofford Dr., Dallas, TX 75227
(877) 886-6222
www.nmbca.com

PROGRESSIVE NATIONAL BAPTISTS CONVENTION

601 50th St. NE, Washington, DC 20019
(202) 396-0558
www.pnbc.org

SOUTHERN BAPTIST CONVENTION

901 Commerce St., Nashville, TN 37203
(615) 244-2355
www.sbc.net

BRETHREN (GERMAN BAPTIST)

BRETHREN OF CHRIST CHURCH

431 Grantham Rd., Mechanicsburg, PA 17055
(717) 697-2634
www.bic-church.org

CHURCH OF THE BRETHREN

1451 Dundee Ave., Elgin, IL 60120
(847) 742-5100
www.brethren.org

BUDDHIST

BUDDHIST CHURCHES OF AMERICA

1710 Octavia St., San Francisco, CA 94109
(415) 776-5600
www.buddhistchurchesofamerica.org

CHRISTIAN CHURCHES (DISCIPLES OF CHRIST)

DISCIPLE CENTER

PO Box 1986, Indianapolis, IN 46206
(317) 635-3100
www.disciples.org

FIRST CHURCH OF CHRIST, THE

210 Massachusetts Ave., Boston, MA 02115
(617) 450-2000
www.christianscience.com

CHURCH OF CHRIST

CHURCH OF CHRIST

PO Box 472, Independence, MO 64051
(816) 833-3995

CHURCH OF THE NAZARENE

Global Ministry Center, 17001 Prairie Star Parkway, Lenexa, KS 66220
(913) 577-0500
www.nazarene.org

CHURCH OF GOD

CHURCH OF GOD

Box 2420, Anderson, IN 46018
(765) 642-0256
www.chog.org

COMMUNITY CHURCH

INTERNATIONAL COUNCIL OF COMMUNITY CHURCHES

21116 Washington Parkway, Frankfort, IL 60423
(815) 464-5690
www.icccusa.com

EASTERN ORTHODOX CHURCH

ANTIOCHAN ORTHODOX CHRISTIAN ARCHDIOCESE OF NORTH AMERICA

PO Box 5238, Englewood, NJ 07630
(201) 871-1355
www.antiochan.org

EPISCOPAL CHURCHES

EPISCOPAL CHURCH

815 Second Ave., New York, NY 10017
(212) 716-6000
www.episcopalchurch.org

ESSENE

ESSENE CHURCH OF JESUS CHRIST

PO Box 516, Elmira, OR 97437

ESSENES OF KORMAN

Route 2, PO Box 26-A, Montrose, CO

FRIENDS | QUAKERS

FRIENDS GENERAL CONFERENCE

1216 Arch St., #2B, Philadelphia, PA 19107
(215) 561-1700
www.fgcquaker.org

RELIGIOUS SOCIETY OF FRIENDS (CONSERVATIVE)

(800) 432-1377
www.quakers.org info@quakers.org

GIDEONS

GIDEONS INTERNATIONAL

PO Box 140800, Nashville, TN 37214
(615) 564-5000
www.gideons.org

GNOSTIC CATHOLIC CHURCH

ECCLESIA GNOSTIC CATHOLICA (EGC)

U.S. Grand Lodge, Ordo Templi Orientis, PO Box 32, Riverside, CA 92502

HARE KRISHNA

ALACHUA HARE KRISHNA TEMPLE

17306 NW 112th Blvd., Alachua, FL 32615
(386) 462-2017
www.alachuatemple.com

HINDU

WORLD HINDU COUNCIL OF AMERICA

PO Box 441505, Houston, TX 77244-1505
(281) 496-5676
www.vhp-america.org office@vhp-america.org

INSTITUTE IN BASIC LIFE PRINCIPLES

IBLP

Mailing address: Box 1, Oak Brook, IL 60522-3001; Physical address: 707 W. Ogden Ave., Hinsdale, IL 60521-3069
(630) 323-9800
www.iblp.org info@iblp.org

JEHOVAH'S WITNESSES

JEHOVAH'S WITNESSES

25 Columbia Heights, Brooklyn, NY 11201
(718) 560-5000
www.jw.org

JUDAISM

AMERICAN JEWISH CONGRESS

260 Madison Ave., 2nd Floor, New York, NY 10016
(212) 879-4500
www.ajcongress.org

B'NAI B'RITH INTERNATIONAL

1120 20th St. NW, Washington, DC 20036
(202) 857-6600
www.bnaibrith.org

CENTRAL CONFERENCE OF AMERICAN RABBIS

355 Lexington Ave., New York, NY 10017
(212) 972-3636
www.ccarnet.org

HADASSAH, WOMEN'S ZIONIST ORGANIZATION OF AMERICA

40 Wall St., New York, NY 10005
(888) 303-3640
www.hadasseh.org

JEWISH RECONSTRUCTIONIST FEDERATION

1299 Church Rd., Wyncote, PA 19095
(215) 576-0800
www.jewishrecon.org

NATIONAL COUNCIL OF JEWISH WOMEN

475 Riverside Dr., Suite 1901, New York, NY 10115
www.ncjw.org

ORTHODOX UNION

11 Broadway, New York, NY 10004

(212) 563-4000
www.ou.org

KABBALA

Kabbala Research Institute, PO Box 670263, Flushing, NY 11365
(800) 540-3234

UNION FOR REFORM JUDAISM

633 3rd Ave., New York, NY 10017
(212) 650-4000
www.urj.org

UNITED SYNAGOGUE OF CONSERVATIVE JUDAISM

820 Second Ave., New York, NY 10017
(212) 533-7800
www.uscj.org

LATTER-DAY SAINTS | MORMONS

COMMUNITY OF CHRIST (REORGANIZED CHURCH OF JESUS CHRIST OF LDS)

1001 W. Walnut, Independence, MO 64050
(816) 933-1000
www.cofchrist.org

CHURCH OF JESUS CHRIST OF LATTER-DAY SAINTS, THE

50 W., North Temple St., Salt Lake City, UT 84150
(801) 240-2640
www.lds.org

LUTHERAN CHURCHES

LUTHERAN CHURCH IN AMERICA

8765 W. Higgins Rd., Chicago, IL 60631
(773) 380-2700
www.elca.org

LUTHERAN CHURCH | MISSOURI SYNOD

1333 S. Kirkwood Rd., St. Louis, MO 63122
(800) 248-1930
www.lcms.org

MENNONITE | AMISH

MENNONITE CENTRAL COMMITTEE

21 S. 12th St., PO Box 500, Akron, PA 17501-0500
(818) 859-1151
www.mcc.org

MENNONITE CHURCH USA

718 N. Main St., Newton, KS 67114
(316) 283-5100
www.mennonitusa.org

METHODIST CHURCHES

AFRICAN METHODIST EPISCOPAL CHURCH

500 8th Ave., South Nashville, TN 37203
(615) 254-0911
www.ame-church.com

AFRICAN METHODIST EPISCOPAL ZION CHURCH

3225 West Sugar Creek Rd., Charlotte, NC 28269
(704) 599-4630
www.amez.org

CHRISTIAN METHODIST EPISCOPAL CHURCH

4466 Elvis Presley Blvd., Memphis, TN 38116
(901) 345-0580
www.c-m-e.org

FREE METHODIST CHURCH USA

770 N. High School Rd., Indianapolis, IN 46214
(317) 244-3660
www.fmcusa.org

UNITED METHODIST CHURCH

100 Maryland Ave. NE, Washington, DC 20002
3(202) 488-5600
www.umc.org

WESLEYAN CHURCH

13300 Olio Rd., Fishers, IN 46037
(317) 774-7900
www.wesleyan.org

MORAVIANS

MORAVIAN CHURCH OF NORTH AMERICA

Northern Prov.: 1021 Center St., PO Box 1245, Bethlehem, PA 18016
(610) 867-7566
Southern Prov.: 459 S. Church St., Winston-Salem, NC 27101
(336) 725-5811
www.moravian.org

MUSLIMS

ISLAMIC SOCIETY OF NORTH AMERICA

6555 S. County Rd. 750 East, Plainfield, IN 46168
(317) 839-8157
www.isna.net

ORGANIZATION OF NORTH AMERICAN SHIA ITHNA-ASHERI MUSLIM COMMUNITIES

PO Box 26961, Minneapolis, MN 55429
(905) 763-7512
www.nasimco.info

NATIVE AMERICANS

BUREAU OF INDIAN AFFAIRS

C Street NW, Washington, DC 20240
www.bia.gov

CHOCTAW NATION OF OKLAHOMA

PO Box 1210, Durant, OK 74702-1210

PENTECOSTAL CHURCHES

ASSEMBLIES OF GOD USA

1445 N. Boonville Ave., Springfield, MO 65802
(417) 862-2781
www.ag.org

CHURCH OF GOD

2490 Keith St. W, Cleveland, TN 37320
(423) 472-3361
www.churchofgod.org

CHURCH OF GOD IN CHRIST MASON TEMPLE

930 Mason St., Memphis, TN 38126
(901) 947-9300
www.cogic.org

PENTECOSTAL ASSEMBLIES OF THE WORLD

3939 N. Meadows Dr., Indianapolis, IN 46205
(317) 547-9541
www.pawinc.org

UNITED PENTECOSTAL CHURCH INTERNATIONAL

8855 Dunn Rd., Hazelwood, MO 63042
(314) 827-7300
www.upci.org

PRESBYTERIAN CHURCHES

CUMBERLAND PRESBYTERIAN CHURCH

8207 Traditional Place, Cordova, TN 38016
(901) 276-4572
www.cumberland.org

PRESBYTERIAN CHURCH USA

100 Witherspoon St., Louisville, KY 40202
(800) 728-7228
www.pcusa.org

RASTAFARIAN

RASTAFARI CENTRALIZATION ORGANIZATION

20 Melody Dr., Kingston 4, Jamaica (West Indies)
(876) 948-1128

REFORMED CHURCHES

UNITED CHURCH OF CHRIST

700 Prospect Ave., Cleveland, OH 44115
(216) 736-2100
www.ucc.org

ROMAN CATHOLIC

NATIONAL CATHOLIC EVANGELIZATION ASSOCIATION

3031 4th St NE, Washington, DC 20017
(202) 832-5022
www.pricea.org

U.S. CONFERENCE OF CATHOLIC BISHOPS

3211 4th St NE, Washington, DC 20017
(202) 541-3000
www.usccb.org

SCIENTOLOGY

CHURCH OF SCIENTOLOGY

65 E. 82nd St., New York, NY 10028
(212) 288-1526
www.scientology.org

SHAKERS

SHAKERS CANTERBURY | SHAKER VILLAGE

288 Shaker Rd., Canterbury, NH 03224
(603) 783-9511
www.shakers.org

SHIITE MUSLIM

ISLAMIC CENTER OF AMERICA

19500 Ford Rd., Dearborn, MI 48128
(313) 593-0000
www.icofa.com admin@icofa.com

SHINTO

INTERNATIONAL SHINTO FOUNDATION

New York Center, 245 E. 58th St., Apt. 29F, New York, NY 10022
(212) 686-9117
www.internationalshinto.org

SIKHS

SIKH TEMPLE GURUDWARA

12070 1st Ave., Cincinnati, OH 45249-1535
www.worldgurudwaras.org

SUNNI MUSLIM

ISLAMIC CENTER, THE

3112 Ridge Ave., Philadelphia, PA 19121
(215) 232-9435

TAOISM | DAOISM

DAOIST ASSOCIATION

6120 Highway 7, Estes Park, CO 80517
(970) 586-8133
www.daousa.org admin@daousa.org

UNITARIANS

UNITARIAN UNIVERSALIST ASSOCIATION OF CONGREGATIONS

24 Farnsworth St., Boston, MA 02210
(617) 742-2100
www.uua.org

VINEYARD

VINEYARD U.S.A. | NATIONAL OFFICE

PO Box 2089, Stafford, TX 77947
(281) 313-8463
www.vineyardusa.org info@vineyardusa.org

WICCA

AQUARIAN TABERNACLE CHURCH

48631 River Park Dr., PO Box 409, Index, WA 98256
(306) 793-1945
www.aquariantabernacle.org atc@aquatabch.org

CHURCH AND SCHOOL OF WICCA

PO Box 297-IN, Hinton, WV 25951-0297
www.wicca.org feedback@wicca.org

NEW WICCAN CHURCH

PO Box 192, Citrus Heights, CA 95611
www.newwiccanchurch.org nwcoutreach@yahoo.com

WOTANISM | ODINISM

VINLAND REGIONAL OFFICE | THE ODINIC RITE

PO Box 351, Brush Prairie, WA 98606
www.odinic-rite.org

ZOROASTRIAN

FEDERATION OF ZOROASTRIAN ASSOCIATIONS OF NORTH AMERICA

5750 Jackson St., Hinsdale, IL 90521
(514) 656-2036
www.fezana.org

Prisoner-Friendly Religious Organizations

Buddhist Resources

AMERICAN BUDDHIST TEMPLE

10515 N. Latson Rd., Howell, MI 48855
www.abtemble.org

ABT practice Ch'an and esoteric Buddhist teachings. They offer Mahayana Buddhist literature, FREE to prisoners, as well as downloads of Buddhist books on their website.

AMITABHA BUDDHIST SOCIETY OF U.S.A

650 S. Bernardo Ave., Sunnyvale, CA 94087
(408) 736-3386
www.amtb-usa.org

AMTB practices Mahayana teachings. They offer a variety of Buddhist information through literature and audio/video media, in both English and Spanish. Write for a catalog of current offerings. They will also send Buddha pictures.

ATLANTA SOTO ZEN CENTER

1167-C, Zonolite Place, Suite C, Atlanta, GA 30306
www.aszc.org

ASZC publishes and distributes the *Gassho* newsletter, FREE to prisoners, written by and for sangha practitioners, containing articles on prison life and Buddhism. They encourage prisoners to send articles, artwork, and any questions.

BUDDHIST BOOKSTORE | JODO SHINSHU BUDDHISM

1710 Octavia St., San Francisco, CA 94109

BB specializes in literature on the Jodo Shinshu lineage and practices. Write for a catalog of current offerings as well as other literature available from the bookstore.

BUDDHIST LIBRARY, THE

Po Box 20101, Fredericton, New Brunswick, Canada E3B 6Y8

BL distributes information and literature on a wide spectrum of Buddhist teachings and disciplines. They will also refer you to other Buddhist sources if needed. Note: Requires international envelope to send correspondence.

BUDDHIST PEACE FELLOWSHIP

PO Box 4650, Berkeley, CA 94704-0650
prisons@bpf.org

BPF publishes the *Turning Wheel* quarterly newsletter, $10 per year for prisoners. ($45/year for others.)

COMPASSION WORKS FOR ALL

PO Box 7708, Little Rock, AR 72217-7708
www.compassionworksforall.org

CWA distributes a variety of Buddhist publications. FREE to prisoners, including their monthly newsletter, *Dharma Friends*. They encourage prisoners to contribute stories of what led them to prison, which they share in book form to juvenile offenders.

DALLAS BUDDHIST ASSOCIATION

515 Apollo Rd., Richardson, TX 75081
www.amtb-dba.org

AMTB practices Mahayana teachings. They offer a variety of Buddhist information through literature and audio/video media, in both English and Spanish. Write for a catalog of current offerings. They will also send Buddha pictures.

DHARMA COMPANIONS

PO Box 762, Cotati, CA 94931
dharmacompanions.wordpress.com

DC is a Buddhist organization that provides information and support to any interested in the Buddhist practices. Volunteers, through correspondence, help prisoners explore meditation and contemplation and discuss aspects of Buddhist philosophy and ethics.

DHARMA PUBLISHING

2910 San Pablo Ave., Berkeley, CA 94702
(510) 548-5407
info@dharmapublishing.org

DP provides Buddhist literature to prison libraries and to prisoners upon request.

DHARMA SEED ARCHIVAL CENTER

PO Box 66, Wendell Depot, MA 03180
dharma@crocker.com

DSAC provides FREE audio and video tapes on Western Vipassana Buddhist teachings. Note: Must send instructions on sending to your prison.

ENGAGED ZEN FOUNDATION

PO Box 213, Sedgwick, ME 04676-0213
www.engaged-zen.org

EZF provides information and FREE resources to anyone interested Zen Buddhism.

FREEING THE MIND | SARAHA BUDDHIST CENTER

PO Box 12037, San Francisco, CA 94112
www.kadampas.org

FTM provides information on the New Kadampa Tradition teachings, as presented by Geshe Kelsang Gyatso. Write for FREE literature, and correspondence program.

HEART MOUNTAIN PROJECT, THE

1223 S. St. Francis Dr., Suite C, Santa Fe, NM 87505

HMP offers information on several styles of meditation, including a 17-page meditation manual, FREE to prisoners. Also available in Spanish.

INSIGHT MEDITATION SOCIETY

1230 Pleasant St., Barre, MA 01005
(978) 355-4378
www.dharma.org/ims ims@dharma.org

IMS publishes and distributes the newsletter *Insight*, FREE to prisoners, covering vipassana meditation.

INTERNATIONAL BUDDHIST MEDITATION CENTER

928 S. New Hampshire Ave., Los Angeles, CA 90006
(213) 384-0850
www.ibmc.org

IBMC focuses on Zen Buddhism, but includes all methods of Buddhism. They provide a quarterly newsletter to prison libraries and up to four prisoners at each institution upon request.

LIBERATION PRISON PROJECT

PO Box 31527, San Francisco, CA 94131
(415) 701-8500
www.liberationprisonproject.org
info@liberationprisonproject.org

LPP provides literature an materials on Tibetan Buddhism, including books, their newsletter *Liberation Magazine* and practice support, FREE to prisoners. Literature available in English, Spanish, Vietnamese, and Chinese.

METTA FOREST MONASTERY

PO Box 1409, Valley Center, CA 92082
www.watmetta.org

MFM offers Dharma literature, including translations from the Pali Canon, and teachers in the Thai Forest tradition, as well as books from Thanissaro Bhikkhu. Write for current titles.

NALJOR PRISON DHARMA SERVICE

www.naljorprisondharmaservice.org

NPDS offers religious resources for prisoners, including a comprehensive prisoner religious resource directory and *The Heart of Dharma Collection*, ten dharma teachings, FREE to anyone with access to their website.

NATIONAL BUDDHIST PRISON SANGHA

PO Box 197, S. Plank Rd., Mount Tremper, NY 12457

NBPS offers a variety of services to prisoners interested in Zen Buddhist practices, including literature, guidance through correspondence, audio tapes, and other training materials.

NOBLE SILENCE PROGRAM | DHARMA INSTRUCTIONS

23611 NE SR26, Melrose, FL 32666

NSP offers Dharma instruction to prisoners. Send SASE for more information.

PARALLAX PRESS

PO Box 7355, Berkeley, CA 94707

PP distributes the Buddhist teachings of Thich Nhat Hanh. Write for a catalogue, or request specific titles.

PRISON MINDFULNESS INSTITUTE

11 S. Angell St., #303, Providence, RI 02906
www.prisonmindfulness.org
info@prisonmindfulness.org

PMI provides non-denominational Buddhist information, including *Sitting Inside: Buddhist Practice in America's Prisons*, FREE to prisoners.

SNOW LION PUBLICATIONS

PO Box 6483, Ithaca, NY 14851-6483
www.snowlionpub.com info@snowlionpub.com

SLP offers a newsletter, *Snow Lion*, and catalog, FREE to prisoners. They also send books to some prisoners in solitary confinement.

SRAVASTI ABBEY

PO Box 30446, Spokane, WA 99223

SA offers Buddhism literature by Ven. Thubten Chodron and other Buddhist teachers, as well as tapes and CDs on meditation and other teachings, FREE to prisoners.

SUTRA TRANSLATION COMMITTEE OF THE U.S. AND CANADA

2611 Davidson Ave., Bronx, NY 10468
(718) 584-0621
www.ymba.org *ymba@ymba.org*

STC offers a wide variety of dharma literature, FREE to prisoners. Write for a current list of available books.

TRICYCLE MAGAZINE | THE BUDDHIST REVIEW

1115 Broadway, Suite 1113, New York, NY 10010
(800) 873-9871

Tricycle Magazine is a quarterly Buddhist magazine, FREE to prisoners.

WILDMIND MEDIATION SERVICES

177 Main St., Newmarket, NH 03857
www.wildmind.org

WMM offers a wide range information on meditation, including guided tapes on *Mindfulness of Breathing*, and the *Metta Bhavana* meditation, FREE to prisoners.

Christian Resources

AMERICAN BIBLE ACADEMY

PO Box 1627, Joplin, MO 64802
www.abarc.org

ABARC offers Christian information and materials, including correspondence courses, bibles, greeting cards and Baptist series FREE to prisoners. See separate listing under FREE Religious Studies.

ARM PRISON OUTREACH | INTERNATIONAL

PO Box 1490, Joplin, MO 64802-1627
(417) 781-9100
www.arm.org

ARM provides prison chaplains with Christian greeting cards, bibles, gospel tracts, in-prison seminar materials, and baptisteries.

CHAPEL LIBRARY | MT. ZION BIBLE CHURCH

2603 W. Wright St., Pensacola, FL 32505
(580) 434-0058
www.chapellibrary.org

CL provides bibles, study courses, and a variety of Christian literature, FREE to prisoners. Write for an order form containing over 100 titles.

HEART OF AMERICA PRISON MINISTRIES

PO Box 1685, Independence, MO 64055
(816) 257-1685
www.heartmin.org

HAPM will provides bibles to prisoners. Write a short testimonial and they will put you on a waiting list to receive a leather-bound study bible, and will add you to their monthly newsletter mailing list.

INSTITUTE OF BASIC LIFE PRINCIPLES

PO Box 2837, Little Rock, AK 72203
(501) 374-1020
prisonseminars@iblp.org

IBLP provides instruction to prisoners on how to find success in life by following conservative biblical principles through video seminars. Ask your chaplain to contact IBLP for more information.

INTERNATIONAL BIBLE STUDY

1820 Jet Stream Dr., Colorado Springs, CO 80921-3696
(719) 488-9200
www.ibsdirect.com

IBS distributes the *New International Reader's Version: Free on the Inside* bible, FREE to prisoners. Request in English or Spanish.

LOVED ONES OF PRISONERS

PO Box 14953, Odessa, TX 79768
(915) 580-5667
www.loopsministries.com *info@loopsministries.com*

LOOP provide information and support to Christians, including correspondence courses and their newsletter *Reflections*, FREE to prisoners. See separate listing under FREE Religious Studies.

MESSIANIC TIMES, THE

PO Box 2190, Niagara Falls, NY 14302
(905) 685-4072

www.messianctimes.com office@messianictimes.com

Messianic Times is a Messianic Jewish newspaper, which includes news, opinion, current events, books and music reviews, teaching articles, and a directory of Messianic Jewish synagogues, FREE to prisoners.

MISSING LINK, THE

PO Box 40031, Cleveland, OH 44140-0031
www.misslink.org office@misslink.org

ML provides a variety of services to Christian prisoners, including counseling, ministering to prisoner's families, encouragement and guidance to ex-offenders.

PRISON FELLOWSHIP MINISTRIES

PO Box 17500, Washington, DC 20041
(703) 478-0100
www.prisonfellowship.org gvt@pfm.org
PFM offers a variety of Christianity-based services, including *Angel Tree,* a gift delivery service for children of incarcerated parents, pen pal programs, in-prison pre-release programs, and their newspaper, *Inside Journal*, FREE to prisoners.

PRISON RESOURCES

59 Industrial Rd., PO Box 649, Addison, IL 60101
(630) 543-1441
www.prisonresources.com

PR provides Christian literature, including bibles, calendars, and publications, FREE to prisoners.

ST. DISMAS GUILD

PO Box 2129, Escondido, CA 92033
www.stdismasguild.org

St. Dismas Guild provides information and literature to prisoners interested in the Catholic faith, including a FREE newsletter.

UNITED BRETHREN JAIL AND PRISON OUTREACH MINISTRY

1278 Glenneyre, Box 219, Laguna Beach, CA 92651
unitedbrethren4god@yahoo.com

UB offers a variety of resources for Christian prisoners, including pen pals, information on medical needs, educational information for parents, a recovery program, and more.

Hindu, Yoga, and Meditation Resources

AHAM MEDITATION CENTER | PRISON MINISTRY

4368 NC Highway 134, Asheboro, NC 27205
www.aham.com

Aham provides meditation aids, FREE to serious-minded prisoners, including *Living Free While Incarcerated* and *Freeing Yourself from the Prison of the Mind.*

AMERICAN GITA SOCIETY, THE

511 Lowell Place, Fremont, CA 94536
www.gita-society.com

AGS offer Hindu information, including correspondence courses, FREE to prisoners, and Bhagavad Gita books to the prisons library or chaplains.

ASSOCIATION OF HAPPINESS FOR ALL MANKIND

4368 NC Highway 134, Asheboro, NC 27203
www.aham.com ahamcetr@asheboro.com

AHAM provides a variety of information to prisoners interested in the practice of Self Inquiry (Atma Vichara) and the awakening of True Nature, including literature, and their newsletter, *Heart to Heart.*

GANGAJI FOUNDATION PRISON PROJECT

505A San Marin Dr., Suite 120, Novato, CA 94925
(800) 267-9205, (415) 899-9855
www.gangaji.org info@gangaji.org

GF provides Gangaji information through volunteer correspondence, literature, audio and video tapes, FREE to prisoners.

INTERNATIONAL PURE BHAKTI YOGA SOCIETY

PO Box 52724, Durham, NC 27717
www.prisonseva.org prisonseva@gmail.com

IPBYS distributes literature from Srila Bhaktivedanta Narayana Gosvani Maharaja, offers a monthly course on his enlightenment, and provides spiritual pan pals. Write for a current listing of books and services.

OSHA VIHA MEDITATION CENTER

PO Box 352, Mill Valley, CA 94942
www.oshaviha.org oshaviha@oshaviha.org

OVMC provides enlightenment form Osha (Bhagwan Sri Rajneesh) through literature and videos, including *Doing Time Doing Vipassana*, FREE to prisoners.

RAM DASS TAPE LIBRARY FOUNDATION

524 San Anselmo Ave., #203, San Anselmo, CA 94960
www.ramdasstapes.org

RD Tape Library provides audio tapes on the Hindu oriented teachings of Ram Dass, FREE to prisoners. Write for a catalog of current titles.

SAI BABA BOOKSTORE

305 W. First St., Tustin, CA 92780

SBB provides books on the teachings of Sai Baba, FREE to prisoners.

SIDDHA YOGA MEDITATION PRISON PROJECT | SYDA FOUNDATION

PO Box 99140, Emeryville, CA 94662
(510) 898-2700
www.siddhayoga.org prisonproject@compuserve.org

SYMPP provides information and support through Siddha Yoga meditation, including volunteers to provide in-prison instruction and a 12-year study correspondence course, called *In Search of Self*, FREE to prisoners.

SIVANANDA YOGA PRISON PROJECT

PO Box 195, Budd Rd., Woodbourne, NY 12788
(845) 434-9242
www.sivananda.org yogaranch@sivananda.org

SYPP provides spiritual guidance through the Swami Vishnu-Davananda's *Complete Illustrated Book of Yoga*, FREE to prisoners.

TRIYOGA PRISON PROJECT

PO Box 6367, Malibu, CA 90264
(310) 589-0600
www.triyoga.com info@triyoga.com

TYPP provides information on prison yoga, including TriYoga instructional videos, meditation music, and teacher manuals, FREE to prison yoga instructors.

WHITE MOUNTAIN EDUCATION ASSOCIATION

543 Eastwood Dr., Prescott, AZ 86303
www.wmea.org staff@wmea-world.org

WMEA provides information on meditation through a monthly newsletter, *Meditation Monthly International*, and through correspondence with prisoners, FREE of charge.

YOGA ON THE INSIDE FOUNDATION

1356 Westwood Blvd., Los Angeles, CA 90024
(888) 859-YOGA, (310) 234-2700
www.yogainside.org info@yogainside.org

YIF provides yoga and meditation information and support to encourage "Freedom from Within" to prisoners. Write for more information and for programs in your region.

Islamic Resources

INTERNATIONAL ASSOCIATION OF SUFISM PRISON PROJECT

PO Box 2382, San Rafael, CA 94912
(415) 382-7834
www.ias.org

IAS is a Muslim organization that provides information and correspondence opportunities to prisoners. They also have a quarterly newsletter, FREE to prisoners.

ISLAMIC SOCIETY OF NORTH AMERICA

PO Box 38, Plainfield, IN 46168
www.isna.net

Provides information and publications to any interested in Islamic teachings. Sends Qurans and other introductory books on Islamic study FREE to prisoners and prison libraries.

ISLAMIC EDUCATION CENTER

2551 Massachusetts Ave., NW, Washington, DC 20008
(202) 332-8343
www.theislamiccenter.org

IEC provides instruction, publications and other information to prisoners interested in Islamic teachings. FREE *Koran* and beginner to advanced study guides are available in English and Arabic.

Jewish Resources

ALEPH INSTITUTE

9540 Collins Ave., Surfside, FL 33154
(305) 864-5553
www.aleph-institute.org

AI offers Jewish instruction, articles, correspondence courses, counseling and other information to prisoners interested in Judaism.

AMERICAN JEWISH COMMITTEE

PO Box 705, New York, NY 10150
(212) 751-2000
www.ajc.org

AJC offers information and support to Jewish prisoners and those who would like to learn more about the Jewish faith.

CHABAD REACHING OUT

383 Kingston Ave., Room 190, Brooklyn, NY 11213
(718) 771-0770, (718) 771-3866
www.jewishprisoner.com

CRO provides information and support to Jewish prisoners and those interested in the Jewish faith.

JEWISH PRISONERS ASSISTANCE FOUNDATION

770 Eastern Pkwy, Brooklyn, NY 11213
(718) 735-2000
www.chabad.org

JPAF provides information and spiritual support to Jewish prisoners. Published the weekly newsletter 'The Scroll', FREE to prisoners.

JEWISH PRISONER SERVICES INTERNATIONAL

PO Box 85840, Seattle, WA 98145-1840
(206) 985-0577
www.jewishprisonerservices.org www.jpsi.org

JPSI provides Jewish materials, information, and support to Jewish prisoners and their family members. Write for FREE literature, including Hebrew texts.

SHALOM CENTER

6711 Lincoln Dr., Philadelphia, PA 19119
(215) 844-8984
Theshalomcenter.org

SC provides information to anyone interested in the Jewish faith.

Krishna Resources

ISKCON PRISON MINISTRY

PO Box 2693, Toledo, OH 43606
(419) 508-2291
www.iskcon.org

IPM provides information and materials on the Krishna consciousness, including literature on yoga, audio tapes, correspondence, japa mala and neck beads, and more. They also have a newsletter, *IPM Freedom*, and a magazine, *Back to Godhead*, available FREE to prisoners.

Native American Resources

METTANOKIT

187 Merriam Hill Rd., Greenville, NH 03048
(603) 878-3201
www.circleway.org mettanokit@yahoo.com

Mettanokit provides programs and services that incorporate the ancestral wisdom of Native Americans, including information on how to start a Native American circle, counseling services through correspondence, literature and tapes. Write for a list of current books, tapes and programs.

NATIVE AMERICAN PRIDE COMMITTEE

33 Bay Shore Dr., Bay City, MI 98706
natam2000@hotmail.com

NAPC provides assistance, education, correspondence and spiritual support to Native American prisoners. Publishes the monthly newsletter '*Native Pride*', FREE to prisoners.

Quaker Resources

AMERICAN FRIENDS SERVICE COMMITTEE

1501 Cherry St., Philadelphia, PA 19102
(215) 241-7000
www.afsc.org

AFC is a Quaker organization that focuses on prison reform and non-violence issues of prisoners. However, they can provide information on the Quaker culture.

Rosicrucian Resources

ROSICRUCIAN FELLOWSHIP

2222 Mission Ave., Oceanside, CA 92054-2399
(760) 757-6600
www.rosicrucian.com, rosfshp@rosicrucian.com

RF provides information on Western Wisdom teachings to prisoners. Offers FREE correspondence courses, including studies in esoteric Christian philosophy and studies in spiritual astrology. Write for introductory package.

ROSICRUCIAN FRATERNITY, THE

PO Box 220, Quakertown, PA 18951
(800) 779-3796
www.soul.org

The RF offers information and correspondence course to prisoners seriously interested in personal growth and final immortality. Write for a comprehensive brochure and application

Wiccan Resources

NEW WICCAN CHURCH

PO Box 192, Citrus Heights, CA 95611
www.newwiccanchurch.org nwcoutreach@yahoo.com

NWC provides prison outreach services, including literature, instruction, and assistance to prison chaplains. Write for current prisoner assistance options.

Other Religion Resources

ANGEL TREE

PO Box 50211, Knoxville, TN 37950-0211
www.angeltree.info

Angel Tree is a prison fellowship program where religious volunteers purchase and send gifts to the children of prisoners and their loved ones. Write for a participation form.

ANTHROPOSOPHICAL PRISON OUTREACH PROJECT

1923 Geddes Ave., Ann Arbor, MI 48104-1797
www.anthroposophy.org
prisonoutreach@anthroposophy.org

APOP provides information on Anthroposophy, which embraces a spiritual view of the human being and the cosmos, emphasizing knowledge instead of faith. Write for their introduction packet containing a booklet, *Self-Development in the Penitentiary,* as well as other articles and meditation exercises.

ART OF LIVING | PRISON SMART PROGRAM

PO Box 3642, Boulder, CO 80307
www.artofliving.org

AL's Prison SMART Program (Stress Management & Rehabilitative Training Program) teaches breathing techniques and cognitive skills to reduce and manage stress levels in order to think more clearly and act smarter. Write for current services in your region.

ASSOCIATION FOR RESEARCH & ENLIGHTENMENT | EDGAR CAYCE

215 67th St., Virginia Beach, VA 23451
(800) 333-4499
www.edgarcayce.org

ARE distributes the teachings of Edgar Cayce, which focus on self-improvement, holistic health, intuition and ancient mysteries. Prisoners can receive two FREE books every other month, EXCEPT for prisoners in Washington, California, and Oregon.

CONTEMPLATIVE OUTREACH

PO Box 767, Butler, NJ 07405
www.contemplativeoutreach.org

CO provides information and teachings on Centering Prayer, also called *Contemplative Prayer,* including their booklet, *Locked Up and Free*, as well as other literature and videos, FREE to prisoners. Write for a current list of options.

CONVERSATIONS WITH GOD FOUNDATION | PRISON OUTREACH

PMB #1150, 2157 Siskiyou Blvd., Ashland, OR 97520
(541) 482-8806
www.cwg.org prisonoutreach@cwg.org

CWG distributes the teachings of Neale Donald Walsh, including the *Conversations with God* books and the newsletter, *Conversations*, FREE to prisoners. They will also provide pen pals to prisoners interested in learning more.

FRIENDS OF PEACE PILGRIM

7350 Dorado Canyon Rd., Somerset, CA 95684
(530) 620-0333
www.peacepilgrim.org peacepilgrim@d-web.com

FPP distributes the teachings and literature of the Peace Pilgrim, a woman who walked 25,000 miles across America to spread the word about peace among the nations, between people, and inner peace. Literature includes the book *Peace Pilgrim, Her Life and Work in Her Own Words,* and the booklet *Steps towards Inner Peace*. They are FREE to prisoners and are available in English and Spanish. They also offer audio and video options to prison chaplains.

HUMAN KINDNESS FOUNDATION | BO LOGOFF

PO Box 61619, Durham, NC 27715
(919) 383-5160
www.humankindness.org

HKF distributes the teachings of Bo Logoff, which encompass three primary principles: Simple living, a dedication to service, and a commitment to personal spiritual practice. FREE to prisoners. They also have a newsletter, which they encourage prisoner submissions for possible inclusion. Write for a current list of books.

INTERNATIONAL ASSOCIATION OF HUMAN VALUES (IAHV)

2401 15th St. NW, Washington, DC 20009
www.iahv.org

IAHC programs enhance clarity of mind, shift attitudes and behaviors, and develop leaders and communities that are resilient, responsible, and inspired.

LARSON PUBLICATIONS

4936 Route 414, Burdett, NY 14818
www.larsonpublications.org

LP distributes books on karma, including *What is Karma?* By Paul Brunton, a positive view of karma and how to get it working for you. FREE to prisoners. Write for a current list of other publications.

LIONHEART FOUNDATION

PO Box 194, Back Bay, Boston, MA 02117
(781) 444-6667
www.lionheaqrt.org questions@lionheart.org

LF provides resources for breaking the cycle of addiction and violence, including the book *Houses of Healing: A Prisoner's Guide to Inner Power and Freedom*, FREE to prison libraries.

MIRACLES PRISONER MINISTRY

501 E. Adams St., Wisconsin Dells, WI 53965
(608) 253-9598
www.miraclesprisonerministry.org www.acimi.org
info@miraclesprisonerministry.org

MPM offers a recover program based on spiritual solutions, including *A Course on Miracles*, the 12-Step program of Alcoholics Anonymous, and the *Spiritual Recovery Correspondence Course*, FREE to prisoners and their families.

SCIENCE OF MIND FOUNDATION

573 Park Point Dr., Golden, CO 80401
www.somfoundation.org

SOM Foundation distributes literature containing SOM teachings by Dr. Ernest Holmes, who teaches that there is a power for good in the universe and you can use it to change your thinking and your life. They offer books and a one subscription to their magazine, *Science of Mind*, FREE to prisoners. Write for a brochure.

SOUNDS TRUE

PO Box 8010, Boulder, CO 80306
(800) 333-9185
www.soundstrue.com
customerrelations@soundstrue.com

ST provides a wide variety of audio resources on transformation and awakening, such as liberal spirituality, mystical Christianity, Buddhism, and others, FREE to prisoners. Write for a list of current titles.

SURVIVING THE SYSTEM

PO Box 1860, Ridgeland, MS 39158
www.survivingthesystem.com

SS works to keep children out of prison through educational outreach. They encourage prisoners to share their stories artwork, poetry, views on current events, and ideas. Write to see how you can get involved.

WORLDWIDE VOICE IN THE WILDERNESS

PO Box 740273, Dallas, TX 75374
(972) 234-6009
www.wviw.com, info@wviw.com

WVIW offers general spiritual support, religious ministry, and family counseling services to prisoners and their loved ones.

Religious Education

NOTE: The following section provides religious education listings under two categories Fee-Based and FREE.

If you would like to learn more about college level religious education, ask us about ou publication:

'Prison Lives Almanac: Prisoner Education Guide.' (See ad later in this book.)

FEE-Based Religious Studies

NOTE: The following schools do not accept transfer credits or grants for study. They do, however, reward a *Certificate of Completion* or Diploma in the course of study. These are good prep options if you are considering taking more advanced religious studies.

FULL GOSPEL BIBLE INSTITUTE

PO Box 1230, Coatesville, PA 19230
(610) 857-2357

Courses: Personal Evangelism, Prayer and Fasting, The Holy Spirit, The Gifts of the Spirit, Tithing, The Trinity I & II, New Testament Survey I, II, and III, Life of Christ I and II, Divine Healing I and II, and Dispensational Truth.

Tuition: $280 per program (for all 16 courses), $160 with partial scholarship (upon request), FREE with a full scholarship (waiting list.)

GLOBAL UNIVERSITY | BEREAN SCHOOL OF THE BIBLE

1211 S. Glenstone Ave., Springfield, MO 65804-0315
(800) 433-0315, (417) 862-9533
www.globaluniversity.edu
berean@globaluniversity.edu

Courses: *Certificates* in/as Ordained Ministry, Certified Minister, or Licensed Minister. *Diplomas* in Ministerial Studies, Specialized Ministries (five areas of study), Bible & Doctrine, Urban Bible Training Center, Church Ministries, and Christian Service.

Tuition: $10 per course for shipping, plus course text fees ($0-82), plus textbook fees ($$12 – 106.50).

MOODY BIBLE INSTITUTE

820 N. La Salle Blvd., Chicago, IL 60610
(800) 758-6352
www.moody.edu mdlc@moody.edu

Courses: *Certificates* in Biblical Studies New Testament, Old Testament, and Personal Ministry and Leadership. *Scofield Certificates* in New Testament, Old Testament, Bible Doctrines, and Bible Studies.

Tuition: $49 per course, $367.50 per program. Scofield courses: $200 per course, $585 per program. Certificate fee: $5.

RHEMA CORRESPONDENCE BIBLE SCHOOL

PO Box 50220, Tulsa, OK 74150-0220
(918) 258-1588 ext. 2216
www.rbtc.org/rbcs

Courses: *Certificates* in Dynamics in Faith, Healing Truth, Life of Prayer, Bible Interpretation, Charismatic Truths, and Christology.

Tuition: $25 per course. (Full prisoner scholarships available.) Application fee: $25 (RHEMA *Diploma* awarded upon completion of all certification programs.)

SEMINARY EXTENSION

901 Commerce St., Suite 500, Nashville, TN 37203-3631
(800) 229-4612, (615) 242-2453
www.seminaryextension.org

Courses: *Certificates* in Church Work, Bi-Vocational Ministry, Lay Ministry, and Women's Ministry. *Diplomas* in Bible Studies, Educational Ministries, Ministries/Pastoral Education, and Theological Foundation.

Tuition: $84 per credit hour (for Level one courses), $28 per hour (Level two courses, which require a proctor).

FREE Religious Studies

NOTE: The following courses are largely designed with prisoners in mind and come recommended by prisoners. There are various levels of study and degrees of difficulty. The more advanced studies are marked as such. All offer *Certificates of Completion* or *Diplomas*, unless marked otherwise.

CHRISTIAN COURSES

AMERICAN BIBLE ACADEMY

PO Box 1627, Joplin, MO 64802-1627
(417) 781-9100
www.abarc.org www.arm.org info@arm.org

Courses: John, Acts, Mark, Galatians, Philippians, and Christian Doctrine.

Difficulty: Advanced

Notes: Bible provided. Courses are also available in Spanish. Their website available on the website in Russian, German, and Khmer.

CATHOLIC HOME STUDY SERVICE

PO Box 363, Perryville, MO 63775
www.amm.org

Courses: Catholic study service.

Difficulty: Easy to moderate

CHRIST FOR ME

PO Box 1694, Tahlequah, OK 74465
(918) 431-1981
www.christforme.org cfm@christforme.org

Courses: Over 1,500 lessons in over 150 topics.

Difficulty: East to moderate.

CROSSROAD BIBLE INSTITUTE

PO Box 900, Grand Rapids, MI 49509-0900
(800) 668-2450, (616) 530-1300
www.crossroadbibleinstitute.org

Courses: *Tier One:* Great Truths of the Bible, Survey of the Bible. *Tier Two*: Ten Men You Should Know (for men), Ten Women You Should Know (for women), In God we Trust, and Sermon on the Mount (59 lessons).

Difficulty: Moderate. These are in-depth courses take, on average, 4-6 years to complete them in their entirety.

Notes: Bible provided. Courses are also available in Spanish.

ECS PRISON MINISTRIES

2570 Asbury Rd. Dubuque, IA 52001
(563) 585-2070
www.ecsministries.org

Courses: Over 65 courses containing Christian and bible-themed subjects.

Difficulty: Moderate. These are in-depth courses.

Notes: Bible provided. Upon completion, ECS awards a new bible. Grades over 90 earn college credit that can be used for degree courses at Louisiana Baptist University.

EXODUS PRISON MINISTRY

PO Box 6363, Lubbock, TX 79493

Exodus Prison Ministry offers 33 moderately difficult in-depth bible study courses. Bible is awarded upon completion.

GLOBAL UNIVERSITY | PRISON MINISTRY

1211 S. Glenstone Ave., Springfield, MO 65804
(800) 443-1083, (417) 862-9533
www.globaluniversity.edu
studentinfo@globaluniversity.edu

Courses: Over 35 Christian-themed courses.

Difficulty: Easy

Notes: Over 30 courses available in Spanish. They also offer college level courses. See their listing in our FEE-based Religious Studies section.

GREAT COMMISSION INSTITUTE AND BIBLE COLLEGE

PO Box 844, 139 Caves Ave., Cave Junction, OR 97523
(541) 692-4775

Courses: Over 40 bible-themed courses.

Difficulty: Easy to difficult. These courses are in-depth.

INMATE DISCIPLER FELLOWSHIP

PO Box 185905, Fort Worth, TX 76118

Courses: 25 Christian and bible-themed courses

Difficulty: Easy to moderate

Notes: Upon completion of all 25 courses, you're eligible to earn a Diploma in Pastoral Ministry.

LAMP AND LIGHT PUBLISHERS

26 Farm Road 5577, Farmington, NM 87401-1436
(505) 632-3521

Courses: 14 courses containing over 140 lessons on Christianity

Difficulty: Easy. Courses take 2-5 years to complete in their entirety.

Notes: Lessons are also available in Spanish, French, German, and Portuguese.

LITTLE LAMBS

PO Box 32, Sebring, FL 33870-0032
(863) 471-2626
www.littlelambsinc.org

Courses: 16 lessons on all parts of the bible.

Difficulty: Moderate. These are in-depth courses.

LOVE BIBLE STUDY

PO Box 299, Madison, TN 37116

Courses: Basic Christian Series, Books of the Bible, Understanding our Christian Faith Series, In-Depth Study Series, Bible Language Series.

Difficulty: Easy to collegiate

Notes: The Bible Language Series offers 180 lessons on the Hebrew and Greek languages. Courses are also available in Spanish.

LOVED ONES OF PRISONERS

PO Box 14953, Odessa, TX 79768
(915) 580-5667
www.loopsministries.com

Courses: Several bible-based courses.

Difficulty: Easy

MESSENGER BIBLE INSTITUTE (MBI)

PO Box 1756, Oakdale, CA 95361
(209) 845-1718
www.prisonministry.net/MBI mbimessenger@aol.com

MBI offers FREE bible correspondence education, ministry diplomas, and pen pal opportunities.

MIRACLES PRISONER MINISTRY

501 E. Adams St., Wisconsin Dells, WI 53965
(608) 253-9568
www.amici.com

Courses: 12-Step Spiritual Recovery

Difficulty: Easy. Requires about 1 year of study.

PAN AMERICAN LITERATURE MISSION

5215 E. Fort Lowell Rd., Tucson, AZ 85712

Courses: Several bible-themed courses.

Difficulty: Easy

PMI CENTER FOR BIBLICAL STUDIES

PO Box 177, Battle Creek, MI 49016-0177
(269) 282-9381
www.pmiministries.com

Courses: Knowing You Are Saved, Everyday Living, Understanding God, The Lordship of Jesus, Fellowship and Church, Giving and Tithing, Praying with Power, Victorious Christian Living

Difficulty: Easy

PRISONERS FOR CHRIST OUTREACH MINISTRIES

PO Box 1530, Woodinville, WA 98072-1530
(425) 483-4151 ext. 1
www.pfcom.org *gvt@pfcom.org*

Courses: One main comprehensive introductory course. Other lessons will follow.

Difficulty: Easy

PRISON MISSION ASSOCIATION | BIBLE CORRESPONDENCE FELLOWSHIP

PO Box 2300, Port Orchard, WA 98366
(360) 876-0918
www.pmabcf.org *pma@pmabcf.org*

Courses: General bible based

Difficulty: Easy

ROCK OF AGES PRISON MINISTRY

PO Box 2308, Cleveland, TN 37320

Rock of Ages offers FREE easy to moderately difficult bible studies to prisoners. Upon completion a bible is awarded.

SALVATION ARMY | CONTINUING EDUCATION CENTER

1032 Metropolitan Pkwy. SW, Atlanta, GA 30310
www.salvationaarmysouth.org/sce/biblecourses.html

Courses: Over 20 Christian and bible-themed courses.

Difficulty: Easy to difficult. Courses are very in-depth.

SET FREE PRISON MINISTRIES

PO Box 5440, Riverside, CA 92517
www.spiritualfreedom-setfree.org

Courses: Several bible-themed courses.

Difficulty: Easy

Notes: Courses available in English and Spanish

SOURCE OF LIGHT MINISTRIES INTERNATIONAL

1011 Mission Rd., Madison, GA 30650
(706) 342-0397
www.sourcelight.org slm@sourcelight.org

Courses: Over 18- lessons on Christianity and the bible.

Difficulty: Easy

Notes: Bible provided. Courses are available in Creole, French, Hungarian, Korean, Portuguese, Romanian, Russian, Spanish, and Tagalog.

TOMORROW'S WORLD

PO Box 3810, Charlotte, NC 28227-8010
www.tomorrowsworld.org

Courses: Bible study subscription.

Difficulty: Easy

TRUE POWER OUTREACH MINISTRY

PO Box 69585, Odessa, TX 79769
(915) 367-9025

Courses: Over 15 Christian-themed courses containing over 140 devotional studies.

Difficulty: Easy. Takes 2-3 years to complete.

UNITED BRETHREN JAIL AND PRISON OUTREACH MINISTRY

1278 Glenneyre, Box 219, Laguna Beach, CA 92651
unitedbrethren4god@yahoo.com

Courses: 12-Step Christ-centered recovery program.

Notes: *Life Recovery Bible* included.

WATER OF LIFE | STEINKAMP PRISON STUDIES

7623 East Ave., Fontana, CA 92336
www.wateroflifecc.org

Courses: 10-lesson course covering the New Testament.

Difficulty: Easy. Course takes about 10 months to complete.

Notes: Bible provided after lesson 7.

VOICE OF GOD RECORDINGS

PO Box 950, Jeffersonville, IN 47131

Voice of God Recordings sends printed Christian-based sermons to prisoners, FREE of charge.

YOU VISITED ME | PRISON MINISTRIES

PO Box 537, Eagle, WI 53119

You Visited Me provides annual quality Christian-themed calendars and other biblical resources to prisoners, FREE of charge.

BUDDHISM COURSES

ASIAN CLASSICS INSTITUTE

7055 Juniper Dr., Colorado Springs, CO 80908
(212) 475-7752
www.world-view.org aci@world-view.org

Courses: 15 studies that parallel the same core information that a Geshe (Doctor of Theology) learns at Tibetan monastery.

BUDDHIST ASSOCIATION OF THE UNITED STATES

1709 Mexico Ave., Tarpon Springs, FL 34689
www.baus.org

Courses: Fundamentals of Buddhism, with a focus on meditation and mindfulness practice.

DHARMA COMPANIONS

PO Box 762, Cotati, CA 94931
www.dharmacompanions.wordpress.com

Courses: Variety of Buddhism-themed courses.

KADAMPA BUDDHISM | SARAH BUDDHIST CENTER

PO Box 12037, San Francisco, CA 94112
www.kadampas.org

Courses: The teachings of a Geshe (Doctor of Theology).

HINDU COURSES

AMERICAN GITA SOCIETY, THE

511 Lowell Place, Fremont, CA 94536
www.gita-society.com

Courses: Various studies on Gita.

Notes: Bhagavad Gita provided.

INTERNATIONAL PURE BHAKTI YOGA SOCIETY

PO Box 52724, Durham, NC 27717
www.prisonseva.org

Courses: Monthly course on spiritual enlightenment.

SIDDHA YOGA MEDITATION PRISON PROJECT

PO Box 99140, Emeryville, CA 94662
(510) 428-1836
www.siddhayoga.org

Courses: 12-year Siddha yoga course, *In Search of Self.*

Notes: Courses available in English and Spanish.

ISLAM COURSES

ISLAMIC EDUCATION CENTER

2551 Massachusetts Ave. NW, Washington, DC 20008
(202) 332-8343
www.theislamiccenter.org

Courses: Islamic study guides.

Difficulty: Easy to difficult.

Notes: Koran provided.

JEWISH COURSES

ALEPH INSTITUTE, THE

9540 Collins Ave., Surfside, FL 33154
(305) 864-5553
www.alephinstitute.org

Courses: Jewish faith studies.

ROSICRUCIAN (WESTERN WISDOM TEACHINGS)

ROSICRUCIAN FELLOWSHIP

222 Mission Ave., Oceanside, CA 92054-2399
(760) 757-6600
www.rosicrucianfellowship.org

Courses: Esoteric Christian Philosophy, Spiritual Astrology, Deeper Biblical Truths.

ROSICRUCIAN FRATERNITY, THE

PO Box 220, Quakertown, PA 18951
(800) 779-3796
www.soul.org

Courses: Unique courses on spiritual development and immortality.

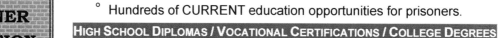

Religious Newsletters & Periodicals

FREE Religious Newsletters & Periodicals

BUDDHIST

DHARMA FRIENDS | COMPASSION WORKS FOR ALL

PO Box 7708, Little Rock, AR 72217-7708

Monthly Newsletter.

DHARMA GARDEN

1 Fairtown Lane, Taneytown, MD 21787
www.facebook.com/DharmaGardenSangha
dharmagardensangha@gmail.com

Quarterly newsletter.

GASSHO | ATLANTA ZOTOT ZEN CENTER

1167-C Zonolite Pl., Atlanta, GA 30306
www.aszc.org

Bi-monthly newsletter.

GAY BUDDHIST FELLOWSHIP

PMPB 456, 2215-R Market St., San Francisco, CA 94114
www.gaybuddhist.org

Bi-monthly newsletter.

INSIGHT | INSIGHT MEDITATION SOCIETY

1230 Pleasant St., Barre, MA 01005
www.dharma.org

Bi-monthly newsletter.

IBMC | INTERNATIONAL BUDDHIST MEDITATION CENTER

928 S. New Hampshire Ave., Los Angeles, CA 90006
www.ibmc.info

Bi-monthly newsletter.

LIBERATION MAGAZINE | LIBERATION PRISON PROJECT

PO Box 31527, San Francisco, CA 94131
www.liberationprisonproject.org

Bi-monthly newsletter.

PURPLE LOTUS JOURNAL

636 San Mateo Ave., San Bruno, CA 94066
www.purplelotus.com

Annual magazine.

SNOW LION

PO Box 6483, Ithaca, NY 14851-6483
www.snowlionpub.com

Bi-monthly newsletter.

TRICYCLE MAGAZINE | THE BUDDHIST REVIEW

1115 Broadway, Suite 1113, New York, NY 10010

Quarterly magazine. Note: Tricycle is a FEE-based magazine, but they will send back issues for FREE.

CATHOLIC

MY PEOPLE | PRESENTATION MINISTRIES

3230 McHenry Ave., Cincinnati, OH 45211

Monthly newsletter.

VOICE OF PROVIDENCE, THE | PIOUS UNION OF ST. JOSEPH

953 E. Michigan Ave., Grass Lake, MI 49240
www.pusj.org

Bi-monthly magazine.

CHRISTIAN (NON-DENOMINATIONAL)

A LITTLE GOOD NEWS | HUMAN KINDNESS FOUNDATION

PO Box 61619, Durham, NC 27715
www.humankindness.com

Quarterly newsletter.

CONVERSATIONS | THE CONVERSATIONS WITH GOD FOUNDATION

PMB 1150m 1257 Siskiyou Blvd., Ashland, OR 97520
www.cwg.org

Bi-monthly newsletter.

CROSSROADS JOURNAL OF THE ARTS

PO Box 900, Grand Rapids, MI 49509

Bi-monthly newsletter.

FISHER OF MEN PRISON MINISTRIES

5403 N. Second St., Loves Park, IL 61111
(815) 633-7508
www.prisonministry.net/fompm

Monthly newsletter.

HEART OF AMERICA

PO Box 1685. Independence, MO 64055
www.heartmin.org

Monthly newsletter.

INSIDE JOURNAL | PRISON FELLOWSHIP

PO Box 17500, Washington, DC 20041
www.prisonfellowship.org insidejournal@pfm.org

Bi-monthly newsletter.

JOY WRITERS GOOD-NEWS LETTER

2001 Liberty Square Dr., Cartersville, GA 30121

Bi-monthly newsletter.

PRESENT TRUTH

PO Box 315, Kansas City, OK 74347
www.presenttruth.com

Monthly newsletter.

REFLECTIONS | LOVED ONES OF PRISONERS

PO Box 164953, Odessa, TX 79768
www.loopsministries.com

Monthly newsletter.

TOMORROW'S WORLD

PO Box 3810, Charlotte, NC 28227-8010
www.tomorrowsworld.org

Bi-monthly magazine.

YARD OUT | PRISONERS FOR CHRIST

PO Box 1530, Woodinville, WA 98072
www.pfcom.org

Three times annually newsletter.

HINDU

HEART TO HEART | THE AMERICAN GITA SOCIETY

515 Lowell Place, Fremont, CA 94536
www.gita-society.com

Bi-monthly newsletter.

JEHOVAH'S WITNESSES

WATCHTOWER & AWAKE

Watchtower Bible & Tract Society, 25 Columbia Heights, Brooklyn, NY 11201
www.jw.org

Bi-monthly magazines.

KRISHNA

IPM FREEDOM NEWSLETTER | ISHKON PRISON MINISTRY

1400 Cherry St., Denver, CO 80220

Bi-monthly newsletter.

MESSIANIC JEWISH

MESSIANIC TIMES

PO Box 2190, Niagara Falls, NY 14302
www.messianictimes.com

Bi-monthly magazine.

NATIVE AMERICAN

NATIVE PRIDE | NATIVE AMERICAN PRIDE COM.

33 Bay Shore Dr., Bay City, MI 48706

Bi-monthly newsletter.

RED WARRIOR | RED HEART WARRIOR'S SOCIETY

PO Box 4362, Allentown, PA 18105

Quarterly newsletter.

OTHER

MEDITATION MONTHLY INTERNATIONAL | WHITE MOUNTAIN EDUCATION ASSOCIATION

543 Eastwood Dr., Prescott, AZ 86303
www.wmea.org

Bi-monthly newsletter.

Fee-Based Religious Periodicals

BUDDHIST

BUDDHADHARMA

Features on Buddhist traditions and disciplines, Eastern history, politics. More. 8 issues/year.

SHAMBHALA SUN

Buddhist magazine. Everything Buddhist. 12 issues/year.

TRICYCLE

Features on the independent voice of Buddhism in western culture. 10 issues/year.

TURNING WHEEL JOURNAL

Features a variety of information on the Buddhist faith. 4 issues/year.

CATHOLIC

AMERICA

Catholic weekly magazine. 52 issues/year.

CATECHIST MAGAZINE

Features article for catechists, DREs and religion teachers working with students pre-school aged to adults. 7 issues/year.

CATHOLIC ANSWER, THE

Easy to read magazine on the teachings of the Catholic faith. 6 issues/year.

CATHOLIC DIGEST

Editorials of inspiration, information, and human interest stories. 12 issues/year.

LIGUORIAN

Catholic guidance, counsel, and moral education for Catholics of all ages. 10 issues/year.

OUR SUNDAY VISITOR

Coverage of important national and international news. 52 issues/year.

PRIEST, THE

For and about the priesthood. 11 issues/year.

SOJOURNERS

A Christian voice that preaches not political correctness but compassion. 10 issues/year.

TAKE OUT-FAMILY FAITH ON GO

Written for today's busy Catholic family. A mini-mag alternative of *Our Sunday Visitor.* 10 issues/year.

CHRISTIAN (NON-DENOMINATIONAL)

ANGELS ON EARTH

Stories of angels and the messages they deliver, filled with profound mystery and faith-affirming hope. 6 issues/year.

BIBLE STUDY MAGAZINE

Tools and methods for bible study and insights. 6 issues/year.

CHARISMA

For the contemporary Christians. 12 issues/year.

CHRISTIAN CENTURY

An ecumenical journal of opinion and news. 26 issues/year.

CHRISTIANITY TODAY

Features on evangelical conviction. Theory. 12 issues/year.

CHURCH EXECUTIVE

For senior pastors and church administrators. Ideas and strategies that address church issues. 12 issues/year.

HOPE TODAY

Editorial on life challenges and opportunities on an inspirational level. 12 issues/year.

KINDRED SPIRIT

Global guide to positive change. 10 issues/year.

MEN OF INTEGRITY

Daily devotionals for the unique challenges men face. 6 issues/year.

MESSAGE MAGAZINE

Features addressing African American issues. 6 issues/year.

MINISTRY TODAY

Hands on magazine for Christian leaders. 6 issues/year.

MY DAILY VISITOR

Pocket sized magazines offering scripture-of-the-day references. 6 issues/year.

RELEVANT

For forward thinking, spiritually passionate people, challenging all people to go beyond the traditional teachings. 6 issues/year.

SPORT'S SPECTRUM

Christian sport's magazine containing exclusive interviews with Christian athletes. 8 issues/year.

HINDU

HINDUISM TODAY

Interviews with spiritual leaders, news, and issues. 8 issues/year.

JEWISH

MINDSTREAM

Focuses on all issues concerning Judaism and Zionism. 6 issues/year.

MOMENT MAGAZINE

Features on the Jewish community. 6 issues/year.

MUSLIM

PRISONWORLD MAGAZINE | DAWAH INTERNATIONAL

PO Box 380, Powder Springs, GA 30127

(678) 233-8286

www.prisonworldmagazine.com

Bi-monthly Muslim-based tabloid featuring entertainment news. Proceeds go towards prison outreach programs. 6 issues/year. $5/issue (or 12 stamps.)

TAO

EMPTY VESSEL

Dedicated to the exploration and dissemination of non-religious Taoist philosophy. 4 issues/year.

OTHER

LIVING SPIRIT

Features material on all aspects of life, with a focus on teaching people to research and learn for themselves. 4 issues/year.

PARABOLA

Explores human question. 4 issues/year.

SACRED HOOP

Explores ancient sacred traditions around the world. 6 issues/year.

SCIENCE OF MIND

Offers a spiritual perspective on world events. 12 issues/year.

SEDONA JOURNAL OF EMERGENCE

Features on self and spiritual awakenings. 12 issues/year.

TATHAASTU

Features on happy and healthy life. 6 issues/year.

VIBRANT LIFE

Features on physical health, mental clarity and spiritual balance. 6 issues/year.

Religious Freedom Restoration Act (RFRA)

2000bb. Congressional findings and declaration of purposes

(a) **Findings**. The Congress finds that--

(1) the framers of the Constitution, recognizing free exercise of religion as an unalienable right, secured its protection in the First Amendment to the Constitution;

(2) laws "neutral" toward religion may burden religious exercise as surely as laws intended to interfere with religious exercise;

(3) governments should not substantially burden religious exercise without compelling justification;

(4) in Employment Division v. Smith, 494 U.S. 872 (1990) the Supreme Court virtually eliminated the requirement that the government justify burdens on religious exercise imposed by laws neutral toward religion; and

(5) the compelling interest test as set forth in prior Federal court rulings is a workable test for striking sensible balances between religious liberty and competing prior governmental interests.

(b) **Purposes**. The purposes of this Act are--

(1) to restore the compelling interest test as set forth in Sherbert v. Verner, 374 U.S. 398 (1963) and Wisconsin v. Yoder, 406 U.S. 205 (1972) and to guarantee its application in all cases where free exercise of religion is substantially burdened; and

(2) to provide a claim or defense to persons whose religious exercise is substantially burdened by government.

2000bb-1. Free exercise of religion protected

(a) **In general**. Government shall not substantially burden a person's exercise of religion even if the burden results from a rule of general applicability, except as provided in subsection (b).

(b) **Exception**. Government may substantially burden a person's exercise of religion only if it demonstrates that application of the burden to the person--

(1) is in furtherance of a compelling governmental interest; and

(2) is the least restrictive means of furthering that compelling governmental interest.

(c) **Judicial relief**. A person whose religious exercise has been burdened in violation of this section may assert that violation as a claim or defense in a judicial proceeding and obtain appropriate relief against a government. Standing to assert a claim or defense under this section shall be governed by the general rules of standing under article III of the Constitution.

2000bb-2. Definitions

As used in this Act--

(1) the term "government" includes a branch, department, agency, instrumentality, and official (or other person acting under color of law) of the United States, or of a covered entity;

(2) the term "covered entity" means the District of Columbia, the Commonwealth of Puerto Rico,

and each territory and possession of the United States;

(3) the term "demonstrates" means meets the burdens of going forward with the evidence and of persuasion; and

(4) the term "exercise of religion" means religious exercise, as defined in section 8 of the Religious Land Use and Institutionalized Persons Act of 2000 [42 USCS 2000cc-5].

2000bb-3. Applicability

(a) **In general**. This Act applies to all Federal law, and the implementation of that law, whether statutory or otherwise, and whether adopted before or after the enactment of this Act [enacted Nov. 16, 1993].

(b) **Rule of construction**. Federal statutory law adopted after the date of the enactment of this Act [enacted Nov. 16, 1993] is subject to this Act unless such law explicitly excludes such application by reference to this Act.

(c) **Religious belief unaffected**. Nothing in this Act shall be construed to authorize any government to burden any religious belief.

2000bb-4. Establishment Clause unaffected

Nothing in this Act shall be construed to affect, interpret, or in any way address that portion of the First Amendment prohibiting laws respecting the establishment of religion (referred to in this section as the "Establishment Clause"). Granting government funding, benefits, or exemptions, to the extent permissible under the Establishment Clause, shall not constitute a violation of this Act. As used in this section, the term "granting", used with respect to government funding, benefits, or exemptions, does not include the denial of government funding, benefits, or exemptions.

Religious Land Use and Institutionalized Persons Act (RLUIPA)

2000cc. Protection of land use as religious exercise

(a) **Substantial burdens**.

(1) General rule. No government shall impose or implement a land use regulation in a manner that imposes a substantial burden on the religious exercise of a person, including a religious assembly or institution, unless the government demonstrates that imposition of the burden on that person, assembly, or institution--

(A) is in furtherance of a compelling governmental interest; and

(B) is the least restrictive means of furthering that compelling governmental interest.

(2) Scope of application. This subsection applies in any case in which--

(A) the substantial burden is imposed in a program or activity that receives Federal financial assistance, even if the burden results from a rule of general applicability;

(B) the substantial burden affects, or removal of that substantial burden would affect, commerce with foreign nations, among the several States, or with Indian tribes, even if the burden results from a rule of general applicability; or

(C) the substantial burden is imposed in the implementation of a land use regulation or system of land use regulations, under which a government makes, or has in place formal or informal procedures or practices that permit the government to make, individualized assessments of the proposed uses for the property involved.

(b) **Discrimination and exclusion**.

(1) Equal terms. No government shall impose or implement a land use regulation in a manner that treats a religious assembly or institution on less than equal terms with a nonreligious assembly or institution.

(2) Nondiscrimination. No government shall impose or implement a land use regulation that discriminates against any assembly or institution on the basis of religion or religious denomination.

(3) Exclusions and limits. No government shall impose or implement a land use regulation that--

(A) totally excludes religious assemblies from a jurisdiction; or

(B) unreasonably limits religious assemblies, institutions, or structures within a jurisdiction.

2000cc-1. Protection of religious exercise of institutionalized persons

(a) **General rule**. No government shall impose a substantial burden on the religious exercise of a person residing in or confined to an institution, as defined in section 2 of the Civil Rights of Institutionalized Persons Act (42 U.S.C. 1997), even if the burden results from a rule of general applicability, unless the government demonstrates that imposition of the burden on that person--

(1) is in furtherance of a compelling governmental interest; and

(2) is the least restrictive means of furthering that compelling governmental interest.

(b) **Scope of application**. This section applies in any case in which--

(1) the substantial burden is imposed in a program or activity that receives Federal financial assistance; or

(2) the substantial burden affects, or removal of that substantial burden would affect, commerce with foreign nations, among the several States, or with Indian tribes.

2000cc-2. Judicial relief

(a) **Cause of action**. A person may assert a violation of this Act as a claim or defense in a judicial proceeding and obtain appropriate relief against a government. Standing to assert a claim or defense under this section shall be governed by the general rules of standing under article III of the Constitution.

(b) **Burden of persuasion**. If a plaintiff produces prima facie evidence to support a claim alleging a violation of the Free Exercise Clause or a violation of section 2 [42 USCS 2000cc], the government shall bear the burden of persuasion on any element of the claim, except that the plaintiff shall bear the burden of persuasion on whether the law (including a regulation) or government practice that is challenged by the claim substantially burdens the plaintiff's exercise of religion.

(c) **Full faith and credit**. Adjudication of a claim of a violation of section 2 [42 USCS 2000cc] in a non-Federal forum shall not be entitled to full faith and credit in a Federal court unless the claimant had a full and fair adjudication of that claim in the non-Federal forum.

(d) [Omitted]

(e) **Prisoners**. Nothing in this Act shall be construed to amend or repeal the Prison Litigation Reform Act of 1995 (including provisions of law amended by that Act).

(f) **Authority of United States to enforce this Act**. The United States may bring an action for injunctive or declaratory relief to enforce compliance with this Act. Nothing in this subsection shall be construed to deny, impair, or otherwise affect any right or authority of the Attorney General, the United States, or any agency, officer, or employee of the United States, acting under any law other than this subsection, to institute or intervene in any proceeding.

(g) **Limitation**. If the only jurisdictional basis for applying a provision of this Act is a claim that a substantial burden by a government on religious exercise affects, or that removal of that substantial burden would affect, commerce with foreign nations, among the several States, or with Indian tribes, the provision shall not apply if the government demonstrates that all substantial burdens on, or the removal of all substantial burdens from, similar religious exercise throughout the Nation would not lead in the aggregate to a substantial effect on commerce with foreign nations, among the several States, or with Indian tribes.

2000cc-3. Rules of construction

(a) **Religious belief unaffected**. Nothing in this Act shall be construed to authorize any government to burden any religious belief.

(b) **Religious exercise not regulated**. Nothing in this Act shall create any basis for restricting or burdening religious exercise or for claims against a religious organization including any religiously affiliated school or university, not acting under color of law.

(c) **Claims to funding unaffected**. Nothing in this Act shall create or preclude a right of any religious organization to receive funding or other assistance from a government, or of any person to receive government funding for a religious activity, but this Act may require a government to incur expenses in its own operations to avoid imposing a substantial burden on religious exercise.

(d) **Other authority to impose conditions on funding unaffected**. Nothing in this Act shall--

(1) authorize a government to regulate or affect, directly or indirectly, the activities or policies of a person other than a government as a condition of receiving funding or other assistance; or

(2) restrict any authority that may exist under other law to so regulate or affect, except as provided in this Act.

(e) **Governmental discretion in alleviating burdens on religious exercise**. A government may avoid the preemptive force of any provision of this Act by changing the policy or practice that results in a substantial burden on religious exercise, by retaining the policy or practice and exempting the substantially burdened religious exercise, by providing exemptions from the policy or practice for applications that substantially burden religious exercise, or by any other means that eliminates the substantial burden.

(f) **Effect on other law**. With respect to a claim brought under this Act, proof that a substantial burden on a person's religious exercise affects, or removal of that burden would affect, commerce with foreign nations, among the several States, or with Indian tribes, shall not establish any inference or presumption that Congress intends that any religious exercise is, or is not, subject to any law other than this Act.

(g) **Broad construction**. This Act shall be construed in favor of a broad protection of religious exercise, to the maximum extent permitted by the terms of this Act and the Constitution.

(h) **No preemption or repeal**. Nothing in this Act shall be construed to preempt State law, or repeal Federal law, that is equally as protective of religious exercise as, or more protective of religious exercise than, this Act.

(i) **Severability**.

If any provision of this Act or of an amendment made by this Act, or any application of such provision to any person or circumstance, is held to be unconstitutional, the remainder of this Act, the amendments made by this Act, and the application of the provision to any other person or circumstance shall not be affected.

2000cc-4. Establishment Clause unaffected

Nothing in this Act shall be construed to affect, interpret, or in any way address that portion of the first amendment to the Constitution prohibiting laws respecting an establishment of religion (referred to in this section as the "Establishment Clause"). Granting government funding, benefits, or exemptions, to the extent permissible under the Establishment Clause, shall not constitute a violation of this Act. In this section, the term "granting", used with respect to government funding, benefits, or exemptions, does not include the denial of government funding, benefits, or exemptions.

2000cc-5. Definitions
In this Act:
(1) Claimant. The term "claimant" means a person raising a claim or defense under this Act.
(2) Demonstrates. The term "demonstrates" means meets the burdens of going forward with the evidence and of persuasion.
(3) Free Exercise Clause. The term "Free Exercise Clause" means that portion of the first amendment to the Constitution that proscribes laws prohibiting the free exercise of religion.
(4) Government. The term "government"--
(A) means--
(i) a State, county, municipality, or other governmental entity created under the authority of a State;
(ii) any branch, department, agency, instrumentality, or official of an entity listed in clause (i); and
(iii) any other person acting under color of State law; and
(B) for the purposes of sections 4(b) and 5 [42 USCS 2000cc-2(b) and 2000cc-3], includes the United States, a branch, department, agency, instrumentality, or official of the United States, and any other person acting under color of Federal law.
(5) Land use regulation. The term "land use regulation" means a zoning or landmarking law, or the application of such a law, that limits or restricts a claimant's use or development of land (including a structure affixed to land), if the claimant has an ownership, leasehold, easement, servitude, or other property interest in the regulated land or a contract or option to acquire such an interest.
(6) Program or activity. The term "program or activity" means all of the operations of any entity as described in paragraph (1) or (2) of section 606 of the Civil Rights Act of 1964 (42 U.S.C. 2000d-4a).
(7) Religious exercise.
(A) In general. The term "religious exercise" includes any exercise of religion, whether or not compelled by, or central to, a system of religious belief.
(B) Rule. The use, building, or conversion of real property for the purpose of religious exercise shall be considered to be religious exercise of the person or entity that uses or intends to use the property for that purpose.

Prisoner Service Center

Prisoner Service Center

Prisoners need to get things done as much as anyone in the real world. But it certainly isn't as easy to do the things you need to do from behind bars.

This is your section if you are looking to accomplish your hopes, dreams, and ambitions from the comfort of your cell. Shopping, services, pen pals finding… Everything you need to get started on any path is here waiting to be used by you.

PRISONER SERVICE CENTER

Prisoner Products & Services

Attention:
The following products and services should be used at your own risk. We do not rate them simply because service providers may be the most professional organization one day and be gone the next.
However, every effort has been made to ensure that at the time of publishing the following service providers were alive and willing helpful resources for prisoners.
As always, if you learn of a resource that is no longer useful to prisoners, or you discover a new one that you would like us to check out and possibly include, please let us know!

BOOKSELLERS

AK PRESS

674-A 23rd St., Oakland, CA 94612
www.akpress.org

Wide variety of titles, with many anarchy listings. 30% discount to prisoners. Thousands of titles. FREE catalog.

AMERICAN CORRECTIONAL ASSOCIATION | PUBLICATIONS DEPARTMENT

206 N. Washington St., Suite 200, Alexandria, VA 22314
www.aca.org

300+ titles on various topics. Many self-help options. FREE catalog.

B.B.P.D.

PO Box 248, Compton, MD 20627
www.bookstoinmates.com

500+ titles on various topics. $3.95 shipping for the entire order. FREE catalog.

BLACK MEDIA FAMILY

PO Box 27514, Lansing, MI 48909-7514
blackmediafamily@gmail.com

Write for a current listing of publications. Catalog features mostly urban/street titles.

BOOKS 'N THINGS WAREHOUSE

PO Box 7330, Shrewsbury, NJ 07702-7330
(800) 681-2740
www.mybntw.com

Books' N Things Warehouse sells a wide variety of books of every genre, as well as calendars, journals, toys, and more. Write for a FREE catalog.

BOOKRAK

PO Box 104720, Jefferson City, MO 65110-4720
(800) 456-1774
www.bookrak.com

All paperback books, in all genres, but are limited in non-fiction. FREE catalog as frequently as monthly.

BUD'S ART BOOKS

PO Box 1689, Grass Valley, CA 95945
www.budplant.com

Comprehensive listing of contemporary art and photography titles. Catalog must be printed from their website.

CLEIS PRESS

101 Hudson St., 37th Floor, Suite 3705, Jersey City, NJ 07302
(646) 257-4343
www.cleispress.com

Cleis Press publishes books for the LGBT community, as well as BDSM, romance, and erotic collections. Write for a catalog.

EDEN PRESS

PO Box 8410, Fountain Valley, CA 92728
www.edenpress.com

Wide variety of topics. Catalog features extensive listing of how-to titles. FREE catalog.

GRADUATE GROUP

PO Box 370351, West Hartford, CT 06137
www.graduategroup.com

Catalog contains mostly prisoner help and reentry titles. Send SASE for current listings.

GROUNDWORK BOOKS

0323 Student Center, La Jolla, CA 92037
(858) 452-9625
groundwork@libertad.ucsd.edu

Specializes in geography, political science, social civics, criminal justice, and history. 40% discount to prisoners. May send up to two FREE books to prisoners who are indigent. Stamp donations are appreciated.

HAYMARKET BOOKS

PO Box 180165, Chicago, IL 60618
(773) 538-7884
www.haymarketbooks.org

Haymarket books publishes and distributes radical-themed titles reflecting the values of social justice reform activists. Discounts are offered to prisoners. Write for a catalog.

HIT POINTE

540 N. Lapeer Rd., Suite 255, Orion Township, MI 48362
(248) 845-8229
www.hitpointe.com services@hitpointe.com

Hit Pointe offers a wide selection of fantasy and roll-playing game-related books, such as D&D, Pathfinder, etc., as well as board games and trading cards. Some used books are available. Write for FREE catalog.

INTELLIGENT SOLUTIONS

4-831 Kuhio Highway, Suite 438-333, Kapaa, HI 96746
(800) 770-8802
www.toolsforfreedom.com

Mostly 'get-rich-quick' and infomercial related titles. Features over 700 titles. FREE catalog.

JAGUAR BOOKS

6881 Stanton Ave., #F, Buena Park, CA 90621

Variety of genres, English and Spanish. Send $1 or 3 stamps for catalog.

ACE LANFRANCO PUBLICATIONS

5447 Van Fleet Ave., Richmond, CA 94804-5929

ACE Lanfranco Publications offers publication and ad-sheets, such as the Bay Area Advertiser. Write for current list of publications.

LEFT BANK BOOKS

92 Pike St., Box A, Seattle, WA 98101
www.leftbankbooks.com

Small family-owned website specializing in small publishers. Catalog must be printed from their website. Accepts stamps for payment.

LOCKDOWN BOOKSTORE, THE

PO Box 215, Moorpark, CA 93020
(888) 858-2676

Limited titles, mostly erotica. Send $1 and SASE for current catalog.

NATIONAL LAWYERS GUILD

132 Nassau St., Suite 922, New York, NY 10038
www.nlg.org

FREE book list. Mostly legal titles.

NOTES & NOVELS

12436 FM 1960 West, PMB 177, Houston, TX 77065
(281) 890-8911
www.notesandnovels.com

Offers a large 70+ page catalog with a wide variety of topics and thousands of titles. Send $5 or 15 stamps for their catalog.

OPEN, INC.

PO Box 472223, Garland, TX 75047
www,openinc.org

FREE book list. Limited selections.

OXFORD UNIVERSITY PRESS

198 Madison Ave., New York, NY 10016
(816) 445-8685
www.oup.com

FREE Oxford University/Oceana book list. Specializes in legal and reference titles.

PAPERBACK SWAP 'N SHOP

1115 FM 517 Road East, Dickinson, TX 77539
(281) 534-3370
www.imailtoprison.com

The Paperback Swap 'n Shop offers 'grab bag' used book specials, such as a three foot stack of books for $30 to $54. They also offer magazine subscriptions. Write for current offerings.

PATHFINDER PRESS

PO Box 167767, Atlanta, GA 30321-2767
(404) 669-0600
www.pathfinderpress.com

Specializes in the "works of revolutionary and world class leaders" in all major languages, as well as Swedish, Farsi, and Indonesian. $3 for entire order. Orders must be placed online. 50% discount for prisoners. FREE catalog.

PM PRESS

Po Box 23912, Oakland, CA 94623
(510) 658-3906
www.pmpress.org

Features mostly counter-culture and anti-incarceration titles. 50% off for prisoners. FREE catalog.

SOUTH END PRESS

PO Box 382132, Cambridge, MA 02238
(718) 955-4841
www.southendpress.org

Specializes in radical topics. 50% discount for prisoners. Free catalog.

SURESHOT BOOKS PUBLISHING

PO Box 924, Nyack, NY 10960
(845) 675-7505
www.sureshotbooks.com

They have a wide variety of subjects, including books, magazines and newspapers. Catalog costs $12.95.

VALLEY MERCHANDISERS

PO Box 1271, Hagerstown, MD 21741-1271

Specialize in hard-to-find and out of print books. They will do searches for books and sell them at discounted prices to prisoners and families.

VENTURA BOOKS

7928 Oak St., Los Molinos, CA 96055

Limited variety, specializing in erotica titles. Send SASE for current catalog.

EYEWEAR/OPTICAL

39DOLLARGLASSES

60 Plant Ave., Suite 4, Hauppauge, NY 11788
(800) 672-6304
www.39dollarglasses.com

39DollarGlasses provides reasonably priced eyewear options, offering a wide selection of frames, lenses, and options. Prices range from $39 to $198.

SAN FRANCISCO OPTICAL

PO Box 281443, San Francisco, CA 94128-1443
(415) 738-4288
www.sanfranciscooptical.com

SFO offers extremely discounted eyewear, starting at $7.98. Catalog is limited. Send SASE for info.

PRISM OPTICAL

10954 NW 7th Ave., Miami, FL 33168
(800) 637-4104, (305) 754-5894
www.prismoptical.com
contact@prismoptical.com

Prism Optical offers an extensive selection of eyeglass frames and lens options, with a money back guarantee. They have been in business since 1959 and are accustomed to supplying prisoners. Send for a FREE catalog.

GIFTS

BASKET BOUTIQUE

PO Box 352, Sparta, TN 38583

Basket Boutique offers unique and affordable gift baskets. Send an SASE for a FREE brochure.

BOTTLE THOUGHTS GIFT STORE

PO Box 596, Wills Point, TX 75169
(877) 705-0425
www.bottlethoughts.com *sales@bottlethoughts.com*
(*Corrlinks* registered.)

Bottle Thoughts offer unique gifts such as messages-in-a-bottle. FREE shipping on all orders. Send SASE for brochure.

CELL SHOP GIFT SHOP

Po Box 1487, Bloomfield, NJ 07003
(973) 770-8100
www.cellshopgiftshop.com

CSGS offers a variety of gifts, including stuffed animals, jewelry, and much more. Send for a FREE catalog.

DIVERSIFIED PRESS

PO Box 135005, Clermont, FL 34713-5005=

Diversified Press offers unique gif solutions such as greeting cards, puzzles, and other products with your pictures and personal messages, background and other photo edit options, and more. Stamps accepted. Send SASE for current products.

ELIJAH RAY GIFTS

PO Box 3008, La Grande, OR 97850
www.elijahray.com

Elijah Ray Gifts offers a wide variety of products, including jewelry, toys, gift baskets, fresh flowers from local florists, and other gifts. Send $2 (or 4 stamps) for catalog.

EXOTIC FRAGRANCES

1645 Lexington Ave., New York, NY 10029
(877) 787-3645
www.exoticfragrances.com

Exotic Fragrances sells fragrance oils, bath and aromatherapy products. Write for a FREE catalog.

FREDA'S THINGS JUST FOR YOU

PO Box 24802, Detroit, MI 48224
fredasthingsjustforyou@yahoo.com

Freda's Things just For You offers a variety of prisoner gift ideas, including flowers, t-shirts, pillows and more. $10 shipping applies to all orders. Shopping service is offered for $10 fee, or 10 percent of item cost.

FREEBIRD PUBLISHERS

Box 541, North Dighton, MA 02764
(774) 406-8682
www.freebirdpublishers.com
diane@freebirdpublishers.com

Freebird Publishers offers a variety of gifts through individual catalogs, which must be purchased. General Card Catalog ($3), Holiday Card & Gift Catalog ($3), Valentine's Day & Gift Catalog ($3), Easter Card & Gift Catalog ($3), Silpada Jewelry Catalog ($7), and Mother's Day Card Brochure ($1). Stamps accepted for catalog purchases.

GIFTS FROM WITHIN

PO Box 5636, Peoria, IL 61601
giftsfromwithin2@yahoo.com

Gifts from Within offers a variety of gift products. Send SASE for catalog.

GOLDSTAR FRAGRANCES

4 West 37th St., New York, NY 10018
(212) 279-4474, (212) 279-4470
www.goldstarfragrances.com
gstarfragrances@gmail.com

Goldstar Fragrances offers over 1,000 perfume oils, soaps, incenses, body lotions, shower gels, bottles, and more. Send for a FREE catalog.

HARVEST 21 GIFTS

PO Box 3472-P, Modesto, CA 95353
harvest21gifts@gmail.com

Harvest 21 Gifts offers a variety of gifts, including jewelry, flowers, shirts, and stuffed animals.

JULIES GIFTS

PO Box 1941, Buford, GA 30515

Julies Gifts offers a wide variety of gifts. Write for FREE 4-page color catalog. Prices range between $20 - $80. Note: They also own/operate Tightwad Magazines.

LOVE IN A GIFT BOX

PO Box 206A, South Loop 336 West, # 239, Conroe, TX 77304

loveinagiftbox@yahoo.com

Love in a Gift Box is a gift buying service, which also offers heirloom gifts, such as baby bonnets and Christian-themed items. Send SASE for more info.

TIME ZONE GIFTS

PO Box 41093, Houston, TX 77241
(800) 731-6726
www.timezonegifts.com

Time Zone Gifts offers a wide variety of gift options, including plush animals, gift baskets, jewelry, greeting cards, and more. Write for a FREE catalog.

JADEN MOORE OF NEW YORK

36 Cottage St., 2nd Floor, Suite 200-West, Poughkeepsie, NY 12601
gifts@jadenmooreofnewyork.com

Jaden Moore offers a variety of high quality gifts, including flowers, desserts, jewelry, gift boxes, gift cards and much more. Gift packages include wrapping, a FREE card of choice and message (your own letter or drawing) and a FREE silk rose (for adults) or candy (for children's.) Prices are competitive. Many items are name brand. Write for FREE well-designed 60+ page color catalog.

OFFICE SERVICES/PERSONAL ASSISTANTS

Prison Lives

PRISONER ASSISTANT SERVICES

PO Box 842, Exeter, CA 93221
www.prisonLives.com
info@prisonlives.com

Our **Prisoner Assistance Services** are designed to directly help you accomplish anything you hope to do from prison, despite your confines. We understand how difficult it can be to get even the simplest tasks done. We provide a range of reliable services at reasonable rates to help you keep moving forward towards your goals.

Our services include, but are not limited to:

Office Assistance
(typing, printing, scanning, email, & more)

Research Assistance
(internet lookups, people location, photo/article finding & more)

Publishing Assistance
(manuscript typing, proofing, editing, cover design, book launch, marketing & more)

Online Shopping Assistance
(books, textbooks, stationary, outside gifts, & more)

Personal Shopper Assistance
(trip to store, gift wrapping, urgent requests & more)

Subscription Assistance
(newspapers, catalogs, newsletters, magazines & more)

Pen Pal Assistance
(sign up/profile placement, Craig's List posting & more)

Web Presence Assistance
(web & graphic design packages, social media & more)

Don't see a service you need listed here? Just ask us.

Custom services available!

Open an account now $100.

No monthly or annual fees!

If you only intend to place occasional orders, we offer individual service packages for several of our services.

Write for a brochure!

OTHER OFFICE SERVICES/PERSONAL ASSISTANTS

A BOOK YOU WANT

PO Box 16141, Rumford, RI 02916
zling13@comcast.net

A Book You Want provides ordering services, including, books, gifts, and more. They will also do internet searches, print out lyrics, etc. Accepts stamps as payment.

ACADIA IMAGING SERVICES BUREAU

2040 Westlake Ave. N, #307, Seattle, WA 98109

Acadia offers document, slide and photo scanning services. They will scan handwritten or printed documents into digital form for 10 cents/page (b&w) or 17 cents/page (color). Great for prison writers.

ACE SERVICES ORGANIZATION

PO Box 1799, Patterson, NJ 07509-17799
aorganization3@aol.com

Ace Services Organization offers general prisoner assistance services such as email, internet research, social media, phone number setup, mail and banking services, typing, copies and more. Send SASE for more information and pricing.

AMBLER DOCUMENTS

PO Box 938, Norwalk, CT 06852
(203) 849-0708
www.protypeexpress.com

Ambler Documents provides typing and layout services. They accept handwritten documents, but not legal paperwork. Prices start at $2 per double-spaced page.

DFL RESEARCH SERVICES

2851 Chloe Dr., Converse, TX 78109
(210) 462-3427
dflresearchservices@gmail.com

DFL provides reasonably-priced legal research and paralegal assistance to prisoners. Send SASE for more info.

COMPUTERZ FOR CONVICTZ

104 Rolling Rock Rd., Tempe, GA 30179-3656

Computerz for Convictz provides computer services for prisoners, including internet research, social media set up, and more. Write for more information.

CYBER HUT DESIGNS

PO Box 541, North Dighton, MA 02764
www.freebirdpublishers.com

Cyber Hut Designs offers web and graphic design services, including web pages, book covers, brochures and more. Write for list of current services.

ELITE PARALEGAL AND PRISONER SERVICES (EPS)

PO Box 1717, Appleton, WI 54912-1717
(920) 749-1060
www.eliteparalegalservices.us

EPS provides a variety of services with a focus on paralegal assistance. Stamps accepted. Send SASE for more information.

FOR THE SCOOP

PO Box 90594, San Antonio, TX 78209
www.forthescoop.com info@forthescoop.com

For the Scoop provides email news service, including world, U.S., and sports news, and TV schedules, direct to *TruLincs* accounts. $2/month. *TruLincs* users only.

HAWKEYE EDITING

PO Box 16406, St. Paul, MN 55116

Hawkeye Editing provides manuscript typing and editing services. Services are available through *CorrLinks*. Send SASE for more information.

HELP FROM BEYOND THE WALLS

PO Box 18, Springvale, ME 04083
helpfrombeyondethewalls@gmail.com

Help From Beyond the Walls provides prisoner assistance services, including copies, email services, *Facebook* setup, internet research, pen pal registry, stamp buying and more. Send SASE for brochure.

HELPING HANDS

PO Box 1793, Gastonia, NC 28054

Helping Hands provides prisoner publishing services, including editing, formatting, cover design, social media setup and more. Payment plans available. Send SASE for more information.

HELP FROM OUTSIDE

2620 Bellevue Way NE, #200, Bellevue, WA 98004
(206) 486-6042
www.helpfromoutside.com
info@helpfromoutside.com

Help From Outside provides a wide range of prisoner assistance services, including administrative, paralegal, internet researching, purchases, email, publishing, and banking services. $200 initial deposit, $25 application fee. $30/hour for most services, charged in 15-minute increments ($7.50). Send for FREE brochure.

IN SCAN DOCUMENT SERVICES

401 Wilshire Blvd., 12th Floor, Santa Monica, CA 90401
(800) 470-5338
www.inmatescan.com

In Scan offers document scanning services. Send you documents, which they will scan, store, and send back your originals to you. One-time storage fee of $59.99, plus the price of scanning, ($0.30/page, up to 500 pages; $0.25/per page, over 500 pages.)

INMATE CONCIERGE SERVICES

450 W. Hanes Mill Rd., Suite 226, Winston-Salem, NC 27105
(336) 926-0079
inmateconciergeservices@gmail.com

Inmate Concierge Services offers a wide range of prisoner assistance services, including photocopies, internet research, book and catalog orders and more. Send SASE for pricing and more information.

INMATE LOVE LINK

4001 Inglewood Ave., Suite 144, Redondo Beach, CA 90278
www.inmatelovelink.com support@inmatelovelink.com

Inmate Love Link offers a variety of basic prisoner assistant services, including photocopies, email, and pen pal services (see separate listing.)

INMATE PHOTO PROVIDER | IPP

PO Box 2451, Forrest City, AR 72336
(870) 317-7561
www.inmatephotoprovider.com
socialmedia@inmatephotoprovider.com

Inmate Photo Provider offers some office assistant-type services including social media monitoring, shopping, copying and photo services (see separate listing under *Photo Providers*.)

INMATE SCRIBES

PO Box 818, Appleton, WI 54912

Inmate Scribes offers a number of individual and packaged services, including email, social media, research, friend finding, photos, personal gifts and more.

INMATE SERVICES

PO Box 535547, Grand Prairie, TX 75053
(214) 298-2603
J161jones@yahoo.com

LENOIR PUBLICATIONS

350 Bay St., Suite 100-361, San Francisco, CA 94133
(877) 786-4290
www.lenoirpublications.com
services@lenoirpublications.com

Lenoir Publications provides prisoner publishing services, including editing, typing, printing, and distribution. Send for FREE information.

LET MY FINGERS DO YOUR TYPING

c/o Sandra Z. Thomas, PO Box 4178, Winter Park, FL 21793-4178
(407) 579-5563

Let My Fingers Do Your Typing provides typing, printing, and copy services for prisoners.

LIFETIME LIBERTY GROUP

122 Lakeshore Dr., Suite 692, Lake Harmony, PA 18624-0692
(570) 580-8861
www.lifetimelibertygroup.org
info@lifetimelibertygroup.org

Out of Business

LLG offers a variety of paid administrative services, including banking, purchases, email, internet research, website development, publishing, writing, typing, and much more. $100 initial deposit, $25 enrollment fee. $24-36 per hour for most services, charged in 15-minute increments. Various additional fees. Send $4.50 for their 32-page brochure.

MIDNIGHT EXPRESS BOOKS

PO Box 69, Berryville, AR 72616
(870) 210-3772
mebooks1@yahoo.com

Midnight Express Books provides prisoner book publishing services, including editing, formatting, cover design, and more. They also offer web design, social media posting, book/magazine search/purchase, and more. Send SASE for more information.

ON DEMAND INMATE SERVICES

PO Box 81, Cheltenham, PA 19012
(318) 277-9712
ondemandis@yahoo.com

On Demand provides general prisoner assistance, including posting personal bios online, intimate photos, gift shopping and more. Send $2, or 4 stamps for catalog and services.

PRISONER PROMOTIONS

691 S. Green Bay Rd., #212, Neenah, WI 54956

Prisoner Promotions provides prisoner social media assistance, including email and social media posting. Send SASE for brochure.

SLAMMER BOOKS

Out of Business

PO Box 941, Lake Elsinore, CA 92531
www.slammerbooks.com info@slammerbooks.com

Slammer Books provides prisoner book publishing services including typing, editing, proofing, promotion, and much more. They offer a variety of publishing packages. Write for more information.

TFL

PO Box 171, Glenham, NY 12527

TFL is a pen pal ad forwarding service. If you have a pen pal ad out there already, they will re-list your ad through other providers. Service fee of $15.

VOICE FREEDOM CALLS

2620 Bellevue Way NE, Box 175, Bellevue, WA 98004
www.voicefreedomcalls.com

Voice Freedom Calls offers voicemail and texting solutions for prisoners. They assign you a phone number which you and your friends and family can use as a drop box for messages. They claim that it works will all prison phone providers, subject to prison restrictions. It can not be used from federal facilities.

PHONE SERVICE PROVIDERS

AFFORDABLE INMATE CALLING SERVICES

(866) 645-9593, (303) 214-0097
www.aicsllc.net inmates@aicsllc.net

AICS is a prisoner phone discounter. They offer vanity numbers and monthly phone plans.

CONS CALL HOME

(855) 266-7225
www.conscallhome.com

Cons Call Home provides monthly calling plans. Offers a FREE hour of talk time upon signup.

FASTER LINKS

(855) 671-LINK (5465)
www.fasterlinks.com go@fasterlinks.com

Faster Links provides local phone number setup, $9.99 for the first number, $1.99 each additional number, $10/month for four numbers. Also offers texting and photo services to/from friends and family, through *Corrlinks*. $20/month text, 50 cents/photo.

FREEDOMLINE

PO Box 7, Connersville, IN 47331
www.freedomline.net

Provides phone numbers for $2.50/month. Rates: 5 cents/minute U.S., 15 cents/minute Mexico. 11 cents/minute Canada, 31 cents/minute other international.

INMATEFONE | SP TELECOM

1220 Broadway, #801-A, New York, NY 10001
(845) 326-5300, (845) 342-8110 (en espanol)
www.inmatefone.com clients@inmatefone.com
soprte@inmatefone.com (en espanol)

Provides month-to-month phone services, including multi-number friends and family packages for as little as $10/month.

INMATE TOLLBUSTERS

(888) 966-8655
www.inmatetollbusters.com

Provides monthly calling plans. Rates: $1.25/month plus 6 cents/minute. International calling available.

JAIL CALLS USA

(888) 726-2012
www.jailcallsusa.com

Jail Calls USA provides a monthly calling plan with no per minute charges. $9.95/month, unlimited usage. Works for *GTL, Securus, V-Connect, VAC, PayTel,* and *ICSolutions.*

SENTEL

9550 S. Eastern Ave., Suite 253, Las Vegas, NV 89123
www.sentel.us sentel.va@gmail.com

Sentel offers a variety of phone discount plans from 6 cents/minute to "unlimited" packages. International calls as low as 10 cents/minute.

PHONE DONKEY

Online Only: www.phonedonkey.com
(855) 420-0880

Phone Donkey offers long distance phone solutions to BOP prisoners. They offer a FREE trial period.

TEXT INMATE

Online Only: www.textinmate.com
(855) 420-0880

Text Inmate offers a text messaging service for CorrLinks, which allows friends and family to text to a personal number dedicated to the prisoner.

PHOTO SELLERS

ACME PUBLICATIONS

PO Box 130398, St. Paul, MN 55113

ACME offers celebrity and other non-nude intimate photo options.
Cost: $0.35 per 4x6; $1.50 per 6x9. Quantity deals.

BRANLETTES BEAUTIES

PO Box 5765, Baltimore, MD 21282

Branlettes Beauties sells intimate girl pictures. Nude or BOP-friendly. Prices start at 45 cents per 4x6 glossy. 5000+ photos earn a 20% discount. Send SASE with 2 stamps for 84-image sample catalog.

BUTTERWATER

PO Box 669, Matthews, NC 28106
www.butterwater.com

Butterwater sells intimate girl pictures. They offer FREE catalog of over 300 photos.
cost: 10 4x6 $5.50

BUZZ PHOTOS

PO Box 255, Webb City, MO 64870
buzzphotos045@yahoo.com

Buzz Photos sell a wide variety of intimate pictures in several categories. Send SASE for brochure.

CNN ENTERTAINMENT | CASEY HALL

PO Box 185, Hitchcock, TX 77563
cnatexas@live.com

CNN Entertainment sells intimate girl pictures. Wide selection, pregnant to porn stars, nude or non-nude. 40-90 cents per photo. Catalogs $1.25 each.

COLD CRIB COMMUNICATIONS

PO Box 602487, Franklin, TN 37068
www.coldcrib.com www.coldcribcommuncations.com

Cold Crib Communications sells intimate girl pictures. They also offer discounted phone services and pen pals.

COSIGN PRO

PO Box 1530, Port Richey, FL 34673
www.cosignentertainment.com

CoSign Pro sells sexy girl pictures. Order through catalog/magazines. $10, includes 4 FREE pictures. Also offers phone services (Jailjack: $10/month), pen pal listings ($39.95).

FIEN MAGAZINE | FEDERAL INSTITUTION ENTERTAINMENT NETWORK

2890 Georgia Highway, Suite A-115, Conyers, GA 30084
orderfienmag@gmail.com

Fein Magazine is a catalog that sells BOP-friendly intimate pictures. Order through catalog, $15/catalog, $50/year (4 issues). Accepts *TruLincs*.

FIYA GIRLS | HOT DREAMS

PO Box 112118, Houston, TX 77293
loveaprisoner.com fiyagirls@yahoo.com (Corrlinks registered)

FIYA Girls sells intimate girls pictures. Wide variety of catalog choices. $15 for up to 4,000 photo options. Nude and non-nude. Send $2 (or 5 stamps) for a starter catalogs.

FOR YOUR EYES ONLY

PO Box 1174, San Angelo, TX 76902
(252) 366-9997

For Your Eyes Only sells intimate girl pictures. Cost: Color catalog: $3; B&W: $1.25

F.O.S.

PO Box 42922, Phoenix, AZ 85080

F.O.S. sells intimate girl pictures, displayed in dozens of nude and non-nude catalog sheets. They also buy stamps.

GHOST PHOTOS

PO Box 1591, Rocky Mount, NC 27802

Ghost Photos sells a wide variety of intimate girl pictures, nude and non-nude. They also offer downloads to Mp3s and tablets. Send SASE for brochure or $2 for a catalog.

HOT DREAMS

PO Box 112118, Houston, TX 77293

Hot Dreams sells intimate girl pictures. Catalogs come with one complimentary 4x6 photo. Cost: Catalogs (450 images): $2 (or 5 stamps)

HOT FLIXX

PO Box 137482, Fort Worth, TX 76136

Hot Flixx sells intimate girl pictures. Nude and non-nude. $5 per catalog (150+ pix).

INMATE SERVICES

PO Box 535547, Grand Prairie, TX 75053
(214) 298-2603
www.inmateservices.biz

Inmate Services sells intimate girl pictures. If photos are rejected by your mailroom, they will offer to swap them. Cost: $0.75 per 4x6 photo; catalogs: $4; 3 for $15; 4 for $25

KILL SHOT KING

PO Box 81074, Corpus Christi, TX 81074
(361) 834-5895
www.killshotking.com killshotking@gmail.com

Kill Shot King sells intimate girl pictures, as well as calendars. Catalogs can be downloaded for FREE from their website. Cost: $0.20 to 0.30 per 4x6, depending on quantity.

KRASNYA LLC

PO Box 32082, Baltimore, MD 21282
krasnyababes@hotmail.com

Krasnya LLC sells intimate girl and guy pictures. Nude or BOP-friendly. Prices as low as 35 cents per glossy photo. Offers heavily discounted "grab bags" full of photos. Send SASE with 2 stamps for a 120-image sample catalog. $4.50 (or 10 stamps) for other catalogs.

MAIL CALL ENTERTAINMENT

8034 Culebra Rd., Suite 526m, San Antonio, TX 78251

Mail Call Entertainment sells intimate girl pictures All photos 50 cents. Send SASE for catalog.

MARSHALL BALDWIN PUBLICATIONS

14801 CR 438, Lindale, TX 75771
Marshall Baldwin Publications sells intimate and fetish pictures in over 15 categories.

MARTYSMILLIONS HOT SHOTS

PO Box 513, Manville, NJ 08835
(908) 256-9635

MartysMillions offers intimate nude and non-nude photos, both print (4x6) and for tablets. Send four Forever stamps or $1.50 for catalog and info.

NICKELS AND DIMEZ

14173 Northwest Freeway 154, Houston, TX 77040
(832) 756-3377
www.nickelsanddimez.com
nickelsanddimex1@gmail.com

Nickels and Dimez sells intimate girl pictures. Send SASE with all correspondence. Cost: catalogs: $2 for color; $0.50 for B&W

NUBIAN PRINCESS ENTERTAINMENT

PO Box 37, Timmonsville, SC 29161
www.writesomeoneinprison.com

Nubian Princess Entertainment sells over 7,000 intimate girl pictures.

PHOTO TRYST

PO Box 10756, Jacksonville, FL 32247

Photo Tryst sells intimate girl pictures. Order through catalogs. 450 images per catalog. $4 (or 10 stamps) per catalog. Send SASE for sample catalog. (Not available in OR, UT, DE, or VA.)

PHOTOWORLD

PO Box 401016, Las Vegas, CA 89140

Photo World sells celebrity photos, non-nude,

magazine-type. $2.50 per photo. FREE shipping on orders of $20 or more. Send SASE for star names.

PICTURE ENTERTAINMENT

PO Box 54806, Los Angeles, CA 90054

Picture Entertainment sells intimate girl pictures. 7-photo pack and catalog for $7.50 (or 20 stamps.) Send $2.75 (or 9 stamps) for catalog. They also buy stamps at 31 cents each.

PINEAPPLE PICTURES

PO Box 7732, Round Rock, TX 78683

Pineapple Pictures offers over 11,000 "pictures of men for men" in 22 different categories. Send SASE for more details.

SB STUDIOS | SUMMER BUNNIES

PO Box 741145, Houston, TX 77274-1145
www.summerbunnies.com

SB Studios sells professional intimate model pictures as individual photos and trading cards. Cost: Trading card sets: 20 for $10 (plus $2 postage)

SOUTH BEACH SINGLES

PO Box 1656, Miami, FL 33238
www.southbechsingles.ning.com

South Beach Singles sells intimate girl pictures and calendars. send $1 to be added to their mailing list. Cost: $1 per 4x6; discounts for quantity.

SENZA

PO Box 5840, Baltimore, MD 21282

Senza offers intimate girl pictures. Nude or non-nude. 4x6 glossy: 1-5 $1 each, 6-15 41.50 each, 16-25 $2 each, plus $1 shipping. 1,000+ at one time, $0.30 each. Order by type: Caucasian, Asian, African American, Hispanic, or mixed. Send SASE with 2 stamps for a 99-image catalog. Other catalogs $2.50 each.

SOILED DOVES

PO Box 2588, Fernley, NV 89408

Soiled Doves sells intimate girl pictures. Nude of non-nude. $0.80 each 4x6 glossy photo. 10-photo minimum. Order by type. They can also send photos through *Access Corrections*. Other catalogs begin at $3. Send SASE for sample catalog.

STABLE ENTERTAINMENT

PO Box 1352, Lancaster, TX 75146
69stable@gmail.com

Stable Entertainment sells intimate non-nude girl pictures.

SURROGATE SISTERS

PO Box 95043, Las Vegas, NV 89123
www.surrogatesisters.com
service@surrogatesisters.com

Surrogate Sisters sells intimate girl pictures. Nude and non-nude. They also offer gifts, pen pal services, erotic stories, and more.

PHOTO SERVICE PROVIDERS

FASTER LINKS

(855) 671-LINK (5465)
www.fasterlinks.com go@fasterlinks.com (Corrlinks)

Faster Links provides photo delivery and texting services for *Corrlinks* customers who use their phone number services. Friends and family text photo to your phone number, which *Faster Links* prints and sends to you. 50 cents/photo. $20/month for texting.

INMATE PHOTO PROVIDER | IPP

PO Box 2451, Forrest City, AR 72336
(870) 317-7561
www.inmatephotoprovider.com
info@inmatephotoprovider.com

Inmate Photo Provider provides photo delivery services. Friends/family email or text photos, which IPP prints and sends to prisoner $0.50 cents/photo. $10 minimum to open a prepaid account. They also provide printing services from Facebook, Instagram and enlargements. Special effects available including alternative backgrounds, clothing and people placement in photos starting at $15. Other services available. See *Office Services* section. Send SASE for more information.

PELIPOST

www.pelipost.com

Pelipost provides photo delivery services. Friends/family upload photos through *Pelipost's* website, which are then printed and sent to prisoner. Photos can also be personalized with captions. They advertise 3-5 day delivery service. 10 for $4.95, 20 for $7.95, 30 for $9.95. FREE trial available.

PRISON PACKAGES

BUST THE MOVE

PO Box 1026, Point Pleasant Beach, NJ 08742
(800) 676-0286
www.bustthemove.com

Bust the Move sells a wide variety of products for prisoners, including clothing, electronics, cosmetics, shoes and more.

SECURE ELECTRONICS

5569 Route 9 West, Building 1, Marlboro, NY 12542
(570) 704-3451
www.s-celectronics.com

Secure Electronics produces and supplies clear electronics and accessories to prisons and prisoners. Send SASE for a catalog and more information.

SHIP A PACKAGE

33 William St., Suite 8A, Auburn, NY 13021
(800) 918-9352
www.shipapackage.net

Ship A Package supplies care packages to the New York area. Write for a FREE catalog.

RELIGIOUS SUPPLIES

AZURE GREEN

16 Bell Rd., PO Box 48, Middlefield, MA 02143
(413) 623-2155
www.azuregreen.net

Azure Green offers a wide variety of spiritual items, including Tarot cards, books, and medallions and other jewelry for various religions. Send $5 for 150+ page catalog.

CRAZY COW TRADING POST

PO Box 847, Pottsboro, TX 75076
(800) 786-6210
www.crazycow.com

Crazy Cow sells American Indian crafts and supplies.

DIAMMA AK HEWEL

934 NE 21st St., Oklahoma City, OK 73105
(405) 521-8817
www.diammaakhewel.com

Diamma Ak Hewel sells a wide variety of religious oils and incense products, as well as healing ointments, soaps, and more. Write for a FREE catalog.

GOLDSTAR FRAGRANCES

4 West 37th St., New York, NY 10018
(212) 279-4474, (212) 279-4470
www.goldstarfragrances.com
gstarfragrances@gmail.com

Goldstar Fragrances offers a wide variety of religious incenses, oils, and more. Send for a FREE catalog.

HALALCO BOOKS & SUPERMARKET

155 Hillwood Ave., Falls Church, VA 22046
(703) 532-3202
www.halalco.com

Halalco offers a wide variety of Muslim items, including body oils and medallions. Write for FREE catalog.

JEWISH SUPPLIES

9540 Collins Ave., Surfside, FL 33154-7127
(305) 866-5875
www.jewishsupply.com sales@jewishsupply.com

Jewish Supply sells a wide array of Jewish items to prisoners, including daily prayer and Sabbath items, a variety of books, DVDs and CDs, and much more. Write for more information.

NOC BAY TRADING COMPANY

PO Box 295, Escanaba, MI 49829
(800) 652-7192
www.nocbay.com

NOC Bay sells a wide variety of Native American crafts and other supplies.

TIBETAN SPIRIT

PO Box 57, Boonsboro, MD 21713-0057
(888) 327-2890, (301) 416-2712
www.tibetanspirit.com shop@tibetanspirit.com

Tibetan Spirit offers a large selection of Buddhist items at competitive prices. Write for a FREE catalog.

STAMP BUYERS

CASH FOR UR STAMPS

PO Box 687, Walnut Creek, CA 91788
tacks1000@yahoo.com

Cash for Ur Stamps buys unused stamps for 60- 70% of their face value.

FRIENDS BEYOND THE WALL

36 Cottage St., Suite 202, Poughkeepsie, NY 12601

Friends Beyond the Wall purchases unused forever stamps for cash, 70% face value -- minimum of 200 stamps., only in books or strips.

GREAT GOODS

PO Box 888, Lake Worth, FL 33460
Greatgoods888@gmail.com

Great Goods buys unused stamps for between 60 and 70% face value, within 24 hours of receipt. $20 minimum.

PRISON LIVES

PO Box 842, Exeter, CA 93221
www.prisonlives.com

Yes, we buy stamps too! 80% face value. No single, stapled, torn or used stamps accepted.

FREE Pen Pal Services

Attention:

The following listings try to provide FREE pen pals to prisoners, with varying degrees of success. Some organizations may find a pen pal for each prisoner they hear from, while others may never be heard from again. (Many do not have staffing necessary to reply to all inquiries.) But they are FREE, so you can't go wrong in trying them out. You never know. You may make the best friend you never knew existed.

Do NOT send SASE unless otherwise noted.

Remember, if they are located outside of the U.S., you'll have to send your letter in an *international* envelope.

ALIVE

Postfach 13 26, 46363 Bocholt, Germany

ALIVE typically provides pen pals to death row prisoners in the U.S., but they have provided assistance to others.

BLACK & PINK

c/o Community Church of Boston, 565 Boylston St., Boston, MA 02116

Black & Pink provides pen pals to LGBT prisoners.

CANADIAN COALITION AGAINST THE DEATH PENALTY

80 Lillington Ave., Toronto, Ontario M1N 3K7, Canada
www.ccadp.org

CCADP provides pan pals for death row prisoners only. Send up to 3 paragraphs for posting on their website.

CHARITY FOUNDATION & LIBRARY

4 Chiou, Chalandri, Athens, Greece 15231

CHRISTIAN PEN PALS

PO Box cpp-ministry.com

CPP provides pen pals to prisoners who would like spiritual support. They assist prisoners, their families, and prison chaplain services. Include your areas of interest and what you want in a pen pal with your inquiry.

CHRISTIAN PEN PALS

Attn: Veteran's Ministry
PO Box 2112, Stateville, NC 28687
Veteransministry.com/registeraninmate.htm

CPP's Veteran's Ministry provides pan pals to incarcerated veterans. Send personal information along with release date, education level, dates of military service, religion, and a statement about what you want out of a pen pal.

CROSSROADS PEN PAL MINISTRY

PO Box 363, Hyde Park, PA 16843

DEATH ROW SUPPORT PROJECT

PO Box 600, Dept. P, Liberty Mills, IN 46946

Offers pen pal assistance to death row prisoners. They can also connect Spanish speakers.

EUROPEAN ASSOCIATION FOR HUMAN RIGHTS

Frankfurter Strasse 106A, 34121 Kassel, Germany

Primarily assists Texas prisoners, but may be worth a try if from other states.

GENDER MUTINY COLLECTIVE

PO Box 0494, Chapel Hill, NC 27514

GMC provides pen pals to LGBT prisoners.

GERMAN COALITION TO ABOLISH THE DEATH PENALTY

Bahnhofstr 40, 97944 Boxberg, Germany

GCADP primarily provides pen pals to death row prisoner in the U.S. They post exactly what you write them on their website.

HEARTS ON A WIRE

PO Box 36831, Philadelphia, PA 19107

HW provides pen pals to LGBT prisoners.

HUMAN WRITES

34 Downsview Crescent, Uckfield, East Sussex, TN22 1UB, United Kingdom
www.humanwrites.org

Human Writes befriends death row prisoners in the U.S. through organized pen pal coordination. They are long-established and one of the more reliable death row pen pal organizations, offering a coordinator for each state's death row. HW has a newsletter, which death row prisoners can submit art and writings to for possible publication. They encourage prisoners to send used stamps with their correspondence, which they can use to raise funds for further HW efforts. Remember to use international postage when corresponding!

INSIGHT PRISON PROJECT

PO Box 169, Woodacre, CA 94973

IPP is based out of the Spirit Rock Meditation Center, a Buddhist organization. They provide Buddhism discussion-based pen pals to all interested.

LIFELINES

63 Forest Rd., Garston, Watford, WD25 7QP, United Kingdom
http://www.lifelines-uk.org.uk/

Lifelines seeks to provide prisoners with international pen pals, especially for those who live on death row. Prisoners are encouraged to send an international SASE with a request for a pen pal, and to be patient -- the process can take 3 to 4 months. Remember to use international postage when corresponding!

LOSTVAULT

PO Box 242, Mascot, TN 37806
www.lostvault.com

LostVault primarily provides pen pals to death row prisoner in the U.S. NOTE: FREE if submitted online, $5 otherwise.

MOVING ON MINISTRY

PO Box 6667, Visalia, CA 93290

Moving on Ministry provides a newsletter pen pal listing.

PEN PAL PROGRAMS

PO Box 17500, Washington, DC 20041

Pen pal program for prisoners with at least 24 months left on their sentence.

PRISONER CORRESPONDENCE PROJECT

C/o Concordia University, 1455 de Maisonneuve O, Montreal, QC H3G 1M8, Canada

PCP provides pen pals to LGBT prisoners in Canada and the U.S.

PRISONERLIFE.COM

PO Box 1664, Voorhees, NJ 08043
www.prisonerlife.com

PrisonerLife.com was created by prisoners and is maintained by prisoner volunteers. Some pay services options (Ad-page with photo, $35/year.) Write for more info.

PRISON MINISTRY PEN PALS

PO Box 73, Syracuse, NY 13206-0073

Christian based ministry program. They request that prisoners send stamps as donation, if possible.

PRISON PEN PALS

PO 120997, Ft. Lauderdale, FL 3312

PPP places your name on a list, which they send out to interested parties. They may take a few months to respond.

REACHING BEYOND THE WALLS

PO Box 6905, Rutland, VT 05702-6905
www.reachingbeyondthewalls.com

RBW offers prisoner pen pal listings on their website. Send what you'd like posted, including, text, photos, poetry, etc. Send SASE for more info.

TIG PRISONER PEN PAL PROJECT

PO Box 1122, Portland, OR 97221

TIG provides pen pals to transgender/transsexual, intersex, and gender questioning prisoners.

WORLDWIDE FRIENDS

PO Box 14, Harrah, OK 73045

WF provides pen pals to Native American prisoners.

WRITE TO WIN COLLECTIVE

2040 N. Milwaukee Ave., Chicago, IL 60647

WWC provides pen pals to LGBT prisoners.

PAY Pen Pal Services

Attention:
The following pen pal services require you to pay a subscription of membership fee, typically monthly, biannually or annually. Always contact the services directly for information and current pricing, but most importantly to find out what you are getting for your money. Use at your own risk.

BLACKFACE PRODUCTIONS

c/o Joseph Doss or Richard Boyd, PO Box 4231, Santa Clara, CA 95056
www.blackfaceinc.com

BlackFace states that they are "the world's first adult-rated "pen pal match-making" dating site. Send SASE and one clean book of USPS Forever stamps or $10 for details, application, and brochure.

CELLPALS

PO Box 13278, Las Cruces, NM 88013
(855) 736-7257
www.cellpals.com

CellPals offers a wide array of packages. Write for current options.

Profile: Varies by package choice

Cost: Varies by package choice ($5 to $50)

CONPALS INMATE CONNECTIONS.COM

465 NE 181st Ave., #308, Portland, OR 97230-6660
www.inmateconnections.com *info@conpals.com (CorrLinks)*

Conpals advertises 75,000+ hits daily to their website and an 89% response rate. Site advertisements start at $45. Offers email forwarding, photo modification, "how-to" info and more. Stamps accepted. Send SASE for more info. Habla espanol.

CONVICT MAILBAG

PO Box 661, Redonda Beach, CA 90277
www.convictmailbag.com

CM prices begin at $40/year. 250 words and photo. Feature ad for $15/month. Send SASE for more info.

CONVICT PEN PALS

465 181st St., #308, Portland, OR 97230
www.convictpenpals.com

Moderate to expensive pricing. Offers site placement, social networking (*Facebook, Twitter*). Stamps accepted for payment.

FRIENDS BEYOND THE WALL

2600 South Rd., Suite 44-244, Poughkeepsie, NY 12601-7003
www.friendsbeyondthewall.com
info@friendsbeyondthewall.com

FBW has been in the pen pal business for over a decade. $39.95 per year for a 250 word profile. Offers FREE newsletter and ad placement tips to prisoner members. Send SASE for brochure and application.

FRIENDSHIPS AND MORE

PO Box 1304, Miami, FL 33265
www.friendshipsandmore.com
webmaster@friendshipsandmore.com

Reasonably-priced option that allows you to add additional elements for small fees. Stamps accepted.

Profile: 50 words; one photo. Additional options can be added, such as 100 words for $5 more.

Cost: $20 per year; additional options will increase the price.

GAY PRISONERS USA (GPUSA)

PO Box 19134, St. Louis, MO 63118
www.gayprisoers.net *gayprisoners@gmail.com*

Requires mail-in registration directly from the prisoner and that the prisoner be gay or bisexual. So long as you let them know each year that you would like to continue the add, no additional annual fees are required.

Profile: 100 words; one photo

Cost: $10 per year; premium ad $25 per year

INMATE CLASSIFIED

PO Box 3311, Granada Hills, CA 91394
(323) 529-8570
www.inmate.com

IC is one of the oldest, yet priciest prisoner pen pal sites around. Pen pal ads on their website range from $10-15/month, $60/6 months, $100/year for 300 word profile and one photo. Premium ads, $120/6 months,

$200/year. Includes weekly messaging service, and *Facebook*. Send SASE for a brochure.

INMATE-CONNECTION.COM

PO Box 83897, Los Angeles, CA 90083
www.inmate-connection.com
info@inmate-connection.com

IC (not to be confused with the next 'Inmate Connections' listing) offers a full web page for each prisoner subscriber. $30 per year, $40/2 years for 100 word profile and one photo. Send SASE for more info.

INMATE LOVE LINK

4001 Inglewood Ave., Suite 144, Redondo Beach, CA 90278
www.inmatelovelink.com

They offer pan pal ads and basic prisoner services (See separate listing). They offer several profile options. Write for current packages.

Profile: 250 words; one photo. $5 for 75 additional words.

Cost: $20 per year; Premium listing: $20 for 6 months/$35 per year.

JAIL MAIL

ONLINE SUBMISSIONS ONLY:www.jailmail.com

Jail Mail is an online only prisoner pen pal site. they offer a variety of options. Outside assistance will be required.

Profile: 200 words; one photo; one poem or artwork. Premium listing; 400 words; three photos; three poems or artwork.

Cost: $30 per year; premium listing $50 per year

J&J HOLDINGS

PO Box 1023, Danville, IL 61834

J&J Holdings provides pen pal address of women for $10 or 40 Forever stamps.

LOVE A PRISONER

PO Box 112118, Houston, TX77293
www.loveaprisoner.com loveaprisoner@gmail.com

Offers a variety of additional options. Send SASE for brochure.

Profile: 250 words; one photo

Cost: $25 per year. VIP service: $65 per year.

LOVELY FRIENDS DIRECT

PO Box 1304, Miami, FL 33465
www.lovelyfriendsdirect.com

Owned and operated by Moonlight Productions 9see separate listing). Stamps accepted.

Profile: 50 words. Additional fee ($5) for 50 more words and one photo

Cost: $20 per year

MEET-AN-INMATE

PO Box 1342, Pendleton, OR 97801
www.meet-an-inmate.com

MIA lists prisoner ads on their site for $20 per 6 months for 250 word profile and two photos. $35 for featured ad on own page, with a link on their homepage. Send SASE for more info.

MYPRISONPENPALS.COM

c/o Mail Call Entertainment, 8034 Culebra Rd., Suite 526 San Antonio, TX 78251
www.myprisonpenpals.com

MPPP advertises they are a part of a network of pen pal sites, so that your ad gets placed on multiple sites. $50/year. Send SASE for more info.

NUBIAN PRINCESS ENTERTAINMENT

PO Box 37, Timmonsville, SC 29161

NPE was established in 1998 and advertises that they guarantee responses. Send $3 and an SASE for more information.

PENACON.COM

Box 533, North Dighton, MA 02764
www.penacon.com penacon@freebirdpublishers.com

PenACon offers annual or lifetime membership. $35/year, $95 lifetime. They print and send emailed messages every 2 weeks. Friends/family may submit profile online for $10 savings. Welcome package for $5, or send SASE for more info.

PENPALCONNECTION.NET

Po Box 1352, Elgin, SC 29045
www.penpalconnection.net
contact@penpalconnection.net (CorrLinks registered)

Prices start at $15. Offers unique services, such as slide shows of your images and background music on your ad page. Send SASE for more info.

PRISONER PAL

PO Box 19689, Houston, TX 77224

www.prisonerpal.com

Prisoner Pal will host an personal ad for you on their website for one year for $9.95. Write for FREE order form and info.

PRISON INMATES.COM

8033 W. Sunset Blvd., #7000, Los Angeles, CA 90046
www.prisoninmates.com info@prisoninmates.com

Prison Inmates.com offers their pen pal services "for life," meaning that so long as you update your profile annually, they will continue to list it. They also offer messaging forwarding services, as well as blogging, poetry, document and YouTube video posting to your profile. For an extra fee they will "Feature" you profile on each page of their site to enhance your chances of being seen. Price for the service is $50 (for life). Their "Featured" service is $30 per month, or $180 per year.

PRISON INMATES ONLINE

8033 W. Sunset Blvd., suite 7000, Los Angeles, CA 90046
www.prisonerinmates.com info@prisonerinmates.com

Site sorts profiles according to several categories to help those 8seeking pen pals to find the most appropriate match. They also offer art, tattoos, poetry classifieds and other posting options.

Profile: 300 words; one photo

Cost: $50 for life. Other prices apply for add-ons.

PRISONER PAL

c/o TIC Interest, PO Box 19689, Houston, TX 77224
www.prisonerpal.com

Offers several levels of service. Send SASE for current package options.

Profile: Ranges from 50 to 300 words, depending on package

Cost: Packages: $9.95; $19.95; $39.95; $79.95 per year.

PRISONPENPALS.COM

PO Box 235, East Berlin, PA 17316
www.prisonpenpals.com ads@prisonpenpals.com

PPP has provided personal and legal assistance ads since 1996. Pricing from $10-100. Offers unique services, such as background music on your ad page. Accepts PayPal.

SURROGATE SISTERS

PO Box 95043, Las Vegas, NV 89123
www.surrogatesisters.com
service@surrogatesisters.com

Surrogate Sisters offers limited pen pal services. Send a SASE for more information.

WRITE4LIFE

613 Bryden Ave., Suite C226, Lewiston, ID 83501
www.write4life.org contactusatwriteforlife@gmail.com

Write4Life advertises that they'll provide you with a "guaranteed fictional pen pal" for $10/month.

WRITEAPRISONER.COM

PO Box 10, Edgewater, FL 32132
(386) 427-5857
www.writeaprisoner.com

WP is the largest pen pal site. Prices begin at $40/year. Offers unique services, such as visitor "subscriptions" to your page to receive auto updates as you post them. FREE resume service to members. Send SASE.

Pen Pals Exclusively For Women Prisoners

BABES BEHIND BARS

4246 Albert St., Suite 403, Regina, Saskatchewan, Canada S4S 3R9
www.babes-behind-bars.com

Send international SASE for more information.

Profile: 100 words; one photo

CAPTIVE ANGELS

PO Box 13152, Las Cruces, NM 88013
www.captiveangels.com info@captiveangels.com

Prices are not listed on their site. Write for a brochure.

FORGOTTEN FEMALES

c/o McLloyd Services, PO Box 3621, Wichita, KS 67201
www.forgottenfemales.tripod.com
forgottenfemales@yahoo.com

The Forgotten Females site is a place for sincere incarcerated women to tell their stories to the world, for whom they allow personal listings on their site. Contact for any guidelines.

Cost: FREE

PAPER DOLLS

PO Box 218, Oregon, WI 53575
www.paperdollspenpals.com paperdolls@mail.com

They may post your profile at no cost, but they suggest that you send $5 for your listing to be guaranteed.

Profile: 100 words; 1 photo

Cost: $5 setup. Email-to-mail forwarding: $5/month; $50/year

PRISON PRINCESSES

c/o Foster-Hansen Holdings, PO Box 864862, Plano, TX 75086-4862
www.prisonprincesses.com

They may place your ad for the cost of 2 Forever stamps, but they recommend that you send $7.50 (18 stamps) for a guaranteed listing and a copy of your page.

Profile: 100 words; one photo

Cost: $7.50 setup; $15 for a premium ad on their homepage

WOMEN BEHIND BARS

c/o Todd Muffoletto, PO Box 284, Hobart, IN 46342
www.womenbehindbars.com

Free to prisoners. Instead they require a small fee ($) from the outside writer for the prisoner's contact information.

Profile: Request an application

Cost: FREE

Outside World Pen Pals

The following pen pal companies (dating sites) are NOT set up exclusively for prisoners, but they do allow prisoner profiles. All of them require online registration and responses will typically come via email, so you will likely need outside assistance.

Note: Some of these sites require that you to disclose that you are incarcerated.

FOREIGN LADIES

ONLINE SUBMISSIONS ONLY:
www.foreignladies.com
(408) 372-2100

This site features women from around the world, including China, Russia, the Philippines and more. They charge for correspondence through their site once you make a connection.

Profile: 100 words; one photo

Cost: FREE to post; Credits required to correspond through their site (credit packages start at $7.50)

FRIENDS WITH PENS

ONLINE SUBMISSIONS ONLY:
www.friendswithpens.com

This site leans on the conservative side, so modest posts are appreciated. Posts include options such as music and video attachments. Have outside assistance request their brochure to be sent to you, which will answer any questions.

Profile: 100 words; photos; other attachments

Cost: FREE

JADE ROSES

ONLINE SUBMISSIONS ONLY: *www.jaderoses.com*

Prisoners must disclose that they are incarcerated.

Profile: 100 words; one photo

Cost: FREE

PEN PAL WORLD

ONLINE SUBMISSIONS ONLY:
www.penpalworld.com

Large pen pal site claiming over one million pen pals. They allow FREE messaging for the first contact. Prices apply thereafter if you continue to correspond though the site.

Profile: 100 words; one photo

Cost: FREE

PEN PAL PARTY

ONLINE SUBMISSIONS ONLY:
www.penpalparty.com

Site claims 20,000 pen pals from over 165 countries. This site does not allow you to post your physical address, so you will need to have access to outside email. They also require you to disclose that you are incarcerated (in the 'occupation' portion of the registration.)

Priofile: 100 words; one photo

Cost: FREE

ZOOSK

ONLINE SUBMISSIONS ONLY: *www.zoosk.com*

(888) 939-6675

Zoosk is a popular dating site, boasting over 50 million members. The service is FREE, but it will require access to the site for correspondence.

Profile: Online registry form

Cost: FREE

Art & Writing

PRISONER ART SELLERS

There are dozens of websites claiming to sell prisoner art. Most of these are "mom & pop" sites that may disappear while your art is in transit. Therefore, below are only sites that have been verified and are most likely to draw the traffic necessary to get your artwork seen. But as always, use at your own risk.

DEVIANT ART

7905 Hollywood Blvd., #788, Hollywood, CA 90028
www.deviantart.com

DA is a large online art dealer that sells "deviant" art. Not specifically a prison art dealer, but prisoners can display and sell their art on the site. Over 4 million *Facebook* followers. Offers art in over 2000 categories. Must contact through their website.

EBAY

www.ebay.com/bhp/prison-art

eBay has a wide variety of prisoner art for sale that friends and family of prisoners can post for profit. Art coalitions are encouraged to expand their marketing through *eBay's* prison art outlet. Must contact through their website.

JAIL SERGEANT.COM (AKA, BIG HOUSE PRISON ART.COM

PO Box 1511, Interlochen, MI 49643
www.jailsergeant.com

JailSergeant.com is a large online seller of prisoner art. You must contact them through their website.

SAFE STREETS ART FOUNDATION

2512 Virginia Ave. NW, #58043, Washington, DC 20037
www.safestreetarts.org
sales@safestreetarts.org

SSA accepts prisoner art for display and sale at various art galleries. Send SASE for more info. General submission guidelines: Simply send your art to them, which they will prepare for display at no cost to you. Include name and address on the back of your art, and description of your piece, and any background or additional info you'd like to include. They pay you 50% of the selling price, less any matting/framing expenses incurred.

SAN QUENTIN PRISON ART

www.sanquentinprisonart.com

San Quentin Prison Art is a site dedicated to the sales of art from prisoners housed on death row in San Quentin. Prisoners housed there are encouraged to display their art, with the possibility of selling it. Must contact through their website.

ART PERIODICALS

AMERICAN ARTIST

770 Broadway, New York, NY 10003
www.myamericanartist.com
4 issues/year

American Artist features artists, their art, and discussions of their techniques.

AMERICAN INDIAN ART

7314 E. Osborn Dr., Scottsdale, AZ 85251
www.aiamagazine.com
4 issues/year

Focuses on contemporary American Indian art.

ARTIST'S MAGAZINE

700 E. Galbraith Rd., Cincinnati, OH 45235
www.artistsmagazaine.com
10 issues/year

How-to info and detailed instruction on various art genres.

BEAD & BUTTON

PO Box 1612, Waukesha, WI 53187
www.beadandbutton.com
6 issues/year

Materials, ideas, and techniques on bead working.

CREATIVE KEEPSAKES

14850 Pony Express Rd., Bluffdale, UT 84065
12 issues/year

Extensive scrapbooking techniques and instruction.

DRAWING | AMERICAN ARTIST

770 Broadway, New York, NY 10003
www.myamericanartist.com
4 issues/year

Learning the art of sketching.

INTERNATIONAL ARTIST

6 issues/year

Profiles the world's greatest artists and their working methods.

JEWELRY ARTIST

300 Chesterfield Pkwy., Suite 100, Malvern, PA 19355
9 issues/year

Formerly the Lapidary Journal. Features articles on gemstones, artist profiles, bead and jewelry arts, and easy-to-follow instructions.

LEATHER CRAFTERS AND SADDLERS JOURNAL

331 Annette Ct., Rhinelander, WI 54501
www.leathercraftersjournal.com
6 issues/year

Leather crafting techniques for all skill levels.

PAPER CRAFTS

14850 Pony Express, Bluffdale, UT 84065
www.papercraftsmagazine.com
10 issues/year

Extensive paper crafting techniques and instruction,

PASTEL JOURNAL

6 issues/year

Leading publication on pastel art instruction for all skill levels.

PROFESSIONAL ARTIST

11 issues/year

Business publication for visual artists. Provides income resources and opportunities.

SUNSHINE ARTIST

4075 L.B. McLead Rd., Suite E, Orlando, FL 32811
www.sunshineartist.com
12 issues/year

Articles on marketing crafts and selling art. Detailed coverage of the nation's art shows.

WATERCOLOR ARTIST

8 issues/year

Profiles the best watercolor artists and discusses their technique.

WATER COLOR | AMERICAN ARTIST

770 Broadway, New York, NY 10003
www.myamericanartist.com
4 issues/year

Tips and tricks on watercolor painting. Also reviews the latest art supplies and instructional books.

PRISONER WRITER RESOURCES

DEVINE BOOKS

PO Box 4026, Flint, MI 48504
www.devinebooks.web.com, devinebooks@ymail.com

Devine Books offers a variety of publishing services, including typing, editing, publication and advertising. Also offers website building services. Send SASE for newsletter and info.

F&W PUBLICATIONS

4700 Gallbraith Rd., Cincinnati, OH 45236
(800) 333-0133
www.writersmarket.com

Publishes *Writer's Market, 4th Edition*, a 919-page book for writers, packed with publishers, trade journals, literary agents, and other helpful resources. $29.95 list, but you can find it new at discount booksellers for as low as $11.95.

FREEBIRD PUBLISHERS

Box 541, North Dighton, MA 02764
(774) 406-8682
www.freebirdpublishers.com
diane@freebirdpublishers.com

Freebird Publishers offers self-publishing services, from the written page to book. Send $3 (or 8 FCS stamps) for and information package.

HOLLYWOOD WRITERS STUDIO

1437 Rising Glen Rd., Las Angeles, CA 90069
www.hollywoodwritersstudio.com

HWS accepts manuscripts for agency representation consideration for potential production in the film industry.

JME WORD PROCESSING

510 State Highway 67, #6, Woodland Park, CO 80863
(720) 416-5208
www.jeanniemay.com jeanniemay@jeanniemay.com

JME provides word processing services for writers, including typing, editing, formatting, and transcriptions.

LENOIR PUBLICATIONS

350 Bay St., Suite 100-361, San Francisco, CA 94133
(877) 786-4290
www.lenoirpublications.com,
services@lenoirpublications.com

LeNoir Publications offers a variety of publishing services, including typing, editing, publication and advertising.

MIDNIGHT EXPRESS BOOKS

PO Box 69, Berryville, AR 72616
(870) 210-3772
www.midnightexpressbooks.com

Midnight Express Books offers a variety of publishing services, including typing, editing, cover design, layout, publication and advertising. They also offer website building and maintenance, and other office services. Send SASE for more info.

NATIONAL ASSOCIATION OF WRITERS AND EDITORS

PO Box 549, Ashland, VA 23005
www.naiwe.com

Provides support services and to aspiring writers to assist them with freelancing, marketing, and publishing.

PEN PRISON WRITING PROGRAM

PEN American Center, 588 Broadway, Suite 303, New York, NY 10012
(212) 334-1660 ext. 117
www.pen.org prisonwriting@pen.org

PEN encourages prisoners to become writers through information and contests. Their FREE publication, *Handbook for Writers in Prison,* is full of resources for the aspiring prisoner writer. Also sponsors annual prisoner writing contests in poetry, fiction, nonfiction, and drama (typically no more than 25 pages in length, deadline: September 1), with cash prizes of $50 - $200 every March. Write for more info.

POETS & WRITERS MAGAZINE

PO Box 422460, Palm Coast, FL 32142

Comprehensive writer's resource magazine for aspiring poets and other writers, including tips, contests, grants, and much more.

PROFESSIONAL PRESS

PO Box 3581, Chapel Hill, NC 27515-3581
(800) 277-8960
www.profpress.com professionalpress1@gmail.com

Professional Press provides book publishing services, including typesetting, formatting, cover design, editing, marketing and more.

WORDSTATION

391 Brick Blvd., Brick, NJ 08723
(800) 538-8206
wordstation@comcast.net

Wordstation provides word processing services for writers, including typing/syntax editing. FREE sample pages on request.

WRITER'S DIGEST MAGAZINE

Editorial: 10151 Carver Rd., Suite 200, Blue Ash, OH 45242
(513) 531-2690
Subscriptions: PO Box 421751, Palm Coast, FL 32142
(800) 333-0133
www.writersdigest.com

Comprehensive writer's resource magazine for aspiring writers of all kinds, including tips, agents, contests and much more.

Writer's Digest Magazine hosts an annual writing competition!

This year's contest will have over 500 winners in 10 writing categories, with prizes as high as $5000 and a chance at agency representation. Subscribe to Writer's Digest, or write their editorial address for more information.

GET PUBLISHED

WRITE FOR US!

Prison Lives is looking for talented writers to join our online blog community:
Writing on the Wall
Find details at the end of the book.

AMERICAN DISSIDENT

217 Commerce Rd., Barnstable, MA 02630

American Dissident accepts poems and essays, up to 650 words, in English, Spanish, or French. They look for works that involve conflicts similar to what prisoners face every day.

AMERICAN PRISON WRITING ARCHIVE (APWA)

198 College Hill Rd., Clinton, NY 13323-1218
www.dhinitiative.org/projects/apwa

APWA accepts non-fiction prisoner written essays focusing on prison conditions for publishing on their website, 5,000-word max. Write for guidelines.

BEAT WITHIN

275 Ninth St., San Francisco, CA 94103
(415) 503-4170
www.thebeatwithin.org

The Beat Within accepts prisoner written essays, commentary, and poetry directed towards teaching, inspiring, and giving hope. Write for submission guidelines. They are unable to provide free subscriptions. Donations are appreciated.

GENERAL MEDIA COMMUNICATIONS (PENTHOUSE)

2 Penn Plaza, 11th Floor, New York, NY 10121
www.penthouse.com

Get published in Penthouse magazine. Seeks erotic submissions. Write for more info.

HASTING'S WOMEN'S LAW JOURNAL

100 McAlister, Suite 2207, San Francisco, CA 94102
hwlsubmissions@gmail.com

Hastings seeks writings from women prisoners. Can be fiction or non-fiction prison related writing, poetry, or sons. Write for submission guidelines.

INSTITUTE OF CHILDREN'S LITERATURE

93 Long Ridge Rd., West Reddington, CT 06896
(800) 243-9645
www.theinstituteofchildrensliterature.com

ICL seeks manuscripts for children's books. Also offers writing tutorials and assists with connections in the field of children's literature. Write for more info.

JOURNAL OF PRISONERS ON PRISONERS

542 King Edward Ave., Ottawa, Ontario, Canada K1N 6N2
www.jpp.org jpp@uottawa.ca

Journal of Prisoners on Prisoners is an annual publication that seeks submissions from prisoner writers, including papers, collaborative essays, interviews, book reviews, and photo or graphic essays. No fiction or poetry. Write for more info. Publishes articles in French and English.

MURIEL RUKYSER POETRY WALL

Cathedral of St. John the Divine, 1047 Amsterdam Ave. New York, NY 10025

Seeks poetry submissions in any language for public display on church walls.

POET'S WORKSHOP | ST. LOUIS COUNTY JAIL

4334 Haines Rd., Duluth, MN 55811

The Poet's Workshop publishes a monthly magazine. They encourage poetry submissions from prisoners. If you are published in their pages, they will provide the magazine to you FREE of charge.

REJECTED QUARTERLY

PO Box 1351, Cobb, CA 95426

Rejected Quarterly seeks writing submissions that have previously been rejected by other publishers. Must submit 5 rejection letters for every piece you submit. Send SASE for more.

PRISONS FOUNDATION

2512 Virginia Ave., NW #58043, Washington, DC 20037
(202) 393-1511
www.prisonsfoundation.org

Seeks prisoner writings for publication on their website, any subject, uncensored. A good source for attracting agents or attention to others interested in prisoner writings. Will scan your handwritten or types pages in (manuscripts: 100 to 600 pages; plays, music, poetry: 20 to 150 pages) and post as-is. Write for more info.

SUN MAGAZINE

107 N. Roberson St., Chapel Hill, NC 27516
(919) 942-5282
www.thesunmagazine.org

Seeks personal essays, short stories, interviews, and poetry from prisoner writers. Write for submission guidelines and/or FREE subscription to their magazine.

TOCSIN MAGAZINE

PO Box 64527, Rochester, NY 14624
www.tocsinmag.com

Tocsin is an urban entertainment magazine for prisoners and their families. They encourage prisoners to submit articles and photos for publication.

X PUBLISHING, INC.

818 SW 3rd Ave., Suite 1324, Portland, OR 97204
(503) 816-4174
www.xmag.com

Seeks true story and fiction erotica. Send SASE for more info. Send 9x12 SASE with 5 stamps for sample magazine.

FREE BOOKS

Keep in Mind...

Most FREE-books-to prisoners programs are sparsely staffed donor-supported organizations. They are generally established out of the kindness of individuals who wish they had the ability to fill all requests as specifically and as quickly as the requestor would like them filled. Therefore, please be patient with them, and keep the following in mind.

They are typically not a library or bookstore, and likely will not have specific titles.

Keep requests generalized, as in 'Dictionary', beginner Spanish, thriller novels, etc. Do not ask for a specific title or author and expect to get it.

Send backup requests, 2nd, 3rd, and 4th options.

If you are looking for education books, specify what grade level, as in High school, college, professional, etc.

Write neatly and be sure to provide you name, prison ID, and address.

Mention any restriction your prison may have, as in paperback only, maximum number allowed per order, whether used is okay, or if an invoice is required.

Take note of the states serviced in the listing.

Above all, BE PATIENT. And, oh yeah, did we mention 'be patient'?

FREE BOOK Topics

Most of the following book providers ask that you request books by topic instead of title. This makes their process much simpler. Unless otherwise noted, the following topic index can be used when requesting books from these providers. Not every book provider will have books on every topic below, so give plenty of options in your request.

addiction
Africa
African American
AIDS/HIV
alternative technology
anthropology
archeology
architecture
art/drawing
Asia/Pacific
astrology
astronomy
biography/Memoir
biology
brain science
business
Caribbean
chemistry
comics
computers
cookbooks/food
death/dying
dictionaries
disease (specify)
drama
dreams
economics
education
engineering
exercise
fantasy
feminism
film
foreign language (specify)
games/puzzles
gardening
geology
global warming
graphic novels
health
historical fiction
history (specify time or locale)
humor
incarceration
large-print
Latino/Chicano
LGBT/gender studies
literature/classics
mathematics
Middle East
music
mysteries/crime
mythology
National Geographic mags
parenting
philosophy
photography
physics
poetry
political science
Prison Legal News mags
psychology
racism
radical 'zines
reading
reference
religion (specify)
research
romance
science fiction
sexual abuse
self-help
short stories
sociology
South America
Spanish (books in)
spirituality
sports
statistics
travel/outdoor
UFO/conspiracy
war
westerns
Wicca
women's health
writing/grammar
yoga

AMERICAN CORRECTIONAL ASSOCIATION

8025 Laurel Lakes, Laurel, MD 20707-5075

Serves: All states except Oregon. No religious or legal books.

APPALACHIAN PRISON BOOK PROJECT

PO Box 601, Morgantown, WV 26507
Aprisonbookproject.wordpress.com
appalachianbp@gmail.com

Serves: KY, MD, OH, TN, VA, and WV.

BEEHIVE BOOKS BEHIND BARS | WELLER BOOK WORKS

607 Trolley Square, Salt Lake City, UT 84102
(801) 319-5051
www.beehivebooksbehindbars.com

Serves: AZ, CA, CO, ID, MT, NM, NV, OR, UT, WA, and WY.

BOOK 'EM

PO Box 7137, Pittsburgh, PA 12513
(412) 251-7302

Serves: Pennsylvania only. Primarily supplies educational and non-fiction books and magazines.

BOOKS THROUGH BARS | NEW SOCIETY PUBLISHERS

4722 Baltimore Ave., Philadelphia, PA 19143
(215) 727-8170
www.booksthroughbars.org

Serves: DE, MD, NJ, NY, PA, VA, and WV.

BOOKS THROUGH BARS NYC | BLUESTOCKINGS BOOKSTORE

172 Allen St., New York, NY 10002
www.booksthroughbarsnyc.com

Serves: ALL states except AL, FL, LA, MA, MI, MS, NC, PA, and OH. Priority is given to NY prisoners. They specialize in history and political books, with some literary fiction and educational books. No religious books.

BOOKS THROUGH BARS ITHACA | AUTUMN LEAVES BOOKSTORE

115 The Commons, 2nd Floor, Ithaca, NY 14850
(607) 645-0250
prisonactivist@gmail.com

Serves: CA, FL, NY, PA, TX, and others. Write to see if your sate is included.

BOOKS TO OREGON PRISONERS

PO Box 11222, Portland, OR 97211
www.bookstooregonprisoners.org

Serves: Oregon only.

BOOKS TO PRISONERS | JOINT EFFORT

PO Box 78005, Vancouver, BC, Canada V5N 5W1

Serves: Canadian prisoners only.

BOOKS TO PRISONS | LEFT BANK BOOKS

92 Pike St., Box A, Seattle, WA 98101
(206) 442-2013
www.bookstoprisoners.net

Serves: ALL states except CA or states that require first class postage or new books. No religious or legal books. Stamps or donations are appreciated

BRAILLE INSTITUTE LIBRARY SERVICE

741 N. Vermont Ave., Los Angeles, CA 90029

FREE Braille books to prisoners who are legally blind.

CHICAGO BOOKS TO WOMEN IN PRISON

PO Box 14778, Chicago, IL 60614
www.chicagobwp.org chicagobwp@gmail.com

Serves: Women prisoners in all states.

CLAREMONT PRISON LIBRARY PROJECT

PMB 128, 915-C W. Foothill Blvd., Claremont, CA 91711

Serves: ALL states. Specializes in self-help personal, and spiritual growth publications. No legal, technical, or GED.

CLEVELAND BOOKS TO PRISONERS

PO Box 602440, Cleveland, OH 44102

Serves: ALL states. They give priority to Ohio prisoners.

CODY'S BOOKSTORE

2454 Telegraph Ave., Berkeley, CA 94704
(800) 995-1180, (510) 845-7852
www.codysbooks.com

Serves: ALL states.

DC BOOKS TO PRISONS PROJECT

PO Box 34190, Washington, DC 20043-4190
www.dcbookstopriosners.org btodc@gmail.com

Serves: ALL states EXCEPT CT, IL, MA, ME, NH, NJ, NY, OH, OR, PA, RI, VT, WA, and WV. They will ship two books per request, one request allowed every 6-month period.

EAST BAY PRISONER SUPPORT

PO Box 22449, Oakland, CA 94609
www.eastbayprisonersupport.wordpress.com

Serves: CA, AZ, NM, TX, UT, and NV. They primarily provide anarchist titles. They will send magazines to LGBT prisoners and women in any state. Write for a catalog.

GROUNDWORK BOOKS

0323 Student Center, La Jolla, CA 92037
(858) 452-9625
groundwork@libertad.ucsd.edu

Serves: ALL states. Specializes in geography, political science, social civics, criminal justice, and history. May send up to two FREE books to prisoners who are indigent. Stamp donations are appreciated. Note: Thy also sell books at a 40% discount to prisoners.

INSIDE BOOKS PROJECT | 12TH STREET BOOKS

827 W. 12th St., Austin, TX 78701
(512) 655-3121
www,insidebooksproject.org
contact@insidebooksproject.org

Serves: Texas only, except Del Valle. No hardcover books, bibles, pulp fiction, or pornography.

INTERNATIONAL PRISON BOOK COLLECTIVE | INTERNATIONALIST BOOKS

405 W. Franklin St., Chapel Hill, NC 27516
www.prisonbooks.info

Serves: AL, MS, and some NC prisons.

LOOMPANICS UNLIMITED

PO Box 1197, Port Townsend, WA 98368

Serves: ALL states. Specializes in legal/prisoner issues books.

LOUISIANA BOOKS TO PRISONERS

1631 Elysian Fields, #117, New Orleans, LA 70117
lab2p@wordpress.com books2prisoners@gmail.com

Serves: Al, AR, FL, GA, KY, LA, MS, NC, SC, TN, VA, and WV. They give priority to women and Louisiana prisoners. No legal books or almanacs.

MIDWEST BOOKS TO PRISONERS | QUIMBY BOOKSTORE

1854 W. North Ave., Chicago, IL 60622
(773) 342-0910
www.freewebs.com/mwbtp

Serves: IA, IL, IN, KS, MN, MO, NE, and WI.

MIDWEST PAGES TO PRISONERS PROJECT | BOXCAR BOOKS AND COMMUNITY CENTER

118 S. Rogers, Suite 2, Bloomington, IN 47404
(866) 598-1543
www.pagestoprisoners.org

Serves: AZ, AR, FL, IA, IN, KS, KY, MN, MO, ND, OH, OK, SD, TN, and WI.

MAOIST INTERNATIONAL MINISTRY OF PRISONS (MIM)

PO Box 40799, San Francisco, CA 94140
www.prisoncensorship.info
mim@prisoncensorship.info

Serves: ALL states. MIM specializes in political, legal, and historical books, as well as some dictionaries and other reference books. They expect work in exchange for books, such as writing articles for their newsletter, sharing literature, leading campaigns and other advocacy. Stamps are appreciated.

OPEN BOOKS PRISON BOOK PROJECT

1040 N. Guillemard St. Pensacola, FL 32501
(850) 453-6774
www.openbookspcola.org

Serves: Florida only.

PRISON BOOK PROGRAM | ASHEVILLE

67 N. Lexington Ave., Ashville, NC 28801
www.main.nc.us/prisonbooks
prisonbooks31@hotmail.com

Serves: GA, NC, SC, and TN. If your institution requires prior approval, you must include approval with your book request. Stamps appreciated.

PRISON BOOK PROGRAM | THE READERS CORNER

31 Montford Ave., Asheville, NC 28801
www.main.nc.us/prisonbooks
prisonbooks31@hotmail.com

Serves: NC, SC, GA, and TN only.

PRISON BOOK PROGRAM QUINCY | LUCY PARSONS BOOKSTORE

1306 Hancock St., Suite 100, Quincy, MA 02169

www.prisonbookprogram.org
info@prisonbookprogram.org

Serves: ALL states EXCEPT CA, IL, MD, MI, NV, and TX.

Note: Allows two free book shipments per year. They also offer a 6-page National Prisoner Resource List and an LGBTQ resource list, FREE to prisoners.

PRISON BOOK PROJECT

PO Box 396, Amherst, MA 01004
(413) 584-8975
www.prisonbooks.org prisonbookproject@riseup.net

Serves: CT, MA, ME, NH, RI, TX, and VT.

PRISON LIBRARY PROJECT

915 W. Foothill Blvd., PMB 128, Claremont, CA 91711
(909) 626-3066
www.claremontforum.org

Serves: ALL states EXCEPT HI, MA, MI, MS, NE, NV, PA, VA, and WI. PLP specializes in self-help, personal and spiritual growth, wellness, and metaphysical books. No law or technical books.

PRISONER'S LITERATURE PROJECT | BOUND TOGETHER BOOKS

1369 Haight St., San Francisco, CA 94117
(415) 672-7858
www.prisonersliteratureproject.com
prisonlit@gmail.com

Serves: ALL states EXCEPT OR and TX. No thrillers, westerns, or romance books. Stamp donations appreciated.

PROVIDENCE BOOKS THROUGH BARS | MYOPIC BOOKS

5 S. Angell St., Providence, RI 02906
(401) 356-0388
www.providencebtb.org info@providencebtb.org

Serves: ALL states.

READ BETWEEN THE BARS | DAILY PLANET PUBLISHING

PO Box 1589, Tucson, AZ 85072-1589
www.readbetweenthebars.com
readbetweenthebars@gmail.com

Serves: Arizona only.

UC BOOKS TO PRISONERS

PO Box 515, Urbana, IL 61803
(708) 782-4608
www.books2prisoners.org

Serves: Illinois only.

WISCONSIN BOOKS TO PRISONERS

426 W. Gilman St., Madison, WI 53703
(608) 262-9026

Serves: Wisconsin and LGBT prisoners nationwide.

WOMEN'S PRISON BOOK PROJECT | BONESHAKER BOOKS

2002 23rd Ave. South, Minneapolis, MN 55404
www.wpbp.com
womensprisonbookproject@gmail.com

Serves: Women and transgender prisoners in ALL states EXCEPT CA, FL, IL, IN, MA, MI, MS, OH, OR, and PA.

Reference Center

Sometimes even the most basic reference information can be hard to come by from behind concrete and bars.

The *Reference Center* is designed to bridge that gap. Each edition of *Prison Lives Almanac : Prisoner Resource Guide* provides you with a building collection of useful information that will come in handy for your everyday life.

Whether making a phone call to an unfamiliar region of the world, sending an unusually sized letter, or just wanting the answer to a question that you've always wondered about during your stay, this section is a ready resource for you.

REFERENCE CENTER

General Reference

Weights & Measures

Frequently Used Conversions

U.S. Customary to Metric				Metric to U.S. Customary			
	If you have:	Multiply by:	To Get:		If you have:	Multiply by:	To Get:
Length	inches	25.4	millimeters	**Length**	millimeters	0.04	inches
	inches	2.54	centimeters		centimeters	0.4	inches
	feet	0.3	meters		meters	3.3	feet
	yards	0.9	meters		meters	1.1	yards
	miles	1.6	kilometers	**Weight**	kilometers	0.6	miles
Weight	ounces	28	grams		grams	0.035	ounces
	pounds	454	grams		grams	0.002	pounds
	pounds	0.45	kilograms		kilograms	2.2	pounds
	tons	0.91	metric tons	**Liquid**	metric tons	1.1	tons
Liquid	ounces	0.03	liters		liters	33.8	ounces
	cups	0.24	liters		liters	4.2	cups
	pints	0.47	liters		liters	2.1	pints
	quarts	0.95	liters		liters	1.1	quarts
	gallons	3.79	liters		liters	0.26	gallons

MATHEMATICAL FORMULAS

Calculating Circumference

Circle	Multiply the diameter by pi (3.1416)

Calculating Area

Circle	Multiply the square of the radius (equal to 1/2 the diameter) by pi.
Rectangle	Multiply the length of the base by the height.
Sphere (surface)	Multiply the square of the radius by pi and multiply by 4.
Square	Square the length of one side.
Trapezoid	Add the length of the two parallel sides, multiply by the height, and divide by 2.
Triangle	Multiply the base by the height and divide by 2.

Calculating Volume

Cone	Multiply the square of the radius of the base by pi, multiply by the height, and divide by 3.
Cube	Cube the length of one edge.
Cylinder	Multiply the square of the radius of the base by pi and multiply by the height.
Pyramid	Multiply the area of the base by the height and divide by 3.
Rectangular prism	Multiply the length by the width by the height.
Sphere	Multiply the cube of the radius by pi, multiply by 4, and divide by 3.

Weight & Measurement Equivalents

Lengths			Areas or Surfaces	
1 angstrom	= .01 nanometer (exactly)		1 acre (a)	= 43,560 square feet (exactly)
	= .0001 micrometer (exactly)			= 4,840 square yards
	= .0000001 Millimeter (exactly)			= .405 hectare
	= .000000004 inch		1 bolt (cloth)	
1 centimeter (cm)	= .3937 inch		length	= 100 yards
1 decimeter (dm)	= 3.937 inch		width	= 45 or 60 inches
1 degree (geographical)	= 364,566.929 feet		1 square centimeter	= .155 square inch
	= 69.047 miles (avg.)		1 square decimeter	= 15.500 square inches
	= 111.123 kilometers (avg.)		1 square foot	= 929.030 square centimeters
of latitude	= 68.708 miles at equator		1 square inch	= 6.45116 centimeters
	= 69.403 miles at poles		1 square kilometer	= 247.104 acres
of longitude	= 69.171 miles at equator			= .0386102 square mile
1 decameter (dam)	= 32,808 feet		1 square meter	= 1.196 square yards
1 fathom (fath)	= 6 feet (exactly)			= 10.764 square feet
	= 1.8288 meters		1 square mile	= 640 acres (exactly)
1 foot (ft)	= 12 inches (exactly)		1 square millimeter	= .002 square inch
	= 0.3048 meters (exactly)		1 square yard	= .836127 square meter
1 furlong (fur)	= 660 feet (exactly)			
	= 201.168 meters		**Weights or Masses**	
1 inch (in)	= 2.54 centimeters (exactly)		1 grain	= 64.79891 milligrams
1 kilometer (km)	= 0.621371 mile		1 gram (g)	= 1532 grains
	= 3280.8 feet			= 0.035 ounce (avoirdupois)
1 meter (m)	= 39.37 inches		1 kilogram (kg)	= 2.20462 pounds
	= 1.09361 yards		1 microgram	= .000001 gram (exactly)
1 mil	= .001 inch (exactly)		1 milligram	= .015 grain
	= .0254 millimeters (exactly)		1 ounce, troy (oz t)	= 480 grains (exactly)
1 mile (mi) (land)	= 5,280 feet (exactly)			= .911 troy ounce
	= 1.609344 kilometers (exactly)			= 31.103 grams
1 nautical mile (nmi)	= 1.151 miles		1 pound, troy (lb)	= 5.760 grains (exactly)
	= 1.852 kilometers (exactly)			= 373.242 grams
1 millimeter (mm)	= .03937 inch			= .823 pound
1 nanometer (nm)	= .00000003937 inch		1 stone (st)	= 14 pounds (exactly)
1 yard (yd)	= 3 feet (exactly)		1 ton, metric (t)	= 2,204.623 pounds
	= .9144 meter (exactly)		1 ton, net (sh ton)	= 2,000 pounds (exactly)

Weight & Measurement Equivalents (continued)

Capacities & Volumes

1 barrel, liquid (bbl)	= 21 to 42 gallons	1 liter (L)	= 1.057 liquid quarts
1 barrel, dry (bbl)	= 7,056 cubic inches		= .980 dry quart
	= 105 dry courts	1 milliliter (mL)	= .271fluid dram
	= 3.281 bushels		= .061 cubic inch
1 bushel, U.S. (struck measure)	= 2,150.42 cubic inches (exactly)	1 ounce, liquid (U.S.)	= 1.805 cubic inches
	= 35.239 liters		= 29.574 milliliters
1 cord (firewood) (cd)	= 128 cubic feet (exactly)	1 pint, dry (pt)	= 33.600 cubic inches
1 cubic centimeter	= .061 cubic inch		= .551 liter
1 cubic decimeter	= 61.024 cubic inches	1 pint, liquid	= 28.875 cubic inches
1 cubic inch	= .554 fluid ounce		= .473 liter
	= 4.433 fluid drams	1 quart, dry (qt)	= 67.201 cubic inches
	= 16.387 cubic centimeters		= 1.101 liters
1 cubic foot	= 7.481 gallons	1 quart, liquid	= 2 pints, liquid (exact)
	= 28.317 cubic decimeters		= 4 cups (exact)
1 cubic meter	= 1.308 cubic yards		= .946 liters
1 cubic yard	= .765 cubic meter	1 tablespoon (T)	= 3 teaspoons (exact)
1 cup, measuring	= 8 fluid ounces (exactly)		= ½ fluid ounce (exact)
	= ½ liquid pint (exactly)	1 teaspoon (t)	= ½ tablespoon (exact)
1 dekaliter (daL)	= 2.642 gallons		
1 gallon, U.S. (gal)	= 4 quarts, liquid (exactly)		
	= 231 cubic inches (exactly)		
	= 3.785 liters		
	= 128 U.S. fluid ounces		

Weather Conversions

Temperature Conversions

Formula: To convert Fahrenheit to Celsius, subtract 32 degrees and divide by 1.8. To convert Celsius to Fahrenheit, multiply by 1.8 and add 32 degrees.

Celsius	Fahrenheit	Celsius	Fahrenheit	Celsius	Fahrenheit	Celsius	Fahrenheit	Celsius	Fahrenheit
-273.15	-459.67	-45.6	-50	-1.1	30	30	86	65.6	150
-250	-418	-40	-40	0	32	32.2	90	70	158
-200	-328	-34.4	-30	4.4	40	35	95	80	176
-184.4	-300	-30	-22	10	50	37	98.6	90	194
-156.7	-250	-28.9	-20	15.6	60	37.8	100	93.3	200
-150	-238	-23.3	-10	20	68	40	104	100	212
-126.9	-200	-20	-4	21.1	70	43.3	110	121.1	250
-101.1	-150	-17.8	0	23.9	75	48.9	120	148.9	300
-100	-148	-12.2	10	25	77	50	122	150	302
-73.3	-100	-10	14	26.7	80	54.4	130	200	392
-50	-58	-6.7	20	29.4	85	60	140	300	572

Wind Chill Temperature

Temperature and wind combine to cause heat loss from body surfaces. For example, a temperature of 5 degrees (F), plus a 10-mph wind, causes body heat loss equal to that which would occur in -10 degrees (F) with no wind. In other words, a 10-mph wind makes 5 degrees feel like -10 degrees.

Wind speeds greater than 45-mph have little additional chilling effects. Direct sunlight can increase the wind chill by 10 to 15 degrees.

Wind Speed (mph)	Air Temperature (F)																	
Calm	40	35	30	25	20	15	10	5	0	-5	-10	-15	-20	-25	-30	-35	-40	-45
	Wind Chill Temperature (F)																	
5	36	31	25	19	13	7	1	-5	-11	-16	-22	-28	-34	-40	-46	-52	-57	-63
10	34	37	21	15	9	3	-4	-10	-16	-22	-28	-35	-41	-47	-53	-59	-66	-72
15	32	25	19	13	6	0	-7	-13	-19	-26	-32	-39	-45	-51	-58	-64	-71	-77
20	30	24	17	11	4	-2	-9	-15	-22	-29	-35	-42	-48	-55	-61	-68	-74	-81
25	29	23	16	9	3	-4	-11	-17	-24	-31	-37	-44	-51	-58	-64	-71	-78	-84
30	28	22	15	8	1	-5	-12	-19	-26	-33	-39	-46	-53	-60	-67	-73	-80	-87
35	28	21	14	7	0	-7	-14	-21	-27	-34	-41	-48	-55	-62	-69	-76	-82	-89
40	27	20	13	6	-1	-8	-15	-22	-29	-36	-43	-50	-57	-64	-71	-78	-84	-91
45	26	19	12	5	-2	-9	-16	-23	-30	-37	-44	-51	-58	-65	-72	-79	-86	-93

Heat Index

The heat index, or apparent temperature, is a measure of how hot it feels when the relative humidity is factored in with the actual air temperature. For example, when air temperature is 100 degrees (F), and relative humidity is 50%, it feels as if it's 118 degrees (F) with no humidity.

Full sunlight can make one feel even hotter.

Relative Humidity (%)	Temperature (F)														
	80	82	84	86	88	90	92	94	96	98	100	102	104	106	108
	Apparent Temperature (F)														
40	80	81	83	85	88	91	94	97	101	105	109	114	119	124	130
45	80	82	84	87	89	93	96	100	104	109	114	119	124	130	137
50	81	83	85	88	91	95	99	103	108	113	118	124	131	137	
55	81	84	86	89	93	97	101	106	112	117	124	130	137		
60	82	84	88	91	95	100	105	110	116	123	129	137			
65	82	85	89	93	98	103	108	114	121	128	136				
70	83	86	90	95	100	105	112	119	126	134					
75	84	88	92	97	103	109	116	124	132						
80	84	89	94	100	106	113	121	129							
85	85	90	96	102	110	117	126	135							
90	86	91	98	105	113	122	131								
95	86	93	100	108	117	127									
100	87	95	103	112	121	132									

Postal Information

First Class Mail

Each ounce is 22 cents more.

Sending to:	1 ounce	2 ounces	3 ounces	3.5+ ounces
Letters (Maximum sizes: length = 11 ½", height = 6 ¼", thickness = ¼")				
U.S.	47 cents	68 cents	89 cents	$1.10
Canada	$1.20	$1.20	$1.67	$2.16
Mexico	$1.20	$1.79	$2.38	$2.97
Other Countries*	$ 1.20	$2.21	$3.24	$4.27
Flats (Maximum sizes: length = 15", height = 12", thickness = ¾")				
U.S.	94 cents	$1.15	$1.36	$1.63 + 0.21 for each addl. ounce
Canada	$2.38	$2.60	$2.82	$3.02 + 0.22 for each addl. ounce
Mexico	$2.38	$3.09	$3.78	$4.49 + 0.69 for each addl. ounce
Other Countries*	$2.38	$3.36	$4.32	$5.30 + 0.98 for each addl. ounce

* This is the maximum postage rate, regardless of country. If you use this rate for mail outside of the U.S., Canada, or Mexico, your mail will be delivered.

Priority Mail

Flat Rate mailers by size. Can hold up to 75 pounds and will take 1-3 days for delivery. Unlimited weight for domestic mail (U.S.), or a maximum of 4 pounds for international mailings.

	U.S.	Canada	Mexico	Other*
Flat Rate Envelopes	$6.45	$23.95	$29.95	$62.50
Regular: 12.5" x 9.5" or smaller				
Legal: 15" x 9.5"				
Small Flat Rate Boxes	$6.80	$24.95	$30.95	$33.95
8 11/16" x 5 7/16" x 1 ¾"				
Medium Flat Rate Boxes	$13.45	$45.95	$66.95	$75.95
Top loading: 11.25" x 8.75" x 6"				
Side loading: 14" x 12" x 3.5"				
Large Flat Rate Boxes	$18.75	$59.95	$86.95	$95.95
12.25" x 12.25" x 6"				
24-1/16" x 11 7/8" x 3 1/8"				

* This is the maximum postage rate for Flat Rate boxes, regardless of country. If you use this rate for mail outside of the U.S., Canada, or Mexico, your mail will be delivered.

Other Postal Services

	Domestic	International
Adult Signature Required	$5.70	
Adult Signature Restricted	$5.95	
Certificate of Mailing		
Individual article (Form 3817)	$1.30	$1.35
Addl. Copy of Form 3817	$1.35	$1.35
Certified Mail (per item)	$3.30	
Certified Mail – Restricted	$8.60	
Certified Mail – Adult Sign	$8.60	
Collect on Delivery (COD)		
$0.01 to $50	$7.25	
$50.01 to 100	$9.05	
For every addl. $100 add	$1.80	
Insurance (amount of insurance coverage desired)		
$0.01 to $50	$2.20	Free
$50.01 to 100	$2.75	Free
$100.01 to 200	$3.50	Free
$200.01 to 300	$4.60	$5.00
$300.01 to 400	$5.80	$6.15
$400.01 to 500	$7.00	$7.30
$500.01 to 600	$9.45	$8.45
$600.01+	$9.45 + $1.30/$100	$9.60 + $1.15/$100
Insurance Restricted	$5.15	
Money Orders		$4.75
$0.01 to 500	$1.25	
$500.01 to $1,000 (max)	$1.65	
Military Money Order	$0.40	
Inquiry Fee	$6.20	$5.95
Registered Mail (in addition to postage)		$13.95
$0.00	$12.20	
$0.01 to $100	$13.00	
$100.01 to 500	$15.15	
$500.01 to 1,000	$16.75	
$1,000+		$18.35 + $1.60/500
Return Receipt		
Request at time of mailing (Form 3811)	$2.80	$3.85
Signature Confirmation		
First-Class Mail	$9.70	
Sunday/Holiday Delivery	$12.50	
10:30 AM Delivery	$5.00	

Area Codes, by number

Area Code	State/Region
52 55	Mexico City area
201	Northern New Jersey
202	DC
203	Connecticut
204	Manitoba, Canada
205	Central Alabama
206	Washington
207	Maine
208	Idaho
209	Stockton, CA area
210	San Antonio, TX area
211	Local community info
212	NYC
213	Los Angeles, CA area
214	Dallas, TX area
215	SE Pennsylvania
216	Cleveland, OH area
217	Springfield, IL area
218	Duluth, MN area
219	Gary, IN area
220	Columbus, OH area
224	N/NE Illinois
225	Louisiana
226	Windsor, Ontario area
227	Maryland
228	Southern Mississippi
229	Albany, GA area
231	Western Michigan
234	NE Ohio
236	British Columbia, Canada
239	Southern Florida
240	Western Maryland
242	Bahamas
246	Barbados
248	Oakland County, Michigan
250	British Columbia, Canada
251	Southern Alabama
252	Eastern North Carolina
253	Southern Washington
254	Central Texas
256	North/East Alabama
260	NE Indiana
262	SE Wisconsin
264	Anguilla
267	SE Pennsylvania
268	Antigua/Barbuda
269	SW Michigan
270	Western Kentucky
272	NE/NC Pennsylvania
274	Wisconsin
276	S/SW Virginia
278	Detroit suburbs, Michigan
281	Houston, Texas area
283	SW Ohio
284	British Virgin Islands
289	S/Central Ontario, Canada
301	Western Maryland
302	Delaware
303	Central Colorado
304	West Virginia
305	SE Florida
306	Saskatchewan, Canada
307	Wyoming
308	Western Nebraska
309	W/Central Illinois
310	Southern California
311	Reserved
312	Chicago, IL area
313	Detroit, MI area
314	SE Missouri
315	N/Central New York
316	Southern Kansas
317	Indianapolis, IN area
318	Northern Louisiana
319	Eastern Iowa
320	Central Minnesota
321	Central Florida
323	Los Angeles, CA area
325	Central Texas
330	NE Ohio
331	W/NE Illinois
332	New York
334	Southern Alabama
336	Central North Carolina
337	SW Louisiana
339	Boston, MA area
340	U.S. Virgin Islands
341	California (overlay 510)
343	SE Ottawa, Canada
345	Cayman Islands
347	New York
351	Massachusetts
352	N/Central Florida
360	Western Washington
361	South Texas
365	S/Central Ontario, Canada
369	Solano County, CA area
380	Central Ohio
385	Salt Lake City, UT area
386	N/Central; Florida
401	Rhode Island
402	Eastern Nebraska
403	Southern Alberta, Canada
404	Atlanta, GA area
405	Oklahoma City, OK area
406	Montana
407	Orlando, FL area
408	San Jose, CA area
409	SE Texas
410	Eastern Maryland
411	Local information
412	Pittsburgh, PA area
412	Western Massachusetts
414	SE Wisconsin
415	San Francisco, CA area
416	S/Central Ontario, Canada
417	Springfield, MO area
418	NE Quebec, Canada
419	NW Ohio
423	Eastern Tennessee
424	Los Angeles, CA area
425	Northern Washington
430	NE Texas
431	Manitoba, Canada
432	Western Texas
434	Eastern Virginia
435	Utah
437	Toronto, Canada area
438	SW Quebec, Canada
440	Cleveland, OH metro area
441	Bermuda
442	San Diego, CA suburbs
443	Eastern Maryland
447	Illinois
450	SE Quebec, Canada
456	Inbound International
458	SC Oregon
463	Indiana
464	Chicago, IL suburbs
469	Dallas, TX metro area
470	Atlanta, GA metro area
473	Grenada
475	Connecticut
478	Central Georgia
479	NW Arkansas
480	East Phoenix, AZ area
481	NE Quebec, Canada
484	SE Pennsylvania
500	Person communication service
501	Central Arkansas
502	Louisville, KY area
503	Northern Oregon
504	New Orleans, LA area
505	New Mexico
506	New Brunswick, Canada
507	Southern Minnesota
508	Central Massachusetts
509	E/Central Washington
510	Oakland/East Bay, CA area
511	Travel info
512	Austin, TX area
513	Cincinnati, OH area
514	Montreal City Quebec area
515	Des Moines, IA area
516	Long Island, NY area
517	Lansing, MI area
518	Albany, NY area
519	Windsor, Ontario, Canada
520	Tucson, AZ area
530	NE California
539	Tulsa, OK area
540	W/SW Virginia
541	SC Oregon
548	SW Ontario, Canada
551	Northern New Jersey
555	Directory assistance
557	St. Louis, MO area
559	Fresno, CA area
561	SC Florida
562	Long Beach, CA area
563	Eastern Iowa
564	Western Washington
567	NW Ohio
570	NE/NC Pennsylvania
571	Northern Virginia
573	SE Missouri
574	Northern Indiana
575	New Mexico
579	SE Quebec, Canada
580	Western Oklahoma

585	Rochester, NY area
586	Macomb County, MI area
587	Alberta, Canada area
600	Canadian services
601	Mississippi
602	Phoenix, AZ area
603	New Hampshire
604	Vancouver, BC Canada area
605	South Dakota
606	Eastern Kentucky
607	S/Central New York
608	Madison, WI area
609	Trenton, NJ area
610	SE Pennsylvania
611	Reserved
612	Minneapolis, MN area
613	Ottawa, Canada area
614	Columbus, OH area
615	Nashville, TN metro area
616	Western Michigan
617	Boston, Ma area
618	Centralia, IL area
619	San Diego, CA area
620	Wichita, KS area
623	West Phoenix, AZ area
626	Pasadena, CA area
628	San Francisco/Marin, CA
629	Nashville, TN metro area
630	Chicago, IL suburbs
631	Easter New York
636	St. Louis, MO metro area
639	Saskatchewan, Canada
641	Iowa
646	NYC, NY mobile
647	Toronto, Ontario, Canada area
649	Turks and Caicos
650	Central California
651	St. Paul, MN area
657	Orange County, California area
660	Northern Missouri
661	Northern Los Angeles, CA area
662	Northern Mississippi
664	Montserrat
669	San Jose, CA area
670	Northern Mariana Islands
671	Guam
678	Atlanta, GA metro area
679	Dearborn, MI area
680	New York
681	West Virginia
682	Fort Worth, TX area
684	American Samoa
689	Orlando, FL metro area
700	Interexchange carrier service
701	North Dakota
702	Southern Nevada
703	Northern Virginia
704	Charlotte, NC area
705	NE Ontario, Canada
706	Northern Georgia
707	NW California
708	Chicago, IL suburbs
709	Newfoundland/Labrador, Canada
710	US Government
711	Telecommunications relay
712	Council Bluffs, IA area
713	Houston, TX area
714	N/W Orange County, CA area
715	Northern Wisconsin
716	Buffalo, NY area
717	Harrisburg, PA area
718	NYC, NY area
719	SE Colorado
720	Denver, CO area
721	Sint Maarten
724	Pittsburgh, PA metro area
725	Clark County, NV area
727	Tampa, FL metro area
730	Illinois
731	Memphis, TN metro area
732	Central New Jersey
734	SE Michigan
737	Austin, TX area
740	Columbus, OH suburbs
743	North Carolina
747	Southern California
754	Ft. Lauderdale, FL area
757	Eastern Virginia
758	St. Lucia
760	San Diego, CA area
762	Northern Georgia
763	Minneapolis, MN area
765	Indianapolis, IN suburbs
767	Dominica
769	Jackson, MS area
770	Atlanta, Georgia suburbs
772	SC Florida
773	Chicago, IL outside loop
774	Central Massachusetts
775	Reno, NV area
778	Vancouver BC, Canada area
779	NW Illinois
780	Northern Alberta, Canada
781	Boston, MA suburbs
782	Nova Scotia/Prince Edward Isle
784	St. Vincent/Grenadines
785	Topeka, KS area
786	SE Florida
787	Puerto Rico
800	U.S./Canada toll free
801	Salt Lake City, UT metro area
802	Vermont
803	South Carolina
804	Richmond, VA area
805	Central California
806	Texas panhandle
807	Western Ontario, Canada
808	Hawaii
809	Dominican Republic
810	Eastern Michigan
811	Reserved
812	Southern Indiana
813	Tampa, FL metro area
814	Erie, PA area
815	NW Illinois
816	Kansas City, MO area
817	Fort Worth, TX area
818	Los Angeles, CA area
819	NW Quebec, Canada
822	U.S./Canada toll free
825	Alberta, Canada
828	Asheville, NC area
829	Dominican Republic
830	San Antonio, TX area
831	Central coast, CA
832	Houston, TX area
833	U.S/Canada toll free
835	SE Pennsylvania
843	South Carolina Coastal region
844	U.S./Canada toll free
845	Upstate New York
847	Chicago, IL NW suburbs
848	Central New Jersey
849	Santo Domingo, Dominican Republic
850	Florida panhandle
855	U.S./Canada toll free
856	SW New Jersey
857	Boston, MA area
858	San Diego, CA area
859	N/C Kentucky
860	Connecticut
862	Northern New Jersey
863	Lakeland, FL area
864	South Carolina, upstate
865	Eastern Tennessee
866	U.S./Canada toll free
867	Northwest Territories, Canada
868	Trinidad/Tobago
869	St. Kitts/Nevis
870	Arkansas
872	Chicago, IL downtown area
873	NW Quebec
876	Jamaica
877	U.S./Canada toll free
878	Pittsburgh, PA area
880	Toll-free service
881	Toll-free service
882	Toll-free service
888	U.S./Canada toll-free
898	VoIP service
900	U.S. Toll calls
901	Memphis, TN metro area
902	Nova Scotia/Prince Edward Isle
903	Tyler, TX area
904	Jacksonville, FL area
905	Toronto, Canada area
906	Michigan, Upper Peninsula
907	Alaska
908	Central New Jersey
909	San Bernardino, CA area
910	South Central South Carolina
911	Emergency services
912	Savannah, GA area
913	Kansas City, KS area
914	Westchester County, NY area
915	El Paso, TX area
916	NE California
917	NYC, NY cellular service
918	Tulsa, OK area
919	Raleigh, NC area
920	NE Wisconsin
925	Contra Costa, CA area
927	Orlando, FL cellular service
928	C/N Arizona
929	NYC and Five Burroughs
931	Nashville, TN area
934	New York
935	San Diego, CA area
936	SE Texas
937	Dayton, Ohio area
939	Puerto Rico
940	N/C Texas
941	SW Florida
947	Oakland County, MI area
949	Orange County, CA area
951	Riverside County, CA area
952	Minnesota
954	Broward County, FL area
956	Texas, valley area

957	New Mexico
959	Connecticut
970	N/W Colorado
971	Oregon
972	Dallas, TX metro area
973	Northern New Jersey
975	Kansas City, MO area
978	Massachusetts
979	SE Texas
980	North Carolina
984	Raleigh, NC area
985	Eastern Louisiana
986	Idaho
989	Upper Central Michigan

International Dialing Codes

To place a call to somewhere outside of the U.S., dial 011, plus the country code, followed by the area code and phone number.

For instance: To place a call to Mexico, dial: 011, then 52, then the area code and number.

Country	Code	Time Differences (E.S.T.)	Country	Code	Time Differences (E.S.T)
Algeria	213	6	Morocco	212	5
Argentina	54	2	Nepal	977	10 ½
Australia	61	15 (Mel/Syd) 13 (Per)	Netherlands	31	6
Austria	43	6	New Caledonia	687	16
Belgium	32	6	New Zealand	64	17
Bosnia &	387	6	Nicaragua	505	-1
Brazil	55	2	Nigeria	234	6
Bulgaria	359	7	Norway	47	6
Canada	1	-2 (Calg.) -3 (Vanc.)	Pakistan	92	10
Chile	56	1	Palestine	970	7
China	86	13	Peru	51	0
Croatia	385	6	Philippines	63	13
Cyprus	357	7	Poland	48	6
Czech Republic	420	6	Portugal	351	5
Denmark	45	6	Puerto Rico	1	1
Dominican Republic	1	1	Republic of Korea	82	14
Egypt	20	7	Romania	40	7
Estonia	372	7	Russian Federation	7	8
Finland	358	7	Saudi Arabia	966	8
France	33	6	Senegal	221	5
Germany	49	6	Serbia	381	6
Greece	30	7	Singapore	65	12
Hong Kong	852	13	Slovakia	421	6
Hungary	36	6	Slovenia	386	6
Iceland	354	5	South Africa	27	7
India	91	10 ½	Spain	34	6
Indonesia	62	12	Sri Lanka	94	10 ½
Iran	98	9 ½	Sweden	46	6
Iraq	964	8	Switzerland	41	6
Ireland	353	5	Syria	963	7
Israel	972	7	Taiwan	886	13
Italy	39	6	Thailand	66	12
Japan	81	14	Tunisia	216	6
Kenya	254	8	Turkey	90	7
Kuwait	965	8	Ukraine	380	7
Latvia	371	7	United Kingdom	44	5
Lithuania	370	7	Uruguay	598	2
Luxembourg	352	6	Uzbekistan	998	10
Malaysia	60	13	Venezuela	58	1
Malta	356	6	Vietnam	84	12
Mexico	52	-1	Zimbabwe	263	7
Montenegro	382	6			

Health Reference

Body Mass Index Chart (BMI Scale)

The BMI scale is used as a gauge to determine if you are fit, overweight or obese. It does not, however, take into account big-bonedness or muscle mass. If you have even a moderate amount of muscle weight, this scale will not accurately measure your body mass.

	Healthy						Overweight					Obese					
BMI	19	20	21	22	23	24	25	26	27	28	29	30	31	32	33	34	35
Height	**Body Weight (pounds)**																
4'10"	91	96	100	105	110	115	119	124	129	134	138	143	148	153	158	162	167
4'11"	94	99	104	109	114	119	124	128	133	138	143	148	153	158	163	168	173
5'	97	102	107	112	118	123	128	133	138	143	148	153	158	163	168	174	179
5'1"	100	106	111	116	122	127	132	137	143	148	153	158	164	169	174	180	185
5'2"	104	109	115	120	126	131	136	142	147	153	158	164	169	175	180	186	191
5'3"	107	113	118	124	130	135	141	146	152	158	163	169	175	180	186	191	197
5'4"	110	116	122	128	134	140	145	151	157	163	169	174	180	186	192	197	204
5'5"	114	120	126	132	138	144	150	156	162	168	174	180	186	192	198	204	210
5'6"	118	124	130	136	142	148	155	161	167	173	179	186	192	198	204	210	216
5'7"	121	127	134	140	146	153	159	166	172	178	185	191	198	204	211	217	223
5'8"	125	131	138	144	151	158	164	171	177	184	190	197	203	210	216	223	230
5'9"	128	135	142	179	155	162	169	176	182	189	196	203	209	216	223	230	236
5'10"	132	139	146	153	160	167	174	181	188	195	202	209	216	222	229	263	243
5'11"	136	143	150	157	165	172	179	186	193	200	208	215	222	229	236	243	250
6'	140	147	154	162	169	177	184	191	199	206	213	221	228	235	242	250	258
6'1"	144	151	159	166	174	182	189	191	199	206	213	221	228	235	242	250	258
6'2"	148	155	163	171	179	186	194	202	210	218	225	233	241	249	256	264	272
6'3"	152	160	168	176	184	192	200	208	216	224	232	240	256	264	264	272	279
6'4"	156	164	172	180	189	197	205	213	221	230	238	246	254	263	271	279	287

Find your BODY FAT Percentage

A better reference to determine if your body is where it should be may be to get a rough idea of your actual body fat percentage. To get the most exact body fat percentage measurement requires calipers and pools of water, which you likely don't have access to. But the following equation can be used to *estimate* your body fat percentage.

	Body Fat % = waist + (½ hips) – (3x forearms) - wrist	
Measure your:	Waist circumference	_______
	Hip circumference, divide by 2	+ _______
	Forearm circumference, multiply by 3 (over 30, by 2.7)	- _______
	Wrist circumference	- _______
	Body Fat %	_________

4-9% = Very fit **10-16%** = Fit **17-24%** = borderline **25-31%** = Not so fit **33+%** = Get help now

Find your Target Heart Rate

Perhaps the best way to gauge your current fitness level is by simply checking your heart rate.

Assuming you're not taking heart regulating medication, you should be able to exercise for at least 20 to 30 minutes at your target heart rate (weight loss range) without difficulty.

The following equation will help you find your target heart rate.

Maximum heart rate = 220 minus your age

Example: If you're 40 years old, **220 – 40 = 180**

At 40 years old, your maximum heart rate is **180**

Target heart rate range = 50% and 80% of your max rate

Example: If you're 40 years old, **180 x 0.5 = 90, 180 x 0.8 = 144**

At 40 years old, your target heart range is **90 to 144**

Now walk briskly for 5 minutes. Once done, take your pulse (count your pulse rate for 10 seconds and multiply by 6 to find your beats per minute.)

If you are near the top of your range, or over it, you are out of shape. You should be able to do this fairly easily for 20-30 minutes. If you can barely do it for 5 minutes, it may be time to make adjustments in your routine.

Calories Burned During Exercise

The following calories burned are estimates for a man who is 5'10" tall and weighs 154 lbs. The more you weigh the more calories you will burn by exercising at the same intensity.

Moderate physical activity	In 1 hr.	In 30 min.	–	Vigorous physical activity	In 1 hr.	In 30 min.
Bicycling (under 10 mph)	290	145		Jogging (5 mph)	550	295
Walking (3 ½ mph)	280	140		Bicycling (over 10 mph)	590	295
Stretching	180	90		Aerobics	480	240
Weight training (light)	220	110		Walking (4 ½ mph)	460	230
				Weightlifting (vigorous)	440	220
				Basketball (vigorous)	440	220

Body Mass Index of Prisoners – by Percentage

	Underweight	Normal	Overweight	Obese	Morbidly Obese
All Prisoners	0.8%	25.6%	45.7%	25.5%	2.4%
Sex					
Male	0.8	25.8	46.5	24.7	2.2
Female	1.0	21.6	34.7	37.2	5.6
Age					
18-24	1.4	42.2	41.2	14.2	1.1
25-34	0.3	29.7	47.3	20.3	2.3
35-49	1.3	18.9	43.6	33.3	3.0
50+	0.5	21.6	50.7	25.3	1.9
Race					
White	0.3	28.0	47.2	22.6	1.9
Black	1.3	25.2	42.7	28.7	2.1
Hispanic	1.0	22.0	47.4	26.4	3.3
Other	0.7	27.6	47.0	23.1	1.7

Source: Bureau of Justice Statistics, National Inmate Survey, 2011-12

How much protein do you need?

Prisoner activity level	% of calories that should come from protein	Grams of protein/pound of body weight	200lb man needs…
Inactive prisoner	10-15%	.39-.59	78-118 g/day
Active prisoner who wants to maintain current mass	15-20%	.59-.79 g/lb.	118-158 g/day
Active prisoner who wants to gain mass	20-35%	.80-1.09 g/lb.	160-218 g/day
Bodybuilder prisoner	25-35%	1.10-2.19 g/lb.	Not recommended

Vitamins & Minerals

Vitamins and minerals are essential to regulate the body and help build healthy blood, bones and muscles. Generally, the best way to ensure that you are getting all of them you need is to eat a wide variety of foods, with emphasis on whole grains, vegetables and fruits, as well as some proteins and good fats. The more colorful your fruit and vegetable choices, usually the more vitamins and minerals you'll receive.

It is a good idea to know what each of the individual vitamins and minerals do for your body so that you can make wise food decisions and be aware of where you may be deficient. Therefore, the following provides a breakdown of the value of these necessary life-sustaining resources.

Vitamins

Vitamin	What it does...	Sources...
A	Promotes good and eyesight and help keep skin and mucous membranes infection-resistant	Liver, sweet potatoes, carrots, kale, cantaloupe, greens, broccoli, and fortified milk.
B-1 thiamine	Prevents beriberi, a disease causing inflammation on the nerves and heart failure. Essential to carbohydrate metabolism and nervous system health.	Eggs, enriched bread, nuts, seeds, organ meat, and whole grains.
B-2 riboflavin	Protects the skin, mouth, eyes and mucous membranes. Essential to growth, red blood cell production and energy metabolism.	Dairy, meat, poultry, broccoli, spinach, eggs, and nuts.
B-3 niacin	Maintains the health of skin, nerves and digestive system.	Poultry, nuts, fish, and eggs.
B-6 Pyridoxine	Important in the regulation of the central nervous system and in protein metabolism.	Whole grains, meat, fish, nuts, avocado, and bananas.
B-9 Folic acid	Required for new cell formation, growth, reproduction, and for important chemical reactions in body cells.	Leafy greens, fruits, dried beans, nuts, peas, enriched breads, and cereals.
B-12 cobalamin	Necessary to form red blood cells.	Meat, shellfish, poultry, eggs, and dairy.
C Ascorbic acid	Maintains collagen, a protein necessary for the formation of skin, ligaments, and bones. Helps heal wounds and mend fractures.	Citric fruits and juices, cantaloupe, broccoli, brussel sprouts, tomatoes, potatoes, and cabbage.
D	Important for bone development.	Sunlight, milk, tuna, salmon, and oysters.
E tocopherol	Helps protect red blood cells.	Vegetable oils, wheat germ, whole grains, eggs, peanuts, margarine, and leafy vegetables.
K	Necessary for formation of prothrombin, which helps blood to clot. Also made by intestinal bacteria.	Green leafy vegetables and tomatoes.

Minerals

Mineral	What it does...	Sources...
Calcium	Works with phosphorus to build and maintain bones and teeth.	Dairy and leafy green vegetables.
Phosphorus	Main function is in the formation of bones and teeth. Performs more functions than any other mineral and plays a part in nearly every chemical reaction in the body.	Dairy, meats, poultry, fish, and tofu.
Iron	Necessary for the formation of myoglobin, a reservoir of oxygen for muscle tissue, and hemoglobin, which transports oxygen to the blood.	Lean meats, beans, green leafy vegetables, shellfish, and whole grains.
Sodium, Potassium, and Chloride	These are electrolytes, which help regulate the water and chemical balance in your body. Potassium is also a major component of muscle.	
Magnesium	Assists calcium and phosphorus with the development and health of bones and teeth.	
Trace Minerals (micro minerals): Chromium, cobalt, copper, fluoride, iodine, manganese, molybdenum, selenium, sulfur, and zinc.		

Water?

While not exactly a food component, water is essential to proper nutritional balance. Water seems so ordinary that you may forget how truly vital it is to your health. But it plays a role in nearly every major body function. For instance, it regulates body temperature, carries nutrients and oxygen to cells, and it removes wastes. Water also helps cushion joints and helps protect organs and tissues.

How much water do you need?

Prisoner type	Daily water intake (in addition to water found in foods)
Average MALE prisoner	3 quarts/day (96oz.)
Average FEMALE prisoner	2 quarts/day (64oz.)
Active prisoner	Same as above, PLUS an extra pint (16oz.) 2 hours pre-workout and 3-6 ounces for every 10 to 20 minutes of exercise. If your workout is unusually intense, you may want to consider an electrolyte, such as Gatorade.

Looking for more health information?

Go to our ***Reference Center*** to find valuable references guides, including a BMI Scale, a Body Fat Calculator, a Calories Burn Chart, a Target Heart Rate finders and more.

The Unhealthy Prisoner

There's a good chance that if you ignore healthful options and let the sedentary life that prison makes so convenient suck you in, you may develop any number of chronic conditions. Maybe you've already developed one of more that you're forced to live with. Prison is a very inhospitable place to have to deal with any chronic condition, but that doesn't mean that you are without access to the information and resources you need to know how to best deal with these conditions.

The following is meant to be used as a warning to encourage a healthier lifestyle or as a resource if you already dealing with a chronic condition while behind bars. It is never too late to make the absolute best of your circumstances, or to prevent worse circumstances from finding their way into your life.

Diabetes

Diabetes is essentially a disease that makes it difficult for the body to turn food into fuel.

Food we eat is broken down in the digestion process into simple sugar called *glucose*. The glucose is absorbed into your blood stream from the stomach, which makes *blood glucose*, also known as blood sugar, levels rise. In order for our cells to use the glucose as fuel, it needs the help of *insulin*, a hormone produced in the pancreas, which is a small gland located behind the stomach. Insulin acts as a bridge to get the glucose from the bloodstream to the cells. Once there, glucose is burned to give the body energy.

In diabetics, the pancreas cannot produce enough insulin. As a result, glucose backs up in the blood and blood sugar levels rise. Over years, this can damage arteries and nerves, and can lead to heart disease, kidney damage, vision problems, and more frequent and serious infections.

To some degree, diabetes is hereditary (known as *Type 1* diabetes), but scientists still don't fully understand why some people get diabetes and others don't. A common denominator, however, is that most people who contract the disease are overweight (which is typically classed as *Type 2* diabetes.)

Am I in danger of becoming a diabetic?

Unfortunately, diabetes develops gradually and produces very few, if any, signs or symptoms. Most often, people are shocked to discover that they have diabetes. Because in this case what you don't know can literally kill you, it's important to do all you can to ensure that you are healthy and diabetes-free.

GET TESTED!

You've undoubtedly seen the long line of prisoners waiting for their turn to get poked to be tested by the nurses. And then poked again to get insulin injections. If you don't want to end up having to stand in line getting daily pokes, ensure you are tested annually to check you're diabetes-free. Because diabetes is such a prevalent problem in prison, it is likely that your prison medical staff will be more than willing to test you for diabetes every year. Kite medical and ask for a screening.

Before you head to medical, here are a few facts to keep in mind:

- The most accurate time to test for blood sugar levels is after 8 hours of fasting, or first thing in the morning before you eat breakfast. Without at least 8 hours of no food, your test will be unreliable.
- A good blood sugar reading is between 70 and 100.
- A consistent reading between 100 and 125 is considered pre-diabetes, which indicates a high risk for developing diabetes.
- A reading of over 125 will require further testing.

I have diabetes. Now what?

If you have diabetes, your life is by no means over. It just means that you have no choice but to watch your diet and fitness levels more carefully than everyone else to ensure that you live a long healthy life. Thanks to there being more than 30 million Americans with diabetes, there are plenty of resources available to help you. Your prison may have information packets and guidance, but we've included several great sources for your convenience at the end of this chapter in our *Health Resources* section.

Diabetes Myths:

Myth: People with diabetes need to follow a special diet.

Fact: People with diabetes benefit from the same healthy diet as everyone else.

Myth: Healthy foods won't raise your blood sugar.

Fact: Eating too much of anything can lead to high blood sugar levels.

Myth: Diabetes is not a serious disease.

Fact: Diabetes can kill you. In fact, it kills more Americans each year than AIDS and breast cancer combined.

Hepatitis C

One of the most common health problems in prison today is hepatitis, specifically the hepatitis C virus, or HCV. The majority of those exposed to HCV will eventually go on to develop some form of liver disease, such as cirrhosis or liver cancer, or may result in liver failure that will require a liver transplant to save their life. Your liver is the largest internal organ in your body and has over 500 important functions. Almost everything we eat, drink, swallow, or absorb through our skin goes through the liver. Since HCV can destroy that functionality, it's an important topic for every prisoner to take seriously.

How do you get it?

HCV is spread through direct blood contact. To get it, your blood has to come into direct contact with infected blood, likely through methods such as the sharing of needles, a razor, nail clippers, or a toothbrush... anything that may have blood on it.

You CANNOT get HCV through kissing, hugging, sharing eating utensils, or sharing a toilet.

How prevalent is it?

In the past, it was estimated that anywhere from 39 to 54% of prisoners were infected with the virus. More recent estimates put the number of infected around 17%. Still, that means that approximately 1 in 5 prisoners may already have HCV! Worse, because there are so few signs or symptoms, relatively few prisoners know that they even have the infection. Therefore, unless you get specifically tested for HCV you may never know you have it.

The good news is that there is now a cure!

Hepatitis C Treatments

Today's HCV treatments are extremely effective.

Drug	Description	Regimen	Term	Cure Rate
Harvoni	Harvoni is the most recent treatment for genotype one diabetics (the most common strain of HCV).	One-a-day pill that is taken in combination with sofosbuvir and lepidasvir.	8-12 weeks	95-99.6%
Sovaldi & Olysio	Sovaldi (aka sofosbuvir) and Olysio (aka simeprevir) is a recent generation regimen that has proven to be highly effective.	One-a-day pill taken in combo with interferon (genotype one) or ribavirin (for genotypes 2 or 3)	12-24 weeks	90-95%

Can I get the latest hepatitis treatment in prison?

Today's treatments are extremely expensive – about $1000 a pill per day. Treatments can easily run up to $100,000. Because of that, many prison systems have been reluctant to adopt the latest treatments. However, more prison administrators are beginning to see the long-term benefits of these treatments and are at least providing them for those who have significant scarring – those with stage 3 or 4 fibrosis. If you are in county jail, the likelihood of treatment is miniscule.

Likewise, in the outside world, many insurance companies are declining to pay for such treatments due to their cost. If you're getting out soon, it may be advisable to start asking your release coordinator/case manager now for patient assistance programs that may help pay for treatment.

So how can I get treatment?

First, ask your health care provider what your options are. It may be that you have a medically progressive prison system and you may in fact be eligible for treatment now. If you are advised to wait, ask questions so that you fully understand why treatment is currently being withheld.

If outright denied treatment, the good news is that HCV is an extremely slow moving virus. If you don't already have significant liver damage, it's likely that you can wait for treatment. However, it is vital that you see your doctor regularly so they can monitor the health of your liver through biopsies and other tests, such as liver enzyme testing or APRI scores.

In the meantime, take care of yourself so that you don't make matters worse. Avoid alcohol, drink plenty of water, eat as well as you can, exercise, and get vaccinated for hepatitis A and B.

If you have hepatitis, there are plenty of resources out there to assist you in understanding your infection and the help available to you. For more information, see you prison medical staff, of write to any of the hepatitis organizations in the *Health Resources* portion of this chapter.

Prisoners & Organ Donation

24 people die every day because they cannot find a suitable organ or tissue donor. More than half of all Americans are prohibited from donating organs, blood, and other parts due to preexisting conditions ranging from infectious diseases to obesity.

However, there is a pool of untapped healthy and willing millions who are effectively banned from donating their healthy parts due to long outdated concerns. Prisoners make up a large chunk of those millions.

Over 20 years ago, the transplant community banned all prisoners from donating their healthy organs and tissues due to the then rampant AIDS crisis in America. However, since that time, considerable advancements have been made in the field of disease detection. These have made ensuring the safety of donor organs a much simpler matter. Yet the transplant community has failed to adjust accordingly.

Today many prisoners have voiced their wish to donate their healthy parts. Some would like to do so right now, while alive, through living kidney and bone marrow donations. Others wish to make sure that their organs are made available to those in need once they have passed away and no longer need them themselves. However, prisons are reluctant to get actively involved in such matters, largely because this is still a controversial topic within the transplant community. Some will allow donation, but almost universally only to an immediate family member. Others simply state that they'll consider such donations on a 'case-by-case' basis.

Lawmakers, however, are beginning to see the value in prisoner donations. In 2013, Utah became the first state to grant prisoners the legal right to donate. Now, once you go through intake in the Utah prison system, you are asked if you would like to become an organ or tissue donor. Other states are considering legislation now.

If you're interested in considering organ or tissue donation, ask you prison system's health department about their donation policies. Make your wish known!

With over 2 million people incarcerated in this country, allowing healthy prisoner donations can have a tremendous impact on the organ and tissue shortage in this country now. There is no longer a reason for those who need an organ or tissue to have to wait and wonder if the parts they need will be available for them in time.

Would you like more information on prisoner organ and tissue donation? Contact:

GAVE

www.gavelife.org   info@gavelife.org (Corrlinks-friendly)

GAVE was founded by a death row prisoner who was denied the ability to donate to a friend in need. After his plea was published by the *New York Times*, many prisons and state legislators began looking at their prisoner donor policies. While some have made adjustments, there are still thousands of people in need who die needlessly every year.

LETHAL REJECTION:

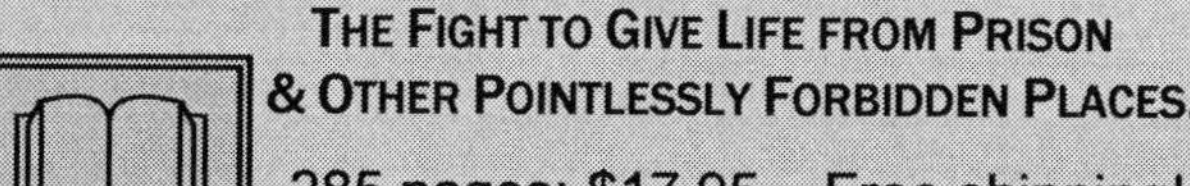

THE FIGHT TO GIVE LIFE FROM PRISON & OTHER POINTLESSLY FORBIDDEN PLACES.

285 pages; $17.95 – Free shipping!

Order through GAVE (see below). You may also order this book directly from Prison Lives.

Lethal Rejection provides a rare look behind prison walls to show why organ and tissue donation from healthy and willing prisoners SHOULD be allowed. It shows how allowing such healthy donations can drastically affect the organ shortage in this country, how those waiting in line now should not have to die needlessly, and how prisoners can get involved right now.

Prisoner Q & A Reference

Am I Eligible for Social Security Income (SSI)?

Social Security is a benefit package paid by the U.S. government to people with inadequate or no income. Since that essentially describes the majority of prisoners in this country, it leaves some questions as to whom, and who does not, qualify for these benefits.

There are two primary forms of Social Security:

- Old-age, Survivors and Disability Insurance (OASDI), commonly referred to as 'Social Security'.
- Supplemental Security Income (SSI).

OASDI – "Social Security":

Benefits that are paid to you and your family upon retirement, disability, or death. It is an insurance program that you paid into if you've worked a job where federal taxes were taken out of your check. Because of those payments, your benefit payouts are based on the amount of your earnings and the taxes you paid.

- Retirees must be 65 years or older to receive full benefits, or 62 or older to receive partial benefits. Generally, you must have worked and paid Social Security taxes to be eligible.
- Disability can be paid to those who have recently worked and paid Social Security taxes and who are unable to now work because of a serious medical condition that is expected to last at least a year or result in death. Note: The fact that a person is a recent parolee or is unemployed does NOT qualify as a disability.

SSI:

Benefits that are paid to those who are 65 or older or to those who are disabled or blind and whose income is below certain limits.

- Low income individuals can receive supplemental income by meeting the same requirements as for OASDI.

Can you get paid while in prison?

No.

Unfortunately, neither OASDI nor SSI are payable while you are in prison, jail, or certain other institutions for commission of a crime. Even when you are released, you are not automatically eligible for benefits.

Who can get paid?

While YOU cannot receive benefits while locked up, your spouse of children may be paid benefits based on your work and tax payment history. Also, if you worked and paid taxes, your survivors may be eligible to receive benefits in the event of your death.

How do you or your family get paid?

If you are about to get out and you think you will qualify for benefits upon release, or if your family may qualify to receive benefits now, contact Social Security and apply for benefits.

SOCIAL SECURITY ADMINISTRATION CONTACT INFO:

SOCIAL SECURITY ADMINISTRATION – OFFICE OF INFORMATION

6401 Security Blvd., Baltimore, MD 21235
1-800-772-1213 (For the deaf or hard of hearing: TTY 1-800-325-0778)
www.socialsecurity.gov

The Importance of your Social Security Card

Upon your release, you may be required to show your Social Security card to obtain some services or to get a job. In many cases, you will be asked to show your card as evidence of your Social Security number (SSN).

If you are over the age of 18 and have never had an SSN before, you will need to apply for one in person at the Social Security Administration office when you get out. If you already have an SSN, but no longer have your card, or if you are under 18 years of age and have never had an SSN before, you can apply for a card prior to your release by writing the Social Security Administration by using the following 'Application Form SS-5'. Complete the application and mail it back with the required paperwork, which the application explains, depending on whether you are applying for an original card or a replacement.

What You'll Need to Apply for a Social Security Card

If you've never had a social security card before...

You'll need to provide at least two documents that prove your age, identity, and U.S. citizenship or current, lawful, work-authorized immigration status.

If you're just replacing your card...

You'll need one document to prove your identity. If born outside the U.S., you must provide documents to prove your U.S. citizenship or current, lawful, work-authorized status.

Evidence Documents

EVIDENCE OF AGE
Birth Certificate
Religious record established prior to age 5
Passport
Final adoption decree

EVIDENCE OF IDENTITY
U.S. Driver's License
U.S. State-issued identity card
U.S. Passport

EVIDENCE OF CITIZENSHIP/IMMIGRATION STATUS
U.S. Birth Certificate
Consular report of birth
Certificate of Citizenship
Certificate of Naturalization
Department of Homeland Security (DHS) forms Form I-551, I-94, or I-766
If an exchange visitor/student, Form I-20, DS-2019, or an authorization from school or work (F-1 or J-1)

Do I Need to Pay Taxes?

The same rules for filing a tax return apply to you outside of prison still apply while you're in prison. You must file a tax return if your gross income for the tax year is over the filing requirements set by law.

For example, some prisoners will need to pay taxes if:

- They worked part of the year and were in prison part of the year.
- They received income while in prison, such as: retirement income, investment income, alimony payments, or prison industries.

Taxable Income	Nontaxable Income
These are only examples. For complete information, see IRS pub 525.	
Employee compensation, such as wages, salaries, commissions, fees, and tips.	Veterans' benefits, such as disability pay, insurance proceeds, dividends, allowances for education, training, and subsistence.
Miscellaneous compensation, such as bonuses, severance pay, and sick pay.	Qualified combat pay.
Business income (partnerships, S Corps, self-employed).	Government benefit payments from a public welfare fund.
Unemployment benefits.	Child support payments received.
Alimony.	Medicare benefits.
Retirement income (distributions, pensions, annuities.)	
Investment income (interest, dividends, capital gains).	
Gambling winnings.	
Some social security benefits.	
Rental property income.	

IRS CONTACT INFO:

1111 Constitution Ave. NW, Washington, DC 20224
(800) 829-1040 (questions); (800) 829-3676 (forms/publications)
www.irs.gov

Can I Vote?

In 48 states, if you have a felony conviction, you are restricted from voting. This is known as "Felony Disenfranchisement." States vary as to whether you can or cannot get your voting privileges upon completion of your prison term. Some states restore them completely, while other states effectively disenfranchise you for life. Today, 5.85 million Americans are unable to vote due to current state disenfranchisement policies.

When can I vote?

This table tells you at what point you'll be allowed to vote in your state. The only two states where there are no restrictions, where prisoners can currently vote, are Maine and Vermont.

States	Now (No voting restriction)	Upon Release	After Parole	After parole and probation	Never
Alabama					⦸
Alaska				☑	
Arizona					⦸
Arkansas				☑	
California			☑		
Colorado			☑		
Connecticut			☑		
Delaware		☑			
Florida					⦸
Georgia				☑	
Hawaii		☑			
Idaho				☑	
Illinois		☑			
Indiana		☑			
Iowa					⦸
Kansas				☑	
Kentucky					⦸
Louisiana				☑	
Maine	☑				
Maryland				☑	
Massachusetts		☑			
Michigan		☑			
Minnesota				☑	
Mississippi					⦸

When Can I Vote? Continued...

States	Now (No voting restriction)	Upon Release	After Parole	After parole and probation	Never
Montana					
Nebraska					⊘
Nevada					⊘
New Hampshire		☑			
New Jersey				☑	
New Mexico				☑	
New York			☑		
North Carolina				☑	
North Dakota		☑			
Ohio		☑			
Oklahoma				☑	
Oregon		☑			
Pennsylvania		☑			
Rhode Island					⊘
South Carolina				☑	
South Dakota				☑	
Tennessee					⊘
Texas				☑	
Utah		☑			
Vermont	☑				
Virginia					⊘
Washington				☑	
West Virginia				☑	
Wisconsin				☑	
Wyoming				☑	

PRISON CONTACT CENTER

Federal Prison Contacts

FEDERAL BUREAU OF PRISONS

HEADQUARTERS

320 First St. NW, Washington, DC 20534
(202) 307-3198

ALABAMA

FCI ALICEVILLE

11070 Highway 14, Aliceville, AL 35442
(205) 373-5000

FPC MONTGOMERY

Maxwell AFB, Montgomery, AL 36112
(256) 315-4100

FCI TALLADEGA

PO Box 1000, Talladega, AL 35160
(256) 315-4100

ARIZONA

FCI PHOENIX

37910 N. 45th Ave., Phoenix, AZ 85086
(623) 465-9757

FCI SAFFORD

1529 West Highway 366, Safford, AZ 85546
(928) 428-6600

FCI TUCSON

8901 Wilmot Rd., Tucson, AZ 85756
(520) 574-7100

ARKANSAS

FCI FORREST CITY (LOW)

1400 Dale Bumpers Rd., Forrest City, AR 72335
(870) 630-6000

FCI FORREST CITY (MEDIUM)

1400 Dale Bumpers Rd., Forrest City, AR 72335
(870) 494-4200

CALIFORNIA

CI TAFT (CONTRACTED CORRECTIONAL)

1500 Cadet Rd., Taft, CA 93268
(661) 763-2510

FCI DUBLIN

5701 8th St., Camps Park, Dublin, CA 94568
(925) 833-7500

FCI HERLONG

741-925 Access Road A-25, Herlong, CA 96113
(530) 827-8000

FCI LOMPOC

3600 Guard Rd., Lompoc, CA 93436
(805) 736-4154

FCI MENDOTA

33500 West California Ave., Mendota, CA 93640
(559) 274-4000

FCI TERMINAL ISLAND

1299 Seaside Ave., San Pedro, CA 90731
(310) 831-8961

FCI VICTORVILLE (MEDIUM 1)

13777 Air Expressway Blvd., Victorville, CA 92394
(760) 246-2400

FCI VICTORVILLE (MEDIUM 2)

13777 Air Expressway Blvd., Victorville, CA 92394
(760) 530-5700

USP ATWATER

1 Federal Way, Atwater, CA 95301
(209) 386-0257

USP LOMPOC

3901 Klein Blvd., Lompoc, CA 93436
(805) 735-2771

USP VICTORVILLE

13777 Air Expressway Blvd., Victorville, CA 92394
(760) 530-5000

COLORADO

ADX FLORENCE

PO Box 8500, Florence, CO 81226
(719) 784-9464

FCI ENGLEWOOD

9595 West Quincy Ave., Littleton, CO 80123
(313) 985-1566

FCI FLORENCE

PO Box 6000, Florence, CO 81226-6000
(719) 784-9100

FPC FLORENCE

PO Box 5000, Florence, CO 81226

USP FLORENCE

PO Box 7000, Florence, CO 81226
(719) 784-9454

CONNECTICUT

FCI DANBURY

33½ Pembroke Rd., Danbury, CT 06811-3099
(203) 743-6471

DISTRICT OF COLUMBIA

DISTRICT OF COLUMBIA | COMMUNITY CORRECTIONS

800 K St., Suite 400, Washington, DC 20001
(301) 317-3280

FLORIDA

FCC COLEMAN (LOW)

PO Box 1031, Coleman, FL 33521-1031
(352) 330-3100

FCC COLEMAN (MEDIUM)

PO Box 1032, Coleman, FL 33521-1032
(352) 330-3003

FCC COLEMAN II

PO Box 1034, Coleman, FL 33521

FCI COLEMAN (MEDIUM)

846 NE 54th Terrace, Coleman, FL 33521-0846
(352) 330-3200

FCI MARIANNA

3625 FCI Rd., Marianna, FL 32446
(850) 526-2313

FCI MIAMI

PO Box 779800, Miami, FL 33177
(305) 259-2100

FCI TALLAHASSEE

501 Capital Cir. NE, Tallahassee, FL 32301-3572
(850) 878-2173

FDC MIAMI

33 NW 4th St., PO Box 019120, Miami, FL 33101-9120
(305) 982-1114

FPC ELGIN

PO Box 600, Elgin AFB, FL 32542-7606
(850) 882-8522

FPC PENSACOLA

110 Raby Ave., Pensacola, FL 32509-5127
(850) 457-1911

USP COLEMAN I

PO Box 1033, Coleman, FL 33521

USP COLEMAN II

PO Box 1034, Coleman, FL 33521
(352) 689-7000

GEORGIA

CI MCRAE

PO Drawer 30, McRae, GA 31055
(229) 868-7778

FCI JESSUP

2680 Highway 301 South, Jessup, GA 31599
(912) 427-0870

FPC ATLANTA

PO Box 150160, Atlanta, GA 30315
(404) 635-5100

HAWAII

FDC HONOLULU

PO Box 30080, Honolulu, HI 96820
(808) 838-4200

ILLINOIS

FCI GREENVILLE

PO Box 5000, Greenville, IL 62246
(618) 664-6200

FCI PEKIN

PO Box 5000, Pekin, IL 61555
(309) 346-8588

MARION FEDERAL PRISON CAMP

PO Box 1000, Marion, IL 62529

MCC CHICAGO

71 West Van Buren, Chicago, IL 60605
(312) 322-0567

INDIANA

USP TERRE HAUTE | PRISON AND FEDERAL DEATH ROW

PO Box 33, Terre Haute, IN 47808-0033
(812) 238-1531

KANSAS

FPC LEAVENWORTH | PRISON AND MILITARY DEATH ROW

PO Box 1000, Leavenworth, KS 66048

KENTUCKY

FCI ASHLAND

PO Box 6001, Ashland, KY 41105-6001
(606) 928-6414

FCI MANCHESTER

PO Box 4000, Manchester, KY 40962-4000
(606) 598-1900

FMC LEXINGTON

PO Box 14500, Lexington, KY 40512
(606) 255-6812

USP BIG SANDY

PO Box 2068, Inez, KY 41224

USP MCCREARY

PO Box 3000, Pine Knot, KY 46235
(606) 354-7000

LOUISIANA

FCI OAKDALE

PO Box 5000, Oakdale, LA 71463
(318) 335-4070

FDC OAKDALE

PO Box 5010, Oakdale, LA 71463
(318) 335-4466

FPC OAKDALE

PO Box 5010, Oakdale, LA 71463
(318) 335-4466

USP POLLOCK

PO Box 2099, Pollock, LA 71467
(318) 561-5300

MASSACHUSETTS

FMC DEVENS

PO Box 879, Devens, MA 01434
(978) 796-1000

MARYLAND

CCM ANNAPOLIS

10010 Junction Dr., Suite 100-N, Annapolis Junction, MD 20701
(301) 317-3142

FCI CUMBERLAND

PO Box 1000, Cumberland, MD 21501
(301) 784-1000

FEDERAL PRISON CAMP | CUMBERLAND

PO Box 1000, Cumberland, MD 21501-1000

MICHIGAN

CCM DETROIT

211 W. Fort St., Suite 620, Detroit, MI 48226
(313) 226-6186

FCI MILAN

PO Box 1000, Milan, MI 48160
(734) 439-1511

MINNESOTA

FCI SANDSTONE

PO Box 1000, Sandstone, MN 55072
(320) 245-2262

FCI WASECA

PO Box 1500, Waseca, MN 56093
(507) 835-8972

FMC ROCHESTER

PMB 4000, Rochester, MN 55903
(507) 287-0674

FPC DULUTH

PO Box 1000, Duluth, MN 55814
(218) 722-8634

MISSOURI

CCM ST. LOUIS

1114 Market St., St. Louis, MO 63101
(314) 539-2376

MCF SPRINGFIELD

PO Box 4000, 1900 W. Sunshine, Springfield, MO 65801-4000
(417) 862-7041

MISSISSIPPI

FCI YAZOO CITY

PO Box 5000, Yazoo City, MS 39194
(662) 751-7800

NEW JERSEY

FCI FAIRTON

655 Fairton-Milville Rd., Fairton, NJ 08320
(856) 453-1177

FCI FORT DIX

5676 Hartford and Pointville Rd., Fort Dix, NJ 08640
(609) 723-1100

NEW MEXICO

FCI LA TUNA

PO Box 3000, Anthony, NM 88201
(915) 886-3422

NEVADA

FPC NELLIS

C.S. 4500, North Las Vegas, NV 89036-4500

NEW YORK

FCI OTISVILLE

Two Mile Dr., Otisville, NY 10963
(845) 386-6700

FCI RAY BROOK

128 Ray Brook Rd., Ray Brook, NY 12977
(518) 897-4000

NORTH CAROLINA

CCM RALEIGH

310 New Bern Ave., Room 303, Raleigh, NC 27611
(919) 856-4548

FCI BUTNER (LOW)

PO Box 999, Butner, NC 27509
(919) 575-5000

FCI BUTNER I (MEDIUM)

Old NC Highway 75, Butner, NC 27509
(919) 575-4541

FCI BUTNER II (MEDIUM)

Old NC Highway 75, Butner, NC 27509
(919) 575-8000

FMC BUTNER

PO Box 999, Old Oxford Highway 75, Butner, NC 27509-1000
(919) 575-3900

FPC SEYMOUR JOHNSON

Caller Box 8004, Goldsboro, NC 27533-8004
(919) 735-9711

N.C. CORRECTIONAL INSTITUTION FOR WOMEN

4287 Mail Service Center, Raleigh, N.C. 27699-4287
(919) 733-4340

OHIO

FCI ELKTON

8730 Scroggs Rd., Lisbon, OH 44432
Mailing Address: PO Box 2, Lisbon, OH 44432
(330) 420-6200

OKLAHOMA

FCI EL RENO

4205 Highway 66 West, P.O. Box 1500,
El Reno, OK 73036
(405) 262-4875

FTC OKLAHOMA CITY | FEDERAL TRANSIT

PO Box 898801, Oklahoma City, OK 73189
(702) 644-5001

FTC OKLAHOMA CITY

PO Box 898802, Oklahoma City, OK 73189
(702) 682-4075

OREGON

FCI SHERIDAN

27072 Ballston Rd., Sheridan, OR 97378
(503) 843-4442

PENNSYLVANIA

FCC ALLENWOOD LOW

PO Box 1000, White Deer, PA 17887

FCI LORETTO

772 St. Joseph St., Loretto, PA 15940
(814) 472-4140

FCI MCKEAN

6975 Route 59, Lewis Run, PA 16738
(814) 362-8900

FCI SCHUYLKILL

Interstate 81 & 901 West, Minersville, PA 17954
Mailing Address: PO Box 759, Minersville, PA 17954-0759
(570) 544-7100

USP CANAAN

3057 Easton Turnpike, PO Box 300, Waymart, PA 18472
(570) 488-8000

USP LEWISBURG

2400 Robert F. Miller Dr., PO Box 1000, Lewisburg PA 17837
(570) 523-1251

SOUTH CAROLINA

ESTILL FEDERAL PRISON CAMP

PO Box 699, Estill, SC 29918

FCI BENNETTSVILLE

696 Muckerman Rd., Bennettsville, SC 29512
(843) 454-8200

FCI EDGEFIELD

501 Gary Hill Rd., PO Box 724, Edgefield, SC 29824
(803) 637-1500

FCI ESTILL

100 Prison Rd., PO Box 699, Estill, SC 29918
(803) 625-4607

FPC EDGEFIELD

501 Gary Hill Rd., PO Box 725, Edgefield, SC 29824
(803) 637-1500

FPC WILLIAMSBURG

PO Box 380, Salters, SC 29590

SOUTH DAKOTA

FPC YANKTON

PO Box 680, Yankton, SD 57078
(605) 665-3262

TENNESSEE

FCI MEMPHIS

1101 John A. Denie Rd., Memphis, TN 38134
(901) 372-2269

TEXAS

CCM HOUSTON

515 Rusk, Room 12102, Houston, TX 77002

FCI BASTROP

PO Box 1010, Bastrop, TX 78602
(512) 321-3903

FCC BEAUMONT | ADMINISTRATIVE

PO Box 26015, Beaumont, TX 77720
(409) 727-8187

FCI BEAUMONT (LOW)

PO Box 26025, Beaumont, TX 77720
(409) 727-8172

FCC BEAUMONT (MEDIUM)

PO Box 26040, Beaumont, TX 77720-6045
(409) 727-0101

FCI BIG SPRING

1900 Simler Drive., Big Spring, TX 79720-7799
(915) 263-6699

FCI SEAGOVILLE

PO Box 9000, Seagoville, TX 75159-9000
(972) 287-2911

FCI TEXARKANA

PO Box 9500, Texarkana, TX 75505
(903) 838-4587

FCI THREE RIVERS

PO Box 4000, Three Rivers, TX 78071
(361) 786-3576

FDC HOUSTON

PO Box 526245, 1200 Texas Ave., 77052-6245
(713) 221-5400

FMC CARSWELL

PO Box 27137, Fort Worth, TX 76127
(817) 782-4000

FMC FORT WORTH

3150 Horton Rd., Fort Worth, TX 76119-5996
(817) 534-8400

FPC BRYAN

PO Box 2149, Bryan, TX 77805
(409) 823-1879

FPC EL PASO

PO Box 16300, SSG Sims Rd., Building 11636, El Paso, TX 79906-0300
(915) 566-1271

FPC TEXARKANA

PO Box 9300, Texarkana, TX 75505

USP BEAUMONT

PO Box 26030, Beaumont, TX 77720-6030
(409) 727-8188

VIRGINIA

CI PETERSBURG (LOW)

PO Box 1000, Petersburg, VA 23804

FCI PETERSBURG

PO Box 90043, Petersburg, VA 23804
(804) 733-7881

USP LEE

Lee County Industrial Park, Hickory Flats Rd., Pennington Gap, VA 24277
(276) 546-0150

USP LEE | CAMP

PO Box 644, Jonesville, VA 24263-0644
(276) 546-0150

WASHINGTON

FDC SEATAC

PO Box 13900, Seattle, WA 98198
(206) 870-5700

WISCONSIN

FCI OXFORD

PO Box 1000, Oxford, WI 52952

WEST VIRGINIA

FCI BERKLEY

PO Box 350, Beaver, WV 25813
(304) 252-9758

FCI GILMER

PO Box 6000, Glenville, WV 26351

FCI MORGANTOWN

Greenbag Rd., PO Box 1000, Morgantown, WV 26507-1000
(304) 296-4416

FPC ALDERSON

Glen Ray Rd., Box B, Alderson, WV 24910
(304) 445-2901

USP HAZELTON

PO Box 2000, Bruceton Mills, WV 26525
(304-379-5000

State Prison Contacts

ALABAMA

ALABAMA DEPARTMENT OF CORRECTIONS
301 S. Ripley St., PO Box 301501, Montgomery, AL 36130-1501
(334) 353-3883
www.doc.state.al.us

ALABAMA ALEX CITY WORK RELEASE

PO Drawer 160, Alex City, AL 35010-0160
(256) 234-7533

ATMORE WORK RELEASE

9947 Highway 21 North, Atmore, AL 36503
(251) 368-9115

BIBB COUNTY CORRECTIONAL FACILITY

565 Bibbs Lane, Brent, AL 35034
(205) 926-5252

BIRMINGHAM WORK RELEASE

1216 25th St. N, Birmingham, AL 35324-3196
(205) 252-2994

BULLOCK CORRECTIONAL FACILITY

PO Box 5107, Union Springs, AL 36089-5107
(334) 738-5625

BULLOCK WORK RELEASE

PO Box 192, Union Springs, AL 36089-0192
(334) 738-5537

CAMDEN WORK RELEASE

Route 2, Box 221, Camden AL 36726-9542
(334) 682-4287

CHILDERSBURG COMMUNITY WORK CENTER

PO Box 368, Childersburg, AL 35044-0368
(205) 368-5034

DECATUR WORK RELEASE

PO Box 5279, Decatur, AL 35601
(256) 350-0876

DONALDSON CORRECTIONAL FACILITY

100 Warrior Lane, Bessemer, AL 35023-7299
(205) 436-3681

DRAPER CORRECTIONAL FACILITY

PO Box 1107, Elmore, AL 36025
(334) 567-2221

EASTERLING CORRECTIONAL FACILITY

PO Box 10, Clio, AL 36017-0010
(334) 397-4471

EDWINA MITCHELL WORK RELEASE

8950 U.S. Highway 231 North, Wetumpka, AL 36092
(334) 567-9182

ELBA WORK RELEASE

PO Drawer 427, Elba, AL 36323-0361
(334) 897-5738

ELMORE CORRECTIONAL FACILITY

PO Box 8, Elmore, AL 36025

FARQUHAR CATTLE RANCH

1132 County Road 73, Greensboro, AL 36744
(334) 624-3383

FOUNTAIN CORRECTIONAL FACILITY

PO Box 3800, Atmore, AL 36503-3800
(251) 638-81223

HAMILTON AGED AND INFIRMED

PO Box 1568, Hamilton, AL 35570-1568
(205) 921-7453

HAMILTON WORK RELEASE

PO Box 1628, Hamilton, AL 35570-1628
(205) 921-9308

HOLMAN CORRECTIONAL FACILITY | PRISON AND DEATH ROW

PO Box 3700, Atmore, AL 36503-3700
(251) 368-8173

J.O. DAVIS CORRECTIONAL FACILITY

PO Box 4000, Atmore, AL 36503

JULIA TUTWILER PRISON FOR WOMEN | PRISON AND WOMEN'S DEATH ROW

8966 U.S. Highway 231 North, Wetumpka, AL 36092
(334) 567-4369

KILBY CORRECTIONAL FACILITY

PO Box 150, Mt. Meigs, AL 36057
(334) 215-6600

LIMESTONE CORRECTIONAL FACILITY

PO Box 66, Capshaw, AL 35742
(256) 233-4600

LOXLEY WORK RELEASE AND COMMUNITY WORK CENTER

PO Box 1030, Loxley, AL 36551-1030

MOBILE WORK RELEASE

PO Box 13150, Eight Mile, AL 36663-0150
(251) 452-0098

MONTGOMERY CCM | MAXWELL AFB 1209

820 Willow St., Montgomery, AL 36112

MONTGOMERY WORK RELEASE

PO Box 75, Mt. Meigs, AL 36057

RED EAGLE HONOR FARM

1290 Red Eagle Rd., Montgomery, AL 36110

ST. CLAIR CORRECTIONAL FACILITY

1000 St. Clair Rd., Springville, AL 36146
(205) 467-6111

STATON CORRECTIONAL FACILITY

PO Box 56, Elmore, AL 36025
(334) 567-2221

VENTRESS CORRECTIONAL FACILITY

PO Box 767, Clayton, AL 36016-0767
(334) 775-3331

ALASKA

ALASKA DEPARTMENT OF CORRECTIONS
802 3rd St., Douglas, AK 99824
(907) 465-4652
www.correct.state.ak.us/corrections

ANVIL MOUNTAIN CORRECTIONAL CENTER

Mile 3.5 Center Creek Rd., PO Box 730, Nome, AK 99762
(907) 443-2271

FAIRBANKS CORRECTIONAL CENTER

1931 Eagan Ave., Fairbanks, AK 99701

HILAND MOUNTAIN CORRECTIONAL CENTER

9101 Hesterberg Rd., Eagle River, AK 99577

KETCHIKAN CORRECTIONAL CENTER

1201 Schoenbar Rd., Ketchikan, AK 99901-6270
(907) 225-9429

LEMON CREEK CORRECTIONAL CENTER

2000 Lemon Creek Rd., Juneau, AK 99801
(908) 465-6200

MAT-SU PRETRIAL

330 E. Dogwood, Palmer, AK 99645
(909) 745-0943

SPRING CREEK CORRECTIONAL CENTER

PO Box 5001, Seward, AK 99664
(907) 224-8200

YUKON-KUSKOKWIM CORRECTIONAL CENTER

1000 Chief Eddie Hoffman Highway, Box 400, Bethel, AK 99559

ARIZONA

ARIZONA DEPARTMENT OF CORRECTIONS
www.az.corrections.gov

ARIZONA STATE PRISON | LEWIS

PO Box 3100, Buckeye, AZ 85326

ARIZONA STATE PRISON

PO Box 3700, Buckeye, AZ 85326

ARIZONA STATE PRISON | FLORENCE WEST

PO Box 1599, Florence, AZ 85323-1599
(520) 868-4251

ARIZONA STATE PRISON | FORT GRANT

PO Box 4399, Fort Grant, AZ 85644-4000

ARIZONA STATE PRISON | PHOENIX WEST

PO Box 18460, Phoenix, AZ 85005
(602) 352-0350

ARIZONA STATE PRISON | BUCKEYE

PO Box 3600, Buckeye, AZ 85326

ARIZONA STATE PRISON COMPLEX | YUMA

PO Box 8940, San Luis, AZ 85349

ARIZONA STATE PRISON | DOUGLAS

PO Box 5003, Douglas, AZ 85608

ARIZONA STATE PRISON | FORT GRANT

PO Box 2500, Fort Grant AZ 85644

ARIZONA STATE PRISON | DOUGLAS

PO Box 3867, Douglas, AZ 85608-3867
(914) 364-7521

ARIZONA STATE PRISON COMPLEX | DOUGLAS (CDU)

PO Box 5006, 85608-5006
(520) 364-7521

ARIZONA STATE PRISON COMPLEX | DOUGLAS (EGGERS)

PO Box 5001, Douglas, AZ 85608-5001
(520) 364-7521

ARIZONA STATE PRISON COMPLEX | DOUGLAS (GILA)

PO Box 5004, Douglas, AZ 85608-5004
(520) 364-7521

ARIZONA STATE PRISON COMPLEX | DOUGLAS (MARICOPA)

PO Box 5000, Douglas, AZ 85608-5000
(520) 634-7521

ARIZONA STATE PRISON COMPLEX | DOUGLAS (MOHAVE)

PO Box 5002, Douglas, AZ 85608-5002
(520) 364-7521

ARIZONA STATE PRISON COMPLEX | DOUGLAS (PAPAGO)

PO Box 5005, Douglas, AZ 85608-5005
(520) 364-7521

ARIZONA STATE PRISON COMPLEX | EYMAN

PO Box 3500, Florence, AZ 85232-3500
(520) 868-0201

ARIZONA STATE PRISON COMPLEX | EYMAN (COOK)

PO Box 3200, Florence, AZ 85232-3200
(520) 868-0201

ARIZONA STATE PRISON COMPLEX | EYMAN (MEADOWS)

PO Box 3300, Florence, AZ 85232-3300
(520) 868-0201

ARIZONA STATE PRISON COMPLEX | EYMAN (RYNNING)

PO Box 3100, Florence, AZ 85232-3100
(520) 868-0201

ARIZONA STATE PRISON COMPLEX | EYMAN (SMU II) | PRISON AND DEATH ROW

PO Box 3400, Florence, AZ 85232-3400
(520) 868-0201

ARIZONA STATE PRISON COMPLEX | FLORENCE

PO Box 6900, Florence, AZ 85232
(520) 868-4011

ARIZONA STATE PRISON COMPLEX | FLORENCE (CB-6)

PO Box 8600, Florence, AZ 85232-8600
(520) 868-4011

ARIZONA STATE PRISON COMPLEX | FLORENCE (CENTRAL UNIT)

PO Box 8200, Florence, AZ 85232-8200
(520) 868-4011

ARIZONA STATE PRISON COMPLEX | FLORENCE (EAST UNIT)

PO Box 5000, Florence, AZ 85232-5000
(520) 868-4011

ARIZONA STATE PRISON COMPLEX | FLORENCE (NORTH UNIT 41)

PO Box 7000, Florence, AZ 85232-7000
(520) 868-4011

ARIZONA STATE PRISON COMPLEX | FLORENCE (NORTH UNIT 42)

PO Box 8000, Florence, AZ 85232-8000
(520) 868-4011

ARIZONA STATE PRISON COMPLEX | FLORENCE (NORTH UNIT 93)

PO Box 7200, Florence, AZ 85232-7200
(520) 868-4011

ARIZONA STATE PRISON COMPLEX | FLORENCE (PICACHO)

PO Box 629, Florence, AZ 85232-0629
(520) 868-4011

ARIZONA STATE PRISON COMPLEX | FLORENCE (SOUTH UNIT)

PO Box 8400, Florence, AZ 85232-8400
(520) 868-4011

ARIZONA STATE PRISON COMPLEX | LEWIS

PO Box 70, Buckeye, AZ 85236
(623) 386-6160

ARIZONA STATE PRISON COMPLEX | LEWIS (BACHMAN)

PO Box 3500, Buckeye, AZ 85236
(623) 386-6160

ARIZONA STATE PRISON COMPLEX | LEWIS (BARCHEY)

PO Box 3200, Buckeye, AZ 85236
(623) 386-6160

ARIZONA STATE PRISON COMPLEX | LEWIS (BUCKLEY)

PO Box 3700, Buckeye, AZ 85236
(623) 386-6160

ARIZONA STATE PRISON COMPLEX | LEWIS (EAGLE POINT)

PO Box 3400, Buckeye, AZ 85236
(623) 386-6160

ARIZONA STATE PRISON COMPLEX | LEWIS (MOREY)

PO Box 3300, Buckeye, AZ 85236
(623) 386-6160

ARIZONA STATE PRISON COMPLEX | LEWIS (STINER)

PO Box 3100, Buckeye, AZ 85236
(623) 386-6160

ARIZONA STATE PRISON COMPLEX | PERRYVILLE

PO Box 3000, Goodyear, AZ 85338-0901
(623) 853-0304

ARIZONA STATE PRISON COMPLEX | PERRYVILLE (CDU)

PO Box 3000, Goodyear, AZ 85338-0901
(623) 853-0304

ARIZONA STATE PRISON COMPLEX | PERRYVILLE (LUMLEY)

PO Box 3300, Goodyear, AZ 85338-0901
(623) 853-0304

ARIZONA STATE PRISON COMPLEX | PERRYVILLE (SAN PEDRO)

PO Box 3100, Goodyear, AZ 85338-0901
(623) 853-0304

ARIZONA STATE PRISON COMPLEX | PERRYVILLE (SANTA CRUZ)

PO Box 3200, Goodyear, AZ 85338-0901
(623) 853-0304

ARIZONA STATE PRISON COMPLEX | PERRYVILLE (SANTA MARIA) | PRISON AND WOMEN'S DEATH ROW

PO Box 3400, Goodyear, AZ 85338-0901
(623) 853-0304

ARIZONA STATE PRISON COMPLEX | PHOENIX

PO Box 52109, Phoenix, AZ 85072-2109
(602) 685-3100

ARIZONA STATE PRISON COMPLEX | PHOENIX (ACW)

PO Box 52112, Phoenix, AZ 85072-2112
(602) 685-3100

ARIZONA STATE PRISON COMPLEX | PHOENIX (ASPEN / SPU)

PO Box 52110, Phoenix, AZ 85072-2110
(602) 685-3100

ARIZONA STATE PRISON COMPLEX | PHOENIX (GLOBE)

PO Box 2799, Globe, AZ 85502-2799

ARIZONA STATE PRISON COMPLEX | PHOENIX (ALHAMBRA / FLAMENCO)

PO Box 52109, Phoenix, AZ 85072-2109
(602) 685-3100

ARIZONA STATE PRISON COMPLEX | SAFFORD

PO Box 2222, Safford, AZ 85548-2222
(520) 428-4698

ARIZONA STATE PRISON COMPLEX | SAFFORD (GRAHAM)

PO Box 2300, Safford, AZ 85548-2300
(520) 428-4698

ARIZONA STATE PRISON COMPLEX | SAFFORD (TONTO)

PO Box 2400, Safford, AZ 85548-2400
(520) 428-4698

ARIZONA STATE PRISON COMPLEX | TUCSON

PO Box 24400, Tucson, AZ 85734-4400

ARIZONA STATE PRISON COMPLEX | TUCSON (CDU)

PO Box 24405, Tucson, AZ 85734-4405

ARIZONA STATE PRISON COMPLEX | TUCSON (CIMARRON)

PO Box 24408, Tucson, AZ 85734-4408

ARIZONA STATE PRISON COMPLEX | TUCSON (ECHO)

PO Box 24402, Tucson, AZ 85734-4402

ARIZONA STATE PRISON COMPLEX | TUCSON (MANZANITA)

PO Box 24401, Tucson, AZ 85734-4001

ARIZONA STATE PRISON COMPLEX | TUCSON (RINCON)

PO Box 24403, Tucson, AZ 85734-4403

ARIZONA STATE PRISON COMPLEX | TUCSON (SACRC)

1275 W. Star Pass Blvd., Tucson, AZ 85734

ARIZONA STATE PRISON COMPLEX | TUCSON (SANTA RITA)

PO Box 24406, Tucson, AZ 85734-4406

ARIZONA STATE PRISON COMPLEX | TUCSON (WINCHESTER)

PO Box 24407, Tucson, AZ 85734-4407

ARIZONA STATE PRISON COMPLEX | WINSLOW

2100 South Highway 87, Winslow, AZ 86047-9799
(928) 289-9551

ARIZONA STATE PRISON COMPLEX | WINSLOW (APACHE)

PO Box 3240, Winslow, AZ 86047-3240

ARIZONA STATE PRISON COMPLEX | WINSLOW (CORONADO)

2100 South Highway 87, Winslow, AZ 86047-9799
(928) 289-9551

ARIZONA STATE PRISON COMPLEX | WINSLOW (KAIBAB)

2100 South Highway 87, Winslow, AZ 86047-9799
(928) 289-9551

ARIZONA STATE PRISON COMPLEX | YUMA

PO Box 13004, Yuma, AZ 85366-3004
(928) 627-8871

ARIZONA STATE PRISON COMPLEX | YUMA (CHEYENNE)

PO Box 13006, Yuma, AZ 85366-3006
(928) 627-8871

ARIZONA STATE PRISON COMPLEX | YUMA (COCOPAH)

PO Box 13005, Yuma, AZ 85366-3005
(928) 627-8871

ARIZONA STATE PRISON COMPLEX | YUMA (DAKOTA)

PO Box 13007, Yuma, AZ 85366-3007
(928) 627-8871

CENTRAL ARIZONA CORRECTIONAL FACILITY (CACF)

PO Box 9600, Florence, AZ 85132-0999
(520) 868-4809

MARANA COMMUNITY CORRECTIONAL TREATMENT FACILITY

12610 W. Silverbell Rd., PO Box 940, Marana, AZ 85653

USP TUCSON

PO Box 24550, Tucson, AZ 85734

WRIGHTSVILLE

PO Box 1000, Wrightsville, AZ 72183-1000
(501) 897-5806

ARKANSAS

ARKANSAS DEPARTMENT OF CORRECTIONS

www.adc.arkansas.gov

BENTON

701 Highway 67, Benton, AR 72015-8488
(501) 315-2252

BOOT CAMP

PO Box 1000, Wrightsville, AR 72813-1000
(870) 897-5806

CUMMINS

PO Box 500, Grady, AR 71644-0500
(870) 850-8899

DELTA REGIONAL

Route 1, Box 12, Dermott, AR 71638-9505
(870) 538-2000

DIAGNOSTIC UNIT

7500 Correctional Cir., Pine Bluff, AR 71603
(870) 267-6410

EAST ARKANSAS REGIONAL

PO Box 180, Brickeys, AR 72320-0180
(870) 295-4700

GRIMES

300 Wackenhut Way, Newport, AR 72112-3493
(870) 523-5877

MAXIMUM SECURITY UNIT | PRISON AND DEATH ROW

2501 State Farm Rd., Tucker, AR 72168-8713
(501) 842-3800

MCPHERSON UNIT

302 Wackenhut Way, Newport, AR 72112
(870) 523-2639

NORTH CENTRAL

HC 62, PO Box 300, Calico Rock, AR 72519-0300
(870) 297-4311

NORTHWEST ARKANSAS WORK RELEASE CENTER

PO Box 1352, Springdale, AK 72765-1352
(501) 756-2037

PINE BLUFF

890 Free Line Dr., Pine Bluff, AR 71603-1498
(870) 267-6510

SOUTHWEST ARKANSAS COMMUNITY CORRECTIONS CENTER

506 Walnut, Texarkana, AR 71854

TEXARKANA REGIONAL CORRECTION CENTER

100 North State Line Ave., Box 21, Texarkana, AR 75502-5952

TUCKER

PO Box 240, Tucker, AR 72618-0240
(501) 842-2519

TUCKER MAX

2501 State Farm Rd., Tucker, AR 72168

VARNER

PO Box 600, Grady, AR 71644-0600
(860) 479-3030

WOMEN'S UNIT | PRISON AND WOMEN'S DEATH ROW

800 W. 7th St., Pine Bluff, AR 71603-1498

CALIFORNIA

CALIFORNIA DEPARTMENT OF CORRECTIONS

www.cdcr.ca.gov

AVENAL STATE PRISON (ARIZONA STATE PRISON)

PO Box 9, Avenal, CA 93204
(559) 386-0587

BUTTE COUNTY

35 County Center Rd., Oroville, CA 95965

CALIFORNIA CORRECTIONAL CENTER (CCC)

PO Box 2500, Susanville, CA 96127-2500
(530) 257-2181

CALIFORNIA CORRECTIONAL INSTITUTE (CCI)

PO Box 1906, Tehachapi, CA 93581
(661) 822-4402

CALIFORNIA DETENTION CENTER (CDC)

PO Box 1011, Imperial, CA 92251

CALIFORNIA INSTITUTE FOR MEN (CIM) | FACILITY B (RECEPTION CENTER CENTRAL)

PO Box 441, Chino, CA 91708

CALIFORNIA INSTITUTE FOR MEN (CIM) | FACILITY D (MINIMUM SUPPORT FACILITY)

PO Box 600, Chino, CA 91708

CALIFORNIA INSTITUTE FOR MEN (CIM) | RECEPTION CENTER FACILITY C (EAST)

PO Box 500, Chino, CA 91708

CALIFORNIA INSTITUTE FOR MEN (CIM) | RECEPTION CENTER FACILITY A (WEST)

PO Box 368, Chino, CA 91708

CALIFORNIA INSTITUTE FOR WOMEN (CIW)

16756 Chino-Corona Rd., Corona, CA 92880-9508

CALIFORNIA MEDICAL FACILITY

PO Box 2000, Vacaville, CA 95696-2000
(707) 448-6841

CALIFORNIA MEN'S COLONY (CMC) | EAST

PO Box 8101, San Luis Obispo, CA 93409-8101
(805) 547-7900

CALIFORNIA MEN'S COLONY (CMC) | WEST

PO Box 8103, San Luis Obispo, CA 93409-8103
(805) 547-7900

CALIFORNIA REHABILITATION CENTER (CRC)

PO Box 3535, Norco, CA 92860-0991
(951) 737-2683

CALIFORNIA STATE PRISON | COALINGA (COA)

PO Box 8501, Coalinga, CA 93210

CALIFORNIA STATE PRISON | LANCASTER

PO Box 4490, Lancaster, CA 93539-4670
(661) 729-2000

CALIFORNIA STATE PRISON | NEW FOLSOM

PO Box 29, Represa, CA 95671

CALIFORNIA STATE PRISON | SACRAMENTO (SAC)

PO Box 290066, Represa, CA 95671
(916) 985-8610

CALIFORNIA STATE PRISON | SOLANO

PO Box 4000, Vacaville, CA 95696-4000
(707) 451-0182

CALIFORNIA SUBSTANCE ABUSE TREATMENT FACILITY (SATF)

Facility A & B: PO Box 5248, Corcoran, CA 93212
Facility C: PO Box 5246, Corcoran, CA 93212
Facility D & E: PO Box 5242, Corcoran, CA 93212
Facility F & G: PO Box 5244, Corcoran, CA 93212

CALIPATRIA STATE PRISON (CAL)

PO Box 5007, Calipatria, CA 92233-5007
(760) 348-7000

CENTINELA STATE PRISON (CEN) | A YARD

PO Box 901, Imperial, CA 92251
(619) 337-7601

CENTINELA STATE PRISON (CEN) | B YARD

PO Box 911, Imperial, CA 92251
(619) 337-7601

CENTINELA STATE PRISON (CEN) | C YARD

PO Box 921, Imperial, CA 92251
(619) 337-7601

CENTINELA STATE PRISON (CEN) | D YARD

PO Box 1011, Imperial, CA 92251
(619) 337-7601

CENTRAL CALIFORNIA WOMEN'S FACILITY (CCWF) | PRISON AND WOMEN'S DEATH ROW

PO Box 1508, Chowchilla, CA 93610-1508
(559) 665-5531

CHUCKWALLA VALLEY STATE PRISON

PO Box 2349, Blythe, CA 92226
(760) 922-5300

COALINGA S.H.

PO Box 5003, Coalinga, CA 95205

CORCORAN STATE PRISON (CSP)

PO Box 3456, Corcoran, CA 93231

CORCORAN STATE PRISON | CSP-C

PO Box 3466, Corcoran, CA 93212-3456
(559) 992-8800

CORCORAN STATE PRISON | SHU

PO Box 3476, Corcoran, CA 93212-3476
(559) 992-8800

CORRECTIONAL TRAINING FACILITY (CTF) | CENTRAL FACILITY

PO Box 689, Soledad, CA 93960-0689
(831) 678-3951

CORRECTIONAL TRAINING FACILITY (CTF) | NORTH FACILITY

PO Box 705, Soledad, CA 93960-0705
(831) 678-3951

CORRECTIONAL TRAINING FACILITY (CTF) | SOUTH FACILITY

PO Box 690, Soledad, CA 93960-0690
(831) 678-3951

DESERT VIEW MSSC

PO Box 4000, Adelanto, CA 92301

DEUEL VOCATIONAL INSTITUTE (DVI)

PO Box 600, Tracy, CA 95378-0004
(209) 835-4141

FOLSOM STATE PRISON (FSP)

PO Box 715071, Represa, CA 95671-5071
(916) 985-2561

HIGH DESERT STATE PRISON (HDSP)

PO Box 3030, Susanville, CA 96127-3030
(530) 251-5100

INTENSIVE CONFINEMENT CENTER (ICC)

4000 Victory Rd., Lompoc, CA 93439

IRONWOOD STATE PRISON (ISP)

PO Box 2199, Blythe, CA 92226
(760) 921-3000

KERN VALLEY STATE PRISON

PO Box 5103, Delano, CA 93216-5102

LANCASTER STATE PRISON

44750 60th St. West, Lancaster, CA 93536

LOMPOC CAMP

3705 Farm Rd., Lompoc, CA 93436

MULE CREEK STATE PRISON (MCSP)

PO Box 409000, Ione, CA 95640
(916) 274-4911

NEW FOLSOM

PO Box 290066, Represa, CA 95671

NORTH KERN STATE PRISON (NKSP)

PO Box 5000, Delano, CA 93216
(661) 721-2345

NORTHERN CALIFORNIA WOMEN'S FACILITY (NCWF)

PO Box 213006, Stockton, CA 95213-9006
(209) 943-1600

PELICAN BAY STATE PRISON (PBSP)

PO Box 7000, Crescent City, CA 95531-7000
(707) 465-1000

PLEASANT VALLEY STATE PRISON (PVSP)

24863 West Jayne Avenue, Coalinga, CA 93210
PO Box 8500, Coalinga, CA 93210
(559) 935-4900

PLEASANT VALLEY STATE PRISON (PVSP) | FACILITY A

PO Box 8501, Coalinga, CA 93210
(559) 935-4900

PLEASANT VALLEY STATE PRISON (PVSP) | FACILITY B

PO Box 8502, Coalinga, CA 93210
(559) 935-4900

PLEASANT VALLEY STATE PRISON (PVSP) | FACILITY C

PO Box 8503, Coalinga, CA 93210
(559) 935-4900

PLEASANT VALLEY STATE PRISON (PVSP) | FACILITY D

PO Box 8504, Coalinga, CA 93210
(559) 935-4900

R.J. DONOVAN CORRECTIONAL FACILITY | ROCK MOUNTAIN (RJD)

PO Box 799004, San Diego, CA 92179-9004

R.J. DONOVAN CORRECTIONAL FACILITY | ROCK MOUNTAIN (RJDCF)

PO Box 799003, San Diego, CA 92179-9003

SALINAS VALLEY STATE PRISON (SVSP)

PO Box 1020, Soledad, CA 93960-1020

SAN QUENTIN STATE PRISON (SQ) | PRISON AND DEATH ROW

San Quentin, CA 94974
(415) 454-1460

SIERRA CONSERVATION CENTER (SCC)

Physical Address: 5100 O'Byrnes Ferry Road
Mailing Address: 5150 O'Byrnes Ferry Road
Jamestown, CA 95327
(209) 984-5291

SIERRA CONSERVATION CENTER (SCC) | CALAVERAS UNIT

PO Box 617, Jamestown, CA 95327
(209) 984-5291

SIERRA CONSERVATION CENTER (SCC) | MARIPOSA UNIT

PO Box 617, Jamestown, CA 95327
(209) 984-5291

SIERRA CONSERVATION CENTER (SCC) | TUOLUMNE UNIT

PO Box 500, Jamestown, CA 95327
(209) 984-5291

VALLEY STATE PRISON FOR WOMEN (VSPW)

PO Box 92, Chowchilla, CA 93610-0099
(559) 665-6100

VICTORVILLE | MEDIUM II

PO Box 5300, Adelanto, CA 92301

WASCO PRISON

PO Box 4400, Wasco, CA 93280

COLORADO

COLORADO DEPARTMENT OF CORRECTIONS

PO Box 777, Canon City, CO 81215 or
2862 South Circle Dr., Colorado Springs, CO 80906
www.doc.state.co.us

ARKANSAS VALLEY CORRECTIONAL FACILITY

12750 Highway 96, Crowley, CO 81034
(719) 267-3520

ARROWHEAD CORRECTIONAL CENTER

PO Box 300, Canon City, CO 81215-0300
(719) 269-5601

BUENA VISTA CORRECTIONAL FACILITY

PO Box 2017, Buena Vista, CO 81211
(719) 395-2404

BUENA VISTA MINIMUM CENTER

PO Box 2005, Buena Vista, CO 81211

CENTENNIAL CORRECTIONAL FACILITY | EAST CANON COMPLEX | PRISON AND DEATH ROW

PO Box 777, Canon City, CO 81215

CHEYENNE MOUNTAIN REENTRY CENTER

2925 East Las Vegas St., Colorado Springs, CO 80906
(719) 390-0125

CLEAR CREEK COUNTY JAIL

PO Box 518, Georgetown, CO 80444

COLORADO CORRECTIONAL ALTERNATIVE PROGRAM (CCAP)

PO Box 1794, Buena Vista, CO 81211

COLORADO CORRECTIONAL CENTER

15000 Old Golden Rd., PO Box 4020, Golden, CO 80401-0020
(303) 273-1620

COLORADO STATE PENITENTIARY

PO Box 777, Canon City, CO 81215
(719) 269-5120

COLORADO TERRITORIAL CORRECTIONAL FACILITY

PO Box 1010, Canon City, CO 81215-1010
(719) 269-4002

COLORADO WOMEN'S CORRECTIONAL FACILITY | PRISON AND WOMEN'S DEATH ROW

3800 Grandview, PO Box 500, Canon City, CO 81215-0500

CROWLEY COUNTY CORRECTIONAL FACILITY

6564 State Highway 96, Olney Springs, CO 81062-8700
(719) 267-3528

DELTA CORRECTIONAL CENTER

11363 Lockhart Rd., Delta, CO 81416
(970) 874-7614

DENVER RECEPTION AND DIAGNOSTIC CENTER

PO Box 392004, Denver, CO 80239-8004
(303) 371-4804

DENVER WOMEN'S CORRECTIONAL FACILITY

PO Box 392005, Denver, CO 80239
(303) 371-4804

FORT LYON CORRECTIONAL FACILITY

PO Box 1000, Ft. Lyon, CO 81038
(719) 456-2201

FOUR MILE CORRECTIONAL CENTER

PO Box 300, Canon City, CO 81215-0300
(719) 269-5601

FREMONT CORRECTIONAL FACILITY | EAST CANON COMPLEX

PO Box 999, Canon City, CO 81215-0999
(719) 269-5002

KIT CARSON CORRECTIONAL CENTER

49777 County Road V, Burlington, CO 80807
(719) 346-9450

LA VISTA CORRECTIONAL FACILITY

PO Box 3, Pueblo, CO 81002
(719) 544-4800

LIMON CORRECTIONAL FACILITY

PO Box 49030, Colorado 71 S., Limon, CO 80826
(719) 775-9221

PUEBLO MINIMUM CENTER

1410 W. 13th St., PO Box 3, Pueblo, CO 81003
(719) 544-4800

RIFLE CORRECTIONAL CENTER

200 County Road 219, Rifle, CO 81650
(970) 625-7578

SAN CARLOS CORRECTIONAL FACILITY

PO Box 3, Pueblo, CO 81002-0003

(719) 544-4800

SKYLINE CORRECTIONAL CENTER (SCC) | EAST CANNON COMPLEX

PO Box 300, Canon City, CO 81215
(719) 269-5450

STERLING CORRECTIONAL FACILITY

PO Box 6000, Sterling, CO 80751
(970) 521-5010

COLORADO TERRITORIAL CORRECTIONAL FACILITY (CTCF)

PO Box 1010, Canon City, CO 81215

TRINIDAD CORRECTIONAL FACILITY

21000 E. Highway 350, Model, CO 81059
(719) 845-3226

USP FLORENCE ADMAX | SATELLITE CAMP

PO Box 8500, Florence, CO 81226

YOUTHFUL OFFENDER SYSTEM (YOS)

1300 W. 13th St., Pueblo, CO 81003

CONNECTICUT

CONNECTICUT DEPARTMENT OF CORRECTIONS
www.ct.gov/doc/

BERGIN CORRECTIONAL INSTITUTION

251 Middle Turnpike, Storrs, CT 06268
(860) 487-2712

BRIDGEPORT CORRECTIONAL CENTER

1106 North Ave., PO Box 6490, Bridgeport, CT 06604
(203) 579-6131

BROOKLYN CORRECTIONAL INSTITUTION

59 Hartford Rd., Brooklyn, CT 06234
(860) 566-2480

CHESHIRE CORRECTIONAL INSTITUTION

900 Highland Ave., Cheshire, CT 06410
(203) 250-2600

CORRIGAN-RADGOWSKI CORRECTIONAL INSTITUTION

986 Norwich-New London Turnpike, Uncasville, CT 06382

ENFIELD CORRECTIONAL INSTITUTION

289 Shaker Rd., PO Box 1500, Enfield, CT 06082
(860) 763-7310

GARNER CORRECTIONAL INSTITUTION

50 Nunnawauk Rd., PO Box 5500, Newtown, CT 06470
(230) 270-2800

GATES CORRECTIONAL INSTITUTION

131 N. Bridebrook Rd., Niantic, CT 06357
(860) 691-4700

HARTFORD CORRECTIONAL CENTER

177 Weston St., Hartford, CT 06120
(860) 240-1800

MACDOUGALL-WALKER CORRECTIONAL INSTITUTE

1152 East Street South, Sutfield, CT 06078
(860) 627-2100

NEW HAVEN CORRECTIONAL CENTER

245 Whaley Ave., PO Box 8000, New Haven, CT 06530
(203) 974-4111

NORTHERN CORRECTIONAL INSTITUTION

287 Bilton Rd., PO Box 665, Somers, CT 06071
860) 763-8600

OSBORN CORRECTIONAL INSTITUTION

100 Bilton Rd., PO Box 100, Somers, CT 06071
(860) 566-7500

ROBINSON CORRECTIONAL INSTITUTION

285 Shaker Rd., PO Box 1400, Enfield, CT 06082
(860) 763-6200

WEBSTER CORRECTIONAL INSTITUTION

111 Jarvis St., Cheshire, CT 06410
(203) 271-5900

WILLARD-CYBULSKI CORRECTIONAL INSTITUTION

391 Shaker Rd., Enfield, CT 06082
(860) 763-6106

YORK CORRECTIONAL INSTITUTION

201 W. Main St., Niantic, CT 06357
(860) 691-6700

DISTRICT OF COLUMBIA

WASHINGTON DISTRICT JAIL

1901 D St. SE, Washington, DC 20003

DELAWARE

DELAWARE DEPARTMENT OF CORRECTIONS

www.doc.delaware.gov

BAYLOR WOMEN'S CORRECTIONAL INSTITUTION (BWCI) | PRISON AND WOMEN'S DEATH ROW

660 Baylor Blvd., New Castle, DE 19720

DELAWARE CORRECTIONAL CENTER (DCC) | PRISON AND DEATH ROW

1181 Paddock Rd., Smyrna, DE 19977

GANDER HILL (MPCJF)

PO Box 9279, Wilmington, DE 19809

JOHN L. WEBB CORRECTIONAL FACILITY (WCF)

200 Greenbank Rd., Wilmington, DE 19808

SUSSEX BOOT CAMP

Route One, Box 500, Georgetown, DE 19947

SUSSEX CORRECTIONAL INSTITUTION (SCI)

Route One, Box 500, Georgetown, DE 19947

FLORIDA

FLORIDA DEPARTMENT OF CORRECTIONS

www.dc.state.fl.us

APALACHEE CORRECTIONAL INSTITUTION | EAST

35 Apalachee Dr., Sneads, FL 32460
(850) 593-6431

APALACHEE CORRECTIONAL INSTITUTION | EAST

52 West Unit Dr., Sneads, FL 32460
(850) 593-6431

AVON PARK CORRECTIONAL INSTITUTION

PO Box 1100, County Road 64 East, Avon Park, FL, 33826-1100

BAKER CORRECTIONAL INSTITUTION

PO Box 500, U.S. 90, Sanderson, FL 32087-0500
(386) 719-4500

BAY CORRECTIONAL FACILITY

54500 Bayline Dr., Panama City, FL 32404
(850) 769-1455

BREVARD CORRECTIONAL INSTITUTION

855 Camp Rd., Cocoa, FL 32927-3709
(321) 634-6000

BROWARD CORRECTIONAL INSTITUTION | PRISON AND WOMEN'S DEATH ROW

20421 Sheridan St., Ft. Lauderdale, FL 33332
(954) 252-6400

CALHOUN CORRECTIONAL INSTITUTION

19562 SE Institution Dr., Unit 1, Blountstown, FL 32424
(850) 674-5901

CENTRAL FLORIDA RECEPTION CENTER | EAST UNIT

7000 H. C. Kelley Rd., Orlando, FL 32831-2518
(407) 207-7777

CENTRAL FLORIDA RECEPTION CENTER | SOUTH UNIT

7000 H. C. Kelley Rd., Orlando, FL 32831-2518
(407) 207-7777

CENTURY CORRECTIONAL INSTITUTION

400 Tedder Rd., Century, FL 32535
(850) 256-2600

CHARLOTTE CORRECTIONAL INSTITUTION

33123 Oil Well Rd., Punta Gordo, FL
(941) 575-2828

COLUMBIA CORRECTIONAL INSTITUTION

216 Correctional Way, U.S. 90 East, Lake City, FL 32055-8767
(386) 758-8090

COLUMBIA WORK CAMP

Route 7, Box 376, U.S. 90, Lake City, FL 32055-8767
(386) 758-8090

CROSS CITY CORRECTIONAL INSTITUTION

PO Box 1500, Veterans Rd., Cross City, FL 32628-1500
(352) 498-5576

DADE CORRECTIONAL INSTITUTION

19000 SW 377th St., Florida City, FL 33034-6409
(305) 242-1900

DADE CORRECTIONAL INSTITUTION | ANNEX

19000 SW 377th St., Florida City, FL 33034
(305) 242-1700

DESOTO CORRECTIONAL INSTITUTION ANNEX

13617 SE Highway 70, Arcadia, FL 34266
(863) 494-3727

EVERGLADES CORRECTIONAL INSTITUTION

1601 SW 187th Ave., PO Box 949000, Miami, FL 33194

FLORIDA STATE PRISON | PRISON AND DEATH ROW

7819 NW 228th St., Raiford, FL 32026
(904) 368-2500

GADSDEN CORRECTIONAL FACILITY

6044 Greensboro Highway, Quincy, FL 323531
(850) 875-9701

GAINESVILLE CORRECTIONAL INSTITUTION

2845 NE 39th Ave., Gainesville, FL 32609-2668
(352) 955-2001

GLADES CORRECTIONAL INSTITUTION

500 Orange Ave. Cir., Belle Glade, FL 33430-5222
(561) 996-5241

GRACELAND CORRECTIONAL FACILITY

5168 Ezell Rd., Graceland, FL 32440

GULF CORRECTIONAL INSTITUTION

500 Ike Steele Rd., Wewahitchka, FL 32465
(850) 639-1000

GULF CORRECTIONAL INSTITUTION | ANNEX

699 Ike Steele Rd., Wewahitchka, FL 32465
(850) 639-1000

HAMILTON CORRECTIONAL INSTITUTION

10650 SW 46th St., Jasper, FL 32052-1360
(904) 792-5151

HAMILTON CORRECTIONAL INSTITUTION | ANNEX

10650 SW 46th St., Jasper, FL 32052-1360
(904) 792-5504

HARDEE CORRECTIONAL INSTITUTION

6901 State Road 62, Bowling Green, FL 33834-9505
(863) 773-2441

HENDRY CORRECTIONAL INSTITUTION

12551 Wainwright Dr., Immokalee, FL 34142-4797
(239) 657-6354

HERNANDO CORRECTIONAL INSTITUTION

16415 Spring Hill Dr., Brooksville, FL 34604-8167
(352) 754-6715

HILLSBOROUGH CORRECTIONAL INSTITUTION

11150 Highway 672, Riverview, FL 33569-8402
(813) 671-5022

HOLMES CORRECTIONAL INSTITUTION

3142 Thomas Dr., Bonifay, FL 32425

HOMESTEAD CORRECTIONAL INSTITUTION

19000 SW 377th St., Florida City, FL 33034-6409
(305) 242-1700

INDIAN RIVER CORRECTIONAL INSTITUTION

7625 17th St. SW, Vero Beach, FL 32968

JACKSON CORRECTIONAL INSTITUTION

5563 10th St., Malone, FL 32445-3144
(850) 569-5260

JEFFERSON CORRECTIONAL INSTITUTION

1050 Big Joe Rd., Monticello, FL 32344
(850) 997-1987

LAKE CITY CORRECTIONAL FACILITY

Route 7, Box 1000, Highway 90 East, Lake City, FL 32055
(386) 755-3379

LAKE CORRECTIONAL INSTITUTION

19225 U.S. Highway 27, Clermont, FL 34715
(352) 394-6146

LANCASTER CORRECTIONAL INSTITUTION

3449 SW State Road 26, Trenton, FL 32693-0158
(352) 463-4100

LARGO ROAD PRISON

5201 Ulmerton Rd., Clearwater, FL 33760
(727) 570-5135

LAWLEY CORRECTIONAL INSTITUTION

7819 228th St., Raiford, FL 32026-2110

LAWTEY CORRECTIONAL INSTITUTION

22298 NE County Road 200B, Lawtey, FL 32058-0229

LIBERTY CORRECTIONAL INSTITUTION

HCR 2, Box 144, County Road 1641, Bristol, FL 32321-9711
(850) 643-2141

LIBERTY CORRECTIONAL INSTITUTION

11064 NW Dempsey Barron Rd., Bristol, FL 32321

LIBERTY WORK CAMP

11064 NW Dempsey Barron Rd., Bristol, FL 32321

LOWELL CORRECTIONAL INSTITUTION

11120 NW Gainesville Rd., Ocala, FL 34482-1479
(352) 401-5301

MADISON CORRECTIONAL INSTITUTION (MCI)

382 SW MCI Way, Madison, FL 32340
(850) 973-5300

MARION CORRECTIONAL INSTITUTION

PO Box 158, 3269 NW 105th St., Lowell, FL 32663-0158
(352) 401-6400

MARTIN CORRECTIONAL INSTITUTION

1150 SW Allapattah Rd., Indiantown, FL 34956-4397
(561) 597-3705

MAYO CORRECTIONAL INSTITUTION

PO Box 448, U.S. Highway North, Mayo, FL 32066-0488
(386) 294-4500

MOORE HAVEN CORRECTIONAL INSTITUTION

PO Box 718501, 1900 East State Road 78 NW, Moore Haven, FL 33471

NEW RIVER CORRECTIONAL INSTITUTION | EAST & WEST

PO Box 333, State Road 16, Raiford, FL 32083-0333

NORTH FLORIDA RECEPTION CENTER | WEST UNIT

PO Box 628, Highway 231, Lake Butler, FL 32054
(386) 496-6002

OKALOOSA CORRECTIONAL INSTITUTION

3189 Little Silver Rd., Crestview, FL 32539-6708
(850) 682-0931

OKEECHOBEE CORRECTIONAL INSTITUTION

3420 NE 168th St., Okeechobee, FL 34972
(863) 462-5474

POLK CORRECTIONAL INSTITUTION

10800 Evans Rd., Polk City, FL 33868-6925
(863) 948-2273

PUTNAM CORRECTIONAL INSTITUTION

128 Yelvington Rd., East Palatka, FL 32131
(386) 325-2857

QUINCY ANNEX

2225 Pat Thomas Parkway, Quincy, FL 32351
(850) 627-5400

RIVER JUNCTION WORK CAMP

300 Pecan Lane, Chattahoochee, FL 32324-3700
(850) 663-3300

SANTA ROSA CORRECTIONAL INSTITUTION

5850 E. Milton Rd., Milton, FL 32583
(850) 983-5800

SOUTH BAY CORRECTIONAL FACILITY

PO Box 7171, South Bay, FL 33493
(561) 992-9505

SOUTH FLORIDA RECEPTION CENTER

PO Box 02-8538, 14000 NW 41st St., Miami, FL 33178
(305) 592-9567

SUMTER CORRECTIONAL INSTITUTION

PO Box 667, 9544 County Road 476B, Bushnell, FL 33513-0667
(386) 793-2525

TAYLOR CORRECTIONAL INSTITUTION

8501 Hampton Springs Rd., Perry, FL 32348

TOMOKA CORRECTIONAL INSTITUTION

3950 Tiger Bay Rd., Daytona Beach, FL 32124-1098
(386) 323-1220

UNION CORRECTIONAL INSTITUTION

7819 NW 228th St., PO Box 1000 Raiford FL 32083-4430
(904) 431-2000

WAKULLA CORRECTIONAL INSTITUTION

110 Melaleuca Dr., Crawfordsville, FL 32327
(850) 421-0777

WALTON CORRECTIONAL INSTITUTION

691 World War II Veterans Lane, De Funiak Springs, FL 32433
(850) 892-6141

WALTON WORK CAMP

301 World War II Veterans Lane, De Funiak Springs, FL 32433
(850) 892-6141

WASHINGTON CORRECTIONAL INSTITUTION

4455 Sam Mitchell Dr., Chipley, FL 82428-3597
(850) 773-6100

ZEPHYRHILLS CORRECTIONAL INSTITUTION

2739 Gall Blvd., Zephyrhills, FL 33541-9701
(813) 782-5521

GEORGIA

GEORGIA DEPARTMENT OF CORRECTIONS

www.dcor.state.ga.us

ALBANY TRANSITIONAL CENTER

304 N. Washington St., Albany, NY 31701
(912) 430-3888

ARRENDALE STATE PRISON (LASP)

PO Box 709, Alto, GA 30510-0709
(706) 776-4700

ATLANTA TRANSITIONAL CENTER

332 Ponce DeLeon Ave. NE, Atlanta, 30308
(404) 206-5075

AUGUSTA STATE MEDICAL PRISON

3001 Gordon Highway, Grovetown, GA 30813
(706) 855-4700

AUGUSTA STATE PRISON

3001 Gordon Highway, Grovetown, GA 30813

AUTRY PRE-TRANSITIONAL CENTER

PO Box 648, Pelham, GA 31779
(912) 294-6530

AUTRY STATE PRISON

PO Box 648, Pelham, GA 31779
(912) 294-2940

BALDWIN BOOT CAMP

PO Box 218, Hardwick, GA 31034
(912) 445-5218

BOSTICK STATE PRISON

PO Box 1700, Hardwick, GA 31034
(912) 445-4623

BURRUS BOOT CAMP

1000 Indian Springs, Forsyth, GA 31029
(912) 994-7511

BURRUS CORRECTIONAL TRAINING CENTER

PO Box 5849, Forsyth, GA 31029
(912) 994-7511

CALHOUN STATE PRISON

PO Box 249, Morgan, GA 39866
(912) 849-5000

CCM ATLANTA

719 McDonough, Atlanta, GA 30315

CENTRAL STATE PRISON

4600 Fulton Mill Rd., Macon, GA 31213
(478) 471-2906

COASTAL STATE PRISON

PO Box 7150, Garden City, GA 31418
(912) 965-6330

COFFEE CORRECTIONAL FACILITY

2760 Harmony Rd., PO Box 650, Nicholls, GA 31554
(912) 345-5059

DODGE STATE PRISON

PO Box 276, Chester, GA 31012
(912) 358-7200

DOOLY STATE PRISON

PO Box 750, Unadilla, GA 31091
(478) 627-2000

GEORGIA DIAGNOSTIC AND CLASSIFICATION PRISON (GDCP) | PRISON AND DEATH ROW

PO Box 3877, Jackson, GA 30233
(912) 504-2000

GEORGIA STATE PRISON

200 Georgia Highway 147, Reidsville, GA 30453
(912) 557-7301

HANCOCK STATE PRISON

PO Box 339, Sparta, GA 31087
(706) 444-1000

HAYS BOOT CAMP

PO Box 668, Trion, GA 30753
(706) 857-0400

HAYS STATE PRISON

PO Box 668, Trion, GA 30753
(706) 857-0400

HOMERVILLE STATE PRISON

PO Box 337, Homerville, GA 31634
(912) 487-3052

JOHNSON STATE PRISON

PO Box 344, Wrightsville, GA 31096
(912) 864-4100

LEE STATE PRISON

153 Pinewood Rd., Leesburg, GA 31763
(912) 759-6453

LONG BOOT CAMP

PO Box 70, Ludowici, GA 31316

LOWNDES STATE PRISON

PO Box 5367, Valdosta, GA 31601
(912) 245-6450

MACON STATE PRISON

PO Box 426, Oglethorpe, GA 31068
(912) 472-3400

MACON TRANSITIONAL CENTER

1100 Second St., Macon, GA 31201
(912) 751-6090

MEN'S STATE PRISON

PO Box 396, Hardwick, GA 31034
(478) 445-4702

METRO STATE PRISON

1301 Constitution Rd., Atlanta, GA 30316
(404) 624-2200

METRO TRANSITIONAL CENTER

1301 Constitution Rd., Atlanta, GA 30316
(404) 624-2380

MILAN STATE PRISON

PO Box 410, Milan, GA 31060
(912) 362-4900

MONTGOMERY BOOT CAMP

PO Box 256, Mount Vernon, GA 30445
(912) 583-3600

MONTGOMERY STATE PRISON

PO Box 256, Mount Vernon, GA 30445
(912) 583-3600

PHILIPS STATE PRISON

2989 W. Rock Quarry Rd., Buford, GA 30518
(770) 932-4500

PULASKI STATE PRISON

PO Box 839, Hawkinsville, GA 31036
(912) 783-6000

PUTNAM STATE PRISON

PO Box 3970, Eatonton, GA 31024
(912) 445-4591

RAY JAMES CORRECTIONAL FACILITY

PO Box 2000, Folkston, GA 31537
(912) 496-6242

RIVERS STATE PRISON

PO Box 1500, Hardwick, GA 31034
(912) 445-4591

ROGERS STATE PRISON

200 Rogers Rd., Reidsville, GA 30453
(912) 557-7771

RUTLEDGE STATE PRISON

7175 Manor Rd., Columbus, GA 31907
(706) 568-2340

SAVANNAH MEN'S TRANSITIONAL CENTER

439 E. Broad St., Savannah, GA 31401
(914) 651-6372

SAVANNAH WOMEN'S TRANSITIONAL CENTER

439 E. Broad St., Savannah, GA 31401
(914) 651-2268

SCOTT BOOT CAMP

PO Box 417, Hardwick, GA 31034
(912) 445-5375

SCOTT STATE PRISON

PO Box 417, Hardwick, GA 31034
(912) 445-5375

SMITH STATE PRISON

PO Box 726, Glennville, GA 30427
(912) 654-5000

TELFAIR STATE PRISON

PO Box 549, Helena, GA 31037
(912) 868-7721

VALDOSTA STATE PRISON

PO Box 310, Valdosta, GA 31601
(912) 333-7900

WALKER STATE PRISON

PO Box 98, Rock Springs, GA 30739
(706) 764-3600

WARE STATE PRISON

3620 Harris Rd., Waycross, GA 31501
(912) 285-6400

WASHINGTON STATE PRISON | MEN

PO Box 128, Davisboro, GA 31018
(912) 348-5814

WASHINGTON STATE PRISON | WOMEN

PO Box 128, Davisboro, GA 31018
(912) 348-5814

WAYNE STATE PRISON

1007 Shed Rd., Odum, GA 31555
(912) 586-2244

WEST CENTRAL STATE PRISON

PO Box 589, Zebulon, GA 30295
(770) 567-0531

WHEELER CORRECTIONAL FACILITY

1100 N. Broad St., Alamo, GA 30411
(912) 568-1732

WILCOX STATE PRISON

PO Box 397, Abbeville, GA 31001
(912) 467-3000

HAWAII

HAWAII DEPARTMENT OF CORRECTIONS
www.hawaii.gov.psd

IDAHO

IDAHO DEPARTMENT OF CORRECTIONS
www.corr.state.id.us

IDAHO CORRECTIONAL CENTER (ICC)

PO Box 70010, Boise, ID 83707
(208) 331-2760

IDAHO CORRECTIONAL INSTITUTION | OROFINO (ICI-O)

23 Hospital Drive North, Orofino, ID 83544

IDAHO MAXIMUM SECURITY INSTITUTION (IMSI) | PRISON AND DEATH ROW

Pleasant Valley Rd., PO Box 51, Boise, ID 83707

IDAHO STATE CORRECTIONAL INSTITUTION

Pleasant Valley Rd., PO Box 14, Boise, ID 83707

NORTH IDAHO CORRECTIONAL INSTITUTION

Star Route #3, Box 147, Cottonwood, ID 83522

POCATELLO WOMEN'S CORRECTIONAL CENTER (PWCC) | PRISON AND WOMEN'S DEATH ROW

1451 Fore Rd., PO Box 6049, Pocatello, ID 83205-6049

SOUTH IDAHO STATE CORRECTIONAL INSTITUTION (SICI)

Pleasant Valley Rd., PO Box 8509, Boise, ID 83707

ST. ANTHONY WORK CAMP (SAWC)

125 8th St. W, St. Anthony, ID 83445
(208) 624-3775

ILLINOIS

ILLINOIS DEPARTMENT OF CORRECTIONS
www.idoc.state.il.us

BIG MUDDY RIVER CORRECTIONAL CENTER

251 N. Illinois Highway 37, PO Box 900, Ina, IL 62846-1000

CENTRALIA CORRECTIONAL CENTER

Shattuc Rd., PO Box 7711, Centralia, IL 62801
(618) 533-4111

CROSSROADS ATC

3210 W. Arthington, Chicago, IL 60624
(312) 533-5000

DANVILLE CORRECTIONAL CENTER

3820 E. Main St., Danville, IL 61834-4001
(217) 446-0441

DECATUR ATC

2175 E. Pershing Rd., Decatur, IL 62526
(217) 429-9198

DECATUR CORRECTIONAL CENTER

2310 E. Mound Rd., PO Box 3066, Decatur, IL 62524-3066
(217) 877-0353

DIXON CORRECTIONAL CENTER

2600 N. Brinton Ave., Dixon, IL 61021
(815) 288-5561

DWIGHT CORRECTIONAL CENTER

Route 17 West, PO 5001, Dwight, IL 60420-5001

(815) 584-2806

EAST MOLINE CORRECTIONAL CENTER

100 Hillcrest Rd., East Moline, IL 61244
(309) 755-4511

FOX VALLEY ATC

1329 N. Lake St., Aurora, IL 60606

FPC GREENVILLE

PO Box 6000, Greenville, IL 62246

GRAHAM CORRECTIONAL CENTER

PO Box 500, Hillsboro, IL 62049
(217) 532-6961

HILL CORRECTIONAL CENTER

600 S. Linwood Rd., Galesburg, IL 61401
(309) 343-4212

ILLINOIS RIVER CORRECTIONAL CENTER

Route 9 West, PO Box 1900, Canton, IL 61520
(309) 647-7030

JACKSONVILLE CORRECTIONAL CENTER

2268 E. Morton Ave., Jacksonville, IL 62650
(217) 245-1481

JESSIE "MA" HOUSTON ATC

14127 Leavitt, Dixmoor, IL 60426
(929) 371-2032

JOLIET ATC

Route 53 and Airport Rd., PO Box 7128, Romeoville, IL 60441
(815) 834-1500

JOLIET CORRECTIONAL CENTER

1125 Collins St., PO Box 515, Joliet, IL 60432
(815) 727-6141

LAWRENCEBURG CORRECTIONAL CENTER

PO Box 900, Sumner, IL 62466-0900
(217) 936-2064

LINCOLN CORRECTIONAL CENTER

1098 1350th St., PO Box 549, Lincoln, IL 62656
(217) 735-5411

LOGAN CORRECTIONAL CENTER

1096 1350th St., PO Box 1000, Lincoln, IL 62656
(217) 735-5581

MENARD CORRECTIONAL CENTER

711 Kaskaskia St., PO Box 1000, Menard, IL 62259-0100
(217) 826-5071

METRO ATC

2020 W. Roosevelt Rd., Chicago, IL 60608
(312) 793-2476

NORTH LAWNDALE ATC

2839 W. Fillmore, Chicago, IL 60624
(312) 638-8491

PEORIA ATC

607-613 N. Main, Peoria, IL 61602
(309) 671-3162

PINCKNEYVILLE CORRECTIONAL CENTER

5835 State Route 154, PO Box 999, Pinckneyville, IL 62274-3410

PONTIAC CORRECTIONAL CENTER

700 W. Lincoln St., PO Box 99, Pontiac, IL 61764
(815) 842-2816

ROBINSON CORRECTIONAL CENTER

13423 E. 1150th Ave., PO Box 900, Robinson, IL 62454

SHAWNEE CORRECTIONAL CENTER

Highway 146 East, Vienna, IL 62995
(618) 658-8331

SHERIDAN CORRECTIONAL CENTER

4017 East 2603 Rd., PO Box 38, Sheridan, IL 60551
(630) 496-2311

SOUTHERN ILLINOIS ATC

805 W. Freeman, PO Box 609, Carbondale, IL 62903
(618) 457-6705

SOUTHWESTERN CORRECTIONAL CENTER

950 Kings Highway St., PO Box 129, East St. Louis, IL 62203-0050

STATEVILLE CORRECTIONAL CENTER

Route 53, PO Box 112, Joliet, IL 60434-0112
(815) 727-3607

TAMMS CORRECTIONAL CENTER

200 E. Supermax Rd., PO Box 2000, Tamms, IL 62988
(618) 747-2042

TAYLORSVILLE CORRECTIONAL CENTER

Route 29 South, PO Box 900, Taylorsville, IL 62568
(217) 824-4004

THOMAS CORRECTIONAL CENTER

214½ Main St., PO Box 1015, Savanna, IL 61074
(815) 273-3969

URBANA ATC

1303 C N. Cunningham, Urbana, IL 61802

VANDALIA CORRECTIONAL CENTER

Route 51 North, PO Box 500, Vandalia, IL 62471
(217) 283-4170

VIENNA CORRECTIONAL CENTER

Highway 146 East, PO Box 100, Vienna, IL 62995
(618) 658-8371

WEST SIDE ATC

121 N. Campbell, Chicago, 60612
(312) 633-3838

WESTERN CORRECTIONAL CENTER

Route 99 South, PO Box 1000, Mount Sterling, IL 62353
(309) 773-4441

WINNEBAGO ATC

315 S. Court St., Rockford, IL 61102
(815) 987-7399

INDIANA

INDIANA DEPARTMENT OF CORRECTIONS
www.in.gov/idoc

ATTERBURY CORRECTIONAL FACILITY

PO Box 95, Edinburgh, IN 46124
(317) 887-0428

BRANCHVILLE CORRECTIONAL FACILITY

PO Box 500, Tell City, IN 47586
(812) 843-5921

CHAIN O'LAKES CORRECTIONAL FACILITY

3516 E-75 South, Albion, IN 46701
(260) 636-3114

CORRECTIONAL INDUSTRIAL FACILITY

PO Box 600, Pendleton, IN 46064
(317) 778-8011

EDINBURGH CORRECTIONAL FACILITY

PO Box 470, Edinburgh, IN 46124
(317) 526-8434

HENRYVILLE CORRECTIONAL FACILITY

PO Box 355, Henryville, IN 47126
(812) 294-4372

INDIANA STATE PRISON | PRISON AND DEATH ROW

PO Box 41, Michigan City, IN 46261
(219) 874-7258

INDIANA WOMEN'S PRISON | PRISON AND WOMEN'S DEATH ROW

401 N. Randolph St., Indianapolis, IN 46201
(317) 639-2671

INDIANAPOLIS MEN'S WORK RELEASE

448 W. Norwood St., Indianapolis, IN 46225
(317) 232-1454

INDIANAPOLIS WOMEN'S WORK RELEASE

512 E. Minnesota St., Indianapolis, IN 46203
(219) 872-8239

MADISON CORRECTIONAL FACILITY

PO Box 1079, Madison, IN 47250
(812) 265-6154

MAXIMUM CONTROL FACILITY

PO Box 557, Westville, IN 46391
(219) 785-2554

MEDARYVILLE CORRECTIONAL FACILITY

5426 East 850 North, Medaryville, IN 47957

MIAMI CORRECTIONAL FACILITY

PO Box 900, Bunker Hill, IN 46914
(765) 689-8920

PENDLETON CORRECTIONAL FACILITY

PO Box 30, Pendleton, IN 46068

PLAINFIELD CORRECTIONAL FACILITY

727 Moon Rd., Plainfield, IN 46168
(317) 839-2513

PUTNAMVILLE CORRECTIONAL FACILITY

1946 West U.S. Highway 40, Greencastle, IN 46135
(765) 653-8441

RECEPTION DIAGNOSTIC CENTER

737 Moon Rd., Plainfield, IN 46168
(317) 839-7728

ROCKVILLE CORRECTIONAL FACILITY

RR #3, Box 281, Rockville, IN 47872

SOUTH BEND WORK RELEASE

2421 S. Michigan St., South Bend, IN 46614
(574) 234-4094

STEUBER COUNTY JAIL

206 E. Gale St., Angela, IN 46703
(260) 668-1000

USP TERRE HAUTE

PO Box 12015, Terre Haute, IN 47801

WABASH VALLEY CORRECTIONAL FACILITY

PO Box 2222, Carlisle, IN 47838
(972) 398-5050

WESTVILLE CORRECTIONAL FACILITY

5501 South 1100 W., Westville, IN 46391

WESTVILLE TRANSITION FACILITY

PO Box 473, Westville, IN 46391

IOWA

IOWA DEPARTMENT OF CORRECTIONS
www.doc.state.ia.us

ANAMOSA STATE PENITENTIARY

406 N. High St., PO Box 10, Anamosa, IA 52205-0010
(319) 462-3504

CLARINDA CORRECTIONAL FACILITY

PO Box 1338, Clarinda, IA 51632
(712) 542-5634

FORT DODGE CORRECTIONAL FACILITY

L St., Fort Dodge, IA 50501
(515) 574-4700

IOWA CORRECTIONAL INSTITUTE FOR WOMEN

300 Elm St. SW, PO Box 700, Mitchellville, IA 50169

IOWA MEDICAL AND CLASSIFICATION CENTER

Highway 965, PO Box A, Oakdale, IA 52319
(319) 626-2391

IOWA STATE PENITENTIARY

PO Box 316, Fort Madison, IA 52627
(319) 372-5432

LUSTER HEIGHTS

481 Luster Heights Rd., Harper's Ferry, IA 52146
(319) 586-2115

MOUNT PLEASANT CORRECTIONAL FACILITY

1200 E. Washington, Mt. Pleasant, IA 52641
(319) 385-3511

NEWTON CORRECTIONAL FACILITY

PO Box 218, 307 S. 60th Ave. W, Newton, IA 50208
(515) 792-7552

NORTH CENTRAL CORRECTIONAL FACILITY

313 Lanedale, Rockwell City, IA 50579
(712) 297-7521

KANSAS

KANSAS DEPARTMENT OF CORRECTIONS
www.dc.state.ks.us

BELOIT COUNTY JAIL | MITCHELL

114 S. Campbell, Beloit, KS 67420

EL DORADO

PO Box 311, El Dorado, KS 67042
(316) 321-7284

ELLSWORTH

PO Box 107, Ellsworth, KS 67439
(785) 472-5501-0107

HUTCHINSON CORRECTIONAL FACILITY

PO Box 1568, Hutchinson, KS 67504-1568
(620) 662-2321

LANSING CORRECTIONAL FACILITY

PO Box 2, Lansing, KS 66043
(913) 727-3235

LARNED CORRECTIONAL MENTAL HEALTH FACILITY

PO Box E, Larned, KS 67550-0280
(620) 285-6249

NORTON

PO Box 546, Norton, KS 67654-0546
(785) 877-3380

TOPEKA

815 SE Rice Rd., Topeka, KS 66607
(785) 296-7220

WICHITA WORK RELEASE

401 S. Emporia, Wichita, KS 67202
(316) 265-5211

WINFIELD

1806 Pinecrest Cir., Winfield, KS 67156
(316) 221-6660

KENTUCKY

KENTUCKY DEPARTMENT OF CORRECTIONS
www.corrections.ky.gov

BELL COUNTY FORESTRY CAMP

560 Correctional Dr., Pineville, KY 40977
(859) 337-7065

BLACKBURN CORRECTIONAL COMPLEX

3111 Spurr Rd., Lexington, KY 40511
(859) 246-2366

EASTERN KENTUCKY CORRECTIONAL COMPLEX

200 Road to Justice, West Liberty, KY 41472
(606) 743-2800

FRANKFORT CAREER DEVELOPMENT CENTER

Coffee Tree Rd., PO Box 538, Frankfort, KY 40602
(502) 564-2120

GREEN RIVER CORRECTIONAL COMPLEX

1200 River Rd., PO Box 9300, Central City, KY 42330
(270) 754-5415

KENTUCKY CORRECTIONAL INSTITUTE FOR WOMEN | PRISON AND WOMEN'S DEATH ROW

3000 Ash Ave., Peewee Valley, KY 40056
(502) 241-8454

KENTUCKY STATE PENITENTIARY | PRISON AND DEATH ROW

266 Water St., Eddyville, KY 42038
(502) 388-2211

KENTUCKY STATE REFORMATORY

3001 West Highway 146, LaGrange, KY 40031
(502) 222-9441

LEE ADJUSTMENT CENTER

PO Box 900, Beattyville, KY 41311
(502) 464-2866

LITTLE SANDY CORRECTIONAL COMPLEX

505 Prison Connector, Sandy Hook, KY 41171
(606) 738-6133

LUTHER LUCKETT CORRECTIONAL COMPLEX

1612 Dawkins Rd., Box 6, LaGrange, KY 40031
(502) 222-0363 / 222-0365

MARION ADJUSTMENT CENTER

95 Raywick Rd., St. Mary, KY 60063

NORTHPOINT TRAINING CENTER

Box 479, Highway 33, 710 Walter Reed Rd., Burgin, KY 40310
(859) 239-7012

ROEDERER CORRECTIONAL COMPLEX

PO Box 69, LaGrange, KY 40031
(502) 222-0170

ROSS-CASH CENTER

374 New Bethel Rd., Fredonia, KY 42411
(270) 388-1057

SOLF

PO Box 45699, Lucasville, KY 45699

WESTERN KENTUCKY CORRECTIONAL COMPLEX

374 New Bethel Rd., Fredonia, KY 42411
(270) 388-9781

LOUISIANA

LOUISIANA DEPARTMENT OF PUBLIC SAFETY AND CORRECTIONS SERVICES
504 Mayflower St., Baton Rouge, LA 70802
(225) 352-9711
www.doc.louisiana.gov

ALLEN CORRECTIONAL CENTER (ALC)

3751 Lauderdale Woodyard Rd., Kinder, LA 70468
(337) 639-2943

AVOYELLES CORRECTIONAL CENTER (AVC)

1630 Prison Rd., Cottonport, LA 71327
(318) 876-2891

DAVID WADE CORRECTIONAL CENTER

670 Bell Hill Road, Homer, LA 71040
(318) 927-0400

DIXON CORRECTIONAL INSTITUTE (DCI)

PO Box 788, Jackson, LA 70748

(225) 634-1200

ELAYN HUNT CORRECTIONAL CENTER

PO Box 174, St. Gabriel, LA 70776
(225) 642-3306

LOUISIANA CORRECTIONAL INSTITUTE FOR WOMEN (LCIW) | PRISON AND WOMEN'S DEATH ROW

PO Box 26, St. Gabriel, LA 70776

LOUISIANA STATE PENITENTIARY (LSP) | PRISON AND DEATH ROW

Angola, LA 70712
(504) 655-4411

C. PHELPS CORRECTIONAL CENTER (CPCC)

PO Box 1056, Dequincy, LA 70633
(337) 786-7963

VERNON CORRECTIONAL FACILITY

2294 Slagle Rd., Leesville, LA 71446

WASHINGTON CORRECTIONAL INSTITUTE

27268 Highway 21, Angie, LA 70426
(337) 986-5000

WINN CORRECTIONAL CENTER (WNC)

PO Box 1260, Winnfield, LA 71483
(318) 628-3971

WORK TRAINING FACILITY | NORTH (WTF/N)

Camp Beauregard, 1453 15th St., Pineville, LA 71360
(318) 640-0351

MAINE

MAINE DEPARTMENT OF CORRECTIONS
www.state.me.us/corrections

BOLDUC CORRECTIONAL FACILITY

516 Cushing Rd., Warren, ME 04864
(207) 273-2036

CHARLESTON CORRECTIONAL FACILITY

1202 Dover Rd., Charleston, ME 04422
(207) 285-0800

DOWN EAST CORRECTIONAL FACILITY

HCR 70, Box 428, Machiasport, ME 04655
(207) 255-1100

MAINE CORRECTIONAL CENTER

PO Box 250, Windham, ME 04062-0250
(207) 893-7000

MAINE CORRECTIONAL INSTITUTION | WARREN

Box A, Thomaston, ME 04860
(207) 273-5200

MAINE STATE PRISON

807 Cushing Rd., #601, Warren, ME 04864-4600
(207) 354-3000

MARYLAND

MARYLAND DEPARTMENT OF CORRECTIONS
www.dpscs.state.md.us

EASTERN CORRECTIONAL INSTITUTION (ECI)

30430 Revells Neck Rd., Westover, MD 21890
(410) 651-9000

MARYLAND CORRECTIONAL ADJUSTMENT CENTER (MCAC)

401 E. Madison St., Baltimore, MD 21202

MARYLAND CORRECTIONAL INSTITUTION | HAGERSTOWN (MCIH)

18701 Roxbury, MD 21746

MARYLAND CORRECTIONAL INSTITUTION | JESSUP (MCIJ)

PO Box 549, Jessup, MD 20794
(410) 799-7610

MARYLAND CORRECTIONAL INSTITUTION | WOMEN (MCIW)

7943 Brockridge Rd., Jessup, MD 20794
(410) 799-5550

MARYLAND CORRECTIONAL TRAINING CENTER (MCTC)

18800 Roxbury Rd., Hagerstown, MD 21746
(240) 791-7200

MARYLAND HOUSE OF CORRECTION | ANNEX (MHCX)

PO Box 534, Jessup, MD 20794
(410) 799-6100

MARYLAND HOUSE OF CORRECTION (MHC)

PO Box 534, Jessup, MD 20794
(410) 799-3100

MARYLAND RECEPTION, DIAGNOSTIC AND CLASSIFICATION

550 E. Madison St., Baltimore, MD 21202
(877) 265-1801

METROPOLITAN TRANSITION CENTER (MTC)

654 Forrest St., Baltimore, MD 21202
(410) 837-2135

NORTH BRANCH CORRECTIONAL INSTITUTION

14100 McMullen Highway SW, Cumberland, MD 21502

PATUXENT INSTITUTION

PO Box 700, Jessup, MD 20794
(877) 650-2211

POPLAR HILL PRERELEASE UNIT

PO Box 14, Quantico, MD 21856
(410) 543-6615

ROXBURY CORRECTIONAL INSTITUTION (RCI)

18701 Roxbury Rd., Hagerstown, MD 21746
(240) 420-3000

SMPRU

14320 Oaks Rd., Charlotte Hall, MD 20622

WESTERN CORRECTIONAL INSTITUTION

13800 McMullen Highway SW, Cumberland, MD 21502

MASSACHUSETTS

MASSACHUSETTS DEPARTMENT OF CORRECTIONS
50 Maple St., Suite 3, Milford, MA 07157
(508) 422-3300
www.mass.gov

BAY STATE CORRECTIONAL CENTER

28 Clark St., PO Box 73, Norfolk, MA 02056

BOSTON PRERELEASE CENTER

PO Box 678, Dorchester Center Station, Dorchester, MA 02124
(617) 727-8130

BRIDGEWATER STATE HOSPITAL

20 Administration Rd., Bridgewater, MA 02324
(508) 279-4500

LEMUEL SHATTUCK HOSPITAL CORRECTIONAL UNIT

180 Morton St., Jamaica Plain, MA 02130

MASSACHUSETTS BOOT CAMP

2 Administration Rd., Bridgewater, MA 02324

MASSACHUSETTS TREATMENT CENTER

30 Administration Rd., Bridgewater, MA 02324

MCI | CEDAR JUNCTION

Route 1A, PO Box 100, South Walpole, MA 02071

MCI | CONCORD

965 Elm St., PO Box 9106, Concord, MA 01742

MCI | FRAMINGHAM

95 Loring Dr., PO Box 9007, Framingham, MA 01701

MCI | LANCASTER

Old Common Rd., PO Box 123, Lancaster, MA 01523

MCI | NORFOLK

2 Clark St., PO Box 43, Norfolk, MA 02056

MCI | PLYMOUTH

Myles Standish Forest, PO Box 207, South Carver, MA 02366

MCI | SHIRLEY (MINIMUM/MEDIUM)

PO Box 1218, Shirley, MA 01464

NORTH CENTRAL CI | GARDNER STATE COLONY

500 Colony Rd., PO Box 466, Gardner, MA 01440

NORTHEASTERN CORRECTIONAL CENTER

PO Box 1069, West Concord, MA 01742

OLD COLONY CORRECTIONAL CENTER

1 Administration Rd., Bridgewater, MA 02324

PONDVILLE CORRECTIONAL CENTER

PO Box 146, Norfolk, MA 02056

SOUTH MIDDLESEX CORRECTIONAL CENTER

135 Western Ave., PO Box 850, Framingham, MA 01701

SOUTHEASTERN CORRECTIONAL CENTER

12 Administration Rd., Bridgewater, MA 02324

SOUZA-BARANOWSKI CORRECTIONAL CENTER

PO Box 8000, Shirley, MA 01464
(978) 514-6500

WORCHESTER HOUSE OF CORRECTION

5 Paul X. Tivnan Dr., West Boylston, MA 01583

MICHIGAN

MICHIGAN DEPARTMENT OF CORRECTIONS

www.michigan.gov/corrections

ALGER MINIMUM CORRECTIONAL FACILITY

PO Box 600, Munising, MI 49862

BARAGA MAXIMUM CORRECTIONAL FACILITY

301 Wadaga Rd., Baraga, MI 49908

BELLAMY CREEK CORRECTIONAL FACILITY

1727 W. Bluewater Highway, Ionia, MI 48846
(616) 527-2510

BOYER ROAD CORRECTIONAL FACILITY

PO Box 5000, Carson City, MI 48811

BROOKS CORRECTIONAL FACILITY

2500 S. Sheridan Dr., Muskegon Heights, MI 49444
(231) 773-9200

CAMP BRIGHTON

PO Box 200, Pinckney, MI 48169

CAMP CUSINO

HCR Space One, Box 120, Shingleton, MI 49884
(906) 452-6248

CAMP KITWEN

M-26 South, PO Box 7, Painedale, MI 49955
(906) 288-3791

CAMP KOEHLER

16463 S. Hugginin Rd., Kincheloe, MI 49738
(906) 495-2215

CAMP LEHMAN

5135 Hartwick Pines Rd., Grayling, MI 49738
(989) 348-8101

CAMP MANISTIQUE

401 N. Maple St., Manistique, MI 49854
(906) 341-8451

CAMP OTTOWA

216 Gendron Rd., Iron River, MI 49935
(906) 265-6431

CAMP PELLSTON

Route 1, Pellston, MI 49769
(231) 526-5177

CAMP SAUBLE

4058 E. Freesoil Rd., Freesoil, MI 49411
(231) 464-7104

CARON CITY CORRECTIONAL FACILITY

Boyer Rd., PO Box 5000, Carson City, MI 48877-5000
(989) 584-3941

CHIPPEWA CORRECTIONAL FACILITY

4269 West M-80, Kincheloe, MI 49784
(906) 495-2275

COOPER STREET CORRECTIONAL FACILITY

3100 Cooper St., Jackson, MI 49201
(517) 780-6175

DEERFIELD CORRECTIONAL FACILITY

1755 Harwood Rd., Ionia, MI 48846
(616) 527-6320

EGELER CORRECTIONAL FACILITY

3855 Cooper St., Jackson, MI 49201-7517
(517) 780-5600

FLORENCE CRANE FACILITY

38 Fourth St., Coldwater, MI 49036
(517) 279-9165

G. ROBERT COTTON CORRECTIONAL FACILITY

3510 N. Elm St., Jackson, MI 49201
(517) 780-5000

GUS HARRISON CORRECTIONAL FACILITY

2727 E. Beecher St., PO Box 1888, Adrian, MI 49221
(517) 265-3900

HIAWATHA CORRECTIONAL FACILITY

4533 W. Industrial Park Dr., Kincheloe, MI 49786-0001
(906) 495-5661

HURON VALLEY CENTER

3511 Bemis Rd., Ypsilanti, MI 48197
(734) 434-5888

HURON VALLEY MEN'S CORRECTIONAL FACILITY

3201 Bemis Rd., Ypsilanti, MI 48197
(734) 572-9900

HURON VALLEY WOMEN'S CORRECTIONAL FACILITY

3201 Bemis Rd., Ypsilanti, MI 48197

IONIA MAXIMUM CORRECTIONAL FACILITY

1576 W. Bluewater Highway, Ionia, MI 48846
(616) 527-6331

KINROSS CORRECTIONAL FACILITY

16770 S. Watertower Dr., Kincheloe, MI 49788
(906) 495-2282

LAKELAND CORRECTIONAL FACILITY

141 First St., Coldwater, MI 49036
(517) 278-6942

MACOMB CORRECTIONAL FACILITY

34625 26 Mile Rd., New Haven, MI 48048
(517) 749-4900

MARQUETTE BRANCH PRISON

1960 U.S. 41 South, Marquette, MI 49855
(906) 226-6531

MICHIGAN REFORMATORY

1342 E. Main, Ionia, MI 48846
(616) 527-2500

MID-MICHIGAN CORRECTIONAL FACILITY

8201 N. Croswell Rd., St. Louis, MI 48880
(989) 681-4361

MOUND CORRECTIONAL FACILITY

17601 Mound Rd., Detroit, MI 48212
(313) 368-8300

MUSKEGON CORRECTIONAL FACILITY

2400 S. Sheridan Dr., Muskegon, MI 49442
(231) 773-3201

NEWBERRY CORRECTIONAL FACILITY

3001 Newberry Ave., Newberry, MI 49868
(906) 293-6200

OAKS CORRECTIONAL FACILITY

1500 Caberfae Highway, Eastlake, MI 49626

OJIBWAY CORRECTIONAL FACILITY

5705 Ojibway Rd., Marenisco, MI 49947
(906) 787-2217

AL FACILITY

1780 E. Parnall, Jackson, MI 49201
(517) 780-6000

PARR HIGHWAY CORRECTIONAL FACILITY

2727 E. Beecher St., Adrian, MI 49221
(517) 263-3500

PINE RIVER CORRECTIONAL FACILITY

320 N. Hubbard, St. Louis, MI 48880
(989) 681-6668

PUGSLEY CORRECTIONAL FACILITY

7401 E. Walton Rd., Kingsley, MI 49649
(231) 363-5253

RICHARD A. HANDLON CORRECTIONAL FACILITY

1728 Bluewater Highway, Ionia, MI 48846

RIVERSIDE CORRECTIONAL FACILITY

777 W. Riverside Dr., Ionia, MI 48846
(616) 527-0110

ROBERT SCOTT CORRECTIONAL FACILITY

47500 Five Mile Rd., Plymouth, MI 48170

RYAN CORRECTIONAL FACILITY

17600 Ryan Rd., Detroit, MI 48212
(313) 368-3200

SAGINAW CORRECTIONAL FACILITY

9625 Pierce Rd., Freeland, MI 48623
(989) 695-9880

SCOTT CORRECTIONAL FACILITY

47500 Five Mile Rd., Plymouth, MI 48170
(313) 459-7400

SOUTHERN MICHIGAN CORRECTIONAL FACILITY

4002 Cooper St., Jackson, MI 49201
(517) 780-6000

ST. LOUIS CORRECTIONAL FACILITY

8585 N. Croswell Rd., St. Louis, MI 48880
(989) 681-6444

STANDISH MAXIMUM CORRECTIONAL FACILITY

4713 West M-61, Standish, MI 48658
(989) 846-7000

STATE PRISON OF SOUTHERN MICHIGAN

4000 Cooper St., Jackson, MI 49201
(517) 780-6000

STRAITS CORRECTIONAL FACILITY

4387 West M-80, Kincheloe, MI 49785
(906) 495-5674

THUMB CORRECTIONAL FACILITY

3225 John Conley Dr., Lapeer, MI 48446

(313) 667-2045

WEST SHORELINE CORRECTIONAL FACILITY

2500 S. Sheridan Dr., Muskegon Heights, MI 49444
(231) 773-1122

WESTERN WAYNE CORRECTIONAL FACILITY

48401 Five Mile Rd., Plymouth, MI 48170
(313) 459-2500

MINNESOTA

MINNESOTA DEPARTMENT OF CORRECTIONS

www.doc.state.mn.us

MCF | FAIRBAULT

1101 Linden Lane, Faribault, MN 55021-6400
(507) 334-0700

MCF | LINO LAKES

7525 Fourth Ave., Lino Lakes, MN 55014
(651) 717-6100

MCF | OAK PARK HEIGHTS

5329 Osgood Ave. N, Stillwater, MN 55082-1117
(651) 779-1400

MCF | 7600 525TH ST., RUSH CITY, MN 55069

(320) 358-0400

MCF | SHAKOPEE | WOMEN

1010 W. Sixth Ave., Shakopee, MN 55379
(612) 496-4440

MCF | ST. CLOUD

2305 Minnesota Blvd. SE, St. Cloud, MN 56304
(320) 240-3000

MCF | STILLWATER

970 Picket St., Bayport, MN 55003-1490
(651) 779-2700

MCF | WILLOW RIVER / MOOSE LAKE

1000 Lake Shore Dr., Moose Lake, MN 55767
(218) 485-5000

PRAIRIE CORRECTIONAL INSTITUTION

PO Box 500, Appleton, MN 56208

MISSISSIPPI

MISSISSIPPI DEPARTMENT OF CORRECTIONS

www.mdoc.state.ms.us

BOLIVAR COUNTY CORRECTIONAL FACILITY

PO Box 539, Cleveland, MS 38732
(662) 843-7478

CAROL / MONTGOMERY CORRECTIONAL FACILITY

Route 2, Box 240, Vaiden, MS 39176
(662) 464-5440

CENTRAL MISSISSIPPI CORRECTIONAL FACILITY | PRISON AND WOMEN'S DEATH ROW (CMCF)IMAGI

PO Box 88550, Pearl, MS 39288-8550
(601) 932-2880

CHICKASAW CCF

130 Lancaster Circle, Houston, MS 38851

DELTA CORRECTIONAL FACILITY

3800 County Road 540, Greenwood, MS 38930
(620) 455-4546

EAST MISSISSIPPI CORRECTIONAL FACILITY

PO Box 10641, Highway 80 West, Meridian, MS 39307
(601) 485-5255

HOLMES / HUMPHREYS COUNTY CORRECTIONAL FACILITY

Highway 12 East, Box 2323, Lexington, MS 39095
(601) 834-5016

ISSAQUENA COUNTY CORRECTIONAL FACILITY

PO Box 220, Mayersville, MS 39113
(601) 873-2153

JEFFERSON / FRANKLIN CORRECTIONAL FACILITY

Route 2, Box 29, Fayette, MS 39069
(601) 786-2284

KEMPER / NESHOBA COUNTY CORRECTIONAL FACILITY

Route 2, Box 300, Industrial Park Rd., DeKalb, MS 39328

LEAKE COUNTY CORRECTIONAL FACILITY

399 C.O. Brooks St., Carthage, MS 39051
(601) 298-9003

MARION / WALTHALL CORRECTIONAL FACILITY

503 S. Main St., Columbia, MS 39429
(601) 736-3621

MARSHALL COUNTY CORRECTIONAL FACILITY

833 West Street, PO Box 5188, Holly Springs, MS 38634

MISSISSIPPI STATE PENITENTIARY | PRISON AND DEATH ROW (MSP)

Post Office Box 1057 - Hwy 49 West, Parchman, MS 38738
(601) 745-6611

SOUTH MISSISSIPPI CORRECTIONAL INSTITUTION (SMCI)

PO Box 1419, Leakesville, MS 39451
(238) 394-5600

STONE COUNTY CORRECTIONAL FACILITY

1420 Industrial Park Rd., Wiggins, MS 39577
(228) 928-7042

TALLAHATCHIE COUNTY CORRECTIONAL FACILITY

PO Box 368, Tutwiler, MS 38963
(662) 345-6567

WALNUT GROVE YOUTH CORRECTIONAL FACILITY

PO Box 389, Walnut Grove, MS 39189

WILKINSON COUNTY CORRECTIONAL FACILITY

2999 Highway 61 North, Woodville, MS 39669
(601) 888-3199

WINSTON / CHOCTAW COUNTY CORRECTIONAL FACILITY

2460 Highway 25 North, Louisville, MS 39339

MISSOURI

MISSOURI DEPARTMENT OF CORRECTIONS
2729 Plaza Dr., Jefferson City, MO 65102
(573) 751-2389
www.doc.state.mo.us

ALGOA CORRECTIONAL CENTER

8501 Fenceline Rd., Jefferson City, MO 65102
(573) 751-3911

BOONVILLE CORRECTIONAL CENTER

1216 E. Morgan St., Boonville, MO 65233-1300
(660) 882-6521

CAMP HAWTHORN

PO Box 140, Kaiser, MO 65047
(573) 348-3194

CENTRAL MISSOURI CORRECTIONAL CENTER

PO Box 539, Jefferson City, MO 65102
(573) 751-2053

CHILLICOTHE CORRECTIONAL CENTER

1500 W. Third St., Chillicothe, MO 64601
(660) 646-4032

CROSSROADS CORRECTIONAL CENTER

1115 E. Pence Rd., Cameron, MO 64429
(816) 632-2727

EASTERN RECEPTION AND DIAGNOSTIC CENTER

2727 Highway K, Bonne Terre, MO 63628

FARMINGTON CORRECTIONAL CENTER

1012 W. Columbia St., Farmington, MO 63640
(573) 756-8001

FULTON RECEPTION AND DIAGNOSTIC CENTER

PO Box 190, Fulton, MO 65251
(573) 592-4040

JEFFERSON CITY CORRECTIONAL CENTER

8200 No More Victims Rd., Jefferson City, MO 65101
(573) 751-3224

MARYVILLE TREATMENT CENTER

30227 U.S. Highway 136, Maryville, MO 64468
(660) 582-6542

MISSOURI EASTERN CORRECTIONAL CENTER

18701 Old Highway 66, Pacific, MO 63069
(314) 257-3322

MOBERLY CORRECTIONAL CENTER

PO Box 7, Moberly, MO 65670
(660) 263-3778

NORTHEAST CORRECTIONAL CENTER

13698 Airport Rd., Bowling Green, MO 63334
(573) 324-9975

OZARK CORRECTIONAL CENTER

929 Honor Camp Lane, Fordland, MO 65652
(417) 767-4491

POTOSI CORRECTIONAL CENTER | PRISON AND DEATH ROW

Route 2, Box 2222, Mineral Point, MO 63660
(573) 438-6000

SOUTH CENTRAL CORRECTIONAL CENTER

255 West Highway 32, Licking, MO 65542
(573) 674-4470

SOUTH EAST CORRECTIONAL CENTER

300 S. Pedro Simmons Dr., Charleston, MO 63834
(573) 683-2461

TIPTON CORRECTIONAL CENTER

619 N. Osage Lane, Tipton, MO 65801
(660) 433-2031

WESTERN CORRECTIONAL CENTER

3401 Faraon, St. Joseph, MO 64506
(816) 387-2158

WESTERN MISSOURI CORRECTIONAL CENTER

609 E. Pence Rd., Cameron, MO 64429
(816) 632-1390

WOMEN'S EASTERN CORRECTIONAL CENTER

PO Box 300, 1101 East Highway 54, Vandalia, MO 63382
(573) 594-6686

MONTANA

MONTANA DEPARTMENT OF CORRECTIONS
www.cor.montana.gov

CASCADE COUNTY REGIONAL PRISON

3800 Ulm North Frontage Rd., Great Falls, MT 59404
(406) 454-6823

CROSSROADS CORRECTIONAL CENTER

75 Heath Rd., Shelby, MT 59474
(406) 434-7055

DAWSON COUNTY REGIONAL PRISON

440 Colorado Blvd., Glendive, MT 59330
(406) 377-7600

MISSOULA COUNTY REGIONAL PRISON

2340 Mullan Rd., Missoula, MT 59808
(406) 829-4071

MONTANA STATE PENITENTIARY (MSP) | PRISON AND DEATH ROW

500 Conley Lake Rd., Deer Lodge, MT 59722
(406) 846-1320

MONTANA WOMEN'S PRISON (MWP) | PRISON AND WOMEN'S DEATH ROW

South 27th St., Billings, MT 59101
(406) 247-5100

NEBRASKA

NEBRASKA DEPARTMENT OF CORRECTIONS
www.corrections.nebraska.gov

COMMUNITY CORRECTIONS CENTER | LINCOLN

PO Box 22800, Lincoln, NE 68542-2800
(402) 471-0740

COMMUNITY CORRECTIONS CENTER | OMAHA

2320 Avenue J, Omaha, NE 68110-2766
(402) 595-2010

DIAGNOSTIC AND EVALUATION CENTER

PO Box 22800, Lincoln, NE 68542-2800
(402) 471-3330

HASTINGS CORRECTIONAL CENTER

PO Box 2048, Hastings, NE 68902-2048
(402) 462-1947

LINCOLN CORRECTIONAL CENTER

PO Box 22800, Lincoln, NE 68542-2800
(402) 471-2861

NEBRASKA CORRECTIONAL CENTER FOR WOMEN

1107 Recharge Rd., York, NE 66467-8003
(308) 362-3317

NEBRASKA CORRECTIONAL TREATMENT CENTER

PO Box 2700, Lincoln, NE 68542-2700
(402) 471-4129

NEBRASKA STATE PENITENTIARY

PO Box 2500, Lincoln, NE 68542-2500
(402) 471-3161

OMAHA CORRECTIONAL CENTER

PO Box 11099. 2323 Avenue J, Omaha, NE 68111-0099
(402) 595-3964

TECUMSEH STATE CORRECTIONAL INSTITUTION (TSCI)

PO Box 900, Tecumseh, NE 68450
(402) 479-5935

WORK ETHIC CAMP (WEC)

2309 North Highway 83, McCook, NE 69001
(308) 345-8405

NEVADA

NEVADA DEPARTMENT OF CORRECTIONS
PO Box 7011, Carson City, NV 89702
(775) 887-3266
www.doc.nv.gov

ELY CONSERVATION CAMP

PO Box 1989, 4569 N. State Route 490, Ely, NV 89301
(775) 289-8800

ELY STATE PRISON | PRISON AND DEATH ROW

PO Box 1989, 4569 N. State Route 490, Ely, NV 89301
(775) 289-8800

FLORENCE MCCLURE WOMEN'S CORRECTIONAL CENTER

4370 Smiley Rd., Las Vegas, NV 89115

HIGH DESERT STATE PRISON

PO Box 650, Indian Springs, NV 89018

INDIAN SPRINGS CONSERVATION CAMP

Cold Creek Rd., PO Box 208, Indian Springs, NV 89018
(702) 486-3888

JEAN CONSERVATION CAMP

1 Prison Rd., PO Box 100, Jean, NV 89026
(702) 874-1626

LOVELOCK CORRECTIONAL CENTER

PO Box 359, Lovelock, NV 89419
(775) 273-1300

NEVADA STATE PRISON

3301 E. 5th St., PO Box 607, Carson City, NV 89702
(775) 882-8588

NEVADA WOMEN'S CORRECTIONAL CENTER | PRISON AND WOMEN'S DEATH ROW

PO Box 7007, Carson City, NV 89702

NORTHERN NEVADA CORRECTIONAL CENTER

PO Box 7000, 1721 E. Snyder Ave., Carson City, NV 89702

NORTHERN NEVADA RESTITUTION CENTER

3301 E. 5th St., PO Box 7007, Carson City, NV 89702
(775) 684-3000

SILVER SPRING CONSERVATION CAMP

3301 E. 5th St., PO Box 7007, Carson City, NV 89702
(775) 684-3000

SOUTHERN DESERT CORRECTIONAL CENTER

Cold Creek Rd., PO Box 208, Indian Springs, NV 89018
(702) 486-3888

SOUTHERN NEVADA CORRECTIONAL CENTER

1 Prison Rd., PO Box 100, Jean, NV 89026
(702) 874-1626

SOUTHERN NEVADA WOMEN'S CORRECTIONAL CENTER

4370 Smiley Rd., Las Vegas, NV 89115
(702) 651-8866

STEWART CONSERVATION CAMP

PO Box 5005, Carson City, NV 89702
(775) 882-9203

WARM SPRINGS CORRECTIONAL CENTER

3301 E. 5th St., PO Box 7007, Carson City, NV 89702
(775) 684-3000

NEW HAMPSHIRE

NEW HAMPSHIRE DEPARTMENT OF CORRECTIONS
www.nh.gov/nhdoc

LAKES REGION FACILITY

1 Right Way Path, Laconia, NH 03246
(603) 528-9203

NEW HAMPSHIRE STATE PRISON FOR MEN

PO Box 14, Concord, NH 03302-0014
(602) 271-18101

NEW HAMPSHIRE STATE PRISON FOR WOMEN

317 Mast Rd., Goffstown, NH 03045
(603) 668-6137

NORTHERN NEW HAMPSHIRE CORRECTIONAL FACILITY (NCF – BERLIN)

138 E. Milan Rd., Berlin, NH 03570
(603) 752-2906

SOUTHERN STATE CORRECTIONAL FACILITY

PO Box 150, Delmont, NJ 08314
(856) 785-1300

NEW JERSEY

NEW JERSEY DEPARTMENT OF CORRECTIONS
www.state.nj.us/corrections

NEW JERSEY ADULT DIAGNOSTIC AND TREATMENT CENTER

PO Box 190, Avenal, NJ 07001
(732) 574-2250

BAYSIDE STATE PRISON

PO Box F-1, Leesburg, NJ 08327

CENTRAL RECEPTION AND ASSIGNMENT FACILITY

PO Box 7450, West Trenton, NJ 08628
(609) 984-6000

EAST JERSEY STATE PRISON

Lock Bag R, Rahway, NJ 07065
(732) 499-5010

MAHAN CORRECTIONAL FACILITY FOR WOMEN

PO Box 4004, Clinton, NJ 08809
(908) 735-7111

MID-STATE CORRECTIONAL FACILITY

PO Box 866, Wrightstown, NJ 08562
(609) 723-4221

NEW JERSEY STATE PRISON

PO Box 861, Trenton, NJ 08625-0861
(609) 292-9700

NORTHERN STATE PRISON

PO Box 2300, Newark, NJ 07114-2300
(973) 465-0068

RIVERFRONT STATE PRISON

PO Box 9104, Camden, NJ 08101-9104
(856) 225-5700

SOUTH WOODS STATE PRISON

215 S. Burlington Rd., Bridgeton, NJ 08302
(856) 459-7000

NEW MEXICO

NEW MEXICO DEPARTMENT OF CORRECTIONS
4104 Pan American Freeway NE, Albuquerque, NM 87107
(505) 841-4289
www.corrections.state.nm.us

CENTRAL NEW MEXICO CORRECTIONAL FACILITY | MINIMUM UNIT

3201 Highway 314 SW, Los Lunas, NM 87031

CENTRAL NEW MEXICO CORRECTIONAL FACILITY

PO Drawer 1328, Los Lunas, NM 87031-1328
(505) 865-1622

GUADALUPE COUNTY CORRECTIONAL FACILITY

PO Box 520, South Highway 54, Santa Rosa, NM 88435
(505) 472-1001

LEA COUNTY CORRECTIONAL FACILITY

6900 W. Millen, Hobbs, NM 88244
575) 392-5681

NEW MEXICO WOMEN'S CORRECTIONAL FACILITY

PO Box 800, Grants, NM 87020
(505) 287-2941

PENITENTIARY OF NEW MEXICO

PO Box 1059, Santa Fe, NM 87504-1059
(505) 827-8200

ROSWELL CORRECTIONAL CENTER

578 W. Chickasaw Rd., Hagerman, NM 88232
(575) 625-3100

SOUTHERN NEW MEXICO CORRECTIONAL FACILITY

PO Box 6391, 983 Joe R. Silva Blvd., Las Cruces, NM 88004-0639

TORRANCE COUNTY DETENTION CENTER

PO Box 837, Estancia, NM 87016

(505) 384-2711

WESTERN NEW MEXICO CORRECTIONAL FACILITY

PO Drawer 250, Grants, NM 87020
(505) 876-8300

NEW YORK

NEW YORK DEPARTMENT OF CORRECTIONS
www.docs.state.ny.us

ADIRONDACK CORRECTIONAL FACILITY

PO Box 110, Ray Brook, NY 12977-0110
(518) 891-1343

ALBION CORRECTIONAL FACILITY

3595 State School Rd., Albion, NY 14411
(585) 589-5511

ALTONA CORRECTIONAL FACILITY

555 Devils Den Rd., Altona, NY 12910
(518) 236-7841

ARTHUR KILL CORRECTIONAL FACILITY

2911 Arthur Kill Rd., Staten Island, NY 10309-1197
(212) 356-7333

ATTICA CORRECTIONAL FACILITY

PO Box 149, Attica, NY 14011-0149
(716) 591-2000

AUBURN CORRECTIONAL FACILITY

PO Box 618, Auburn, NY 13024
(315) 253-8401

BARE HILL CORRECTIONAL FACILITY

Caller Box 20, 181 Brand Rd., Malone, NY 12953
(518) 483-8411

BAYVIEW CORRECTIONAL FACILITY

550 W. 20th St., New York, NY 10011-2878
(212) 255-7590

BEACON CORRECTIONAL FACILITY

PO Box 780, Beacon, NY 12508-0780
(845) 831-4200

BEDFORD HILLS CORRECTIONAL FACILITY

247 Harris Rd., Bedford Hills, NY 10507-2499
(914) 241-3100

BUFFALO CORRECTIONAL FACILITY

PO Box 300, Alden, NY 14004
(716) 937-3786

BUTLER ASACTC

PO Box 400, Red Creek, NY 13143

BUTLER CORRECTIONAL FACILITY

Route 370, PO Box 388, Red Creek, NY 13143

CAMP GABRIELS

PO Box 100, Gabriels, NY 12939-0100

CAMP GEORGETOWN

PO Box 48, Georgetown, NY 13072-9307

CAMP PHARSALIA

496 Center Rd., South Plymouth, NY 13844-6777

CAPE VINCENT CORRECTIONAL FACILITY

Route 12E, PO Box 739, Cape Vincent, NY 13618

CAYUGA CORRECTIONAL FACILITY

PO Box 1186, Moravia, NY 13118
(315) 497-1110

CCM NY | COMMUNITY CORRECTIONS OFFICE

100 29th St., Brooklyn, NY 11232

CCM NY | BRONX

2534 Creston Ave., Bronx, NY 10468

CCM NY | BROOKLYN

PO Box 329014, Brooklyn, NY 11232

CHATEAUGAY CORRECTIONAL FACILITY

PO Box 320, Route 11, Chateaugay, NY 12920
(518) 497-3300

CLINTON CORRECTIONAL FACILITY | ANNEX

PO Box 2002, Dannemora, NY 12929
(518) 492-2511

CLINTON CORRECTIONAL FACILITY | MAIN | PRISON AND DEATH ROW

PO Box 2001, Dannemora, NY 12929
(518) 492-2511

COLLINS CORRECTIONAL FACILITY

PO Box 340, Collins, NY 14034-0340

COXSACKIE CORRECTIONAL FACILITY

PO Box 999, West Coxsackie, NY 12051-0999

(518) 731-2781

DOWNSTATE CORRECTIONAL FACILITY

122 Red Schoolhouse Rd., Box F, Fishkill, NY 12524
(745) 831-6600

EASTERN CORRECTIONAL FACILITY

PO Box 338, Napanoch, NY 12458-0338
845) 647-7400

EDGECOMBE CORRECTIONAL FACILITY

611 Edgecombe Ave., New York, NY 10032-4398
(212) 923-2575

ELMIRA CORRECTIONAL FACILITY

PO Box 500, Elmira, NY 14902-0500
(607) 734-3901

FISHKILL CORRECTIONAL FACILITY

PO Box 1245, Beacon, NY 12508
(845) 831-4800

FIVE POINTS CORRECTIONAL FACILITY

Caller Box 119, Romulus, NY 14541

FRANKLIN CORRECTIONAL FACILITY

PO Box 10, Malone, NY 12953
(518) 483-6040

FULTON CORRECTIONAL FACILITY

1511 Fulton Ave., Bronx, NY 10457-8398
(212) 583-8000

GOUVERNEUR CORRECTIONAL FACILITY

Scotch Settlement Rd., PO Box 370, Gouverneur, NY 13642-0370

GOWANDA CORRECTIONAL FACILITY

PO Box 311, South Rd., Gowanda, NY 14070-0311
(716) 532-0177

MEADOW CORRECTIONAL FACILITY

PO Box 51, Comstock, NY 12821

GREAT MEADOW CORRECTIONAL FACILITY

11739 State Route 22, Comstock, NY 12821-0051

GREEN HAVEN CORRECTIONAL FACILITY

PO Box 4000, Stormville, NY 12582

GREENE CORRECTIONAL FACILITY

PO Box 975, Coxsackie, NY 12051-0975
(518) 731-2741

GROVELAND CORRECTIONAL FACILITY | ANNEX

PO Box 46, Sonyea, NY 14556

GROVELAND CORRECTIONAL FACILITY | MAIN

PO Box 104, Sonyea, NY 14556

HALE CREEK ASACTC

279 Maloney Rd., PO Box 950, Johnstown, NY 12095
(518) 736-2094

HUDSON CORRECTIONAL FACILITY

PO Box 576, Hudson, NY 12534-0576
(518) 828-4311

LAKEVIEW ANNEX CORRECTIONAL FACILITY

PO Box W, Brocton, NY 14716-0679

LAKEVIEW SHOCK INCARCERATION CORRECTIONAL FACILITY

PO Box T, Brocton, NY 14716
(716) 792-7100

LINCOLN CORRECTIONAL FACILITY

31-33 West 110th St., New York, NY 10026-4398
(212) 860-9400

LIVINGSTON CORRECTIONAL FACILITY

PO Box 1991, Sonyea, NY 14556

LYON MOUNTAIN CORRECTIONAL FACILITY

PO Box 276, Lyon Mountain, NY 12952-0276

MARCY CORRECTIONAL FACILITY

PO Box 3600, Marcy, NY 13403-3600

MDC BROOKLYN

PO Box 329002, Brooklyn, NY 11232

METROPOLITAN CORRECTIONAL CENTER

150 Park Row, New York, NY 10007

MID-ORANGE CORRECTIONAL FACILITY

900 Kings Highway, Warwick, NY 10990-0900
(845) 986-2291

MID-STATE CORRECTIONAL FACILITY

PO Box 2500, Marcy, NY 13403
(315) 768-8581

MOHAWK CORRECTIONAL FACILITY

PO Box 8451, Rome, NY 16442-8451
(315) 339-5232

MONTEREY SHOCK INCARCERATION CORRECTIONAL FACILITY

2150 Evergreen Hill Rd., Beaver Dams, NY 14812-9718

MORIAH SHOCK CORRECTIONAL FACILITY

PO Box 999, Mineville, NY 12956-0999
(518) 942-7561

MT. MCGREGOR CORRECTIONAL FACILITY

1000 Mt. McGregor Rd., Wilton, NY 12831
(518) 587-3960

NASSAU COUNTY CORRECTIONAL FACILITY

100 Carmen Ave., East Meadow, NY 11554

OGDENSBURG CORRECTIONAL FACILITY

One Correction Way, Ogdensburg, NY 13669-2288
(315) 393-0281

ONEIDA CORRECTIONAL FACILITY

PO Box 4580, Rome, NY 13442-4580
(315) 339-6880

ORLEANS CORRECTIONAL FACILITY

35-31 Gaines Basin Rd., Albion, NY 14411
(585) 589-6820

OTISVILLE CORRECTIONAL FACILITY

PO Box 8, Otisville, NY 10963-0008
(845) 386-1490

QUEENSBORO CORRECTIONAL FACILITY

47-04 Van Dam St., Long Island City, NY 11101-3081
(718) 361-8920

RIVERVIEW CORRECTIONAL FACILITY

PO Box 247, Ogdensburg, NY 13669
(315) 393-8400

ROCHESTER CORRECTIONAL FACILITY

470 Ford St., Rochester, NY 14608-2499
(585) 454-2280

SHAWANGUNK CORRECTIONAL FACILITY

PO Box 700, Wallkill, NY 12589
(845) 895-2081

SING CORRECTIONAL FACILITY

354 Hunter St., Ossining, NY 10562-5442
(914) 941-0108

SOUTHPORT CORRECTIONAL FACILITY

PO Box 2000, Pine City, NY 14781-2000

SULLIVAN CORRECTIONAL FACILITY

PO Box 116, Fallsburg, NY 12733-0116
(845) 434-2080

SUMMIT SHOCK INCARCERATION CORRECTIONAL FACILITY

R.F.D., Dibbles Rd., Summit, NY 12175-9608

TACONIC CORRECTIONAL FACILITY

250 Harris Rd., Bedford Hills, NY 10507-2498
(845) 241-3010

ULSTER CORRECTIONAL FACILITY

PO Box 800, Berme Rd., Napanoch, NY 12458
(845) 647-1670

UPSTATE CORRECTIONAL FACILITY

PO Box 2001, Malone, NY 12953
(518) 483-6997

WALLKILL CORRECTIONAL FACILITY

PO Box G, Wallkill, NY 12589-0286
(845) 895-2021

WASHINGTON CORRECTIONAL FACILITY

PO Box 180, Comstock, NY 12821-0180

WATERTOWN CORRECTIONAL FACILITY

23147 Swan Rd., Watertown, NY 13601-9340
(315) 782-7490

WENDE CORRECTIONAL FACILITY

PO Box 1187, 3622 Wende Rd., Alden, NY 14004-1187
(716) 937-4000

WILLARD DRUG TREATMENT CENTER

PO Box 303, 7116 County Road 132, Willard, NY 14588

WOODBOURNE CORRECTIONAL FACILITY

Riverside Dr., Woodbourne, NY 12788
(845) 434-7730

WYOMING CORRECTIONAL FACILITY

PO Box 501, Dunbar Rd., Attica, NY 14011
(716) 591-1010

NORTH CAROLINA

NORTH CAROLINA DEPARTMENT OF CORRECTIONS

www.doc.state.nc.us

ALBEMARLE CORRECTIONAL INSTITUTION

PO Box 458, Badin, NC 28009
(704) 422-3036

ALEXANDER CORRECTIONAL INSTITUTION

PO Box 909, Taylorsville, NC 28681
(828) 632-1161

ANSON CORRECTIONAL CENTER

Route 1, Box 160-C, Polkton, NC 28135
(704) 694-7500

AVERY / MITCHELL CORRECTIONAL CENTER

PO Box 608, 600 Amity Park Rd., Spruce Pine, NC 28777
(828) 765-0229

BLACK MOUNTAIN CORRECTIONAL CENTER FOR WOMEN

PO Box 609, Black Mountain, NC 28711-0609
(828) 669-9165

BLADEN CORRECTIONAL CENTER

5853 U.S. 701 North, Elizabethtown, NC 28337
(910) 862-3107

BROWN CREEK CORRECTIONAL INSTITUTION

PO Box 310, Polkton, NC 28135
(704) 694-2622

BUNCOMBE CORRECTIONAL CENTER

PO Box 18089, Asheville, NC 28814
(828) 645-7630

CABARRUS CORRECTIONAL CENTER

PO Box 158, Mt. Pleasant, NC 28124

CALDWELL CORRECTIONAL CENTER

PO Box 609, Hudson, NC 28638
(828) 726-2509

CALEDONIA CORRECTIONAL INSTITUTION

PO Box 137, Tillery, NC

CARTERET CORRECTIONAL CENTER

PO Box 220, Newport, NC 28570
(252) 223-5100

CASWELL CORRECTIONAL CENTER

PO Box 217, Yanceyville, NC 27379
(336) 694-4531

CATAWBA CORRECTIONAL CENTER

PO Box 520, Newton, NC 28658
(828) 466-5521

CENTRAL PRISON | PRISON AND DEATH ROW

1300 Western Blvd., Raleigh, NC 27606
(919) 733-0800

CHARLOTTE CORRECTIONAL CENTER

4100 Meadow Oak Dr., 28208
(704) 357-6030

CI RIVERS CORRECTIONAL INSTITUTE

PO Box 630, Winton, NC 27986
(252) 358-5200

CLEVELAND CORRECTIONAL CENTER

260 Kemper Rd., Shelby, NC 28150
(704) 480-5428

COLUMBUS CORRECTIONAL INSTITUTE

PO Box 8, Brunswick, NC 28424
(910) 642-3285

CRAVEN CORRECTIONAL INSTITUTE

PO Box 839, Vanceboro, NC 28586
(252) 244-3337

DAN RIVER PRISON WORK FARM

PO Box 820, Yanceyville, NC 27379
(336) 694-1583

DAVIDSON CORRECTIONAL CENTER

1400 Thomason St., Lexington, NC 27292
(336) 249-7528

DUPLIN CORRECTIONAL CENTER

PO Box 780, Kenansville, NC 28349
(919) 296-0315

DURHAM CORRECTIONAL CENTER

PO Box 2567, Durham, NC 27705
(919) 471-4341

EASTERN CORRECTIONAL INSTITUTE

PO Box 215, Maury, NC 28554
(252) 747-8101

FOOTHILLS CORRECTIONAL INSTITUTE

5150 Western Ave., Morgantown, NC 28655
(828) 438-6021

FORSYTH CORRECTIONAL CENTER

307 Craft Dr., Winston-Salem, NC 27105
(336) 896-7041

FOUNTAIN CORRECTIONAL CENTER FOR WOMEN

PO Box 1435, Rocky Mount, NC 27802
(252) 442-9712

FRANKLIN CORRECTIONAL CENTER

PO Box 155, Bunn, NC 27508

GASTON CORRECTIONAL CENTER

1025 Cherryville Highway, Dallas, NC 28034
(704) 922-7628

GATES CORRECTIONAL CENTER

Route 1, Box 84, Gatesville, NC 27938
(252) 357-0778

GREENE CORRECTIONAL CENTER

2699 Highway 903, PO Box 39, Maury, NC 28554
(919) 747-3676

GUILFORD CORRECTIONAL CENTER

4250 Camp Burton Rd., McLeansville, NC 27301
(336) 375-5024

HARNETT CORRECTIONAL INSTITUTE

PO Box 1569, Lillington, NC 24546
(910) 893-2751

HAYWOOD CORRECTIONAL CENTER

PO Box 218, Hazelwood, NC 28738
(828) 452-5141

HIGHPOINT DETENTION CENTER

507 E. Green Dr., High Point, NC 27626

HOKE CORRECTIONAL INSTITUTE

PO Box 700, Raeford, NC 28376-0700
(910) 944-7612

HYDE CORRECTIONAL CENTER

PO Box 278 Swan Quarter, NC 278853
(252) 926-1494

JOHNSTON CORRECTIONAL INSTITUTE

2465 Highway 70 West, Smithfield, NC 27577

LANESBORO CORRECTIONAL INSTITUTE

PO Box 280, Polkton, NC 28135
(828) 632-1161

LINCOLN CORRECTIONAL CENTER

464 Prison Camp Rd., Lincolntown, NC 28092
(704) 735-0485

LUMBERTON CORRECTIONAL INSTITUTE

Sanchez Drive, Box 1649, Lumberton, NC 28359
(910) 618-5574

MARION CORRECTIONAL INSTITUTE

PO Box 2405, Marion, NC 28752
(828) 659-7810

MCCAIN CORRECTIONAL HOSPITAL

PO Box 5118, McCain, NC 28631-5118
(910) 944-2351

MORRISON CORRECTIONAL INSTITUTE

PO Box 169, Hoffman, NC 28347

MOUNTAIN VIEW CORRECTIONAL INSTITUTE

PO Box 708, Spruce Pine, NC 28777
(828) 765-0956

NEUSE CORRECTIONAL INSTITUTE

701 Stevens Mill Rd., Goldsboro, NC 27530

NEW HANOVER CORRECTIONAL CENTER

PO Box 240, Wilmington, NC 28402
(910) 251-2666

NORTH CAROLINA CORRECTIONAL INSTITUTION FOR WOMEN | PRISON AND WOMEN'S DEATH ROW

1034 Bragg St., Raleigh, NC 27610
(336) 733-4340

NORTH PIEDMONT CORRECTIONAL CENTER FOR WOMEN

PO Box 1277, Lexington, NC 27292
(336) 242-1259

ODOM CORRECTIONAL INSTITUTE

Route 1, Box 36, Jackson, NC 27845
(252) 534-5611

ORANGE CORRECTIONAL CENTER

2110 Clarence Walters Rd., Hillsborough, NC 27278
(919) 732-9301

PAMLICO CORRECTIONAL INSTITUTE

601 N. Third St., Bayboro, NC 28515
(252) 745-3074

PASQUOTANK CORRECTIONAL INSTITUTE

527 Commerce Dr., Caller Box 5005, Elizabeth City, NC 27906
(252) 331-4881

PENDER CORRECTIONAL INSTITUTE

PO Box 1058, Burgaw, NC 28425
(910) 259-8735

PIEDMONT CORRECTIONAL INSTITUTE

977 Prison Camp Rd., Salisbury, NC 28147
(704) 639-7540

POLK CORRECTIONAL

PO Box 2500, Butner, NC 27509

POLK YOUTH INSTITUTION

PO Box 2500, Butner, NC 27509
(919) 575-3070

RALEIGH CORRECTIONAL CENTER FOR WOMEN

1201 S. State St., Raleigh, NC 27610
(919) 733-4248

RANDOLPH CORRECTIONAL CENTER

PO Box 4128, Asheboro, NC 27204
(336) 625-2578

ROBESON CORRECTIONAL CENTER

PO Box 1979, Lumberton, NC 28359
(910) 618-5535

ROWAN CORRECTIONAL CENTER

PO Box 1207, Salisbury, NC 28144
(704) 639-7552

RUTHERFORD CORRECTIONAL CENTER

PO Box 127, Spindale, NC 28160
(919) 286-4121

SAMPSON CORRECTIONAL INSTITUTE

PO Box 999, Highway 421 North, Clinton, NC 28328
(910) 592-2151

SANDHILLS YOUTH CENTER

PO Box 5088, McCain, NC 28361

SANFORD CORRECTIONAL CENTER

PO Box 2490, Sanford, NC 27330
(919) 776-4325

SCOTLAND CORRECTIONAL INSTITUTE

PO Box 1808, Laurinburg, NC 28353
(919) 844-3078

SOUTHERN CORRECTIONAL INSTITUTE

PO Box 786, Troy, NC 27371
(336) 572-3784

TABOR CORRECTIONAL INSTITUTION

PO Box 730, Tabor City, NC 28463
(910) 653-6413

TILLERY CORRECTIONAL CENTER

PO Box 222, Tillery, NC 27887

TYRRELL PRISON WORK FARM

PO Box 840, Columbia, NC 27925
(252) 796-1085

UMSTEAD CORRECTIONAL CENTER

PO Box 106, Butner, NC 27509
(919) 575-3174

UNION CORRECTIONAL CENTER

200 S. Sutherland Ave., Monroe, NC 27112
(704) 283-6142

WAKE CORRECTIONAL CENTER

1000 Rock Quarry Rd., Raleigh, NC 27610
(919) 733-7988

WARREN CORRECTIONAL CENTER

PO Box 399, Manson, NC 27553
(704) 456-3400

WAYNE CORRECTIONAL CENTER

Caller Box 8011, Goldsboro, NC 24533-8011
(919) 734-5580

WESTERN YOUTH INSTITUTION

Drawer 1439, Morgantown, NC 28655
(828) 438-6037

WILKES CORRECTIONAL CENTER

404 Statesville Rd., North Wilkesboro, NC 28659
(252) 667-4533

WILMINGTON RESIDENTIAL FACILITY FOR WOMEN

76 Darlington Ave., Wilmington, NC 28403
(910) 257-2671

NORTH DAKOTA

NORTH DAKOTA DEPARTMENT OF CORRECTIONS

www.nd.gov/docr

JAMES RIVER CORRECTIONAL CENTER

2521 Circle Dr., Jamestown, ND 58401
(701) 253- 3660

MISSOURI RIVER CORRECTIONAL CENTER

PO Box 5521, Bismarck, ND 58506-5521
(701) 328-9696

NORTH DAKOTA STATE PENITENTIARY

PO Box 5521, Bismarck, ND 58506-5521
(701) 328-6100

OHIO

OHIO DEPARTMENT OF CORRECTIONS

www.doc.ohio.gov

ALLEN CORRECTIONAL INSTITUTION (ACI)

PO Box 4501, Lima, OH 45802
(419) 224-8000

BELMONT CORRECTIONAL INSTITUTION (BECI)

PO Box 540, St. Clairsville, OH 43950
(740) 695-5769

CAMP REAMS | SOUTHEASTERN CORRECTIONAL INSTITUTION

5900 B.I.S. Rd., Lancaster, OH 43130
(740) 653-4324

CCM CINCINNATI

36 E. 7th St., Suite 2107-A, Cincinnati, OH 45202

CHILLICOTHE CORRECTIONAL INSTITUTION (CCI)

PO Box 5500, Chillicothe, OH 45601
(740) 773-2616

CORRECTIONAL RECEPTION CENTER (CRC)

PO Box 300, Orient, OH 43146
(614) 877-2441

CORRECTIONS MEDICAL CENTER

1990 Harmon Ave., Columbus, OH 43223
(614) 445-5960

DAYTON CORRECTIONAL INSTITUTION (DCI)

PO Box 17249, Dayton, OH 45417
(937) 263-0058

GRAFTON CORRECTIONAL INSTITUTION (GCI)

2500 S. Avon Beldon Rd., Grafton, OH 44044
(440) 748-1161

HOCKING CORRECTIONAL FACILITY (HCF)

PO Box 59, Nelsonville, OH 45764
(740) 753-1917

LAKE ERIE CORRECTIONAL INSTITUTION

501 Thompson Rd., PO Box 8000, Conneaut, OH 44030
(440) 599-5000

LEBANON CORRECTIONAL INSTITUTION (LECI)

PO Box 56, Lebanon, OH 45036
(513) 932-1211

LIMA CORRECTIONAL INSTITUTION (LCI)

PO Box 4571, Lima, OH 45802
(419) 225-8060

LONDON CORRECTIONAL INSTITUTION (LOCI)

PO Box 69, London, OH 43140
(740) 852-2454

LORAIN CORRECTIONAL INSTITUTION (LORCI)

2075 S. Avon Beldon Rd., Grafton, OH 44044
(440) 748-1049

MADISON CORRECTIONAL INSTITUTION (MACI)

PO Box 740, London, OH 43140-0740
(740) 852-9777

MANSFIELD CORRECTIONAL INSTITUTION (MANCI) | PRISON AND DEATH ROW

PO Box 788, Mansfield, OH 44901
(419) 525-4455

MARION CORRECTIONAL INSTITUTION (MCI)

PO Box 57, Marion, OH 43302
740) 382-5781

MONTGOMERY EDUCATION AND PRERELEASE CENTER (MEPRC)

PO Box 17399, Dayton, OH 45418
(937) 262-9853

NOBLE CORRECTIONAL INSTITUTION (NCI)

15708, State Route 78, Caldwell, OH 43724
(740) 732-5788

NORTH CENTRAL CORRECTIONAL INSTITUTION (NCCI)

PO Box 1812, Marion, OH 43302
(740) 387-7040

NORTH COAST CORRECTIONAL TREATMENT FACILITY (NCCTF)

2000 S. Avon Beldon Rd., Grafton, OH 44044

NORTHEAST PRERELEASE CENTER (NEPRC)

2675 E. 30th St., Cleveland, OH 44115
(216) 771-6460

OAKWOOD CORRECTIONAL FACILITY (OCF)

2100 N. West St., Lima, OH 45801
(419) 225-8052

OHIO REFORMATORY FOR WOMEN (ORW) | PRISON AND WOMEN'S DEATH ROW

1479 Collins Ave., Marysville, OH 43040
(937) 642-1065

OHIO STATE PENITENTIARY (OCI)

878 Coitsville-Hubbard Rd., Youngstown, OH 44505
(330) 743-0700

ORIENT CORRECTIONAL INSTITUTION (OCI)

PO Box 511, Columbus, OH 43216
(614) 877-4367

PICKAWAY CORRECTIONAL INSTITUTION

PO Box 209, Orient, OH 43146
(614) 877-4362

RICHLAND CORRECTIONAL INSTITUTION

1001 Olivesburg Rd., PO Box 8107, Mansfield, OH 44901

ROSS CORRECTIONAL INSTITUTION

PO Box 7010, Chillicothe, OH, 45601
(740) 653-4324

SOUTHERN OHIO CORRECTIONAL FACILITY

PO Box 45699, Lucasville, OH 45699
(740) 259-5544

TOLEDO CORRECTIONAL INSTITUTION

PO Box 80033, Toledo, OH 43608

TRUMBULL CORRECTIONAL INSTITUTION

PO Box 901, Leavittsburg, OH 44430
(330) 898-0820

WARREN CORRECTIONAL INSTITUTION

PO Box 120, Lebanon, OH 45036
(513) 932-3388

OKLAHOMA

OKLAHOMA DEPARTMENT OF CORRECTIONS
www.doc.state.ok.us

ALTUS COMMUNITY WORK CENTER

301 W. Broadway, Altus, OK 73521-3806
(580) 482-0790

ARDMORE COMMUNITY WORK CENTER

Ardmore Air Park, Building 315, PO Box 68, Gene Autry, OK 73436-0068

BEAVER COMMUNITY WORK CENTER

215 Avenue E, PO Box 1210, Beaver, OK 73932-1210
(580) 625-4608

BILL JOHNSON CORRECTIONAL CENTER

Route 1, Box 48, Alva, OK 73717-9744
(850) 327-8000

CIMARRON CORRECTIONAL FACILITY

3700 SW Kings Highway, Cushing, OK 74023
(918) 225-3336

CLARA WATERS COMMUNITY CORRECTIONS CENTER

9901 Northeast Expressway, Oklahoma City, OK 73131-5299

DAVIS CORRECTIONAL FACILITY

6888 East 133rd Rd., Holdenville, Ok 74848-9295
(405) 379-6400

DIAMONDBACK CORRECTIONAL FACILITY

PO Box 460, Watonga, OK 73772
(580) 614-2000

DICK CORNER CORRECTIONAL CENTER

PO Box 220, Hominy, OK 74035-0220
(918) 885-2192

DR. EDDIE WARRIOR CORRECTIONAL CENTER

PO Box 315, Taft, OK 74463-0315

EARL A. DAVIS CORRECTIONAL CENTER

Route 4, Box 36B, Holdenville, OK 74848
(405) 379-7296

ELK CITY COMMUNITY WORK CENTER

1309 Airport Industrial Rd., PO Box 1142, Elk City, OK 73644-1142

ENID COMMUNITY CORRECTIONS CENTER

2020 E. Maine, PO Box 2245, Enid, OK 73702-2245
(405) 234-2115

FREDERICK COMMUNITY WORK CENTER

421 W. Gladstone, Frederick, OK 73542-4219

(405) 335-2142

GREAT PLAINS CORRECTIONAL FACILITY

700 Sugar Creek Rd., PO Box 1018, Hinton, OK 73047
(405) 542-3711

HEALDTON COMMUNITY WORK CENTER

110 N. 4th St., Healdton, OK 73438-1612
(580) 229-2633

HOBART COMMUNITY WORK CENTER

311 S. Washington, PO Box 674, Hobart, OK 73651-4023
(580) 726-3341

HOLLIS COMMUNITY WORK CENTER

106 W. Jones, PO Box 171, Hollis, OK 73550-0171
(580) 688-3331

HOWARD MCLEOD CORRECTIONAL CENTER

HC 82, Box 612, Atoka, OK 74542-9152
(580) 889-6651

ISABEL COMMUNITY WORK CENTER

1800 W. Martin Luther King St., Isabel, OK 74745-4000
(918) 286-7286

JACKIE BRANNON CORRECTIONAL CENTER

PO Box 1999, McAlester, OK 74502-1999
(918) 426-4470

JAMES CRABTREE CORRECTIONAL CENTER

Route 1, Box 8, Helena, OK 73741-9606
(580) 852-3221

JAMES E. HAMILTON CORRECTIONAL CENTER

53468 Mineral Springs Rd., Hodgen, OK 74939-3064

JESS DUNN CORRECTIONAL CENTER (JDCC)

PO Box 316, Taft, OK 74463-0316

JOHN LILLEY CORRECTIONAL CENTER

PO Box 308, Boley, OK 74829-0308
(405) 667-3381

JOSEPH HARP CORRECTIONAL CENTER

PO Box 548, Lexington, OK 73051-0548
(405) 527-5593

KATE BARDS COMMUNITY CORRECTIONAL CENTER

3200 NW 39th St., Oklahoma City, OK 73112-6298

LAWTON COMMUNITY CORRECTIONAL CENTER (LCCC)

605 SW Coombs Rd., Lawton, OK 73501-8294

LAWTON CORRECTIONAL FACILITY

8607 SE Flower Mound Rd., Lawton, OK 73501
(580) 351-2778

LEXINGTON ASSESSMENT AND RECEPTION CENTER

PO Box 576, Lexington, OK 73051
(405) 527-5676

LEXINGTON CORRECTIONAL CENTER

PO Box 260, Lexington, OK 73051-0260
(405) 527-5676

MABEL BASSETT CORRECTIONAL CENTER | PRISON AND WOMEN'S DEATH ROW

PO Box 11491, Oklahoma City, OK 73136-0491
(405) 425-2900

MABEL BASSETT MINIMUM UNIT

315 West I-44 Service Rd., Oklahoma City, OK 73118-7634
(405) 848-3895

MACK ALFORD CORRECTIONAL CENTER

PO Box 220, Stringtown, OK 74569-0220

MAGNUM COMMUNITY WORK CENTER

119 E. Jefferson, PO Box 277, Magnum, OK 73554-0277
(580) 782-3315

MARSHALL COUNTY COMMUNITY WORK CENTER

205 N. 4th St., Madill, OK 73446-2215
(580) 795-7348

MUSKOGEE COMMUNITY CORRECTIONAL CENTER (MCCC)

3031 N. 32nd St., Muskogee, OK 74401-2246
(918) 682-3394

NORTH FORK CORRECTIONAL FACILITY

PO Box 209, Sayre, OK 73662
(580) 928-8200

NORTHEAST OKLAHOMA CORRECTIONAL CENTER (NOCC)

PO Box 887, Vinita, OK 74301-0887
(918) 256-3392

OKLAHOMA STATE PENITENTIARY (OSP)

PO Box 97, McAlester, OK 74502-0097
(918) 423-4700

OKLAHOMA STATE REFORMATORY (OSR)

PO Box 514, Granite, OK 73547-0514
580) 535-2186

SAYRE COMMUNITY WORK CENTER

1107 N. Broadway, PO Box 424, Sayre, OK 73662-0424
(580) 928-5211

WALTERS CITY COMMUNITY WORK CENTER

Rural Route 3, Box 9, Walters, OK 73572-9602
(580) 875-2885

WAURIKA COMMUNITY WORK CENTER

107 W. Anderson, Waurika, OK 73572-9602
(580) 228-3521

WILLIAM S. KERR CORRECTIONAL CENTER

PO Box 61, Fort Supply, OK 73841-9718
(580) 766-2224

OREGON

OREGON DEPARTMENT OF CORRECTIONS

2575 Center St. NE, Salem, OR 97301
(503)945-9090
www.oregon.gov/doc

COFFEE CREEK CORRECTIONAL FACILITY | INTAKE CENTER (CCCF - INTAKE)

PO Box 9000, Wilsonville, OR 97070
(503) 582-9683

COFFEE CREEK CORRECTIONAL FACILITY | WOMEN'S CORRECTIONAL CENTER (CCCF) | PRISON AND WOMEN'S DEATH ROW

PO Box 9000, Wilsonville, OR 97070
(503) 582-9683

COLUMBIA RIVER CORRECTIONAL INSTITUTION (CRCI)

9111 NE Sunderland Ave., Portland, OR 97211-1708

EASTERN OREGON CORRECTIONAL INSTITUTION (EOCI)

2500 Westgate, Pendleton, OR 97801-9699
(541) 276-0700

MILL CREEK CORRECTIONAL FACILITY (MCCF)

5465 Turner Rd., Salem, OR 97301-9400
(503) 378-2600

OREGON STATE CORRECTIONAL INSTITUTION (OSCI)

3405 Deer Park Dr. SE, Salem, OR 97310-9302

OREGON STATE PENITENTIARY (OSP) | PRISON AND DEATH ROW

2605 State St., Salem, OR 97310
(503) 378-2453

POWDER RIVER CORRECTIONAL FACILITY (PRCF)

3600 13th St., Baker City, OR 97814-1346
(541) 523-6680

SANTIAM CORRECTIONAL INSTITUTION (SCI)

4005 Aumsville Highway SE, Salem, OR 97301-3112
(503) 378-2144

SHUTTER CREEK CORRECTIONAL INSTITUTION (SCCI)

95200 Shutters Landing Lane, North Bend, OR 97549-0303

SNAKE RIVER CORRECTIONAL INSTITUTION (SRCI)

777 Stanton Blvd., Ontario, OR 97914-0595
(541) 881-5000

SOUTH FORK FOREST CAMP (SFFC)

48300 Wilson River Highway, Tillamook, OR 97141-9799
(503) 842-2811

TWO RIVERS CORRECTIONAL INSTITUTION (TRCI)

82911 Beach Access Rd., Umatilla, OR 97882
(541) 922-2001

PENNSYLVANIA

PENNSYLVANIA DEPARTMENT OF CORRECTIONS

www.cor.state.pa.us

CCC

600 E. Luzerne St., Philadelphia, PA 19124

CCM PHILADELPHIA

PO Box 562, Philadelphia, PA 19105

CCM PITTSBURGH COMMUNITY CORRECTION'S OFFICE

1000 Liberty Ave., Suite 1315, Pittsburgh, PA 15222

CI MOSHANNON VALLEY

555 George Dr., Philipsburg, PA 16866

FPC SCHUYLKILL

PO Box 670, Minersville, PA 17954

LEC LEWISBURG CAMP

PO Box 2000, Lewisburg, PA 17837

QUEHANNA BOOT CAMP

HC Box 32, Karthaus, PA 16845

SCI ALBION

10745 Route 18, Albion, PA 16475-0001
(814) 756-5778

SCI CAMBRIDGE SPRINGS

451 Fullerton Ave., Cambridge Springs, PA 16403-1238
(814) 398-5400

SCI CAMP HILL

PO Box 200, Camp Hill, PA 17001-0200
(717) 737-4531

SCI CHESTER

500 E. Fourth St., Chester, PA 19013
(610) 490-5412

SCI COAL TOWNSHIP

1 Kelley Dr., Coal Township, PA 17866-1020
(814) 644-7890

SCI DALLAS

1000 Follies Rd., Dallas, PA 18612
(570) 675-1101

SCI FAYETTE

50 Overlook Drive, P.O. Box 9999 (mail),
LaBelle, PA 15450-1050
(724) 364-2200

SCI FOREST

1 Woodland Dr., PO Box 307, Marienville, PA 16239-0307

SCI FRACKVILLE

1111 Altamont Blvd., Frackville, PA 17931
(570) 874-4516

SCI GRATERFORD | PRISON AND DEATH ROW

PO Box 244, Graterford, PA 19426-0244
(215) 489-4151

SCI GREENE | PRISON AND DEATH ROW

175 Progress Dr., Wayneburg, PA 15370
(724) 852-2902

SCI HOUTZDALE

PO Box 1000, Houtzdale, PA 16698-1000
(814) 378-1000

SCI HUNTINGTON

1100 Pike St., Huntington, PA 16654-1112
(814) 643-2400

SCI LAUREL HIGHLANDS

5706 Glades Pike, PO Box 631, Somerset, PA 15501-0631
(814) 445-6501

SCI MAHONEY

301 Morea Rd., Frackville, PA 17932
(570) 773-2158

SCI MUNCY | PRISON AND WOMEN'S DEATH ROW

PO Box 180, Muncy, PA 17756-0180
(570) 546-3171

SCI PITTSBURGH

PO Box 99901, Pittsburgh, PA 15233
(412) 761-1955

SCI RETREAT

660 State Route 11, Hunlock Creek, PA 18621-3136

SCI ROCKVIEW

Box A, Bellefonte, PA 16823-0820
(814) 355-4874

SCI SMITHFIELD

1120 Pike St., PO Box 999, Huntingdon, PA 16652-0999
(814) 643-6520

SCI SOMERSET

1600 Walters Mill Rd., Somerset, PA 15510
(814) 443-8100

SCI WAYMART

PO Box 256, Route 6, Waymart, PA 18472-0256
(570) 488-5811

SCI WAYNESBURG

375 Prison Rd., Waynesburg, PA 15370

(724) 627-6185

SCI MERCER

801 Butler Pike, Mercer, PA 16137
(814) 662-1837

USP LEWISBURG | SATELLITE CAMP

PO Box 2000, Lewisburg, PA 17837

RHODE ISLAND

RHODE ISLAND DEPARTMENT OF CORRECTIONS

40 Howard Ave., Cranston, RI, 02920
(401) 462-1000
www.doc.ri.us

ANTHONY P. TRAVISONO INTAKE SERVICE CENTER

PO Box 8249, Cranston, RI 02920
(401) 462-2285

BERNADETTE BUILDING WOMEN'S FACILITIES

PO Box 8312, Cranston, RI 02920
(401) 462-0787

HIGH SECURITY CENTER (HSC)

PO Box 8200, Cranston, RI 02920
(401) 462-2028

MAXIMUM SECURITY FACILITY

PO Box 8273, Cranston, RI 02920
(401) 462-2054

JOHN J. MORAN MEDIUM SECURITY FACILITY

PO Box 8274, Cranston, RI 02920
(401) 462-3771

MINIMUM SECURITY

PO Box 8212, Cranston, RI 02920
(401) 462-2162

MCDONALD MEDIUM SECURITY FACILITY

Cranston, RI, 02920
(401) 462-2366

SOUTH CAROLINA

SOUTH CAROLINA DEPARTMENT OF CORRECTIONS

PO Box 21787, Columbia, SC 29210
(803) 896-8500
www.doc.sc.gov corrections.info@doc.state.sc.us

ALLENDALE CORRECTIONAL INSTITUTION

PO Box 1151, Highway 47, Fairfax, SC 29827
(803) 632-2561

BROAD RIVER CORRECTIONAL INSTITUTION

4460 Broad River Rd., Columbia, SC 29210
(803) 896-2200

CAMPBELL PRERELEASE CENTER

4530 Broad River Rd., Columbia, SC 29210
(803) 896-8560

CATAWBA PRERELEASE CENTER

1030 Milling Rd., Rock Hill, SC 29730
(803) 324-5361

COASTAL PRERELEASE CENTER

3765 Leeds Ave., North Charleston, SC 29405
(803) 740-1630

EVANS CORRECTIONAL INSTITUTION

PO Box 2951202, Bennettsville, SC 29512-5202
(803) 734-0652

GOODMAN CORRECTIONAL INSTITUTION

4556 Broad River Rd., Columbia, SC 29210
(803) 896-8565

KERSHAW CORRECTIONAL INSTITUTION

4848 Gold Mine Highway, Kershaw, SC 29067
(803) 896-3300

KIRKLAND CORRECTIONAL INSTITUTION

4344 Broad River Rd., Columbia, SC 29210
(803) 896-8572

LEATH CORRECTIONAL INSTITUTION

2829 Airport Rd., Greenwood, SC 29649
(803) 229-5709

LEE CORRECTIONAL INSTITUTION

1204 E. Church St., Bishopville, SC 29010
(803) 896-2400

LIEBER CORRECTIONAL INSTITUTION | PRISON AND DEATH ROW

PO Box 205, Ridgeville, SC 29472
(843) 875-3332

LIVESAY PRERELEASE CENTER

104 Broadcast Dr., Spartanburg, SC 29303-4711
(864) 594-4921

Lower Savannah Prerelease Center

361 Wire Rd., Aiken, SC 29801
(803) 648-8865

MacDougall Correctional Institution

1516 Old Gilliard Rd., Ridgeville, SC 29742
(843) 737-3036

Manning Correctional Institution

502 Beckman Rd., PO Box 3173, Columbia, SC 29230-3173
(803) 935-7248

McCormick Correctional Institution

Route 2, Box 100, McCormick, SC 29899
(803) 443-2114

Northside Correctional Institution

504 Broadcast Dr., Spartanburg, SC 29303-9702
(864) 594-4915

Palmer Prerelease Center

2012 Pisgah Rd., Florence, SC 29501
(843) 661-4770

Perry Correctional Institution

430 Oaklawn Rd., Pelzer, SC 29669

Ridgeland Correctional Institution

PO Box 2039, Ridgeland, SC 29936
(843) 726-6888

State Park Correctional Center

PO Box 98, State Park, SC 29147

Stevenson Correctional Institution

4546 Broad River Rd., Columbia, SC 29210
(803) 896-8575

Trenton Correctional Institution

84 Greenhouse Rd., Trenton, SC 29847

Turbeville Correctional Institution

PO Box 252, Turbeville, SC 29162
(843) 659-4800

Tyger River Correctional Institution

100 Prison Rd., Enoree, SC 29335-9308
(803) 583-6017

Walden Correctional Institution

4340 Broad River Rd., Columbia, SC 29210
(803) 896-8580

Wateree River Correctional Institution

PO Box 189, Rembert, SC 29128-0189

Watkins Prerelease Center

1700 St. Andrews Terrace Rd., Columbia, SC 29210
(803) 896-8584

Women's Correctional Institution | Prison and Women's Death Row

4450 Broad River Rd., Columbia, SC 29210-4096
(803) 896-8590

South Dakota

South Dakota Department of Corrections
www.doc.sd.gov

Mike Durfee State Prison

PO Box 428, Springfield, SD 57062

Redfield Trustee Unit

Rural Route 3, PO Box 500, Redfield, SD 57469-0410

South Dakota State Penitentiary | Prison and Death Row

1600 North Dr., PO Box 5911, Sioux Falls, SD 57117-5911
(605) 367-5051

South Dakota State Penitentiary | Jameson Annex

1600 North Dr., PO Box 5911, Sioux Falls, SD 57117-5911
(605) 367-5051

South Dakota Women's Prison | Prison and Women's Death Row

500 E. Capitol Ave., Pierre, SD 57501-5070
(605) 773-6636

Yankton Trustee Unit

PO Box 76, Yankton, SD 57078-0076
(605) 668-3354

Tennessee

Tennessee Department of Corrections
www.state.tn.gov/corrections

BRUSHY MOUNTAIN CORRECTIONAL COMPLEX (BMCX)

PO Box 1000, Petros, TN 37845
(865) 324-4011

BRUSHY MOUNTAIN CORRECTIONAL COMPLEX | MORGAN (MCRC)

PO Box 2000, Wartburg, TN 37887
(865) 346-6641

CARTER COUNTY WORK CAMP (CCWC)

Caller Box 1, Roan Mountain, TN 37887
(423) 772-3231

DEBERRY SPECIAL NEEDS FACILITY (DSNF)

7575 Cockrill Bend Industrial Rd., Nashville, TN 37209-1057

HARDEMAN COUNTY CORRECTIONAL FACILITY (HCCF)

PO Box 549, Whiteville, TN 38075
(731) 231-0465

LAKE COUNTY REGIONAL CORRECTIONAL FACILITY (LCRCF)

Route 1, Box 330, Tiptonville, TN 38079
(731) 253-5000

LUTTRELL CORRECTIONAL CENTER (MLCC)

6000 State Rd., Memphis, TN 38134
(901) 372-2080

MIDDLE TENNESSEE CORRECTIONAL COMPLEX (MTCX)

7177 Cockrill Bend Industrial Rd., Nashville, TN 37243-0470

NASHVILLE COMMUNITY SERVICE CENTER (NCSC)

7466 Centennial Blvd., Nashville, TN 37243-0466

NASHVILLE CORRECTIONAL COMPLEX (NECX)

PO Box 5000, Mountain City, TN 37683-5000
(423) 727-7387

NORTHWEST CORRECTIONAL COMPLEX (NWCX)

960 State Route 212, Tiptonville, TN 38079
(731) 253-5000

RIVERBEND MAXIMUM SECURITY INSTITUTION (RMSI) | PRISON AND DEATH ROW

7575 Cockrill Bend Industrial Rd., Nashville, TN 37243-0471

RUTHERFORD COUNTY WORKHOUSE

1710 S. Church St., Murfreesboro, TN 37130

SOUTH CENTRAL CORRECTIONAL CENTER (SCCF)

PO Box 279, Clifton, TN 38425-0279
(865) 676-5372

SOUTHEASTERN REGIONAL CORRECTIONAL FACILITY (STSRCF)

1045 Horsehead Rd., Pikeville, TN 37367
(423) 881-3251

TENNESSEE PRISON FOR WOMEN (TPFW) | PRISON AND WOMEN'S DEATH ROW

3881 Stewarts Lane, Nashville, TN 37243-0468
(615) 880-7100

TURNEY CENTER INDUSTRIAL PRISON AND FARM (TCIP)

Route 1, Only, TN 37140

WAYNE COUNTY BOOT CAMP (WCBC)

PO Box 182, Clifton, TN 38425
(865) 676-3345

WEST TENNESSEE STATE PENITENTIARY (WTSP)

PO Box 1150, Henning, TN 38041-1150

WHITEVILLE CORRECTIONAL FACILITY

PO Box 679, Whiteville, TN 38075

TEXAS

TEXAS DEPARTMENT OF CRIMINAL JUSTICE

209 W. 14th St., Austin, TX 78770
(512) 463-9988
www.tdcj.state.tx.us

JAMES V. ALLRED UNIT

2101 FM 369 North, Iowa Park, TX 76367
(640) 855-7477

BARRY B. TELFORD UNIT

3899 State Highway 98, New Boston, TX 75570-9200

BARTLETT STATE JAIL

1018 Arnold Dr., Bartlett, TX 76511
(512) 527-3300

BATEN INTERMEDIATE SANCTION FACILITY

1995 Hilton Rd., Pampa, TX 79065

(806) 665-7070

BETO ONE UNIT

PO Box 128, Tennessee Colony, TX 75880
(817) 928-2217

BILL CLAYTON DETENTION CENTER

2600 S. Sunset, Littlefield, TX 79339
(806) 385-1302

BILL CLEMENTS UNIT

9601 Spur 591, Amarillo, TX 79107

BOYD UNIT PRISON

Route 2, Box 500, Teague, TX 75860-5174
(254) 739-5555

BRADSHAW STATE JAIL

PO Box 9000, Henderson, TX 75653-9000
(903) 655-0880

BRIDGEPORT PRE-PAROLE TRANSFER FACILITY

222 Lake Rd., Bridgeport, TX 76426
(817) 683-2162

BYRD UNIT

21FM 247, Huntsville, TX 77320
(936) 295-5768

CENTRAL PRISON

One Circle Dr., Sugarland, TX 77478
(713) 491-2146

C BIG SPRINGS CORRECTIONAL INSTITUTE

2001 Rickabaugh Dr., Big Springs, TX 79720
(432) 264-0060

CLEMENS PRISON

11034 Highway 36, Brazoria, TX 77422
(979) 798-2188

CLEMENTS UNIT

9601 Spur 591, Amarillo, TX 79107-9606
(806) 381-7080

CLEVELAND PRISON

PO Box 1678, Cleveland, TX 77328
(713) 592-9559

COFFIELD UNIT PRISON

Route 1, Box 150, Tennessee Colony, TX 75884
(817) 928-2211

COLE STATE JAIL

3801 Silo Rd., Bonham, TX 75418
(903) 583-1100

CONNALLY PRISON

899 FM 632, Kennedy, TX 78119
(361) 583-4003

COTULLA TRANSFER FACILITY

HC 62, Box 100, Cotulla, TX 78014
(210) 879-3077

DALHART PRISON

HCR 4, Box 4000, Dalhart, TX 79022
(806) 249-8655

DANIEL UNIT

938 South FM 1673, Snyder, TX 79549
(432) 573-1114

DARRINGTON PRISON

59 Darrington Rd., Rosharon, TX 77583
(281) 595-3465

DAWSON STATE JAIL

PO Box 650051, Dallas, TX 75365-0051
(214) 744-4422

DIBOLL PRISON

1604 S. First St., Diboll, TX 75941
(409) 829-8895

DOLPH BRISCOE UNIT

1459 West Highway 85, Dilley, TX 78017
(210) 965-4444

DOMINGUEZ STATE JAIL

6535 Cagnon Rd., San Antonio, TX 78252-2202
(210) 675-6620

DUNCAN TRANSFER FACILITY

1502 S. First St., Diboll, TX 75941
(409) 829-2616

EASTHAM UNIT

PO Box 16, Lovelady, TX 75851-0016

ELLIS UNIT

1697 FM 980, Huntsville, TX, 77343
(936) 295-5756

ESTELLE UNIT

264 FM 3478, Huntsville, TX 77320
(936) 291-4200

ESTES PRISON

1100 Highway 1807, Venus, TX 76084
(817) 366-3334

FORMBY STATE JAIL

970 County Road AA, Plainview, TX 79072
(806) 296-2448

FORT STOCKTON TRANSFER FACILITY

1500 IH-10, Fort Stockton, TX 79735
(915) 336-7676

FRENCH ROBERTSON UNIT

12071 Farm Rd., #3522, Abilene, TX 79601
(915) 548-9035

GARZA EAST TRANSFER FACILITY

HC 02, Box 985, Beeville, TX 78102
(361) 358-9880

GATESVILLE PRISON

1500 State School Rd., Gatesville, TX 76598
(254) 865-8431

GIST STATE JAIL

3925 FM 3514, Beaumont, TX 77705
(409) 727-8400

GLOSSBRENNER SUBSTANCE ABUSE FELONY PUNISHMENT FACILITY

623 South FM 1329, San Diego, TX 78384

GOODMAN TRANSFER FACILITY

Route 1, Box 273, Jasper, TX 75951
(409) 383-0012

GOODMAN UNIT

349 Private Road 8430, Jasper, TX 75951

GOREE CORRECTIONAL INSTITUTE

7405 Highway 75 South, PO Box 38, Huntsville, TX 77344
(936) 295-6331

GURNEY TRANSFER FACILITY

PO Box 6400, Tennessee Colony, TX 75861
(817) 928-3118

HALBERT SUBSTANCE ABUSE FELONY PUNISHMENT FACILITY

PO Box 923, Burnet, TX 78611
(512) 756-6171

HAVENS SUBSTANCE ABUSE FELONY PUNISHMENT FACILITY

PO Box 90401, Brownwood, TX 76804-4401

HENLEY SUBSTANCE ABUSE FELONY PUNISHMENT FACILITY

Route 3, Box 7000B, Dayton, TX 77535
(936) 258-2476

HIGHTOWER PRISON

Route 3, Box 9800, Dayton, TX 77535
(936) 258-8013

HILLTOP PRISON

1500 State School Rd., Gatesville, TX 76598-2996
(254) 865-8901

HILLTOP TRUSTEE UNIT

1500 State School Rd., Gatesville, TX 76598-2996
(254) 865-8901

HOBBY UNIT

742 FM 712, Marlin, TX 76661
(254) 883-5561

HODGE MENTALLY RETARDED OFFENDER PROGRAM

PO Box 999, Rusk, TX 75785
(936) 683-5781

HOLLIDAY TRANSFER FACILITY

295 IH-45 North, Huntsville, TX 77320-8443
(936) 295-8200

HUGHES PRISON

Route 2, Box 4400, Gatesville, TX 76597
(254) 865-6663

HUNTSVILLE PRISON

PO Box 99, Huntsville, TX 77342-0099
(936) 437-1975

HUTCHINS STATE JAIL

1500 E. Langdon Rd., Dallas, TX 75241
(214) 225-1304

J.R. LINDSEY UNIT

1620 Post Oak Rd., Jacksboro, TX 76548

JESTER SUBSTANCE ABUSE FELONY PUNISHMENT FACILITY

Jester I, Richmond, TX 77469
(713) 277-3030

JESTER III PRISON

Jester III, Richmond, TX 77469
(713) 277-7000

JESTER IV PSYCHIATRIC FACILITY

Jester IV, Richmond, TX 77469
(713) 277-3700

JOHN B. CONNALLY UNIT

899 FM 632, Kenedy, TX 75701

JOHNSTON SUBSTANCE ABUSE FELONY PUNISHMENT FACILITY

703 Airport Rd., Winnsboro, TX 75494

JORDAN PRISON

1992 Hilton Rd., Pampa, TX 79065
(806) 655-7070

KEGANS STATE JAIL

707 Top St., Houston, TX 77002
(713) 224-6584

KYLE PRISON

701 IH-35 South, Kyle, TX 78640
(512) 268-0079

LANE MURRAY UNIT

1916 N. Highway 36 Bypass, Gatesville, TX 76596

LEBLANC PRISON

3695 FM 3514, Beaumont, TX 77705
(409) 724-1515

LEWIS PRISON

PO Box 9000, Woodville, TX 75990
(409) 283-8181

LINDSEY UNIT

1620 Post Oak Rd., Jacksboro, TX 76458
(817) 567-2272

LOPEZ STATE JAIL

1203 El Cibolo Rd., Edinburg. TX 78539-9334
(956) 316-3810

LUTHER PRISON

1800 Luther Dr., Navasota, TX 77869
(979) 825-7547

LYCHNER STATE JAIL

2350 Atascocita Rd., Humble, TX 77396
(713) 454-5036

LYNAUGH PRISON

900 FM 2037, Fort Stockton, TX 79735
(432) 395-2938

MARK W. STILES UNIT

3060 FM 3514, Beaumont, TX 77705
(409) 722-5255

MCCONNELL PRISON

3001 S. Emily Dr., Beeville, TX 78102
(361) 362-2300

MICHAEL PRISON

PO Box 4500, Tennessee Colony, TX 75886
(817) 928-2311

MICHAEL UNIT

2664 FM 2054, Tennessee Colony, TX 75885

MIDDLETON TRANSFER FACILITY

13055 FM 3522, Abilene, TX 79601
(325) 548-9075

MONTFORD PSYCHIATRIC FACILITY

8602 Peach St., Lubbock, TX 79404

MOORE PRISON

8500 North FM 3053, Overton, TX 75684
(936) 834-6186

MOORE TRANSFER FACILITY

1700 North FM 87, Bonham, TX 75418
(903) 583-4464

MOUNTAIN VIEW UNIT | PRISON AND WOMEN'S DEATH ROW

2305 Ransom Rd., Gatesville, TX 76528
(254) 865-7226

MURRAY UNIT

1916 N. Highway 36 Bypass, Gatesville, TX 76596
(254) 865-2000

NEAL PRISON

9055 Spur 591, Amarillo, TX 79107-9696
(806) 383-1175

NEY SUBSTANCE ABUSE FELONY PUNISHMENT FACILITY

114 Private Road 4303, Hondo, TX 78861-3812

OHIO LUTHER PRISON

1800 Luther Lane, Navasota, TX 77868-4714

PACK UNIT

2400 Wallace Pack Rd., Navasota, TX 44869
(979) 825-3728

PLANE UNIT

904 FM 686, Dayton TX, 77535
(713) 258-2476

POLUNSKY UNIT | PRISON AND DEATH ROW

3872 FM 350 South, Livingston, TX 77351
(936) 967-8082

POWLEDGE PRISON

Route 2, Box 2250, Palestine, TX 75882
(903) 723-5074

PRESTON SOUTH UNIT

1313 County Road 19, Lamesa, TX 79331
(806) 872-6741

PRICE DANIEL UNIT

938 South FM 1673, Snyder, TX 79546

RAMSEY I UNIT

1100 FM 655, Rosharon, TX 77583

RAMSEY II UNIT

1200 FM 655, Rosharon, TX 77583

RAMSEY III UNIT

1300 FM 655, Rosharon, TX 77583

REAVES COUNTY DETENTION CENTER

PO Box 1560, Pecos, TX 79772

RETRIEVE PRISON

Route 5, Box 1500, Angleton, TX 77515
(979) 849-9306

ROACH PRISON

Route 2, Box 500, Childress, TX 79201
(940) 937-6364

ROBERTSON PRISON

12071 FM 3522, Abilene, TX 79601
(325) 548-9035

RUDD TRANSFER FACILITY

2004 Lamesa Highway, Brownfield, TX 79316
(806) 637-4470

SANCHEZ STATE JAIL

3901 State Jail Rd., El Paso, TX 79938-8456
(915) 856-0046

SAYLE SUBSTANCE ABUSE FELONY PUNISHMENT FACILITY

4176 FM 1800, Breckinridge, TX 76424-7301

SEGOVIA TRANSFER FACILITY

1201 El Cibolo Rd., Edinburg, TX 78539
(956) 316-2400

SKYVIEW PSYCHIATRIC FACILITY

PO Box 999, Rusk, TX 75785
(936) 683-5781

STEVENSON PRISON

1525 FM 766, Cuero, TX 77954
(361) 275-2075

STILES PRISON

3060 FM 3514, Beaumont, TX 77705
(409) 722-5255

T.L. ROACH

15845 FM 164, Childress, TX 79201

TELFORD UNIT

PO Box 9200, New Boston, TX 75570
(903) 628-3171

TEXAS MEDICAL FACILITY

Route 4, Box 1174, Dickenson, TX 77539
(281) 948-0024

TORRES PRISON

125 Private Road 4303, Hondo, TX 78861
(210) 426-5325

TRAVIS COUNTY STATE JAIL

8101 FM 969, Austin, TX 78724
(512) 926-4482

TULIA TRANSFER FACILITY

4000 Highway 86 West, Tulia, TX 78724
(806) 995-4109

VANCE PRISON | CAROL VANCE UNIT

Route 2, Richmond, TX 77469
(713) 277-3030

WALLACE UNIT

1675 South FM 3525, Colorado City, TX 79512
(432) 728-2162

WARE TRANSFER FACILITY

PO Box 2500, Colorado City, TX 79512

(432) 728-2162

WHEELER SUBSTANCE ABUSE FELONY PUNISHMENT FACILITY

986 County Road AA, Plainview, TX 79072

WILLACY COUNTY STATE JAIL

1695 S. Buffalo Dr., Raymondville, TX 78580
(965) 689-4900

WILLIAM P. CLEMENTS JR. UNIT

9601 Spur 591, Amarillo, TX 79107-9606

WOODMAN STATE JAIL

1210 Coryell City Rd., Gatesville, TX 76528
(254) 865-9398

WYNNE PRISON

Huntsville, TX 77349
(936) 295-9126

UTAH

UTAH DEPARTMENT OF CORRECTIONS
www.corrections.utah.gov

BONNEVILLE COMMUNITY CORRECTIONAL CENTER

1141 South 2475 West, Salt Lake City, UT 84104

CENTRAL UTAH CORRECTIONAL FACILITY

PO Box 550, Gunnison, UT 84634
(801) 528-6000

FREMONT COMMUNITY CORRECTIONAL CENTER (FCCC)

2588 West 2365 S., West Valley City, UT 84116

NORTHERN UTAH COMMUNITY CORRECTIONAL CENTER

2445 S. Water Tower Way, 1125 W, Ogden, UT 84401

ORANGE STREET COMMUNITY CORRECTIONAL CENTER

80 S. Orange St., 1900 W, Salt Lake City, UT 84116

UTAH STATE PRISON (USP) | PRISON AND DEATH ROW

PO Box 250, Draper, UT 84020
(801) 576-7000

VERMONT

VERMONT DEPARTMENT OF CORRECTIONS
www.doc.state.vt.us

ADDISON COUNTY SHERIFF'S OFFICE

35 Court St., Middlebury, VT 05753

CALEDONIA COUNTY WORK CAMP

St. Johnsbury, VT 05819
(802) 748-6628

CHITTENDEN REGIONAL CORRECTIONAL FACILITY

South Burlington, VT 05403
(802) 863-7356

DALE WOMEN'S FACILITY

Waterbury, VT 05676
(802) 241-1311

MARBLE VALLEY REGIONAL CORRECTIONAL FACILITY

Rutland, VT 05701
(802) 786-5830

NORTHEAST STATE CORRECTIONAL FACILITY

Newport, VT 05855
(802) 334-3364

NORTHWEST STATE CORRECTIONAL FACILITY

3649 Lower Newton Rd., Swanton, VT 05488
(802) 524-6771

SOUTHEAST STATE CORRECTIONAL FACILITY

Windsor, VT 05089
(802) 674-6711

ST. JOHNSBURY REGIONAL CORRECTIONAL FACILITY

St. Johnsbury, VT 05819
(802) 748-8151

WOODSTOCK REGIONAL CORRECTIONAL FACILITY

Woodstock, VT 05091
(802) 457-2310

VIRGINIA

VIRGINIA DEPARTMENT OF CORRECTIONS

6900 Atmore Dr., Richmond, VA 23255
(804) 674-3244
www.vadoc.virginia.gov

AUGUSTA CORRECTIONAL CENTER

1821 Estaline Valley Rd., Craigsville, VA 24430
(540) 997-7000

BASKERSVILLE CORRECTIONAL CENTER

4150 Hayes Mill Rd., Baskerville, VA 23915

BLAND CORRECTIONAL CENTER

Route 2, Box 143, Bland, VA 24315-9615
(540) 688-3318

BOTETOURT CORRECTIONAL CENTER

PO Box 250, Troutville, VA 24175
(540) 857-7021

BRUNSWICK CORRECTIONAL CENTER

PO Box 207C, Lawrenceville, VA 23822
(804) 848-4131

BUCKINGHAM CORRECTIONAL CENTER

PO Box 430, Dillwyn, VA 23936

CAROLINE CORRECTIONAL UNIT

31285 Camp Rd., Hanover, VA 23069
(804) 994-2161

COFFEEWOOD CORRECTIONAL CENTER

12352 Coffeewood Dr., PO Box 500, Mitchells, VA 22729

COLD SPRINGS CORRECTIONAL UNIT

221 Spitler Cir., Greenville, VA 24440
(540) 337-1818

COLD SPRINGS CORRECTIONAL UNIT

192 Spitler Cir., Greenville, VA 24440
(540) 337-2913

DEEP MEADOW CORRECTIONAL CENTER

State Farm, VA 23160

DEERFIELD CORRECTIONAL CENTER

21360 Deerfield Dr., Capron, VA 23829

DILLWYN CORRECTIONAL CENTER

PO Box 670, Dillwyn, VA 23936

DINWIDDIE CORRECTIONAL UNIT

PO Box 40, 13510 Cox Rd., Church Road, VA 23833
(804) 265-5744

FLUVANNA CORRECTIONAL CENTER FOR WOMEN

PO Box 1000, Troy, VA 22974

GREENSVILLE CORRECTIONAL CENTER

901 Corrections Way, Jarratt, VA 23870-9614
(804) 535-7000

HALIFAX CORRECTIONAL UNIT

PO Box 1789, Halifax, VA 24588
(434) 572-2683

HAYNEVILLE CORRECTIONAL CENTER

PO Box 129, Hayneville, VA 22472

INDIAN CREEK CORRECTIONAL CENTER

801 Sanderson, PO Box 16481, Chesapeake, VA 23328-6481

JAMES RIVER CORRECTIONAL CENTER

State Farm, VA 23160

KEEN MOUNTAIN CORRECTIONAL CENTER

PO Box 860, Oakwood, VA 24631

LADC

PO Box 6018, Lynchburg, VA 24505

LAWRENCEVILLE CORRECTIONAL CENTER

1607 Planters Rd., Lawrenceville, VA 23686
804) 848-9349

LUNENBURG CORRECTIONAL CENTER

PO Box Y, Victoria, VA 23974-0650
(434) 696-2045

MARION CORRECTIONAL TREATMENT CENTER

PO Box 1027, Marion, VA 24354
(540) 783-7154

MECKLEBURG CORRECTIONAL CENTER

PO Box 500, Boydton, VA 23917
(804) 738-6114

MIDDLE RIVER REGIONAL JAIL

PO Box 2727, Staunton VA 24402
540-245-5420

NOTTOWAY CORRECTIONAL CENTER

PO Box 488, Burkeville, VA 23922

PATRICK HENRY CORRECTIONAL CENTER

PO Box 1090, Ridgeway, VA 24148

(540) 957-2234

POCAHONTAS CORRECTIONAL UNIT

6900 Courthouse Rd., Chesterfield, VA 23832
(804) 796-4277

POWHATAN CORRECTIONAL CENTER

State Farm, VA 23160

PULASKI CORRECTIONAL UNIT

PO Box 1188, Dublin, VA 24084
(540) 831-5840

RAPPAHANNOCK REGIONAL JAIL

PO Box 3300, Stafford, VA 22555

RED ONION STATE PRISON

PO Box 1900, Pound, VA 24279
(540) 796-7510

RUSTBURG CORRECTIONAL UNIT

PO Box 340, Rustburg, VA 24588

SCP LEE COUNTY

PO Box 644, Jonesville, VA 24263

SOUTHAMPTON CORRECTIONAL CENTER

14545 Old Belfield Rd., Capron, VA 23829

ST. BRIDES CORRECTIONAL CENTER

701 Sanderson Rd., PO Box 16482, Chesapeake, VA 23328-6482

STAUNTON CORRECTIONAL CENTER

PO Box 3500, Staunton, VA 24402-3500
(540) 332-7500

SUSSEX I STATE PRISON | PRISON AND DEATH ROW

24414 Musselwhite Dr., Waverly, VA 23891-1111
(804) 834-9967

SUSSEX II STATE PRISON

24427 Musselwhite Dr., Waverly, VA 23891-1111
(804) 834-2678

TAZEWELL CORRECTIONAL UNIT

Route 3, Box 472, Tazewell, VA 24651
(540) 988-4701

VIRGINIA CORRECTIONAL CENTER FOR WOMEN | PRISON AND WOMEN'S DEATH ROW

PO Box 1, Goochland, VA 23063
(840) 784-3582

WALLENS RIDGE STATE PRISON

PO Box 759, Big Stone Gap, VA 24219
(540) 523-3310

WISE CORRECTIONAL UNIT

PO Box 1198, Coeburn, VA 24230-1198
(540) 395-2384

WASHINGTON

WASHINGTON DEPARTMENT OF CORRECTIONS
www.doc.wa.gov

AHTANUM VIEW CORRECTIONS CENTER

2009 S. 64th St Ave., Yakima, WA 98903
(509) 573-6300

AIRWAY HEIGHTS CORRECTIONS CENTER

PO Box 1839, Airway Heights, WA 99001
(509) 244-6700

CEDAR CREEK CORRECTIONS CENTER

1 Bordeaux Rd., PO Box 37, Littlerock, WA 98556
(360) 753-7278

CLALLAM BAY CORRECTIONS CENTER

1830 Eagle Crest Way, Clallam Bay, WA 98326-9723
(360) 963-2000

COYOTE RIDGE CORRECTIONS CENTER

PO Box 769, Connell, WA 99326-0769
(509) 573-6312

LARCH CORRECTIONS CENTER (LCC)

15314 NE Dole Valley Rd., Yacolt, WA 98675-9531
(360) 260-6300

MCNEIL ISLAND CORRECTIONS CENTER (MCC)

1403 Commercial St., PO Box 881000, Steilacoom, WA 98388-1000

MONROE CORRECTIONS COMPLEX | MINIMUM SECURITY UNIT (MSU)

16446 177th Ave. SE, PO Box 7001, Monroe, WA 98272

MONROE CORRECTIONS COMPLEX | SPECIAL OFFENDER UNIT

16700 177th Ave. SE, PO Box 777, Monroe, WA 98272-0777

OLYMPIC CORRECTIONS CENTER (OCC)

11235 Hoh Mainline, Forks, WA 98331

(360) 374-6181

PINE LODGE PRERELEASE

PO Box 300, 751 S. Pine St., Medical Lake, WA 99022-0300
(509) 299-2300

STAFFORD CREEK CORRECTIONS CENTER (SCCC)

191 Constantine Way, Aberdeen, WA 98520-9504
(360) 537-1800

TACOMA PRERELEASE

PO Box 881038, Steilacoom, WA 98388-0530
(253) 761-7610

TWINS RIVER CORRECTIONS CENTER (TRU)

167740 170th Dr. SE, PO Box 888, Monroe, WA 98272-0888
(360) 794-2400

WASHINGTON CORRECTIONS CENTER

2321 Dayton Airport Rd., PO Box 900, Shelton, WA 98584
(360) 426-4433

WASHINGTON CORRECTIONS CENTER FOR WOMEN

9601 Bujacich Rd. NW, Gig Harbor, WA 98332-8300
(253) 858-4200

WASHINGTON STATE PENITENTIARY | PRISON AND DEATH ROW

1313 N. 13th St., Walla Walla, WA 99362-8817
(509) 525-3610

WASHINGTON STATE REFORMATORY (WSRU)

PO Box 777, Monroe, WA 98272-0777
(360) 794-2600

WEST VIRGINIA

WEST VIRGINIA DIVISION OF CORRECTIONS

1409 Greenbrier St., Charleston, WV 25311
(304) 558-2036
www.wv.doc.com/wvdoc

ANTHONY CORRECTIONAL CENTER (ACC)

Box N-1, HC 70, White Sulphur Springs, WV, 24986

BECKLEY CORRECTIONAL CENTER (BCC)

111 S. Eisenhower Dr., Beckley, WV 25801
(304) 256-6780

CHARLESTON WORK RELEASE CENTER (CWRC)

607 Brooks St., Charleston, WV 25301-1319
(304) 558-2763

DENMAR CORRECTIONAL CENTER (DCC)

HC 64, Box 125, Hillsboro, WV 24946

HUNTINGTON WORK RELEASE CENTER (HWRC)

1236 Fifth Ave., Huntington, WV 25701
(304) 529-6885

HUTTONSVILLE CORRECTIONAL CENTER (HCC)

PO Box 1, Huttonsville, WV 26273
(304) 335-2291

MOUNT OLIVE CORRECTIONAL COMPLEX (MOCC)

1 Mountainside Way, Mt. Olive, WV 25185
(304) 442-7213

NORTHERN CORRECTIONAL CENTER (NCC)

RR 2, Box 1, Moundsville, WV 26041

OHIO COUNTY CORRECTIONAL CENTER (OCCC)

1501 Eoff St., Wheeling, WV 26003
(304) 238-1007

PRUNTYTOWN CORRECTIONAL CENTER (PCC)

PO Box 159, Grafton, WV 26354
(304) 265-6111

ST. MARYS CORRECTIONAL CENTER (SMCC)

RR 2, Box 383B, St. Marys, WV 26170
(304) 684-5500

TYGART VALLEY REGIONAL JAIL

400 Abbey Rd., Belington, WV 26250

WISCONSIN

WISCONSIN DEPARTMENT OF CORRECTIONS

www.wi-doc.com

COLUMBIA CORRECTIONAL INSTITUTION

PO Box 900, Portage, WI 53901-0950
(608) 742-9100

DODGE CORRECTIONAL INSTITUTION

PO Box 700, Waupun, WI 53963-0700
(920) 324-5577

FOX LAKE CORRECTIONAL INSTITUTION

10237 Lake Emily Rd., PO Box 147, Fox Lake, WI 53933-0147

GREEN BAY CORRECTIONAL INSTITUTION

2833 Riverside Dr., PO Box 19033, Green Bay, WI 54307-9033

JACKSON CORRECTIONAL INSTITUTION

PO Box 233, Black River Falls, WI 54615
(715) 284-4550

KCDC

4777 88th Ave., Kenosha, WI 53144

KETTLE MORRAINE CORRECTIONAL INSTITUTION

9071 Forest Dr., PO Box 31, Plymouth, WI 53073-0031

MILWAUKEE SECURE DETENTION FACILITY

1015 N. 10th St., PO Box 05740, Milwaukee, WI 53205-0740

NEW LISBON CORRECTIONAL INSTITUTION

New Lisbon, WI
(608) 566-5066

OAKHILL CORRECTIONAL INSTITUTION

PO Box 938, Oregon, WI 53575-0938
(608) 935-3101

OSHKOSH CORRECTIONAL INSTITUTION

PO Box 3310, Oshkosh, WI 54903-3310
(920) 231-4010

PRAIRIE DU CHIEN CORRECTIONAL INSTITUTION

500 E. Parrish St., Prairie du Chien, WI 53821

RACINE CORRECTIONAL INSTITUTION

2019 Wisconsin St., PO Box 900, Sturtevant, WI 53177
(414) 886-3214

RED GRANITE CORRECTIONAL INSTITUTION (RGCI)

1006 County Road EE, PO Box 925, Red Granite, WI 54970-0925

SANGER B. POWERS CORRECTIONS CENTER

N8375 County Line Rd., Oneida, WI 54155
(920) 869-1095

STANLEY CORRECTIONAL INSTITUTION

100 Corrections Dr., Stanley, WI 54768-6500

SUPERMAX CORRECTIONAL INSTITUTION

PO Box 9900, Boscobel, WI 53805-9900
(608) 375-5656

TAYCHEEDAH CORRECTIONAL INSTITUTION

751 County Road K, PO Box 1947, Fond du Lac, WI 54936-1947
(920) 929-3800

WAUPUN CORRECTIONAL INSTITUTION

PO Box 351, Waupun, WI 53963
(920) 324-5571

WISCONSIN RESOURCE CENTER

PO Box 220, Winnebago, WI 54985

WYOMING

WYOMING DEPARTMENT OF CORRECTIONS

www.doc.wy.us

WYOMING HONOR CONSERVATION PROGRAM

PO Box 160, 40 Pippen Rd., Newcastle, WY 82701-0160
(307) 746-4436

WYOMING HONOR FARM

40 Honor Farm Rd., Riverton, WY 82501-9411
(307) 856-9578

WYOMING STATE PENITENTIARY | PRISON AND DEATH ROW

PO Box 400, 2900 S. Higley Blvd., Rawlins, WY 82301-0400
(307) 328-1441

WYOMING WOMEN'S CENTER | DEATH ROW

PO Box 20, 1000 W. Griffith, Lusk, WY 82225
(307) 334-3693

2017 CALENDAR

JANUARY

Sun	Mon	Tue	Wed	Thu	Fri	Sat
1	2	3	4	5	6	7
8	9	10	11	12	13	14
15	16	17	18	19	20	21
22	23	24	25	26	27	28
29	30	31				

JANUARY

1
New Year's Day; Rose Bowl, Sugar Bowl, Fiesta Bowl

9
College National Football Championship

16
Martin Luther King Jr. Day

29
NFL Pro Bowl

31
Time to order your new SPRING *Prisoner Entertainment Guide*!

FEBRUARY

Sun	Mon	Tue	Wed	Thu	Fri	Sat
			1	2	3	4
5	6	7	8	9	10	11
12	13	14	15	16	17	18
19	20	21	22	23	24	25
26	27	28				

FEBRUARY

2
Groundhog Day

5
NFL Super Bowl

14
Valentine's Day

15
SPRING Prisoner Entertainment Guide released

20
President's Day

26

Daytona 500

Academy Awards

MARCH

Sun	Mon	Tue	Wed	Thu	Fri	Sat
			1	2	3	4
5	6	7	8	9	10	11
12	13	14	15	16	17	18
19	20	21	22	23	24	25
26	27	28	29	30	31	

MARCH

1
Ash Wednesday

12
Daylight Saving Time Begins

17
St. Patrick's Day

20
First Day of Spring

21
Benito Jaurez Birthday

31
NCAA Women's Basketball Final Four Games Begin

APRIL

Sun	Mon	Tue	Wed	Thu	Fri	Sat
						1
2	3	4	5	6	7	8
9	10	11	12	13	14	15
16	17	18	19	20	21	22
23	24	25	26	27	28	29
30						

APRIL

1
April Fools' Day

NCAA Men's Basketball Final Four Begins

3
Master's Golf Tournament

14
Good Friday

16
Easter Sunday

30
Time to order your new SUMMER *Prisoner Entertainment Guide*!

MAY

Sun	Mon	Tue	Wed	Thu	Fri	Sat
	1	2	3	4	5	6
7	8	9	10	11	12	13
14	15	16	17	18	19	20
21	22	23	24	25	26	27
28	29	30	31			

MAY

1
Cinco De Mayo

3
Buddha's Birthday

6
Kentucky Derby

14
Mother's Day

15
SUMMER *Prisoner Entertainment Guide* released

27
Ramadan Begins

28
French Open Tennis Tourney

29
Memorial Day

JUNE

Sun	Mon	Tue	Wed	Thu	Fri	Sat
			1	1	2	3
4	5	6	7	8	9	10
11	12	13	14	15	16	17
18	19	20	21	22	23	24
25	26	27	28	29	30	

JUNE

10
Belmont Stakes

15
U.S. Open Golf Tourney

18
Father's Day

21
First Day of Summer

31
Time to order your new 2017/2018 *Prisoner Education Guide*!

JULY

Sun	Mon	Tue	Wed	Thu	Fri	Sat
						1
2	3	4	5	6	7	8
9	10	11	12	13	14	15
16	17	18	19	20	21	22
23	24	25	26	27	28	29
30	31					

JULY

3
Wimbledon Tennis Tourney

4
Independence Day

6
Running of the Bulls

15
2017/2018 *Prisoner Education Guide* Released!

20
British Open Golf Tourney

31
Time to order your new FALL *Prisoner Entertainment Guide!*

AUGUST

Sun	Mon	Tue	Wed	Thu	Fri	Sat
		1	2	3	4	5
6	7	8	9	10	11	12
13	14	15	16	17	18	19
20	21	22	23	24	25	26
27	28	29	30			

AUGUST

7
PGA Championship

15
FALL
Prisoner Entertainment Guide
Released

SEPTEMBER

Sun	Mon	Tue	Wed	Thu	Fri	Sat
					1	2
3	4	5	6	7	8	9
10	11	12	13	14	15	16
17	18	19	20	21	22	23
24	25	26	27	28	29	30

SEPTEMBER

4
Labor Day

16
Mexican Independence Day

21
Islamic New Year
Rosh Hashanah Begins

22
First Day of Autumn

30
Yom Kippur

OCTOBER

Sun	Mon	Tue	Wed	Thu	Fri	Sat
1	2	3	4	5	6	7
8	9	10	11	12	13	14
15	16	17	18	19	20	21
22	23	24	25	26	27	28
29	30	31				

OCTOBER

2
U.S. Supreme Court Session Begins

9
Columbus Day

31
Time to order your new WINTER *Prisoner Entertainment Guide*!

November

Sun	Mon	Tue	Wed	Thu	Fri	Sat
			1	2	3	4
5	6	7	8	9	10	11
12	13	14	15	16	17	18
19	20	21	22		24	25
26	27	28	29	30		

November

5
Daylight Saving Time Ends

7
Election Day

10
Veteran's Day

23
Thanksgiving Day

15
WINTER
Prisoner Entertainment Guide
Released

Time to order your 2018
Prisoner Resource Guide!

December

Sun	Mon	Tue	Wed	Thu	Fri	Sat
					1	2
3	4	5	6	7	8	9
10	11	12	13	14	15	16
17	18	19	20	21	22	23
24	25	26	27	28	29	30
31						

December

1
2018
Prisoner Resource Guide
Released!

13
Hanukkah Begins

21
First Day of Winter

25
Christmas Day

INDEX

Alphabetical Listing of Resources

2

3

4

7

A

B

C

D

E

F

G

H

I

J

K

L

M

N

O

P

Q

R

S

T

U

V

W

X

Y

Z

Writing on the Wall

DO YOU HAVE SOMETHING TO SAY?

SHOUT IT OUT!

Join Prison Lives social media circle by becoming a guest writer on our blog: **Writing on the Wall**

We are on the lookout for talented prisoner-writers to join our online community. Speak your mind about virtually any topic related to prison life.

Write Us for guidelines.
Tell us a little about yourself and any special interests you wish to write about. If you have been published online, or anywhere else before, let us know where.

Write us at:
PRISON LIVES
PO Box 842, Exeter, California
info@prisonlives.com (CorrLinks-friendly)

Thank you for purchasing

Prison Lives Almanac

Prisoner Resource Guide – 2016 Edition

Prison Lives Almanac: Prisoner Resource Guide is updated **every year**.

Information and resources for prisoners are constantly changing. For you to find the most comprehensive, up-to-date, and dependable information you need, *Prison Lives* keeps up with these changes and refreshes our *Prisoner Resource Guide* annually.

WE WANT YOUR FEEDBACK!

Our resource guides are designed to make your time in prison a more productive experience by bringing the outside world inside to you. Your input matters to us.

Please feel free to contact us anytime with your thoughts or suggestions on how we can make this an even better product. We will promptly respond to these, as well as any questions or concerns you may have.

PRISON LIVES

PO BOX 842, EXETER, CA 93221

WWW.PRISONLIVES.COM

INFO@PRISONLIVES.COM *(CORRLINKS FRIENDLY)*

Remember, *Prison Lives Almanac* is updated every year.

Our new edition will be available in November 2016. Reserve your copy now!

In the meantime, send your suggestions for our next guide and consider the other products in our *Prison Lives Almanacs* line.

Enjoy Yourself While in Prison!

Your one-stop reference guide to enhance your entertainment options.

TV / MOVIES / SPORTS / BOOKS / MAGAZINES / MUSIC / GAMES / COOKING / HOW-TO / WRITING / ART... AND MUCH MUCH MORE!

- TV. Movies. DVDs. Sports

COMPLETE SEASONAL SCHEDULE AND PROGRAMMING GUIDE

EVERY MAJOR PRO & COLLEGE TEAM SCHEDULE IN THAT SEASON COMPLETE WITH EACH TEAM'S STARTING LINE-UP!

- Books and Magazines

MAGAZINE GUIDE COMPLETE WITH DESCRIPTIONS AND COMPARATIVE PRICING CHART OF THE TOP PRISON MAG DISTRIBUTERS.

BOOK REVIEWS FROM/FOR PRISONERS

- Art & Writing Resources and Contests. Origami. Guitar Riffs. Canteen Recipes. Game rules & Ideas. Pen Pals. Prison Info from Around the World...

TOO MUCH TO TELL YOU ABOUT HERE. THERE'S NOTHING ELSE LIKE IT!

Prison Lives *Almanac*

PRISONER ENTERTAINMENT GUIDE

$20
FREE Shipping

All New EVERY Season
4 TIMES/Year

Subscriptions Available
$70/year

Prison Lives Almanac: Prisoner ENTERTAINMENT Guide

500+ pages, 8½ x 11" paperback

Prison Lives *Almanac*

PRISONER EDUCATION GUIDE

Educate Yourself from Prison!

- Hundreds of CURRENT education opportunities for prisoners.

HIGH SCHOOL DIPLOMAS / VOCATIONAL CERTIFICATIONS / COLLEGE DEGREES

- Everything you need to know to go to school while behind bars.

HOW-TO GUIDES / SCHOOLS / COURSES / TUITION RATES / RESOURCES

- Choose your path, any path.

GENERAL STUDIES \ PARALEGAL \ BUSINESS MANAGEMENT \ MARKETING \ RELIGION \ TRUCK DRIVING \ TAX CONSULTING \ PHYSICAL THERAPY \ ELECTRONICS TECH...

$25
FREE Shipping

Prison Lives Almanac: Prisoner EDUCATION Guide

500+ pages, 8½ x 11" paperback

Updated for EVERY Fall Semester

2017/18 EDITION RELEASES AUGUST 1

Order Form

Please indicate your choice(s) below:

Package Deals

○ **Take No Prisoners $75**
($15 off!) Includes 4 Almanacs: 2017 Resource Guide, 2016/2017 Education Guide, and 2 Entertainment (Spring and Summer)

○ **Not Just Fun & Games Package $58**
($7 off!) Includes 3 Almanacs: 2017 Resource Guide and 2 Entertainment Guides (Spring and Summer)

○ **Enlightenment Package $45**
($5 off!) Includes 2 Almanacs: 2017 Resource Guide and 2016/2017 Education Guide

○ **Live & Learn Package $58**
($7 off!) Includes 3 Almanacs: 2016/2107 Education Guide and 2 Entertainment Guides (Spring and Summer)

○ **Heaps of Fun Package $70**
($10 off!) Includes 4 Almanacs: An entire year's worth of Entertainment Guides!

○ **Prison Lives Full Assault Package $130**
($25 off) Includes 7 Almanacs: 2017 Resource Guide, 2016/207 Education Guide, and a full year's worth of Entertainment Guides!

Individual Almanacs

○ Resource Guide 2016 Sale! Only $15!

○ Resource Guide **2017**

○ Entertainment Guide Spring 2017

○ Entertainment Guide Summer 2017

○ Entertainment Guide fall 2017

○ Education Guide 2016/2017

Prisoner Assistance Services

To order Prisoner Assistance Services, please complete this form and mail it together with a **detailed** explanation of the services you need on a separate piece of paper.

Include payment or request a quote.

f.y.i.

All books and services can be ordered online.
www.PrisonLives.com

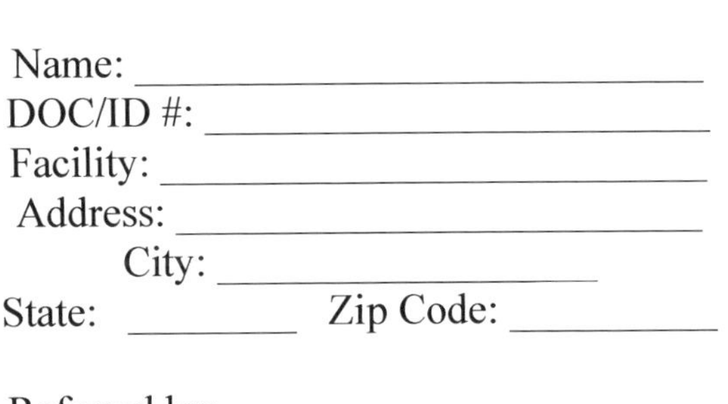

Name: ____________________
DOC/ID #: ____________________
Facility: ____________________
Address: ____________________
City: ____________________
State: ________ Zip Code: ________

Referred by: ____________________

Complete and mail with your **money order** payment to:

Prison Lives
PO Box 842
Exeter, CA 93221

All books are in paperback. Guides will be shipped within approximately two weeks of receipt of payment or once published, whichever comes first.

Made in the USA
Lexington, KY
05 April 2017